Evolution of Cross-Sector Cyber Intelligent Markets

Eugene J. Lewis
Capitol Technology University, USA

A volume in the Advances in Business Information
Systems and Analytics (ABISA) Book Series

Published in the United States of America by
    IGI Global
    Business Science Reference (an imprint of IGI Global)
    701 E. Chocolate Avenue
    Hershey PA, USA 17033
    Tel: 717-533-8845
    Fax: 717-533-8661
    E-mail: cust@igi-global.com
    Web site: http://www.igi-global.com

Library of Congress Cataloging-in-Publication Data

Names: Lewis, Eugene, 1978- editor.
Title: Evolution of cross-sector cyber intelligent markets / edited by
  Eugene Lewis.
Description: Hershey, PA : Business Science Reference, [2024] | Includes
  bibliographical references and index. | Summary: "The primary objective
  of the evolution of cross-sector cyber intelligent markets is to enhance
  the collective cybersecurity posture across industries and sectors. This
  evolution seeks to foster collaboration and information sharing among
  organizations and stakeholders to effectively combat the growing
  sophistication of cyber threats"-- Provided by publisher.
Identifiers: LCCN 2023050949 (print) | LCCN 2023050950 (ebook) | ISBN
  9798369319703 (hardcover) | ISBN 9798369319710 (ebook)
Subjects: LCSH: Computer crimes--Prevention. | Computer networks--Security
  measures. | Computer security.
Classification: LCC HV6773 .E96 2024 (print) | LCC HV6773 (ebook) | DDC
  364.16/8--dc23/eng/20231220
LC record available at https://lccn.loc.gov/2023050949
LC ebook record available at https://lccn.loc.gov/2023050950

This book is published in the IGI Global book series Advances in Business Information Systems and Analytics (ABISA) (ISSN: 2327-3275; eISSN: 2327-3283)

British Cataloguing in Publication Data
A Cataloguing in Publication record for this book is available from the British Library.

All work contributed to this book is new, previously-unpublished material. The views expressed in this book are those of the authors, but not necessarily of the publisher.

For electronic access to this publication, please contact: eresources@igi-global.com.

Advances in Business Information Systems and Analytics (ABISA) Book Series

Madjid Tavana
La Salle University, USA
ISSN:2327-3275
EISSN:2327-3283

MISSION

The successful development and management of information systems and business analytics is crucial to the success of an organization. New technological developments and methods for data analysis have allowed organizations to not only improve their processes and allow for greater productivity, but have also provided businesses with a venue through which to cut costs, plan for the future, and maintain competitive advantage in the information age.

The **Advances in Business Information Systems and Analytics (ABISA) Book Series** aims to present diverse and timely research in the development, deployment, and management of business information systems and business analytics for continued organizational development and improved business value.

COVERAGE

- Data Governance
- Legal information systems
- Business Models
- Business Information Security
- Business Process Management
- Strategic Information Systems
- Performance Metrics
- Data Strategy
- Business Intelligence
- Data Analytics

> IGI Global is currently accepting manuscripts for publication within this series. To submit a proposal for a volume in this series, please contact our Acquisition Editors at Acquisitions@igi-global.com or visit: http://www.igi-global.com/publish/.

Titles in this Series

For a list of additional titles in this series, please visit: www.igi-global.com/book-series

Data Envelopment Analysis (DEA) Methods for Maximizing Efficiency

Adeyemi Abel Ajibesin (American University of Nigeria, Nigeria) and Narasimha Rao Vajjhala (University of New York Tirana, Alania)

Business Science Reference • © 2024 • 389pp • H/C (ISBN: 9798369302552) • US $250.00

Intersecting Environmental Social Governance and AI for Business Sustainability

Cristina Raluca Gh. Popescu (University of Bucharest, Romania & The Bucharest University of Economic Studies, Romania & The National Institute for Research and Development in Environmental Protection, Romania & INCDPM, Bucharest, Romania & National Research and Development Institute for Gas Turbines (COMOTI), Bucharest, Romania) and Poshan Yu (Soochow University, China & European Business Institute, Luxembourg & Australian Studies Centre of Shanghai University, hina)

Business Science Reference • © 2024 • 371pp • H/C (ISBN: 9798369311516) • US $275.00

Human-Centered Approaches in Industry 5.0 Human-Machine Interaction, Virtual Reality Training, and Customer Sentiment Analysis

Ahdi Hassan (Global Institute for Research Education and Scholarship, The Netherlands) Pushan Kumar Dutta (Amity University Kolkata, India) Subir Gupta (Swami Vivekanand University, India) Ebrahim Mattar (College of Engineering, University of Bahrain, Bahrain) and Satya Singh (Sharda University, Uzbekistan)

Business Science Reference • © 2024 • 369pp • H/C (ISBN: 9798369326473) • US $275.00

Educational Perspectives on Digital Technologies in Modeling and Management

G. S. Prakasha (Christ University, India) Maria Lapina (North-Caucasus Federal University, Russia) Deepanraj Balakrishnan (Prince Mohammad Bin Fahd University, Saudi Arabia) and Mohammad Sajid (Aligarh Muslim University, India)

Engineering Science Reference • © 2024 • 348pp • H/C (ISBN: 9798369323144) • US $360.00

Big Data Analytics Techniques for Market Intelligence

Dina Darwish (Ahram Canadian University, Egypt)

Engineering Science Reference • © 2024 • 512pp • H/C (ISBN: 9798369304136) • US $355.00

Digital Twin Technology and AI Implementations in Future-Focused Businesses

Sivaram Ponnusamy (Sandip University, Nashik, India) Mansour Assaf (University of the South Pacific, Fiji) Jilali Antari (Ibn Zohr Agadir University, Morocco) Satyanand Singh (Fiji National University, Nasinu, Fiji) and Swaminathan Kalyanaraman (University College of Engineering, Pattukkottai, India)

Business Science Reference • © 2024 • 331pp • H/C (ISBN: 9798369318188) • US $285.00

701 East Chocolate Avenue, Hershey, PA 17033, USA
Tel: 717-533-8845 x100 • Fax: 717-533-8661
E-Mail: cust@igi-global.com • www.igi-global.com

Table of Contents

Detailed Table of Contents

Chapter 1
Critical Analysis on the Challenges of Product Distribution in Global Infrastructure and Value-
Added Systems in Logistics and Supply Chain Management 1
    Helen MacLennan, Lindsey Wilson College, USA
    Eugene J. Lewis, Capitol Technology University, USA
    Jessica Roman, Florida Institute of Technology, USA

In this critical analysis, the focus is on the nation's maritime port operations and international mode of transportation for Fixing America's Surface Transportation (FAST) Act of 2015 surrounding port distribution and logistics. The FAST Act requires the Bureau of Transportation and Statistics to report statistical data highlighting the challenges in global product distribution within infrastructure and value-added systems in logistics and supply chain management. The transportation costs estimate costs accounted for approximately 50% of the total logistics costs for businesses. Furthermore, fluctuations in fuel prices and increased demands for e-commerce shipping further emphasized the significance of cost challenges in global distribution. These disruptions underscored the complexity of managing a global network of suppliers, distributors, and customers. In this study, the researchers analyze 76% of companies still struggling with forecasting accuracy along with ongoing challenges in inventory management due to fluctuating consumer demand.

Chapter 2
Marketing Information Systems (MkIS) Parts Shortage Challenges in the Aviation Industry:
Foreign Military Sales (FMS) Legacy System in Cross-Sector Markets 18
    Eugene J. Lewis, Capitol Technology University, USA
    Danica F. Abejon, Athens State University, USA

The qualitative focus group research utilizes the theory of constraints and supply chain management (SCM) framework to review over 179 emails discoveries in obsolescence issues surrounding the Chinook/Cargo Helicopter-47 Delta-Model (CH-47 D-Model) helicopter. In the early part of 2010, there were 66 vendors who manufactured long-lead D-Model parts; now, only 13 remain. As foreign military sale (FMS) customers upgrade to more advanced systems, a critical challenge focuses on customer-centric, predictive business models, and smart automation to understand the value of military and defense operations for legacy systems. The researchers utilized participant data from focus group discussions, emails, and written correspondence to develop a comprehensive spotlight into the Chinook/Cargo community within FMS. The purpose is to determine if there is value in servicing country needs for CH-47 D-Model parts. Shortages of critical components and a lack of access to authentic, certified spare parts affect the safety and performance of the helicopters.

Chapter 3

In this era of rapid technological advancement, government leaders must expertly navigate intricate policies, including artificial intelligence, cybersecurity, and telehealth. Proficiency in these domains is paramount, requiring a steadfast commitment to enhancing leadership competencies. By investing in executive coaching and holistic leadership development, government agencies can proactively tackle modern challenges. This study, grounded in descriptive phenomenology, examines 22 thematic motifs, unveiling the effectiveness of leadership coaching for government leaders managing complex technologies and addressing pivotal policy issues in artificial intelligence, cybersecurity, and telehealth.

Chapter 4

Securing the networks underpinning industrial control systems (ICS), mainly supervisory control and data acquisition (SCADA) systems, holds paramount significance, with far-reaching implications for public health, safety, and national security. This chapter delves into the intricate landscape of cybersecurity vulnerabilities within critical infrastructures, including managing electrical grids, oil pipelines, and water distribution systems, which remain susceptible to cyber threats and attacks across diverse technological vectors in the United States. Through an exhaustive examination of contemporary and emerging literature, this research elucidates the multifaceted security risks afflicting domains crucial to the U.S. infrastructure.

Chapter 5

Childhood obesity has long-term consequences, emphasizing the need for comprehensive intervention. Research highlights a strong link between childhood obesity and adult obesity. Globally, the World Health Organization notes that overweight and obesity now claim more lives than underweight conditions. In 2016, an astonishing 41 million children under 5 were classified as overweight worldwide. In the United States, childhood obesity prevalence tripled since 1970, affecting 1 in 5 school-aged children by 2015-2016. This chapter advocates innovative technology-driven solutions to address childhood and adolescent obesity. The authors propose leveraging low-cost mobile health, remote monitoring, and wearable technologies, empowering individuals and healthcare providers to effectively manage obesity, offering personalized support and real-time data. Embracing these technologies can foster a transformative shift in obesity management, ensuring a healthier future for the next generation.

Darrell Norman Burrell, Marymount University, USA
Danielle Gervacio Graf, Marymount University, USA
Michelle D. Espinoza, Marymount University, USA
Maria Mondala-Duncan, Marymount University, USA
Arden E. Servidio, Marymount University, USA
Tiffany Weitoish, Capitol Technology University, USA
Marlena Daryousef, Colorado Technical University, USA

Amidst the prevailing scarcity of personnel and leaders within healthcare cybersecurity and technology management, the demand for bolstering the ranks of professionals in these domains has reached unprecedented significance and urgency. Enlisting women leaders and those from diverse backgrounds is imperative to address the deficiencies in workforce development and devise pioneering business strategies. The endeavor to effectively confront the most formidable issues about organizational technology management strategies necessitates women's active participation and contributions. This chapter embarks on a comprehensive exploration of the hurdles, intricacies, and innovative methodologies pertinent to the advancement of women into executive and supervisory positions within the domains of information technology and healthcare cybersecurity.

Eugene J. Lewis, Capitol Technology University, USA
Ramona R. Cruz, Oakwood University, USA

The cyber health deficiencies from customer patient advocacy did not exist until September 2021. The exploratory research focuses on a recent conference advancing in healthcare equity through policy and practice from the lenses of the University of Washington Continuing Education Conference held on 19-20 October 2023. The conference consisted of professionals in the state of Washington who are physicians, nurses, and other medical personnel. It provided insights into the general trends and issues related to patient advocacy in the healthcare industry. In this research study, the authors discuss the statistical challenges and lack of aid in resolving disputes within healthcare providers, understanding insurance coverage, and ensuring that informed consent is obtained for medical procedures for prospective customers.

Quatavia McLester, Capitol Technology University, USA
Darrell Norman Burrell, Capitol Technology University, USA

In recent years, the United States has confronted an escalating public health and safety challenge brought about by the proliferation of driving under the influence (DUI) of marijuana. This predicament has arisen due to the legalization of marijuana for medicinal and recreational purposes across several states, engendering a substantial rise in the presence of marijuana-impaired drivers on the nation's roadways. This scholarly work explores the contemporary landscape of marijuana DUI legislation, the pervasiveness of marijuana-impaired driving incidents, and the consequential health and safety hazards.

The analysis underscores the exigency for pioneering healthcare technologies and strategic interventions to enhance the detection and deterrence of marijuana-impaired driving. This chapter posits that such healthcare technological advancements, combined with comprehensive strategies, promise to ameliorate the burgeoning menace of cannabis-related DUI and its impact on public health and safety in the United States by exploring current literature.

    Quatavia McLester, Capitol Technology University, USA
    Darrell Norman Burrell, Capitol Technology University, USA & The Pellegrino Center,
        Georgetown University, USA

In the United States (U.S.), the COVID-19 outbreak is still ongoing. As a result, medical professionals are increasingly turning to new forms of technology and innovation to provide therapy to patients requiring medical assistance. This pattern is anticipated to maintain its prevalence well into the foreseeable future. The standard wait time for a new patient to be seen by a dermatologist in the United States is 33 days; however, the standard wait time in rural areas is 96 days. By conducting a content analysis of the pertinent published literature, this research aims to study the potential of telemedicine technology to serve the growing demand for dermatology among patients. Tele-dermatology is a crucial tool to expand healthcare access and reduce health disparities by enabling timely and equitable dermatological care, especially in underserved and remote areas through emerging and innovative healthcare technologies.

    Sharon L. Burton, Capitol Technology University, USA
    Darrell Norman Burrell, Marymount University, USA
    Calvin Nobles, Illinois Institute of Technology, USA
    Laura Ann Jones, Capitol Technology University, USA
    Yoshino W. White, Florida State University, USA
    Dustin I. Bessette, Mt. Hood Community College, USA
    Amalisha Aridi, Capitol Technology University, USA

It is necessary to reassess the allocation of resources, questioning traditional notions of return on investment (ROI) and focusing, in particular on the critical area of cybersecurity. Anticipated damages from cybercrime are increasing 15% per year globally, totaling an estimated $10.5 trillion by 2025. In addition to the financial benefits, the ROI for these cybersecurity efforts may be measured in terms of retaining user confidence and guaranteeing the seamless running of online learning platforms. In the age of remote learning, the goal is to enhance educational effectiveness while wisely controlling expenses, given the increasing importance of cybersecurity in online commerce. Although past data guides initiatives, it is crucial to continuously examine new data to improve strategy, particularly in the ever-changing field of cybersecurity. This understanding through qualitative inquiry gives practitioners the knowledge to understand the component parts required for the ROI calculation in the cybersecurity investment environment.

The cyber intelligence and security sector faces a growing number of threats and attacks that are increasing in complexity, but reports indicate that the current workforce lacks the qualified professionals needed to combat them. The U.S. Government and the educational community have been increasing efforts to help grow and diversify a workforce that continues to be primarily white male dominated. However, there are organization-level tactics that can be leveraged to increase and enhance the talent pool. Diversity, equity, and inclusion (DEI) initiates should be viewed not only as opportunities to engender equality but also as an opportunity to help recruit and develop the talent pool necessary to strategically heighten cyber intelligence and security capabilities. Consequently, the author reviews the benefits that DEI can bring to cybersecurity and discuss practical recommendations for moving forward with DEI initiative that can help support the industry's growing challenges.

Multifaceted ramifications of integrating connected and autonomous vehicles (CAVs) into the transportation systems pose a complex puzzle, with no easily discernible solutions regarding their impact on traffic efficiency and safety. Arriving at a clearer understanding requires exhaustive assessments of the performance of mixed traffic involving AI and CAVs is imperative, as it holds the potential to furnish invaluable insights. The role of connectivity looms large in this context, as it wields the power to substantially enhance both road safety and traffic management, with spill-over advantages affecting congestion mitigation and, conceivably, air quality improvement. It is essential to recognize that the adoption of connectivity also ushers in a new set of challenges. These challenges encompass issues related to technology compatibility, safeguarding data privacy, and fortifying defenses against cyber threats. The knowledge generated from this comprehensive evaluation of CAVs can be harnessed to benefit stakeholders within the automotive industry, academia, and policymakers.

This study investigates the utility of ethnography and artificial intelligence as a valuable tool for understanding the multifaceted nature of job-seeking experiences across four generations: Baby Boomers, Generation X, Millennials, and Generation Z. Ethnography design offers insight into the creative thought processes, expressions, and lived experiences integral to the job-seeking process. Explored is the impact of the COVID-19 pandemic on the job market, highlighting the global economic downturn and the resultant loss of millions of jobs, revealing systemic vulnerabilities. This research investigates the obstacles faced by job seekers, including those without specific qualifications or degrees, who often need help to gain visibility in a competitive job market. Addressed is the issue of online applications needing to align with job criteria. This chapter provides valuable insights into the contemporary job-seeking landscape, stressing the need for adaptable strategies such as Artificial intelligence in the face of evolving challenges and opportunities.

The increasing prevalence of illnesses, particularly Salmonella infections, presents a significant public health challenge. Traditional surveillance and outbreak management methods are resource-intensive and often must catch up to real-time occurrences. This chapter explores the application of artificial intelligence (AI) within a systems thinking framework to revolutionize public health surveillance and outbreak response for Salmonella. By harnessing AI-driven tools for data analysis, early detection, source attribution, and intervention planning, public health agencies can enhance their capacity to prevent and mitigate Salmonella outbreaks. This chapter discusses the potential of AI-driven systems to transform the landscape of public health. The chapter proposes AI as a holistic approach integrating technology, data, and human expertise for more effective Salmonella outbreak control based on actual life outbreaks and the historical contexts of the of a real outbreak event.

The integration of artificial intelligence (AI) into recruitment processes has promised to revolutionize and optimize the hiring landscape. However, recent legal proceedings have shed light on the alarming implications of AI algorithms in the employment sector. This chapter delves into a significant case study where African American, Latina American, Arab American, and other marginalized job applicants and employees filed a 100-million-dollar class action lawsuit against a prominent organization, Context Systems. The suit alleges that AI screening tools, entrusted with the crucial task of selecting candidates, have been marred by programming bias, leading to discriminatory outcomes. This case study critically examines the multifaceted problems arising from bias in AI algorithms, revealing their detrimental effects on marginalized communities in the employment sector. By scrutinizing this pivotal case, the authors aim to provide insights into the urgent need for transparency, accountability, and ethical considerations in the development and deployment of AI-driven recruitment tools.

Studies establish that cybersecurity executives face complex difficulties from constantly shifting risks due to the role's scalability and increasing responsibilities in this cyber-revolution. Cognitive and emotional aspects can influence change and decision-making, especially during times of heightened anxiety and evolving change. Through qualitative study and interpretative phenomenological analysis design, this research offers how leaders' 16-hour or more per-day working schedules affect the companies' readiness, how working hours affect leaders' resilience, and whether leadership traits like longevity, tenure, and other similar characteristics should be considered when estimating cyber risk insurance. This study aims to strengthen the defense-in-depth perimeter by providing a means to proactively identify factors that align with an enhanced approach to better estimate appropriate cyber liability coverage. Beneficiaries of this research are cybersecurity leaders and practitioners, academia, organizations that employ cybersecurity, and cyber risk insurance brokerages.

Chapter 17

Jesse Singleton Sr., Capitol Technology University, USA
Kevin Richardson, Capitol Technology University, USA

This chapter examines the role of emotional intelligence (EI) in supply chain leadership. It begins by providing an overview of EI, its components and its relevance in leadership. The supply chain landscape is then explored, highlighting the complexities and challenges faced in the global marketplace. The importance of EI in supply chain leadership and its impact on decision-making are discussed. Case studies and examples are provided to illustrate the application of EI in supply chain leadership. The chapter also delves into how EI can help navigate supply chain challenges, such as disruptions and stakeholder relationships. Real-world examples of organizations integrating EI into supply chain leadership are provided, along with the outcomes. The future outlook and implications of EI in supply chain management are explored, including emerging trends and potential areas for further research. The chapter concludes with a summary of the broader implications for supply chain leadership and a call to action for organizations and leaders to embrace and incorporate EI into their practices.

Chapter 18

Tiffany Weitoish, Capitol Technology University, USA
Darrell Norman Burrell, Capitol Technology University, USA

In an era characterized by rapidly evolving threats to cybersecurity, public health, and public safety, the imperative for nuclear power organizations to adapt and excel has never been more pronounced. This inquiry delves into the critical journey of transforming nuclear power organizations into learning organizations that are resilient and highly effective in safeguarding against cybersecurity threats and adeptly managing incidents, planning, and recovery. Leveraging the rich insights derived from qualitative focus group research, this study unveils a comprehensive framework of best practices tailored to the unique challenges nuclear power organizations face. Moreover, the study highlights the significance of organizational commitment to the principles of organizational learning, the seamless integration of learning into daily operations, regular assessments of organizational capacity and competence, and the unequivocal expression of an organizational commitment to learning.

Chapter 19

Amalisha Sabie Aridi, Capitol Technology University, USA
Darrell Norman Burrell, Marymount University, USA
Aikyna Finch, American Public University, USA
Sharon L. Burton, Capitol Technology University, USA
William Quisenberry, Purdue University Global, USA
Laura Ann Jones, Capitol Technology University, USA
Marlena Daryousef, Colorado Technical University, USA
Danielle Gervacio Graf, Marymount University, USA
Michelle Espinoza, Marymount University, USA
Maria Mondala-Duncan, Marymount University, USA

This inquiry emphasizes executive coaching as an indispensable leadership development tool in cybersecurity project management, encompassing cyber engineering and offensive operations. Effective cybersecurity project management is crucial in today's digital landscape, characterized by ever-evolving cyber threats and vulnerabilities. It extends beyond administrative tasks, serving as the linchpin for resource allocation, risk mitigation, and aligning security measures with organizational objectives. With the evolving cyber threat landscape, cybersecurity project management leaders require technical expertise, effective leadership skills, and a commitment to continuous professional development. This chapter underscores the pivotal role of executive coaching in developing leaders capable of navigating the cybersecurity landscape effectively and ensuring the resilience of critical organizational assets against sophisticated cyber threats.

Chapter 20

Darrell Norman Burrell, Marymount University, USA
Cedric Dewayne Webber, Trevecca Nazarene University, USA

The demand for specialized computer science degrees, particularly cybersecurity, has surged within educational institutions, presenting a significant challenge in the quest for well-qualified instructors. These emerging dynamics underscore the critical role of instructors in shaping and delivering relevant and comprehensive course experiences to mold adept security technologists. This chapter delves into the contemporary educational landscape, marked by the rapid expansion of the digital domain and an escalating need for cybersecurity professionals. Historically Black Colleges and Universities (HBCUs) are at the epicenter of an imperative. To meet the burgeoning demand for cybersecurity expertise, they must cultivate a new generation of cybersecurity faculty and graduates equipped to navigate the challenges of the digital age. The chapter explores innovative faculty development approaches in cybersecurity, addressing the need for educators to align their teaching with industry practices and equip students with the skills to thrive in this dynamic field.

Foreword

In the rapidly evolving landscape of the twenty-first century, the intersection of technology and industry has given rise to unprecedented challenges and opportunities. As we witness the dynamic transformation of cross-sector cyber intelligent markets, this book delves into the intricate web of developments that shape the future of various industries. One of the key focal points is the profound impact of Artificial Intelligence in the Auto Industry, where innovation is redefining not only the vehicles, we drive but the entire ecosystem surrounding them.

The pages within unfold a comprehensive exploration of diverse realms, ranging from Consumer Behavior in Intelligent Markets to the intricate nuances of Cyber Intelligence. In an era marked by digital connectivity, understanding consumer behavior in intelligent markets becomes imperative for businesses seeking to navigate the intricacies of an ever-changing market landscape. Cyber Intelligence, a cornerstone in this digital age, is dissected to unravel the complexities of safeguarding sensitive information and infrastructure. The narrative extends beyond the realms of technology to address essential societal aspects, such as Diversity, Equity, and Inclusion. In a world increasingly reliant on interconnected systems, ensuring a diverse and inclusive approach to cyber intelligence is vital for the well-being of global networks.

The Evolution of Electronic Vehicle Technology takes center stage as we embark on a journey through the transformative advancements in transportation. From electric vehicles to autonomous driving, the book navigates the technological milestones that are reshaping the automotive industry. The Global Infrastructure & Value-Added Systems emerge as critical considerations, providing insights into the interconnectedness of nations and industries. The book sheds light on the intricate dance between nations, corporations, and systems that collectively drive progress and innovation.

HealthCare Cybersecurity emerges as a critical discourse, recognizing the paramount importance of securing the sensitive health information in an increasingly digital healthcare landscape. Marketing Information Systems (MkIS) are explored as powerful tools in the hands of businesses navigating the complexities of modern marketing landscapes. The exploration extends into Multi-functional Business Challenges in Industry, recognizing the multifaceted obstacles that businesses encounter in a rapidly changing environment. Operations Maritime & Supply Chain Production Impacts complete the tapestry, emphasizing the interconnectedness of global operations and the far-reaching consequences of technological disruptions.

As we embark on this intellectual journey through the Evolution of Cross-Sector Cyber Intelligent Markets, each chapter presents a unique lens through which we can comprehend the intricate tapestry of technology, industry, and society. This book serves as a compass, guiding readers through the multifaceted landscape of a digital era where innovation and adaptability are the keys to success. May the insights within these pages inspire thought, spark dialogue, and contribute to the ongoing dialogue surrounding the evolution of our interconnected world.

Darrell Norman Burrell
Capitol Technology University, USA & Marymount University, USA & Georgetown University, USA

Preface

AN OVERVIEW OF THE SUBJECT MATTER

An overview of the subject matter into the *Evolution of Cross-Sector Cyber Intelligent Markets*:

1. Artificial Intelligence in the Auto Industry: Examines how AI is transforming the automotive sector, including applications in autonomous vehicles, predictive maintenance, and personalized driving experiences.
2. Consumer Behavior in Intelligent Markets: Studies how consumers interact with intelligent markets, considering factors like purchasing decisions, brand loyalty, and the influence of AI-driven recommendations.
3. Cyber Intelligence: Involves gathering, analyzing, and interpreting information related to cybersecurity threats, aiming to proactively prevent and respond to cyber incidents.
4. Diversity, Equity, and Inclusion (DEI): Focuses on promoting diversity, equity, and inclusion in workplaces, emphasizing the importance of a diverse workforce for innovation and overall organizational success.
5. Evolution of Electronic Vehicle Technology: Tracks the advancements in electric vehicle technology, including developments in battery technology, charging infrastructure, and energy efficiency.
6. Global Infrastructure and Value-Added Systems (VAS): Examines the development and management of global infrastructure, including the role of value-added systems in enhancing operational efficiency.
7. Health Care Cybersecurity: Addresses the unique challenges and solutions in securing healthcare information systems and protecting sensitive patient data from cyber threats.
8. Marketing Information Systems (MkIS): Involves the use of information systems to support marketing activities, including data analytics, customer relationship management, and market research.
9. Multi-functional Business Challenges: Encompasses the complex challenges faced by businesses, considering factors such as globalization, technology integration, and changing consumer expectations.
10. Operations Maritime and Supply Chain Production Impacts: Examines the impact of operations in maritime and supply chain industries, considering factors such as logistics, production efficiency, and sustainability.

In the contemporary world, these diverse topics collectively represent the dynamic and rapidly evolving landscape of technology, business, and cybersecurity. The auto industry's adoption of artificial intelligence signals a transformative shift towards autonomous vehicles and smart transportation solutions. Understanding consumer behavior in intelligent markets is crucial for businesses adapting to the digital era, where data-driven insights shape marketing strategies. Cyber intelligence is at the forefront of safeguarding digital assets, addressing the escalating threats in cyberspace. Diversity, equity, and inclusion have become integral components of organizational success, recognizing the value of diverse perspectives in driving innovation. The evolution of electronic vehicle technology mirrors the global push towards sustainable transportation solutions. Health care cybersecurity has become paramount in protecting sensitive patient data amidst the digitization of healthcare. Marketing information systems enable businesses to navigate the complex landscape of consumer data and market trends. Multi-functional business challenges encapsulate the multifaceted nature of contemporary enterprises, addressing issues from globalization to technological integration. Operations maritime and supply chain production impacts underscore the significance of efficient logistics and sustainable practices. Together, these topics paint a comprehensive picture of the challenges, innovations, and transformative forces shaping our world today.

The evolution of Cross-Sector Cyber Intelligent Markets has given rise to a specific target audience composed of a diverse range of stakeholders, each with distinct interests and needs. At the core of this audience are cybersecurity professionals and experts, including Chief Information Security Officers (CISOs), security analysts, and ethical hackers, who seek advanced threat intelligence solutions to bolster their organizations' cyber defenses. Additionally, executives and decision-makers in various industries, especially those in critical infrastructure sectors such as energy, healthcare, and finance, constitute another key segment. They are interested in investing in cyber intelligence to safeguard their operations from cyber threats and regulatory compliance risks. Government agencies and law enforcement entities are also crucial participants, aiming to enhance national security through cross-sector collaboration and intelligence sharing. Lastly, technology vendors and solution providers catering to the growing demands of this market are pivotal, as they develop innovative products and services to meet the evolving cybersecurity challenges across sectors. In essence, the target audience for Cross-Sector Cyber Intelligent Markets encompasses a multidisciplinary community striving to create a safer digital landscape through collaborative intelligence and innovative solutions. The evolution of Cross-Sector Cyber Intelligent Markets promises to bring about significant benefits for a wide range of stakeholders. Firstly, businesses across various industries will benefit from enhanced cybersecurity solutions, enabling them to better protect their digital assets, customer data, and critical operations. Chief Information Security Officers (CISOs) and IT professionals will find advanced threat intelligence tools and services that empower them to stay ahead of cyber threats. Government agencies and regulatory bodies stand to gain improved visibility into cyber risks across sectors, enabling more effective policy-making and regulatory enforcement. Ethical hackers and cybersecurity researchers will have access to richer data sources and collaborative platforms, facilitating the identification and mitigation of vulnerabilities. Additionally, consumers will experience increased confidence in digital services, knowing that their data and privacy are better safeguarded. Ultimately, the evolution of Cross-Sector Cyber Intelligent Markets has the potential to create a safer and more resilient digital ecosystem, benefiting society by reducing the impact of cyberattacks and bolstering overall cybersecurity posture.

(1) Critical Analysis on the Challenges of Product Distribution in Global Infrastructure and Value-Added Systems in Logistics and Supply Chain Management

This book chapter focuses on the critical analysis of challenges in product distribution within the global infrastructure and value-added systems in logistics and supply chain management. The book chapter involves a comprehensive examination of the complex issues and obstacles faced by businesses operating in a highly interconnected and dynamic environment are challenged by traverse regulatory frameworks, cultural nuances, and infrastructural differences. Coordinating these intricate networks demands a robust understanding of the local and international logistics systems.

(2) Marketing Information Systems (MkIS) Parts Shortage Challenges in the Aviation Industry: Foreign Military Sales (FMS) Legacy System in Cross-Sector Markets

The book chapter discusses the CH-47 D-model spare part issues within the Aviation Industry. Although, foreign military sales (FMS) part shortage challenges stem across multiple spectrums. The CH-47 legacy system aircraft is still used by some countries and organizations within industry. The researchers focus on ways in which obsolescence affects the global supply chain and the impacts of a lack of marketing information system (MkIS) infrastructure across multiple segments of the defense and aviation market.

(3) Leadership Learning and Leadership Coaching for Government Leaders in Cybersecurity, Artificial Intelligence, and Technology

The book chapter titled "Leadership Learning and Leadership Coaching for Government Leaders in Cybersecurity, Artificial Intelligence (AI), and Technology" demonstrate how shaping effective governance and decision-making amongst leaders is increasingly complex in today's digital landscape. In the realm of leadership theory in cybersecurity, leaders must continually enhance their understanding of evolving cyber threats, regulatory frameworks, and technological solutions. Leadership learning programs can provide insights into the latest trends, threat intelligence, and best practices, enabling government leaders to develop proactive strategies for safeguarding critical infrastructure and sensitive information.

(4) SCADA Systems and Threats to Critical Infrastructure

The book chapter titled "Supervisory Control and Data Acquisition (SCADA) Systems and Threats to Critical Infrastructure" play a crucial role in monitoring and controlling critical infrastructure such as power plants, water treatment facilities, and transportation systems. These systems are designed to collect and analyze data in real-time, allowing operators to make informed decisions and ensure the smooth operation of essential services. However, the increasing connectivity of SCADA systems to the internet and other networks has exposed them to various cybersecurity threats, posing significant risks to critical infrastructure. Cybercriminals may exploit vulnerabilities in the software or hardware components of SCADA systems to gain control over the infrastructure they monitor. Once inside, attackers can manipulate operational processes, disrupt services, or cause physical damage, leading to severe consequences for public safety and the economy. Another common threat to SCADA systems is malware and ransomware attacks. Malicious software can be designed to infiltrate and compromise SCADA networks, leading to data theft, system malfunctions, or even complete shutdowns.

(5) Addressing Childhood Obesity Through Technology Innovation

The book chapter addresses childhood obesity through technology innovation presenting both opportunities and challenges. The researchers focus on how technological advancements offer innovative solutions to encourage healthier lifestyles among children. Mobile apps, wearable devices, and interactive gaming platforms have the potential to make physical activity more engaging and enjoyable, fostering a habit of exercise from an early age. Additionally, smart devices can help monitor dietary habits, providing real-time feedback and personalized recommendations for healthier food choices. However, challenges arise in ensuring equitable access to these technologies, as socio-economic disparities may limit some children's ability to benefit from such innovations. Moreover, concerns about data privacy and security must be carefully addressed to protect the sensitive health information of young users. The risk of excessive screen time and sedentary behavior also poses a dilemma, as the very technologies designed to combat obesity could inadvertently contribute to a more sedentary lifestyle if not used mindfully. Striking a balance between leveraging technology for positive health outcomes and avoiding unintended consequences requires a comprehensive and thoughtful approach that involves collaboration among technology developers, healthcare professionals, educators, and policymakers.

(6) Barricades and Hindrances Concerning Women Managers in Healthcare Cybersecurity and Technology

The research involving barricades and hindrances facing women managers in healthcare cybersecurity and technology refer to the various challenges and obstacles that impede the professional advancement and representation of women in leadership roles within these sectors. Despite progress in promoting gender diversity, there remains a notable underrepresentation of women managers in the fields of healthcare cybersecurity and technology. Structural barriers such as gender bias, stereotyping, and unequal opportunities often hinder women's career progression. Discrimination, whether overt or subtle, can limit their access to leadership roles and stifle their contributions to decision-making processes. Addressing these barricades requires a concerted effort from organizations to foster inclusive cultures, promote diversity initiatives, and provide mentorship programs that support the professional development of women in healthcare cybersecurity and technology. By dismantling these barriers, organizations can unlock the full potential of their workforce and ensure that women have equal opportunities to excel and lead in these critical and rapidly evolving sectors.

(7) Healthcare Information Systems (HCIS) Customer Patient Advocacy: Cyber Health Deficiencies in the State of Washington

This chapter focuses Health Care Information Systems (HCIS) Customer Patient Advocacy in the State of Washington pertaining to the efforts and initiatives aimed at addressing cybersecurity deficiencies within health care information systems to ensure the protection and privacy of patient information. With the increasing reliance on digital technologies in healthcare, the need for robust cybersecurity measures has become paramount. Patient advocacy within HCIS involves advocating for the implementation of advanced cybersecurity protocols and technologies to safeguard sensitive health information from cyber threats. In the context of the State of Washington, acknowledging and rectifying cyber health deficiencies is critical for maintaining the integrity of health care information systems. This may involve advocating for improved encryption methods, regular security audits, and the adoption of best practices to mitigate vulnerabilities. Additionally, HCIS customer patient advocacy in Washington seeks to enhance public awareness about the importance of cybersecurity in healthcare and empower patients to actively engage in the protection of their own health information. By addressing cyber health deficiencies, the state can contribute to building a more secure and resilient healthcare information infrastructure, ensuring the confidentiality and trustworthiness of patient data in the digital era.

(8) Healthcare Technologies to Address Driving Under the Influence (DUI) of Marijuana

The chapter aimed at addressing Driving Under the Influence (DUI) of marijuana and healthcare innovative technological tools to assess impairment levels and promote road safety. Given the increasing legalization of marijuana in various jurisdictions, concerns about impaired driving have grown, necessitating technological solutions. Additionally, healthcare technologies may include mobile applications that offer educational resources, cognitive assessments, and impairment monitoring tools to help individuals make informed decisions about their fitness to drive after marijuana consumption. Telehealth platforms could play a role in providing counseling and support services for individuals struggling with substance abuse issues, contributing to prevention efforts. Integrating these technologies into broader public health initiatives and law enforcement strategies can enhance efforts to mitigate the risks associated with marijuana-impaired driving, promote safer roadways, and reduce the potential for accidents and injuries related to DUI incidents involving marijuana.

(9) Tele-Dermatology Through Telehealth and Healthcare Internet Technologies

In this study it pertains to tele-dermatology, facilitated by Telehealth and Healthcare Internet Technologies, representing a transformative approach to delivering dermatological care and services. This innovative application of telemedicine allows patients to remotely consult with dermatologists, providing timely access to expertise and diagnosis without the need for in-person visits. Through secure online platforms, patients can share images and descriptions of skin conditions, enabling dermatologists to assess and diagnose various dermatological issues remotely. Healthcare Internet Technologies play a crucial role in ensuring the seamless transmission of high-quality images and data while maintaining patient privacy and confidentiality. This approach enhances accessibility to dermatological care, particularly in underserved or remote areas where access to specialized healthcare may be limited. Tele-dermatology also promotes efficiency in the healthcare system by reducing wait times and minimizing the need for unnecessary in-person appointments. Overall, this integration of technology into dermatological care not only improves patient outcomes but also contributes to the optimization of healthcare resources, making quality skin health services more accessible and convenient for a broader population.

(10) Cyber Leadership Excellence: Bridging Knowledge Gaps, Maximizing Returns

This chapter focuses on cyber leadership excellence an adept management of cybersecurity initiatives with a focus on bridging knowledge gaps and maximizing returns. A cyber leader excels in understanding the dynamic and complex landscape of cybersecurity, identifying gaps in knowledge within their team, and implementing strategies to address those deficiencies. This includes staying abreast of the latest developments in cybersecurity threats, technologies, and regulations. By fostering a culture of continuous learning and professional development, a cyber leader ensures that the team is well-equipped to handle emerging challenges. Moreover, cyber leadership excellence extends to maximizing returns on cybersecurity investments, ensuring that resources are strategically allocated to achieve the highest impact. Ultimately, a cyber leader who excels in bridging knowledge gaps and maximizing returns contributes to a resilient and adaptive cybersecurity strategy that safeguards the organization against evolving cyber threats.

(11) Maximizing Cyber Intelligence and Security Team Capabilities Through DEI: The Hidden Benefits of Diversity as a Strategic Defense

This chapter emphasizes maximizing cyber intelligence and security team capabilities through Diversity, Equity, and Inclusion (DEI) represents the strategic recognition of the hidden benefits that diverse perspectives bring to the field of cybersecurity. DEI initiatives aim to foster a workforce that reflects a broad spectrum of backgrounds, experiences, and expertise. In the context of cyber intelligence and security, a diverse team can offer a range of insights, innovative approaches, and unique problem-solving strategies that a homogenous group may overlook. This strategic approach not only strengthens the organization's defense against cyber threats but also contributes to a more inclusive and supportive work environment. In essence, maximizing cyber intelligence and security team capabilities through DEI is a recognition that diversity is not just a matter of social responsibility but a critical component of a robust and resilient defense against evolving cyber challenges.

(12) Cybersecurity in Connected Autonomous Vehicles: Navigating the Future of Transportation

The connected autonomous vehicles is a paramount consideration as we navigate the future of transportation. The integration of advanced technologies into vehicles, such as sensors, communication systems, and autonomous driving capabilities, introduces new complexities and vulnerabilities. Ensuring the security of these connected systems is critical to safeguarding both passenger safety and the integrity of transportation infrastructure. Cyber threats, ranging from unauthorized access to data manipulation and remote control of vehicles, pose significant risks that demand comprehensive cybersecurity measures. Protective strategies may include robust encryption protocols, secure software development practices, and continuous monitoring of vehicle networks for anomalies. Collaborative efforts between automotive manufacturers, cybersecurity experts, and regulatory bodies are essential to establish industry standards and guidelines that prioritize the resilience of connected autonomous vehicles against cyber threats. As we forge ahead into a future of increasingly interconnected transportation, cybersecurity remains a fundamental pillar in shaping a safe, efficient, and reliable autonomous driving experience.

(13) Generations in Transition: Navigating in the Cybersecurity-Infused Job Market

The research is based on generations of transition significantly influencing the navigation of cybersecurity-infused job market as each generation brings unique perspectives, skills, and expectations to the evolving landscape. Younger generations, such as Millennials and Generation Z, often possess a natural affinity for technology and digital platforms, making them well-suited to the demands of the cybersecurity field. They may bring a fresh approach to problem-solving and a keen awareness of emerging cyber threats. On the other hand, older generations, like Generation X and Baby Boomers, contribute valuable experience, leadership skills, and a deeper understanding of the historical evolution of technology. Bridging the generational gap is crucial for effective collaboration, knowledge transfer, and building cohesive cybersecurity teams.

(14) Using Artificial Intelligence as a Public Health Surveillance Tool During Salmonella Outbreaks

The chapter focuses on the utilization of artificial intelligence (AI) as a public health surveillance tool during salmonella outbreaks presents both opportunities and challenges for society. AI can significantly enhance the efficiency and speed of identifying and tracking salmonella outbreaks, allowing for more prompt responses and interventions. AI algorithms can analyze vast amounts of data from various sources, including social media, healthcare records, and food distribution networks, to detect patterns and signals indicative of a potential outbreak. However, the challenge lies in ensuring the accuracy and reliability of AI-driven surveillance systems. False positives or misinterpretations of data could lead to unnecessary public alarm, resource misallocation, or unwarranted regulatory actions. Moreover, the ethical considerations surrounding data privacy and the responsible use of AI in public health surveillance require careful attention. Striking the right balance between leveraging the benefits of AI for timely outbreak detection and addressing the associated challenges is essential to maximize the positive impact of these technological advancements on societal well-being.

(15) Organizational Dynamics and Bias in Artificial Intelligence (AI) Recruitment Algorithms

This chapter highlights organizational dynamics in bias within artificial intelligence (AI) recruitment algorithms refer to the systemic influences and inherent biases that can emerge during the development and implementation of AI systems used in the hiring process. When crafting and training recruitment algorithms, organizations may inadvertently introduce biases based on historical hiring patterns, demographic trends, or subjective human decision-making processes. If historical data used to train these algorithms contains biases, such as gender or racial disparities, the AI system may perpetuate and even amplify these biases, leading to unfair and discriminatory outcomes.

(16) Influence of Cybersecurity Leadership Resiliency on Organizational Readiness: Exploring Intersectionality With Cyber Risk Liability Valuation

This chapter focuses influence of cybersecurity leadership resiliency on organizational readiness is a critical aspect that plays a central role in navigating the complex landscape of cyber threats. Leadership resiliency in the cybersecurity domain involves the ability of leaders to adapt, respond, and recover effectively in the face of evolving cyber risks and challenges. The valuation process becomes more nuanced, considering not only technical vulnerabilities but also the leadership's capability to lead proactive strategies, response plans, and foster a cybersecurity culture. A resilient cybersecurity leadership not only enhances the organization's overall readiness but also contributes to a more accurate and comprehensive cyber risk liability valuation, aligning strategic priorities with the evolving landscape of cyber threats and ensuring a robust defense against potential cyber risks.

(17) Supply Chain Management: The Role of Emotional Intelligence in Supply Chain Leadership

This chapter focuses supply chain management is a multifaceted discipline that relies heavily on effective leadership to navigate complexities, disruptions, and ensure the seamless flow of goods and services. The role of emotional intelligence in supply chain leadership is increasingly recognized as crucial for success. Emotional intelligence, encompassing self-awareness, empathy, and effective interpersonal skills, enables leaders to navigate the intricate web of relationships within the supply chain. Leaders with high emotional intelligence can foster collaboration, build strong relationships with suppliers and stakeholders, and effectively manage conflicts. Understanding and managing one's emotions and those of others become instrumental in decision-making, negotiation, and crisis management within the dynamic and often unpredictable realm of supply chain operations. Moreover, emotional intelligence contributes to building a resilient and adaptive supply chain, fostering a culture of innovation and continuous improvement. Recognizing the human element in supply chain processes, emotional intelligence in leadership enhances communication, trust, and overall team dynamics, ultimately optimizing supply chain performance and responsiveness to ever-changing market demands.

(18) Nuclear Power Organizations as Learning Organizations Around Cybersecurity, Public Health, Public Safety, and Critical Infrastructure Protection

The chapter emphasizes nuclear power organizations, as learning organizations, play a crucial role in addressing challenges related to cybersecurity, public health, public safety, and critical infrastructure protection. In the context of cybersecurity, these organizations recognize the ever-evolving nature of cyber threats and continuously strive to enhance their capabilities to safeguard sensitive information and systems. Learning from past incidents and staying abreast of technological advancements is integral to their approach. In essence, nuclear power organizations function as dynamic learning organizations that prioritize continuous improvement in cybersecurity, public health, public safety, and critical infrastructure protection. By fostering a culture of adaptability and knowledge-sharing, these organizations contribute to the overall safety, security, and sustainability of nuclear power operations.

(19) Coaching Cybersecurity Project Managers and Cybersecurity Engineers

In this book chapter, it explores coaching cybersecurity project managers and cybersecurity engineers offering a multitude of benefits within the dynamic and rapidly evolving landscape of cybersecurity. For project managers, coaching enhances leadership skills, strategic thinking, and risk management capabilities. It helps them navigate complex projects, ensuring effective communication, stakeholder engagement, and efficient resource allocation. It facilitates the acquisition of advanced cybersecurity knowledge, such as threat intelligence and ethical hacking, enabling engineers to stay ahead of cyber adversaries. Overall, coaching for cybersecurity project managers and engineers not only bolsters individual professional growth but also strengthens the overall cybersecurity posture of an organization by cultivating adaptive, skilled, and collaborative teams capable of navigating the complexities of the cybersecurity landscape.

(20) Why Historically Black Colleges and Universities (HBCUs) Should Employ New Approaches to Cybersecurity Faculty Development

In this book chapter it discusses Historically Black Colleges and Universities (HBCUs) adoption of new approaches to cybersecurity faculty development for several compelling reasons. In the rapidly evolving field of cybersecurity, staying abreast of emerging technologies, threats, and teaching methodologies is crucial. By implementing innovative faculty development programs, HBCUs can empower their instructors with the latest knowledge and skills, ensuring they provide high-quality and up-to-date education to students. Additionally, new approaches can foster diversity in the cybersecurity workforce by encouraging the recruitment and retention of underrepresented groups. Creating mentorship opportunities, promoting industry partnerships, and offering continuous professional development can enhance the effectiveness of cybersecurity faculty and contribute to the overall competitiveness of HBCU graduates in the rapidly changing cybersecurity landscape. By embracing new strategies, HBCUs can play a pivotal role in bridging the diversity gap in cybersecurity and equipping students with the skills needed for success in this critical field.

In conclusion, this comprehensive book encompasses a myriad of topics that collectively define the intricate tapestry of our contemporary world. The diverse array of subjects, ranging from logistics and supply inventory and production challenges reflects the multifaceted nature of today's global landscape. By delving into these domains, the book not only captures the essence of current technological and business trends but also contributes to advancing knowledge and understanding in each respective field. The critical discussions on cyber intelligence, DEI, Health Care Cybersecurity, and Telehealth underscore the pressing need for resilient solutions in the face of evolving challenges. The exploration of artificial intelligence in the auto industry, machine learning, and app development elucidates the transformative impact of technology on traditional sectors. Moreover, the focus on operations maritime, supply chain production impacts, and global infrastructure sheds light on the pivotal role of efficient logistics in our interconnected world. As we navigate the complexities of multi-functional business challenges, the book serves as a valuable resource for academics, practitioners, and professionals alike, offering insights that resonate with the ever-changing dynamics of our society. Ultimately, this compilation not only captures the pulse of our contemporary existence but also paves the way for future exploration and innovation in these vital spheres.

Eugene J. Lewis
Capitol Technology University, USA

Acknowledgment

The completion of this book, *Evolution of Cross-Sector Cyber Intelligent Markets*, has been a life-long dream to share in a collaborative effort with fellow academics, researchers, and practitioners alike. This opportunity would not have been possible without the support of the IGI Global Community. As I reflect on this work, I am deeply grateful to those who have played pivotal roles in bringing this project to fruition.

First and foremost, I extend my heartfelt gratitude to the dedicated researchers, industry experts, and professionals who generously shared their insights and expertise. Your contributions have enriched the content of this book and provided valuable perspectives on the intricate dynamics of cross-sector cyber intelligent markets.

I would like to express my sincere appreciation to the editorial team whose meticulous efforts have shaped the narrative into its final form. Your commitment to excellence and attention to detail have been instrumental in ensuring the quality of this work.

To the academic institutions, organizations, and industry partners that have supported and encouraged this endeavor, I extend my deepest thanks. Your collaboration has been instrumental in bridging the gap between theory and practice, enriching the content with real-world relevance. I am indebted to my colleagues and peers who have provided invaluable feedback and constructive criticism throughout the writing process. Your input has been instrumental in refining the ideas presented in this book.

My gratitude extends to my family and friends for their unwavering support and understanding during the demanding phases of this project. Your encouragement and belief in the importance of this work have been a constant source of motivation.

Lastly, I would like to acknowledge the readers who embark on this intellectual journey. Your interest in the evolution of cross-sector cyber intelligent markets is a testament to the significance of the topics covered in this book. I hope the insights shared within these pages contribute to a deeper understanding of the complexities and opportunities inherent in our hyper-macro and micro-level digital interconnected world.

This book stands as a collective effort, and I am profoundly thankful to everyone who has been a part of this endeavor. Your contributions have left an invaluable impression on this work, and I am honored to share it with the broader academic community.

Chapter 1
Critical Analysis on the Challenges of Product Distribution in Global Infrastructure and Value-Added Systems in Logistics and Supply Chain Management

Helen MacLennan
https://orcid.org/0000-0002-0795-5008
Lindsey Wilson College, USA

Eugene J. Lewis
https://orcid.org/0000-0002-2956-0760
Capitol Technology University, USA

Jessica Roman
Florida Institute of Technology, USA

ABSTRACT

In this critical analysis, the focus is on the nation's maritime port operations and international mode of transportation for Fixing America's Surface Transportation (FAST) Act of 2015 surrounding port distribution and logistics. The FAST Act requires the Bureau of Transportation and Statistics to report statistical data highlighting the challenges in global product distribution within infrastructure and value-added systems in logistics and supply chain management. The transportation costs estimate costs accounted for approximately 50% of the total logistics costs for businesses. Furthermore, fluctuations in fuel prices and increased demands for e-commerce shipping further emphasized the significance of cost challenges in global distribution. These disruptions underscored the complexity of managing a global network of suppliers, distributors, and customers. In this study, the researchers analyze 76% of companies still struggling with forecasting accuracy along with ongoing challenges in inventory management due to fluctuating consumer demand.

DOI: 10.4018/979-8-3693-1970-3.ch001

INTRODUCTION

The United States is one of the world's largest global markets with nearly $6 trillion in exports and imports of goods and services (BLS, 2022; USDOT, 2022). Recent growth in the United States international trade and transportation continued at a phenomenal pace following the shift in consumer spending due to the COVID-19 pandemic (Lee & Song, 2017; BLS, 2022; USDOT, 2022). The nation's ports have been burdened by workforce, equipment shortages, and container vessel backups. These challenges have created monumental domestic and global-supply chain disruptions (Loh et al., 2017; Inkinen, Helminen, & Saarikoski, 2019; Agrawal, Narain, & Ullah, 2019; BLS, 2022; USDOT, 2022). However, there has been several altered landscapes within the logistics and supply chain management industry that have major implications as ports handle unprecedented amounts of cargo (Agrawal, Narain, & Ullah, 2019; BLS, 2022; USDOT, 2022). According to BLS (2022; USDOT, 2022), total trade in goods amounted to more than $4.6 trillion (77 percent) in 2021. Moreover, statistics show an increase year after year of $835 billion annually amounting to 22 percent (BLS, 2022; USDOT, 2022). Additionally, US imports of goods growing by almost $506 billion (22 percent) while exporting of goods increased by more than $329 billion (23 percent) between 2020 and 2021 (BLS, 2022; USDOT, 2022; WEF, 2023). US and international trade modes for distribution of goods has moved by 41% percent in trade value in international markets (BLS, 2022; USDOT, 2022). In Figure 1 below it demonstrates the two-thirds of containerized freight still needing to go through the appropriate distribution channels (Perego, Perotti, & Mangiaracina, 2011). See Figure 1. Number of Containerized Freight-Cranes at the Top 25 Container Ports in FY2020.

Product distribution has anchored challenge in the United States, as $1.1 trillion (43 percent) of freight value is either containerized or non-containerized awaiting product distribution (Fabiano et al., 2010; USDOT, 2022). Around the world, transportation costs accounted for about 15% to 20% of the total product value in developing countries and up to 30% in some developing countries (Cazzanti, Davoli, & Millefiori, 2017; Lee & Song, 2017). According to Cazzanti, Davoli, & Millefiori, (2017) reported 71% of companies cited managing complexity in global supply chains as a significant challenge (Agrawal, Narain, & Ullah, 2019). Report indicated cost of carrying excess inventory in the United States was estimated at $471 billion, while the cost of stockouts was around $634 billion annually (Cazzanti, Davoli, & Millefiori, 2017).

Technology integration is increasingly important (Chen, Das, & Ivanov, 2019). According to digital supply chain investments implementing technologies (Cazzanti, Davoli, & Millefiori, 2017; Lee & Song, 2017). The study aims to identify and analyze barriers associated with port logistics for emerging economies. The results highlight non-supportive policy ecosystem, lack of research and development as the major barriers, and reducing the price interdependence of sustainability, environmental, and supply chains shifts (Jothimani, Shankar, & Yadav, 2016; Cazzanti, Davoli, & Millefiori, 2017; Lee & Song, 2017). The purchase preference toward sustainable products, pressuring supply chains to adopt more environmentally friendly practices (Jothimani, Shankar, & Yadav, 2016). The supplier vendor management maintaining strong relationships with suppliers and vendors was critical. The BLS and USDOT (2022) indicated that 62% of procurement leaders viewed supplier collaboration as a significant challenge.

Businesses now operate on a global scale (WEF, 2023). Organizations must impose a highly efficient product distribution network to meet the evolving demands of this complex global infrastructure, organizations must navigate a myriad of challenges in their value-added systems (Inkinen, Helminen, & Saarikoski, 2019). The critical analysis explores the key challenges faced in global product distribution, with a focus on infrastructure and value-added systems in logistics and supply chain management

(Agrawal, Narain, & Ullah, 2019). These encounters focus on a litany of ever-changing fears and challenges such as: transportation costs, global network complexity, infrastructure development, regulatory compliance, demand forecasting, and challenges in value-added systems (Lee & Song, 2017; Inkinen, Helminen, & Saarikoski, 2019).

Figure 1. Number of containerized freight-cranes at the top 25 container ports in FY2020 (BLS, 2022; USDOT, 2022)

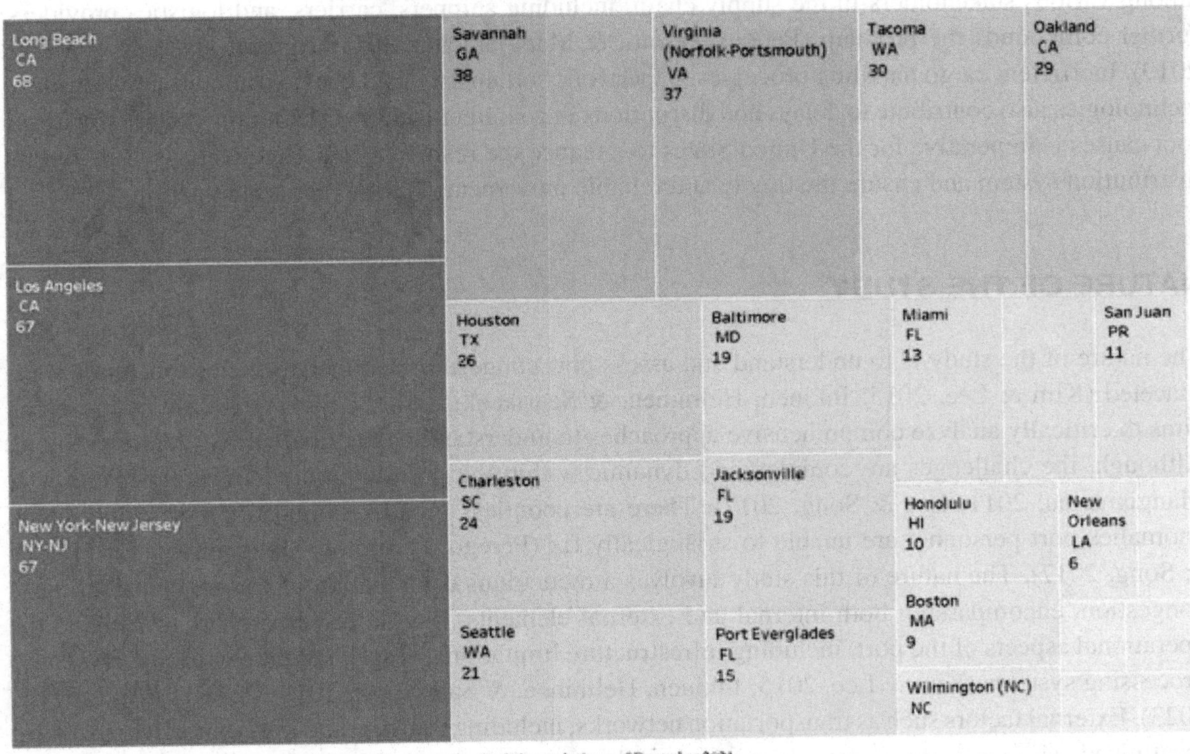

Number of Container Cranes at the Top 25 Container Ports: 2020

Long Beach CA 68	Savannah GA 38	Virginia (Norfolk-Portsmouth) VA 37	Tacoma WA 30	Oakland CA 29
Los Angeles CA 67	Houston TX 26	Baltimore MD 19	Miami FL 13	San Juan PR 11
New York-New Jersey NY-NJ 67	Charleston SC 24	Jacksonville FL 19	Honolulu HI 10	New Orleans LA 6
	Seattle WA 21	Port Everglades FL 15	Boston MA 9 / Wilmington (NC) NC	

SOURCE: U.S. Department of Transportation, Bureau of Transportation Statistics analysis, as of December 2021.

PROBLEM STATEMENT

The United States is currently grappling with a myriad of challenges in its freight distribution system, particularly at its ports, which play a pivotal role in facilitating the movement of goods across the country (Perego, Perotti, & Mangiaracina, 2011; Agrawal, Narain, & Ullah, 2019). The influx of containerized cargo has surged in recent years, placing immense strain on port infrastructure, causing delays, and hindering the smooth flow of goods through the supply chain (Perego, Perotti, & Mangiaracina, 2011; Agrawal, Narain, & Ullah, 2019). This bottleneck is exacerbated by an inadequate transportation network, outdated technology, and insufficient capacity to handle the growing volume of container traffic.

The problem statement for this critical analysis study is the following:

(1)   Why is there escalating congestion and inefficiencies witnessed at these crucial gateways of product distribution? What are the root causes of the influx of challenges surrounding goods and services?

Several root causes contribute to the lack of container freight distribution efficiency (WEF, 2023). First and foremost, aging port infrastructure struggles to cope with the modern demands of increased cargo volumes and larger vessels, leading to congestion and longer turnaround times (Perego, Perotti, & Mangiaracina, 2011; Agrawal, Narain, & Ullah, 2019). Additionally, the trucking and rail networks connecting ports to inland distribution points face their own set of challenges, including outdated routes, limited capacity, and insufficient investment in upgrades. The lack of synchronization and coordination among various stakeholders in the supply chain, including shippers, carriers, and logistics providers, further compounds the problem (Perego, Perotti, & Mangiaracina, 2011; Agrawal, Narain, & Ullah, 2019). Inefficient cargo handling processes, paperwork bottlenecks, and the slow adoption of advanced technologies also contribute to delays and disruptions in container freight distribution. Addressing these root causes is imperative for the United States to enhance the resilience and effectiveness of its freight distribution system and ensure the timely and reliable movement of goods across the nation.

NATURE OF THE STUDY

The nature of the study is to understand and assess port congestion and inefficiencies inherently multifaceted (Kim & Lee, 2015; Inkinen, Helminen, & Saarikoski, 2019; USDOT, 2022). The research aims to critically analyze comprehensive approaches to understanding a global infrastructure problem. Although, the challenges are complex and dynamic within the port environment (Perego, Perotti, & Mangiaracina, 2011; Lee & Song, 2017). There are countless broader implications of supply chain anomalies port personnel are unable to strategically fix (Perego, Perotti, & Mangiaracina, 2011; Lee & Song, 2017). The nature of this study involves a meticulous examination of factors contributing to congestion, encompassing both internal and external elements. Internally, researchers investigate the operational aspects of the port, including infrastructure limitations, vessel handling capacity, and cargo processing systems (Kim & Lee, 2015; Inkinen, Helminen, & Saarikoski, 2019; USDOT, 2022; WEF, 2023). External factors such as transportation networks, including trucking and rail connectivity, are also scrutinized. Moreover, the study delves into the role of various stakeholders, such as government agencies, port authorities, shipping companies, and logistics providers, to identify coordination challenges and potential points of collaboration (Kim & Lee, 2015; Inkinen, Helminen, & Saarikoski, 2019; USDOT, 2022). Data collection methods may require quantitative analyses of cargo throughput, turnaround times, and transportation efficiency, complemented by qualitative assessments through interviews and surveys with key industry participants (Kim & Lee, 2015; Inkinen, Helminen, & Saarikoski, 2019; USDOT, 2022). The goal of such a study is to provide a comprehensive understanding of the root causes of port congestion and inefficiencies, enabling the formulation of targeted strategies and policy recommendations to enhance the overall effectiveness of the freight distribution system.

GLOBAL SUPPLY CHAINS

Global supply chain fluctuations in fuel prices, coupled with the increased demands for e-commerce shipping, have significantly impacted the landscape of global distribution (Perego, Perotti, & Mangiaracina, 2011; Agrawal, Narain, & Ullah, 2019). The volatility in fuel prices, driven by geopolitical events and market dynamics, has introduced uncertainty and cost challenges into the supply chain (Agrawal, Narain, & Ullah, 2019; Inkinen, Helminen, & Saarikoski, 2019). Fluctuations in fuel costs affect transportation expenses, which are a dire component of global distribution (Perego, Perotti, & Mangiaracina, 2011; Lee & Song, 2017). Additionally, the surge in e-commerce has led to a higher demand for efficient shipping and delivery services (Lee & Song, 2017). Companies are striving to meet customer expectations for faster, more flexible, and cost-effective shipping options (Lee & Song, 2017; Inkinen, Helminen, & Saarikoski, 2019). As a result, supply chain stakeholders are increasingly investing in technologies and strategies to optimize their distribution networks, reduce transportation emissions, and enhance their ability to adapt to changing market conditions (Lee & Song, 2017; Agrawal, Narain, & Ullah, 2019). These shifts in global distribution reflect the ongoing evolution of the industry in response to these interconnected challenges (Inkinen, Helminen, & Saarikoski, 2019).

Product distribution within the global infrastructure and value-added systems in logistics and supply chain management remains a subject of ongoing scrutiny and debate within the industry for several reasons (Agrawal, Narain, & Ullah, 2019). First, the increasing complexity of global supply chains due to globalization, e-commerce, and consumer demands for fast and reliable delivery has raised questions about the efficiency and resilience of existing distribution networks (Agrawal, Narain, & Ullah, 2019). The need to balance cost-effectiveness with responsiveness has become a persistent challenge (Lee & Song, 2017; Inkinen, Helminen, & Saarikoski, 2019). Second, the advent of new technologies, such as advanced analytics, automation, and blockchain, has transformed the logistics landscape. These innovations offer opportunities for more transparent and efficient distribution systems, but their integration and potential disruption to existing processes raise questions about the best strategies and investments (Loh et al., 2017). Third, environmental and sustainability concerns playing an increasingly significant role (Jothimani, Shankar, & Yadav, 2016). Stakeholders scrutinizing distribution methods to reduce the carbon footprint and minimize waste, which has led to the exploration of alternative transportation modes and more environmentally friendly packaging solutions (Jothimani, Shankar, & Yadav, 2016; Lee & Song, 2017). Finally, geopolitical factors, trade disputes, and changing regulations contribute to the uncertainty in global product distribution. Companies must navigate these complexities to maintain secure and efficient supply chains while managing risks associated with potential disruptions (Loh et al., 2017; Agrawal, Narain, & Ullah, 2019). See Figure 2. 20-Foot Equivalent Units (TEUs) handled by the Top 10 US Container Ports.

Global supply chain fluctuations in fuel prices significantly impact the landscape of global distribution, especially in the context of increased demands for e-commerce shipping (Agrawal, Narain, & Ullah, 2019; WEF, 2023). As fuel prices fluctuate, they directly influence transportation costs, affecting the entire supply chain network (Lee & Song, 2017; Agrawal, Narain, & Ullah, 2019). Higher fuel costs can escalate shipping expenses, impacting the pricing of goods, transportation methods chosen, and overall operational costs for businesses involved in global distribution (Lee & Song, 2017). Additionally, the surge in e-commerce has intensified these effects, as more goods are being shipped across longer distances to meet the demands of online consumers worldwide (Jothimani, Shankar, & Yadav, 2016; Lee & Song, 2017; Agrawal, Narain, & Ullah, 2019). The combination of these factors has forced companies to reevaluate their logistical strategies (Jothimani, Shankar, & Yadav, 2016; Lee & Song, 2017; Agrawal, Narain, & Ullah, 2019). Companies must pursue more fuel-efficient transportation methods, optimizing routes, and rethinking inventory placement to mitigate the impact of rising fuel prices while maintaining timely and cost-effective global distribution services for e-commerce customers (Lee & Song, 2017).

Figure 2. 20-foot equivalent units (TEUs) handled by the top 10 US container ports

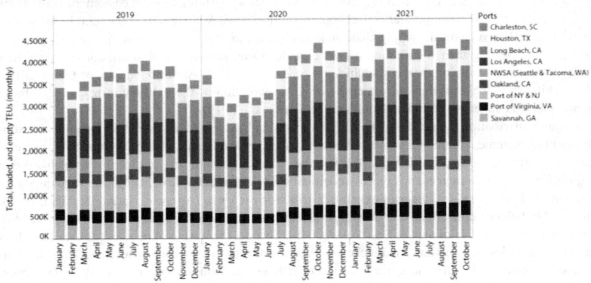

SOURCES: U.S. Department of Transportation, Bureau of Transportation Statistics analysis; based upon TEU volumes at the ports of Charleston, SC, http://scspa.com/about/statistics/; Houston, https://porthouston.com/; Long Beach, https://www.polb.com/; Los Angeles, https://www.por-toflosangeles.org/; Northwest Seaport Alliance (Seattle / Tacoma), https://www.nwseaportalliance.com/; Oakland, https://www.oaklandseaport.com/; New York/New Jersey, https://www.panynj.gov/; Port of Virginia, http://www.portofvirginia.com/; and Savannah, https://gaports.com/; as of December 2021.

REVIEW OF THE LITERATURE

Some common themes in recent literature on port disruptions might include the impact of events like the COVID-19 pandemic on global ports, strategies for mitigating port disruptions, the role of technology and automation in enhancing port resilience, and the implications of port disruptions for various industries and global trade (Loh et al., 2017; Agrawal, Narain, & Ullah, 2019). Within the field of supply chain and logistics dynamic research in this area is ongoing. The delay in product distribution at ports in the United States can be attributed to several root causes. Firstly, a major factor is the ongoing global supply chain disruptions, which have been exacerbated by the COVID-19 pandemic (Loh et al., 2017; Agrawal, Narain, & Ullah, 2019). These disruptions have led to congestion at ports due to a shortage of labor, social distancing protocols, and quarantine requirements, affecting the smooth flow of goods (Loh et al., 2017). Additionally, there has been a surge in demand for imported goods, driven by the growth of e-commerce and the need for supplies and equipment during the pandemic. This increased demand has overwhelmed the capacity of many ports, leading to backlogs and delays. Other contributing factors include the shortage of shipping containers, logistical challenges, and vessel congestion (Fabiano et al., 2010; Inkinen, Helminen, & Saarikoski, 2019). The imbalance in trade, with more goods arriving in the U.S. than leaving, has caused an imbalance in the availability of containers, which is crucial for the transportation of goods (Fabiano et al., 2010; Lee & Song, 2017). Ports have struggled with limited infrastructure and capacity constraints, making it difficult to handle the surge in incoming shipments. Severe weather events, such as hurricanes or winter storms, further disrupt port operations (WEF, 2023). Moreover, the shortage of truck drivers and distribution center labor in the U.S. has made it challenging to transport goods from the ports to their final destinations (Lee & Song, 2017). This bottleneck in the inland distribution process contributes to the delay in products reaching companies across the country. In short, product distribution problems in the United States at ports are primarily the result of global supply chain disruptions, increased demand for imported goods, container shortages, logistical challenges, and a lack of infrastructure investment (Fabiano et al., 2010; Loh et al., 2017; Inkinen, Helminen, & Saarikoski, 2019; Agrawal, Narain, & Ullah, 2019).

Such encounters have all converged, leading to significant delays in product distribution and creating a complex problem that require multifaceted solutions to resolve, such as:

(1) overwhelming surge in container cargo volume (Fabiano et al., 2010),
(2) exacerbated by a shortage of labor due to pandemic-related restrictions,
(3) leading to a backlog in processing and unloading containers at ports (Fabiano et al., 2010)
(4) In addition, a shortage of truck drivers and chassis,
(5) combined with warehouse and distribution center labor shortages.

These outcomes have further compounded the problem, hindering the swift movement of goods once they leave the ports (Inkinen, Helminen, & Saarikoski, 2019). The situation has been aggravated by the imbalanced flow of goods, with more imports arriving than exports leaving, creating congestion and further delays (Ye & Wang, 2023). Moreover, pandemic-related disruptions, including intermittent lockdowns, have disrupted the predictability and stability of global supply chains, affecting the timely distribution of goods (Loh et al., 2017; Agrawal, Narain, & Ullah, 2019). These factors have culminated in a perfect storm, with products piling up at ports, awaiting processing, and subsequently delaying the distribution to companies across the country. The interplay of these multifaceted issues has led to the current bottleneck in the distribution of products at ports, creating a major challenge for the timely receipt of goods by companies nationwide.

CRITICAL ANALYSIS AND METHODOLOGY FRAMEWORK

The critical analysis framework is a qualitative study utilizing multiple sources. The concepts further identified and explained theoretically providing the relevance of the evaluation through methodology (Douvan, 1997; Thompson, 2019; Nicola, 2023). The goal of product distribution in global infrastructure and value-added systems in logistics and supply chain management is to provide analysis of the following paradigms:

(1) Identifying and explaining the argument
(2) Accessing with clarity the argument
(3) Analyze the authenticity of the facts and figures.
(4) Identifying potential limitations
(5) Determine biases or conflicts of interests.
(6) Provide an existing argument about the value of another argument.

Critical analysis in this context provides a detailed evaluation of another perspective not yet realized. This study provides an interpretation of the work by assessing and studying multiple aspects of the challenge (Douvan, 1997; Thompson, 2019; Nicola, 2023). The significance of the subject matter is well established considering the complexities within the realm of Fixing America's Surface Transportation (FAST) Act of 2015, particularly focusing on Port Distribution and Logistics statistical data, reporting cycles of container distribution, research articles, periodic reviews, and commentary outlining systematic problems (Douvan, 1997; Thompson, 2019; Nicola, 2023). Traditional qualitative or qualitative research methods critically analyzes these ideals through research in the following areas for this topic:

(1) Research Articles,
(2) Reviews, and
(3) Commentaries.

Research Articles: Research articles are the cornerstone of academic publishing, representing original research in a specific field (Luo et al., 2023). These manuscripts undergo a rigorous peer-review process and are expected to adhere to the highest standards of scientific rigor. They typically present the outcomes of scientifically sound experiments, providing a substantial amount of new information that advances the knowledge base within the field (Douvan, 1997; Thompson, 2019; Nicola, 2023). Research articles should not only describe the research methods and findings but also place them within the context of existing literature, demonstrating an awareness of the most recent and relevant references. The critical analysis of this paper utilizes this key distinction of research articles to contribute novel insights, methodologies, or discoveries to the scientific community, thereby pushing the boundaries of knowledge in the field (Douvan, 1997; Thompson, 2019; Nicola, 2023).

Reviews: Additionally, the authors used review articles serving as a comprehensive analysis of existing literature within the field of study. Reviews play a pivotal role in synthesizing and critically evaluating the current body of knowledge, identifying gaps, controversies, and areas in need of further exploration (Luo et al., 2023). Reviews should be both critical and constructive, providing a nuanced understanding of the subject matter. While they do not present new, unpublished data, they do offer valuable recommendations for future research directions (Douvan, 1997; Thompson, 2019; Nicola, 2023). The significance of review articles lies in their ability to guide researchers toward fruitful areas of investigation and to offer a holistic perspective on the state of knowledge within a specific domain, fostering a deeper understanding of complex subjects in this topical area.

Commentary: Lastly, commentaries serve as a vital genre of academic literature, frequently employed in the humanities and social sciences, to offer provocative arguments and viewpoints aimed at challenging established perspectives and prompting readers to reevaluate specific issues (Luo et al., 2023). These articles are characterized by their ability to provoke thought and stimulate intellectual discourse within a given field. Commentaries often delve into topics that are of considerable societal or scholarly interest, addressing contemporary issues or long-standing debates. Authors of commentaries are encouraged to present original and persuasive arguments, providing readers with fresh insights and alternative viewpoints. The primary objective of a commentary is to encourage critical thinking and spark discussions among scholars, practitioners, and the broader audience, ultimately contributing to the ongoing development of ideas and the evolution of thought within a particular discipline.

These articles challenge established norms and paradigms, inviting readers to question prevailing assumptions and re-examining their own beliefs and perspectives (Luo et al., 2023). Commentaries often take on timely or contentious topics, providing a space for authors to express their informed opinions and propose novel solutions or approaches (Douvan, 1997; Thompson, 2019; Nicola, 2023). They are an essential medium for fostering intellectual diversity and stimulating healthy debate within academia. Furthermore, commentaries play a crucial role in addressing issues of societal relevance, offering fresh insights into complex challenges, and encouraging interdisciplinary dialogue. By presenting compelling arguments and thought-provoking perspectives, commentaries contribute to the ongoing refinement and enrichment of scholarly discourse, ensuring that academic fields remain dynamic and responsive to evolving realities and perspectives. These contents of these three topical areas provide the methodology for how the critical analysis was conducted and used throughout the research study.

THE CHALLENGES OF PRODUCT DISTRIBUTION IN GLOBAL INFRASTRUCTURE

The challenges of product distribution in global infrastructure are port capacity. Port capacitty is a measure of maximum distribution throughout port terminals handling over time (Kim & Lee, 2015; US-DOT, 2022). The communication channels of products and services on a global scale presents physical constraints (USDOT, 2022). The factors including terminals, length of berths, depth of access channels, and the amount and type of cargo handling equipment several significant challenges in the context of the global infrastructure (Kim & Lee, 2015; Inkinen, Helminen, & Saarikoski, 2019; USDOT, 2022). One major challenge is the complexity of international regulations and trade barriers, which vary from one country to another (USDOT, 2022). Port capacity influenced by operational factors not currently measured in this program, and economic factors, including labor availability and cost (USDOT, 2022). These factors typically proprietary, less likely to be available for public use. Port features that influence capacity are summarized (USDOT, 2022). Navigating customs, tariffs, and compliance with different regulatory standards can be a cumbersome and time-consuming process for companies engaged in global distribution (Ye & Wang, 2023). Furthermore, infrastructure disparities between regions can lead to uneven transportation and logistical capabilities (Lee & Song, 2017). While some areas boast modern and efficient transportation networks, others may lack adequate roads, ports, or distribution facilities, resulting in delays and added costs. Additionally, geopolitical factors and unexpected events, such as political instability or natural disasters, can disrupt global supply chains, affecting the timely movement of goods (Agrawal, Narain, & Ullah, 2019). Climate change and environmental concerns have also brought sustainability and carbon emissions reduction to the forefront of global distribution challenges (Jothimani, Shankar, & Yadav, 2016; Inkinen, Helminen, & Saarikoski, 2019). These factors necessitate increased focus on environmentally responsible transportation methods and practices (Jothimani, Shankar, & Yadav, 2016). Finally, the growth of e-commerce and changing consumer preferences require more agile distribution networks capable of accommodating shorter delivery times, which is a notable challenge in remote or less developed regions.

The Port Performance Freight Statistics Program (PPFSP) provides port performance measures for port capacity and throughout at the nation's top ports (Perego, Perotti, & Mangiaracina, 2011). The program shows change in distribution from extent of changes in cargo handled. According to BTS (2022), criteria for selecting capacity measurements features:

(1)   data availability
(2)   national consistency
(3)   timeliness
(4)   relevance and clarity
(5)   accuracy and transparency

In summary, product distribution in the context of global infrastructure is fraught with challenges ranging from regulatory complexities to infrastructure disparities, geopolitical risks, environmental concerns, and the evolving demands of modern consumers (Jothimani, Shankar, & Yadav, 2016; Inkinen, Helminen, & Saarikoski, 2019). Businesses involved in global distribution must adapt and innovate to overcome these challenges and remain competitive in the international marketplace (Inkinen, Helminen, & Saarikoski, 2019). Global product distribution in logistics and supply chain management is an intricate endeavor, impacted by a myriad of challenges within infrastructure and value-added systems (Agrawal, Narain, & Ullah, 2019; Inkinen, Helminen, & Saarikoski, 2019). To overcome these challenges, organizations must adopt a proactive and strategic approach (Inkinen, Helminen, & Saarikoski, 2019). They should invest in technology, promote sustainability, foster collaboration, and remain adaptable in the face of a rapidly changing global environment (Jothimani, Shankar, & Yadav, 2016; Chen, Das, & Ivanov, 2019). Continuous assessment, innovation, and optimization of supply chain operations are essential to thrive in the dynamic world of global logistics and supply chain management (Agrawal, Narain, & Ullah, 2019).

Product distribution within the framework of global infrastructure presents a myriad of challenges for businesses (Inkinen, Helminen, & Saarikoski, 2019). Firstly, the complexity of navigating diverse regulations, trade policies, and customs procedures across different countries creates substantial logistical hurdles. This involves understanding and adhering to varying compliance standards, which can lead to delays, added costs, and complexities in ensuring seamless product movement. Furthermore, the vast distances involved in global distribution led to increased transportation costs and longer lead times (Ye & Wang, 2023). These extensive logistics networks also face the challenge of effectively managing inventory across multiple locations, striking a balance between demand, storage costs, and transportation expenses. Geopolitical instability, natural disasters, or global events can disrupt supply chains, leading to unpredictability and risk (Ye & Wang, 2023). The rise of e-commerce and the demand for faster delivery further intensifies these challenges, necessitating a rethinking of traditional distribution models to meet consumer expectations for speed and efficiency while managing the associated costs (Inkinen, Helminen, & Saarikoski, 2019). Balancing cost-effectiveness, compliance, resilience, and the need for swift delivery poses ongoing challenges in the realm of global product distribution within the infrastructure (Inkinen, Helminen, & Saarikoski, 2019).

VALUE-ADDED SYSTEMS

Value-added systems in logistics and supply chain management play a crucial role in enhancing the efficiency and effectiveness of global infrastructure and product distribution (Agrawal, Narain, & Ullah, 2019). These systems are designed to create additional value for customers and stakeholders by optimizing various processes within the supply chain (Agrawal, Narain, & Ullah, 2019). Here's how value-added systems contribute to the success of global infrastructure and product distribution. See Table 1. Success of Global Infrastructure and Product Distribution.

In summary, value-added systems in logistics and supply chain management are essential for enhancing the performance and competitiveness of global infrastructure and product distribution. They contribute to improved efficiency, customization, risk mitigation, and cost reduction, enabling companies to thrive in the complex and dynamic world of global supply chains.

Table 1. Success of global infrastructure and product distribution

	Success of Global Infrastructure and Product Distribution	
1	Improved Efficiency	Value-added systems streamline various supply chain activities, such as inventory management, transportation, and order processing. By reducing waste, minimizing delays, and optimizing resource allocation, they help companies move products from manufacturing facilities to consumers more efficiently, ultimately reducing costs and lead times (WEF, 2023).
2	Enhanced Visibility	These systems provide real-time visibility into the entire supply chain, allowing businesses to monitor the movement of goods, track inventory levels, and respond promptly to disruptions. This visibility is essential in global distribution, where products often traverse long distances and encounter multiple touchpoints (Loh et al., 2017; Agrawal, Narain, & Ullah, 2019).
3	Customization and Personalization	Value-added systems enable companies to tailor their products and services to the specific needs and preferences of customers. This level of customization is increasingly important in global markets, where consumer demands can vary significantly from one region to another (WEF, 2023).
4	Risk Mitigation:	With global supply chains susceptible to various risks, including geopolitical factors, natural disasters, and economic fluctuations, value-added systems help companies assess and mitigate these risks. By diversifying sourcing, optimizing inventory, and having contingency plans in place, organizations can better manage uncertainty 9 Agrawal, Narain, & Ullah, 2019).
5	Cost Reduction	These systems help identify opportunities for cost reduction through process optimization, demand forecasting, and transportation management. By minimizing expenses, companies can offer competitive pricing and still maintain healthy profit margins (WEF, 2023).
6	Regulatory Compliance	Global distribution often involves navigating complex international regulations and trade restrictions. Value-added systems can assist in ensuring compliance with these regulations, reducing the risk of costly penalties and delays (WEF, 2023).
7	Data-Driven Decision-Making	Value-added systems collect and analyze vast amounts of data, enabling companies to make informed decisions. This data-driven approach is especially valuable in a global context, where market conditions and consumer behavior can vary widely (WEF, 2023).
8	Sustainability	Sustainable practices are becoming increasingly important in global supply chain management. Value-added systems can help companies reduce their carbon footprint by optimizing transportation routes, minimizing waste, and making environmentally responsible sourcing decisions (Jothimani, Shankar, & Yadav, 2016).
9	Competitive Advantage	In a global marketplace, companies that leverage value-added systems gain a competitive edge. They can respond faster to changing market dynamics, offer better customer experiences, and outperform competitors in terms of cost-efficiency and product quality.

PORT LOGISTICS

Globalization prompted a massive demand for transporting chemicals, foods, and commodities from one country to another (UNCTAD, 2016; Sarkar & Shankar, 2021). The 80% of the goods involved in global trade shifted through sea routes (UNCTAD, 2016; Pacific Merchant Shipping Association, 2021). Port logistics is the term used to describe logistics distribution services based at the port where goods arrive (UNCTAD, 2016; Maldonado et al., 2021). Port logistics consist of a wide range of operations like cargo handling, loading/unloading, custom paperwork, and port security (Maldonado et al., 2021; Sarkar & Shankar, 2021; Pacific Merchant Shipping Association, 2021). Some insights into the challenges that were prevalent at that time, and you may find more recent data by consulting industry reports and reputable sources (Inkinen, Helminen, & Saarikoski, 2019). See Table 2. Insights into the Challenges of Port Logistics.

The integration of decision making to optimal solutions require organizations to evaluate port logistic hubs (Dragovic, Chen, & Papadimitriou, 2023; Wang & Wu, 2023). In summary, a combination of simulation and analytical solutions is used to integrate handling processes on the quay and yard areas with transfer of container inventory management (Dragovic, Chen, & Papadimitriou, 2023; Wang & Wu, 2023). Shipping line deployment of ship capacity, improve economic efficiencies, expand market share, user clear cleaner fuels, and assess potential impacts of the macro-environment within port operations (Dragovic, Chen, & Papadimitriou, 2023).

Table 2. Insights into the challenges of port logistics

		Insights into the Challenges of Port Logistics
1	Transportation Costs	High transportation costs were a significant challenge in global product distribution (WEF, 2023).
2	Infrastructure Development	Infrastructure disparities between regions and countries persisted as a challenge. The World Economic Forum's Global Competitiveness Report 2019 noted that infrastructure quality varies significantly worldwide, with some countries having more developed infrastructure than others (WEF, 2023).
3	Regulatory Compliance	Regulatory changes and trade disruptions were common in global supply chains. Trade barriers, tariffs, and sanctions were dynamic issues. For instance, the United Nations Conference on Trade and Development (UNCTAD) reported in 2020 that global non-tariff measures continued to rise, affecting trade flows (Loh et al., 2017).
4	Inventory Management	Inventory management challenges included overstocking and understocking (Inkinen, Helminen, & Saarikoski, 2019)

ORGANIZATIONAL GOALS

Organizational goals in product orientation, implementation, and distribution within the logistics and supply chain management (SCM) framework are intrinsically linked to achieving efficiency, cost-effectiveness, and customer satisfaction. The ports of Los Angeles and Long Beach, California specifically must coordinate with the local Vessel Traffic Control System implemented a queuing system to reduce congestion and emissions at the ports (BLS, 2020; USDOT, 2022). In the product orientation phase, the primary goal is to align the ports strategy with product design, features, and quality with customer demands and market trends (Ye & Want, 2023). This means understanding consumer preferences and needs to create products that are desirable and competitive. But ensuring port operators, that containerships can be proper communication flow to disembark cargo to its respective areas (Fabiano et al., 2010). Otherwise, containerships are forced to be at sea 50 to 150 miles away from port to prevent congestion (Fabiano et al., 2010; BLS, 2022; USDOT, 2022). In the implementation phase, the focus shifts to optimizing production, quality control, and inventory management, with the goal of producing products at a reasonable cost and in a timely manner. Efficiency and productivity are key objectives here.

Finally, in the distribution phase, the primary goal is to ensure that products reach customers on time and in the right condition. This entails establishing an efficient network of transportation, warehousing, and distribution channels. Key objectives include minimizing lead times, reducing shipping costs, and providing accurate order fulfillment. Overall, the overarching goal of product orientation, implementation, and distribution within the SCM framework is to create a streamlined, customer-centric, and cost-effective process that delivers high-quality products to the right place at the right time, ultimately enhancing customer satisfaction and driving organizational success. See Table 3. SCM Framework in High-Quality Products

Table 3. SCM framework in high-quality products

	Supply Chain Management (SCM) Framework in High-Quality Products	
1	Inventory Management	Managing inventory across the supply chain is a delicate balancing act. Overstocking leads to higher holding costs, while understocking can result in stockouts, lost sales, and dissatisfied customers (WEF, 2023).
2	Demand Forecasting	Accurate demand forecasting is crucial for efficient supply chain management. Unpredictable shifts in consumer demand, influenced by factors like trends, seasonality, and economic conditions, make forecasting a challenging task (WEF, 2023).
3	Technology Integration	Integrating and maintaining advanced technologies, such as IoT, AI, and blockchain, into value-added systems can be complex and costly. Compatibility issues, cybersecurity threats, and the need for skilled personnel add to the challenge (Chen, Das, & Ivanov, 2019).
4	Sustainability and Environmental Concerns	Customers and regulatory bodies are increasingly concerned about the environmental impact of supply chain operations. Implementing sustainable practices, such as reducing emissions and minimizing waste, requires careful planning and investment (Jothimani, Shankar, & Yadav, 2016).
5	Supplier and Vendor Management	Collaborating effectively with suppliers and vendors is crucial. Ensuring quality, reliability, and adherence to ethical and social responsibility standards can be a constant challenge, especially when dealing with a diverse global network.

RECOMMENDATIONS FOR FUTURE INVESTIGATIONS

Port operations recommendations to enhance efficiency and effectiveness include investments in advanced technology and automation for cargo handling, improved infrastructure, and equipment maintenance to reduce downtime, and optimizing labor and staffing levels to match the fluctuating demands (Chen, Das, & Ivanov, 2019). Port authorities should also prioritize sustainability by adopting eco-friendly practices and reducing emissions to meet environmental standards (Jothimani, Shankar, & Yadav, 2016). Enhancing security measures is crucial to safeguard against potential threats and ensure smooth operations. Collaboration and coordination among various stakeholders, such as customs, logistics providers, and shipping lines, can further streamline processes at the port.

In terms of supplier and vendor management on a global scale, companies should establish clear and transparent communication channels to foster strong relationships with suppliers (Ye & Fang, 2023). A robust vendor evaluation system, considering factors like quality, reliability, and compliance, should be implemented. Diversifying sources of supply and reducing dependence on a single vendor or region is advisable to mitigate risks. Continuous monitoring of supplier performance and compliance with regulations, especially in international trade, is vital. Implementing contingency plans and redundancy measures to address potential disruptions in the supply chain is essential for risk management (Loh et al., 2017). In a global context, understanding cultural differences and international regulations is crucial, as well as staying informed about global economic and political trends that could impact the supplier landscape.

Table 4. Key steps for possible action contributions and strategic insights into future investigations

Key Steps for Possible Action Contributions and Strategic Insights Into Future Investigations	
Investment in Infrastructure	Advocate for increased funding and investment in port infrastructure to accommodate growing cargo volumes and larger vessels.
	Prioritize projects that enhance port capacity, dredging capabilities, and terminal efficiency to alleviate congestion.
Modernization of Transportation Networks	Support the modernization and expansion of trucking and rail networks to improve connectivity between ports and inland distribution points.
	Promote the integration of advanced technologies, such as GPS tracking and smart logistics systems, to optimize transportation routes and enhance overall efficiency.
Collaborative Stakeholders	Encourage collaboration among key stakeholders, including port authorities, government agencies, shipping companies, and logistics providers, to streamline coordination and information sharing.
	Establish task forces or working groups to address specific issues and foster a collective approach to problem-solving.
Regulatory Reforms	Advocate for regulatory reforms that promote streamlined processes, reduce paperwork bottlenecks, and facilitate smoother cargo handling.
	Explore innovative regulatory approaches, such as pilot programs for new technologies, to improve efficiency without compromising safety and security.
Data-Driven Decision-Making	Emphasize the importance of data-driven decision-making by promoting the collection and analysis of key performance indicators related to port operations and freight distribution.
	Develop a comprehensive data-sharing platform to enhance visibility and enable stakeholders to make informed decisions.
Workforce Development	Invest in workforce development programs to ensure that the industry has the skilled personnel needed to operate and maintain modernized infrastructure and technology.
	Collaborate with educational institutions and industry partners to address the skills gap in the transportation and logistics sector.
Resilience Planning	Develop and implement resilience plans to mitigate the impact of disruptions, such as natural disasters or unforeseen events, on port operations and the supply chain.

CONCLUSION

In conclusion, the study focuses on maritime port operations and international transportation aligning with Fixing America's Surface Transportation (FAST) Act. However, to improve current regulatory factors global infrastructure plays a key role in addressing the escalating congestion and inefficiencies at crucial gateways for product distribution, several actionable contributions, and strategic insights can be considered. Global product distribution in logistics and supply chain management is an intricate endeavor, impacted by a myriad of challenges within infrastructure and value-added systems (Inkinen, Helminen, & Saarikoski, 2019). The growing number of TEU handled may result in more container-ships waiting to dock and prolonged vessel turn times especially at ports such Los Angeles and Long Beach, California which account for nearly 34% of United States imports (BLS, 2022; USDOT, 2022). According to (BLS, 2022; USDOT, 2022), 90 containerships wait at port to dock across the country the number of ships and days vary at selected ports (Fabiano et al., 2010). To overcome these challenges, organizations must adopt a proactive and strategic approach (Inkinen, Helminen, & Saarikoski, 2019). They should invest in technology, promote sustainability, foster collaboration, and remain adaptable in the face of a rapidly changing global environment (Jothimani, Shankar, & Yadav, 2016; Chen, Das, & Ivanov, 2019). Continuous assessment, innovation, and optimization of supply chain operations are essential to thrive in the dynamic world of global logistics and supply chain management. See Table 4. Key Steps for possible Action Contributions and Strategic Insights into Future Investigations.

These components in the broader landscape of logistics and supply chain management function provide innate vantage points of infrastructure needs. The capacity of transportation costs accounting for approximately 50% of total logistics costs resonates with the practical concerns faced by businesses and adds a layer of economic context to the discussion (USDOT, 2022; WEF, 2023). Moreover, through the intricate web of challenges posed by fuel price fluctuations and the surging demands of e-commerce, thereby showcasing a keen understanding of the contemporary dynamics affecting global distribution. The container vessel cargo has been a primary focal point of port challenges in recent years (Fabiano et al., 2010; Inkinen, Helminen, & Saarikoski, 2019). The dilemmas comprise mostly of consumer goods imported into the United States. The following figures show the nation's Top 10 Container Ports handled relatively low numbers of monthly twenty-foot equivalent units (TEU) in the first half of 2020 (BLS, 2020; USDOT, 2022). Meanwhile, dropping to a lower point of 2.8 million TEU by third quarter of the same year (BLS, 2020; USDOT, 2022). Ports continue to handle an unprecedented amount of cargo with the challenge of product distribution. The global infrastructure and value-added systems in logistics and supply chain management are multifaceted, encompassing issues of complexity, technological advancement, sustainability, and geopolitical considerations. Addressing these challenges require continuous adaptation and innovation in the ever-evolving world of logistics and supply chain management.

REFERENCES

Agrawal, P., Narain, R., & Ullah, I. (2019). Analysis of barriers in implementation of digital transformation of supply chain using interpretive structural modeling approach. *Journal of Modelling in Management*, *15*(1), 297–317. doi:10.1108/JM2-03-2019-0066

Bureau of Transportation Statistics. (2022). *US Ports work through daunting Challenges to Deliver the Goods*. https://www.bts.gov/data-spotlight/us-ports-work-through-daunting-challenges-deliver-goods

Cazzanti, L., Davoli, A., & Millefiori, L. M. (2017). Automated port traffic statistics: from raw data to visualization. *Science and Technology Organization Center for Maritime Research and Experimentation*. *CMRE-PR-2017-010. IEEE International Conference on Big Data*, 1-6.

Chen, H. Y., Das, A., & Ivanov, D. (2019). Building resilience and managing post-disruption supply chain recovery: Lessons from the information and communication technology industry. *Ocean and Coastal Management*, *165*, 244–257. doi:10.1016/j.ocecoaman.2018.08.031

Douvan, E. (1997). Erik Erikson: Critical Times, Critical Theory. *Child Psychiatry and Human Development*, *28*(1), 15–21. doi:10.1023/A:1025188901554 PMID:9256525

Dragović, B., Chen, G., & Papadimitriou, S. (2023). Editorial: The time factor in maritime and port logistics. *Maritime Business Review*, *8*(4), 298–300. doi:10.1108/MABR-11-2023-092

Fabiano, B., Curro, F., Reverbreri, A. P., & Pastorino, R. (2010). Port safety and the container revolution: A statistical study on human factor and occupational accidents over the long period. *Safety Science*, *48*(8), 980–990. doi:10.1016/j.ssci.2009.08.007

Inkinen, T., Helminen, R., & Saarikoski, J. (2019). Port digitalization with Open Data: Challenges, Opportunities, and Integrations. *Journal of Open Innovation*, *5*(30), 1–16. doi:10.3390/joitmc5020030

Jothimani, D., Shankar, R., & Yadav, S. S. (2016). Modeling hierarchical relationships among enablers of supply chain coordination in flexible environment. In *Managing flexibility* (pp. 171–186). Springer. doi:10.1007/978-81-322-2380-1_13

Kim, K. H., & Lee, H. (2015). Container terminal operation: current trends and future challenges. In *Handbook of Ocean Container Transport Logistics* (pp. 43–73). Springer. doi:10.1007/978-3-319-11891-8_2

Lee, C. Y., & Song, D. P. (2017). Ocean container transport in global supply chains: Overview and research opportunities. *Transportation Research Part B: Methodological*, *95*, 442–474. doi:10.1016/j.trb.2016.05.001

Loh, H. S., Zhou, Q., Thai, V. V., Wong, Y. D., & Yuen, K. F. (2017). Fuzzy comprehensive evaluation of port-centric supply chain disruption threats. *Ocean and Coastal Management*, *148*, 53–62. doi:10.1016/j.ocecoaman.2017.07.017

Luo, G., Serrão, C., Liang, D., & Zhou, Y. (2023). A Relevance-Based Technology–Organisation–Environment Model of Critical Success Factors for Digital Procurement Adoption in Chinese Construction Companies. *Sustainability (Basel)*, *15*(16), 12260. doi:10.3390/su151612260

Maldonado, S., Gonzalez-Ramirez, R. G., Quijada, F., & Ramirez-Nafarrate, A. (2019). Analytics meets port logistics: A decision support system for container stacking operations. *Decision Support Systems*, *121*, 84–93. doi:10.1016/j.dss.2019.04.006

Nicola, F. G. (2023). Failures of comparability in global governance: Exploring the practical dimension of the redress of law. *European Law Open*, *2*(1), 173–183. doi:10.1017/elo.2023.20

Pacific Merchant Shipping Association. (2021). *New Queuing Process for Container Vessels Bound for Ports of LA/Long Beach to Improve Safety and Air Quality Off California Coast*. https://www.pmsaship.com/wp-content/uploads/2021/11/Container-Vessel-Queuing-Release-FINAL.pdf

Perego, A., Perotti, S., & Mangiaracina, R. (2011). ICT for logistics and freight transportation: A literature review and research agenda. *International Journal of Physical Distribution & Logistics Management*, *41*(15), 457–483. doi:10.1108/09600031111138826

Sarkar, B.D. & Shankar, R. (2021). Understanding the barriers of port logistics for effective operation in the Industry 4.0 era: Data-driven decision making. *International Journal of Information Management Data Insights, 1.*

Thompson, M. J. (2019). Critical theory in critical times: Transforming the global political and economic order. *Contemporary Political Theory, 18*(S4, Suppl.4), 284–289. doi:10.1057/s41296-018-0229-0

UNCTAD. (2016). *Review of maritime transport 2016.* Available at: https://unctad.org/transportnews

U.S. Department of Transportation. (2022a). *Bureau of Transportation Statistics analysis of U.S. Census Bureau, U.S. Import & Export Merchandise Trade Statistics.* https://www.census.gov/foreign-trade/data/index.html

U.S. Department of Transportation. (2022b). *Bureau of Transportation Statistics, Freight Facts & Figures, available at Freight Facts and Figures.* https://data.bts.gov/stories/s/45xw-qksz

U.S. Department of Transportation. (2022c). *Bureau of Transportation Statistics analysis of U.S. Department of Commerce, Census Bureau, USA Trade Online.* https://www.census.gov/foreign-trade/data/index.html

U.S. Department of Transportation. (2022d). *Bureau of Transportation Statistics; analysis based on data sources cited in Port Profiles, available at Port Performance Freight Statistics Program.* Bureau of Transportation Statistics. https://explore.dot.gov/views/FreightIndicators/ContainershipsAwaiting?%3Aembed_code_version=3&%3Aembed=y&%3AloadOrderID=8&%3Adisplay_spinner=no&%3AshowAppBanner=false&%3Adisplay_count=n&%3AshowVizHome=n&%3Aorigin=viz_share_link#1

U.S. Department of Transportation (USDOT). (2022). *Bureau of Transportation Statistics, based upon USDOT, Maritime Administration, Office of Policy & Plans / U.S. Customs & Border Protection, Vessel Monitoring System, special tabulation.* Author.

Wang, W., & Wu, Q. (2023). Research on the Coordinated Development of Coastal Port Logistics and International Trade: Based on Six Coastal Provinces of China. *Sustainability (Basel), 15*(1), 121. doi:10.3390/su15010121

World Economic Forum. (2023). *Annual Report 2022-2023.* https://www3.weforum.org/docs/WEF_Annual_Report_2022-23.pdf

Ye, L., & Fang, X. (2023). Analysis on Integration of Logistics Trade Resources and Global Competition of Ports Along the Belt and Road Based on Fuzzy Algorithm. *Revista Ibérica De Sistemas e Tecnologias De Informação,* 526-536. https://www.proquest.com/scholarly-journals/analysis-on-integration-logistics-trade-resources/docview/2828438621/se-2

Chapter 2
Marketing Information Systems (MkIS) Parts Shortage Challenges in the Aviation Industry:
Foreign Military Sales (FMS) Legacy System in Cross-Sector Markets

Eugene J. Lewis
https://orcid.org/0000-0002-2956-0760
Capitol Technology University, USA

Danica F. Abejon
Athens State University, USA

ABSTRACT

The qualitative focus group research utilizes the theory of constraints and supply chain management (SCM) framework to review over 179 emails discoveries in obsolescence issues surrounding the Chinook/Cargo Helicopter-47 Delta-Model (CH-47 D-Model) helicopter. In the early part of 2010, there were 66 vendors who manufactured long-lead D-Model parts; now, only 13 remain. As foreign military sale (FMS) customers upgrade to more advanced systems, a critical challenge focuses on customer-centric, predictive business models, and smart automation to understand the value of military and defense operations for legacy systems. The researchers utilized participant data from focus group discussions, emails, and written correspondence to develop a comprehensive spotlight into the Chinook/Cargo community within FMS. The purpose is to determine if there is value in servicing country needs for CH-47 D-Model parts. Shortages of critical components and a lack of access to authentic, certified spare parts affect the safety and performance of the helicopters.

DOI: 10.4018/979-8-3693-1970-3.ch002

INTRODUCTION

The part shortage challenges on CH-47 D-Model aircraft can be primarily attributed to their age and the evolving nature of the aviation industry (Bachman, Goldsmith, & Nix, 2023). These helicopters have been in service for several decades, and many original manufacturers of specific components have ceased production or gone out of business over time (Marchet et al., 2018). It is important to note, research in this area was very challenging as much of the references focus on military documents that are not accessible to the public. As a result, locating authentic, certified spare parts that meet the stringent quality and safety standards required for military aircraft can be increasingly difficult (Pedrosa, Näslund, & Jasmand, 2012; Abdul, Kharoufeh, & Maillart, 2019). The complexity of the aircraft's systems and the need for specialized components further exacerbate these trials. Additionally, the military's stringent procurement processes and budget constraints can hinder the timely acquisition of replacement parts, as they often involve a rigorous certification and qualification procedure (Russo, Masorgo, & Gligor, 2022; Bachman, Goldsmith, & Nix, 2023). This combination of factors creates a significant obstacle to ensuring the availability of necessary components for the CH-47 D-Model helicopters, potentially affecting their operational readiness and safety.

The issue of MkIS from vendors for parts shortages on CH-47 D-Model helicopters can be attributed to several factors. First and foremost, the CH-47 D-Model helicopters are a specialized and relatively older aircraft, which may not be as widely used as more militaries modernize their aircraft. This results in a limited market for spare parts, making it less economically attractive for vendors to invest in comprehensive marketing information systems (MkIS) for these helicopters (Öner, Scheller-Wolf, & van Houtum, 2013; Abdul, Kharoufeh, & Maillart, 2019). Additionally, the procurement process in the defense industry is often complex and subject to rigorous regulations. Vendors may encounter bureaucratic obstacles and lengthy approval processes when trying to market their products and services for military aircraft (Bachman, Goldsmith, & Nix, 2023). This can discourage vendors from actively promoting parts for the CH-47 D-Model helicopters. Furthermore, the military's stringent quality and safety standards mean vendors must meet specific requirements to provide parts for these helicopters. Ensuring compliance with these standards can be costly and time-consuming, further discouraging vendors from investing in marketing efforts for these aircraft.

Finally, these essential components provide mission-capable accessories and resources that support the transporting of troops, equipment, and supplies for operations. As such, maintaining the operational readiness for this aircraft has become significantly difficult due to new innovations and upgrades to this legacy system. The qualitative study will discuss some of the economic challenges for customers. Moreover, address the budget constraints faced by military agencies limiting their ability to procure spare parts, leading to a reduced demand for such products (Abdul, Kharoufeh, & Maillart, 2019; Arts, Basten, & Van Houtum, 2016). Consequently, vendors might find it more lucrative to focus on other, more widely used aircraft systems, diverting their marketing resources away from the CH-47 D-Model helicopters (Öner, Scheller-Wolf, & van Houtum, 2013; Morgan et al., 2018). In summary, the issue of marketing information systems (MkIS) from vendors for parts shortages on CH-47 D-Model helicopters can be attributed to a combination of factors, including the limited market, complex procurement processes, stringent quality standards, and budget constraints within the defense sector, which collectively make it less appealing for vendors to invest in marketing efforts for these specific aircraft (Pedrosa, Näslund, & Jasmand, 2012).

However, the aircraft is still valuable today in industry as several customers still utilize this legacy system. MkIS challenges consist of the availability of vendors to provide spare parts for these aging aircraft continues to be a major challenge (Abdul, Kharoufeh, & Maillart, 2019; Aggarwal et al., 2023). One significant aspect of this issue is the advanced age of the CH-47 D-Model helicopters with a historical timeline consisting of several decades, and many of the original manufacturers and suppliers having gone out of business or phased out of production for specific parts (Marchet et al., 2018). In the next section, marketing information systems (MkIS) further defined, implemented, and explained.

MARKETING INFORMATION SYSTEMS (MkIS)

What is Marketing Information Systems (MkIS)? MkIS can provide essential logistical supply chain support for cross-sector markets in several ways (Parrish & Blazer, 2008; Rosalinda & Ali, 2023; Aho & Cirillo, 2023; Goldsby et al., 2023; Aggarwal et al., 2023). Marketing information systems is a continuing and interacting structure of people, equipment, and processes for gathering, sorting, analyzing, evaluating, and distributing products and services (Öner, Scheller-Wolf, & van Houtum, 2013; Rosalinda & Ali, 2023). The meticulous planning and extensive research for developing marketing strategies is vital in collecting relevant data to ensure data is processed, organized, evaluated, and communicated appropriately (Rosalinda & Ali, 2023). The application of MkIS can be explained in the context of the CH-47 D-Model aircraft for the following purpose.

(1) MkIS offers real-time visibility and tracking capabilities, allowing organizations to monitor the movement of goods and components across various sectors and regions (Farhan, Krejci, & Cantor, 2023; Goldsby et al., 2023; Aggarwal et al., 2023). For organizations gaining visibility the concept is vital for ensuring that products reach their intended destinations promptly and efficiently (Rahman et al., 2022; MacDonald & Neeley, 2022).
(2) Additionally, MkIS can optimize inventory management by helping organizations maintain adequate stock levels and anticipate fluctuations in demand, thus reducing the risk of shortages or overstocking (Scala et al., 2013; Arts, Basten, & Van Houtum, 2016; Khademi & Eksioglu, 2018; Pakocs & Lupulescu, 2015; Aggarwal et al., 2023).
(3) Furthermore, MkIS can facilitate communication and collaboration among different sectors, fostering efficient open-source information and coordination (Rasool et al., 2023; Aggarwal et al., 2023; Rosalinda, & Ali, 2023).

These concepts are particularly valuable in cross-sector markets where multiple stakeholders are involved in the supply chain (Aho & Cirillo, 2023; Aho & Cirillo, 2023; Goldsby et al., 2023). MkIS can serve as a central platform for sharing data, forecasts, and market insights, enhancing the overall efficiency of the supply chain (Randall et al., 2014; Aho & Cirillo, 2023; Rahman et al., 2022; Aggarwal et al., 2023). Moreover, MkIS can support decision-making by providing data-driven insights, market analysis, and performance metrics (Aggarwal et al., 2023; Rosalinda, & Ali, 2023). The paradigm aids organizations in making informed choices regarding suppliers, logistics providers, and distribution strategies, leading to cost savings and improved supply chain performance (Pedrosa, Näslund, & Jasmand, 2012; Forslund, 2012; MacDonald & Neeley, 2022; Aho & Cirillo, 2023). In conclusion, MkIS serves as a valuable tool for cross-sector markets by enhancing visibility, inventory management, communication, and decision-making within the supply chain (Randall et al., 2014; Khademi & Eksioglu, 2018; Aho & Cirillo, 2023; Goldsby et al., 2023). This, in turn, helps streamline operations, reduce costs, and ensure the seamless flow of goods and components across different sectors and markets. In the next sections, discussions on the gap in the research and problem statement revealed.

GAP IN THE RESEARCH

The gap in research consists of discovering ways to sustain CH-47 Cargo-Chinook D-Model transport helicopters (Freedberg, 1999; Judson, 2023). The CH-47 aircraft is an important aircraft for military operations. Although, the airframe has a unique build, maintenance practices and spare parts the aviation platform still require improvements (Freedberg, 1999; Judson, 2023). The primary issue is obsolescence. As the aircraft matures over time so do its parts (BFS, 2021; Judson, 2023). The production of each rotorcraft comes with the manufacture and assembly of each component (BFS, 2021).

The gap consists of providing all the collective components for manufacturing and producing important spare parts such as: powerplant, drivetrain, dynamic, hydraulic, electrical, avionics, fuel, airframe, and accessory packages (BFS, 2021). Over time parts wear down and must be replaced with specific parts prior to components reaching their term life, pre-defined time life, time before overhaul (TBO), or no longer meet expected performance (leaking, seized, cracked, non-functioning, inaccurate, over-temp) (BFS, 2021). A valuable aspect of the research is to ensure the CH-47 Chinook continues to fly (BFS, 2021). The research study seeks to uncover ways in which the aircraft can remain viable while new innovations of future upgrades of the aircraft are being developed.

PROBLEM STATEMENT

Funding shortfalls for parts shortage challenges on CH-47 D-Model aircraft can be attributed to a combination of factors. One of the key primary reasons is cost, schedule, and performance goals for the development phase in accordance with the age and obsolescence of these helicopters (Marchet et al., 2018; MacDonald & Neeley, 2022). The CH-47 D-Model helicopters have been in service for several decades, and as they age, it becomes increasingly difficult to source replacement parts, especially for components that are no longer in production or whose original manufacturers have gone out of business (Marchet et al., 2018; MacDonald & Neeley, 2022). The stringent military specifications and regulations further compound the problem. Military aircraft, including the CH-47 D-Model, must meet rigorous safety and performance standards (Parrish & Blazer, 2008). These arduous standards impose the use of certified and high-quality parts, which may have limited suppliers due to the demanding nature of military procurement (Arts, Basten, & Van Houtum, 2016). The problem statement question for this research is the following:

(1) How can marketing information systems (MkIS) support the demand for parts and shortage challenges in the Aviation Industry for Foreign Military Sales (FMS) Legacy System in Cross-Sector Markets?

The low-rate production constraints within military organizations contribute to the part shortage challenges. Allocating resources for procuring spare parts and retrofitting older aircraft can be expensive, and competing priorities may lead to delays in addressing these shortages (Abdul, Kharoufeh, & Maillart, 2019; Morgan et al., 2018). Overall, the part shortage challenges on CH-47 D-Model aircraft stem from the combination of the aircraft's aging status, strict military standards, and budget limitations, which collectively make it a complex issue to resolve and maintain the operational readiness of these helicopters (Bachman, Goldsmith, & Nix, 2023). The research further delves into the significance of the study and the attributes emerging as essential.

SIGNIFICANCE OF THE STUDY

The significance of the study assesses CH-47 D-Model aircraft and growing concerns due to the crucial role these helicopters play in military operations. The CH-47 D-Model is a versatile and vital aircraft used for troop transport, cargo logistics, and a wide range of mission-critical tasks (Forslund, 2012; Islam, Mahmud, & Pritom, 2020; Gabaldon et al., 2021). Any shortage of indispensable parts can lead to decreased operational readiness, potentially resulting in mission failures, compromised of troop safety, and increased maintenance downtime. Additionally, the CH-47 D-Model is often deployed in support of disaster relief and humanitarian efforts, where rapid and dependable transportation are vital (Islam, Mahmud, & Pritom, 2020; Goldsby et al., 2023). Manufacturing readiness to ensure a sufficient level of parts available to avoid shortages of critical components can hinder the helicopter's ability to respond effectively in these situations. Therefore, addressing the part shortage challenges is imperative to maintain the reliability and effectiveness of these aircraft in military and civilian contexts, ensuring the safety and success of various missions and operations (Wu et al., 2022).

The part shortage challenges on CH-47 D-Model aircraft hold significant implications, both for military readiness and budget considerations. These helicopters play a crucial role in military operations, including troop transport and logistics, making their availability essential for mission success (Pedrosa, Näslund, & Jasmand, 2012; Forslund, 2012; Gabaldon et al., 2021). Part shortages can lead to grounded aircraft, reduced operational capacity, and potential mission failures, which could have severe consequences for national defense and security. Additionally, the need to source rare or specialized parts may result in increased maintenance costs and extended downtime, straining already limited military budgets. Therefore, addressing these part shortage challenges is essential to maintain the reliability, readiness, and effectiveness of the CH-47 D-Model helicopters in military service (Wu et al., 2022). The application of theory in correlation with the spare parts issues will be discussed in the next section.

THEORETICAL FRAMEWORK

A theoretical framework is a foundational review of existing theories that serves as a roadmap into developing reasonable arguments for future works. The theoretical framework utilized in this study, is the "theory of constraints" which follows a multi-paradigm understanding of phenomena in "supply chain value and finance (Sale & Sale, 2013; Almansoori, Al-Emran, & Shaalan, 2023; Shashi, 2023)." The theoretical concept covers the "why" in the interaction between conceptual "constraints" in the supply chain (Randall et al., 2014; Pirasteh & Kannappan, 2013; Shashi, 2023). Although logistically the theory of constraints (TOC) is a management paradigm focused on limitations in the system (Sale & Sale, 2013; Shashi, 2023). The concept frames problems, issues, and challenges as the constraints defining the reason for inability to achieve one's goals (Garvanova et al., 2023). The value-chain analysis focuses on boundaries in meeting objectives due to various margins and constraints (Sale & Sale, 2013; Shashi, 2023). The embedded perception of at least one constraint causes challenges in re-structuring strategies to organize solutions (Almansoori, Al-Emran, & Shaalan, 2023). The correlation or the link between marketing information systems (MkIS) and parts shortage challenges with the Theory of Constraints in the Aviation Industry are the constraints in procuring materials (Sale & Sale, 2013; Pirasteh & Kannappan, 2013; Shinde, 2014). Within the Foreign Military Sales (FMS) environment legacy systems in cross-sector markets suffer tremendously from constraints limiting systematic improvements to solve obstacles in attaining parts procurement and acquisition (Öner, Scheller-Wolf, & van Houtum, 2013; Sale & Sale, 2013; Garvanova et al., 2023).

Theory of Constraints identify the most significant constraint that is preventing the whole system from reaching its full potential (Randall et al., 2014; Sale & Sale, 2013; Shinde, 2014). One of the tools utilized in the theoretical framework are the five-step process of supply chain valuation:

1. <u>Identify the constraint</u> = targeting a single aspect of the process limiting achievement of a goal
2. <u>Exploit the constraint</u> = making quick improvements using existing resources
3. <u>Subordinate and synchronize to the constraint</u> = reviewing all other activities in the process to ensure that they support the needs of the constraint
4. <u>Elevate the performance of the constraint</u> = considering further actions as needed; at this point, further resources such as capital investment may be required
5. <u>Repeat the process</u> = moving immediately to the next constraint

The theory of constraints brings value to this research study as it provides the exact constraint related to the concept of limitations with the spare parts industry for CH-47 D-Model aircraft (Sale & Sale, 2013; Shinde, 2014). The theoretical framework depicts the behavior of organizations and other entities as MkIS aims to improve conceptually the constant challenge of removing obstacles (Shashi, 2023; Sun et al., 2023). The obstacles often affect industry's ability to open production and manufacturing of parts distribution because supporting a small group of customers with CH-47 D-Model aircraft is not cost effective in the grand scheme of business intelligence (Almansoori, Al-Emran, & Shaalan, 2023; Bertolini et al., 2023). Industry must determine if re-opening production lines has the potential to be profitable (Spector, 2011; Bertolini et al., 2023). If industry cannot determine if the constraints can potentially lead to profitability, then the concept cannot be sustained (Pirasteh & Kannappan, 2013; Sale & Sale, 2013). These organizations must ask themselves, "does it make sense for us to do develop or reverse engineer old systems and parts?"

In conclusion, the supply chain context, the constraint likely to be identified would be its "weakest link (Spector, 2011)." If one component moves through the supply chain at a significant slower pace than all the others, the entire process is stalled (Garvanova et al., 2023). But if one constraint effectively managed, there is an across-the-board benefit (Spector, 2011; Sun et al., 2023). Theory of constraints does not support diverting optimization efforts toward components not identified as constraints (Spector, 2011; Sale & Sale, 2013; Shinde, 2014). Instead, it evaluates the motives and behaviors of organizations and other entities regarding financial aspects of supply chain management, constructed with research design adopting a focus group methodology (Randall et al., 2014; Pirasteh & Kannappan, 2013; Sun et al., 2023). The next section explores focus groups discussions, emails, and correspondence aimed at understanding the meaning and interpretations of thematic patterns related to possible causes of constraints.

METHODOLOGY

The supply chain management (SCM) framework incorporates supply chain planning and execution processes from demand management to customer delivery (Randall et al., 2014; Arts, Basten, & Van Houtum, 2016; MacDonald & Neeley, 2022; Aho & Cirillo, 2023; Cheah et al., 2023). The methodology used for this study is a qualitative focus group study. This study to review over 179 emails discoveries in obsolescence issues surrounding the Chinook/Cargo. The researchers will utilize participant data from focus group discussions, emails, and written correspondence concerning the D-Model spare parts issue. The analysis is based on qualitative research where researchers review the lived experiences of individuals working in the Chinook/Cargo environment. The research leans on the expertise of these individuals as the discussions purpose for the determination of the usefulness of continued service for legacy systems. A holistic view begins by matching supply with demand to create a feasible plan defining the operating levels and resources needed to meet customer requirements (Arts, Basten, & Van Houtum, 2016; Goldsby et al., 2023). The Supply Chain Management (SCM) framework methodology can be applied to address part shortages on the CH-47 D-Model aircraft in several ways (Aho & Cirillo, 2023; Cheah et al., 2023).

The location of the research is a military installation in the State of Alabama. Also, the respondents from the CH-47 aviation civilian community for the United States military (Svanberg, 2020). The respondents totaled fifteen (15) participants utilizing a constructivist focus group approach with discussion points over six (6) months with vendors, government, and commercial entities. Researchers led spare part discussions in an office area, WebEx, or MS Teams embodied by Chief Program Integrators, Program Integrators, Chief Logistic Specialist, Logistics Specialist, International Program Manager (IPM), and Security Assistance Specialist (SAS). The technical experts in the CH-47 aviation field provided the following data:

STEP 1: Involved end-to-end coordination and integration of the supply chain, from suppliers to end-users, which help ensure a steady flow of critical components. SCM methodologies can identify and evaluate suppliers capable of providing the required parts and establish robust relationships with them, reducing the risk of shortages caused by supplier-related issues (Pakocs & Lupulescu, 2015; Aho & Cirillo, 2023).

STEP 2: Researchers utilized the SCM framework to review spare parts on the CH-47 D-Model aircraft to demand forecasting and inventory management (Arts, Basten, & Van Houtum, 2016; Khademi & Eksioglu, 2018). Researchers logistical analysis, historical data, and usage patterns SCM framework that can accurately predict future demand for specific parts (Arts, Basten, & Van Houtum, 2016). The SCM framework allows for proactive procurement and appropriate inventory levels to mitigate shortages (Abdul, Kharoufeh, & Maillart, 2019; Durach, Kembro, & Wieland, 2021).

STEP 3: The researchers analysis, implementing just-in-time inventory strategies, and optimize the use of limited storage space and reduce the carrying costs of excess inventory (Scala et al., 2013; Khademi & Eksioglu, 2018; Shi et al., 2023). The SCM framework emphasizes transparency and communication throughout the supply chain (Aho & Cirillo, 2023; Cheah et al., 2023). In the context of CH-47 D-Model aircraft, this can include information sharing with original equipment manufacturers (OEMs), suppliers, and maintenance crews, facilitating quick identification and resolution of part shortages (Durach, Kembro, & Wieland, 2021). Collaboration and shared data can lead to more effective inventory management and distribution (Manuj & Pohlen, 2012; Öner, Scheller-Wolf, & van Houtum, 2013).

STEP 4: Additionally, researchers addressed part shortages with vendors, government, and contractor personnel by implementing robust quality control and certification processes, ensuring that the procured parts meet stringent military and safety standards (Scala et al., 2013; Svanberg, 2020). Researchers continuously monitor the quality of parts and supplier performance, SCM can minimize the risk of receiving substandard components that could lead to shortages due to frequent replacements or repairs (Pedrosa, Näslund, & Jasmand, 2012; Durach, Kembro, & Wieland, 2021; Cheah et al., 2023).

In summary, the application of the SCM framework methodology for part shortages on the CH-47 D-Model aircraft involves efficient supplier management, demand forecasting, inventory optimization, transparency, and quality control (Durach, Kembro, & Wieland, 2021; MacDonald & Neeley, 2022; Cheah et al., 2023). All of which collectively contribute to mitigating and managing shortages effectively in a critical and complex supply chain environment (Randall et al., 2014; Arts, Basten, & Van Houtum, 2016; Aho & Cirillo, 2023; Goldsby et al., 2023).

LITERATURE REVIEW

The research associated with the CH-47D aircraft primarily revolves around military and aviation publications, as the contents of the topic are government-centric (Svanberg, 2020). Historically, these sources have documented the challenges faced by CH-47D operators in sourcing spare parts for aging helicopters (Abdul, Kharoufeh, & Maillart, 2019). They have often highlighted the impact of the aircraft's extended service life, the obsolescence of components, and the difficulties in maintaining supply chains for essential parts (Petreski et al., 2014; Aho & Cirillo, 2023). These sources also discuss the critical need for sustainable solutions to address these challenges, which can involve measures like reverse engineering, procurement strategies, and the involvement of third-party suppliers (Durach, Kembro, & Wieland, 2021; Shi et al., 2023). The literature not only provides a historical perspective, but also offers insights into ongoing efforts to mitigate part shortages and sustain the operational readiness of CH-47D aircraft, making it a valuable resource for military aviation and defense professionals, as well as researchers in the field (Morgan et al., 2018; MacDonald & Neeley, 2022).

The literature on the history of parts shortage challenges on CH-47D aircraft primarily focuses on documenting the experiences and lessons learned by military organizations and aviation experts. While there may not be a vast amount of scholarly literature, there are government reports, military publications, and anecdotal accounts that shed light on this issue. These sources often discuss the aging status of the CH-47D, its service history, and the difficulties in sourcing spare parts due to obsolescence and strict military standards (Abdul, Kharoufeh, & Maillart, 2019; Islam, Mahmud, & Pritom, 2020). They also address the financial implications and budget constraints associated with retrofitting and maintaining these helicopters. Additionally, some publications may delve into the efforts made to mitigate these challenges, such as the development of supply chain strategies, partnerships with vendors, or the exploration of alternative solutions to keep these aircraft operational (Aho & Cirillo, 2023; Shi et al., 2023). Overall, the literature on parts shortage challenges for CH-47D aircraft serves as a valuable resource for understanding the historical context and complexities of maintaining aging military aircraft in service (Morgan et al., 2018).

FINDINGS AND RESULTS

The findings and results, depict MkIS as an essential logistical supply chain support for cross-sector markets through various means. The contents are separated into six thematic categories based on the CH-47 Aviation Participants-Respondents.

- Theme Category 1 – Table 2. Real-Time Data Collection of Spare Parts and Inventory.
- Theme Category 2 – Table 3. Collaboration and Communication Among Stakeholders.
- Theme Category 3 – Table 4. Integrating Marketing Insights and Historical Data.
- Theme Category 4 – Table 5. Track and Trace Data.
- Theme Category 5 – Table 6. Risk Management.
- Theme Category 6 – Table 7. Optimizing Transportation and Logistics.

The contents of findings and results is from the database of 179 emails discoveries in obsolescence issues surrounding the Chinook/Cargo Helicopter-47 Delta-Model (CH-47 D-Model) helicopter. The emails derive from participant data in focus group discussions, emails, and written correspondence developed as a comprehensive spotlight into the Chinook/Cargo community challenge within FMS. Enclosed is a restatement of the problem statement question below. Furthermore, the initial Table 1 provides the aviation participant response for significance and position type description to develop the phenomena based on each participant experience in the field. See Table 1. CH-47 Aviation Participants-Respondents.

(1) How can marketing information systems (MkIS) support the demand for parts and shortage challenges in the Aviation Industry for Foreign Military Sales (FMS) Legacy System in Cross-Sector Markets?

In response to the <u>problem statement question</u>:

First, MkIS provides real-time data collection and analysis capabilities, allowing for the continuous monitoring of supply chain activities across different sectors (Aho & Cirillo, 2023; Aggarwal et al., 2023; Rosalinda, & Ali, 2023). This data-driven approach enables organizations to make informed decisions, optimize inventory levels, and streamline distribution processes to meet the diverse demands of various markets (Manuj & Pohlen, 2012; Arts, Basten, & Van Houtum, 2016). See Table 2. Real-Time data collection of spare parts and inventory. See Table 2. Real-Time Data Collection of Spare Parts Inventory.

Second, MkIS facilitates collaboration and communication among stakeholders involved in cross-sector markets (Rasool et al., 2023; Rosalinda, & Ali, 2023). It acts as a central platform for sharing information, coordinating activities, and aligning supply chain strategies (Shi et al., 2023). This promotes synergy among different sectors, which can be especially beneficial when dealing with parts and products that are used across multiple industries. See Table 3. Collaboration and Communication Among Stakeholders.

Third, MkIS helps in demand forecasting by integrating market insights and historical data from various sectors (Aggarwal et al., 2023; Rosalinda, & Ali, 2023). This predictive capability assists in anticipating and responding to changes in demand, ensuring that the supply chain remains agile and adaptable (Aho & Cirillo, 2023). See Table 4. Integrating Marketing Insights and Historical Data.

Table 1. CH-47 aviation participants-respondents

	Participant #'s	Position Type Descriptions	Years of Service
CH-47 Aviation Participants-Respondents			
1	Participant 1	Chief Program Integrator (CPI)	35 years
2	Participant 2	Program Integrator	11 years
3	Participant 3	Program Integrator	17 years
4	Participant 4	Program Integrator	23 years
5	Participant 5	Program Integrator	27 years
6	Participant 6	Program Integrator	14 years
7	Participant 7	Program Integrator	11 years
8	Participant 8	Chief Logistics Specialist	32 years
9	Participant 9	Logistics Specialist	32 years
10	Participant 10	Logistics Specialist	14 years
11	Participant 11	Logistics Specialist	24 years
12	Participant 12	Logistics Specialist	8 years
13	Participant 13	International Program Manager	13 years
14	Participant 14	Security Assistant Specialist	9 years
15	Participant 15	Security Assistant Specialist	2 years

Table 2. Real-time data collection of spare parts and inventory

	Participant	Thematic Patterns	Percentage of Participant Thematic Patterns	Concurrence / Non-Concurrence of Participant Evaluation
Real-Time Data Collection of Spare Parts and Inventory				
1	13 out of 15	Continuous monitoring of supply chain activities	0.867	Based on the respondent participation 13 of the participants agreed that continuous monitoring is necessary for legacy systems as challenges still arise when trying to procure spare parts
2	15 out of 15	Data-driven approaches enabling informed decisions	1.000	All participants concurred that data-driven approaches enable decisions as many government and contractor personnel use systems such as FEDLOG or I2LOG or WWRD to find the necessary parts needed to accommodate customers
3	9 out of 15	Optimization of inventory levels	0.600	Some participants believe that the optimization of inventory levels is the greatest challenge as the U.S. military no longer keeps inventory for CH-47 D-Model having divested of much of these spare parts during FY2015-2016
4	14 out of 15	Streamline distribution processes to meet diverse demands	0.933	All most of the respondents shared and concurred that streamlining processes to meet diverse demands is necessary; redundancy and repetition is often needed as even if parts are available; they are distributed to customers on a first-come first-serve basis
5	7 out of 15	Diverse demands of various markets	0.388	Half of the respondents believe diverse demands of various markets are essential; the other believe the issues stem from economies of scales. Does it make sense for commercial vendors to re-open production lines just to accommodate a few customers still using a legacy system? The supply does not always meet the demand.

Table 3. Collaboration and communication among stakeholders

Collaboration and Communication Among Stakeholders				
	Participant	**Thematic Patterns**	**Percentage of Participant Thematic Patterns**	**Concurrence / Non-Concurrence of Participant Evaluation**
1	15 out of 15	Collaboration and communication among stakeholders in cross-sector markets	1.00	All participants believe communication across Life Cycle Management Commands (LCMCs) is the only means for developing a cross-sector market system to streamline opportunities for spare parts for legacy systems
2	3 out of 15	Central platform for sharing information	0.200	Most of the participants did not concur with a centralized platform for sharing information as many believe customers need to strongly consider upgrading to newer more innovative systems.
3	10 out of 15	Aligning supply chain strategies	0.667	Some participants believe industry will have to find ways to support FMS customers as they try to gauge support for legacy systems no longer being used in military operations

Table 4. Integrating marketing insights and historical data

Integrating Marketing Insights and Historical Data				
	Participant	**Thematic Patterns**	**Percentage of Participant Thematic Patterns**	**Concurrence / Non-Concurrence of Participant Evaluation**
1	4 out of 15	Predictive capability assists in anticipating and responding to changes in demand	0.266	Some participants do not understand the benefits of predictive capability in anticipation of demand especially sense legacy systems are considered obsolete and no longer viable for military operations.
2	6 out of 15	Ensuring the supply chains remain agile and adaptable	0.400	Some disagree that organizations whether vendors, government, or commercial entities should invest in supply chains to ensure they are agile and adaptable especially because cost-benefit analysis provides a clear assessment that maintaining is not economical for any parties.

Fourth, MkIS can be employed to track and trace products as they move through the supply chain (Watson & Wu, 2022; Rosalinda, & Ali, 2023). This traceability is crucial for cross-sector markets, where products may have different use cases or end-users. It ensures product visibility, quality control, and compliance with regulatory requirements (Pedrosa, Näslund, & Jasmand, 2012). See Table 5. Track and Trace Data.

Fifth, MkIS plays a significant role in risk management by identifying potential disruptions or vulnerabilities in the supply chain across sectors (Pakocs & Lupulescu, 2015; Watson & Wu, 2022; Rosalinda, & Ali, 2023). It allows organizations to develop contingency plans and implement risk mitigation strategies, thereby enhancing supply chain resilience (Pakocs & Lupulescu, 2015; Shi et al., 2023). See Table 6. Risk Management.

Table 5. Track and trace data

Track and Trace Products				
	Participant	**Thematic Patterns**	**Percentage of Participant Thematic Patterns**	**Concurrence / Non-Concurrence of Participant Evaluation**
1	8 out of 15	Traceability is crucial for cross-sector markets especially to the end-user	0.533	A little over half of the participants believe traceability is key in determining parts acquisition. However, entities responsible whether agencies, item managers, or logistics specialist often cannot determine if the items are truly available for FMS customers.
2	9 out of 15	Product visibility, quality control, and compliance with regulatory requirements are key performance factors	0.600	More than half of the participant share the responsibility of quality controls, more regulations, and compliance measurements for process improvement. But all believe the job should consider transitioning focus on legacy systems that are not feasible or economical for distribution.

Table 6. Risk management

Risk Management				
	Participant	**Thematic Patterns**	**Percentage of Participant Thematic Patterns**	**Concurrence / Non-Concurrence of Participant Evaluation**
1	9 out of 15	Identifying disruptions or vulnerabilities within the supply chains across sectors	0.600	A little over half of the participants state identifying disruptions and vulnerabilities prior to program acceptance could alleviate some of the struggle concerning supply chain challenges and issues.
2	8 out of 15	Develop contingency plans and implement risk mitigation strategies, thereby enhancing supply chain resilience	0.533	Contingency plans are the daily expectations of personnel working in an FMS environment on legacy systems. However, many personnel have difficulty finding plausible solutions for customers without the means to support obsolescence challenges and issues. Mitigating risk is one of the most difficult drawbacks of supply chain resilience and aptitude.

Lastly, MkIS can help in optimizing transportation and logistics by providing data on the most cost-effective and efficient routes for cross-sector market distribution (Forslund, 2012; Islam, Mahmud, & Pritom, 2020; Gabaldon et al., 2021; Goldsby et al., 2023). This leads to reduced lead times, lower operational costs, and improved overall supply chain performance.

See Table 7. Optimizing Transportation and Logistics.

In summary, MkIS serves as a vital tool for logistical supply chain support in cross-sector markets by offering data-driven insights, fostering collaboration, enhancing demand forecasting, ensuring traceability, managing risks, and optimizing transportation and logistics (Pedrosa, Näslund, & Jasmand, 2012; Islam, Mahmud, & Pritom, 2020; Gabaldon et al., 2021; Rintala et al., 2021). MkIS enables organizations to navigate the complexities of operating in multiple sectors effectively, ensuring the smooth flow of goods and services across diverse markets.

Table 7. Optimizing transportation and logistics

Optimizing Transportation and Logistics				
	Participant	Thematic Patterns	Percentage of Participant Thematic Patterns	Concurrence / Non-Concurrence of Participant Evaluation
1	13 out of 15	Cost-effective and efficient routes for cross-sector market distribution	0.866	Many of the participants believe cost-effective measurements are highly important for legacy system procurement. However, these routes need to be disseminated to users to appropriately create cross-sector distribution channels.
2	11 out of 15	Reduced lead times, lower operational costs, and improved overall supply chain performance	0.733	The participants spoke at length about lead time challenges, back ordered items, and transportation/ distribution of repair and return items which is still a highly sensitive issue and challenge. Performance must be improved to create a robust system that maximizes optimization of transportation and logistics.

RECOMMENDATIONS FOR FUTURE INVESTIGATIONS

Several key recommendations can be considered for the parts shortage challenges on CH-47D aircraft:

- First, establishing a robust supply chain management system that includes proactive forecasting, demand planning, and rigorous inventory control is essential. This ensures that spare parts are readily available when needed (Abdul, Kharoufeh, & Maillart, 2019).
- Second, fostering collaboration between military agencies and private sector suppliers can help in diversifying the sources of spare parts, reducing reliance on a limited number of vendors (Petreski et al., 2014; Rasool et al., 2023).
- Third, investing in technology, such as 3D printing and reverse engineering capabilities, can be employed to produce critical components that are no longer in production (Russo, Masorgo, & Gligor, 2022).
- Fourth, allocating adequate budgets and resources for spare parts procurement, maintenance, and modernization programs is crucial for addressing the long-term sustainability of the CH-47D fleet (Morgan et al., 2018).
- Finally, exploring opportunities for international cooperation and information sharing with allies can further enhance the availability of spare parts, as well as contributing to mutual support in times of need (Abdul, Kharoufeh, & Maillart, 2019; Durach, Kembro, & Wieland, 2021).

The above recommendations collectively work toward mitigating parts shortage challenges and ensuring the continued operational readiness of CH-47D aircraft. Minimizing parts shortage challenges on CH-47D aircraft is crucial to ensure their operational readiness and safety. Here are some possible recommendations to address this issue. See Table 8. Possible Recommendations for Future Investigations.

Furthermore, researchers applying action research design, case study, correlation research design and content design analysis would be extremely beneficial for future investigations. By implementing these recommendations, military organizations can enhance their readiness and resilience in the face of parts shortage challenges for CH-47D aircraft, ultimately ensuring the continued effectiveness and safety of these essential assets. To address and improve parts shortage issues in the future for CH-47D aircraft, several recommendations can be considered (McKinnon, 2013; Durach, Kembro, & Wieland, 2021). Firstly, continued investment in modernization programs is crucial to replace aging components with more readily available and standardized parts, thereby reducing reliance on obsolete items. Secondly, embracing emerging technologies like additive manufacturing (3D printing) for on-demand production of critical components can help mitigate shortages (Arts, Basten, & Van Houtum, 2016; Totin & Connor, 2019). Collaboration with private industry partners and international allies to share resources, information, and solutions can enhance parts availability (Morgan et al., 2018; Rasool et al., 2023). Predictive analytics and data-driven maintenance can be further integrated to forecast parts requirements accurately (Sodero, Jin, & Barratt, 2019). Proactive research into alternative materials and designs for components can lead to more sustainable and accessible solutions (Obaze, Manuj, & Farris, 2016; Svanberg, 2020). Lastly, the development of an agile and responsive supply chain that can adapt to changing demands and market conditions can help in managing and mitigating parts shortages more effectively in the future (McKinnon, 2013; Arts, Basten, & Van Houtum, 2016).

Table 8. Possible recommendations for future investigations

	Possible Recommendations for Future Investigations	
1	Supply Chain Diversification	Explore multiple suppliers and manufacturers for critical parts. Diversifying the supply chain reduces dependence on a single source, making it more resilient to shortages caused by supplier issues (Durach, Kembro, & Wieland, 2021).
2	Reverse Engineering	Invest in reverse engineering capabilities to recreate essential components when original manufacturers are no longer in operation. This can be a cost-effective way to maintain a supply of critical parts (Russo, Masorgo, & Gligor, 2022).
3	Stockpile Critical Parts	Create a strategic stockpile of critical and hard-to-find parts to ensure a readily available inventory for maintenance and repairs. Regularly assess and update this stockpile based on usage and component lifecycles (Forslund, 2012; Scala et al., 2013).
4	Technology Upgrades	Consider upgrading certain systems and components to more modern, readily available alternatives, reducing reliance on outdated or obsolete parts.
5	Collaboration with Manufacturers	Engage with the original manufacturers or authorized suppliers to explore options for re-producing or providing substitute components for the CH-47D fleet (Öner, Scheller-Wolf, & van Houtum, 2013; Rasool et al., 2023).
6	Standardization	Promote standardization of parts and components within the military aircraft fleet to facilitate interchangeability and reduce the unique components specific to the CH-47D.
7	Continuous Monitoring and Forecasting	Implement a robust monitoring and forecasting system to predict which parts are likely to become scarce and plan procurement accordingly.
8	Budget Allocation	Ensure adequate budget allocation for spare parts procurement and maintenance to prevent shortages caused by funding constraints.
9	Maintenance and Overhaul Programs	Develop comprehensive maintenance and overhaul programs to extend the lifespan of existing components and minimize the need for replacement.
10	Research and Development	Invest in research and development efforts to design and manufacture 3D-printed or advanced composite parts, which can be produced on-demand and reduce reliance on traditional manufacturing (Arts, Basten, & Van Houtum, 2016; Svanberg, 2020).
11	International Cooperation	Collaborate with international defense partners to share resources, information, and procurement strategies to mitigate parts shortages collectively (Morgan et al., 2018).
12	Legislation and Policy	Advocate for legislation or policy changes that facilitate the acquisition and replacement of critical parts for aging military aircraft

CONCLUSION

In conclusion, MkIS can play a significant role in supporting the demand for parts and addressing shortage challenges in the Aviation Industry, especially for FMS Legacy Systems in Cross-Sector Markets. See Table 9. FMS Legacy Systems in Cross-Sector Markets.

Table 9. FMS legacy systems in cross-sector markets

1	Data Analytics and Forecasting	MkIS can gather and analyze data on part demand, usage patterns, and historical procurement data (Arts, Basten, & Van Houtum, 2016). By applying predictive analytics, MkIS can forecast future demand for specific parts, allowing for proactive procurement and inventory management to mitigate shortages (McKinnon, 2013; Swanson et al., 2017; Sodero, Jin, & Barratt, 2019).
2	Supply Chain Visibility	MkIS can provide real-time visibility into the entire supply chain, including suppliers, manufacturers, and distributors, facilitating efficient tracking and monitoring of parts. This transparency helps identify potential shortages and bottlenecks early, allowing for timely intervention (MacDonald & Neeley, 2022; Rosalinda, & Ali, 2023).
3	Supplier Management	MkIS can assist in identifying reliable suppliers and vendors, not only for original equipment but also for aftermarket and legacy parts. It can assess supplier performance, certification, and quality to ensure a stable supply source (Pedrosa, Näslund, & Jasmand, 2012; Obaze, Manuj, & Farris, 2016).
4	Inventory Optimization	MkIS can support inventory optimization by helping maintain an appropriate stock of critical parts without overstocking. It can suggest reorder points, safety stock levels, and automated procurement triggers to ensure parts availability (Öner, Scheller-Wolf, & van Houtum, 2013; Khademi, & Eksioglu, 2018).
5	Customization and Compatibility	For legacy systems like FMS, MkIS can maintain a database of compatible components and their variations. This information can help in identifying substitute parts or custom manufacturing options to address shortages when original parts are no longer available (Totin & Connor, 2019; Rintala et al., 2021).
6	Market Research and Trend Analysis	MkIS can continuously monitor market trends, technological advancements, and industry developments, enabling organizations to adapt to changing conditions and anticipate parts challenges (Svanberg, 2020; Watson & Wu, 2022).
7	Cost Management	MkIS can provide cost analysis tools, allowing organizations to compare pricing, quality, and lead times from different suppliers. This can help in making informed decisions regarding cost-effective procurement (Pedrosa, Näslund, & Jasmand, 2012).
8	Regulatory Compliance	MkIS can keep track of evolving regulatory standards and certifications, ensuring that parts acquired meet the necessary quality and safety requirements (Pedrosa, Näslund, & Jasmand, 2012).
9	Collaboration and Information Sharing	MkIS can facilitate collaboration between military organizations and international partners involved in FMS Legacy Systems. Shared data and insights can lead to better coordination, pooled resources, and a collective effort to address parts shortages more effectively (Farhan, Krejci, & Cantor, 2023; Rasool et al., 2023).
10	Risk Management	MkIS can assess potential risks associated with parts shortages, helping organizations develop contingency plans and alternative sourcing strategies in advance (Pakocs & Lupulescu, 2015).

MkIS can provide crucial logistical supply chain support for cross-sector markets through several key functionalities (Rosalinda, & Ali, 2023). Firstly, MkIS enables real-time tracking and monitoring of the supply chain, ensuring that organizations can swiftly identify and address any disruptions or delays (Farhan, Krejci, & Cantor, 2023). This is particularly valuable in cross-sector markets where diverse industries and partners are involved. Secondly, MkIS helps in demand forecasting and inventory management, optimizing the allocation of resources and inventory levels to meet the requirements of different sectors (Arts, Basten, & Van Houtum, 2016; Rosalinda, & Ali, 2023). Thirdly, it facilitates supplier relationship management by assessing supplier performance, certifications, and compliance with industry standards, ensuring that the supply chain remains reliable and efficient (Scala et al., 2013). Additionally, MkIS offers data analytics to identify cost-effective sourcing options, helping organizations make informed decisions on procurement across various sectors (Sodero, Jin, & Barratt, 2019; Watson & Wu, 2022). Overall, by enhancing transparency, efficiency, and collaboration in the supply chain, MkIS supports organizations in effectively navigating the complexities of cross-sector markets (Rasool et al., 2023). MkIS can be a valuable tool in addressing parts shortage challenges in the Aviation Industry, particularly for FMS Legacy Systems in Cross-Sector Markets. By leveraging data, analytics, supply chain visibility, and collaboration, organizations can better manage and meet the demand for critical parts, ensuring the operational readiness and safety of legacy aviation systems (Arts, Basten, & Van Houtum, 2016; Rasool et al., 2023).

REFERENCES

Abdul, M. D. T., Kharoufeh, J. P., & Maillart, L. M. (2019). Maintaining systems with heterogeneous spare parts. *Naval Research Logistics*, *66*(6), 485–501. doi:10.1002/nav.21864

Aggarwal, K., Khoa, B. T., Sagar, K. V. D., Agrawal, R., Dhingra, M., Dhingra, J., & R, L. K. (2023). Marketing information system based on unsupervised visual data to manage transportation industry using signal processing. *Expert Systems, 1*. https://doi-org.captechu.idm.oclc.org/10.1111/exsy.13384

Aho, J., & Cirillo, M. (2023). Let's Talk Weapon System Supply Chain Risk Strategy: Logistics as the pacing function requires a Service supply chain risk management strategy. *The Marine Corps Gazette*, *107*(6), 78–81.

Almansoori, A., Al-Emran, M., & Shaalan, K. (2023). Exploring the Frontiers of Cybersecurity Behavior: A Systematic Review of Studies and Theories. *Applied Sciences (Basel, Switzerland)*, *13*(9), 5700. doi:10.3390/app13095700

Arts, J., Basten, R., & Van Houtum, G.-J. (2016). Repairable Stocking and Expediting in a Fluctuating Demand Environment: Optimal Policy and Heuristics. *Operations Research*, *64*(6), 1285–1301. doi:10.1287/opre.2016.1498

Bachman, T., Goldsmith, J., & Nix, J. (2023). Readiness-Based Sparing Models: What You See May Not Be What You Get. *Military Operations Research*, *28*(1), 55–71. https://doi-org.captechu.idm.oclc.org/10.5711/1082598328155

Bertolini, M., Leali, F., Mezzogori, D., & Renzi, C. (2023). A Keyword, Taxonomy and Cartographic Research Review of Sustainability Concepts for Production Scheduling in Manufacturing Systems. *Sustainability (Basel)*, *15*(8), 6884. doi:10.3390/su15086884

Billings Flying Service (BFS). (2021). *Chinook Helicopter Parts (2021): Comprehensive Breakdown of CH-47D Parts*. https://billingsflyingservice.com/chinook-helicopter-parts-guide-2021/

Cheah, J.-H., Kersten, W., Ringle, C. M., & Wallenburg, C. (2023). Guest editorial: Predictive modeling in logistics and supply chain management research using partial least squares structural equation modeling. *International Journal of Physical Distribution & Logistics Management, 53*(7/8), 709–717. doi:10.1108/IJPDLM-08-2023-552

Durach, C. F., Kembro, J. H., & Wieland, A. (2021). How to advance theory through literature reviews in logistics and supply chain management. *International Journal of Physical Distribution & Logistics Management, 51*(10), 1090–1107. doi:10.1108/IJPDLM-11-2020-0381

Farhan, M., Krejci, C. C., & Cantor, D. E. (2023). Do a non-core worker's procedural justice concerns influence their engagement in helping behavior? A multi-method study. *International Journal of Physical Distribution & Logistics Management, 53*(9), 1015–1042. doi:10.1108/IJPDLM-02-2022-0044

Forslund, H. (2012). Performance management in supply chains: Logistics service providers' perspective. *International Journal of Physical Distribution & Logistics Management, 42*(3), 296–311. doi:10.1108/09600031211225972

Freedberg, S. J., Jr. (1999). *Military personnel struggle with spare parts.* https://www.govexec.com/federal-news/1999/12/military-personnel-struggle-with-spare-parts/5403/

Gabaldon, J., Farris, M. T. II, Manuj, I., & Ekezie, U. (2021). Sixth Logistics Faculty Salary Survey. *Transportation Journal, 60*(3), 239–257. doi:10.5325/transportationj.60.3.0239

Garvanova, M., Garvanov, I., Jotsov, V., Razaque, A., Alotaibi, B., Alotaibi, M., & Borissova, D. (2023). A Data-Science Approach for Creation of a Comprehensive Model to Assess the Impact of Mobile Technologies, *Humans. Applied Sciences (Basel, Switzerland), 13*(6), 3600. doi:10.3390/app13063600

Goldsby, T. J., Hoang, T. T., Stank, T. P., & Bell, J. E. (2023). A Modernized Framework for Transportation Decision-Making in a Hyper-Integrated Global Supply Chain Environment. *Transportation Journal, 62*(1), 16–42. doi:10.5325/transportationj.62.1.0016

Islam, M. R., Mahmud, M. R., & Pritom, R. M. (2020). Transportation scheduling optimization by a collaborative strategy in supply chain management with TPL using chemical reaction optimization. *Neural Computing & Applications, 32*(8), 3649–3674. doi:10.1007/s00521-019-04218-5

Judson, J. (2023). *US Army replaces problematic engine part on Chinooks.* https://www.defensenews.com/land/2023/02/15/us-army-replaces-problematic-engine-part-on-chinooks/

Khademi, A., & Eksioglu, B. (2018). Spare Parts Inventory Management with Substitution-Dependent Reliability. *INFORMS Journal on Computing, 30*(3), 507–521. doi:10.1287/ijoc.2017.0794

MacDonald, M. G., & Neeley, R. (2022). Supply Chain Management in a Data-driven World: Army Logistics University's Approach to Supply Chain Education. *Army Sustainment, 54*(2), 60–63.

Manuj, I., & Pohlen, T. L. (2012). A reviewer's guide to the grounded theory methodology in logistics and supply chain management research. *International Journal of Physical Distribution & Logistics Management, 42*(8/9), 784–803. doi:10.1108/09600031211269758

Marchet, G., Melacini, M., Perotti, S., Rasini, M., & Tappia, E. (2018). Business logistics models in omni-channel: A classification framework and empirical analysis. *International Journal of Physical Distribution & Logistics Management, 48*(4), 439–464. doi:10.1108/IJPDLM-09-2016-0273

McKinnon, A. C. (2013). Starry-eyed: Journal rankings and the future of logistics research. *International Journal of Physical Distribution & Logistics Management, 43*(1), 6–17. doi:10.1108/09600031311293228

Morgan, T. R., Tokman, M., Richey, R. G., & Defee, C. (2018). Resource commitment and sustainability: A reverse logistics performance process model. *International Journal of Physical Distribution & Logistics Management, 48*(2), 164–182. doi:10.1108/IJPDLM-02-2017-0068

Obaze, Y., Manuj, I., & Farris, I. I. T. II. (2016). Fifth Logistics Faculty Salary Survey. *Transportation Journal, 55*(2), 208–223. doi:10.5325/transportationj.55.2.0208

Öner, K. B., Scheller-Wolf, A., & van Houtum, G.-J. (2013). Redundancy Optimization for Critical Components in High-Availability Technical Systems. *Operations Research, 61*(1), 244–264. doi:10.1287/opre.1120.1133

Pakocs, R., & Lupulescu, N. B. (2015). Risk Management and Assessment of the Manufacturing and Marketing Risk-Factors within Industrial Companies. *Scientific Research & Education in the Air Force - AFASES, 2*, 575–580.

Parrish, T., & Blazer, D. J. (2008). Modifying the Supply Chain. *Air Force Journal of Logistics, 32*(1), 76–79.

Pedrosa, A. da M., Näslund, D., & Jasmand, C. (2012). Logistics case study based research: Towards higher quality. *International Journal of Physical Distribution & Logistics Management, 42*(3), 275–295. doi:10.1108/09600031211225963

Petreski, D. T., Iliev, A. P., Gjurov, L. M., & Petreska, A. D. (2014). Logistics Supply Chains and Their Application. *Military Technical Courier / Vojnotehnicki Glasnik, 62*(4), 104–119. https://doi-org.captechu.idm.oclc.org/10.5937/vojtehg62-6207

Pirasteh, R. M., & Kannappan, S. (2013). The synergy of continuous process improvement. *Industrial Engineering (American Institute of Industrial Engineers)*, 41–46.

Rahman, S., Ahsan, K., Sohal, A., & Oloruntoba, R. (2022). Guest editorial: The "new normal": rethinking supply chains during and post-COVID-19 global business environment. *International Journal of Physical Distribution & Logistics Management, 52*(7), 481–490. doi:10.1108/IJPDLM-08-2022-518

Randall, W. S., Wittmann, C. M., Nowicki, D. R., & Pohlen, T. L. (2014). Service-dominant logic and supply chain management: Are we there yet? *International Journal of Physical Distribution & Logistics Management, 44*(1/2), 113–131. doi:10.1108/IJPDLM-11-2012-0331

Rasool, F., Greco, M., Morales-Alonso, G., & Carrasco-Gallego, R. (2023). What is next? The effect of reverse logistics adoption on digitalization and inter-organizational collaboration. *International Journal of Physical Distribution & Logistics Management, 53*(5/6), 563–588. doi:10.1108/IJPDLM-06-2022-0173

Rintala, O., Solakivi, T., Laari, S., Töyli, J., & Ojala, L. (2021). Drivers of logistics outsourcing: Examining transaction costs, core competences and planned behavior. *International Journal of Physical Distribution & Logistics Management, 51*(3), 259–280. doi:10.1108/IJPDLM-08-2019-0244

Rosalinda, U. U., & Ali, H. (2023). Analysis of Factors Influencing the Marketing Information System: CRM, Customer Satisfaction and Sales Effectiveness. *Dinasti International Journal of Digital Business Management (DIJDBM), 4*(2), 264–270. https://doi-org.captechu.idm.oclc.org/10.31933/dijdbm.v4i2

Russo, I., Masorgo, N., & Gligor, D. M. (2022). Examining the impact of service recovery resilience in the context of product replacement: The roles of perceived procedural and interactional justice. *International Journal of Physical Distribution & Logistics Management, 52*(8), 638–672. doi:10.1108/IJPDLM-07-2021-0301

Sale, M. L., & Sale, R. S. (2013). Theory of Constraints as related to improved Business Unit Performance. *Journal of Accounting and Finance, 13*(1), 108–115.

Scala, N. M., Rajgopal, J., & Needy, K. L. (2013). A Base Stock Inventory Management System for Intermittent Spare Parts. *Military Operations Research (Alexandria, Va.), 18*(3), 63–77. doi:10.5711/1082598318363

Shashi, M. (2023). Sustainable Digitalization in Pharmaceutical Supply Chains Using Theory of Constraints: A Qualitative Study. *Sustainability (Basel), 15*(11), 8752. doi:10.3390/su15118752

Shi, Y., Venkatesh, V. G., Venkatesh, M., Fosso Wamba, S., & Wang, B. (2023). Guest editorial: Digital transformation in supply chains: challenges, strategies, and implementations. *International Journal of Physical Distribution & Logistics Management, 53*(4), 381–386. doi:10.1108/IJPDLM-05-2023-550

Shinde, A. J. (2014). Application of Thinking Process tools of Theory of Constraints to initiate a business. *Academy of Management Annual Meeting Proceedings, 2014*(1), 1. https://doi-org.captechu.idm.oclc.org/10.5465/AMBPP.2014.10675abstract

Sodero, A., Jin, Y. H., & Barratt, M. (2019). The social process of Big Data and predictive analytics use for logistics and supply chain management. *International Journal of Physical Distribution & Logistics Management, 49*(7), 706–726. doi:10.1108/IJPDLM-01-2018-0041

Spector, Y. (2011). Theory of constraint methodology where the constraint is the business model. *International Journal of Production Research, 49*(11), 3387–3394. doi:10.1080/00207541003801283

Sun, J., Zhang, Y., Chen, H., & Qiao, J. (2023). Optimization Model and Application for Agricultural Machinery Systems Based on Timeliness Losses of Multiple Operations. *Agriculture, 13*(10), 1969. doi:10.3390/agriculture13101969

Svanberg, M. (2020). Guidelines for establishing practical relevance in logistics and supply chain management research. *International Journal of Physical Distribution & Logistics Management, 50*(2), 215–232. doi:10.1108/IJPDLM-11-2018-0373

Swanson, D., Goel, L., Francisco, K., & Stock, J. (2017). Applying Theories from Other Disciplines to Logistics and Supply Chain Management: A Systematic Literature Review. *Transportation Journal, 56*(3), 299–356. doi:10.5325/transportationj.56.3.0299

Totin, A. N., & Connor, B. P. (2019). Evaluating Business Models Enabling Organic Additive Manufacturing for Maintenance and Sustainment. *Defense Acquisition Research Journal: A Publication of the Defense Acquisition University, 26*(4), 379–417. https://doi-org.captechu.idm.oclc.org/10.22594/dau.18-815.26.04

Watson, F., & Wu, Y. (2022). The Impact of Online Reviews on the Information Flows and Outcomes of Marketing Systems. *Journal of Macromarketing, 42*(1), 146–164. doi:10.1177/02761467211042552

Wu, J., Ding, W., Zhang, Y., & Zhao, P. (2022). On reliability improvement for coherent systems with a revelation. *Naval Research Logistics, 69*(4), 654–666. doi:10.1002/nav.22036

Chapter 3
Leadership Learning and Leadership Coaching for Government Leaders in Cybersecurity, Artificial Intelligence, and Technology

Amalisha Sabie Aridi

iD https://orcid.org/0000-0002-7869-5530

Capitol Technology University, USA

ABSTRACT

In this era of rapid technological advancement, government leaders must expertly navigate intricate policies, including artificial intelligence, cybersecurity, and telehealth. Proficiency in these domains is paramount, requiring a steadfast commitment to enhancing leadership competencies. By investing in executive coaching and holistic leadership development, government agencies can proactively tackle modern challenges. This study, grounded in descriptive phenomenology, examines 22 thematic motifs, unveiling the effectiveness of leadership coaching for government leaders managing complex technologies and addressing pivotal policy issues in artificial intelligence, cybersecurity, and telehealth.

INTRODUCTION

Over the past decade, we have witnessed an extraordinary technological revolution in various domains, including smart learning, and the operational paradigms of organizations. This transformative wave was driven by the advent of smartphones and tablets, marking the nascent stage of the big data era. Cloud computing, once an experimental concept, now plays a pivotal role in shaping our digital landscape. As we anticipate more life-altering innovations on the horizon, it has become evident that archaic technical systems and approaches within the federal government have led to frustration among both employees

DOI: 10.4018/979-8-3693-1970-3.ch003

and the American public. Now, more than ever, there is an urgent need for a paradigm shift in policy design and implementation, coupled with the infusion of artificial intelligence, digital, technological, and innovation expertise into federal government agencies.

- Policy Revolution: Virtually every national priority hinges on a precise, comprehensive, and contemporary comprehension of how to harness and leverage modern technology. Federal policies and programs that underpin the welfare of American citizens, including crucial domains like Medicare and national defense, are intricately interwoven with digital services and information technology platforms. Looking to the future, the cornerstone policies of any administration will invariably be influenced by, if not fundamentally contingent upon, the dynamics of existing and emergent technologies such as artificial intelligence and machine learning. Crafting and executing these policies without active involvement of technologists at the decision-making table would be a grave omission.

- Digital Empowerment: The federal government must markedly enhance its capacity to deliver services to the public in a digital format. Veterans should be able to conveniently access their benefits through online and mobile channels. The successful rollout of the next-generation air traffic system should occur on schedule and within the allocated budget. Furthermore, government agencies must ensure that their systems and data remain impervious to the ever-looming cyber threats. Regrettably, we have witnessed numerous instances where significant federal information technology projects either failed or fell short of expectations, often incurring substantial costs.

- Championing Innovation: Some of the most monumental innovations in the United States have been pioneered by federal institutions, spanning domains such as space exploration and the establishment of the patent system. In order for the government to furnish top-tier services, it must continually experiment with and adopt fresh practices, methodologies, and technologies, particularly those that have demonstrated effectiveness in other sectors. The innovations of the forthcoming decades, encompassing realms like automation, artificial intelligence, bioengineering, quantum computing, and novel materials, will surpass the breakthroughs of the past. Therefore, it is imperative to ensure that the federal government continues to formulate policies that champion the positive facets of innovation, mitigate associated risks, and fortify the nation's leadership in technology.

In essence, the demand for adept technical managers who embody effective leadership traits has never been more pressing. Government leaders bear the responsibility of efficiently managing vast sums of taxpayer funds and resources (White, 2016). Effective and judicious leadership, combined with sound managerial decision-making acumen, is pivotal in guaranteeing the appropriate and efficient utilization of these resources. The landscape of government management is in a perpetual state of flux, characterized by dynamic changes (Goldsmith & Levensaler, 2016). These transformations pose formidable challenges to the essence and impact of leadership decision-making and leadership development (Goldring, 2015; White, 2016). As we journey into the future, the intersection of technology and governance necessitates visionary leadership capable of navigating uncharted waters and steering the course towards a more technologically empowered and resilient government.

The Merit Services Protection Board has underscored a critical inadequacy within most government agencies pertaining to the identification and cultivation of proficient supervisors, as revealed by the disheartening statistic that merely 6 out of every 1,000 supervisors fail to meet the standards required to pass their supervisory probationary period (Katz, 2018b). This revelation by Katz (2018b) illuminates the persisting issue of government organizations grappling with ineffective strategies to address supervisors with subpar performance. The federal government grapples with glaring deficiencies in the realm of manager training and development (Katz, 2018b). Therefore, it is incumbent upon organizational leaders to pivot their focus toward championing leadership development initiatives, and proactively immersing themselves in leadership development programs. This shift is imperative in order to counteract the detrimental and deleterious ramifications of inadequate leadership practices (Center for Leadership Studies, 2017; Ciporen, 2015; Gaddis & Foster, 2015).

In an era characterized by relentless technological innovation and paradigm-shifting transformations, it becomes palpable that government policies must be recalibrated to accommodate the dynamic technological landscape. Artificial intelligence, cybersecurity, and telehealth are the cornerstones of this technological revolution, demanding innovative government policies to not only adapt but also to proactively guide and regulate these burgeoning domains. The confluence of these technologies is reshaping governance, healthcare, and security. Therefore, the imperative for leadership within government agencies to bolster their capacity for effective decision-making and policy formulation becomes all the more pressing. An effective response to this need lies in the concerted cultivation of adept leaders who are well-versed in the complexities of these technologies and capable of navigating the intricate web of their implications.

The Center for Leadership Studies (2017), Ciporen (2015), and Gaddis & Foster (2015) all emphasize the profound importance of strategic engagement in leadership development programs, particularly in the context of contemporary governance. As our society becomes increasingly reliant on artificial intelligence, as cyber threats escalate in sophistication, and as telehealth transforms healthcare delivery, leaders must grapple with multifaceted challenges. The development of these innovative government policies cannot be achieved without a deep understanding of these technologies and the capacity to make informed, forward-thinking decisions. Thus, a reinvigorated focus on leadership development serves as a linchpin in the pursuit of effective, responsive governance in this rapidly evolving technological era.

PROBLEM STATEMENT

The consequences of poor management behaviors experienced by employees can reverberate on an individual level, often manifesting as distressing stress-related health issues, as illuminated by Miller-Jones (2020). An alarming study by Gallup (2015) revealed that merely 30% of employees in the United States find themselves actively engaged in their work, with a corresponding engagement rate of just 35% for managers. This disconcerting reality underscores the urgency for leaders to address the pervasive issue of poor management through the cultivation of more effective leadership competencies, a measure that can potentially curtail up to 32% of an organization's voluntary turnover (Center for Leadership Studies, 2017).

Traditionally, many organizations have sought to rectify the issue of subpar management through training interventions, as highlighted by Gallup (2015). However, there is an evolving trend in the federal sector, which is increasingly turning to executive coaching as an instrumental approach to augment the leadership skills of government supervisors. This shift reflects a growing emphasis on both managerial and organizational effectiveness, a shift elucidated by Censer (2011) and Katz (2018a). Executive coaching has surged to prominence on a global scale as a leading trend for achieving organizational effectiveness, enhancing business capacity, and fostering leadership development, in alignment with the insights provided by Lebihan (2011) and McCarthy (2011).

In this era characterized by rapid technological advancements, government leaders are confronted with the imperative to understand and navigate the complexities of innovative government policies related to artificial intelligence, cybersecurity, and telehealth. These domains are at the forefront of reshaping governance, security, and healthcare, demanding leaders who are well-versed in their intricacies. The development of government leaders who can adeptly steer policy formulation in these evolving landscapes necessitates a commitment to enhancing leadership competencies. By investing in executive coaching and leadership development initiatives that encompass these contemporary challenges, government agencies can harness the potential to proactively guide their organizations through the complex and dynamic technological terrain.

LITERATURE REVIEW

An in-depth exploration of the literature unfurls a comprehensive understanding of Kilburg's (2000) executive coaching, delineating its multifaceted components across six system factors, namely input, throughput, output, structure, process, and content. These facets converge with four psychological factors encompassing conscience, idealized self, instinctual self, and rational self, further intertwined with four internal elements of individual function: emotion, cognition, defense, and conflict. Additionally, the paradigm of executive coaching interfaces with three distinct categories of relationships, spanning the dimensions of past, present, and focal. This holistic comprehension underscores the intricacies of executive coaching's theoretical foundation and practical application.

The scholarly discourse within this literature review advances the proposition that executive coaching is inherently interwoven with mentoring, organizational culture, leadership development, and management development. These domains wield significant influence over the outcomes associated with efficiency, productivity, and engagement, as established by Kilburg (1996) within the context of his six system factors, four psychological factors, four internal components of individual function, and three types of relationships. In the modern organizational landscape, the relentless cadence and unrelenting pressures of the business environment impose a continuous strain on employees, subjecting their physical and emotional resources to rigorous testing.

In the wake of Kilburg's (1996) seminal study, theorists have increasingly associated executive coaching with a myriad of constructs, each serving as critical tenets of the overarching conceptual model. These constructs encompass mentoring, organizational culture, leadership development, and management development, as expounded upon by Rekalde et al. (2015). This amalgamation of ideas underscores the dynamic and interconnected nature of executive coaching, illuminating its pivotal role in shaping the competencies and effectiveness of contemporary government leaders, particularly within the ever-evolving domains of artificial intelligence, cybersecurity, and telehealth.

EFFECTS OF TECHNOLOGY

In the contemporary realm of virtual work environments, the dynamics of leadership necessitate alternative strategies and methodologies, especially given the limited opportunities for face-to-face interactions with teams (Elkhouly et al., 2014). This transformative landscape, steered by groundbreaking technologies, exerts a profound influence on organizational strategic planning, shaping the trajectory of leadership efforts (Elkhouly et al., 2014). These innovative technologies are seamlessly woven into organizational strategies, thereby yielding outcomes marked by resounding successes (Elkhouly et al., 2014). In the present epoch, the technology revolution has bestowed upon leaders a new source of power and governance, serving as an indispensable compass for managers as they navigate the path to enhanced performance.

Anderson (2017), in collaboration with the PEW Research Center, conducted extensive research that highlighted the existence of technology usage gaps across generations. This study underscored the imperative for managers and organizations to exhibit adaptability, effectively leveraging technology to optimize their processes. Short (2014) emphasized the notion that technology deployment translates to heightened efficiency and effectiveness. As elucidated by Zveglich and Lacina (2014), the integration of technology augments the efficacy of coaching, underpinned by the potential for immediate feedback and assessment. These innovative technological solutions offer a precious commodity—time saved, an invaluable asset that appreciates in significance as economies progress (Bishop et al., 2013).

To foster the development of more proficient leaders, organizations must harness technological tools, imbuing the leadership coaching and development process with newfound potency. Prominent among these tools are teleconferencing, web conferencing, collaboration, and software video conferencing (Harris et al., 2015; Zveglich & Lacina, 2014). Effective utilization of these IT resources serves as a linchpin in the monitoring process, further enhancing leadership coaching, mentoring, and leadership development initiatives. The ultimate outcome is an upswing in organizational effectiveness, catalyzed by the harmonious amalgamation of technology and leadership in the domains of artificial intelligence, cybersecurity, and telehealth.

EXECUTIVE COACHING

As articulated by the United States Government Office of Personnel Management (OPM), with specific reference to the Center for Leadership Studies (2017), it is manifest that coaching serves as a potent catalyst for an organization's triumphant journey towards excellence. In this context, executive coaching emerges as a paradigm of leadership development, unfolding through a sequence of meticulously orchestrated one-on-one dialogues with proficient coaches (deHaan et al., 2013). Rooted in a Western cultural philosophy that reveres the maximization of individual potentials, both in personal and professional realms, executive coaching has evolved as an integral and celebrated intervention, intricately woven into the fabric of modern leadership development (Nangalia & Nangalia, 2010; Sperry, 2013).

In recent times, executive coaching has surged in prominence, asserting itself as a transformative and indispensable developmental practice, meticulously calibrated to enhance organizational effectiveness and nurture the growth of astute leaders (Mithiotis & Argirou, 2016). However, the intrinsic value of learning and development, epitomized by coaching, often faces relegation to a secondary status during periods of fiscal restraint, as elucidated by Brennand (2017). It is crucial to perceive executive coaching as a fusion of behavioral techniques and processes, orchestrated to bolster the coachee's quest for the realization of jointly identified objectives. These objectives encompass the augmentation of professional prowess and personal contentment, culminating in a synergistic enhancement of the coachee's organizational efficacy, all meticulously codified within a formal coaching agreement (Kilburg, 2000).

RESEARCH DESIGN

The study, adhering to a qualitative research paradigm, sought to delve into the nuanced and intricate tapestry of participants' lived experiences, thereby unraveling the multifaceted layers that underpin executive coaching practices and their associated themes. In the pursuit of this comprehension, the research espoused the rigorous methodology of Descriptive Phenomenology, an approach known for its richness and depth in explicating the intricacies of human experiences (Creswell, 2017).

Descriptive Phenomenology serves as an invaluable tool in qualitative research, enabling a profound exploration of the phenomena at hand. It unfurls the subtleties and nuances embedded within human experiences, offering a comprehensive lens through which to examine the intricacies of executive coaching practices. This approach is inherently suited to illuminate the tacit knowledge and unarticulated dimensions of the lived experiences of participants, ensuring a holistic and multi-dimensional understanding of the phenomenon (Creswell, 2017).

Furthermore, the research process actively fostered participants' engagement and involvement, a hallmark of qualitative inquiry. By encouraging participants to share their perspectives and insights, the study harnessed the power of collaborative knowledge generation. This approach not only enriched the depth of the findings but also ensured that the research was firmly grounded in the authentic voices and narratives of those intimately familiar with executive coaching practices (Creswell, 2017).

POPULATION AND SAMPLING (QUALITATIVE)

The study's geographical demarcation targeted a select cohort of seasoned governmental supervisors. These individuals had undergone executive coaching as an integral component of their leadership development endeavors within the expansive precincts of Washington, D.C. The recruitment process was meticulously orchestrated through affiliations with prominent government professional associations, including but not limited to The Partnership for Public Service, National Federation of Federal Employees, National Association of Hispanic Federal Executives, Blacks in Government, Federal Managers Association, Senior Executives Association (SEA), Young Government Leaders (YGL), Society of American Indian Government Employees (SAIGE), and Asian American Government Executives Network (AAGEN).

The stringent criteria adhered to in participant selection were grounded in the imperative of attaining data that reflected the contemporary landscape of coaching practices within the U.S. Federal Government. This was particularly salient due to the nascent nature of coaching practices in this domain, as underscored by Bartlett et al. (2014) and Turner (2010). The research hewed to the wisdom imparted by Creswell (2013), who expounded that a sample size of 10 participants was deemed adequate for potentially gleaning phenomenological insights, given the purposeful nature of phenomenological research, which seeks to unearth intricate and specific insights from the collected data. Notably, the study boasted a robust cohort of 20 participants, thereby bolstering the robustness and depth of the findings.

RESULTS

Population and Demographics

The study included 20 participants who were supervisors in the federal government that had experienced executive coaching as an aspect of their own leadership development as a federal employee.

Table 1. Demographic information for interview participants

Category	Percent
Gender	
Male	60% (12 Men)
Female	40% (8 Women)
Age	
Age 20-30	10%
Age 31-40	40%
Age 41-50	30%
Age 51-60	20%
Years' Government Work Experience	
3-5 years	10%
6-10 years 30%	30%
11-15 years 30%	30%
16-20 years 40%	40%
Years' Government Management Experience	
3-5 years 20%	20%
6-10 years 30%	30%
11-15 years 30%	30%
16-20 years 20%	20%
Ethnicity	
Caucasian 40% (8)	40% (8)
African American 30% (6)	30% (6)
Latino/Hispanic 10% (2)	10% (2)
Asian/Pacific Islander 20% (4)	20% (4)

RESEARCH FINDINGS

Interview Data Collection Questions

1. In what ways do you feel executive coaching impacted you as a leader?
2. What coaching tools and processes did you find most valuable, and why?
3. What do you see as the benefit, if any, of coaching as an aspect of a formal leadership development?

The three data collection questions, together generated a total of 22 themes, discussed in the following sections under each question topic in descending order of frequency of mention among the 20 participants.

QUESTIONS AND THEMES

Question Topic 1: Ways in Which Executive Coaching Impacted Participants as Leaders

Theme 1: Coaching "Improved Self-Awareness" (Stated by 20 Participants out of 20)

This recurrent theme aligns harmoniously with the assertion made by Kim (2014) that such an outcome could be attributed to the instrumental roles played by mentoring and coaching. The cultivation of self-awareness stands as a linchpin in augmenting leaders' capacities to assert control over their personal lives and, by extension, make judicious decisions in their roles as organizational stewards (Kim, 2014).

Kim's (2014) insights provide valuable underpinnings for comprehending the intricate relationship between self-awareness, leadership efficacy, and the invaluable contributions of mentoring and coaching. The cultivation of self-awareness instills leaders with the ability to navigate the complexities of their personal lives, which, in turn, begets a profound impact on their competence as leaders presiding over organizational domains (Kim, 2014).

Moreover, the study at hand augments these notions by underscoring the multifaceted benefits that accrue from the interplay of self-awareness, mentoring, and coaching in shaping not only individual leadership trajectories but also the broader outcomes within organizational settings. The confluence of these elements is postulated to foster an environment conducive to astute decision-making, enhanced leadership efficacy, and, by extension, the achievement of organizational objectives, echoing the sentiments espoused by Kim (2014). Thus, this study delves into the intricate interplay of self-awareness, mentoring, and coaching, further enriching the discourse on the development of effective leaders.

Theme 2: Coaching "Improved Emotional Intelligence" (Stated by 19 Participants, out of 20)

Emotional intelligence is a component of the intelligent leadership model (Keikha et al., 2017). This recurrent theme seamlessly aligns with the assertion posited by Kim (2014), affirming that the outcome in question can be attributed, in substantial part, to the interplay of mentoring and coaching. Within this context, the cultivation of self-awareness emerges as a pivotal lever that not only enhances the capacity of leaders to assert agency over the trajectory of their lives but also equips them with the acumen requisite for rendering more efficacious decisions in their roles as stewards of their respective organizations (Kim, 2014).

The thematic prominence ascribed to the concept of self-awareness is intrinsically linked to its transformative potential within the domain of leadership. In consonance with the insights of Kim (2014), this thematic underpinning underscores that the confluence of mentoring and coaching plays a substantial role in shaping the discussed outcome. Central to this dynamic is the notion that self-awareness empowers leaders, endowing them with the agency to navigate the course of their lives with a heightened sense of purpose and direction. This, in turn, catalyzes a ripple effect, wherein leaders become more adept at orchestrating effective decisions and strategies in their capacities as stewards of their organizations, thereby enhancing the overarching effectiveness and dynamism of their leadership tenures (Kim, 2014).

Furthermore, the resonant resonance of this recurring theme underscores the intrinsic link between self-awareness and leadership efficacy, as posited by Kim (2014). Within the purview of this discussion, the interplay of mentoring and coaching assumes a central role in yielding the outcome under examination. Self-awareness is revealed as the catalyst that empowers leaders to seize the reins of their lives with intentionality and to exercise discerning judgment in their roles as custodians of their organizations. Kim's (2014) insights further corroborate the idea that this transformation can have a far-reaching impact on leadership practices, ultimately contributing to organizational growth and sustainability.

Theme 3: Coaching "Improved [Participant's] Time and Priority Management as a Supervisor" (Stated by 15 Participants out of 20)

This recurring thematic motif elucidates the profound significance ascribed to the cultivation of self-development, particularly in the domains of priority and time management. Notably, enhancements in time and priority management, when situated within Kilburg's nuanced framework, emerge as tangible outputs stemming from the coaching process. These enhancements are intrinsically intertwined with the rational self, comprising the cognitive dimension, and bear direct relevance to the dynamics of the present and the focal relationships at play. Recent scholarship, as exemplified by Trevillion's (2018) exploration, sheds light on this thematic terrain.

Intriguingly, the work of Nosheen (2013) introduces an additional layer of insight by underscoring that the dividends of improved time management skills extend not only to those in the mentee role but also encompass mentors in the context of peer mentoring engagements. This insight underscores the cascading effects of effective time and priority management, wherein the benefits of such skill refinement reverberate through mentor-mentee relationships, fostering heightened efficiency, productivity, and effectiveness.

The thematic currents observed in this discourse resonate with the evolving landscape of self-development, underscoring that proficiency in managing time and priorities constitutes a crucial facet of leadership and personal growth. These competencies, as discerned through Kilburg's taxonomy, represent an outcome of the coaching process, chiefly attributed to the rational self's cognitive dimensions, and notably, they exert a substantial influence on the dynamics of the present and the focal relationships that define the contemporary professional landscape. The insights encapsulated in Trevillion's (2018) work, complemented by Nosheen's (2013) perspective, shed light on the far-reaching ramifications of these competencies, demonstrating that their cultivation can transcend individual development and foster collective growth in mentoring scenarios.

Theme 4: Coaching "Improved [Participant's] Communication Skills" (Stated by 15 participants out of 20)

This recurrent thematic motif distinctly underscores the paramount significance of cultivating and honing managerial communication competencies. It is conspicuously aligned with the fundamental objective of coaching, which is to augment "interpersonal effectiveness," as eloquently articulated by Dean and Meyer (2002). Within this thematic domain, the intricacies of communication patterns among employees assume a central role, representing a pivotal dimension of organizational culture (Plavin-Masterman, 2015). Furthermore, these patterns of communication serve as a reflection of the underlying values held by employees, an assertion corroborated by the insightful work of Isopeskul et al. (2016).

The crux of this thematic exploration centers on the development and refinement of managerial communication skills. It resonates with the core mission of coaching, which is to elevate "interpersonal effectiveness," thereby enabling leaders to navigate the intricate dynamics of human interaction with acumen and finesse (Dean & Meyer, 2002). Within the organizational context, the discourse on communication patterns among employees is intrinsically intertwined with the broader tapestry of organizational culture (Plavin-Masterman, 2015). This thematic dimension underscores the profound impact of communication dynamics on shaping the ethos and identity of an organization.

Intriguingly, Isopeskul et al. (2016) extend this conversation by postulating that the tenor and tenets of employee communications not only mirror but also coalesce with the prevailing values within the organizational milieu. In this sense, effective managerial communication transcends the exchange of words; it becomes a conduit through which the organization's values, ethos, and cultural identity are channeled and perpetuated. This thematic exploration, therefore, underscores the critical role of communication as a linchpin in the intricate fabric of organizational culture and interpersonal efficacy.

Theme 5: Coaching Provided "an Objective External Viewpoint" (Stated by 15 Participants out of 20)

The thematic strand that illuminates coaching's role in furnishing an external vantage point proves to be profoundly enlightening. In alignment with Kilburg's (2000) taxonomy of categorizations, this objective external perspective may be aptly construed as an input factor. It pertains to the realm of the rational self, comprising cognitive dimensions, and wields influence over the immediate and focal relationships within the organizational milieu. Recent scholarly endeavors that delve into this thematic tapestry encompass the scholarly contributions of Benavides (2008) and Bennett (2021).

This thematic exploration underscores the invaluable dimension of coaching whereby it offers a detached and unprejudiced viewpoint, impervious to internal biases or groupthink dynamics. Kilburg's prescient delineation of the rational self as a vital component in this process underscores the cognitive and analytical facets involved in providing an external perspective. It is within this cognitive landscape that the rational self operates, rigorously analyzing and evaluating the subject matter with judicious objectivity.

The temporal and relational dimensions of this thematic exploration are also of paramount significance. In the immediate context, this external viewpoint serves as a catalytic input, sparking the wheels of introspection, deliberation, and contemplation. Simultaneously, it shapes the dynamics of focal relationships, both within the individual's sphere of influence and within the broader organizational context. Benavides (2008) and Bennett (2021), through their recent scholarly work, have artfully woven the intricate threads of this theme, shedding light on the pivotal role of external perspectives in fostering insight, sound decision-making, and the cultivation of effective relationships.

Theme 6: Coaching "Made [Participant] a More Knowledgeable and Effective Supervisor" (Stated by 15 participants out of 20)

This thematic strand eloquently underscores the enduring significance of leadership acumen, proficiencies, and the perpetual journey of professional leadership development, which remains an ever-essential pursuit even for seasoned supervisors. Aligned with Kilburg's (2000) nuanced categories, a supervisor's evolution into a more erudite and adept leader can be aptly perceived as an outcome engendered by the coaching process. This transformative journey delves into the realms of both the rational and ideal selves, encompassing a harmonious interplay of emotion and cognition, all of which synergistically contribute to the augmentation of leadership prowess. This evolution is not confined to the individual's self but reverberates through the intricate tapestry of present and focal relationships, shaping the very essence of the organizational ecosystem.

The theme extols the idea that leadership is an ever-unfolding odyssey, one that demands continuous refinement and enhancement. Kilburg's schema, which delineates the rational and ideal selves as pivotal facets of this journey, encapsulates the cognitive and aspirational dimensions entailed in leadership growth. The emotional and cognitive elements are inextricably intertwined, shaping not only how a leader thinks but also how they feel, inspiring them to aspire to loftier ideals.

Furthermore, the ripple effects of this evolution are extensive, reaching far beyond the confines of individual self-improvement. The immediate relationships within the leader's sphere of influence, as well as the broader organizational dynamics, are notably influenced by this growth. The synthesis of emotion and cognition, guided by an aspiration for the ideal, imparts transformative powers that reverberate throughout the organization, nurturing an environment conducive to progress, innovation, and success.

Question Topic 2: Coaching Tools and Processes Found Most Valuable

Theme 7: "Relationship With Coach" (Mentioned by 20 Participants out of 20)

This thematic strand underscores the pivotal role of social learning within the tapestry of leadership development, illuminating how the coach emerges as the catalyst for this indispensable facet of the learning journey. A crucial hallmark of this process, as accentuated by Dean and Meyer, is the cultivation of a profound rapport between the coach and the executive. Dean and Meyer, in their seminal work, underscore this interpersonal connection as the foremost of the competencies that a coach should master (Dean & Meyer, 2002, p. 11).

In the wake of Dean and Meyer's influential contributions, there has been a perceptible evolution in the landscape of coaching techniques and skills. A notable shift has transpired, with heightened emphasis on psychological methodologies, particularly the cognitive-behavioral coaching (CBC) paradigm. This psychological orientation, oftentimes intertwined with other conceptual frameworks such as the GROW model (Goal, Reality, Options, Will), offers an enriched and more holistic approach to executive coaching (Lai & Palmer, 2019).

This development underscores the dynamic and evolving nature of coaching practices, where a multidimensional approach aligns seamlessly with the complex and multifaceted dimensions of leadership growth. The acknowledgment of social learning as a cornerstone of leadership development heralds a profound transformation in the understanding of how leaders evolve, expand their horizons, and realize their full potential. As the field of coaching continually evolves, these shifts in emphasis and the integration of various frameworks contribute to a more comprehensive, effective, and multifaceted landscape of leadership development.

Theme 8: "Help in Interpreting Behavioral Assessments" (Mentioned by 20 Participants out of 20)

This thematic strand meticulously underscores the paramount significance of harnessing leadership and preference assessment tools, complemented by the invaluable role played by the coach in facilitating the participant's profound comprehension of the results. This multifaceted approach is instrumental in empowering participants to glean profound insights and leverage the strengths revealed by each assessment tool. In this nuanced dimension, the alignment of leadership development with self-assessment emerges as a transformative facet, albeit one that has received limited attention in recent research.

What sets this theme apart is its uniqueness and the paucity of exploration within contemporary research. This uncharted territory delves into the orchestration of assessments, aiming not only to illuminate the coachee's behavioral proclivities but also considering the possibility of assessing the behavior of the coachee's team members. While this interpretation may appear somewhat speculative, it offers an intriguing perspective that enriches the discourse surrounding leadership development practices.

This theme serves as a testament to the evolving landscape of executive coaching, where novel dimensions are continually unveiled, offering fresh insights and opportunities for a more comprehensive understanding of leadership development. It underscores the need for more in-depth exploration and empirical scrutiny, as the potential ramifications of team-based assessments within the context of executive coaching are of undeniable significance.

Theme 9: "A Mechanism [for] Goal Setting and Planning" (Mentioned by 20 Participants out of 20)

This thematic strand meticulously delineates the pivotal role undertaken by a coach in catalyzing leaders' self-directed cultivation of their leadership development objectives. Through the prism of Kilburg's (2000) categorical framework, this profound engagement may be construed as both an input and a structural facet, predominantly resonating with the rational self. It chiefly comprises cognitive elements and exerts its influence on present relationships. Recent scholarship encapsulating this thematic essence is discerned in the scholarly endeavors of Gavin (2018) and Roelofs (2019).

Central to this theme is the acknowledgement of coaching's profound agency in empowering leaders to embark upon a personalized odyssey of leadership development. It is a sophisticated interplay that involves not just the acquisition of leadership proficiency but also the internalization of ambitions and objectives. It represents a vital dimension that shapes leadership trajectories and underpins the transformative dynamics of contemporary coaching practice.

As we traverse the uncharted terrain of leadership development, this thematic strand assumes a paramount role in the dialogue. The inclusion of recent research investigations serves as a testament to the ongoing evolution of leadership coaching, where the coach's function expands beyond traditional boundaries, becoming a facilitator and enabler of leaders' self-authored leadership aspirations. Further exploration and empirical inquiry in this domain promise to unravel the nuances of this multifaceted process, thereby enhancing our comprehension of leadership development in the modern context.

Theme 10: "Authentic Conversations" (Mentioned by 19 Participants out of 20)

This thematic perspective underscores the profound significance of dialogues that exhibit qualities of reflection, constructive discourse, and formative interactions within the pivotal domain of leadership development, under the vigilant guidance of a proficient coach. The profound ability to engage in authentic conversations, unburdened by apprehensions of potential repercussions, stands as an indispensable foundation for fostering trust within the intricate tapestry of the coach-coachee relationship. Such an atmosphere of trust and candor constitutes an integral facet of what is referred to as a critical of a critical thinking or reflective environment.

Within the taxonomy delineated by Kilburg in 2000, this communication paradigm may be aptly classified as a structural element encompassing the entirety of the four core psychological factors: conscience, idealized self, instinctual self, and rational self. It is a complex amalgamation of emotional and cognitive dimensions, which, uniquely, provides a platform where contentious issues and defense mechanisms can be openly broached. In essence, this nuanced interplay between emotion and cognition bears the potential to exert a discernible influence on the dynamics of contemporaneous relationships, as well as the overarching focus of the individuals involved.

Theme 11: "Enthusiastic Support" (Mentioned by 19 Participants out of 20)

The central motif revolving around the integral role of the coach within a critical framework of learning and emotional sustenance emerges as a compelling and intellectually resonant discourse. The cultivation of an emotionally supportive environment stands as a key aspiration within the tenets of the "thinking environment," as elucidated by the Time to Think framework in the year 2020. This framework explicitly prescribes a compositional structure for feedback that is characterized by an embrace of positivity, wherein a ratio of five affirmative elements is tendered for each challenging facet, thereby fostering an environment brimming with constructive affirmation and gentle critique.

In a parallel vein, Gavin's work draws upon the insights of Crane (2002), underscoring the efficacy of maintaining an 80-20 ratio, where a preponderance of positive elements, constituting 80%, harmoniously intertwines with 20% allocated to the introduction of constructive ideas for enhancement. This strategic ethos, as exemplified in the revitalization efforts led by Douglas Conant at Campbell's Soup, as documented by Gavin in 2018 (p. 143), serves as a testament to its practical application and transformative potential within organizational contexts.

From the vantage point of Kilburg's 2000 classification schema, this modality of interaction may be perceived as an input mechanism, adeptly engaging the conscience and instinctual self, ultimately fortifying the rational self's cognitive prowess. This intricate fusion of emotion and the subtle undercurrents of defense mechanisms manifests itself in a profound manner, actively reshaping the dynamics of contemporaneous relationships and focal points of intellectual focus. It is imperative to recognize the import of recent scholarship that continues to probe this thematic domain, such as the research conducted by Boysen et al. in 2018, thereby adding further nuance and depth to our understanding of this intricate terrain.

Theme 12: "Help With Focus, Redirection, and Clarity" (Mentioned by 19 Participants out of 20)

This theme is essential for the change process that is the goal of all coaching. In terms of Kilburg's (2000) categories, this help can be considered an input that works with the rational self and the conscience, consists of processes of cognition and perhaps, to some extent, emotion, and affects present and possibly focal relationships. Recent research that touches upon this theme includes the work of Benavides (2008), Trevillion (2018), and Bennett (2021).

Theme 13: Coaching "Challenged [Participant's] Approaches and [Their] Own Thinking" (Mentioned by 19 participants out of 20)

The underlying motif concerning the coach's multifaceted role as both the devil's advocate and an empathetic sounding board, ceaselessly goading participants towards their optimal selves, is both prescient and philosophically resonant. As artfully expounded by Kim in 2014, mentors, in their role as guides and mentors, play an indispensable part in not only offering reassurance but also in the art of challenging mentees to transcend their existing boundaries. It is this dialectic of encouragement and confrontation that forges the crucible of profound personal development and growth.

In the scholarly work of Boysen, Arya, and Page, notably in their 2021 publication, the quintessence of coaching finds one of its fundamental pillars in the act of challenging entrenched thinking patterns. It is amidst this intellectual crucible that the very foundations of the coaching process are erected. The practice of challenging these ingrained cognitive paradigms, as underscored by these erudite authors, is central to the overarching objective of effecting transformative change, which is the ultimate aspiration of all coaching endeavors. Devoid of such incisive challenges to ingrained thought and behavioral patterns, the impetus for embarking upon the arduous journey of change, the quintessence of coaching's raison d'être, would be nullified. Moreover, without the persistent challenge to erroneous patterns of thought, coachees may find themselves ensnared in a cocoon of resistance against the very metamorphosis they themselves seek. It is in this juxtaposition of mentorship's dual role, encompassing both gentle guidance and vigorous confrontation, that the crucible for personal evolution finds its most potent alchemy.

Theme 14: "Ask Questions" (Mentioned by 19 Participants out of 20)

The thematic essence encapsulating the role of the coach in proffering incisive and challenging inquiries assumes a pivotal stature in the cultivation of leaders characterized by a profound penchant for reflection. A nuanced interpretation of this theme yields a dichotomy, potentially encompassing two distinct dimensions of this dialectical process. The first pertains to the coach's adeptness in posing pointed or Socratic queries, drawing from the lexicon of Kline's ten components of a thinking environment, which, in the parlance of Time to Think (2020) adherents, are known as "Incisive Questions." This dimension is emblematic of a mentor-driven inquiry, and while its precise purview within the thematic landscape remains indeterminate, it appears to resonate with the contours of Theme 13, thus signifying a distinctive strand of inquiry.

In consonance with Kilburg's classification scheme of 2000, the former case entails an input modality that engages all four psychological factors, encompassing elements of emotion and cognition, and potentially invoking all four internal constituents. This intricate interplay of cognitive and emotional dimensions exerts a discernible impact upon present relationships and the focus of contemplation.

The alternative dimension, in this interplay, pivots on the freedom accorded to the coachee to pose questions to the coach, thereby bestowing upon the theme an association with Theme 10. In this context, the focus is predominantly upon the structural underpinnings, where the rational self occupies the forefront, and cognition and emotion coalesce to form its primary constituents. This dynamic interplay primarily affects present relationships, although with a distinct emphasis on the cognitive and emotional domains.

In a rich tapestry of scholarly discourse, this theme finds resonance within the recent research endeavors of Benavides (2008), Boysen et al. (2018), Roelofs (2019), Bennett (2021), Boysen et al. (2021), and Johnston (2021), each contributing to the ever-evolving understanding of this nuanced facet of coaching, thereby enriching the intellectual discourse with a kaleidoscope of perspectives and insights.

Theme 15: "Challenge Assumptions" (Mentioned by 18 Participants out of 20)

This thematic contour revolves around the coach's distinctive capacity to engage in a perspicacious examination of the participants' assumptions, achieved through a multifaceted spectrum of pedagogical instruments encompassing questions, assignments, assessments, and other forms of coaching interactions. Mirroring the insights advanced by Kim in 2014, the act of challenging mentees emerges as one of the pivotal facets that mentors, in their sagacious role, undertake in their stewardship. The boundaries delineating this thematic terrain and Theme 13 remain an intricate conundrum, for the tenets ascribed to the latter theme find themselves equally germane and seamlessly transposed to this nuanced discourse.

Theme 16: "Provide Resources" (Mentioned by 18 Participants out of 20)

This thematic paradigm elucidates the coach's intrinsic capacity to serve as a wellspring of knowledge and bestow resources that might have previously eluded the awareness of the participants within the coaching engagement process. The brevity of this thematic encapsulation belies the intricate expanse of its potential interpretations, as "resources" encompasses a wide spectrum, ranging from casual recommendations to online hyperlinks, comprehensive compendiums of printed and audiovisual instructional materials, or even the coaches themselves, serving as founts of wisdom.

Within the framework articulated by Kilburg in 2000, this theme ostensibly assumes the character of an input, predominantly engaging the rational self, with the cognitive and emotional facets occupying a prominent position. The ramifications of this thematic element primarily reverberate within the confines of present relationships, exerting their influence in a manner that is palpable and immediate.

Regrettably, the richness of this theme's implications extends beyond the confines of specific recent research endeavors, rendering it elusive to pinpoint precise scholarly works that have grappled with the multifaceted dimensions encapsulated therein. The expansive range of meanings inherent to the notion of resources serves as a testament to the fertile ground that remains ripe for exploration and illumination within the scholarly discourse of coaching.

Theme 17: "Provide Advice" (Mentioned by 18 Participants out of 20)

In terms of Kilburg's (2000) categories, this theme could be described as an input that engages primarily the rational self and possibly the conscience and ideal self, consisting primarily of cognition, and affecting present relationships. Among recent research, this theme is explicitly mentioned by Boysen et al. (2018), but it runs implicitly throughout the coaching literature.

Theme 18: "Objective Assessment and Feedback" (Mentioned by 18 Participants out of 20)

This thematic underpinning delineates the paramount significance of equitably delivered, transparent, punctual, uniform, and constructive feedback as an invaluable facet of the coaching process. In many respects, this theme parallels the characteristics of Themes 13 and 15, yet it deviates in substantial ways. Within the framework of Kilburg's 2000 classifications, this form of input invokes the instinctual self and encompasses elements of emotion, defense, and conflict, albeit to a lesser extent than the aforementioned themes. This divergence arises from the fundamental premise that the feedback proffered in this context is underpinned by an unwavering trust in its objectivity, distinguishing it from the potentially antagonistic implications that might be associated with an attack on the coachee's established thought patterns.

The scholarly landscape resonates with explicit examinations of this theme, as exemplified by the discerning insights offered by Benavides in 2008 and Roelofs in 2019. These researchers have delved into the intricate dynamics of coaching, elucidating the nuances of feedback, thereby enriching our understanding of this pivotal facet within the realm of professional development and personal growth.

Question Topic 3: Perceived Benefits of Coaching as an Aspect of a Formal Leadership Development Program

Theme 19: Coaching "Improved the Way That a Participant Approached Being a Supervisor" (Mentioned by 20 Participants out of 20)

This thematic exploration delves into the profound transformation of a participant's approach and comprehension regarding the roles and responsibilities inherent in the capacity of a supervisor as a result of being coached effectively. While the interplay of this theme exhibits a certain conceptual resonance with Theme 6, the precise demarcations that separate these thematic territories remain elusive, as gleaned from the succinct formulations of these themes. This thematic landscape, much like its counterpart, aligns with Kilburg's categorization of an "output." It evokes the realms of the ideal and rational selves, and the discerning conscience, entailing a preponderance of cognitive and emotional dimensions. This intricate dynamic reverberates predominantly within the sphere of present relationships, while concurrently holding the potential to influence the focal relationships that may come to the fore.

Recent scholarship, emblematic of a burgeoning scholarly discourse in this domain, converges upon this theme, exemplified by the illuminating contributions of Taconis in 2018, Trevillion in 2018, Roelofs in 2019, and Boysen et al. in 2021. These erudite scholars have embarked upon a nuanced exploration of this thematic canvas, unraveling the multifaceted dimensions of transformation within the context of supervisory roles, thus enriching our collective understanding of this pivotal facet in the arena of leadership and professional growth.

Theme 20: Coaching "Increased Confidence" (Mentioned by 19 Participants out of 20)

This thematic thread illuminates the transformative power of an efficacious and captivating coaching relationship in the augmentation of a participant's self-assurance. As Kim perceptively articulates in 2014, mentors orchestrate the gradual construction of mentees' confidence by adeptly shepherding them through the intricate choreography of intention, commitment, preparation, development, and ultimate accomplishment. This meticulous process is akin to a carefully composed symphony, where each note and movement contributes to the crescendo of self-belief.

Within this contemporary milieu of scholarly exploration, other noteworthy research endeavors resonate with this thematic harmony. Taconis, in 2018, Trevillion, in 2018, Roelofs, in 2019, and Brown et al., in 2021, have probed the depths of this thematic tapestry, shedding light on the multifaceted dimensions of confidence cultivation within the dynamic landscape of coaching.

Furthermore, the concept of "self-efficacy," which forms a salient component of psychological capital (PsyCap), is eloquently synonymous with "confidence," as expounded by Luthans et al. in 2007. This alignment underscores the interplay between the domains of psychological capital and coaching, adding to the robust foundation of research surrounding this theme. Even studies such as that of Zuberbuhler et al. in 2020, which may not explicitly mention "confidence" but explore the relationship between PsyCap and coaching, are inherently linked to the rich tapestry of this thematic terrain. As such, the scholarly discourse is rendered even more profound and intricate, elucidating the multifarious dimensions of confidence development within the realm of coaching.

Theme 21: Coaching [Helped] "Establish Better Career Development Goals" (Mentioned by 19 Participants out of 20)

This thematic exploration delineates the instrumental role of coaches in actively cultivating career development-oriented thought patterns, aspirations, and strategic plans. The incisive observations of Gavin in 2018 explicitly underscore the significance of this theme. It is noteworthy that this facet has occasionally received less emphasis, possibly because coaching is traditionally perceived, by both coaches and the employers who finance coaching interventions, as a means to enhance the coachee's performance within their existing job roles. However, the prevalence of its mention by a substantial number of coachees within this context underscores its inherent importance to them.

Within the conceptual framework articulated by Kilburg in 2000, this theme resonates as an "output," engrossing primarily the rational self, characterized by an intricate interplay of cognitive and emotional dimensions. Its reverberations primarily manifest within the ambit of existing relationships, while concurrently bearing the potential to influence more focal interpersonal dynamics. In essence, this thematic terrain acts as a crucible for nurturing and fine-tuning career-oriented cognitive processes and emotions, which are deeply intertwined with the aspirations and strategic objectives of the individuals under the mentorship of coaches.

It is worth noting that the scholarly discourse, although comprehensive, could further benefit from continued exploration of the multifaceted dimensions encompassed by this theme, thereby enriching the collective understanding of the intricate landscape of career development within the purview of coaching.

Theme 22: Coaching "Improved the Comprehension of Strengths and Ways to Leverage Those Strengths" (Mentioned by 19 Participants out of 20)

This thematic vista spotlights the pivotal role of coaching in the process of participants' self-discovery, strength assessment, and the subsequent identification of pathways and activities for harnessing these strengths to their utmost potential. It is essential to note that the statement of this theme, like several others, is inherently broad in scope, encompassing the possibility of addressing both the strengths inherent to the coachee and, in the context of a leader, the strengths inherent in the coachee's team members. The versatility of this theme underscores the profound range of its applications, which can have a transformative impact on diverse facets of professional development.

Within Kilburg's categorization framework, this thematic phenomenon assumes the character of an "output," predominantly engaging the rational self, and, to the extent that it pertains to the coachee's inherent strengths, invoking the conscience and the ideal self. The cognitive dimension forms the lynchpin of this thematic construct, where the act of introspection and the strategic deployment of strengths is paramount. The ripple effects of this process are primarily felt within the precincts of existing relationships, wielding the potential to reshape the dynamics of these relationships in the present moment.

Recent scholarship serves as a testament to the ongoing exploration of this theme, notably with the insightful contributions of Boysen et al. in 2018 and Trevillion in 2018. These erudite works have illuminated the multifaceted dimensions of strength exploration and deployment within the context of coaching, thus expanding our comprehension of this pivotal facet of professional growth and development. The expansiveness of this theme invites continued scholarly inquiry and exploration, promising further depths of understanding in the nuanced arena of strength-based coaching.

SYNTHESIS AND SUMMARY OF DATA

The amalgamation of three distinct lines of inquiry yielded a corpus of 22 salient thematic motifs, meticulously expounded in the ensuing sections. These themes are presented in descending order of prominence as conveyed by the discourse of the 20 participants.

The imperativeness of cultivating technical managers with the acumen and sagacity to effectively lead has never assumed a more paramount standing, particularly in light of the burgeoning presence of artificial intelligence technologies, the proliferation of nascent cybersecurity risks, and the compelling need for comprehensive policy formulations. Within the government's purview, leaders bear the solemn responsibility of adroitly stewarding vast reservoirs of taxpayer dollars and an array of resources, as noted by White in 2016. In this high-stakes milieu, the mantle of effective and efficient leadership assumes a definitive significance, enshrining the meticulous management of these resources to ensure their judicious and efficacious allocation.

Moreover, the ever-evolving landscape of governmental management, as delineated by Goldsmith and Levensaler in 2016, underscores the protean nature of leadership decision-making in the contemporary governmental milieu. These transformations beget an intricate web of challenges that extend across the landscape of leadership decision-making, as underscored by Goldring in 2015 and White in 2016. The advent of social networks and media platforms has ushered in an era of heightened accountability and transparency, thereby amplifying the intricacies of leadership and managerial decision-making, as delineated by Goldring in 2015.

In this labyrinthine terrain, novel technologies, the labyrinthine dynamics of human resource management, the specter of revenue scarcities, and the kaleidoscope of political dynamics collectively underscore the intricate tapestry of challenges that beset effective leadership and managerial decision-making within the federal government, as cogently elucidated by White in 2016. The implications of these multifarious challenges are profound, for they inform and shape the trajectory of leadership and decision-making within the complex arena of federal governance, adding new dimensions of nuance to this critical discourse.

REFERENCES

Al-Asfour, A., & Lettau, L. (2014). Strategies for leadership styles for multi-generational workforce. *Journal of Leadership, Accountability and Ethics, 11*(2), 58–69. http://www.na-businesspress.com/jlaeopen.html

Al-Hindawi, F. H., & Abdulmajeed, R. K. (2017). The Cognitive Principle of Relevance and its application to anti-Iraq war posters. *The Cognitive Principle of Relevance and its Application. Adab Al-Kufa College of Arts Kufa University,* 9-30. Retrieved from https://www.researchgate.net/publication/313928362_The_Cognitive_Principle_of_Relevance_and_its_Application_to_Anti_Iraq_War_Posters

Al Saifi, S. A. (2015). Positioning organisational culture in knowledge management research. *Journal of Knowledge Management, 19*(2), 164–189. doi:10.1108/JKM-07-2014-0287

Alasuutari, P., Bickman, L., & Brennan, J. (Eds.). (2010). *The sage handbook of social research methods.* Sage.

Alexander, D. F. A. (2015). *Effect of leadership facilitation and support on turnover intention in the United States federal workforce: The influence of demographic dimensions* (Doctoral dissertation). Retrieved from ProQuest Dissertations & Theses Global (Order No. 3684889).

Allen, M. (2014). Catching the bug: How virtual coaching improves teaching. *Educational Horizons, 92*(4), 25–27. doi:10.1177/0013175X1409200408

American Management Association. (2017). *Leading four generations at work.* Retrieved from https://www.amanet.org/training/articles/leading-the-four-generations-at-work.aspx

American Management Association. (2018). AMA training helps you meet executive core qualification (ECQs). Retrieved from https://www.amanet.org/government/govt-leadership-competencies.aspx

Amerson, R. (2011). Making a case for the case study for the case study method. *Journal of Nursing Education, 50,* 427-428-.doi:10.3928.01484834-20110719-0

Anderson, M. (2017). Key trends shaping technology in 2017. *Pew Research Center FACTANK.* Retrieved from https://www.pewresearch.org/fact-tank/2017/12/28/key-trends-shaping-technology-in-2017/

Asencio, H., & Mujkic, E. (2016). Leadership behaviors and trust in leaders: Evidence from the U.S. Federal Government. *Public Administration Quarterly, 40*(1), 156. doi:10.18356/0b18c57f-en

Asif, M., & Searcy, C. (2014). Towards a standardised management system for corporate sustainable development. *The TQM Journal, 26*(5), 411–430. doi:10.1108/TQM-08-2012-0057

Athar, R. S. (2015). Impact of Training on Employee Performance Banking Sector Karachi. *IOSR Journal of Business and Management, 17*(11). https://pdfs.semanticscholar.org/89ad/c568261ad273b-1c6e00c7161b191885d9d80.pdf

Bacha, E., & Walker, S. (2013). The relationship between transformational leadership and followers' perceptions of fairness. *Journal of Business Ethics, 116*(3), 667680. doi:10.1007/s10551-012-1507-z

Ballhaus, R., & Miller, S. (2014, Nov 24). U.S. New obituary: Washington's 'mayor for life'. *Wall Street Journal.* Retrieved from https://proxy.cecybrary.com/login?url=https://search.proquest.com/docview/1627006847?accountid=144459

Baron, L., Morin, L., & Morin, D. (2011). Executive coaching. *Journal of Management Development, 30*(9), 847–864. doi:10.1108/02621711111164330

Barondees, J. A. (1997). On mentoring. *Journal of the Royal Society of Medicine, 90*(6), 347–349. doi:10.1177/014107689709000617 PMID:9227389

Bartlett, J. II, Boylan, R., & Hale, J. (2014). Executive coaching: An integrative literature review. *Journal of Human Resource and Sustainability Studies, 2*(4), 188–195. doi:10.4236/jhrss.2014.24018

Bartlett, J. A. (2013). New and noteworthy: Paying it forward, giving it back: The dynamics of mentoring. *mLibrary Leadership & Management , 27,* 1-6.

Belias, D., & Koutelios, A. (2014). The impact of leadership and change management strategy on organizational culture. *European Scientific Journal, 10*(7), 451–470. https://www.eujournal.org/index.php/esj/article/viewFile/2996/2822

Bell, R. L. (2009). Dialing in to the hidden hierarchy: An analysis of culture as content in popular press business books. *Journal of Leadership, Accountability and Ethics, 7*(3), 1–20. https://proxy.cecybrary.com/login?url=https://search.proquest.com/docview/608439443?accountid=144459

Benavides, L. (2008). *The relationship between executive coaching and organizational performance of female executives as a predictor for organizational success.* Doctoral dissertation, University of San Francisco, CA. Retrieved from https://repository.usfca.edu/diss/194

Bennett, K. (2021). Leaders' adaptive identity development in uncertain contexts: Implications for executive coaching. *International Journal of Evidence Based Coaching and Mentoring, 19*(2), 54–69.

Berg, B. L., & Lune, H. (2013). *Qualitative research methods for the social sciences, Plus myresearchkit without etext by Bruce L. Berg.* Pearson.

Berg, M., & Karlsen, J. (2011). An evaluation of management training and coaching. *Journal of Workplace Learning, 24*(3), 177–199. doi:10.1108/13665621211209267

Biggeman, S. (2015). Modeling the structure of business-to-business relationships. In A. Woodside (Ed.), *Organizational culture, business-to-business relationships, and interfirm networks* (pp. 27–177). Emerald Group Publishing.

Bishop, T. F., Press, M. J., Mendelsohn, J. L., & Casalino, L. P. (2013). Electronic communication improves access, but barriers to its widespread adoption remain. *Health Affairs, 32*(8), 1361–1367. doi:10.1377/hlthaff.2012.1151 PMID:23918479

Blau, M., & Simon, D. (2016, October 28). Former PA Attorney General Kathleen Kane gets prison term. *CNN Politics*. Retrieved from https://www.cnn.com/2016/10/24/politics/pennsylvania-attorney-general-sentencing/index.html

Bowles, C., & Flynn, E. (2015). Sports stadiums: What's in a name? *American Bankruptcy Institute Journal, 34*(7), 38-39, 71. Retrieved from https://proxy.cecybrary.com/login?url=https://search.proquest.com/docview/1695789756?accountid=144459

Boysen, S., Cherry, M., Amerie, W., & Takagawa, M. (2018). Organisational coaching outcomes: A comparison of a practitioner survey and key findings from the literature. *International Journal of Evidence Based Coaching and Mentoring, 16*(1), 159–166.

Boysen, S. M., Arya, T., & Page, L. (2021). Creating a coaching culture in a non-profit. *International Journal of Evidence Based Coaching and Mentoring, 19*(2), 115–132.

Brennand, C. (2017, February). Unlocking a Federal Coaching Culture. *Association for Talent Development (ATD)*. Retrieved from https://www.td.org/Publications/Magazines/The-Public-Manager/Archives/2017/02/Unlocking-a-Federal-Coaching-Culture

Brown, M. E., & Treviño, L. K. (2014). Do role models matter? An investigation of role modeling as an antecedent of perceived ethical leadership. *Journal of Business Ethics, 122*(4), 587-598. doi:http://dx.doi.org.proxy.cecybrary.com/10.1007/s10551-013-1769-0

Brown, R. P., Varghese, L., Sullivan, S., & Parsons, S. (2021). The impact of professional coaching on emerging leaders. *International Journal of Evidence Based Coaching and Mentoring, 19*(2), 24–37.

Brunhart, A. D. (2013). *The relationship between felt accountability and perceived overall organizational performance in federal agencies* (Doctoral dissertation). Retrieved from ProQuest Dissertations & Thesis Global (Order No. 3554024).

Burgess, J., & Dyer, S. (2009). Workplace mentoring for indigenous Australians: A case study. *Equal Opportunities International, 28*(6), 465–485. doi:10.1108/02610150910980774

Burkus, D. (2014). How to tell if your company has a creative culture. *Harvard Business Review*. Retrieved from https://hbr.org/2014/12/how-to-tell-if-your-company-has-a-creative-culture

Burton, S. L. (2007). *Quality customer service; Rekindling the art of service to customers*. Lulu Publications.

Caillier, J. G. (2016). Toward a better understanding of the relationship between transformational leadership, public service motivation, mission valence, and employee performance: A preliminary study. *Public Personnel Management, 43*(2), 218–239. doi:10.1177/0091026014528478

Cameron, E., & Green, M. (2015). *Making Sense of Change Management: A Complete Guide to the Models, Tools and Techniques of Organizational Change* (1st ed.). Kogan Page.

Cato Institute. (2017). Downsizing the federal government. Department of Education. *Downsizing Government*. Retrieved from https://www.downsizinggovernment.org/education

Caulfield, M., Collier, A., & Halawa, S. (2013). Rethinking online community in MOOCS used for blended learning. *Educause Review Online*. Retrieved from https://www.educause.edu/ero/article/rethinking-online-community-moocs-used-blended-learning

Censer, M. (2011, October 30). Executive coaching contracts pick up speed. *The Washington Post*.

Center for Leadership Studies. (2017). *The Cost of Poor Leadership On Your Revenue And Culture*. Retrieved from: https://www.gbscorporate.com/blog/the-cost-of-poor-leadership-on-your-revenue-and-culture

Chingching, C. (2016). Methodological issues in advertising research: Current status, shifts, and trends. *Journal of Advertising*, *46*(1), 2–20. doi:10.1080/00913367.2016.1274924

Chong, D. (2013). The relevance of management to society: Peter Drucker's oeuvre from the 1940s and 1950s. *Journal of Management History*, *19*(1), 55–72. doi:10.1108/17511341311286196

Chong, W. C., Yuen, Y. Y., Tan, B. C., Zarim, Z. A., & Hamid, N. A. (2016). Managerial coaches, are they ready? The case of Malaysian telecommunications industry. *The Learning Organization*, *23*(2/3), 121–140. doi:10.1108/TLO-03-2015-0016

Ciporen, R. (2015). The emerging field of executive and organizational coaching: An overview. *New Directions for Adult and Continuing Education*, *2015*(148), 5–15. Advance online publication. doi:10.1002/ace.20147

Coach, U. (2005). *Coach U; About Coach U and corporate Coach U*. Retrieved from http://www.coachu-hq.com/

Cowie, K. (2008, May/June). The HR challenge: leadership development for ordinary heroes. *Ivey Business Journal*. Retrieved from https://iveybusinessjournal.com/publication/the-hr-challenge-leadership-development-for-ordinary-heroes/

Cox, E. (2013). *Coaching understood. A pragmatic inquiry into the coaching process*. Sage Publications Ltd. doi:10.4135/9781446270134

Crabtree, S., Kasperowicz, P., King, R., Lawler, J., Russell, J., Siciliano, J., Takala, R., & Westwood, S. (2016, February 20). These 8 federal agencies are the worst. Here's how to fix them. *The Washington Examiner*. Retrieved from http://www.washingtonexaminer.com/these-8-federal-agencies-are-the-worst-heres-how-to-fix-them/article/2583708

Creswell, J. W. (2013). *Qualitative Inquiry and Research Design: Choosing Among Five Approaches*. Sage Publishing.

Creswell, J. W. (2017). *Qualitative inquiry and research design: Choosing among five approaches*. Sage Publications.

Cummings-White, I. (2013). *Preparing for the boomer exodus: An exploration of knowledge transfer in a municipality* (Order No. 3573953). Available from ABI/INFORM Collection. (1438049225). Retrieved from https://proxy.cecybrary.com/login?url=https://search.proquest.com/docview/1438049225?accountid=144459

Cunningham, J., & Hillier, E. (2013). Informal learning in the workplace: Key activities and processes. *Education + Training, 55*(1), 37–51. doi:10.1108/00400911311294960

Dalati, S. (2014). *Universal leadership across social culture: Theoretical framework, design, and measurement.* Retrieved from https://proxy.cecybrary.com/login?url=https://search.proquest.com/docview/1781570423?accountid=144459

Dartey-Baah, K. (2015). Resilient leadership: A transformational-transactional leadership mix. *Journal of Global Responsibility, 6*(1), 99–112. doi:10.1108/JGR-07-2014-0026

Dasgupta, M. (2015). Exploring the relevance of case study research. *Vision, 12*(2), 147-160. doi:10.1177/0972262915575661

Daveron, J. (2017). Organizational Culture & Employee Performance. *Chronicles of Small Business.* Retrieved from https://smallbusiness.chron.com/organizational-culture-employee-performance-25216.html

de Haan, E., Duckworth, A., Birch, D., & Jones, C. (2013). Executive coaching outcome research: The contribution of common factors such as relationship, personality match, and self-efficacy. *Consulting Psychology Journal, 65*(1), 40–57. doi:10.1037/a0031635

de Haan, E., & Nieb, C. (2015). Differences between critical moments for clients, coaches, and sponsors of coaching. *International Coaching Psychology Review, 10*(1), 1750–2764. doi:10.53841/bpsicpr.2015.10.1.38

de Vires, M. F. R. K. (2014). Dream journeys: A new territory for executive coaching. *Consulting Psychology Journal, 66*(2), 77–92. doi:10.1037/cpb0000004

Deal, J. J., Stawiski, S., Graves, L., Gentry, W. A., Weber, T. J., & Ruderman, M. (2013). Motivation at work: Which matters more, generation or managerial level? *Consulting Psychology Journal, 65*(1), 1–16. doi:10.1037/a0032693

Dean, M. L., & Meyer, A. A. (2002). Executive coaching: In search of a model. *Journal of Leadership Education, 1*(2), 3–17. doi:10.12806/V1/I2/RF1

Diedrich, R. (1996, Spring). An iterative approach to executive coaching. *The Hay Group Consulting Psychology Journal: Practice and Research, 48*(2), 61-66. http://members.aoaorg/ftdocs/cpb/1996/spring/cpb48261.html pp. 1-6.

Dolezalek, H. (2006). The dark side: When good leaders go bad. *Training (New York, N.Y.), 43*(6), 20–26. https://proxy.cecybrary.com/login?url=https://search.proquest.com/docview/203401737?accountid=144459

Douglas, A., Lubbe, B., & Inger, F. R. (2013). Travel or technology? Business factors influencing management decisions. *Suid-Afrikaanse Tydskrif vir Ekonomiese en Bestuurswetenskappe, 16*(3), 279–297. doi:10.4102/sajems.v16i3.362

Dutton, G. (1997, February). Executive coaches call the plays. *Management Review, 86*(2).

Eliades, A. B. (2017). Mentoring practice and mentoring benefit 6: Equipping for leadership and leadership readiness: An overview and application to practice using mentoring activities. *Pediatric Nursing, 43*(1), 40–42. https://www.ncbi.nlm.nih.gov/pubmed/29406666 PMID:29406666

Elkhouly, S., Ossman, M., Selim, M., & Zaghloul, M. (2014). Impact of E-leadership on leadership styles within the Egyptian government sector. *Competition Forum, 12*(1), 131-140. Retrieved from https://proxy.cecybrary.com/login?url=https://search.proquest.com/docview/1640568232?accountid=144459

Emelo, R. (2011). Group mentoring best practices. *Industrial and Commercial Training, 43*(4), 221–227. doi:10.1108/00197851111137898

Fischer, E., & Parmentier, M. A. (2010). Doing Qualitative Research With Archival Data: Making Secondary Data a Primary Resource. In M. C. Campbell, J. Inman, & R. Pieters (Eds.), *NA - Advances in Consumer Research* (Vol. 37, pp. 798–799). Association for Consumer Research.

Fragouli, E., & Ibidapo, B. (2015). Leading in crisis: Leading organizational change & business development. Journal of Information. *Business and Management, 7*(3), 71–90.

Francis, M. (2014, May 30). Four leadership observations from Eric Shinseki's tenure at the Department of Veterans Affairs. *The Oregonian/OregonLive*. Retrieved from https://www.oregonlive.com/business/index.ssf/2014/05/four_leadership_observations_f.html

Fry, R. (2015). Millennials surpass Gen Xers as the largest generation in U.S. labor force. *Pew Research Center*. Retrieved from https://www.pewresearch.org/fact-tank/2015/05/11/millennials-surpass-gen-xers-as-the-largest-generation-in-u-s-labor-force/

Fry, R. (2016). Millennials overtake Baby Boomers as America's largest generation. *Pew Research Center*. Retrieved from https://www.pewresearch.org/fact-tank/2016/04/25/millennials-overtake-baby-boomers/

Furimsky, I., Arts, K., & Lampson, S. (2014). Developing a successful peer-to-peer mentoring program. *Applied Clinical Trials, 22*(12), 27–30. https://proxy.cecybrary.com/login?url=https://search.proquest.com/docview/1477195588?accountid=144459

Gable, R. A. (2014). Teaching students with emotional disabilities: Challenges and opportunities. *Special Education Past, Present, and Future: Perspectives from the Field. Advances in Learning and Behavioral Disabilities, 27*, 117–140. doi:10.1108/S0735-004X20140000027008

Gaddis, B. H., & Foster, J. L. (2015). Meta-analysis of dark side personality characteristics and critical work behaviors among leaders across the globe: Findings and implications for leadership development and executive coaching. *Applied Psychology, 64*(1), 25–54. doi:10.1111/apps.12017

Gallagher, S., Brown, C., & Brown, L. (2008). A strong market culture drives organizational performance and success. *Employment Relations Today, 35*(1), 25–31. doi:10.1002/ert.20185

Gallup. (2015). *The State of the American Manager*. The Gallup Organization. Retrieved from https://www.gallup.com/services/182138/state-american-manager.aspx

Gan, G. C., & Chong, C. W. (2015). Coaching relationship in Executive Coaching: A Malaysian study. *Journal of Management Development*, *34*(4), 476–494. doi:10.1108/JMD-08-2013-0104

Gavin, C. S. (2018). The impact of leadership development using coaching. *Journal of Practical Consulting*, *6*(1), 137–147.

Gehlert, K. M., Ressler, T. H., Anderson, N. H., & Swanson, N. M. (2013). A method to improve the coach participant match in executive coaching. *The Coaching Psychologist*, *9*(2), 78–85. doi:10.53841/bpstcp.2013.9.2.78

Geiman, M. (2016). *A Multiple Case Study of the Influence of Positive Organizational Behavioron Human Resources* (Doctoral dissertation or master's thesis). Retrieved from ProQuest. (10129957)

Gerard, J. A., & Weber, C. M. (2015). Compliance and corporate governance: Theoretical analysis of the effectiveness of compliance based on locus of functional responsibility. *International Journal of Global Business*, *8*(1), 15–26. https://proxy.cecybrary.com/login?url=https://search.proquest.com/docview/1680769364?accountid=144459

Girardin, L. (2015). Eight essential books on government leadership. *GovLoop*. Retrieved from https://www.govloop.com/community/blog/8-essential-books-government-leadership/

Goldring, C. C. (2015). *A design for federal government leaders: Succession planning through knowledge management* (Doctoral dissertation). Available from ProQuest Dissertations & Theses Global. (UMI No. 1688688202)

Goldsmith, A., & Levensaler, L. (2016, February). Build a great company culture with help from technology. *Harvard Business Review*. Retrieved from https://hbr.org/2016/02/build-a-great-company-culture-with-help-from-technology

Grant, A. (2014). Troubling 'lived experience': A post-structural critique of mental health nursing qualitative research assumptions. *Journal of Psychiatric and Mental Health Nursing, 21*, 21-24.doi:. 1213 doi:10. 1111/jpm

Grant, A.M. & O'Connor, S.A. (2010). The differential effects of solution-focused and problem-focused coaching questions: A pilot Study with implications for practice. *Industrial and Commercial Training, 42*, 102-111. doi:10.1108/00197851011026090

Gray, D. (2013). Learning from our mistakes. *Training Journal*, 23-26. Retrieved from https://proxy.cecybrary.com/login?url=https://search.proquest.com/docview/1469704072?accountid=144459

Green, D. D., & Roberts, G. E. (2012). Impact of postmodernism on public sector leadership practices: Federal government human capital development implications. *Public Personnel Management*, *41*(1), 79–96. doi:10.1177/009102601204100105

Gursoy, D., Chi, C. G., & Karadag, C. G. (2013). Generational differences in work values and attitudes among frontline and service contact employees. *International Journal of Hospitality Management*, *33*, 1–9. doi:10.1016/j.ijhm.2012.04.002

Gusfield, J. (1957). The problem of generations in an organizational structure. *Social Forces*, *35*(4), 323–330. doi:10.2307/2573321

Hannafey, F. T., & Vitulano, L. A. (2012). Ethics and executive coaching: An agency theory approach. *Journal of Business Ethics, 115*(3), 599–603. doi:10.1007/s10551-012-1442-z

Harakas, P. (2013). Resistance, motivational interviewing, and executive coaching. *Consulting Psychology Journal, 65*(2), 108–127. doi:10.1037/a0033196

Harris, B., Cheng, K. F., & Gorley, C. (2015). Benefits and barriers. *Journal of Workplace Learning, 27*(3), 193–206. doi:10.1108/JWL-07-2014-0053

Harris, L. C., & Crane, A. (2002). The greening of organizational culture: Management views on the depth, degree and diffusion of change. *Journal of Organizational Change Management, 15*(3), 214–234. doi:10.1108/09534810210429273

Hennink, M. M., Hutter, I., & Bailey, A. (2011). *Qualitative Research Methods*. SAGE. Print

Henry, R., Otto, T., & Wood, M. (2013). Ethnographic artifacts and value transformations. *HAU, 3*(2), 33–51. doi:10.14318/hau3.2.004

Hicks, R. P., & McCracken, J. P. (2010). Three hats of a leader: Coaching, mentoring and teaching. *Physician Executive, 36*(6), 68–70. PMID:21140733

Higginbottom, K. (2017, March 17). The challenges of managing a multi-generational workforce. *Forbes Magazine.* Retrieved from https://www.forbes.com/sites/karenhigginbottom/2016/03/17/the-challenges-of-managing-a-multi-generational-workforce/#6be0a41b7d6a

Hillman, D. R. (2014). Understanding multigenerational work-value conflict resolution. *Journal of Workplace Behavioral Health, 29*(3), 240–257. doi:10.1080/15555240.2014.933961

Holland, J. M., Major, D. A., & Orvis, K. A. (2012). Understanding how peer mentoring and capitalization link STEM students to their majors. *The Career Development Quarterly, 60*(4), 343–354. doi:10.1002/j.2161-0045.2012.00026.x

Holt, D. T., Markova, G., Dhaenens, A. J., Marler, L. E., & Heilmann, S. G. (2016). Formal or informal mentoring: What drives employees to seek informal mentors? *Journal of Managerial Issues, 28*(1), 67-82. Retrieved from https://proxy.cecybrary.com/login?url=https://search.proquest.com/docview/1815961188?accountid=144459

Hughes, O. E. (2003). *Public management and administration: An introduction.* Palgrave.

Hunt, D. M., & Michael, M. C. (1983). Mentorship: A career training and development tool. *Academy of Management Review, 8*(3), 475–485. doi:10.2307/257836

Hunter, A., Lewis, N., & Ritter-Gooder, P. (2011). Constructive developmental theory: An alternative approach to leadership. *Journal of the American Dietetic Association, 111*(12), 1804–1808. doi:10.1016/j.jada.2011.10.009 PMID:22117653

Ibarra, H. (2014, Apr 28). Leadership in human resources (A special report) --- why managers are stuck in their 'silos': Companies want employees to take on new responsibilities; but they aren't teaching them how. *Wall Street Journal* Retrieved from https://proxy.cecybrary.com/login?url=https://search.proquest.com/docview/1519234993?accountid=144459

International Coaching Federation. (2021). *About the ICF*. Retrieved from: https://coachingfederation.org/thought-leadership-institute

Isopeskul, O., Shakina, M., & Georgieva, N. (2016). *Influence of stakeholders on organizational culture development*. Retrieved from https://proxy.cecybrary.com/login?url=https://search.proquest.com/docview/1779263332?accountid=144459

Jabeen, F., Behery, M., & Abu Elanain, H. (2015). Examining the relationship between the psychological contract and organisational commitment. *The International Journal of Organizational Analysis*, *23*(1), 102–122. doi:10.1108/IJOA-10-2014-0812

Jansen, H. (2010). The logic of qualitative survey research and its position in the field of social research methods. *Forum: Qualitative Research*, *11*(2). Retrieved from http://nbn-resolving.de/urn:nbn:de:0114-fqs1002110

Johnson, S. (2017). The disadvantages of corporate culture. *Chronicles of Small Business*. Retrieved from https://smallbusiness.chron.com/disadvantages-corporate-culture-67042.html

Johnston, D. (2021). How do coaches and clients create and experience thinking environments? *International Journal of Evidence Based Coaching and Mentoring*, *S15*, 198–211.

Jones, R. A., Rafferty, A. E., & Griffin, M. A. (2006). The executive coaching trend: Towards more flexible executives. *Leadership and Organization Development Journal*, *27*(7), 583–596. doi:10.1108/01437730610692434

Jones, R. J., Woods, S. A., & Hutchinson, E. (2014). The influence of the Five Factor Model of personality on the perceived effectiveness of executive coaching. *International Journal of Evidence Based Coaching and Mentoring*, *12*(2), 109–118.

Joo, B., Sushko, J. S., & McLean, G. N. (2012). Multiple faces of coaching: Manager-as-coach, executive coaching, and formal mentoring. *Organization Development Journal*, *30*(1), 19-38. Retrieved From http://blogs.wayne.edu/ioadventures/files/2013/12/Multiple-Faces-of-Coaching-Manager-as-coach-Executive-Coaching-and-Formal-Mentoring.pdf

Joo, B. K. (2005). Executive Coaching: A Conceptual Framework From an Integrative Review of Practice and Research. *Human Resource Development Review*, *4*(4), 462–488. doi:10.1177/1534484305280866

Kafle, N. (2011). Hermeneutic phenomenological research method simplified. *Bodhi: An Interdisciplinary Journal*, *5*, 181–198.

Katz, E. (2018a, October 3). *OPM Calls on Agencies to Implement Coaching Programs for Employees*. Government Executive.

Katz, E. (2018b, January 10). *Agencies Aren't Catching Bad Supervisors Early Enough*. Government Executive.

Kavoura, A., & Bitsani, E. (2014). Considerations for qualitative communication research. *Procedia: Social and Behavioral Sciences*, *147*, 544–549. doi:10.1016/j.sbspro.2014.07.156

Keikha, A., Hoveida, R., & Nour, M. Y. (2017). The development of an intelligent leadership model for state universities. *Foresight and STI Governance, 11*(1), 66–74. doi:10.17323/2500-2597.2017.1.66.74.

Keller, J. M. (2010). *Motivational Design for Learning and Performance: The ARCS model approach.* Springer. doi:10.1007/978-1-4419-1250-3

Kellis, D. S., & Ran, B. (2015). Effective leadership in managing NPM-based change in the public sector. *Journal of Organizational Change Management, 28*(4), 614–626. doi:10.1108/JOCM-11-2013-0229

Kerrigan, H. (2015). Eight Tips for changing culture in the federal government. *GovLoop.* Retrieved from https://www.govloop.com/community/blog/8-tips-culture-change/

Khosla, R. (2013). A case study of mentoring at ONGC. *Review of HRM, 2,* 290–298. https://proxy.cecybrary.com/login?url=https://search.proquest.com/docview/1655997777?accountid=144459

Khulumane, M. (2013). Instilling safety culture in the passenger rail transport industry within the South African context. *Journal of Transport and Supply Chain Management, 7*(1). Advance online publication. doi:10.4102/jtscm.v7i1.84

Kilburg, R. R. (1996). Toward a conceptual understanding and definition of executive coaching. *Consulting Psychology Journal, 48*(2), 134–144. doi:10.1037/1061-4087.48.2.134

Kilburg, R. R. (1996). Toward a conceptual understanding and definition of executive coaching. *Consulting Psychology Journal, 48*(2), 134–144. doi:10.1037/1061-4087.48.2.134

Kilburg, R. R. (2000). *Executive coaching: Developing managerial wisdom in a world of chaos.* American Psychological Association. doi:10.1037/10355-000

Kim, S. E. (2014). The mentor-protégé affinity on mentoring outcomes: The mediating effect of developmental networking. *International Review of Public Administration, 19*(1), 91–106. doi:10.1080/12294659.2014.887368

Kissinger, H. (2014). *World order.* Penguin Press.

Knouse, S. B. (2013). Mentoring for Hispanics. *Review of Business, 33*(2), 80–90. https://proxy.cecybrary.com/login?url=https://search.proquest.com/docview/1471854143?accountid=144459

Koonce, R. (2010). Executive coaching: Leadership development in the federal government. *Public Manager, 39*(2), 44-51. Retrieved from https://proxy.cecybrary.com/login?url=https://search.proquest.com/docview/733013948?accountid=144459

Kuula, A. (2010). Methodological and ethical dilemmas of archiving qualitative data. *IASSIST Quarterly, 34*(3), 12–17.

LaFraniere, S. (1990, January). Barry Arrested on cocaine charges in undercover FBI, police operation. *The Washington Post.* Retrieved from https://www.washingtonpost.com/wp-srv/local/longterm/tours/scandal/barry.htm

Lai, Y.-L., & Palmer, S. (2019). Psychology in executive coaching: An integrated literature review. *Journal of Work-Applied Management, 11*(2), 143–164. doi:10.1108/JWAM-06-2019-0017

Lebihan, R. (2011). Business schools tap coaching trend. *Australian Financial Review*, *14*, 27–28.

Lee, D., Choi, Y., Youn, S., & Chun, J. U. (2017). Ethical leadership and employee moral voice: The mediating role of moral efficacy and the moderating role of leader-follower value congruence. *Journal of Business Ethics*, *141*(1), 47–57. doi:10.1007/s10551-015-2689-y

Lee, R. J. & Frisch, M. H. (2015). Legacy reflections: ten lessons about becoming an executive coach, *Consulting Psychology Journal: Practice and Research, 67*(1), 3 – 1. Doi.org/10.1037cpb00000033

Lewis, L. & Wescott, H. (2017). Multi-Generational Workforce: Four Generations United In Lean. *Journal of Business Studies Quarterly*, 8.

Lindblom, A., Kajalo, S., & Mitronen, L. (2016). Does a retailer's charisma matter? A study of frontline employee perceptions of charisma in the retail setting. *Journal of Services Marketing*, *30*(3), 266–276. doi:10.1108/JSM-05-2015-0160

Loy, S. L., Brown, S., & Tabibzadeh, K. (2014). South Carolina department of revenue: Mother of government dysfunction. *Journal of the International Academy for Case Studies*, *20*(2). http://www.alliedacademies.org/articles/jiacsvol20no22014.pdf#page=81

Luthans, F., Avolio, B. J., Avey, J. B., & Norman, S. M. (2007). Positive psychological capital: Measurement and relationship with performance and satisfaction. *Personnel Psychology*, *3*(60), 541–572. doi:10.1111/j.1744-6570.2007.00083.x

Lyons, S., & Kuron, L. (2014). Generational differences in the workplace: A review of the evidence and directions for future research. *Journal of Organizational Behavior*, *35*(S1), 139–157. doi:10.1002/job.1913

Lyons, S., Urick, M., Kuron, L., & Schweitzer, L. (2015). Generational differences in the workplace: There is complexity beyond the stereotypes. *Industrial and Organizational Psychology: Perspectives on Science and Practice*, *8*(3), 346–356. doi:10.1017/iop.2015.48

Maldonado, M. L. (2015). Withstanding the tests of time. *Leadership Excellence Essentials, 32*(1), 9-10. Retrieved from https://proxy.cecybrary.com/login?url=https://search.proquest.com/docview/16489815 52?accountid=144459

Marshall, C., & Rossman, G. (2016). *Designing qualitative research* (6th ed.). Sage. Retrieved from: https://books.google.com/books?hl=en&lr=&id=qTByBgAAQBAJ&oi=fnd&pg=PT8&dq=Marshall, +C.,+%26+Rossman,+G.+(2016).+Designing+qualitative+res earch+(6th+ed.).+Thousands+&ots= xhzaGEZZe2&sig=z9mLUoXC9R0Sb6VJgN2w5T_8tig#v=onepage&q&f=false

Mastrangelo, A., Eddy, E. R., & Lorenzet, S. J. (2014). The relationship between enduring. leadership and organizational performance. *Leadership and Organization Development Journal*, *35*, 590–604. doi:10.1108/LODJ-08-2012-0097

Maxwell, J. (2013). *5 Levels of leadership*. Center Street Publishing.

McKeown, A., & Bates, J. (2013). Emotional intelligent leadership. *Library Management, 34*(6), 462-485. doi:http://dx.doi.org.proxy.cecybrary.com/10.1108/LM-10-2012-0072

Mendez, M. J., Howell, J. P., & Bishop, J. W. (2015). Beyond the unidimensional collective leadership model. *Leadership and Organization Development Journal, 36*(6), 675–696. doi:10.1108/LODJ-11-2013-0141

Merit Services Protection. (2018). *Barriers to effectively using the supervisory probationary period* (Issues of Merit). *Merit Services Protection Board.* Retrieved from: https://www.mspb.gov/MSPBSEARCH/viewdocs.aspx?docnumber=1477762&version=1483321&application=ACROBAT

Merriam, S. (2014). *Qualitative research: A guide to design and implementation.* John Wiley & Sons.

Mezirow, J. (1997). Transformative Learning Theory to Practice. *New Directions for Adult and Continuing Education, 74*(74), 5–12. doi:10.1002/ace.7401

Miller-Jones, G. (2020, February 25). Ineffective Leadership and The Devastating Individual And Organizational Consequences. *Forbes.*

Ming-Chu, Y., & Meng-Hsiu, L. (2015). Unlocking the black box: Exploring the link between perceive organizational support and resistance to change. *Asia Pacific Management Review, 20*(3), 177–183. doi:10.1016/j.apmrv.2014.10.003

Mithiotis, A., & Argirou, N. (2016). Coaching: From challenge to opportunity. *Journal of Management Development, 35*(4), 448–463. doi:10.1108/JMD-10-2014-0139

Morse, A. L., & McEvoy, C. D. (2014). Qualitative research in sport management. *CASE (Philadelphia, Pa.).*

Mustafa, G., & Lines, R. (2016). The emergence and effects of culturally congruent leadership: Current status and future developments. *Entrepreneurial Business and Economics Review, 4*(1), 161–180. doi:10.15678/EBER.2016.040110

Naikal, A., & Chandra, S. (2013). Organisational culture: A case study. *International Journal of Knowledge Management and Practices, 1*(2), 17–24. https://proxy.cecybrary.com/login?url=https://search.proquest.com/docview/1845265395?accountid=144459

Nangalia, L., & Nangalia, A. (2010). The Coach in Asian Society: Impact of social hierarchy on the coaching relationship. *International Journal of Evidence Based Coaching and Mentoring, 8*(1), 51–66.

NASA Shared Services Center. (2016). *What are executive core qualifications (ECQs)?* Retrieved from https://answers.nssc.nasa.gov/app/answers/detail/a_id/5631/~/what-are-executive-core-qualifications-(ecqs)%3F

National Defense University. (n.d.). *Strategic leadership and decision making: Organizational culture.* Retrieved from http://www.au.af.mil/au/awc/awcgate/ndu/strat-ldr-dm/pt4ch16.html

Newsom, G., & Dent, E. B. (2011). A work behaviour analysis of executive coaches. *International Journal of Evidence Based Coaching and Mentoring, 9*(2), 1–22.

Nickerson, J. (2014). How to lead change when you are a middle manager. *Excellence in Government.* Retrieved from https://www.govexec.com/excellence/promising-practices/2014/05/how-lead-change-when-youre-middle-manager/84190/

Noble, H., & Smith, J. (2015). Issues of validity and reliability in qualitative research. *Evidence-Based Nursing, 18*(2), 34–35. doi:10.1136/eb-2015-102054 PMID:25653237

Nosheen, R. N. (2013). Peer mentoring: Enhancing social cohesion in Pakistani Universities. *Higher Education, Skills and Work - Based Learning, 3*(2), 130-140. doi:10.1108/20423891311313162

O'Reilly, M., & Parker, N. (2012). Unsatisfactory saturation: A critical examination of the notion of saturated sample size in qualitative research. *Qualitative Research, 13*(2), 190–197. doi:10.1177/1468794112446106

Office of Alcoholism and Substance Abuse Services. (2017). *Creating a healthy organizational culture: From assessment to change.* Retrieved from https://www.oasas.ny.gov/admed/documents/OWEwork-book.pdf

Office of Personnel Management. (2017). *Center for leadership development.* Retrieved from https://leadership.opm.gov/index.aspx

Onwuegbuzie, A., Leech, N., & Collins, K. (2010). Innovative data collection strategies in qualitative research. *The Qualitative Report, 15*(3), 696–726. http://www.nova.edu/ssss/QR/QR15-3/onwuegbuzie.pdf

Oppong, N. Y. (2017). Still the Dark Continent? Towards contextual methodological approaches to management development research in foreign multinational firms in Africa. *International Journal of Cross Cultural Management, 17*(2), 237–256. doi:10.1177/1470595817706384

Otter, K. (2017). Leadership coaching 2.0: Improving the marriage between leadership and coaching. *Philosophy of Coaching, 2*(2), 69–82. doi:10.22316/poc/02.2.05

Palinkas, L., Horowitz, S., Green, C., Wisdom, J., Duan, N., & Hoagwood, K. (2013). *Purposive sampling in qualitative data collection and analysis in mixed method implementation research.* Admin Policy Ment Health. doi:10.1007/s10488-013-0528-y

Passmore, J. (2007). An integrative model for Executive Coaching. *Consulting Psychology Journal, 59*(1), 68–78. doi:10.1037/1065-9293.59.1.68

Passmore, J., & Fillery-Travis, A. (2011). A critical review of executive coaching research: A decade of progress and what's to come. *Coaching (Abingdon, UK), 4*(2), 70–88. doi:10.1080/17521882.2011.596484

Pavgi, K. (2012, October 10). Congressional Republicans call for resignation of VA chief of staff. *Government Executive.* Retrieved from https://www.govexec.com/oversight/2012/10/congressional-republicans-call-resignation-va-chief-staff/58688/?oref=relatedstories

Peg, B. S., & Single, R. M. (2007). E-mentoring for social equity: Review of research to inform program development. *Mentoring & Tutoring,* 301–320. https://www.tandfonline.com/doi/citedby/10.1080/1361 1260500107481?scroll=top&needAccess=true

Performance Coaching International. (2012). *History of coaching.* Retrieved from PCI: http://www.performancecoachinginternational.com/resources/articles/historyofcoaching.php

Performance Consultants International. (2018). *GROW Model: GROWing people, performance, and purpose.* Retrieved from https://www.coachingperformance.com/wp-content/uploads/2018/10/GROW-Model-Guide.pdf

Phipps, K. (2010). Servant leadership and constructive development theory: How servant leaders make meaning of service. *Journal of Leadership Education, 9*(2), 151–169. doi:10.12806/V9/I2/TF1

Pinho, J. C., Ana, P. R., & Dibb, S. (2014). The role of corporate culture, market orientation and organisational commitment in organisational performance. *Journal of Management Development, 33*(4), 374–398. doi:10.1108/JMD-03-2013-0036

Plavin-Masterman, M. (2015). Are Walls Just Walls? Organizational culture emergence in a virtual firm. *Journal of Organizational Culture, Communications and Conflict, 19*(2), 43-68. Retrieved from https://proxy.cecybrary.com/login?url=https://search.proquest.com/docview/1750418352?accountid=144459

Qian, J., Lin, X., Han, Z. R., Chen, Z. X., & Hays, J. M. (2015). What matters in the relationship between mentoring and job-related stress? The moderating effects of prote'ge's' traditionality and trust in mentor. *Journal of Management & Organization, 20*(5), 608–623. doi:10.1017/jmo.2014.46

Qin, Q., Wen, B., Ling, Q., Zhou, S., & Tong, M. (2014). How and when the effect of ethical leadership occurs? A multilevel analysis in the Chinese hospitality industry. *International Journal of Contemporary Hospitality Management, 26*(6), 974–1001. doi:10.1108/IJCHM-02-2013-0073

Rainie, L. (2017). 10 fact about jobs in the future. *Pew research Center, Internet & Technology*. Retrieved from https://www.pewinternet.org/2017/10/10/10-facts-about-jobs-in-the-future/

Rekalde, I., Landeta, J., & Albizu, E. (2015). Determining factors in the effectiveness of executive coaching as a management development tool. *Management Decision, 53*(8), 1677–1697. doi:10.1108/MD-12-2014-0666

Rekalde, I., Landeta, J., & Albizu, E. (2015). Determining factors in the effectiveness of executive coaching as a management development tool. *Management Decision, 53*, 1677-1697. doi:10.1108/MD-12-2014-0666

Rhodes, J. (2015). Top 25 mentoring relationships in history. *The Chronicle of Evidence-Based Mentoring*. Retrieved from https://chronicle.umbmentoring.org/top-25-mentoring-relationships-in-history/

Richardson, M. (2015). Mentoring for a Dispersed Workforce. *Training & Development, 42*(5), 18–19. https://proxy.cecybrary.com/login?url=https://search.proquest.com/docview/1726692601?accountid=144459

Robinson, D. M., & Reio, T. G. Jr. (2012). Benefits of mentoring African-American men. *Journal of Managerial Psychology, 27*(4), 406–421. doi:10.1108/02683941211220207

Roelofs, B. (2019). How shadow coaching helps leaders to improve their performance on the job in real-time. *International Journal of Evidence Based Coaching and Mentoring, S13*, 49–62.

Rolfe, A. (2014). Taking mentoring to the next level in organisations. *Training & Development, 41*(2), 26–27. https://proxy.cecybrary.com/login?url=https://search.proquest.com/docview/1527341167?accountid=144459

Rosha, A. (2014). Peculiarities of manifestation of coaching in organizations. *Procedia: Social and Behavioral Sciences, 110*, 852–860. doi:10.1016/j.sbspro.2013.12.930

Rowland, K. N. (2011). *E-mentoring: Benefits to the workplace* (Order No. 3493777). Available from ABI/INFORM Collection. (919692070). Retrieved from https://proxy.cecybrary.com/login?url=https://search.proquest.com/docview/919692070?accountid=144459

Rutti, R. M., Helms, M. M., & Rose, L. C. (2013). Changing the lens: Viewing the mentoring relationship as relational structures in a social exchange framework. *Leadership and Organization Development Journal, 34*(5), 446–468. doi:10.1108/LODJ-11-0097

Saini, D. (2015). Integral leadership style: A new perspective. *International Journal on Leadership, 3*(2), 40–47. doi:10.21863/ijl/2015.3.2.007

Saldana, J. (2012). *The coding manual for qualitative researchers.* Sage.

Salem, I. E. (2015). Transformational leadership: Relationship to job stress and job burnout in five-star hotels. *Tourism and Hospitality Research, 15*(4), 240-253. http://dx.doi.org.proxy.cecybrary.com/10.1177/1467358415581445

Sargeant, J. (2012). Qualitative research part II: Participants, analysis, and quality assurance. *Journal of Graduate Medical Education, 4*(March), 1–3. doi:10.4300/JGME-D-11-00307.1 PMID:23451297

Scalia, A., Calabresi, S. G., Harrison, J., & Reynolds, W. B. (2013). In memoriam: Robert H. Bork. *Harvard Journal of Law & Public Policy, 36*(3), 1231–1243, 1245–1256. https://proxy.cecybrary.com/login?url=https://search.proquest.com/docview/1415163652?accountid=144459

Schein, E. (2004). *Organizational culture and leadership* (3rd ed.). John Wiley and Sons.

Schueths, A. M., & Carranza, M. A. (2012). Navigating around educational road blocks: Mentoring for pre-K to 20+ Latino/a students. *Latino Studies, 10*(4), 566–586. doi:10.1057/lst.2012.43

Seaton, H. V. (2007). *The financial implications and organizational cultural perceptions of implementing a performance management system in a government enterprise* (Order No. 3294734). Available from ABI/INFORM Collection. (304699669). Retrieved from https://proxy.cecybrary.com/login?url=https://search.proquest.com/docview/304699669?accountid=144459

Semiyu, A. A., & Folorunso, A. A. (2013). Peer coaching as an institutionalised tool for professional development. *Journal of Workplace Learning, 25*(2), 125–140. doi:10.1108/13665621311299807

Short, T. W. (2014). Workplace mentoring: An old idea with new meaning (part 1). *Development and Learning in Organizations, 28*(1), 8–11. doi:10.1108/DLO-09-2013-0077

Siegel, P. H., Schultz, T., & Landy, S. (2011). Formal versus informal mentoring of MAS professionals. *Journal of Applied Business Research, 27*(2), 5–11. doi:10.19030/jabr.v27i2.4135

Silva, P., & Cooray, R. (2014). Building human capital in organizations through corporate social responsibility – a holistic coaching approach. *Procedia: Social and Behavioral Sciences, 159*, 753–758. doi:10.1016/j.sbspro.2014.12.443

Skinner, M. E., & Welch, F. C. (1996). Peer coaching for better teaching. *College Teaching, 44*(4), 153–156. doi:10.1080/87567555.1996.9932346

Solaja, O. M., Idown, F. E., & James, A. E. (2015). Exploring the relationship between leadership communication style, personality trait and organizational productivity. *Serbian Journal of Management, 11*(1), 99–117. doi:10.5937/sjm11-8480

Sooley, K. (2016). *Examining Supervisor Emotional Intelligence and Employee Organizational Commitment* (Doctoral dissertation). Retrieved from ProQuest Dissertation and Thesis database. (UMI No. 10248026)

Sperber, D., & Wilson, D. (1986). *Relevance: Communication and cognition.* Blackwell Publishers ltd.

Sperber, D., & Wilson, D. (1995). *Relevance: Communication and Cognition* (2nd ed.). Blackwell Publishers Ltd.

Sperry, L. (2013). Executive coaching and leadership assessment: Past, present, and future. *Consulting Psychology Journal, 65*(4), 284–288. doi:10.1037/a0035453

Strategy, A. (2017). *IT cost reduction: Exploiting new technologies to reduce cost and gain agility.* Retrieved from https://www.accenture.com/us-en/insight-it-cost-reductions-new-technologies

Swensen, S., Gorringe, G., Caviness, J., & Peters, D. (2016). Leadership by design: Intentional organization development of physician leaders. *Journal of Management Development, 35*(4), 549–570. doi:10.1108/JMD-08-2014-0080

Taconis, M. (2018). How high potential coaching can add value – for participants and the organization. *International Journal of Evidence Based Coaching and Mentoring, S12,* 61–72.

Tannenbaum, N. (2014). Talent management: Managing the multigenerational workplace. *University of North Carolina Kenan-Flagler Business School.* Retrieved from http://execdev.kenan-flagler.unc.edu/blog/managing-the-multigenerational-workplace-0

Tareef, A. (2013). The relationship between mentoring and career development of higher education faculty members. *College Student Journal, 47*(4), 703–710.

Terblanche, N. H. D., Albertyn, R. M., & van Coller-Peter, S. (2017). Designing a coaching intervention to support leaders promoted into senior positions. *SA Journal of Human Resource Management, 15*(0). doi:10.4102/sajhrm.v15i0.842

The Global Leadership Forecast 2014-2015. (2015). *Ready-now leaders: 25 Findings to meet tomorrow's business challenges* (DDI publication No.7th). Retrieved from the Conference Board Organization: https://www.ddiworld.com/DDI/media/trend-research/global-leadership-forecast-2014-2015_tr_ddi.pdf

Thursfield, D., & Kellie, J. (2013). Unitary practice or pluralist empowerment? *Personnel Review, 42*(4), 488–504. doi:10.1108/PR-08-2011-0124

Time to Think. (2020). *The ten components.* Retrieved from https://www.timetothink.com/thinking-environment/the-ten-components/

Tkaczyk, B. (2016, November/December). Coaching by numbers. *Ivey Business Journal.* Retrieved from https://iveybusinessjournal.com/coaching-by-numbers/

Tobias, R. M. (2015). When the executive core qualifications aren't enough. *Excellence in Government*. Retrieved from https://www.govexec.com/excellence/promising-practices/2015/01/when-executive-core-qualifications-arent-enough/103992/

Toit, A., & Reissner, S. (2012). Experiences of coaching in team learning. *International Journal of Mentoring and Coaching in Education*, *1*(3), 177–190. doi:10.1108/20466851211279448

Trevillion, F. M. H. (2018). Executive coaching outcomes: An investigation into leadership development using five dyadic case studies illustrating the impact of executive coaching. *International Journal of Evidence Based Coaching and Mentoring*, *S12*, 21–40.

Turner, C., & McCarthy, G. (2015). Coachable moments: Identifying factors that influence managers to take advantage of coachable moments in day-to-day management. *International Journal of Evidence Based Coaching and Mentoring*, *13*(1), 1–13.

Turner, D. (2010). Qualitative interview design: A practical guide for novice investigators. *The Qualitative Report*, *15*(3), 754–760.

Tyran, K. L., & Garcia, J. E. (2015). Reciprocal learning and management education: The example of using university alumni and other business executives as "virtual" mentors to business students. *Journal of the Academy of Business Education*, *16*, 54–72. https://proxy.cecybrary.com/login?url=https://search.proquest.com/docview/1713929835?accountid=144459

U. S. Census Bureau. (2016). American Fact Finder. *United States Census Bureau*. Retrieved from https://factfinder.census.gov/faces/tableservices/jsf/pages/productview.xhtml?pid=PEP_2016_PEPSYASEXN&prodType=table

United States Office of Personnel Management (OPM). (2017). *Training and development policy wiki: Mentoring in government*. Retrieved from https://www.opm.gov/wiki/training/mentoring-and-coaching.ashx

University of New Mexico. (2014). The history of mentorship part 1. *The University of New Mexico*. Retrieved from https://mentor.unm.edu/blog/2014/04/10/the-history-of-mentorship-part-1

Uzkurt, C., Kumar, R., Kimzan, H. S., & Eminoglu, G. (2013). Role of innovation in the relationship between organizational culture and firm performance. *European Journal of Innovation Management*, *16*(1), 92–117. doi:10.1108/14601061311292878

van Thiel, J. P. (2016). *A quantitative analysis of supervisor leadership effectiveness: The perception of federal employees* (Doctoral dissertation). Retrieved from ProQuest Dissertations & Thesis Global (Order No. 10140357).

Velsor, E. V., Turregano, C., Adams, B. Fleenor, J. (2016). Creating tomorrow's government leaders an overview of top leadership challenges and how they can be addressed. *Center for Creative Leadership*. Retrieved from file:///C:/Users/Dr.%20B/Desktop/creating-government-leaders-and-addressing-challenges-center-for-creative-leadership.pdf

Waaland, T. (2013). Job characteristics and mentoring in pre-schools. *Journal of Workplace Learning*, *25*(5), 310–327. doi:10.1108/JWL-Mar-2012-0027

Walker-Fraser, A. (2011). An HR perspective on executive coaching for organisational learning. *International Journal of Evidence Based Coaching and Mentoring*, 2(9), 67–79.

Ward, G., van de Loo, F. E., & Ten Have, S. (2014). Psychodynamic group e6xecutive coaching: A literature review. *International Journal of Evidence Based Coaching and Mentoring*, 12(1), 63–78.

Washington, N. J. (2015). *Servant leadership characteristics among senior executive service leaders in the U.S. federal government: A phenomenological study* (Order No. 3714421). Retrieved from https://proxy.cecybrary.com/login?url=https://search.proquest.com/docview/1708991087?accountid=144459

Westwood, S. (2016, February 20). These 8 federal agencies are the worst. Here's how to fix them. *The Washington Examiner*. Retrieved from http://www.washingtonexaminer.com/these-8-federal-agencies-are-the-worst-heres-how-to-fix-them/article/2583708

White, H. D. (2016). Relevance theory and distributions of judgments in document retrieval. *Information Processing & Management*, 5(53), 1080–1102.

Wiles, R. (2012). *What are qualitative research ethics?* Bloomsbury Academic.

Wolgemuth, J., Moody, Z., Ospal, T., Cross, J., Kaanta, T., Dickman, E., & Colomer, S. (2014). Participants' experiences of the qualitative interview: Considering the importance of research paradigms. *Qualitative Research*, 15(3), 351–372. doi:10.1177/1468794114524222

Yang, Y. (2014). Principals' transformational leadership in school improvement. *The International Journal of Educational Management*, 28(3), 279-288. http://dx.doi.org.proxy.cecybrary.com/10.1108/IJEM-04-2013-0063

Yongcheng, L. (2015). Beyond offensive realism: Why leadership matters more than structure in the security environment of East Asia. *International Journal of China Studies*, 6(2), 159–173. https://proxy.cecybrary.com/login?url=https://search.proquest.com/docview/1719405439?accountid=144459

Zuberbuhler, M. J. P., Salanova, M., & Martinez, I. M. (2020). Coaching-based Leadership Intervention Program: A controlled trial study. *Frontiers in Psychology*, 10, 3066. doi:10.3389/fpsyg.2019.03066 PMID:32116873

Zveglich, L., & Lacina, R. (2014). *Powering up coaching by blending human factor with technology*. https://proxy.cecybrary.com/login?url=https://search.proquest.com/docview/1552708249?accountid=144459

Chapter 4
SCADA Systems and Threats to Critical Infrastructures

Tiffany Weitoish

https://orcid.org/0009-0005-4386-0451
Capitol Technology University, USA

Darrell Norman Burrell

https://orcid.org/0000-0002-4675-9544
Capitol Technology University, USA

ABSTRACT

Securing the networks underpinning industrial control systems (ICS), mainly supervisory control and data acquisition (SCADA) systems, holds paramount significance, with far-reaching implications for public health, safety, and national security. This chapter delves into the intricate landscape of cybersecurity vulnerabilities within critical infrastructures, including managing electrical grids, oil pipelines, and water distribution systems, which remain susceptible to cyber threats and attacks across diverse technological vectors in the United States. Through an exhaustive examination of contemporary and emerging literature, this research elucidates the multifaceted security risks afflicting domains crucial to the U.S. infrastructure.

INTRODUCTION

Critical infrastructures encompass energy production, water supply, transportation networks, healthcare facilities, fuel supply, food supply, and more that are the essence of our communities, economies, and survival. Supervisory Control and Data Acquisition (SCADA) systems are crucial to the efficient functioning of many critical infrastructures, facilitating real-time monitoring and control of vital processes (Beggs & Warren, 2014; Mingo & Burrell, 2023). The current landscape is witnessing a notable upsurge in the integration of Internet of Things (IoT) technologies within critical industrial infrastructures. Consequently, it becomes imperative to assess the implications of cybersecurity within SCADA environments, as highlighted by previous research (Beggs & Warren, 2014; Mingo & Burrell, 2023).

DOI: 10.4018/979-8-3693-1970-3.ch004

As defined in previous studies, IoT encompasses an array of autonomous, intelligent, interconnected objects, each uniquely identifiable and endowed with embedded processors that support them with sensing, computational, and communicative capabilities. These intelligent entities are equipped with microcontrollers to facilitate data processing, digital communication transceivers for seamless connectivity, and a comprehensive protocol stack that facilitates communication both among objects and between objects and users (Beggs & Warren, 2014; Mingo & Burrell, 2023).

In essence, the growing integration of IoT technologies within critical industrial systems necessitates a thorough examination of the security implications. The references to Beggs and Warren (2014) and Mingo and Burrell (2023) underscore the importance of this consideration and serve as a foundation for further investigation into the intersection of IoT and SCADA security, ensuring that the integrity and reliability of critical infrastructure systems are maintained in this evolving technological landscape.

Automation plays an indispensable role in modern industrial systems, significantly enhancing operational efficiency. Across various industries, the adoption of remote operational techniques facilitated by Supervisory Control and Data Acquisition (SCADA) systems is nearly ubiquitous (Johnsen, 2014; Marković-Petrović, 2020; Stojanović & Boštjančič Rakas, 2022). These systems find applications in a wide range of sectors, exemplifying their versatility and significance.

For instance, within the oil industry, SCADA systems are instrumental in the remote control and management of gas and oil flow through pipelines, ensuring the safe and efficient transportation of these valuable resources (Johnsen, 2014; Marković-Petrović, 2020; Stojanović & Boštjančič Rakas, 2022). In the realm of water and sewage systems, SCADA systems are pivotal in regulating and optimizing water flow, thereby contributing to the efficient management of these critical utilities (Mingo & Burrell, 2023). Similarly, in the power generation sector, SCADA systems facilitate the precise management of electrical output from power plants, seamlessly integrating them into the broader power grid (Mingo & Burrell, 2023).

Furthermore, SCADA systems play an indispensable role in chemical plants, where they enable real-time process control, ensuring the precise execution of complex chemical processes (Johnsen, 2014; Marković-Petrović, 2020; Stojanović & Boštjančič Rakas, 2022). In manufacturing units, these systems are essential for overseeing the transmission and distribution of products, streamlining production processes, and enhancing overall productivity (Mingo & Burrell, 2023). Additionally, within transportation infrastructure, such as railways, SCADA systems underpin the signaling networks that govern the safe and efficient movement of trains and other vehicles. The references to Johnsen (2014), Marković-Petrović (2020), and Stojanović & Boštjančič Rakas (2022) collectively affirm the pervasive use of SCADA systems across diverse industries. However, it is imperative to acknowledge that as these systems become increasingly integral to critical infrastructure, the imperative for robust cybersecurity measures to protect them from emerging threats becomes ever more apparent.

In many organizations, the susceptibility of field devices to malware attacks is a pressing concern, primarily attributed to their inherent structural vulnerabilities (Upadhyay & Sampalli, 2020). Notably, a significant portion of SCADA controllers and field devices currently in use were designed and manufactured during an era when cybersecurity threats were not a primary consideration (Upadhyay & Sampalli, 2020). Consequently, these legacy systems are ill-equipped to withstand the complexities of modern cyber threats, rendering them susceptible to disruptions caused by high network traffic or potential malware intrusions. To bolster the security posture of these critical components, it becomes imperative to institute a routine regimen of security updates (Upadhyay & Sampalli, 2020). The daily maintenance and application of security updates stand out as pivotal measures in safeguarding both the integrity of processes and the confidentiality of data within the organization.

In conventional IT networks, the management of vulnerabilities often relies on automated tools that systematically scan all network devices to discern the prerequisites for security enhancements (Ismail, Sitnikova, & Slay, 2020). These tools play a crucial role in identifying vulnerabilities, allowing organizations to promptly prioritize and execute the necessary security upgrades. The susceptibility of field devices to malware attacks due to their structural limitations, coupled with the legacy nature of many SCADA controllers and field devices, necessitates a proactive approach to cybersecurity (Mingo & Burrell, 2023). Regular security updates and the utilization of automated vulnerability management tools, as emphasized by Upadhyay and Sampalli (2020) and Ismail, Sitnikova, and Slay (2020), are vital strategies to fortify the security of these critical components in the face of evolving cyber threats.

PROBLEM STATEMENT

Recent cybersecurity incidents in the United States have prompted government officials to emphasize the importance of enhancing security measures within critical infrastructure sectors, particularly in water utilities and industrial facilities (Mingo & Burrell, 2023). These incidents underscore the need to implement fundamental security practices because these industries rely heavily on Supervisory Control and Data Acquisition (SCADA) systems facilities (Mingo & Burrell, 2023).

The cyberattacks, believed to be linked to Iran, targeted both drinking and wastewater systems in the U.S., shedding light on a persistent concern regarding the vulnerability of under-resourced, local entities that rely on operational technology. This includes small utilities, manufacturers, and healthcare organizations (Jones, 2023). Notably, the United States hosts approximately 150,000 public water systems and 16,000 publicly owned wastewater systems, with a significant majority serving communities of fewer than 10,000 customers (Jones, 2023).

Remarkably, these systems collectively provide drinking water to nearly 80% of the population (Jones, 2023). However, these facilities often grapple with limited operational budgets, a sparse workforce, and minimal access to on-site security personnel or forensic experts. This unique set of challenges underscores the urgency of improving cybersecurity resilience within this critical infrastructure sector. Moreover, within the context of cybersecurity, the delineation of responsibilities and the effective mapping of stakeholders represent intricate challenges that warrant careful examination. This paper seeks to delve into these complex dynamics by drawing insights from both current and emerging literature.

PURPOSE AND NATURE OF THE STUDY

This research study will include a literature review of existing material available on cybersecurity risks, threats, and vulnerabilities; provide definitions and terminology related to SCADA systems and critical infrastructures; types of critical infrastructures; SCADA system architecture; explore current issues and case examples that are related to issues of SCADA systems connected to critical infrastructures; and what recommendations and actions can be taken to protect not only the SCADA systems but also the critical infrastructures. This study concentrates on investigating and analyzing existing qualitative literature from 2015 – 2023 that are shown in figures that describe statistical analysis over the years on whether cybersecurity attacks on SCADA systems related to critical infrastructures have increased or decreased and what has changed over time. The results from this research study and recommendations may be used to assist researchers, professionals, security experts, high-ranking officials, private companies, and government agencies in resolving issues related to SCADA systems connected to critical infrastructures.

SIGNIFICANCE OF THE STUDY

The significance and novelty of this study lie in its profound implications for national security, public health, public safety, and the resilience of the nation's critical infrastructure sectors. Recent cybersecurity incidents in the United States have brought to the forefront the pressing need to address security vulnerabilities within critical infrastructure, with a particular focus on water utilities and industrial facilities such as (Mingo & Burrell, 2023):

- National Security - Cyberattacks targeting critical infrastructure can have far-reaching consequences for national security. As underscored by these incidents, adversaries with the capability to disrupt SCADA systems can jeopardize the integrity of essential services, potentially causing widespread disruption and economic damage.
- Public Health - The safety and availability of clean drinking water are paramount to public health. The fact that these cyberattacks targeted drinking and wastewater systems highlights the potential risks to public health in the event of a successful breach. Ensuring the security of these systems is vital to safeguarding public health.
- Public Safety - The reliability of critical infrastructure directly impacts public safety. Attacks on these systems can compromise their operational integrity, potentially leading to hazardous situations, accidents, or even intentional harm. Therefore, enhancing cybersecurity in critical infrastructure is imperative for public safety.
- Economic Stability - The United States is home to a vast network of public water and wastewater systems, serving a significant portion of the population (Jones, 2023). The nation's economic stability is closely tied to the uninterrupted functioning of these systems. Cyberattacks on critical infrastructure can disrupt economic activities, affecting businesses, jobs, and livelihoods.
- Resource-Strapped Entities - Small utilities, manufacturers, and healthcare organizations, often reliant on operational technology, are particularly vulnerable to cyber threats (Jones, 2023). As these entities constitute a significant portion of the critical infrastructure landscape, addressing their cybersecurity challenges is paramount.
- Cybersecurity Resilience - This study's focus on cybersecurity resilience in the face of limited budgets, staffing constraints, and a lack of dedicated security personnel and forensic experts is pioneering. Developing strategies and best practices tailored to the unique challenges faced by such entities is crucial to building resilience.
- Complex Dynamics - The delineation of responsibilities and stakeholder mapping within the context of cybersecurity represents a complex and underexplored area. Investigating these intricacies through current and emerging literature adds a novel dimension to the study.
- Cybersecurity Research & Advancements - The study can contribute to advancements in the field of cybersecurity by addressing the unique challenges posed by SCADA systems, and the knowledge can be applied to improve security practices in other areas.

- <u>Policy & Regulation</u> - Research in SCADA systems and critical infrastructures can inform the development of policies and regulations requiring stricter cybersecurity measures, creating a more secure environment for critical infrastructure operations.
- <u>International Cooperation</u> - Critical infrastructures span international borders, and addressing threats to SCADA systems will promote international collaboration in methods to safeguard global security and stability.

The study on SCADA Systems and Threats to Critical Infrastructures is significant due to its far-reaching impact on national security, public safety, economic stability, technological advancements, and international cooperation. SCADA systems play a critical role in securing foundational systems that modern-day society relies upon daily. The significance of the study is that it provides the potential to influence policies, practices, and technological advancements that contribute toward a more secure and resilient future for SCADA systems and critical infrastructures.

LITERATURE REVIEW

Discovered Security Issues

Since the 1960s, there have been noted issues with security systems and computer networks. These security issues can best be shown in two articles. The first article, titled "Security and Privacy in Computer Systems" by Willis H. Ware (1967), detailed many examples that showed that there were and continue to be security and privacy risks, threats, and vulnerabilities in the design of typical remote access, the multi-user resource- sharing computer systems, accidental or intentional divulgence of information, and suggestive designs for protecting private information by computer systems. The other areas of concern are the risks of damaged or corrupted information from one user or program that can be spread to other users or programs. These risks, threats, and vulnerabilities of linking users or programs can be seen on networked computers as well (Ware, 1967, p. 5).

"Cybersecurity: A Pre-History" by Michael Warner (2012) discusses the history of cyber network computers and cybersecurity risks and issues discovered in the 1960s. Michael Warner pointed out that Bernard Peters of NSA's RYE system stated "that security could not be obtained with a multi-programming system equipped with remote terminals and capabilities" (Warner, 2012, pp. 783–785). Later, the Defense Science Board concluded in October 1967 that there were no resolutions to the problem of computer security, and it was unwise to integrate classified or sensitive information in a system functioning in an open environment unless a significant risk of accidental disclosure can be accepted (Weitoish, 2014). This discovery of risks, threats, and vulnerabilities also holds true for Supervisory Control and Data Acquisition (SCADA) systems.

What Are SCADA Systems?

"Industrial control systems are supervisory control and data acquisition (SCADA) systems" (Thilmany, 2012, p. 26). SCADA systems use coded signals over telecommunication channels to regulate remote equipment frequently 24 hours, seven days a week. SCADA systems are reliable and flexible but may lack security, which can cause issues with services needed for everyday life, such as energy, water treatment plants, and the telecommunication industry. According to Stouffer, K., et al. (2023), SCADA systems are used in distribution systems, such as water distribution and wastewater collection systems, oil and natural gas pipelines, electrical utility transmission and distribution systems, and rail and other public transportation systems" (Stouffer et al., 2023, p. 12). Control systems like SCADA systems are essential to operations for U.S. critical infrastructures because they are interconnected and dependent upon each other.

SCADA systems are made up of hardware, software, and networks. The hardware for SCADA systems may include but are not limited to "maximum transmission units (MTU) placed at control centers; communication equipment such as radios, telephone lines, cables, or satellites; and field sites that have a remote terminal unit (RTU) or program logic controllers (PLC) to control actuators or monitor sensors" (Stouffer et al., 2023, p. 12). The software that is used tells the SCADA systems what and when to monitor operations, what are acceptable limitation ranges, and what responses must be carried out if parameter ranges exceed acceptable values. Networks are used to link a SCADA system with other systems and communicate information. The basic setup for a SCADA system is shown below:

Figure 1. Basic SCADA system
Basic SCADA System (Inductive Automation, 2018, Figure 1)

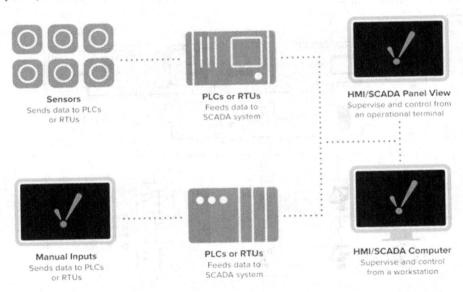

Inductive Automation (2018) states that "SCADA systems allow industrial organizations to monitor, gather, and process data; directly interact with control machines and devices; and record events in a log file" (Inductive Automation, 2018, para. 1). Effective SCADA systems are used for many things, and can save time and money for businesses.

How Are SCADA Systems Used?

According to The White House (2021), ninety percent of the United States' critical infrastructures are privately owned and operated over thousands of miles by being used for electrical grids, water, and many other life-sustaining assets and services (The White House, 2021, para. 38). SCADA systems are integral to various industries and control critical processes. SCADA control centers can monitor, collect, and log information over long distances through communication networks (Stouffer et al., 2023, p. 13). These communication networks can permit automated or better known as "operator-driven" supervisory commands to field sites and devices. The field sites and devices can control local operations such as switching over power disbursement, opening and closing water valves and gates, diverting rail transportation, and controlling gas flow through pipelines. Figure 2 is the general setup of a SCADA system over a wide area network. The picture shows that HMI, engineering workstations, data historians, control servers, and communication routers all work together and send coded signals through the wide area network (WAN) to the field sites and devices that allow for water systems, transportation systems, and communication systems to function correctly (Stouffer et al., 2023, p. 13).

Figure 2. General SCADA system
Stouffer et al. (2023)

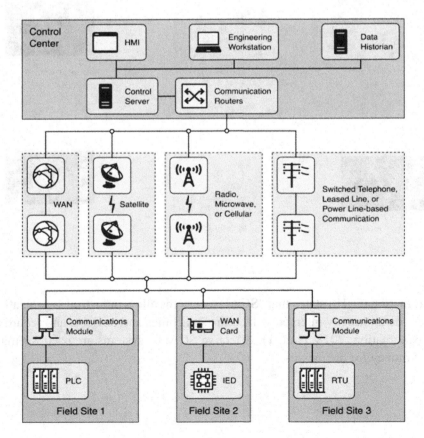

The SCADA system functionality enhances efficiency, reduces downtime, and provides proactive decision-making. The ability to monitor and control processes from a centralized location significantly improves the overall performance of industrial systems. As a result of how SCADA systems are set up, if one component of the SCADA system is attacked, it can cause failures in functionality for output production or could be destroyed. SCADA systems showcase their versatility and essential role in optimizing processes across diverse industries. However, based on how SCADA systems are used, there are many security concerns for SCADA systems.

Security Concerns for SCADA Systems

The security of SCADA systems is a paramount concern due to their vulnerability to cyber threats. There have been many instances of SCADA system breaches that have been reported, including the notorious Stuxnet malware that targeted Iran's nuclear facilities. According to Nate Kube (2013), many times manufacturers, owners, and operators have little knowledge about possible weaknesses in their critical infrastructures (Kube, 2013, para. 10). "Potential weaknesses are but not limited to testing on systems is not guaranteed for accuracy; embedded devices used in SCADA systems are not Windows or UNIX based platforms and the vulnerabilities are not available in security vulnerability lists; and SCADA system operators are unable to make informed decisions for security policies" (Kube, 2013, paras. 8-11). Andrew Hildick-Smith (2021) stated that SCADA systems are vulnerable to malware such as viruses, worms, Trojans, and spyware (Hildick-Smith, 2021, pp. 6–7). Malware on SCADA systems could corrupt the data, overwhelm communication from denial-of-service attacks (DDoS), and allow back doors or keystroke loggers to be installed. In addition, "SCADA systems can be left unpatched due to the operational nature of the system" (Alanazi et al., 2023, p. 9). In fact, according to SynSaber (2023), "there were approximately 34% of security vulnerabilities that impacted industrial controls systems (ICSs) that were reported in the first half of 2023 that did not have patches or remediations, which was a 13% increase compared to 2022." The two most impacted critical infrastructures for the first half of 2023 were manufacturing and energy, as shown in the chart below from the SynSaber ICS Vulnerability Report (SynSaber, 2023).

These security breaches show a critical need for robust cybersecurity measures to protect SCADA systems and their environment. Vulnerabilities and malware (i.e., viruses, worms, trojans, and spyware) can compromise the integrity and functionality of SCADA systems, posing risks to critical infrastructures. Vulnerabilities in SCADA systems pose operational risks and threats to public safety and national security. By recognizing the gravity of these security concerns, it is imperative to implement advanced cybersecurity protocols; comprehensive cybersecurity strategies such as regular updates, intrusion detection systems, employee training, conduct regular audits, and foster collaboration between industry experts and cybersecurity professionals to strengthen the resilience and mitigate the potential impact of SCADA systems against evolving threats on industrial control systems.

In addition to external malware threats, SCADA systems face internal and deliberate risks from insider threats, hackers, and potential terrorist activities. Insider threats, hackers, and cyber terrorism can be defined as follows:

1. <u>Insider Threat</u> - According to the Cybersecurity & Infrastructure Agency (CISA) (2023), an "insider threat is the potential for an insider to use their authorized access or understanding of an organization to harm that organization. CISA further explains that insiders use their authorized access

wittingly or unwittingly to harm the organization and its personnel, equipment, information, and customers. The threat can manifest as damage through the insiders' behaviors, such as but not limited to espionage, terrorism, unauthorized disclosure of information, corruption, organized crime, sabotage, workplace violence, and intentional or unintentional loss or degradation of organization resources or capabilities (Cybersecurity & Infrastructure Security Agency [CISA], 2023c, paras. 10-12).

2. Hackers - The National Institute of Standards and Technology (NIST) (2023) states "Hackers are unauthorized users who attempt to or gain access to an information system" (National Institute of Standards & Technology [NIST], 2023, para. 1). The NIST Special Publication 800-12 Rev.1 details a "malicious hacker as an individual or group who uses and understands systems, networks, and programming to access systems, cause damage, or steal information illegally" (National Institute of Standards and Technology, 2017, p. 22). Hackers are individuals who are on the outside of a company and may probe, intrude, or try to control a system because of the challenge or gratification through monetary gain or revenge (Eisenfeld, 2019, p. 69).

3. Cyber Terrorism – "The U.S. Federal Bureau of Investigations (FBI) defines cyberterrorism as any "premeditated, politically motivated attack against information, computer systems, computer programs, and data which results in violence against noncombatant targets by subnational groups or clandestine agents" (Sheldon & Hanna, 2022, para. 2). Cyber terrorists are politically motivated attackers that use computers, networks, and the public Internet to cause destruction or harm for personal gain. Cyber terrorists that determine and locate critical infrastructures will attempt to disable SCADA systems to disrupt monitoring or take control of SCADA systems in order to give false values or damage physical critical infrastructure systems.

Figure 3. Critical infrastructure sectors most likely impacted by CISA ICS advisory
SynSaber (2023, p. 8)

Critical Infrastructure Sector Most Likely to be Impacted by the CISA ICS Advisory	1H23 CISA ICS Advisory Count (note that some advisories impact multiple sectors)
Chemical	7
Commercial Facilities	11
Communications	10
Critical Manufacturing	69
Dams	2
Energy	45
Food & Agriculture	6
Government Facilities	4
Healthcare & Public Health	7
Information Technology	3
Multiple Critical Sectors*	66
Transportation Systems	8
Water & Wastewater Systems	16

The critical infrastructure sectors most likely to be impacted by CVEs reported in the first half of 2023 were Manufacturing (37.3% of total reported CVEs) and Energy (24.3% of the total reported).

There are instances where insiders with authorized access intentionally manipulate SCADA systems, emphasizing the need to address organizational vulnerabilities. At the same time, hackers and terrorists pose external threats by attempting unauthorized access or launching targeted attacks. Understanding these dynamics is essential for developing a comprehensive security strategy for SCADA systems. Combating threats to SCADA systems will require a holistic approach that includes monitoring internal accesses, implementing stringent access controls, and collaborating with cybersecurity experts to stay ahead of evolving hacking and cyber terroristic tactics.

Based on the information for insider threats, hackers, and cyber terrorists; some experts have considered that the first SCADA attack took place in 1982 when computer chips were found in Soviet military equipment and flawed turbines were installed on the Trans-Siberian gas pipeline, which led to an explosion (Dickman, 2009, para. 1). Other people argue that the first SCADA attack was with the Stuxnet worm. Since then, there have been unconfirmed attacks. Cyber-attacks have increased over the years. In fact, according to Mike Lennon (2015), "Dell Sonic WALL discovered global SCADA attacks against its customer base from 91,676 in January 2012 to 163,228 in January 2013, and 675,186 in January 2014" (Lennon, 2015, para. 1). The following pie chart is based on Dell's SCADA attack methods from the Dell Security Annual Threat Report.

Figure 4. SCADA attack methods
Paganini (2015), Figure 2

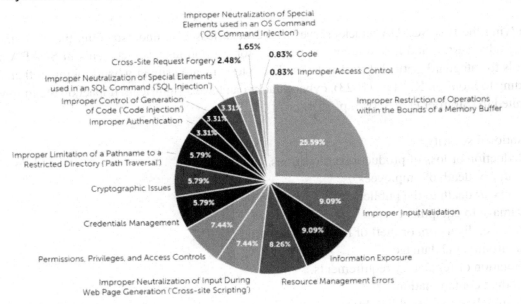

Dell Security Annual Threat Report showed the methodology used to attack SCADA systems. In addition, as shown in the pie graph, 25.59% of the attacks were from improper restrictions of operations within the bounds of a memory buffer, and 9.09% were from improper input validation and information exposure (Paganini, 2015, para. 4). These types of attack methods are at the heart of SCADA attacks and how cybercriminals attack and exploits targeted areas. In comparison, Eduard Kovacs (2022) stated in 2022 that SCADA systems were named the top cybersecurity vulnerability of U.S. ports and terminals, as shown from the survey and data analysis below (Kovacs, 2022, para. 6).

Figure 5. Report from blue and brown water facilities across the U.S.
Kovacs (2022), Figure 1

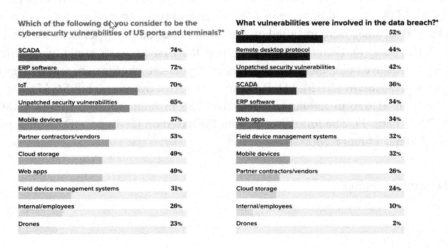

Studying the first SCADA attacks serves as a crucial lesson in understanding the evolving tactics of cyber adversaries, and it reinforces the urgency for continuous advancements in SCADA security protocols to safeguard critical infrastructures. These lessons are critical when looking at their impact. According to Stouffer, K., et al. (2023), cyber-attacks can have a significant impact on the following but not limited to (Stouffer et al., 2023, p. 35):

1. National security.
2. Reduction or loss of production at locations.
3. Injury or death of employees.
4. Injury or death to the public.
5. Damage to equipment.
6. Release, diversion, or theft of hazardous materials.
7. Environmental damage.
8. Violation of regulatory requirements.
9. Product contamination.
10. Criminal or civil legal liabilities.
11. Loss of proprietary or confidential information.
12. Loss of brand image or customer confidence in the product or company.

Theories and Motives Behind Hacking SCADA Systems

As the frequency of SCADA system breaches continues to raise concerns among cybersecurity professionals, delving into the theories and motives behind hacking these critical systems becomes imperative. Various theories suggest motives ranging from industrial espionage, financial gain, ideological, and political. Examples include but are not limited to attempting to disrupt critical infrastructures for strategic advantage or to damage national security. According to Finklea & Theohary (2012), the motives behind cyber criminals committing cybercrimes range from gaining profit, notoriety, political gain, or gratification from activities such as terrorism (Finklea & Theory, 2012, p. 7). These motives are best described in Robert Agnew's Strain Theory. According to Robert Agnew et al. (1996), the classic strain theories of Merton (1968), Cloward, and Ohlin (1960) stated that individuals who cannot achieve monetary success through legitimate channels are more likely than others to engage in crime such as drug use and other types of crimes. Another theory that is related to why criminals commit crimes is the theory called "Social Learning Theory," which was developed by Ronald Akers. Social learning theory is based on differential association, definitions, and attitudes attached to one's behaviors, differential reinforcement, and imitation through engagement of behaviors in others. Social learning theory states that criminal behavior can be learned through interaction with social groups through exposure, long periods of duration, and with more intensity to law-violating actions than law-abiding actions (Paternoster et al., 2001). Based on strain theory and social learning theory, people will find other methods through crime to achieve rewards or gratifications if they cannot attain the rewards or gratifications through legitimate means (Chen et al., 2023, p. 7). This can be seen in motivated criminals. Motivated cyber criminals will do what it takes to acquire or get the tasks or jobs done in order to achieve the reward or gratification (Chen et al., 2023, p. 7). Understanding these theories provides a new perspective on cyber threats to SCADA systems by depicting the complexity of motives, emphasizing the need for cybersecurity strategies to address diverse threat vectors.

The Cost of Cybercrime and Breaches to SCADA Systems

The financial repercussions of cybercrime and breaches targeting SCADA systems are substantial, imposing significant costs on industries and societies. Many victims of cyber criminals do not know that their computer systems were hacked until well after the cybercriminals have already stolen money or information, sabotaged computer systems, or destroyed information and businesses (Senate Homeland Security and Governmental Affairs Subcommittee on Federal Spending Oversight and Emergency Management Hearing, 2020). In 2015, cybercrime costs the average U.S. firm approximately $15 million annually. For example, launching a denial of service (DDoS) attack costs $38 per hour, which resulted in an unmitigated attack costing approximately $40,000 per hour for businesses (Griffiths, 2015, para. 5). In comparison, Steve Morgan (2022) of Cybercrime Magazine stated that cybercrime is predicted to cost the world $8 trillion in 2023 and the cybercrime damage cost is expected to grow by 15 percent per year over the next three years (Morgan, 2022, paras. 1-2). Critical infrastructures are among the highest cyber risk exposures. In another study, IBM (2023) stated that "the global average cost of a data breach reached an all-time high in 2023 of 4.45 million USD, which is a 2.3% increase since 2022 with a cost of 4.35 million USD" (IBM, 2023, p. 5). The U.S. is #1 in 2023 for costs of data breaches with $9.48 million (IBM, 2023, p. 11). "The global total costs measured in USD millions from data breaches from 2017 – 2023 can be seen in Figure 6 (IBM, 2023)". This also applies to cyber criminals hacking into

ICS or SCADA systems, and the costs also include system restoration, legal ramifications, and damage to the company or organization's reputation. The increases in SCADA system attacks have many experts concerned about how those attacks threaten critical infrastructures and the costs of recovering from cybersecurity attacks. However, what is more devastating is the cost of data breaches by industry, as shown by the IBM Cost of Data Breaches Report 2023 in Figure 7. The financial impact shows the urgent need for solid cybersecurity measures in safeguarding SCADA systems from monetary losses; the long-term consequences emphasize the importance of proactive risk management to mitigate the effects of cyber incidents. By recognizing the substantial costs associated with cybercrime and SCADA breaches, it details the importance of ongoing investment in cybersecurity, regulatory compliance, and collaboration to protect critical infrastructures.

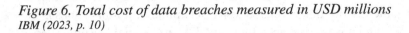

Figure 6. Total cost of data breaches measured in USD millions
IBM (2023, p. 10)

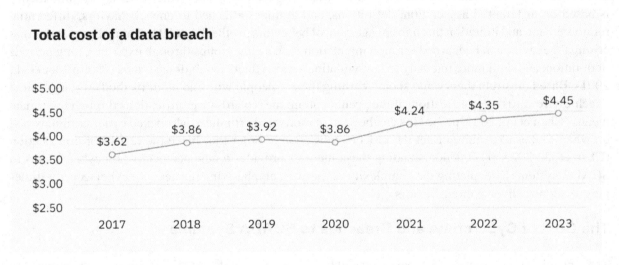

Total cost of a data breach

Military and Federal Government Response to Cyber Attacks on SCADA Systems

The military and federal government play a pivotal role in responding to cyber-attacks on SCADA systems by ensuring national security and safeguarding critical infrastructures. SCADA system attacks that are connected to critical infrastructures put the safety of millions of people at risk and compromise homeland security by bringing an "asymmetrical war" to the United States' doorstep. This issue has brought about a need for change to defend the United States from cyber-attacks.

On December 17, 2003, the "Homeland Security Presidential Directive 7 (HSPD-7) was created that outlines measures to identify, prioritize, and enhance the resilience of the United States' critical infrastructures and protect them from terroristic attacks, emphasizing the importance of critical infrastructure protection" (Cybersecurity & Infrastructure Security Agency [CISA], 2003, para. 1). The HSPD-7 identified 17 critical infrastructures including but not limited to energy, transportation, and water, which emphasized their vital role in maintaining national security and public well-being. The directive established

Figure 7. Cost of data breach by industry in USD millions
IBM (2023, p. 13)

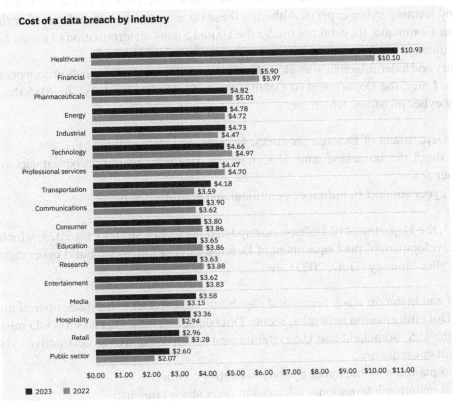

a framework for collaboration between the government and private sectors to develop and implement comprehensive plans for protecting critical infrastructures. The directive also created the EINSTEIN Program in 2003, which was designed to "provide the U.S. Government with an early warning system for intrusions to Federal Executive Branch civilian networks and provided near real-time identification of malicious activity and automated disruption of that malicious activity" (Cybersecurity & Infrastructure Security Agency [CISA], 2010, para. 8). This approach recognizes the interconnectedness of the critical infrastructure sectors and the shared responsibility in safeguarding them. By addressing vulnerabilities and promoting a unified effort to enhance the security of critical infrastructures, HSPD-7 aimed to fortify the nation's ability to prevent, respond to, and recover from potential terrorist threats while contributing to a more resilient and secure homeland.

On June 23, 2009, the U.S. Cyber Command was created to defend computer networks and carry out offensive attacks. The U.S. Cyber Command is a military command that consists of service elements from the Army, Marines, Air Force, and Navy that work closely with the National Security Agency (NSA) (U.S. Cyber Security Policy, 2010). Since the creation of the U.S. Cyber Command, there have been many issues when dealing with cyber-attacks and SCADA system attacks. The first issue was determining the rules during peacetime, wartime, and when America was under attack. The second issue that was discovered was a need for real-time situational awareness in the United States' networks to have the ability to adapt and operate to any situation at Internet speed in order to make appropriate decisions. The coordination between the military service elements and agencies was an issue for situational awareness due to issues with communication and sharing information. The third issue discovered was recruiting, educating, and training cyber experts. Although these three issues were problems after the creation of the U.S. Cyber Command, they did not hinder the United States' determination to create cyber warriors and a cyber strategy.

The military and federal agencies developed and began utilizing communication networks, procedures, and protocols. Later, the Department of Defense created a "Cyber Strategy" in 2015 that outlined the three primary cyber missions, which are:

- Defend Department of Defense networks, systems, and information.
- Defend the U.S. homeland and U.S. national interests against cyber-attacks of significant consequences.
- Provide cyber support to military operational and contingency plans.

Since 2015, the Department of Defense has updated the Cyber Strategy for 2023, which was created to guide the development of the Department of Defense's cyber forces and build cyber capabilities. The goals in the Cyber Strategy (DoD, 2023) are:

- To build and maintain ready forces and capabilities to conduct cyberspace operations.
- Defend DoD information networks, secure DoD data, and mitigate risks to DoD missions.
- Defend the U.S. homeland and U.S. vital interests from disruptive or destructive cyber-attacks of significant consequence.
- Build and maintain viable cyber options to control conflict.
- Build and maintain international alliances to deter shared threats.
- Leverage all legally available contractual mechanisms, resources, and operational arrangements to improve the cybersecurity of U.S. critical infrastructure systems.
- Expand public-private partnerships to ensure that DoD resources, expertise, and intelligence are available to support critical private sector initiatives.

The Cyber Strategy's mission and goals inform and guide the Department of Defense's military branches on building cyber forces and capabilities to defend DoD networks while securing data and information. The Department of Defense will defend the U.S. homeland and vital interests while also planning and exercising to operate with damaged or disrupted cyber environments in the event of an attack on the Department of Defense's networks or critical infrastructure. While the military improved its cyber forces and capabilities, the Federal Government also began improving its cyber abilities and posture.

The U.S. Federal Government introduced the "International Strategy for Cyberspace" in 2011, which detailed a strategy to prioritize and improve security in cyberspace in the United States and the international community. The objectives for cyberspace are to create principles of responsible behaviors in the international community; strengthen partnerships in the domestic and international community; dissuade and deter cyber-attacks on its networks; develop prosperity and security through enhanced connectivity to end-users; and create policy relationships. These objectives outlined a cyberspace policy in the international community and set the stage for domestic policies to be developed, such as the National Infrastructure Protection Plan (NIPP) 2013 and the Cyber Intelligence Sharing and Protection Act (CISPA).

According to the Department of Homeland Security (2013), "the National Infrastructure Protection Plan (NIPP) 2013 detailed that the state, local, tribal, and territorial governments are responsible for implementing the homeland security mission of protecting public safety and welfare; and ensuring essential services to its communities and industries within their jurisdiction" (Department of Homeland Security [DHS], 2013). This includes managing the risks from significant threats and hazards to physical and cyber critical infrastructures through physical and cyber security planning, which correlates with Executive Order 13636, Improving Critical Infrastructure Cybersecurity. Executive Order 13636, Improving Critical Infrastructure Cybersecurity, states that the Federal Government is directed to coordinate with critical infrastructure owners and operators in order to improve information sharing and collaboration and implement risk-based approaches to cybersecurity (Department of Homeland Security [DHS], 2019).

The Cyber Intelligence Sharing and Protection Act (CISPA) proposed sharing Internet traffic information between the U.S. government and technology and manufacturing companies. The CISPA applies to certified entities (corporations, nonprofits, and government agencies) that have or can acquire a security clearance and can appropriately protect classified cyber threat intelligence. The certified entities can then share cyber threat intelligence with other certified entities (Wofford, 2015). The CISPA promoted information sharing between the Federal Government and private companies. The military and federal agencies actively monitor and respond to cyber threats that target SCADA systems. Their collaborative efforts to share threat intelligence and conduct cybersecurity exercises assist with training personnel, check for security gaps, and help improve cybersecurity skills and technologies. For example, the Cybersecurity & Infrastructure Security Agency (CISA) "partners with other government agencies to protect the United States' cyber and physical critical infrastructures provides tools, training, and information materials to prevent, protect against, and mitigate security incidents" (Cybersecurity & Infrastructure Security Agency [CISA], 2023d, para. 1). This proactive approach is essential for mitigating risks, enhancing resilience, and maintaining the functionality of critical infrastructures while staying ahead of evolving threats and ensuring a strong defense against potential disruptions to vital systems. However, these are steps forward in reaction to the cyber-attacks that create consequences for SCADA systems and critical infrastructures. These consequences can be mitigated if the proper steps are taken.

Mitigation of SCADA System Concerns and Threats

Mitigating concerns and threats to SCADA systems will require a comprehensive strategy that addresses vulnerabilities and enhances the overall cybersecurity program for businesses and organizations. SCADA system owners are responsible for protecting what they manage; however, if they need help, there are tools and support to communicate with each other and the federal government. It is advisable to reference the National Institute of Standards and Technology (NIST) SP 800-82 Rev. 3: Guide to Operational Technology (OT) Security, National Institute of Standards and Technology (NIST) SP 800-53 Rev. 5: Security and Privacy Controls for Information Systems and Organizations, and National Institute of Standards and Technology (NIST) SP 800-207: Zero Trust Architecture to assist with following cybersecurity best practices for SCADA systems and critical infrastructures while adhering to Zero Trust Architecture (ZTA). Zero Trust Architecture (ZTA) uses zero trust principles where there is no implicit trust granted to assets or user accounts based solely on their physical network location or on asset ownership (National Institute of Standards and Technology [NIST] et al., 2020, p. 4). Zero trust is a cybersecurity plan encompassing component relationships, workflow planning, and access policies to protect enterprise resources and assets.

SCADA system vendors, academia, SCADA consultants, the military, the federal government, and many other organizations are all working to safeguard SCADA systems from risks, threats, and vulnerabilities. Organizations should provide training that is specific to operational topics such as spear-phishing, zero-day activities, denial-of-service (DDoS) attacks, and many other cyber threats. Organizations and businesses should develop a comprehensive security program that defines the goals and scope of the program, creates, and implements defined SCADA system policies and procedures, determines SCADA system assets, continually utilizes risk and vulnerability assessments, adheres to Zero Trust Architecture (ZTA), and determine mitigation controls (Stouffer et al., 2023). Lastly, organizations and businesses should provide training by raising security awareness through education, certifications, and conducting mock drills and tabletop exercises. An example of actions taken to mitigate SCADA system and critical infrastructure risks, threats, and vulnerabilities can be seen in the Department of Energy's twenty-one-step guide to improving the cyber security of SCADA networks (Department of Energy, 2015). All businesses and organizations that use SCADA systems or critical infrastructure services should review this twenty-one-step guide and develop a guide that encompasses their specific business or organization's objectives and services while focusing on keeping SCADA systems secure. Organizations and businesses can also work with the Cybersecurity & Infrastructure Security Agency (CISA). CISA works closely with law enforcement agencies, the intelligence community, federal, state, local, and tribal governments, and the Department of Homeland Security's U.S. Computer Emergency Readiness Team (CISA, 2023d). The Department of Homeland Security's U.S. Computer Emergency Readiness Team conducts ICS vulnerability analysis, provides support for cyber-attacks, and conducts forensic analysis. CISA provides ICS advisories for SCADA systems, which have an assigned alert code, CVSS, vendor information, equipment affected, type of vulnerability, risk evaluation, and additional technical details (Cybersecurity & Infrastructure Security Agency [CISA], 2023b, para. 1). When ICS advisories are released, businesses and companies need to check if their SCADA systems have those vulnerabilities and then work to fix or patch those vulnerabilities. In addition to securing SCADA systems, organizations should also evaluate and investigate service providers, vendor security controls, enterprise switching costs, and securing their supply chains to SCADA systems and critical infrastructures (NIST et al., 2020, p. 30). Lastly, SCADA system regulations that are developed can be used to monitor and follow proper security procedures that will ensure all businesses and organizations are compliant with those regulations. This will prevent businesses and organizations from getting supplies and products that have been tampered with and pose a threat to SCADA systems and critical infrastructures from having malware, key loggers, and other malicious software and hardware attached to supplies and products.

RECOMMENDATIONS

The following practical recommendations on addressing cybersecurity risks for Supervisory Control and Data Acquisition (SCADA) systems, based on current research in the field (Ismail, Sitnikova, Slay, 2020; Mingo & Burrell; 2023; Stojanović & Boštjančič Rakas, 2022) include:

- Patch and Update Regularly - Ensure that your SCADA system software and hardware are up to date with the latest security patches and updates. This helps fix known vulnerabilities.
- Network Micro-Segmentation - Divide your network into micro-segments, separating your SCADA systems from other parts of your network. This limits access to critical systems.

- <u>Access Control</u> - Implement strict access controls, ensuring only authorized personnel can access and modify SCADA systems. Use strong passwords and consider multi-factor authentication.
- <u>Firewalls and Intrusion Detection</u> - Install firewalls and intrusion detection systems to monitor network traffic and detect any suspicious or unauthorized activity.
- <u>Regular Back-ups</u> - Regularly back up your SCADA system data. In case of a cyberattack, having recent backups can help restore operations quickly.
- <u>Employee Training</u> - Train your staff on cybersecurity best practices and make them aware of potential threats like phishing emails or social engineering attacks.
- <u>Incident Response Plan</u> - Develop a clear incident response plan outlining what to do in the case of a cybersecurity breach. Test and update this plan regularly.
- <u>Encryption</u> - Encrypt data transmitted between SCADA devices to prevent eavesdropping and tampering.
- <u>Vendor Security</u> - Ensure that your SCADA system vendors prioritize security and provide regular updates and patches for their products.
- <u>Security Audits</u> - Conduct regular security audits and vulnerability assessments of your SCADA systems to identify and remediate potential weaknesses. Vendors should be included in these audits.
- <u>Physical Security</u> - Protect physical access to SCADA equipment to prevent unauthorized tampering or theft.
- <u>Monitoring and Logging</u> - Set up monitoring and logging systems to track activities within your SCADA environment. This can help in detecting anomalies and investigating incidents.
- <u>Regulatory Compliance</u> - Ensure that your SCADA systems comply with relevant industry and regulatory standards for cybersecurity.
- <u>Tabletop Exercises, Practice Drills, and Simulations</u> - Tabletop exercises, practice drills, and simulations are invaluable readiness tools for organizations seeking to enhance their ability to manage cybersecurity risks in utilities and industrial settings. These exercises provide a controlled and structured environment in which teams can simulate real-world cybersecurity incidents and responses. During tabletop exercises, participants engage in collaborative discussions, often led by a facilitator, to assess their preparedness, identify vulnerabilities, and refine their incident response strategies. Practice drills involve practical exercises, such as mock cyberattacks or data breaches, allowing teams to apply their knowledge and skills in a hands-on manner. Simulations take these exercises a step further by creating realistic scenarios with varying degrees of complexity, enabling organizations to test their response capabilities under simulated stress conditions. These readiness tools not only help organizations uncover weaknesses and gaps in their cybersecurity defenses, but also foster teamwork, improve decision-making, and enhance overall preparedness for the ever-evolving landscape of cybersecurity threats in critical infrastructure sectors.

DISCUSSION

The impact of threats on SCADA systems is significant. SCADA system information can be stolen or changed, and systems can be damaged or shut down. The impact of cyber threats on SCADA systems can best be seen in the example of the 2007 Estonia attack case. Distributed denial-of-service (DDoS) attacks caused Estonia's computer systems to lag after the attacks targeted government websites, banks, universities, and newspapers. The DDoS attacks took place over three weeks, making the country and the people in Estonia helpless. This type of cyber-attack can and has affected SCADA systems due to their vulnerabilities. It is for this reason that the Estonia attack should be used as an example and viewed as a learning point to determine what the risks, threats, and vulnerabilities are in SCADA systems.

SCADA systems generally have many vulnerabilities in hosts, nodes, networks, and services, and the increase in cyber threats doesn't help keep information secure. Cyber threats and attacks on SCADA systems can be done through Internet connections; business and enterprise network connections, and then through the layered control networks that will lead to field devices. As cyber threats increase, everyone will need to work in concert to protect vital information through securing and encrypting information, creating strong authentication, creating policies and procedures that are specific to SCADA systems, and following cybersecurity standards while conducting periodic risk assessments to ensure SCADA systems are secure from vulnerabilities, utilizing intrusion detection systems, patching, and updating software, and implement Zero Trust Architecture (ZTA).

Overall, SCADA systems connected to critical infrastructures must be secured through cybersecurity methods such as encryption, authentication, privilege management, strong passwords, creating and utilizing cybersecurity policies and procedures that detail mitigation procedures, and the ability to update and upgrade software and hardware. The cost is too great if SCADA systems are not secured. It is, therefore, imperative for SCADA system owners to understand the risks and threats of not securing SCADA systems. SCADA system owners should be educated and provided with information and support in order to acquire the best tools to protect their SCADA systems. SCADA system owners need to consult with Federal Government cybersecurity and Information Technology professionals in order to safeguard SCADA systems, learn best practices, and ensure compliance with policies and regulations.

Cyber-attacks have changed and increased over the years, and they will not stop, as shown below in the screenshot from AO Kaspersky Lab, 2021. This type of system tracks and records live attack points of origin and targets and would be beneficial in determining attacks for attribution for companies, organizations, the Federal Government, and the military. Tracing inbound attacks and utilizing intrusion detection systems can allow information technology and cyber security professionals to prepare and ensure there are no breaches to computer systems connected to networks, SCADA systems, and critical infrastructures. The United States must be diligent in safeguarding SCADA systems that are connected to critical infrastructures, especially with the threats and vulnerabilities that may result from cyber-attacks.

RECOMMENDATIONS FOR FUTURE RESEARCH

It is recommended that The Administration address cybersecurity standards for SCADA systems and educate SCADA system owners about the risks, threats, and vulnerabilities to SCADA systems to mitigate SCADA systems from being attacked and potentially incapacitating the U.S. critical infrastructures. In order to improve SCADA systems and critical infrastructures, SCADA systems and critical infrastructure facilities should be upgraded and improved from aging structures and equipment. SCADA systems and critical infrastructure facilities cannot be protected with their sensitive information if the structures and equipment are in poor condition. Next, cybersecurity is paramount in protecting SCADA systems and critical infrastructures. In order to provide the best protection, computer systems' hardware and software need to be upgraded regularly. Software needs to be updated, and security scans should be run continuously, along with weekly patch maintenance and daily CISA cybersecurity alerts, advisory reviews, and

Figure 8. Example of cyber attacks
AO Kaspersky Lab. (2021)

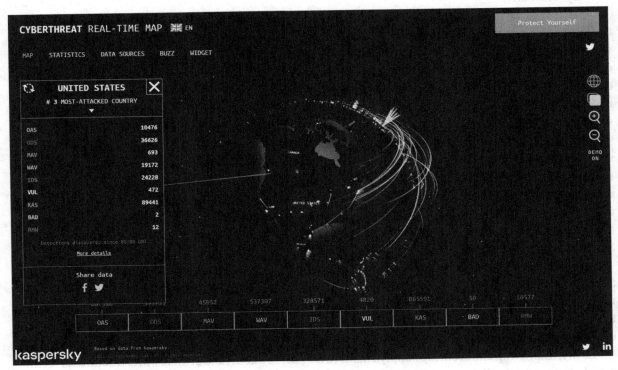

investigations. If there is a breach in the system, that intrusion needs to be handled immediately with the use of security AI and automation to contain breaches. Computer systems connected to SCADA systems or critical infrastructures cannot wait weeks for someone to check on an intrusion. Waiting or not having intrusion detection systems could result in information being stolen, machinery stopping production, or causing a cascade effect on our critical infrastructures. It is also recommended to explore future research in the following areas:

1. Advanced Threat Modeling covers cyber and physical threats to critical infrastructures.
2. Human-Centric Security Measures: for training programs, user awareness, and the impact of insider threats.
3. Resilience and Recovery Strategies: through recovery frameworks, incident response plans, and rapid system restoration that minimizes disruptions.
4. Integration of Artificial Intelligence (AI) and Machine Learning: to leverage anomaly detection, predictive maintenance, and adaptive security measures with automation.
5. Investigate the effectiveness of existing regulatory frameworks and policy measures to ensure SCADA security.
6. Incorporate and utilize "Action Research" methodologies to address real-time issues and challenges securing critical infrastructures. Action research allows for the direct involvement of practitioners, policymakers, and stakeholders in identifying and resolving security vulnerabilities. This can provide

a valuable bridge between theoretical insights and practical solutions in ICS and SCADA system cybersecurity

Therefore, it is also recommended that a SCADA security policy should be developed that defines what the controls, behaviors, and expectations are for users and processes and also encompasses details on how to effectively secure SCADA, control systems (CS), and critical infrastructures. Second, physical security should be established and utilized to protect SCADA and CS in order to prevent damage and unauthorized access to equipment and information. Third, it is advisable to lock down perimeter security by eliminating any unnecessary external connections that connect to the perimeter of CS. This will prevent cyber criminals from attempting to hack into control systems to either damage, control, or steal information. Next, provide security to operational and management communication traffic while managing features and configurations. This will prevent information from being leaked and will assist in preventing insider threats. Next, SCADA risk and vulnerability assessments should be developed and utilized on a periodic basis to determine risks, threats, and vulnerabilities. This will aid organizations, the federal government, and the military in determining if any changes need to be made to better secure SCADA systems and critical infrastructures.

It is also recommended to protect the networks and telecommunication lines through the Internet Service Providers (ISPs) by placing intrusion detection devices and security on all networks and telecommunication lines. This security initiative could then extend to SCADA systems and critical infrastructures to deter cyber-attacks before they hit their targets and reduce the costs for damaged equipment and any other costs that may result from attacks.

Lastly, improving and securing supply chains to SCADA systems and critical infrastructures is recommended to prevent utilizing supplies and products that have been tampered with or imported from other countries. All supply chains should have tracking and receipt verifications on supplies and products. It is also advisable to stop having electronics and software manufactured outside of the United States due to the risk of backdoors, logic bombs, or any other device that can be placed on manufactured electronic goods that can lie dormant until turned on and used against U.S. citizens, the government, or military; or have all electronics and software checked for any issues or threats such as backdoors or logic bombs prior to the electronics and software entering the United States. This preventative measure will help reduce the potential for malicious devices being hidden in manufactured electronic goods that could threaten SCADA systems and critical infrastructures. Businesses and organizations all need to identify and evaluate high-value assets, high-priority items, the business impact, and resource allocation, conduct tabletop mock drills, and test if high-value assets or high-priority items go down are there back-up or recovery systems to keep the business running.

In addition to these recommendations, it is advisable to provide funding and increase research and development for SCADA systems connected to critical infrastructures. Proper funding can provide for testing new hardware and software to discover new ways to protect SCADA systems and critical infrastructures, especially since CISA notes SCADA systems vulnerabilities are found through software vulnerabilities. Research and development will also promote interest in Information Technology by presenting ideas, hardware, and software to stakeholders to increase technological innovations from a security standpoint. As cyber threats increase, individuals and organizations will demand better hardware, software, and technological skills to protect their information and intellectual property to ensure their companies run uninterrupted for routine daily management. In order to help these businesses operate at optimal levels, cost-effective methods must be sought through technological advancement and security.

As a result of the current status of increased cyber threats, it is, therefore, imperative to increase funding for research and development so people can become educated and qualified personnel can mitigate cybersecurity threats and protect SCADA systems and critical infrastructures.

REFERENCES

Agnew, R., Cullen, F. T., Burton, V. S. Jr, Evans, T., & Dunaway, R. (1996). A new test of classic strain theory. *Justice Quarterly*, *13*(4), 681–704. doi:10.1080/07418829600093151

Al-Muntaser, B., Mohamed, M., Tuama, A., & Rana, I. (2023). Cybersecurity advances in SCADA systems. *International Journal of Advanced Computer Science and Applications*, *14*(8). Advance online publication. doi:10.14569/IJACSA.2023.0140835

Alanazi, M., Mahmood, A., & Chowdhury, M. (2023). SCADA vulnerabilities and attacks: A review of the state-of-the-art and open issues. *Computers & Security*, *125*, 103028. doi:10.1016/j.cose.2022.103028

Alqudhaibi, A., Albarrak, M., Aloseel, A., Jagtap, S., & Salonitis, K. (2023). Predicting cybersecurity threats in critical infrastructure for industry 4.0: A proactive approach based on attacker motivations. *Sensors (Basel)*, *23*(9), 4539. doi:10.3390/s23094539 PMID:37177743

AO Kaspersky Lab. (2021). *Kaspersky Cyberthreat Real-Time Map*. Retrieved October 29, 2023, from https://cybermap.kaspersky.com/

Beggs, C., & Warren, M. (2014). Safeguarding Australia from Cyber-Terrorism: A SCADA Risk Framework. In I. Management Association (Ed.), Cyber Behavior: Concepts, Methodologies, Tools, and Applications (pp. 282-297). IGI Global. doi:10.4018/978-1-4666-5942-1.ch016

Chen, S., Hao, M., Ding, F., Jiang, D., Dong, J., Zhang, S., Guo, Q., & Gao, C. (2023). Exploring the global geography of cybercrime and its driving forces. *Humanities & Social Sciences Communications*, *10*(1), 71. Advance online publication. doi:10.1057/s41599-023-01560-x PMID:36852135

Cybernews. (2023, October 12). *SCADA: the invisible backbone of modern industry*. Retrieved October 28, 2023, from https://cybernews.com/security/scada-systems-vulnerabilities-explained/

Cybersecurity & Infrastructure Security Agency. (2003, December 17). *Homeland Security Presidential Directive 7*. Retrieved November 5, 2023, from https://www.cisa.gov/news-events/directives/homeland-security-presidential-directive-7

Cybersecurity & Infrastructure Security Agency. (2010, September). *Preventing and Defending Against Cyber Attacks*. CISA.gov. Retrieved November 11, 2023, from https://www.cisa.gov/sites/default/files/publications/defending-against-cyber-attacks-september-2010.pdf

Cybersecurity & Infrastructure Security Agency. (2023a). *Critical Infrastructure Sectors*. Cybersecurity & Infrastructure Security Agency (CISA). Retrieved October 29, 2023, from https://www.cisa.gov/topics/critical-infrastructure-security-and-resilience/critical-infrastructure-sectors

Cybersecurity & Infrastructure Security Agency. (2023b). *Cybersecurity Alerts & Advisories*. Retrieved November 11, 2023, from https://www.cisa.gov/news-events/cybersecurity-advisories?f%5B0%5D=advisory_type%3A95

Cybersecurity & Infrastructure Security Agency. (2023c). *Defining Insider Threats*. Retrieved November 7, 2023, from https://www.cisa.gov/topics/physical-security/insider-threat-mitigation/defining-insider-threats

Cybersecurity & Infrastructure Security Agency. (2023d). *Federal Government: CISA Partners with Other Government Agencies to Help Them Manage Their Cyber Risk*. Retrieved November 11, 2023, from https://www.cisa.gov/audiences/federal-government

Dell. (2015, December). *2015 Dell Annual Threat Report*. Silicon. Retrieved September 20, 2015, from https://www.silicon.es/wp-content/uploads/2015/12/2015-dell-security-annual-threat-report-white-paper-15657.pdf

Department of Energy. (2015). *21 Steps to Improve Cyber Security of SCADA Networks*. Energy.gov. Retrieved November 11, 2023, from https://www.energy.gov/ceser/articles/21-steps-improve-cyber-security-scada-networks

Department of Homeland Security. (2010). *DHS Risk Lexicon: 2010 Edition*. Retrieved November 19, 2015, from https://www.dhs.gov/xlibrary/assets/dhs-risk-lexicon-2010.pdf

Department of Homeland Security. (2013). *NIPP 2013: Partnering for Critical Infrastructure Security and Resilience (Rev. 2020)*. Cybersecurity & Infrastructure Security Agency (CISA). Retrieved November 11, 2023, from https://www.cisa.gov/sites/default/files/publications/national-infrastructure-protection-plan-2013-508.pdf

Department of Homeland Security. (2019, April 2). *Improving Critical Infrastructure Cybersecurity*. DHS.gov. Retrieved November 11, 2023, from https://www.dhs.gov/sites/default/files/publications/cisa_-_improving_critical_infrastructure_cybersecurity.pdf

Dickman, F. (2009). Hacking The Industrial SCADA Network. *Pipeline & Gas Journal, 236*(11). Retrieved November 9, 2023, from https://pgjonline.com/magazine/2009/november-2009-vol-236-no-11/features/hacking-the-industrial-scada-network

Eisenfeld, B. L. (2019). *National Security's Triple Threat: Terrorists', Spies', and Hackers' Covernging Motivations* (Order No. 27542473). ProQuest On Academic (2309521885). Retrieved November 9, 2023, from https://www.proquest.com/dissertations-theses/national-security-s-triple-threat-terrorists/docview/2309521885/se-2

Finklea, K. M., & Theory, C. A. (2012). Cybercrime: conceptual issues for Congress and U.S. law enforcement. *Journal of Current Issues in Crime, Law and Law Enforcement, 5*(1/2).

Gao, X., Shang, T., & Liu, J. (2022). *Quantitative Risk Assessment of Threats on SCADA Systems Using Attack Countermeasure Tree*. IEEE. doi:10.1109/PST55820.2022.9851965

Genge, B., Haller, P., & Roman, A.-S. (2023). E-aptdetect: Early advanced persistent threat detection in critical infrastructures with dynamic attestation. *Applied Sciences (Basel, Switzerland), 13*(6), 3409. doi:10.3390/app13063409

Griffiths, J. (2015). *CNN: Money – Cybercrime costs the average U.S. firm $15 million a year.* CNN: Money. Retrieved October 15, 2015, from https://money.cnn.com/2015/10/08/technology/cybercrime-cost-business/

Henrie, M. (2013). Cyber security risk management in the SCADA critical infrastructure environment. *Engineering Management Journal, 25*(2), 38–45. doi:10.1080/10429247.2013.11431973

Hildick-Smith, A. (2021). *Security for Critical Infrastructure SCADA Systems.* SANS Institute. Retrieved November 5, 2023, from https://sansorg.egnyte.com/dl/ZQfkrN71w7

IBM. (2023). *Cost of a Data Breach Report 2023.* Retrieved October 30, 2023, from https://www.ibm.com/downloads/cas/E3G5JMBP

Inductive Automation. (2018, September 12). *SCADA: Supervisory Control and Data Acquisition - What is SCADA, Who Uses it and How SCADA Has Evolved?* Retrieved November 10, 2023, from https://inductiveautomation.com/resources/article/what-is-scada

Ismail, S., Sitnikova, E., & Slay, J. (2020). SCADA Systems Cyber Security for Critical Infrastructures: Case Studies in Multiple Sectors. In I. Management Association (Ed.), Cyber Warfare and Terrorism: Concepts, Methodologies, Tools, and Applications (pp. 446-464). IGI Global. doi:10.4018/978-1-7998-2466-4.ch028

Johnsen, S. O. (2014). Safety and Security in SCADA Systems Must be Improved through Resilience Based Risk Management. In I. Management Association (Ed.), Crisis Management: Concepts, Methodologies, Tools, and Applications (pp. 1422-1436). IGI Global. doi:10.4018/978-1-4666-4707-7.ch071

Jones, D. (2023, December 5). *Water utility cyberattacks underscore ongoing threat to OT.* Cybersecurity Dive. Retrieved from: https://www.cybersecuritydive.com/news/water-utility-cyberattacks-threat-ot/701577/

Kovacs, E. (2022, October 5). *SCADA Systems Involved in Many Breaches Suffered by U.S. Ports, Terminals.* Security Week. Retrieved November 10, 2023, from https://www.securityweek.com/scada-systems-involved-many-breaches-suffered-us-ports-terminals/

Kube, N. (2013). Cybersecurity and SCADA in critical infrastructure. *Pipeline & Gas Journal, 240*(2), 46–47. Retrieved November 9, 2023, from https://pgjonline.com/magazine/2013/february-2013-vol-240-no-2/features/cyber-security-and-scada-in-critical-infrastructure

Lennon, M. (2015). *Attacks against SCADA systems doubled in 2014: Dell.* Security Week. Retrieved November 2, 2015, from https://www.securityweek.com/attacks-against-scada-systems-doubled-2014-dell

Less than 5% of critical industrial infrastructure is monitored for threats. (2023). *Communications Today; Noida.* Retrieved October 28, 2023, from http://ezproxy.apus.edu/login?qurl=https%3A%2F%2Fwww.proquest.com%2Ftrade-journals%2Fless-than-5-critical-industrial-infrastructure-is%2Fdocview%2F2806176802%2Fse-2%3Faccountid%3D8289

Macaulay, T., & Singer, B. L. (2011). *Cybersecurity for industrial control systems: SCADA, dcs, plc, hmi, and sis* (1st ed.). Auerbach Publications.

Marković-Petrović, J. D. (2020). Methodology for Cyber Security Risk Mitigation in Next Generation SCADA Systems. In M. Stojanović & S. Boštjančič Rakas (Eds.), *Cyber Security of Industrial Control Systems in the Future Internet Environment* (pp. 27–46). IGI Global. doi:10.4018/978-1-7998-2910-2.ch002

Miles, G., Wiles, J., Claypoole, T., Drake, P., Henry, P. A., & Johnson, L. J. (2008). *Techno Security's Guide to Securing SCADA* (1st ed.). Syngress.

Mingo, H. C., & Burrell, D. N. (2023). Cybersecurity Risks With Supervisory Control and Data Acquisition (SCADA) Systems is a Public Health and National Security Issue. In F. Adedoyin & B. Christiansen (Eds.), *Handbook of Research on Cybersecurity Risk in Contemporary Business Systems* (pp. 149–167). IGI Global. doi:10.4018/978-1-6684-7207-1.ch008

Morgan, S. (2022, October 17). *Cybercrime to Cost the World 8 Trillion Annually in 2023*. Cybercrime Magazine. Retrieved November 9, 2023, from https://cybersecurityventures.com/cybercrime-to-cost-the-world-8-trillion-annually-in-2023/#:~:text=Our%20report%20provides%20a%20breakdown,%24667%20billion%20a%20Month

National Institute of Standards & Technology. (2023). *NIST: Information Technology Laboratory Computer Security Resource Center*. NIST Computer Security Resource Center. Retrieved November 7, 2023, from https://csrc.nist.gov/glossary/term/hacker

National Institute of Standards and Technology. (2017). *An introduction to information security: NIST SP 800-12 rev 1*. CreateSpace Independent Publishing Platform. doi:10.6028/NIST.SP.800-12r1

National Institute of Standards and Technology. (2020). NIST SP. 800-207: Zero Trust Architecture. *National Institute of Standards and Technology*. Retrieved November 11, 2023, from https://doi.org/doi:10.6028/NIST.SP.800-207

National Security Agency. (2010). *U.S. Cybersecurity Policy and the Role of U.S. Cybercom*. Center for Strategic and International Studies, Cybersecurity Policy Debate Series. Retrieved November 6, 2015, from https://www.nsa.gov/Press-Room/Speeches-Testimony/Article-View/Article/1620145/center-for-strategic-and-international-studies-csis-csis-cybersecurity-policy-d/

OPSWAT. (2021). *Securing ICS and SCADA Updates in OT Environments: Best Practice for SCADA System Protection*. Retrieved October 28, 2023, from https://info.opswat.com/hubfs/Demand%20Gen%20Assets%20by%20Wilson/White%20Papers/OPSWAT-Securing-ICS+SCADA-Updates-in-OT-Whitepaper.pdf?hsLang=en&submissionGuid=23e9b3d4-38e9-4653-84fb-69ef7da9ece5

Paganini, P. (2015, April 15). *Dell Report Revealed Attacks on SCADA System are Doubled*. Security Affairs. Retrieved November 7, 2015, from https://securityaffairs.co/35967/hacking/dell-attacks-on-scada-doubled.html

Paternoster, R., & Bachman, R. (2000). *Essays in contemporary criminological theory: Explaining criminals and crime* (1st ed.). Roxbury Publishing Company.

Senate Homeland Security and Governmental Affairs Subcommittee on Federal Spending Oversight and Emergency Management Hearing. (2020). *State and Local Cybersecurity: Defending Our Communities from Cyber Threats amid COVID-19*. Federal Information & News Dispatch, LLC. https://www.govinfo.gov/content/pkg/CHRG-116shrg43278/pdf/CHRG-116shrg43278.pdf

Sheldon, R., & Hanna, K. T. (2022, January). *Cyberterrorism*. TechTarget. Retrieved November 10, 2023, from https://www.techtarget.com/searchsecurity/definition/cyberterrorism#:~:text=The%20U.S.%20Federal%20Bureau%20of,subnational%20groups%20or%20clandestine%20agents.%22

Söğüt, E., & Erdem, O. (2023). A multi-model proposal for classification and detection of DDoS attacks on SCADA systems. *Applied Sciences (Basel, Switzerland), 13*(10), 5993. Retrieved October 28, 2023, from. doi:10.3390/app13105993

Stojanović, M. D., & Boštjančič Rakas, S. V. (2022). Challenges in Securing Industrial Control Systems Using Future Internet Technologies. In I. Management Association (Ed.), Research Anthology on Business Aspects of Cybersecurity (pp. 561-586). IGI Global. doi:10.4018/978-1-6684-3698-1.ch026

Stouffer, K., Pease, M., Tang, C., Zimmerman, T., Pillitteri, V., Lightman, S., Hahn, A., Saravia, S., Sherule, A., & Thompson, M. (2023). NIST SP 800-82 Rev. 3: Guide to Operational Technology (OT) Security. *National Institute of Standards and Technology*. doi:10.6028/NIST.SP.800-82r3

SynSaber. (2023). *SynSaber and ICS Advisory Project Identify Vulnerability Trends Within The Critical Infrastructure Sector*. Retrieved October 29, 2023, from https://14520070.fs1.hubspotusercontent-na1.net/hubfs/14520070/Collateral/SynSaber+ICS-Advisory-Project_ICS-Vulnerabilities_First-Half-2023.pdf

The Department of Defense. (2023). *2023 DOD Cyber Strategy Summary (Unclassified)*. U.S. Department of Defense News. Retrieved November 10, 2023, from https://media.defense.gov/2023/Sep/12/2003299076/-1/-1/1/2023_DOD_Cyber_Strategy_Summary.PDF

The White House. (2011). *International Strategy for Cyberspace*. Retrieved November 12, 2015, from https://obamawhitehouse.archives.gov/sites/default/files/rss_viewer/international_strategy_for_cyberspace.pdf

The White House. (2021, July 28). *Background Press Call on Improving Cybersecurity of U.S. Critical Infrastructure*. Retrieved November 10, 2023, from https://www.whitehouse.gov/briefing-room/press-briefings/2021/07/28/background-press-call-on-improving-cybersecurity-of-u-s-critical-infrastructure/

Thilmany, J. (2012). SCADA security? *Mechanical Engineering (New York, N.Y.), 134*(6), 26–31. Retrieved November 14, 2015, from. doi:10.1115/1.2012-JUN-1

Upadhyay, D., & Sampalli, S. (2020). SCADA (Supervisory Control and Data Acquisition) systems: Vulnerability assessment and security recommendations. *Computers & Security, 89*, 101666. doi:10.1016/j.cose.2019.101666

Ware, W. H. (1967, April). *Security and Privacy in Computer Systems*. The RAND Corporation. Retrieved October 28, 2015, from https://www.rand.org/content/dam/rand/pubs/papers/2005/P3544.pdf

Warner, M. (2012). Cybersecurity: A Pre-History. *Intelligence and National Security, 27*(5), 781–799. doi:10.1080/02684527.2012.708530

Weitoish, T. (2014). Cybersecurity risks that impact national security and intelligence today [Unpublished manuscript]. APUS: American Military University.

Wofford, T. (2015, January 14). *Meet the new CISPA, same as the old CISPA.* Newsweek. Retrieved November 20, 2015, from https://www.newsweek.com/meet-new-cispa-same-old-cispa-299375

Zhang, Y., Wang, L., Xiang, Y., & Ten, C.-W. (2015). Power system reliability evaluation with SCADA cybersecurity considerations. *IEEE Transactions on Smart Grid, 6*(4), 1707–1721. Retrieved October 27, 2015, from. doi:10.1109/TSG.2015.2396994

Chapter 5
Addressing Childhood Obesity Through Technology Innovation

Quatavia McLester
iD https://orcid.org/0000-0003-1596-0517
Capitol Technology University, USA

Darrell Norman Burrell
iD https://orcid.org/0000-0002-4675-9544
Capitol Technology University, USA

ABSTRACT

Childhood obesity has long-term consequences, emphasizing the need for comprehensive intervention. Research highlights a strong link between childhood obesity and adult obesity. Globally, the World Health Organization notes that overweight and obesity now claim more lives than underweight conditions. In 2016, an astonishing 41 million children under 5 were classified as overweight worldwide. In the United States, childhood obesity prevalence tripled since 1970, affecting 1 in 5 school-aged children by 2015-2016. This chapter advocates innovative technology-driven solutions to address childhood and adolescent obesity. The authors propose leveraging low-cost mobile health, remote monitoring, and wearable technologies, empowering individuals and healthcare providers to effectively manage obesity, offering personalized support and real-time data. Embracing these technologies can foster a transformative shift in obesity management, ensuring a healthier future for the next generation.

INTRODUCTION

The COVID-19 pandemic has unleashed a multifaceted crisis that extends beyond the realm of infectious diseases, with its repercussions profoundly affecting children and adolescents. Research has unveiled a disturbing association between the pandemic and a spectrum of adverse outcomes, including anxiety, depression, and impaired social development. To this already concerning list, we must add another concern: obesity. Obesity is defined as having a Body Mass Index (BMI) exceeding the 95th percentile of one's peers of the same age and sex (Centers for Disease Control, 2018). Even before the pandemic, the

DOI: 10.4018/979-8-3693-1970-3.ch005

global prevalence of overweight children had surged, surpassing a staggering 41 million in 2016 (World Health Organization, 2019). Recent studies have uncovered a disconcerting escalation in obesity rates among children and teenagers during the pandemic, intensifying an existing alarming trend (Burrell et al., 2021). Traditionally a cornerstone for promoting proper nutrition and physical education, schools could play a pivotal role in mitigating this crisis (Burrell et al., 2021). However, addressing this issue competes for educators' attention amid the ongoing pandemic, staffing shortages, and the pressing need to address learning loss (Prothero, 2022).

The closure of school buildings increased screen time and reduced physical activity during the initial pandemic, which likely contributed to the surge in childhood obesity (Prothero, 2022). As a result, it is imperative to recognize that simply returning students to in-person learning will not suffice to tackle this complex problem. Moreover, the pandemic has diverted precious resources away from schools, impacting the capacity of school nurses to conduct health screenings and develop programs promoting healthy lifestyles (Prothero, 2022). Children's increased screen time, consumption of processed foods, and reduced physical activity during school closures have likely compounded the issue. The global rise in childhood overweight and obesity carries profound implications, encompassing heightened cardiometabolic risk in childhood, diminished self-esteem, and reduced quality of life in adolescence. Excess weight constitutes a significant risk factor for numerous diseases, including more than a dozen types of cancer. Regrettably, individuals are often unfairly held solely responsible for their weight, and individuals who are overweight or obese frequently endure stigmatization and discrimination (Burrell et al., 2021; Aris & Block, 2022). Childhood obesity frequently sets the stage for adult obesity, with its associated risks of chronic ailments, such as cardiometabolic disease, sleep apnea, nonalcoholic fatty liver disease, type 2 diabetes, kidney disease, and more (Burrell et al., 2021; Aris & Block, 2022). The proportion of deaths attributed to non-communicable diseases, such as diabetes and heart disease, is projected to increase from 59% in 2002 to 69% in 2030 (Stroup et al., 2009). In this context, addressing the complex interplay of factors contributing to childhood obesity during and beyond the pandemic remains a pressing public health challenge that necessitates multifaceted, community-wide interventions and new technology-driven approaches.

PROBLEM STATEMENT

The prevalence of childhood and adolescent obesity witnessed a concerning surge, escalating from 19% to 22% in just a single year between 2020 and 2021 (Prothero, 2022). To contextualize this alarming trend, it is worth noting that in 2019, the United States already grappled with a significant obesity burden, affecting approximately 13.7 million children and adolescents, accounting for 18.5% of the population (Centers for Disease Control, 2019). Notably, disparities exist within this context, with higher prevalence rates among Hispanics (25.8%) and non-Hispanic blacks (22.0%) compared to non-Hispanic whites (14.1%) (Centers for Disease Control, 2019).

The consequences of childhood obesity extend beyond adolescence and into adulthood, forming a disconcerting continuum. Research by Anderson and Butcher (2006) has underscored a strong correlation between childhood obesity and the likelihood of becoming obese adults. This linkage between early-life obesity and long-term health outcomes emphasizes the urgency of addressing this issue comprehensively.

On a global scale, the World Health Organization (2019) has highlighted the sobering reality that in most parts of the world, overweight and obese now claim more lives than underweight. This dire situation is further exemplified by the staggering statistic that, in 2016, the number of children under the age of 5 classified as overweight reached a staggering 41 million (World Health Organization, 2019). In the United States, the prevalence of childhood obesity has tripled since 1970, culminating in a situation where 1 in 5 school-aged children grapples with this health concern, according to data from 2015-2016 (Centers for Disease Control, 2018).

While it is a well-recognized fact that obesity and overweight conditions often result from increased calorie and fat consumption, this complex phenomenon demands a closer examination. This paper delves into the multifaceted dynamics of this issue, seeking innovative technology-driven approaches to address the intricacies of childhood and adolescent obesity, recognizing the need for a holistic and community-driven response to this pressing public health challenge.

THE OBJECT OF RESEARCH AND RESEARCH METHOD

Childhood obesity is a multifaceted concern influenced by many factors and determinants. This research endeavors to provide a comprehensive and innovative approach to combat this issue, leveraging existing literature and research insights. Central to this endeavor is exploring intervention strategies, focusing on harnessing healthcare technologies to facilitate effective solutions. Through a methodical content analysis of academic literature and relevant theories, this paper aims to shed light on the intricate dynamics underlying childhood obesity. By delving into the complexities surrounding this health challenge, we aspire to contribute to developing evidence-based strategies and interventions that can make a meaningful impact in addressing this critical public health issue.

PREVIOUS RESEARCH

Childhood obesity is a multifaceted issue influenced by a diverse array of factors. Sahoo et al. (2015) identified several key contributors, including genetics, consumption of sugary beverages, snack foods, portion sizes, activity levels, environmental factors, socio-cultural influences, family dynamics, and psychological aspects. These factors collectively shape the lives of young children and significantly impact their health and well-being. While genetics substantially predisposes individuals to obesity, it is not the sole determinant of its prevalence (Sahoo et al., 2015).

Physical activity emerges as a crucial factor in promoting health, with research by Lee et al. (2012) highlighting its potential to reduce the risk of chronic diseases and premature mortality. Aligning with this, the World Health Organization (2010) recommends that children and adolescents aged 5-17 engage in daily moderate- to vigorous-intensity physical activities. However, disparities in access to physical activity opportunities and resources persist, particularly in low-income communities.

The impact of childhood obesity is exacerbated in such communities, where outdoor play spaces are limited and readily available, and inexpensive and unhealthy fast-food options often replace fresh, nutritious meals (Burrell et al., 2021; Aris & Block, 2022). The environment in which families reside, work, play, and attend school profoundly influences their choices regarding nutrition and physical activity (Easterling et al., 2018). Notably, social disparities prevail in these communities, contributing significantly to the epidemic of overweight and obesity. As we explore the complexities of childhood obesity, it is evident that a comprehensive approach is essential, one that addresses these multifaceted factors and strives to create equitable environments that support healthier choices and lifestyles.

Obesity is classified as a non-communicable disease in epidemiology, yet its impact on health is just as profound as that of a biological virus. The causes of obesity are multifaceted, reflecting a complex interplay of factors encompassing dietary choices, physical activity levels, genetic predisposition, family and social influences, behavioral and cultural aspects, environmental conditions, socioeconomic status, and media marketing (Easterling et al., 2018). Children who grapple with overweight and obesity often carry this burden into adulthood, increasing their susceptibility to a spectrum of non-communicable diseases (Sahoo et al., 2015). The long-term consequences of this condition set the stage for younger generations to face elevated health risks, including conditions such as high blood pressure and high cholesterol, which are linked to cardiovascular disease (Burrell et al., 2021; Aris & Block, 2022). Obesity is also associated with respiratory issues like asthma and sleep apnea, as well as metabolic disturbances such as type 2 diabetes, impaired glucose tolerance, and insulin resistance (Burrell et al., 2021; Aris & Block, 2022).

Additionally, it can lead to conditions such as fatty liver disease, gallstones, and gastroesophageal reflux. On the psychological front, obesity can contribute to problems like anxiety and depression, while musculoskeletal disorders and joint issues are also common (Burrell et al., 2021; Aris & Block, 2022). Social challenges, including bullying, often accompany obesity, and there is a heightened risk of developing certain cancers (Easterling et al., 2018). The multifaceted nature of obesity underscores the importance of comprehensive interventions to address this significant public health concern and its far-reaching consequences (Burrell et al., 2021; Aris & Block, 2022).

SOCIAL COGNITIVE THEORY

One of the prevailing theories in nutritional education is the Social Cognitive Theory (SCT), as Hall (2016) noted. SCT posits that an individual's behavior is shaped by their ability to regulate their actions and influence their environment (Knol, 2016). Understanding the intricate relationship between knowledge, self-efficacy, and behavior among children can be a cornerstone for developing and enhancing nutritional programs (Hall, 2016).

In the pursuit of assessing the effectiveness of SCT interventions in nutritional programs targeting children from low-income communities, Branscum (2013) embarked on a critical evaluation. The "Food Fit" program, initially piloted in five schools with children in the 3rd through 4th grade, was anchored in specific behaviors. These behaviors included selecting lower-calorie snack options, opting for beverages low in sugar, and embracing a diet rich in fruits and vegetables – all essential elements in preventing childhood obesity (Branscum, 2013).

The program's curriculum comprised 14 distinct modules designed to allow children to participate even if they missed previous sessions. Each lesson spanned 30 to 45 minutes and adhered to a consistent format encompassing Introduction, Benefits and Consequences, Modeling and Taste Testing, Role Playing, and a Wrap-up (Branscum, 2013). These sessions actively engaged children through activities that illustrated the impacts of healthy behaviors or demonstrated those by the facilitators. Role-playing served as a powerful tool for reinforcing the targeted behaviors.

To gauge the program's effectiveness, Body Mass Index (BMI) and self-efficacy were employed as pre- and post-program evaluation measures (Branscum, 2013). A total of 85 children participated in the study, ranging in age from 8 to 13 years old, with approximately half of them classified as overweight or obese (Branscum, 2013).

While the school environment provides an ideal platform for imparting knowledge and instilling desired behaviors in children, SCT underscores the importance of repeated and consistent behaviors in achieving lasting outcomes. As such, parental involvement becomes imperative in reinforcing the behaviors taught in schools; without this ongoing support, the impact of such programs may yield minimal or negligible results.

HEALTH BELIEF MODEL

The Health Belief Model (HBM) is a frequently utilized framework that delves into an individual's readiness to modify health-related behaviors predicated on their beliefs. This social-psychological theory comprises five core components, as outlined by Woods (2018): benefits, barriers, severity, susceptibility, and health value. Central to the HBM is the premise that an individual must be willing to initiate change, implying a perception of susceptibility to a specific health condition and understanding its potentially grave consequences (Woods, 2018).

Moreover, the model emphasizes that the perceived benefits of the desired action must outweigh both psychological and tangible costs. It also underscores the importance of an individual's perception of the severity of the condition. Woods (2018) expounds upon this by proposing a model that employs the HBM to evaluate parental weight classification, problem recognition, and behavior change. This comprehensive analysis drew from 18 distinct studies to discern which components of the HBM exerted the most significant influence. The primary drivers of change identified were severity, barriers, and benefits.

Woods (2018) posits that parents who clearly understand perceived barriers, susceptibility, and severity can accurately assess their child's weight and recognize when it becomes problematic. This, in turn, fosters behavior change, as individuals must comprehend the true nature of the situation to initiate meaningful change when the benefits outweigh the psychological or physical costs. Conversely, a lack of knowledge diminishes the perceived severity, leading to inertia and resistance to change.

Alarming data revealed by Woods (2018) shows that only 26% of parents of overweight children were concerned about the health risks associated with their child's condition. Some studies even indicated that not only did parents fail to grasp the ramifications of childhood obesity, but they also shielded their children from the associated negativity. As Woods (2018) demonstrated, self-efficacy plays a pivotal role in prevention efforts, with parents possessing high self-efficacy more effectively influencing their child's behavior, translating into improved sleep and reduced media consumption.

From an intervention perspective, prevention is more cost-effective and yields superior outcomes. A 3-year study highlighted that parental self-efficacy contributes to a positive home environment that fosters healthy child development (Woods, 2018). While the HBM model efficiently illustrates the significance of knowledge in enabling parents to assess their child's weight accurately, behavioral changes depend on the perceived severity of the issue.

However, applying the Health Belief Model in communities facing various disparities can be challenging. For many, the immediate cost of living precedes future perceived health problems. Healthy habits may not be a priority for families grappling with day-to-day survival. In this context, the determinants of an individual's ability to progress toward increased self-efficacy and the capacity to attain that level are best understood through Maslow's Hierarchy of Needs (Liken, 2018). This broader perspective acknowledges that basic survival needs must be met before individuals can prioritize and invest in health-related behaviors.

LABELING THEORY

For obese teenagers, societal labels and stigmas related to obesity can influence their self-perception and actions (Ciciurkaite & Perry, 2018; Mustillo et al., 2013).

Labeling Theory, a concept in sociology, provides a valuable perspective to understand the elements related to childhood and adolescent obesity described in the provided information. Labeling Theory posits that societal labels and stigmas can significantly influence an individual's self-concept and subsequent behaviors (Ciciurkaite & Perry, 2018; Mustillo et al., 2013). In the context of childhood and adolescent obesity, these labels can have profound effects on how individuals perceive themselves and how they navigate the challenges associated with their weight (Ciciurkaite & Perry, 2018; Mustillo et al., 2013).

The prevalence of childhood and adolescent obesity, as highlighted in the data from Prothero (2022) and the Centers for Disease Control (2019), can contribute to the labeling process. When a significant portion of the population is affected by a particular condition, such as obesity, it can normalize certain stereotypes and associated labels (Ciciurkaite & Perry, 2018; Mustillo et al., 2013). Obese children and adolescents may find themselves labeled as "overweight" or "obese," which can shape their self-perception and influence how they view their bodies (Ciciurkaite & Perry, 2018; Mustillo et al., 2013).

Disparities in obesity rates, particularly among different racial and ethnic groups, as noted in the data (Centers for Disease Control, 2019), can exacerbate labeling and stigmatization. Labeling Theory recognizes that individuals from marginalized or stigmatized groups are often subjected to more negative labels and stereotypes. Therefore, Hispanic and non-Hispanic Black children and adolescents facing higher prevalence rates may be more susceptible to experiencing the detrimental effects of labeling, including lower self-esteem and psychological distress (Ciciurkaite & Perry, 2018; Mustillo et al., 2013). Labeling Theory posits that societal labels and stigmas can significantly shape an individual's self-concept and behaviors, often with far-reaching consequences (Ciciurkaite & Perry, 2018; Mustillo et al., 2013).

Teen obesity often leads to labeling and stigmatization, as peers may use terms like "fat" or "overweight" to describe their classmates. This labeling can affect a teenager's self-esteem and body image, potentially leading to negative emotional consequences (Ciciurkaite & Perry, 2018; Mustillo et al., 2013). Bullying can be a direct consequence of labeling related to teen obesity. Labeling Theory suggests that when an individual is labeled as "fat" or "obese," it may lead to social exclusion, ridicule, and even verbal or physical harassment. Bullying behaviors can further deepen the emotional impact on teenagers struggling with obesity, potentially leading to anxiety, depression, and a reluctance to engage in social activities or seek help for their weight management (Ciciurkaite & Perry, 2018; Mustillo et al., 2013).

The long-term consequences of childhood obesity, including the increased risk of becoming obese adults, as discussed in the information referencing Anderson and Butcher (2006), can perpetuate labeling and stigmatization. Individuals labeled obese during their formative years may carry that label into adulthood, impacting their self-image and influencing how they engage with healthcare, physical activity, and dietary choices (Ciciurkaite & Perry, 2018; Mustillo et al., 2013).

The global perspective on childhood obesity provided by the World Health Organization (2019) underscores the widespread nature of this issue. Labeling Theory suggests that when a condition, such as obesity, is considered a global health concern, the associated labels and stigmas can become even more pervasive, affecting how individuals perceive themselves and their place in society (Ciciurkaite & Perry, 2018; Mustillo et al., 2013).

Labeling Theory offers insights into how societal labels and stigmas related to childhood and adolescent obesity can shape self-concept, influence behaviors, and contribute to the complex dynamics of this public health challenge. Recognizing the role of labeling is essential when developing holistic and community-driven strategies to address childhood and adolescent obesity effectively.

SOCIAL SUPPORT THEORY

The availability of social support, including emotional, informational, and instrumental support from family, friends, or support groups, can significantly impact the behaviors and motivation of obese teenagers in their weight management efforts (Reifegerste et al., 2017; Simpson et al., 2020). Social Support Theory provides a relevant framework to understand the elements related to childhood and adolescent obesity described in the provided information (Reifegerste et al., 2017; Simpson et al., 2020). This theory suggests that the availability of social support, including emotional, informational, and instrumental support, can significantly influence an individual's behavior and well-being (Reifegerste et al., 2017; Simpson et al., 2020). In the context of childhood obesity, social support plays a crucial role in addressing this complex public health challenge.

Social support can come from various sources, including family members, friends, teachers, and healthcare professionals. These individuals can offer emotional support by encouraging, empathizing, and understanding obese children and adolescents as they navigate their weight management journey (Reifegerste et al., 2017; Simpson et al., 2020). Social Support Theory acknowledges that practical support must consider the unique needs and challenges individuals from diverse backgrounds face. Tailored interventions and support networks that understand and respect cultural differences can be instrumental in addressing obesity within these communities (Reifegerste et al., 2017; Simpson et al., 2020).

The long-term consequences of childhood obesity, including the increased risk of obesity in adulthood, as discussed in the information referencing Anderson and Butcher (2006), emphasize the need for sustained social support. This support can involve ongoing guidance on healthy lifestyle choices, access to nutritious food, and opportunities for physical activity. Consistent social support throughout an individual's life course can improve weight management and overall health (Reifegerste et al., 2017; Simpson et al., 2020).

Lastly, the global perspective on childhood obesity provided by the World Health Organization (2019) highlights the need for a collective and community-driven response. Social Support Theory emphasizes the role of community and societal support structures in promoting healthy behaviors and addressing health challenges. Communities that provide resources, education, and opportunities for children and adolescents to make healthier choices can play a vital role in combating the global obesity epidemic.

TECHNOLOGY TO THE RESCUE

In light of the alarming prevalence of obesity as a significant public health issue, there is a pressing need to incorporate innovative technologies into healthcare and the promotion of healthy living. Electronic health (eHealth), which involves utilizing information and communication technologies in healthcare, has played a pivotal role in digitizing medical records and facilitating efficient information exchange among healthcare professionals and between them and patients. This transformation has been cost-effective and instrumental in advancing healthcare (Ghelani et al., 2020; Houser et al., 2019; Marmett et al., 2018; McMullan et al., 2020).

Within eHealth, Mobile Health (mHealth) stands out as a subset that leverages mobile wireless technologies for health-related purposes. mHealth applications exhibit varying degrees of specialization, some tailored to assist patients coping with complex medical conditions, while others target healthy individuals seeking to maintain a well-balanced lifestyle. The proliferation of mHealth products on the market has raised awareness among patients and consumers about healthy lifestyle choices. This empowerment enables individuals to continuously monitor and reflect on their health behaviors (Ghelani et al., 2020; Houser et al., 2019; Marmett et al., 2018; McMullan et al., 2020).

In the past decade, the rapid advancement of portable digital technologies has ushered in a new era of preventive strategies and interactive support systems that offer personalized access to relevant information. These technologies have become widely accessible and are instrumental in promoting health awareness, as they enable the monitoring of health parameters and the collection of data for specialized analysis, thereby aiding in the formulation of tailored treatment strategies (Ghelani et al., 2020; Houser et al., 2019; Marmett et al., 2018; McMullan et al., 2020).

These innovative interventions are smart digital health solutions designed to address diverse health concerns. These interventions encompass weight management programs accessible through websites, social media platforms, and mobile applications. They also include wearable devices seamlessly integrating into individuals' lives, offering convenience and real-time health monitoring (Ghelani et al., 2020; Houser et al., 2019; Marmett et al., 2018; McMullan et al., 2020). Significantly, these technology-driven strategies can be adapted to various settings, making them cost-effective and time-saving. Moreover, they excel in keeping children motivated and engaged while affording them the comfort of their own homes.

The realm of technology-based interventions for childhood obesity is characterized by several distinct categories, including (1) active video games, often referred to as exergaming; (2) web-based, social media-driven activities and mobile application-based programs; and (3) machine learning (ML)-based strategies. These innovations promise to revolutionize childhood obesity management, offering practical and engaging solutions (Ghelani et al., 2020; Houser et al., 2019; Marmett et al., 2018; McMullan et al., 2020).

RECOMMENDATIONS

The global obesity epidemic is a significant public health challenge, demanding multifaceted interventions to prevent and manage this complex condition effectively. The rising prevalence of obesity and related health concerns underscores the need for innovative approaches to support weight loss, healthy eating, and diet management. Internet of Things (IoT) and connected device technologies have emerged as powerful tools in healthcare, offering real-time monitoring, personalized interventions, and enhanced patient engagement.

IoT and connected devices offer a novel approach by leveraging technology to provide continuous monitoring, data collection, and real-time interventions, enhancing weight loss, healthy eating, and dieting outcomes.

IOT AND CONNECTED DEVICES TECHNOLOGIES

IoT encompasses a network of interconnected physical objects equipped with sensors, enabling data collection, analysis, and communication. Connected devices, including wearable fitness trackers, smart scales, and smart kitchen appliances, are integral components of this ecosystem. These technologies facilitate seamless data exchange between devices, users, healthcare providers, and caregivers, creating a dynamic and interactive healthcare environment.

REAL-TIME MONITORING FOR WEIGHT MANAGEMENT

Connected devices, such as wearable fitness trackers and smart scales, offer real-time monitoring of physical activity, calorie expenditure, and weight fluctuations. This data enables users to track progress, set achievable goals, and adjust their weight loss strategies accordingly. Real-time feedback and alerts can motivate individuals to stay active and adhere to dietary plans.

PERSONALIZED DIETARY INTERVENTIONS

IoT-enabled kitchen appliances and dietary apps can provide personalized dietary recommendations based on users' preferences, dietary restrictions, and health goals. These devices can track food consumption, offer nutritional guidance, and suggest healthier alternatives, fostering mindful eating habits. The ability to customize dietary plans enhances adherence and long-term success.

REMOTE PATIENT MONITORING AND HEALTHCARE INTEGRATION

IoT and connected devices enable remote patient monitoring, allowing healthcare providers to track patients' progress, provide timely interventions, and adjust treatment plans. These technologies enhance the continuity of care and facilitate seamless communication between patients, caregivers, and healthcare professionals.

ENHANCED PATIENT ENGAGEMENT AND MOTIVATION

Gamification, social sharing features, and rewards systems integrated into IoT applications can boost patient engagement and motivation. Interactive challenges, peer support, and virtual communities create a supportive environment for individuals on their weight loss and dietary journeys.

TEXTING APPS FOR OBESITY MANAGEMENT

Texting apps, often integrated with artificial intelligence (AI) and behavioral psychology principles, provide a convenient and personalized means of supporting teens and children in weight management. These apps offer several key advantages:

- Personalized Guidance-Texting apps can deliver tailored advice, reminders, and encouragement based on an individual's health goals, preferences, and progress.
- Accessibility- They are accessible through smartphones, making them readily available to a broad audience, including underserved populations.
- Behavior Tracking- Users can log dietary habits, physical activity, and weight, enabling self-monitoring and fostering awareness.
- Timely Interventions- Apps can send timely messages to prevent unhealthy behaviors like sedentary periods or overeating.
- Peer Support- Some apps incorporate social features, allowing users to connect with peers, share experiences, and provide mutual support.

REMOTE MONITORING TECHNOLOGIES

Remote monitoring technologies encompass a range of devices and sensors that track health metrics, providing real-time data to users and healthcare professionals. These technologies offer unique advantages for managing teen and childhood obesity:

- Wearable Devices- Wearable fitness trackers and smartwatches can monitor physical activity, heart rate, and sleep patterns, encouraging increased activity levels and improved sleep hygiene.
- Smart Scales- Wi-Fi-enabled scales can measure weight and body composition, providing users with data to track their progress.
- Mobile Health Apps- Health apps integrated with remote monitoring devices can aggregate and visualize data, helping users and healthcare providers make informed decisions.
- Telehealth -Telehealth platforms facilitate remote consultations with healthcare professionals, allowing personalized guidance and monitoring.

RECOMMENDATIONS FOR FUTURE RESEARCH

Researching the impact, effectiveness, and usefulness of mobile health, wearable health technologies, and remote monitoring technologies presents a compelling avenue for advancing our understanding of their potential in addressing childhood and adolescent obesity.

ACTION RESEARCH

Employing action research methodologies can facilitate collaboration among researchers, healthcare practitioners, and communities to implement and assess the practical implications of mobile health, wearable health technologies, and remote monitoring solutions. Action research offers a dynamic approach to studying the impact of these technologies within real-world contexts, enabling iterative improvements based on user feedback and outcomes.

COMMUNITY-BASED PUBLIC HEALTH RESEARCH

Engaging in community-based research initiatives allows for a holistic examination of the societal and environmental factors that influence the adoption and effectiveness of mobile health technologies. Collaborating with local communities can inform the design and implementation of culturally tailored interventions that resonate with diverse populations.

INTERPRETATIVE PHENOMENOLOGICAL ANALYSIS (IPA)

Employing IPA can illuminate the lived experiences of individuals using these technologies for weight management and healthy eating. IPA provides a framework for understanding users' meaning-making processes and subjective perspectives, shedding light on the psychosocial aspects of technology adoption.

Future research should also focus on specific outcomes and applications, such as the long-term sustainability of interventions, the impact on physical and mental health, and integrating these technologies into existing healthcare systems. Additionally, evaluating the cost-effectiveness and scalability of these interventions in diverse healthcare settings is essential to inform policy decisions and ensure equitable access to effective obesity management strategies. By embracing diverse research methodologies and focusing on comprehensive evaluation, we can advance the evidence base surrounding mobile health, wearable health technologies, and remote monitoring solutions, ultimately contributing to more effective and tailored approaches to combat childhood and adolescent obesity.

REFERENCES

Anderson, P. M., & Butcher, K. F. (2006). Childhood obesity: Trends and potential causes. *The Future of Children*, *16*(1), 19–45. doi:10.1353/foc.2006.0001 PMID:16532657

Aris, I. M., & Block, J. P. (2022). Childhood obesity interventions—Going beyond the individual. *JAMA Pediatrics*, *176*(1), e214388–e214388. doi:10.1001/jamapediatrics.2021.4388 PMID:34747988

Behavioral Economics in Child Nutrition Programs (BEN). (2018). *Smarter Lunchroom Movement. The Cornell Center for Behavioral Economics in Child Nutrition Programs*. Cornell University. Retrieved from: http://www.ben.cornell.edu/index.html

Branscum, P., Kaye, G., & Warner, J. (2013). Impacting Dietary Behaviors of Children from Low-Income Communities: An Evaluation of a Theory-Based Nutrition Education Program. *California Journal of Health Promotion, 11*(2), 43–52. Retrieved from: https://www.cjhp.org/Volume11Issue2_2013/documents/43-52_BranscumP.pdf

Burrell, D. N., Wright, J. B., Taylor, C., Shockley, T., Reaves, A., & Mairs, J. (2021). Addressing the Public Health Epidemic of Childhood Obesity Using Public Schools as Health Education Learning Laboratories. In I. Management Association (Ed.), Research Anthology on Public Health Services, Policies, and Education (pp. 230–243). IGI Global. doi:10.4018/978-1-7998-8960-1.ch011

Carlson, S., Rosenbaum, D., Keith-Jennings, B., & Nchako, C. (2016). *SNAP Works for America's Children. Center on Budget and Policy Priorities.* Retrieved from: https://www.cbpp.org/research/food-assistance/snap-works-for-americas-children

Carter, R. (2002). The impact of Public Schools on Childhood Obesity. Published: November 6, 2002. *Journal of the American Medical Association, 288*(17), 2180. doi:10.1001/jama.288.17.2180-JMS1106-6-1 PMID:12413386

Center for Disease Control and Prevention. (2019). *Childhood obesity.* Retrieved from https://www.cdc.gov/obesity/data/childhood.html

Centers for Disease Control. (2018). *Obesity. CDC Healthy Schools.* Centers for Disease Control and Prevention. Retrieved from: https://www.cdc.gov/healthyschools/obesity/index.htm

Ciciurkaite, G., & Perry, B. L. (2018). Body weight, perceived weight stigma and mental health among women at the intersection of race/ethnicity and socioeconomic status: Insights from the modified labeling approach. *Sociology of Health & Illness, 40*(1), 18–37. doi:10.1111/1467-9566.12619 PMID:28980335

Cornell. (2019). *Agriculture and Food Systems.* Cornell Cooperative Extension. Retrieved from: http://cce.cornell.edu/program/agriculture

Easterling, T., Kerley, K., & Wright, J. (2018). *Overweight and obesity in children and adolescents in schools – The role of school nurse.* Retrieved from: https://www.nasn.org/advocacy/professional-practice-documents/position-statements/ps-overweight

Fakhouri, T., Hughes, J., Burt, V., Song, M., Fulton, J., & Ogden, C. (2014). *Physical Activity in U.S. Youth Aged 12-15 Years, 2012.* NCHS Data Brief. Retrieved from: https://permanent.access.gpo.gov/gpo77970/db141.pdf

Gatto, N., Martinez, L., Spruijt-Metz, D., & Davis, J. (2015). LA Sprouts randomized controlled nutrition, cooking and gardening programme reduces obesity and metabolic risk in Hispanic/Latino youth. *Pediatric Obesity.* Retrieved from: https://onlinelibrary-wiley-com.portal.lib.fit.edu/doi/epdf/10.1111/ijpo.12102

Ghelani, D. P., Moran, L. J., Johnson, C., Mousa, A., & Naderpoor, N. (2020). Mobile Apps for Weight Management: A Review of the Latest Evidence to Inform Practice. *Frontiers in Endocrinology, 11,* 412. doi:10.3389/fendo.2020.00412 PMID:32670197

Greene, K., Gabrielyan, G., Just, D., & Wansink, B. (2017). Fruit-Promoting Smarter Lunchrooms Interventions: Results From a Cluster RCT. *American Journal of Preventive Medicine, 52*(4), 451–458. Retrieved from: https://www-sciencedirect-com.portal.lib.fit.edu/science/article/pii/S0749379716306961

Hall, E., Chai, W., & Albrecht, J. (2016). *Relationships between nutrition-related knowledge, self-efficacy, and behavior for fifth-grade students attending Title I and non-Title I schools. Science Direct* (Vol. 96). Retrieved from https://www-sciencedirect-com.portal.lib.fit.edu/science/article/pii/S0195666315300441

Houser, S. H., Joseph, R., Puro, N., & Burke, D. E. (2019). Use of technology in the management of obesity: A literature review. *Perspectives in Health Information Management, 16*(Fall). PMID:31908626

Katzmarzyk, P. T., Denstel, K. D., Beals, K., Bolling, C., Wright, C., Crouter, S. E., McKenzie, T. L., Pate, R. R., Saelens, B. E., Staiano, A. E., Stanish, H. I., & Sisson, S. B. (2016). Results From the United States of America's 2016 Report Card on Physical Activity for Children and Youth. *Journal of Physical Activity & Health, 13*(11, Suppl 2), S307–S313. doi:10.1123/jpah.2016-0321 PMID:27848726

Knol, L., Myers, H., Black, S., Robinson, D., Awololo, Y., Clark, D., & Higginbotham, J. C. (2016). Development and Feasibility of a Childhood Obesity Prevention Program for Rural Families: Application of the Social Cognitive Theory. *American Journal of Health Education, 47*(4), 204–214. doi:10.1 080/19325037.2016.1179607 PMID:28392882

Lake, A. A. (2011). Obesity. *Perspectives in Public Health, 131*(4), 154. doi:10.1177/1757913911413188 PMID:21888112

Lee, I. M., Shiroma, E. J., Lobelo, F., Puska, P., Blair, S. N., Katzmarzyk, P. T., & the Lancet Physical Activity Series Working Group. (2012). Effect of physical inactivity on major non-communicable diseases worldwide: an analysis of burden of disease and life expectancy. *Lancet (London, England), 380*(9838), 219–229. Retrieved from: https://www.ncbi.nlm.nih.gov/pmc/articles/PMC3645500/ doi:10.1016/S0140-6736(12)61031-9

Liken, M. (2018). *How Teachers and Schools Can Address Childhood Obesity.* Concordia University – Portland. Published on November 16, 2018. Retrieved from: https://education.cu-portland.edu/blog/classroom-resources/teachers-schools-childhood-obesity/

McKenzie, J. F., Pinger, R. R., & Seabert, D. (2018). An introduction to community and public health. Jones & Bartlett Learning.

McMullan, M., Millar, R., & Woodside, J. V. (2020). A systematic review to assess the effectiveness of technology-based interventions to address obesity in children. *BMC Pediatrics, 20*(1), 1–14. doi:10.1186/s12887-020-02081-1 PMID:32438908

Mustillo, S. A., Budd, K., & Hendrix, K. (2013). Obesity, labeling, and psychological distress in late-childhood and adolescent black and white girls: The distal effects of stigma. *Social Psychology Quarterly, 76*(3), 268–289. doi:10.1177/0190272513495883

Prothero, A (2022, February 1). Child Obesity Grew During the Pandemic. How Schools Can Help Reverse the Trend. *Education Week.*

Reifegerste, D., Wasgien, K., & Hagen, L. M. (2017). Online social support for obese adults: Exploring the role of forum activity. *International Journal of Medical Informatics, 101*, 1–8. doi:10.1016/j.ijmedinf.2017.02.003 PMID:28347439

Ryan, P. (2009). Integrated theory of health behavior change: Background and intervention development. *Clinical Nurse Specialist CNS, 23*(3), 161–172. doi:10.1097/NUR.0b013e3181a42373 PMID:19395894

Sahoo, K., Sahoo, B., Choudhury, A. K., Sofi, N. Y., Kumar, R., & Bhadoria, A. S. (2015). Childhood obesity: causes and consequences. *Journal of Family Medicine and Primary Care, 4*(2), 187–192. Retrieved from: https://www.ncbi.nlm.nih.gov/pmc/articles/PMC4408699/ doi:10.4103/2249-4863.154628

Simpson, S. A., Matthews, L., Pugmire, J., McConnachie, A., McIntosh, E., Coulman, E., Hughes, K., Kelson, M., Morgan-Trimmer, S., Murphy, S., Utkina-Macaskill, O., & Moore, L. A. R. (2020). An app-, web-and social support-based weight loss intervention for adults with obesity: The 'HelpMeDoIt!' feasibility randomised controlled trial. *Pilot and Feasibility Studies, 6*(1), 1–14. doi:10.1186/s40814-020-00656-4 PMID:32968544

Story, M., Nanney, M. S., & Schwartz, M. B. (2009). Schools and obesity prevention: Creating school environments and policies to promote healthy eating and physical activity. *The Milbank Quarterly, 87*(1), 71–100. doi:10.1111/j.1468-0009.2009.00548.x PMID:19298416

Stroup, D. F., Johnson, V. R., Hahn, R. A., & Proctor, D. C. (2009). Reversing the trend of childhood obesity. *Preventing Chronic Disease, 6*(3). PMID:19527599

Tsukayama, H. (2015). Teens spend nearly nine hours every day consuming media. *The Washington Post.* Retrieved from: https://www.washingtonpost.com/news/the-switch/wp/2015/11/03/teens-spend-nearly-nine-hours-every-day-consuming-media/

Woods, T., & Nies, M. (2018). Conceptual Application of the Adapted Health Belief Model to Parental Understanding of Child Weight. *Journal of Health Science & Education, 2*(4), 1–6. Retrieved from: https://www.researchgate.net/publication/327230594_Conceptual_Application_of_the_Adapted_Health_Belief_Model_to_Parental_Understanding_of_Child_Weight

World Health Organization. (2010). *Global Recommendations on Physical Activity for Health.* Retrieved from: https://www.who.int/dietphysicalactivity/global-PA-recs-2010.pdf

World Health Organization. (2019). *Childhood overweight and obesity.* World Health Organization. Retrieved from: https://www.who.int/dietphysicalactivity/childhood/en/

Chapter 6
Barricades and Hindrances Concerning Women Managers in Healthcare Cybersecurity and Technology

Darrell Norman Burrell
iD https://orcid.org/0000-0002-4675-9544
Marymount University, USA

Danielle Gervacio Graf
iD https://orcid.org/0009-0003-4570-1193
Marymount University, USA

Michelle D. Espinoza
iD https://orcid.org/0009-0009-5213-6974
Marymount University, USA

Maria Mondala-Duncan
Marymount University, USA

Arden E. Servidio
iD https://orcid.org/0009-0003-1780-0610
Marymount University, USA

Tiffany Weitoish
iD https://orcid.org/0009-0005-4386-0451
Capitol Technology University, USA

Marlena Daryousef
iD https://orcid.org/0000-0001-9513-501X
Colorado Technical University, USA

ABSTRACT

Amidst the prevailing scarcity of personnel and leaders within healthcare cybersecurity and technology management, the demand for bolstering the ranks of professionals in these domains has reached unprecedented significance and urgency. Enlisting women leaders and those from diverse backgrounds is imperative to address the deficiencies in workforce development and devise pioneering business strategies. The endeavor to effectively confront the most formidable issues about organizational technology management strategies necessitates women's active participation and contributions. This chapter embarks on a comprehensive exploration of the hurdles, intricacies, and innovative methodologies pertinent to the advancement of women into executive and supervisory positions within the domains of information technology and healthcare cybersecurity.

DOI: 10.4018/979-8-3693-1970-3.ch006

OVERVIEW

The global health crisis has compelled healthcare institutions to reevaluate their digital approaches and craft innovations that enable remote healthcare provision (Balasubramanian, 2023). The landscape of healthcare has witnessed a transformative shift, with digital health companies introducing an array of convenient and easily accessible solutions, including telehealth services, at-home testing options, and prescription delivery services (Balasubramanian, 2023). These advancements have not only expanded patients' access to top-notch healthcare but have also empowered individuals to take greater control of their well-being.

During the pandemic, healthcare organizations have been prompted to embrace novel digital strategies that cater to the evolving needs of patients and the healthcare landscape (Balasubramanian, 2023). The emergence of telehealth, at-home testing, and prescription delivery services has ushered in a new era of healthcare accessibility and convenience, transcending geographical barriers (Balasubramanian, 2023). These innovations have allowed patients to receive high-quality care from the comfort of their homes, marking a significant transformation in the way healthcare is delivered and managed.

In 2024, digital health technologies are expected to face heightened scrutiny regarding their effectiveness in delivering value and measuring success. Despite this scrutiny, the digital health sector continues to gather momentum, propelling the adoption of innovative solutions. Many of these technologies are anticipated to concentrate on broadening access to healthcare through integrated experiences and generating data that can enhance both individual patient outcomes and overall population health (Balasubramanian, 2023). These advancements hold the potential to foster the development of comprehensive digital health ecosystems, facilitating critical connections among diverse stakeholders and the meaningful utilization of health data (Balasubramanian, 2023).

As digital health continues to flourish, healthcare innovation, telehealth solutions, and remote monitoring capabilities have become integral parts of the healthcare landscape, characterized by technology and internet-driven care delivery (Balasubramanian, 2023). However, this transition to cloud-based and internet-centric applications has also significantly elevated the risk of cyberattacks and security breaches, rendering the entire healthcare system highly susceptible to these threats (Balasubramanian, 2023). The interplay between digital health's potential for transformation and the need for robust cybersecurity measures presents a complex challenge that healthcare organizations must address to ensure the integrity and security of patient data and healthcare delivery systems.

In recent years, a notable incident garnered public attention in which cybersecurity experts demonstrated their ability to introduce malware into a wireless pacemaker. While this demonstration was conducted for educational purposes, it underscored a disconcerting concept: through a relatively straightforward effort, hackers could remotely control a pacemaker (Balasubramanian, 2023). This revelation presents a deeply unsettling prospect, particularly for the millions of individuals worldwide who rely on such life-saving devices for their well-being (Balasubramanian, 2023). For many decades, cybersecurity concerns were primarily associated with the potential loss of data or breaches of privacy. However, as life-saving medical devices increasingly connect to the internet, security breaches now carry tangible and potentially life-threatening risks to patients' well-being and health outcomes (Balasubramanian, 2023).

As the global landscape witnesses a relentless surge in cyber threats, governmental agencies and businesses find themselves engaged in an ongoing struggle to secure the requisite talent needed to combat threat actors' ever-evolving tactics, techniques, and procedures (Osborne, 2023). Bereft of adequate in-house expertise, organizations often find themselves at a disadvantage in this high-stakes battle. This predicament is further exacerbated by the grim forecast that cybercrime is poised to wreak havoc on a global scale, with anticipated damages estimated to soar to an astounding 8 trillion USD in 2023 (Osborne, 2023). The assertion by Magid (2014) underscores that cybersecurity transcends individual roles; instead, it is an all-encompassing responsibility that permeates an entire organization. The criticality of augmenting the workforce in this context cannot be overstated, as it directly impacts the successful execution of business strategies, seamless business operations, and safeguarding sensitive business information and customer data (Magid, 2014).

Notably, statistics reveal a stark reality that 3.5 million cybersecurity positions remain vacant on a global scale in the year 2023, with this alarming shortage projected to persist until 2025 (Osborne, 2023). The gravity of the situation is compounded by the intense pressure of existing skilled teams, which significantly elevates the risk of burnout (Osborne, 2023). This pervasive strain has, regrettably, prompted some security leaders to opt for brief tenures or even exit the industry altogether in search of respite (Osborne, 2023). The imperative to address these workforce deficits has never been more pressing as the relentless onslaught of cyber threats redefines the contemporary healthcare cybersecurity landscape.

The solution lies readily before us. Embracing inclusivity and enticing a larger contingent of women to join the cybersecurity arena can unlock a vast reservoir of untapped potential (Burrell, 2019; Burrell, 2020). The need of the hour is to dismantle the barriers that have long obstructed entry into this field (Burrell, 2020). We must embark on a comprehensive industry-wide campaign that transcends all echelons beyond technical roles. Moreover, we must instigate a cultural shift in cybersecurity discourse that resonates with female and inclusive talent, encouraging them to envision cybersecurity as their chosen career path (Burrell, 2020).

PROBLEM STATEMENT

In 2023, a substantial global workforce gap looms with an estimated 3.5 million unfilled positions, and this deficiency is anticipated to persist until 2025 (Osborne, 2023). Job vacancies have soared 350% since 2013 (Osborne, 2023). This growth rate is exceptional, particularly when juxtaposed with the typical expansion rate of a mere five percent observed across all occupations. More notably, from 2021 to 2031, the profession of information security analysts is projected to sustain an impressive growth rate of approximately 35 percent (Osborne, 2023).

To effectively counteract these glaring workforce deficiencies, organizations must proactively tap into hitherto underrepresented talent pools, encompassing minority groups, particularly women. Notably, the representation of women in cybersecurity roles displayed a positive trajectory, with women holding 25 percent of such positions globally in 2022, compared to 20 percent in 2019 and a mere 10 percent in 2013 (Osborne, 2023). The trajectory is expected to continue upward, with women projected to constitute 30 percent of the global cybersecurity workforce by 2025, further surging to 35 percent by 2031 (Osborne, 2023). As the demand for information security analysts (ISAs) is slated to surge by 18% through 2024, the imperative for a more diversified and expert workforce in information technology becomes evident (Morgan, 2016). However, a conspicuous deficiency in diversity and female representation persists within the cybersecurity domain, with the gender gap most starkly reflected in the hierarchy of leadership roles (Burrell, 2020). Notably, a study by Cybersecurity Ventures illuminated the extent of this gender disparity, indicating that women occupied a mere 17 percent of chief information security officer (CISO) positions within Fortune 500 companies, constituting a mere 85 of the available 500 CISO roles

(Osborne, 2023). This article delves into the crucial significance of increasing the influx of women into the healthcare cybersecurity field and facilitating their ascent to supervisory roles, thereby exploring innovative avenues to address this pressing issue.

SIGNIFICANCE OF THE INQUIRY

The unprecedented demand for professionals in the fields of healthcare cybersecurity and technology management underscores the significance and novelty of this inquiry. Recently, these sectors have grappled with a severe shortage of employees and managers. This critical workforce deficit highlights the urgent and essential need for increased representation from all genders and backgrounds within these industries. As organizations strive to address these workforce development shortfalls and navigate the complexities of the rapidly evolving technology landscape, it becomes increasingly clear that leadership diversity is not merely a matter of equality but a strategic imperative.

One of the key factors that elevate the significance of this study is its emphasis on the pivotal role that women can play in addressing the most pressing concerns related to organizational technology management strategy. Historically, women have been underrepresented in executive and supervisory roles within the information technology and cybersecurity sectors. This study aims to dismantle the barriers and complexities perpetuating this gender disparity and explores innovative approaches to increasing the number of women in leadership positions and empowering them to drive transformative change within these fields. By shedding light on these issues and advocating for gender-inclusive leadership, this study offers a fresh perspective that is both timely and essential in the contemporary technology-driven landscape, making it a pioneering contribution to the discourse on diversity and leadership within the industry.

NATURE AND APPROACH OF THE INQUIRY

The nature of this study is rooted in a perspective approach driven by the current and emerging literature in cybersecurity and technology management. Perspective articles like this provide a valuable platform for authors to offer insightful and forward-looking assessments of the latest developments and recommendations for policy within a specific domain of study. In line with this tradition, this study employs a perspective-driven methodology that strongly emphasizes the author's unique viewpoint and personal assessment of the subject matter.

This approach allows the author to critically and critically analyze the most recent advancements, trends, policies, challenges, and opportunities within healthcare cybersecurity and technology management. Drawing from the current literature and scholarly discourse, this study aims to provide readers with an in-depth understanding of the evolving landscape in these disciplines. Moreover, it seeks to offer a visionary perspective on future directions, innovative policy approaches, and potential breakthroughs in these domains.

Perspective articles, such as this one, are instrumental in fostering discussion and debate among scholars, researchers, and practitioners. They play a pivotal role in guiding professionals in the field and shaping the trajectory of the discipline based on the recommendations of real-world solutions to real-world problems. In this context, the nature of this study aligns with the tradition of perspective articles, offering a thoughtful and comprehensive exploration of the challenges and opportunities in healthcare cybersecurity and technology management while providing valuable insights that others can use as foundations for the exploration in future empirical studies.

The persistent challenges surrounding the representation of women in senior managerial positions within technology-based organizations and businesses have a long-standing history (Vafaei, Ahmed, & Mather, 2015; Ely, Stone, & Ammerman, 2014; Rincón, González, & Barrero, 2017). Research conducted in the United States by Cardador (2017) has shed light on women's manifold challenges when transitioning from employee roles to managerial positions within the technical sphere. As more women ascend to supervisory roles, they frequently grapple with increasing isolation from their female peers. Furthermore, they confront pervasive stereotypes and gender biases rooted in assumptions that certain job positions and roles are more aptly suited for men rather than women.

Meiksins et al. (2017) have articulated the profound impact of public revelations concerning sexual harassment and sexual abuse and the rise of movements like #MeToo, which have unveiled instances of sexual misconduct that often foster hostile, unhealthy, and uncivil work environments for women engaged in technical careers or within technical organizations. Given that men overwhelmingly occupy supervisory and leadership positions in these technical domains, the organizational culture tends to be predominantly shaped by male perspectives, leaving women in a marginalized position with limited influence to voice their concerns and advocate for gender equity (Meiksins et al., 2017).

IN-GROUP AND OUT-GROUP BIAS

In the context of women in male-dominated industries like healthcare cybersecurity and information technology, the theory of in-group and out-group bias plays a crucial role in understanding their dynamics and challenges. In-group bias refers to the tendency of individuals to favor and show a preference for members of their own social group, while out-group bias involves a negative bias or discrimination against individuals from different social groups (McNamara et al., 2016; Molenberghs, 2013).

In male-dominated industries, men often form the dominant in-group. They share everyday experiences, perspectives, and, at times, biases that can inadvertently create an environment where women are viewed as outsiders. This in-group bias can manifest in various ways, including preferential treatment, access to opportunities, and shared camaraderie among in-group colleagues (McNamara et al., 2016; Molenberghs, 2013). Women, who may be perceived as outside the in-group, can face challenges in gaining acceptance and recognition.

Out-group bias, on the other hand, can lead to the stereotyping of women in these industries. Women may be subjected to negative stereotypes that portray them as less competent or less suited for roles traditionally held by men by being members of the out-group. Such biases can hinder women's career progression and opportunities for leadership positions. Out-group bias can also lead to excluding those in the out-group from informal networks and decision-making processes within these organizations (McNamara et al., 2016; Molenberghs, 2013).

In-group and out-group biases can significantly impact women's career advancement. The preference for individuals within the dominant group can result in women being overlooked for promotions, leadership roles, or challenging assignments. It may also create a hostile work environment where women feel excluded or marginalized, further hindering their professional development.

Another element of out-group bias is the imposition of double standards (McNamara et al., 2016; Molenberghs, 2013). Women may be held to different or higher standards than their male counterparts, making succeeding or gaining recognition for their accomplishments more challenging. This double standard can create a sense of unfairness and frustration among women in these industries. Recognizing and addressing in-group and out-group biases is essential for creating more inclusive workplaces (McNamara et al., 2016; Molenberghs, 2013). Organizations can implement diversity and inclusion initiatives, mentorship programs, and unconscious bias training to mitigate biases and provide equal opportunities for women. Also, fostering a diversity and inclusion culture can help break down these barriers and enable women to thrive in male-dominated fields.

The in-group and out-group bias theory highlights women's challenges in male-dominated industries like healthcare cybersecurity and information technology. Understanding these biases and their impact is crucial for organizations and individuals to work toward greater gender equality and inclusivity in these fields.

HYPERVISIBILITY

Visibility at work, being seen fully and accurately by others, is essential for individual self-determination, authenticity, and organizational outcomes such as commitment and a sense of belonging (Newton, 2023). Although there has been increasing attention in the organizational literature on marginalized groups' workplace experiences of harassment, discrimination, and identity-based microaggressions, little attention has been given to issues of invisibility and hypervisibility (Newton, 2023).

In male-dominated industries, women often find themselves navigating a complex landscape where they may be considered outcasts due to the phenomenon of hypervisibility. In this context, hypervisibility refers to being extremely visible, which can be a double-edged sword (Newton, 2023). While hypervisibility can be a positive attribute for dominant group members, positioning them as valued and active contributors, it can have a markedly different impact on women, particularly those marginalized in such environments (Newton, 2023).

For women in male-dominated fields, hypervisibility can take on a negative connotation. It often arises from women's unique challenges, including stereotypes and biases that persist in these industries (Burrell et al., 2020). These negative stereotypes and preconceived notions can result in women being perceived as different or even deviant from the norm, further intensifying their hypervisibility. In essence, they become conspicuous not for their achievements or contributions but for their perceived divergence from the dominant group, typically composed of men.

Consequently, women in these industries may be constantly scrutinized, and their actions and behaviors may be subjected to heightened observation (Burrell et al., 2020). This increased visibility can manifest as a form of isolation, as women struggle to fit into a male-dominated culture that may not fully recognize their talents, experiences, or perspectives. Being seen as different or deviant can exacerbate feelings of exclusion and make it challenging for women to fully integrate into these professional spaces (Burrell et al., 2020).

According to Newton (2023), hypervisibility is the state of being extremely visible, which can be a positive for dominant group members (i.e., visible as a valued and active contributor). For groups that are marginalized, negative stereotypes, along with being considered as different, result in them being perceived as deviant (Newton, 2023). This hypervisibility, combined with being perceived as deviant, leads to increased scrutiny for members of marginalized social groups (Newton, 2023). Under the conditions of hypervisibility, mistakes are used to confirm negative stereotypes and evidence that could counter negative perceptions is minimized or held suspect (e.g., when the person does superior work, dominant group members assume they must have had help) (Buchanan & Settles, 2019). Equally, when individuals are hypervisible, their identities are invisible as they are seen only in terms of their marginalized group membership (e.g., being the token person of color to represent diversity in a workgroup) (Buchanan & Settles, 2019).

Hypervisibility can create a challenging dynamic for women in male-dominated industries, where they are often perceived as outcasts due to negative stereotypes and biases. While hypervisibility may be favorable for dominant group members, for marginalized females, it can contribute to feelings of isolation and a sense of being perpetually scrutinized for their perceived differences (Anderson, 2023). Recognizing and addressing these challenges is crucial for fostering inclusivity and diversity in such environments.

INVISIBILITY

Invisibility is the state or condition where a person feels unvalued or fully recognized (Anderson, 2023). It could be a woman who feels her voice is valued among a group of female peers at work but then feels like she is being dismissed when she is in a meeting with a group of men at the workplace (Anderson, 2023). The dominant group members with the power are the ones who create policies and practices, and there is little to no representation of those in marginalized groups at that level (Anderson, 2023). As a result, invisibility places those in marginalized groups at a disadvantage because they are rendered invisible and are denied recognition, power, and a voice (Anderson, 2023).

In a 2019 qualitative study by Settles, Buchanan, and Dotson, the researchers looked at the concept (of)visibility for women of color. Six themes emerged from the data: tokenism, social and professional exclusion, epistemic exclusion, strategic invisibility, working harder, and disengagement (Settles et al., 2019). The women in the study expressed feelings of (in)visibility in various ways, including being offered fewer opportunities for advancement, leadership roles, and acknowledgment of accomplishments (Settles et al., 2019).

Several themes emerged from the invisibility literature. One theme that emerged is the vital role that the intersection of race and gender plays in the negative experiences of women of color (i.e., discrimination, marginalization, and being overlooked) in the workplace (Anderson, 2023). Another theme that emerged is that women are utilizing various coping strategies to counter negative experiences at work (Anderson, 2023). Additionally, perceived discrimination is another theme that emerged from the literature. Perceived discrimination seems to influence how women of color experience invisibility and exclusion in the workplace setting. As stated previously in all of the cited studies, women, especially women of color, experienced negative stressors in the workplace as a result of their multiple stigmatized identities (Anderson, 2023). Women's expertise, knowledge, education, experience, and professional capabilities are often questioned, overlooked, and sometimes excluded (Anderson, 2023).

GENDER ALLEGORIES

One of the most widely recognized metaphors that depict the challenges faced by women in career advancement within organizational cultures that are not conducive to gender diversity is the concept of the "glass ceiling" (Sabharwal, 2013). This metaphor symbolizes the invisible barriers that hinder women's progress in such environments. Alongside the glass ceiling, several other allegories have been employed to depict the various obstacles women encounter in their pursuit of career advancement, including the "glass cliff," "maternal wall," "glass escalator," "sticky floor," and the "labyrinth" (Carli & Eagly, 2016; Sabharwal, 2013). These allegories are descriptive tools to articulate the circumstances impeding women's leadership opportunities.

Among these allegories, the "glass cliff" represents a specific organizational barrier women often face when aspiring to leadership positions (Elliott & Stead, 2017). The concept of the glass cliff alludes to the tendency for women to be appointed to leadership roles that offer limited opportunities for success or have a limited shelf life (Ryan, 2016). Following the analysis of interviews conducted with 62 women who held leadership roles within technical organizations, Yaghi (2017) determined that men often deliberately place women in challenging and precarious positions with a high likelihood of failure. When women find themselves in high-risk leadership roles, their competence is often questioned, further perpetuating stereotypical assumptions (Yaghi, 2017).

The "maternal wall" is a concept that characterizes the unique and unfair challenges that working mothers often encounter in the workplace (Carli & Eagly, 2016). This term highlights the biases and stereotypes that can come into play when a woman becomes pregnant, visibly appears pregnant, or requests parental leave (Carli & Eagly, 2016). Instead of being celebrated for bringing new life into the world, working mothers may face subtle or overt discrimination that can hinder their career advancement (Williams, 2005).

Research has shown that when women become mothers, they are often perceived as less competent for the workforce compared to their male counterparts who become fathers (Carli & Eagly, 2016). This bias can manifest in various ways, such as being overlooked for promotions, receiving lower pay raises, or being excluded from important projects. The maternal wall not only affects individual women but also perpetuates gender inequality in the workplace, as it discourages women from pursuing leadership roles and reinforces traditional gender roles (Cuddy et al., 2004).

To address the challenges posed by the maternal wall, organizations need to actively work toward creating inclusive and supportive workplace cultures (Burrell et al., 2020). Addressing this occurrence of inequity includes implementing policies that promote work-life balance, offering flexible work arrangements, and educating employees about unconscious biases (Hultin, 2003). By recognizing and addressing the maternal wall, organizations can create a more equitable work environment where women can thrive in their careers without facing unjust obstacles (Hultin, 2003).

The concept of the "sticky floor" allegory sheds light on the discriminatory practices that women often encounter early in their careers, which can lead to them being confined to low-paying, low-status occupations and hinder their career advancement (Carli & Eagly, 2016). Researchers have examined the patterns that show women are less likely to be considered for career progression than their male counterparts (Baert et al., 2016). The research findings reveal that when women apply for their initial job promotions, they receive, on average, 33% fewer interview invitations and 19% fewer positive callbacks than men (Baert et al., 2016).

The sticky floor allegory underscores the persistent challenges women face in their early career stages, where they often find themselves stuck in positions that offer limited opportunities for advancement. These early disparities in job promotions and callbacks have long-term implications for women's career trajectories and contribute to the gender wage gap and underrepresentation of women in leadership roles. Addressing the sticky floor phenomenon requires proactive efforts from organizations to eliminate biases and create fair and equitable promotion processes that enable talented women to rise through the ranks based on their skills and qualifications.

The "glass escalator" concept is a sociological phenomenon related to gender dynamics in the workplace, particularly as it applies to men in female-dominated fields. It describes the often-unnoticed advantage that men experience when working in professions traditionally associated with women. In such settings, men enjoy quicker career advancement and higher positions than their female counterparts (Shiri et al., 2018).

One key aspect of the glass escalator concept is that men in female-dominated fields tend to be channeled into leadership roles more rapidly than women (Shiri et al., 2018). This phenomenon can be attributed to the societal perception that leadership roles are more suitable for men, even in professions where women predominate (Shiri et al., 2018). As a result, men on the "glass escalator" may ascend the organizational hierarchy at a faster pace, benefiting from promotions and career advancements, while women face a "glass ceiling" that limits their upward mobility (Shiri et al., 2018).

Additionally, the glass escalator concept underscores the importance of recognizing and addressing gender biases in the workplace (Shiri et al., 2018). It highlights the need for organizations to actively work toward creating more equitable environments by promoting diversity and inclusion (Shiri et al., 2018). Understanding and challenging the glass escalator effect is crucial for achieving gender balance in leadership positions across various industries and dismantling the barriers that hinder women's career advancement (Shiri et al., 2018).

As Carli and Eagly (2016) highlighted, the concept of the labyrinth allegory illustrates the challenging journey women frequently undertake to attain managerial positions, navigating through a complex maze of obstacles and barriers often less prevalent for their male peers. The labyrinth concept encapsulates the diverse and intricate pathways women must navigate to pursue organizational leadership roles (Bruckmüller et al., 2013). Effectively addressing issues related to organizational culture necessitates a concerted organizational effort to engage employees in activities that foster cultural transformation and emphasize the significance of diversity and inclusion (Burrell, 2015).

The labyrinth allegory underscores women's multifaceted challenges on their path to leadership roles, highlighting the need for organizations to address gender disparities and create inclusive environments proactively. This journey often requires women to demonstrate exceptional resilience, determination, and skill to overcome the various barriers they face. To promote diversity and inclusion, organizations should implement initiatives to dismantle systemic obstacles and promote equal opportunities for all employees, irrespective of gender. Recognizing the labyrinthine nature of the journey toward leadership is the first step in fostering a more equitable and inclusive organizational culture.

MENTORSHIP AND ROLE MODELS

Scholars have underscored the significant impact that mentoring and role models can have on women's career trajectories in leadership positions (Ely et al., 2014; Gipson et al., 2017). Mentoring is an enduring and intensive developmental relationship, typically of extended duration, in which protégés receive a comprehensive spectrum of career guidance and psychosocial support, often exclusively from senior managers (Whitely et al., 1991). On the other hand, role models are individuals whose behaviors within a specific role are emulated by others (Hill & Wheat, 2017). To excel as an influential leader, it is essential to possess a deep understanding of the organizational culture and political dynamics (Hill & Wheat,

2017). Mentors play a pivotal role in assisting women in navigating complex power structures, while role models serve as exemplars, demonstrating how to advance despite prevailing negative stereotypes concerning women in leadership roles (Hill & Wheat, 2017).

SPONSORSHIP

Another facet of mentorship that has garnered scholarly attention is "sponsorship" (Gipson et al., 2017; Hewlett, 2013). Sponsors distinguish themselves from mentors by leveraging their network connections and influence to actively support the individuals they sponsor (Gipson et al., 2015). Sponsors function as staunch advocates for their protégés, proactively seeking opportunities to propel their careers and foster professional growth (Hewlett et al., 2013). Sponsorship is particularly effective due to its enduring and far-reaching advantages (Hewlett, 2013; Hill et al., 2016). Unlike mentors who primarily offer guidance and feedback, sponsors utilize their resources to personally champion those they sponsor, potentially leading to promotions and expanded career development prospects (Hewlett et al., 2013).

NETWORKS AND MENTORS

Professional networks play a pivotal role in nurturing the development of women leaders, granting them access to valuable relationships that can lead to career advancements, coveted job assignments, and enhanced professional credibility (Gipson et al., 2017). These networks encompass an array of connections with fellow professionals within a specific field who can offer guidance, facilitate introductions to influential individuals, and recommend job opportunities (Linehan & Scullion, 2008). For women navigating male-dominated fields and organizations, networks also serve as a source of emotional support, countering the isolation often accompanying such career paths (Gipson et al., 2017; Hill et al., 2016).

To aid women in attaining senior leadership roles, two key strategies come to the fore: cultivating multiple mentors and expanding their professional networks (Gamble & Turner, 2015). The research underscores the pivotal role mentors and networks play in helping women surmount barriers that frequently hinder their progression from staff positions to managerial roles (Linehan & Scullion, 2008). The researchers uncovered a glaring disparity in a study involving interviews with 50 senior female managers aimed at unraveling the role of mentoring and networking in the development of global female leaders. Female managers often miss out on global assignments due to the need for mentors, role models, sponsorships, or networking opportunities that are on par with their male counterparts (Linehan & Scullion, 2008). The study's findings pointed to a potential transformation in women's careers if they were afforded the same networking and mentoring opportunities as men (Linehan & Scullion, 2008). Nevertheless, when women secure mentors, they are frequently paired with male mentors, a practice that can introduce gender and power dynamics that influence the effectiveness of these relationships (Gipson et al., 2017).

In response to the challenges posed by gender bias, Hopkins et al. (2008) conducted a non-empirical study centered on the needs of women in leadership development practices. The findings underscored the importance of women leaders having both male and female mentors and encouraged them to engage as mentors and mentees (Hopkin et al., 2008). This multifaceted approach aims to provide a more balanced and comprehensive support system for women navigating leadership roles, recognizing the unique insights and experiences that individuals of different genders can offer in mentorship and development.

RECOMMENDATIONS AND SOLUTIONS

There are strategies to help channel more women into tech-related leadership professions. The following solutions include:

- Recommendation 1: Create more programs in middle school and high school that encourage women into technical careers, especially in private and charter schools for women. An example is "Girls Who Code," a summer camp coding program that teaches women about coding.
- Recommendation 2- Make diversity goals a performance evaluation goal of all managers, especially senior-level managers. These goals include listing and cataloging the results of activities focused on recruiting and retaining more women in the organization.
- Recommendation 3- Promoting a better vision of today's technical paths within the organization to leadership roles.
- Recommendation 4- Create formal mentoring programs where other women can mentor women, even those outside the organization.
- Recommendation 5- Creating partnerships with women's colleges. These partnerships can lead internship programs and professional development workshops.
- Recommendation 6- Partner with professional organizations like:
  Women in the Enterprise of Science and Technology (WEST)
  Women in Science & Engineering (WiSE)
  The European Association for Women in Science, Technology, Engineering and Mathematics (STEM)
  Society of Women Engineers (SWE)
  To sponsor events, conferences, and activities held by professional organizations and associations that support women in computing, Information technology, and healthcare cybersecurity .
- Recommendation 7- Creating leadership development programs that create pipelines for highly qualified women to move from staff jobs to managerial roles.
- Recommendation 8- Create women-oriented advisory boards that assist organizations with focusing on best practices around recruiting and retaining women in IT roles.
- Recommendation 9- Create developmental programs in the corporate world that mimic those offered by the federal government, including:
  The Presidential Management Fellows (PMF), www.pmf.gov, is a two-year leadership development program for people with advanced degrees to be recruited into permanent job positions in the federal government. The PMF program offers 160 hours of training and even student loan repayment of up to $60,000 (10K a year for up to 6 years), including a service commitment of 3 years for every payment year.
  The "Cyber-corps for Service" program provides scholarship money for healthcare cybersecurity students to pay two years of undergraduate or two years of graduate tuition. Each year of tuition paid requires a year of government service.
- Recommendation 10- Improve recruiting practices. Implement blind recruitment processes that remove gender-related information from job applications to ensure fair evaluation. Include diverse interview panels to minimize bias during the hiring process. Ensure that job descriptions and communications use inclusive language to attract diverse candidates.
- Recommendation 11- Create community college, government-developed, and industry-developed re-skill and upskill Programs. Develop training and certification programs specifically designed

to attract and support women in acquiring new IT and healthcare cybersecurity skills and those in leadership roles in other industries looking to change careers. Offer "return-ship" programs for women who have taken career breaks, providing a pathway to re-enter the workforce.

RECOMMENDATIONS FOR FUTURE RESEARCH

Narrative Research

Narrative qualitative research explores personal stories and experiences through in-depth interviews, narratives, or storytelling. It aims to uncover individuals' unique journeys, challenges, and motivations in healthcare cybersecurity . Future research endeavors could leverage narrative qualitative research to explore the personal stories and experiences of women and minority professionals in healthcare cybersecurity . By collecting and analyzing their narratives, researchers can uncover the intricate details of their journeys, highlighting the barriers they faced, the strategies they employed to overcome obstacles, and the factors that motivated them to pursue careers in this field. Narrative research allows a rich exploration of individual perspectives, shedding light on the unique challenges and triumphs.

Steps in Deployment

Data Collection- Conduct interviews or collect narratives from women and minorities in cybersecurity. Data Analysis- Analyze narratives to identify recurring themes, patterns, and insights.

Benefits

Provides rich and contextual insights into the lived experiences of underrepresented individuals. Offers a platform for participants to share their stories, fostering empowerment and engagement.
Supports the development of targeted strategies for increasing diversity and inclusion.

ETHNOGRAPHY

Ethnography involves immersive fieldwork and participant observation within the healthcare cybersecurity environment. Researchers aim to understand cultural dynamics, workplace interactions, and contextual factors shaping diversity. Ethnography provides an immersive approach to research, allowing investigators to embed themselves within the healthcare cybersecurity environment. Researchers can observe workplace dynamics, interactions, and cultural nuances that may influence the experiences of women and minorities. Ethnographic studies can reveal implicit biases, informal networks, and organizational cultures that impact career progression and retention. Additionally, ethnography can explore the role of mentorship, support systems, and informal practices in shaping the career trajectories of underrepresented groups.

Steps in Deployment

Fieldwork- Embed researchers within healthcare cybersecurity organizations to observe daily practices, cultures, and social interactions.

Data Collection- Gather data through observations, interviews, and document analysis.

Data Analysis- Interpret field notes and qualitative data to uncover themes and patterns.

Benefits

Offers an in-depth understanding of workplace cultures, norms, and informal networks.

Reveals implicit biases and structural barriers that hinder diversity efforts.

Provides actionable insights for organizational change and inclusivity initiatives.

GROUNDED THEORY

Grounded theory research aims to develop theories grounded in empirical data. It involves systematic data collection and analysis to generate concepts and theories that explain diversity phenomena in healthcare cybersecurity . Grounded theory research is well-suited for exploring the emergent themes and patterns within the cybersecurity workforce. Researchers can employ this method to systematically analyze qualitative data and develop theoretical frameworks that elucidate the experiences of women and minorities. Grounded theory research can help identify key factors contributing to the gender gap, barriers to leadership roles, and practical strategies for promoting diversity. The iterative nature of grounded theory research allows for ongoing refinement and validation of emerging theories.

Steps in Deployment

Data Collection- Collect qualitative data from multiple sources, such as interviews, surveys, and documents.

Open Coding- Begin with open coding, where data is broken down into categories and concepts.

Axial Coding- Organize categories and establish relationships between them.

Selective Coding- Develop a theoretical framework that explains diversity dynamics in healthcare cybersecurity .

Benefits

Generates evidence-based theories that explain workforce shortages, diversity challenges, and opportunities. Provides a structured approach to theory development, enhancing rigor and validity. Supports the identification of strategic interventions and policies to promote diversity.

These recommended research methods offer complementary approaches to understanding and addressing the gender gap and diversity challenges in healthcare cybersecurity . Researchers can choose or combine these methods to gain a comprehensive view of the field, inform policy and practice, and contribute to advancing diversity and inclusion in the industry.

REFERENCES

Alfrey, L., & Winddance Twine, F. (2017). Gender Fluid Geek Girls: Negotiating Inequality Regimes in the Tech Industry. *Gender & Society*, *31*(1), 28–50. doi:10.1177/0891243216680590

Anderson, P. (2023). Exploring the Noteworthy Experiences of African American Female Mid-Level Leaders in the United States. In D. Burrell (Ed.), *Applied Research Approaches to Technology, Healthcare, and Business* (pp. 55–72). IGI Global. doi:10.4018/979-8-3693-1630-6.ch005

Baert, S., De Pauw, A. S., & Deschacht, N. (2016). Do employer preferences contribute to sticky floors? *Industrial & Labor Relations Review*, *69*(3), 714–736. doi:10.1177/0019793915625213

Balasubramanian, S. (2023, April 29). With Increasing Reliance On Healthcare Technology, Cybersecurity Is A Growing Concern. *Forbes*. Retrieved from: https://www.forbes.com/sites/saibala/2023/04/29/with-increasing-reliance-on-healthcare-technology-cybersecurity-is-a-growing-concern/?sh=241d1f8f26ee

Blair, E. E., Miller, R. B., Ong, M., & Zastavker, Y. V. (2017). Undergraduate STEM Instructors' Teacher Identities and Discourses on Student Gender Expression and Equity. *Journal of Engineering Education*, *106*(1), 14–43. doi:10.1002/jee.20157

Bruckmüller, S., Ryan, M., Haslam, S., & Peters, K. (2014). Ceilings, cliffs, and labyrinths: Exploring metaphors for workplace gender discrimination. In M. Ryan & N. Branscombe (Eds.), The SAGE handbook of gender and psychology (pp. 450-464). SAGE Publications Ltd.

Buchanan, N. T., & Settles, I. H. (2019). Managing (in) visibility and hypervisibility in the workplace. *Journal of Vocational Behavior*, *113*, 1–5. doi:10.1016/j.jvb.2018.11.001

Burrell, D. (2015, March). As the country becomes more international and diverse, it is critical to develop healthcare professional expertise in diversity and inclusion. In *Interdisciplinarian* (Vol. 2). The Association of Interdisciplinary Doctors of Health Science.

Burrell, D. N. (2019). How Hiring Baby Boomers Can Assist with the Global Cybersecurity Employee Shortage. *International Journal of Hyperconnectivity and the Internet of Things*, *3*(2), 1–10. doi:10.4018/IJHIoT.2019070101

Burrell, D. N. (2020). An Exploration of the Cybersecurity Workforce Shortage. In I. Management Association (Ed.), Cyber Warfare and Terrorism: Concepts, Methodologies, Tools, and Applications (pp. 1072-1081). IGI Global. doi:10.4018/978-1-7998-2466-4.ch063

Burrell, D. N. (2022). Assessing the Value of Executive Leadership Coaches for Cybersecurity Project Managers. In I. Management Association (Ed.), Research Anthology on Business Aspects of Cybersecurity (pp. 349-362). IGI Global. doi:10.4018/978-1-6684-3698-1.ch016

Burrell, D. N., Diperi, D. L., & Weaver, R. M. (2020). Creating Inclusive Cultures for Women in Automation and Information Technology Careers and Occupations. *International Journal of Business Strategy and Automation*, *1*(2), 37–51. doi:10.4018/IJBSA.2020040104

Cardador, M. T. (2017). Promoted Up But Also Out? The Unintended Consequences of Increasing Women's Representation in Managerial Roles in Engineering. *Organization Science*, 28(4), 597–617. doi:10.1287/orsc.2017.1132

Carli, L. L., & Eagly, A. H. (2016). Women face a labyrinth: An examination of metaphors for women leaders. *Gender in Management*, 31(8), 514–527. doi:10.1108/GM-02-2015-0007

Cross, K. J., & Cutler, S. (2017). *Engineering Faculty Perceptions of Diversity in the Classroom*. American Society for Engineering Education Annual Conference, Columbus, Ohio. 10.18260/1-2--28253

Cuddy, A. J. C., Fiske, S. T., & Glick, P. (2004). When professionals become mothers, warmth doesn't cut the ice. *The Journal of Social Issues*, 60(4), 701–718. doi:10.1111/j.0022-4537.2004.00381.x

Eagly, A. H., & Heilman, M. E. (2016). Gender and leadership: Introduction to the special issue. *The Leadership Quarterly*, 3(27), 349–353. doi:10.1016/j.leaqua.2016.04.002

Elliott, C., & Stead, V. (2017). The effect of media on women and leadership. Handbook of Research on Gender and Leadership, 344.

Ely, R. J., Stone, P., & Ammerman, C. (2014). Rethink what you "know" about high-achieving women. *Harvard Business Review*, 92(12), 100–109.

Fidleman, M. (2012, June 5). Here's the Real Reason There Are Not More Women in Technology. *Forbes*.

Gamble, E. D., & Turner, N. J. (2015). Career ascension of African American women in executive positions in postsecondary institutions. *Journal of Organizational Culture, Communications and Conflict*, 19(1), 82.

Gipson, A. N., Pfaff, D. L., Mendelsohn, D. B., Catenacci, L. T., & Burke, W. W. (2017). Women and leadership: Selection, development, leadership style, and performance. *The Journal of Applied Behavioral Science*, 53(1), 32–65. doi:10.1177/0021886316687247

Gröschl, S., & Arcot, S. (2014). Female hospitality executives and their effects on firm performance. *Tourism and Hospitality Research*, 14(3), 143–151. doi:10.1177/1467358414538997

Hewlett, S. A. (2013). *Forget a mentor, find a sponsor: The new way to fast-track your career*. Harvard Business Review Press.

Hill, C., Miller, K., Benson, K., & Handley, G. (2016). *Barriers and bias: The status of women in leadership*. Academic Press.

Hill, L. H., & Wheat, C. A. (2017). The influence of mentorship and role models on university women leaders' career paths to university presidency. *The Qualitative Report*, 22(8), 2090. doi:10.46743/2160-3715/2017.2437

Hopkins, M. M., O'Neil, D. A., Passarelli, A., & Bilimoria, D. (2008). Women's leadership development strategic practices for women and organizations. *Consulting Psychology Journal*, 60(4), 348–365. doi:10.1037/a0014093

Hultin, M. (2003). Some take the glass escalator, some hit the glass ceiling? Career consequences of occupational sex segregation. *Work and Occupations*, 30(1), 30–61. doi:10.1177/0730888402239326

Lennon, T. (2013). *Benchmarking women's leadership in the United States*. Colorado Women's College at the University of Denver.

Linehan, M., & Scullion, H. (2008). The development of female global managers: The role of mentoring and networking. *Journal of Business Ethics*, *83*(1), 29–40. doi:10.1007/s10551-007-9657-0

Magid, L. (2014, October 1). Why Cyber Security Matters to Everyone. *Forbes*. https://www.forbes.com/sites/larrymagid/2014/10/01/why-cyber-security-matters-to-everyone/#61f9e7ae5a71

McNamara, T. K., Pitt-Catsouphes, M., Sarkisian, N., Besen, E., & Kidahashi, M. (2016). Age bias in the workplace: Cultural stereotypes and in-group favoritism. *International Journal of Aging & Human Development*, *83*(2), 156–183. doi:10.1177/0091415016648708 PMID:27199491

Meiksins, P., Layne, P., Beddoes, K., Acton, B., Masters, A., & Roediger, M. (2017). *Tech Women in Engineering: A Review of the 2017 Literature*. Society of Women Engineer Magazine.

Molenberghs, P. (2013). The neuroscience of in-group bias. *Neuroscience and Biobehavioral Reviews*, *37*(8), 1530–1536. doi:10.1016/j.neubiorev.2013.06.002 PMID:23769813

Morgan, S. (2016, March 28). Calling All Women: The Cybersecurity Field Needs You, and There's A Million Jobs Waiting. *Forbes*. https://www.forbes.com/sites/stevemorgan/2016/03/28/calling-all-women-the-cybersecurity-field-needs-you/#2470db2a381c

National Science Board. (2014). *Science and Engineering Indicators 2014. Arlington VA: National Science Foundation Science and Engineering Indicators 2014: Earned Bachelor's degrees by citizenship, field, race, or ethnicity: 2014*. Retrieved from https://www.nsf.gov/statistics/seind14/index.cfm/appendix/tables.htm

National Science Foundation, National Center for Science and Engineering Statistics Directorate for Social, Behavioral and Economic Sciences. (2015). *Women, minorities, and persons with disabilities in science and engineering 2015 report*. Retrieved from www.nsf.gov/statistics/wmpd/

National Science Foundation, National Center for Science and Engineering Statistics. (2013). Women, Minorities, and Persons with Disabilities in Science and Engineering: 2013. Special Report NSF 17-310.

Newton, V. A. (2023). Hypervisibility and Invisibility: Black Women's Experiences with Gendered Racial Microaggressions on a White Campus. *Sociology of Race and Ethnicity (Thousand Oaks, Calif.)*, *9*(2), 164–178. doi:10.1177/23326492221138222

Osborne, C. (2023, September 27). Women To Hold 30 Percent Of Cybersecurity Jobs Globally By 2025. *Cybercrime Magazine*. Retrieved from: https://cybersecurityventures.com/women-in-cybersecurity-report-2023/#:~:text=Women%20held%2025%20percent%20of,to%2035%20percent%20by%202031

Rincón, V., González, M., & Barrero, K. (2017). Women and leadership: Gender barriers to senior management positions. *Intangible Capital*, *13*(2), 319–386. doi:10.3926/ic.889

Ryan, M. K., Haslam, S. A., Morgenroth, T., Rink, F., Stoker, J., & Peters, K. (2016). Getting on top of the glass cliff: Reviewing a decade of evidence, explanations, and impact. *The Leadership Quarterly*, *27*(3), 446–455. doi:10.1016/j.leaqua.2015.10.008

Sabharwal, M. (2013). From glass ceiling to glass cliff: Women in senior executive service. *Journal of Public Administration: Research and Theory*, *25*(2), 399–426. doi:10.1093/jopart/mut030

Schuster, C., & Martiny, S. (2017). Not Feeling Good in STEM: Effects of Stereotype Activation and Anticipated Affect on Women's Career Aspirations. *Sex Roles*, *76*(1/2), 40–55. doi:10.1007/s11199-016-0665-3

Settles, I. H., Buchanan, N. T., & Dotson, K. (2019). Scrutinized but not recognized:(In) visibility and hypervisibility experiences of faculty of color. *Journal of Vocational Behavior*, *113*, 62–74. doi:10.1016/j.jvb.2018.06.003

Shiri, A., Faraji, E., & Yasini, A. (2018). Gender inequality experience in organizational promotions: A metaphorical reading of glass escalator effect. *Women's Studies*, *9*(24), 1–31.

Tellhed, U., Bäckström, M., & Björklund, F. (2017). Will I Fit in and Do Well? The Importance of Social Belongingness and Self-Efficacy for Explaining Gender Differences in Interest in STEM and HEED Majors. *Sex Roles*, *77*(1–2), 86–96. doi:10.1007/s11199-016-0694-y PMID:28725103

Thornton, G. (2013). Women in senior management: Setting the stage for growth. Grant Thornton International Business Report.

Vafaei, A., Ahmed, K., & Mather, P. (2015). Board diversity and financial performance in the top 500 Australian firms: Board diversity and financial performance. *Australian Accounting Review*, *25*(4), 413–427. doi:10.1111/auar.12068

Van Dijk, H., Van Engen, M. L., & Van Knippenberg, D. (2012). Defying conventional wisdom: A meta-analytical examination of the differences between demographic and job-related diversity relationships with performance. *Organizational Behavior and Human Decision Processes*, *119*(1), 38–53. doi:10.1016/j.obhdp.2012.06.003

Whitely, W., Dougherty, T. W., & Dreher, G. F. (1991). Relationship of career mentoring and socioeconomic origin to managers' and professionals' early career progress. *Academy of Management Journal*, *34*(2), 331–350. doi:10.2307/256445

Williams, J. C. (2005). The glass ceiling and the maternal wall in academia. *New Directions for Higher Education*, *2005*(130), 91–105. doi:10.1002/he.181

Yaghi, A. (2017). Glass cliff or glass prison: Think evil-think men in organizational leadership. *International Journal of Public Administration*, 1–11.

Chapter 7
Healthcare Information Systems (HCIS) Customer Patient Advocacy:
Cyber Health Deficiencies in the State of Washington

Eugene J. Lewis
ⓘ https://orcid.org/0000-0002-2956-0760
Capitol Technology University, USA

Ramona R. Cruz
Oakwood University, USA

ABSTRACT

The cyber health deficiencies from customer patient advocacy did not exist until September 2021. The exploratory research focuses on a recent conference advancing in healthcare equity through policy and practice from the lenses of the University of Washington Continuing Education Conference held on 19-20 October 2023. The conference consisted of professionals in the state of Washington who are physicians, nurses, and other medical personnel. It provided insights into the general trends and issues related to patient advocacy in the healthcare industry. In this research study, the authors discuss the statistical challenges and lack of aid in resolving disputes within healthcare providers, understanding insurance coverage, and ensuring that informed consent is obtained for medical procedures for prospective customers.

INTRODUCTION

The challenge in the healthcare cyber market is the complexities of achieving equitable healthcare in North America (Kohan et al., 2023). The goal of the research is to demonstrate a correlation between "healthcare equity" and the industry's current utilization of healthcare information systems (HCIS) disparities (Choi, 2015; Water et al., 2016; Gil Manso et al., 2023). Establishing a relationship between

DOI: 10.4018/979-8-3693-1970-3.ch007

these two mutually exclusive concepts provides additional information into the discovery of the issues surrounding patient advocacy and the impact of a lack of healthcare information systems (HCIS) within the industry (Martin & Shannon, 2023; Choi, 2015; Water et al., 2016; Gil Manso et al., 2023). There is mounting evidence declaring a positive correlation between both mutually exclusive concepts in the wake of growing concerns about patient advocacy, especially amongst minority ethnic groups in disadvantaged communities (Choi, 2015; Water et al., 2016; Gil Manso et al., 2023). The research aims to maximize the utilization of HCIS to generate a more robust patient advocacy system that is more transformational (Choi, 2015; Water et al., 2016; Gil Manso et al., 2023). Currently, the health care system contextually still needs to resolve an analytical fundamental challenge within the industry (Kohan et al., 2023). The significance of this research is to understand why these issues still exist despite technological advances critically.

The primary mission of healthcare providers is to preserve life and provide comfort (Kohan et al., 2023). Unfortunately, there are ethical questions surrounding patient advocacy for "people of color in underserved communities (Martin & Shannon, 2023)." The discomfort of continued healthcare advocacy has developed into a significant health challenge in the State of Washington (Hussain et al., 2023). Especially given the State of Washington's continued challenges as one of the highest "homeless populations" in the country. According to DSHS and DBR (2022), client counts and service costs for the State of Washington are approximately 40% as of FY2017. The need for patient advocacy is to understand the deficiencies within the healthcare field that are undeniable (Choi, 2015). The most common Ethnicity among patient advocates. See Table 1. Most Common Ethnicity among Patient Advocates (Zippia, 2023).

Understanding the data provides an overall landscape of the challenges of accessing equitable health-

Table 1. Most common ethnicity among patient advocates (Zippia, 2023)

Ethnicity Among Patient Advocates	Percentage
White	53.2%
Hispanic or Latino	23.6%
Black or African-American	10.5%
Asian	6.8%
Unknown	5.2%
American Indian and Alaska Native	0.7%

care (Martin & Shannon, 2023). Many clients of patient advocates are from ethnic groups living in underserved communities where individuals receive limited resources, especially about mental health. Healthcare providers offer minimal care for severe ailments and traumas (Hussain et al., 2023; Kohan et al., 2023). The healthcare entities in these communities must expand their creativity with patients' need for advocacy. These perceptual norms within the healthcare industry change governing ordinances to make healthcare equity and accessibility of telemedicine innovations more apparent (Kohan et al., 2023). Customer patient advocacy in healthcare is a critical component of ensuring that patients receive the best possible care and have their rights protected. Patients often rely on advocacy from organizations. However, regulatory services and legal support must address current concerns and navigate the complexities of the healthcare system (Choi, 2015). In the State of Washington, as in many other states, patient advocacy is influenced by healthcare policies, patient demographics, and the availability of advocacy services (Hussain et al., 2023). The State's healthcare system may have seen variations in patient advocacy efforts of patients living in economically challenged areas. Individuals seeking equitable care need reassurance that healthcare entities put the customer first.

Over the past four decades, patient advocacy has become central to health care information system (HCIS) professional identity (Choi, 2015; Water et al., 2016; Gil Manso et al., 2023). Advocacy is seen by the International Council of Nurses (ICN) as central to nurses' contribution to the development of robust and resilient healthcare systems, thereby contributing to achieving optimal sustainable development goals (SDG) (Martin & Shannon, 2023). To facilitate this, healthcare professionals need to advocate for the populations whom they work with, those most vulnerable and at risk; advocate for the development of a strong healthcare workforce; and contribute to the development of policy that supports the goals of ensuring healthy lives and promoting wellbeing for all ages (Martin & Shannon, 2023).

There are growing challenges in health care all over the country. According to recent surveys and reports, a significant percentage of patients in Washington face difficulties in accessing adequate advocacy and support during their healthcare journeys (Hussain et al., 2023). Organizations must consider group representations to coordinate care for patients needing additional support. Many of the patient care support can be accessible using technology. Moreover, many of the technological resources are not up-to-date or do not have the appropriate security systems in place to ensure patients are protected. Studies indicate that a notable portion of patients express dissatisfaction with the information they receive regarding their treatment options and the associated risks and benefits.

In some cases, as many as 30% of patients may feel that their healthcare providers do not adequately involve them in decision-making processes (Emrich et al., 2015; DBR, 2022). Across different demographics with underserved communities and marginalized populations, reports show lower satisfaction levels (DSHS, 2018); aside from the pressures of source mandates, other competing factors, such as determining optimal resources regarding patient vulnerability, are still an issue. Additionally, there is a concerning disparity in patient advocacy experiences across different demographics, with underserved communities and marginalized populations often reporting lower levels of satisfaction (DSHS, 2018). This data underscores the need for improved patient advocacy initiatives and better communication between healthcare providers and patients in Washington to ensure everyone receives the support and information they require to make informed decisions about their healthcare (Choi, 2015).

Along with decreased provider-patient relationships, healthcare information systems (HCIS) and customer-patient advocacy encounter escalating cyberhealth deficiencies (Choi, 2015; Gil Manso et al., 2023). The interplay of these factors has given rise to a significant problem within the State's healthcare system. One of the central issues is the vulnerability of HCIS to cyber threats. (Gil Manso et al., 2023). As healthcare organizations increasingly rely on digital systems to manage patient records and clinical data, they become attractive targets for cybercriminals. Washington, like many other states, has seen a surge in cyberattacks on healthcare facilities, leading to breaches of sensitive patient information. These breaches not only compromise patient privacy but also disrupt the efficient functioning of healthcare systems (Emrich et al., 2015). Customer patient advocacy has faced challenges in Washington due to the lack of transparency and accountability in the healthcare system (Choi, 2015). Patients often need help navigating complex billing procedures, insurance claims, and medical decisions. The determining factors result in confusion, dissatisfaction, and even financial hardship. Advocacy services aim to support patients in understanding and asserting their rights, but they face an uphill battle in a system marred by opacity and complexity. The convergence of these issues exacerbates the problems in Washington's healthcare landscape. Patients, already dealing with a complicated healthcare bureaucracy, must now also worry about the security of their personal and medical information. The compromised trust in the healthcare system further undermines efforts to deliver quality care and maintain patient satisfaction.

To address these challenges, Washington must invest in robust cybersecurity measures to protect HCIS and patient data (Gil Manso et al., 2023). It must also work on improving transparency and simplifying the healthcare experience for patients through better customer advocacy services. Additionally, the State should consider regulatory and legislative measures to ensure that healthcare organizations take cybersecurity and patient advocacy seriously. In the next section, the problem statement will define how the results discussed in this critical analysis address these interconnected issues, "can the State of Washington provide a secure and patient-centered healthcare system?"

PROBLEM STATEMENT

The problem statement surrounding customer patient advocacy in the State of Washington is closely linked to the statistical data supporting Health Care disparities in the State and the national statistics. The issue is unequal access to quality healthcare and the lack of effective patient advocacy, which results in disparities in healthcare outcomes and experiences (Choi, 2015). According to Zippia (2022), statistical data highlights nationally in the fiscal year of 2021 (FY2021) customer advocacy based on race and Ethnicity had Whites (53.18%), Blacks (10.53%), Asians (6.79%), and Latinos (23.65%). Blacks, Asians, and Latinos, particularly in underserved communities, face a disproportionate burden of health disparities. For instance, these communities often exhibit higher rates of chronic illnesses, lower life expectancies, and reduced access to necessary medical services.

The problem statement for this research study seeks to discuss the following questions:

1. How can customer patient advocacy be maximized by utilizing Health Care Information Systems?
2. Finally, what are the interconnected issues from the State of Washington with the national statistical data surrounding a secure patient-centered healthcare system?

These problem statement questions provide a screenshot of patient advocacy deficiencies, as data shows that many patients, particularly in these disadvantaged groups, receive inadequate information and support from healthcare providers to make informed decisions about their health (Nguyen et al., 2022). This discrepancy in the level of care and advocacy received by different population segments underscores the urgent need for healthcare reform and initiatives to address these disparities, ultimately ensuring that all residents in the State of Washington receive equitable and patient-centered healthcare. The following section will discuss the significance of the project in this area.

SIGNIFICANCE OF THE PROJECT

The significance of the study lies in the understanding that healthcare information systems (HCIS) play a pivotal role in enhancing patient advocacy, and this is influenced by a multitude of factors, including healthcare policies, patient demographics, and the availability of advocacy services within the State of Washington (Gil Manso et al., 2023). HCIS, when effectively designed and implemented, can improve patient advocacy by facilitating better communication, informed decision-making, and care coordination among healthcare providers and patients (Gil Manso et al., 2023). The study can shed light on how the State's healthcare system may have experienced variations in patient advocacy efforts, potentially impacting the quality of care received by different patient groups.

By examining the relationship between HCIS and patient advocacy, the study can provide insights into how healthcare policies in Washington have influenced the adoption of technology to support patient-centered care (Siripurapu et al., 2023; Nguyen et al., 2022; Gil Manso et al., 2023). Moreover, it can help identify disparities in patient advocacy across various patient demographics, such as racial and ethnic groups or socioeconomic backgrounds, highlighting where improvements are most needed. Understanding the availability and utilization of advocacy services can reveal gaps in the system that hinder equitable access to care.

The significance of the study lies in its exploration of the complex interplay between Health Care Information Systems (HCIS) and patient advocacy in the context of healthcare policies, patient demographics, and the availability of advocacy services in the State of Washington (Gil Manso et al., 2023). By examining these factors, the study can shed light on how HCIS can influence patient advocacy efforts and their impact on the healthcare system (Nguyen et al., 2022; Gil Manso et al., 2023).

1. **Improved Patient Advocacy**: Understanding how HCIS can enhance or hinder patient advocacy efforts is crucial for improving the quality of care. Effective HCIS can streamline access to patient information, making it easier for healthcare providers to engage in meaningful dialogue with patients, thereby improving patient advocacy.
2. **Healthcare Policies and Equity**: The study can help identify the role of healthcare policies in shaping patient advocacy initiatives. Analyzing how policies impact advocacy services can contribute to the development of policies that promote equitable access to care and reduce disparities in healthcare outcomes.
3. **Tailored Patient Support**: By considering patient demographics, the study can reveal how different groups experience patient advocacy. This information can guide healthcare providers and policymakers in tailoring advocacy services to meet the unique needs of various patient populations, ultimately leading to more equitable healthcare delivery.
4. **Safeguarding Patient Rights**: Understanding how HCIS can contribute to safeguarding patient rights is essential. In an age of increasing data breaches and privacy concerns, this study can help identify vulnerabilities in the system and inform efforts to enhance patient data security.

Customer patient advocacy has become a significant problem due to issues related to patient rights, informed consent, and access to quality care (Kohan et al., 2023; Gil Manso et al., 2023). Many patients in Washington need to be fully aware of their rights, and healthcare providers may not consistently provide information and support to help patients make informed decisions about their treatment. This lack of advocacy leaves patients vulnerable to suboptimal care and can lead to disparities in healthcare outcomes (Rubenstein et al., 2023; Gil Manso et al., 2023).

Furthermore, cyber health deficiencies have increased in Washington, with many healthcare organizations falling victim to cyberattacks (Nguyen et al., 2022). The consequences of these attacks are dire, including data breaches, ransomware incidents, and even disruptions in critical healthcare services. Patients' personal and medical information is at risk, and these breaches erode trust in the healthcare system.

PATIENT ENGAGEMENT

The healthcare system in the State of Washington exhibits unique variations in patient advocacy efforts, focusing on ensuring equitable access to care, addressing disparities, and safeguarding patient rights (Richardson-Parry et al., 2023). A review of the existing literature reveals several key insights into the State's healthcare landscape. Washington is known for its progressive healthcare policies, emphasizing expanding access to care and promoting patient-centered services (Anderson et al., 2023). The State's adoption of the Affordable Care Act (ACA) of 2010 and Medicaid expansion has substantially increased the number of insured individuals, thereby reducing disparities in access to care. These policy initiatives have been instrumental in improving healthcare equity (Creapeau, 2023).

Moreover, the State has prioritized the integration of Health Information Exchange (HIE) systems and electronic health records (EHRs) to enhance patient advocacy. By leveraging technology, healthcare providers in Washington can access comprehensive patient data, enabling more informed decision-making and personalized care plans (Siripurapu et al., 2023; Broughton et al., 2023). In turn, it contributes to equitable healthcare delivery (Kohan et al., 2023; Anderson et al., 2023). Washington's diverse demographics have also driven patient advocacy initiatives that recognize the unique needs of various communities (Anderson et al., 2023). In response to health disparities among different racial and ethnic groups, there has been a collaborative effort to address social determinants of health and promote cultural competence in healthcare delivery. These efforts aim to reduce disparities by ensuring that healthcare services are culturally sensitive and accessible.

The State's commitment to safeguarding patient rights is further exemplified by robust data privacy regulations and security measures (Nguyen et al., 2022). In an era of increasing cyber threats, Washington has implemented stringent policies to protect patient information, bolstering trust in the healthcare system (Creapeau, 2023). In essence, the literature within Washington's healthcare system highlights a strong emphasis on patient advocacy, driven by progressive policies, advanced healthcare technologies, attention to diverse demographics, and a commitment to safeguarding patient rights (Emrich et al., 2015; Anderson et al., 2023). These unique variations in patient advocacy efforts collectively contribute to a more equitable, inclusive, and patient-centric healthcare system in the State.

However, within healthcare information systems, patient engagement creates a separate issue. The essential factor is how to assist healthcare facilities in developing relationships with prospective customers (Martin & Shannon, 2023). Cultural competence has a significant effect on an organization's ability to provide patient advocacy, as disadvantaged communities are often forgotten concerning their healthcare concerns. Although conferences, lectures, and research discuss improvements in health outcomes with underserved communities' little dissemination of information to patients is defined (Martin & Shannon, 2023). See Table 3. Patient Advocate Age by Race and Gender (Zippia, 2022).

According to a Harvard Researcher, the State of Washington sells patient-level health data for $50 (Sweeney, 2013). The publicly available dataset matches health records virtually in all hospital sectors annually, including patient demographics, diagnoses, procedures, attending physicians, hospitals, a summary of charges, and how the bill is paid (Sweeney, 2013; Thai & Mai, 2023). Employers, financial organizations, and others know the same kind of information as reported in news stories for identifying medical records of employees, debtors, and others (Thai & Mai, 2023). See Table 2—patient Advocate Age by Race and Gender (Zippia, 2022).

Table 2. Patient advocate age by race and gender (Zippia, 2022)

Race	Men (Minimum Age)	Women (Minimum Age)
Black or African-American	37	39
Unknown	34	36.5
Asian	38	42
Hispanic or Latino	33	35
White	37	44
American Indian and Alaska Native	38	42

In summary, the significant statistical data from Table 3 provides a range of the minimum-maximum age based on race/Ethnicity for patient advocacy for men is 33 with a maximum of 38. Meanwhile, women are 35 with a maximum of 44. Furthermore, Hispanic/Latino men have the lowest minimum age of 33. Moreover, Hispanic/Latino women have the lowest minimum age of 35. In comparison, Asian and American Indian/Alaska natives have the highest age minimum of 38, and white women have the highest age minimum of 44. The following section provides a more in-depth view into patient advocacy as the literature provides more insight into some of the challenges discussed during the Conference for *Advancing in Healthcare Equity Through Policy and Practice.*

PATIENT ADVOCATE

Customer patient advocacy has become a significant problem due to issues related to patient document security, patient rights, informed consent, and access to quality care (Kohan et al., 2023; Gil Manso et al., 2023). Many patients in Washington need to be fully aware of their rights, and healthcare providers may not consistently provide information and support to help patients make informed decisions about their treatment or who has access to their data (WaTech, 2023). This lack of advocacy leaves patients vulnerable to suboptimal care and can lead to disparities in healthcare outcomes (Rubenstein et al., 2023; Gil Manso et al., 2023). Cyberhealth deficiencies have increased in Washington, with many healthcare organizations falling victim to cyberattacks (Nguyen et al., 2022; WaTech, 2023). Specific to Washington State, The State Office of Privacy and Data Protection (OPDP) was created by the state Legislature in 2016 to help mitigate these deficiencies in cyber health. According to the OPDP website, *"The OPDP serves as a central point of contact for state agencies on policy matters involving data privacy and data protection, and as a resource for consumer privacy issues (WaTech, 2023)."*

The office's duties include:

- Conducting an annual privacy review.
- Providing privacy training for state agencies and employees.
- Articulate privacy principles and best practices for state agencies to coordinate data.

Protection.

- Participate in the review of significant state agency projects involving personally identifiable information.

In addition, the privacy office serves as a resource to local governments and the public on data privacy and protection concerns (WaTech, 2023). The office develops and promotes the dissemination of best practices for the collection and storage of personally identifiable information (WaTech, 2023). According to Zippia (2022), patient advocate demographics research summary estimates statistics in the United States by using a database of 30 million profiles. Our patient advocate estimates are verified against BLS, Census, and current job openings data. A data science team reviewed these critical facts about patient advocates after extensive research and analysis (Zippia, 2023):

- 71,668 patient advocates are currently employed in the United States.
- 82.5% of all patient advocates are women, while men are 17.5%.
- The average patient advocate age is 40 years old.
- Most common patient advocates based on Ethnicity are White (53.2%), Hispanic or Latino. (23.6%), Black or African American (10.5%) and Asian (6.8%).
- Patient advocates in Omaha, Nebraska, have the highest demand.
- The Health Care Industry is the highest paying for patient advocates.
- In 2022, women patient advocates earned 97% of what men earned.
- Patient advocates are 82% more likely to work at private companies in comparison to public companies.

Also, patient advocate gender pay gap income between women ($36,784) and men ($37,920) consists of a three-cent difference between sexes (Zippia, 2022). See Table 3. Patient Advocate Gender Ratio by Year (Zippia, 2022).

Table 3. Patient advocate gender ratio by year (Zippia, 2022)

Year	2016	2017	2018	2019	2020	2021
Men	18.22%	18.51%	17.63%	17.35%	17.77%	17.52%
Women	81.78%	81.49%	82.37%	82.65%	82.23%	82.48%

Even with continued attacks, these challenges are inevitable, but they can be avoided (WaTech, 2023; WSOAG, 2023). Privacy and data protection have dire consequences for patient security when subject to attacks, including data breaches, ransomware incidents, and even disruption to critical healthcare services (WSOAG, 2023). Mitigating risk to patient's personal and medical information should be of the utmost importance to healthcare providers as they seek to gain consumer trust (DBR, 2022; WSOAG, 2023). An example of an incident was evidence of these consequences revealed by the Attorney General's Office highlighting *"a 200 percent increase in the number of breaches impacting more than 50,000 Washingtonians compared to 2020 in the 2021 Data Breach Report (WSOAG, 2023)."* Furthermore, other evidence provided numerous incidents reporting 206 breaches, representing nearly three-quarters (74%) of all breaches in the State of Washington (DBR, 2022; WSOAG, 2023). Many of the breaches resulted in name and date of birth data compromises as the security of patient data was exposed (WaTech, 2023; WSOAG, 2023). Additionally, social security numbers were the second most compromised personally identifiable component, with reported impacts in 40% (113) of breaches (WaTech, 2023; WSOAG, 2023). Of the new elements added to the definition of personal information in 2020 — aside from date of birth — username in combination with a password and passport numbers saw significant increases compared to last year's report, growing by 425% (21) and 450% (22), respectively (WSOAG, 2023; DBR, 2022).

Regardless of these policy efforts to protect patient health information, healthcare entities like the Veteran's Administration and their staff (e.g., Hospital Operators, Clinical staff, and community care nurses) often use the patient's last four digits of social security numbers as their first means of verifying personally identifiable information (PII) via telephone and other modes of communication. It is known within local healthcare entities and Veteran families themselves to use the last four digits of a patient's last four digits of their social security number as a preferred way of sharing and verifying patient health information between all parties. The electronic health record's various methods mean more outstanding patient advocacy and care between healthcare entities and their patient clientele.

METHODOLOGY

The methodology utilized by the researchers in this study is an exploratory qualitative research methodology using ethnography triangulation (Van Maanen, 1988). The critical elements of the ethnographic methodology section defined the following as the method for gathering information:

(1)   the logic of the inquiry,
(2)   research setting and participants,
(3)   methods and procedure of data collection,
(4)   methods and procedure of data analysis, and
(5)   ethical issues.

Researchers used the following method to source data for the research findings and results:

STEP 1: The logic of the research inquiry critically analyzes data based on *Advancing Healthcare Equity Through Policy and Practice.*

STEP 2: The research settings and participants from the study are from the University of Washington Continuing Education Conference held on 19-20 October 2023 at the Bell Harbor Conference Center, 2211 Alaskan Way, Seattle, WA 98121, in front of about 300+ registered attendees. In attendance were MDs (Medical Doctors), DNP/ARNP (Doctor of Nursing/Advanced Practice), MSN/RN/LPN (Nurses), PharmD (Pharmacists), and MSW/LICSW (Social Workers). The speakers' areas of expertise include Legislative Ordinances, Academia, Pediatric, Adult, Gerontology, Family Nurse Practice (FNP), Acute Care, Critical Care, Home Health, Sexual Reproductive Health (SRH), and Psychiatric Mental Health. These industry leaders collectively presented talks to advance the industry's understanding of emerging trends affecting equitable service provided to Washington State patients (Rubenstein et al., 2023).

STEP 3: <u>The methods and procedures of data collection</u> is a conceptual review of the conference lectures and discussions provided by keynote speakers, doctors, nurse practitioners, registered nurses, social workers, psychiatric consultants, and many other professionals in the public health sector.

STEP 4: <u>The procedure of data analysis</u> was to develop a critical analysis based on the contents of the information provided, along with improving transparency and simplifying the healthcare experience for patients through quality customer advocacy services discussed.

STEP 5: <u>Ethically,</u> the research hopes to present three qualitative research findings from the Conference intended to effectively advance Washington State healthcare workforce out of the current ethnic, racially divided system designed to create barriers for non-white patients.

Using the social constructivist approach, the triangulation of the findings and results of this paper will provide a more detailed critical critique of the information provided (Stake, 1995). The qualitative research methodology will explore thoughts, patterns, and ideas of how healthcare information systems can be utilized (Spradley, 1979; Stake, 1995; Van Maanen, 1988). Ethnography can be a valuable research method when used at an academic conference to collect data, especially when the aim is to understand the behaviors, interactions, and cultural dynamics of participants (Denzin, 1978; Fern, 1982). The researchers in the table below list ethnography research methodology for each area. Ethnography applies these specific data points in this context from the Conference. See Table 4—implementation of Ethnography Research Methodology.

The researchers used an ethnographic qualitative approach defined for collecting data often used in the social and behavioral sciences (Stake, 1995). However, triangulation provides explicitly a comprehensive understanding of the phenomena (Patton, 1999). Triangulation, viewed as a qualitative research strategy, tests the validity by converging information from different sources. Most of the data collected through observations and interviews were drawn from conclusions about how societies and individuals function (Van Maanen, 1988). In this study, the researchers chose two of the four triangulation types used by Denzin (1978) and Patton (1999), consisting of (a) method triangulation, (b) investigator triangulation, (c) theory triangulation, and (d) data source triangulation. The two selected in this methodology were the (b) investigator triangulation, as much of the State of Washington's challenges stem from further investigation into patient advocacy needs. They, furthermore, determined the challenges surrounding the subject.

1. Dismantle the convergence of systemic racial issues in healthcare, compounding the advocacy for equitable care of Indigenous, Black, and Brown patient demographics. Quantitative and qualitative studies were used to disseminate the origins of discord in these communities where the healthcare workforce remains structurally racist in providing care despite the best competencies, patient care expertise, and ethical intent.

2. Effectively break the strongholds of Structural Racism embedded in the Healthcare education of its workforce by updating RCWs (Revised Code of Washington) that govern two areas:
   a. Curriculum and Graduation Requirements of Medical Doctors
   b. Requirements to obtain and maintain licensure as a practicing healthcare provider (i.e., DNP, FNP, RN, LPN, MSN, LICSW).

3. Illuminate on technological advancements in the Washington State HCIS that are current and effective at reducing opacity and complexity of delivering care in marginalized communities (i.e., predominantly non-white patients whose care is funded by Dept. of Health and Social Services, patients seeking care from Title X, Rural Clinics, federally funded State Hospitals and Community Health Clinics, and patients with neurodiverse abilities needing advocacy in their care navigation).

Table 4. Implementation of ethnography research methodology

		IMPLEMENTATION OF ETHNOGRAPHY RESEARCH METHODOLOGY Data Collection, Observation, Behaviors, Interactions, & Cultural Dynamics	
(1)	Participant Observation	Ethnographers can attend academic conferences as active participants or observers. They immerse themselves in the conference environment, attending sessions, workshops, and social events. By taking field notes, ethnographers can document the interactions, behaviors, and discussions of participants. This data can reveal how participants engage with conference content, how they network, and what topics generate the most interest.	*Examples during the Conference:* Researchers gathered notes from the guest speakers; focus group discussions demonstrated the vulnerability of the State of Washington's systemic customer patient advocacy needs and discrepancies.
(2)	Informal Interviews	Ethnographers can engage in informal interviews with conference attendees during breaks, meals, or social gatherings. These interviews can provide deeper insights into the motivations, expectations, and experiences of the participants. By talking to a diverse range of attendees, researchers can gain a more comprehensive understanding of the Conference's impact.	*Examples during the Conference:* Researchers had informal discussions with doctors and nurses to understand the State of Washington's growing patient advocacy needs. The individuals expressed how the statistical data was skewed in some areas but entirely accurate in others.
(3)	Document Analysis	Ethnographers can collect and analyze conference materials, such as programs, posters, presentation slides, and handouts. These documents can offer insights into the themes, topics, and trends within the academic community and how they are disseminated at the Conference. It can also help in understanding the official discourse and narratives of the Conference.	*Examples during the Conference:* Researchers collected brochures, handouts, slides, and other documentation to gain a thematic framework of possible patterns in the healthcare industry.
(4)	Ethnographic Notebooks and Reflexivity	Ethnographers often maintain reflective fieldwork journals where they record their own experiences, thoughts, and emotions during the Conference. This reflexivity can be critical in understanding the researcher's positionality and how it may influence data collection and interpretation.	*Examples during the Conference:* Researchers did not use this methodology in this study.
(5)	Research Design	Define the research objectives, select the research site or group, and determine the research questions. Researchers should also consider ethical issues and obtain informed consent from participants.	*Examples during the Conference:* The research design was exploratory. However, much of the data is causal.
(6)	Field Entry	Researchers gain access to the research site or group, establish rapport, and build trust with participants. The guidance often involves building relationships and explaining the research purpose.	*Examples during the Conference:* Researchers spoke with significant benefactors and influencers in this area. Relationships were formed, and an exchange of personal contact information was provided to have further discussions on healthcare efficacy and challenges.
(7)	Data Collection	Researchers begin collecting data through participant observation, which involves attending events, activities, and interactions within the group. Researchers may also conduct interviews and collect documents or artifacts as part of their data collection.	*Examples during the Conference:* Researchers obtained data from the Conference through observations and separate activities such as many session focus groups to detail experiences some industry health care professionals had experienced in the field.
(8)	Field Notes	Detailed field notes are taken during and after observations and interactions. These notes include descriptions, quotes, and researcher reflections. Field notes capture the richness of the context and the participants' experiences.	*Examples during the Conference:* Many notes were taken while Academics and Researchers took to the podium to discuss several issues about healthcare discrepancies amongst people of color and the lack of patient protection. Other notes taken discussed underserved communities and the need for process centers to assist consumers with health care information and potential benefits

continues on following page

Table 4. Continued

IMPLEMENTATION OF ETHNOGRAPHY RESEARCH METHODOLOGY
Data Collection, Observation, Behaviors, Interactions, & Cultural Dynamics

(9)	Data Analysis	Researchers analyze the collected data to identify themes, patterns, and critical cultural elements. The analysis involves coding and categorizing the data to draw out meaningful insights.	*Examples during the Conference:* Researchers defined themes and patterns that were consistent with the State of Washington's current dilemma from health care information systems to customer-patient advocacy. These results and analysis will be provided in the findings and results section.
(10)	Interpretation	Ethnographers interpret the data in the context of the group's culture. This process involves understanding the meaning and significance of observed behaviors, practices, and social interactions.	*Examples during the Conference:* Researchers were able to clearly define the data and the group culture surrounding behaviors, practices, and interactions, as many daunting statistics were given during each presentation
(11)	Triangulation	Ethnographers often use multiple data sources and methods to cross-check and validate their findings. Triangulation helps ensure the reliability and credibility of the study.	*Examples during the Conference:* Researchers utilized this method as three key personnel were identified during the Conference in some data sources provided with validation from research and the field to provide credibility and reliability amongst the peers.
(12)	Writing Ethnographic Reports	Researchers document their findings in written ethnographic reports. These reports provide a comprehensive account of the group's culture, including descriptions, analysis, and interpretation. They typically include rich narratives and examples to illustrate key points.	*Examples during the Conference:* Researchers did not utilize this method during the Conference.
(13)	Reflexivity	Researchers engage in reflexivity, which involves reflecting on their own role in the study and how their presence and biases may have influenced the data collection and interpretation.	*Examples during the Conference:* Researchers spent many days pondering the information provided while being introspective about past experiences in the field where customer-patient advocacy presented real challenges. Furthermore, reflexivity really enhanced personal biases and colorism as a perspective on the root causes of specific actions within the field of health care in the State of Washington.
(14)	Ethical Considerations	Ethnographers must uphold ethical standards throughout the study, ensuring that the rights and privacy of participants are respected.	*Examples during the Conference:* Researchers provide additional information in the methodology concerning the ethical dilemmas and essential steps, outcomes, and instances for future investigation.
(15)	Peer Review and Validation	Researchers engage in peer review and validation to substantiate thoughts, ideas, and patterns related to the subject matter.	*Examples during the Conference:* Researchers utilized peer-reviewed documentation to further the conversation on patient engagement and advocacy as members within the community still discuss the reliability and validity of the conference material in the State of Washington; meanwhile, many healthcare professionals will research statistical data that potentially provide a valuable explanation for ongoing problems.

143

Any conflicts of interest related to biases in the information provided to attendees were disclosed at the beginning of each speaker segment. Attendees of this Conference are currently part of the healthcare workforce within and outside the State of Washington. The list also included those enrolled at Washington State University or Seattle University. Other aspects of the methodology equally important were discussions on healthcare information systems and their potential value to healthcare facilities and personnel around the State. The indication was that healthcare inequality was not inherited but a result of a continuum of structural racism in Washington State. The ethnographic qualitative research method will help provide incidences and key points discussed for future investigations to define themes, patterns, ideas, and experiences helpful to the healthcare community (Spradley, 1979). The methodology is utilized in the critical research analysis as a baseline for future works in healthcare information systems and customer-patient advocacy.

THEORIES FROM THE LITERATURE

The theoretical framework empirically explores the research study in institutional theory (Covaleski et al., 1993). The institutional theory extends to issues of power and decoupling unfinished processes affected by misguided information (Bhattacharya et al., 2023; Thai & Mai, 2023). Employing perspectives of institutional theory develops strategies for reducing the perceived level of corruption by assessing the interaction between regulatory, cognitive, and normative practices (Bhattacharya et al., 2023; Ma et al., 2023). The institutional theory stems from social perspectives versus reality-based perspectives of issues, challenges, and actions that exist (Ra et al., 2023). Institutional theory pioneers the thought process that "what you see is not necessarily what you get." Highlighting areas in which organizations hide, misinterpret, or mislead their audience about what they should know about the consistencies or inconsistencies of action-based outcomes (Covaleski et al., 1993; Ma et al., 2023). The concept is valuable to the research community because it provides academic researchers a baseline into the reality of observations, phenomena, and realities existing in the current lens of systemic perspectives (Bhattacharya et al., 2023).

The application of institutional theory to the topic of healthcare information systems is an invaluable conversation. The reference has a solid correlation to customer patient advocacy and health care disparities as academics, researchers, and practitioners' consistent data substantiate challenges within the specific area of health care (Ra et al., 2023). It is common knowledge that the healthcare community suffers from a lack of transparency among people of color (Ma et al., 2023). People of color or cultural diversity experience misinformation about healthcare resources and must possess the patient advocacy aptitude to understand their basic needs (Anderson et al., 2023; Broughton et al., 2023). Institutionalization provides a litany of challenges and issues, as in a healthcare context, social structure and interest-oriented activity are ignored for intrinsic or extrinsic reasons (Ra et al., 2023). Consequently, this causes a need for greater despondency using health care information systems (HCIS) to support patient advocates without knowing what a person looks like but instead on the health care needs (Ma et al., 2023; Gil Manso et al., 2023). The institutional theory provides the means of a strong correlation between healthcare organizations and their consumers (patient advocates), along with the public health resources allotted to everyone (Creapeau, 2023; Broughton et al., 2023).

The ethnographic methodology supports an institutional theory examination because it measures behavior that takes place within specific social situations, including behavior that is shaped and constrained by these situations, plus people's understanding and interpretation of those experiences (Wolcott, 1995; Jones & Smith, 2017; Arnout et al., 2020). The use of theoretical frameworks in conducting and writing an ethnographic critical analysis makes the research process more insightful, and it makes the process and thoughts of the researcher, the participants, and the potential stakeholders more transparent (Wolcott, 1995; Jones & Smith, 2017).

In recent years, it has become increasingly clear that interventions designed to encourage patient advocacy have yet to have the desired impacts, especially amongst groups with a lower socioeconomic background (Jones & Smith, 2017; Stebbins, 2001; Broughton et al., 2023). To understand why interventions are so valuable and essential is to impact the embedded social and cultural reform to improve opportunities for families that lack opportunities (Visser et al., 2016; Jones & Smith, 2017). HCIS is an invaluable resource due to the use of technology to mitigate the risk of profiling based on socioeconomic background and provide social factors influenced by decision-making (Siripurapu et al., 2023; Gil Manso et al., 2023).

FINDINGS AND RESULTS

Guidelines for conducting ethnographic fieldwork. Arnout (2020), Stebbins (2001), and Wolcott (1995) identified many directions for researchers to develop an ethnographic field study, including the following:

1. Collect a variety of information from different perspectives and different sources.
2. Use notes, open interviews, site documents, and audio-visual materials, such as recordings and photos.
3. Researchers will write descriptive and detailed field notes.
4. They were representing participants on their terms of use and short stories.
5. Gather participant's opinions on their own experiences in their own words.

The findings and results of the critical analysis utilizing a qualitative ethnographic approach through the lens of the exploratory research M.D.s (Medical Doctors), DNP/ARNP (Doctor of Nursing/Advanced Practice), MSN/RN/LPN (Nurses), PharmD (Pharmacists), and MSW/LICSW (Social Workers) focused on the recent Conference *Advancing in Healthcare Equity Through Policy and Practice* from the lenses of the University of Washington Continuing Education Conference held on 19-20. October 2023.

The contents will answer the following two problem statement questions from the research study:

1. How can customer patient advocacy be maximized by utilizing Health Care Information Systems?
2. Finally, what are the interconnected issues from the State of Washington with the national statistical data surrounding a secure patient-centered healthcare system?

Imagine personal health information flowing seamlessly between organizations and devices as needed (Sweeney, 2013). This liquidity in personal health information is the norm according to the American Recovery and Reinvestment Act (ARRA) of 2009, which provides financial compensation to healthcare providers and hospitals for using electronic records (Sweeney, 2013). The ARRA provides patient measurements, diagnoses, procedures, medications, and demographics along with results that will no longer be stored on paper but in digital format (Sweeney, 2013). Therefore, HCIS provides essential data sharing and exchange for repositories, networks, and comprehensive databases (Gil Manso et al., 2023). A broad range of concerns about these initiatives has been previously raised as concerns about these initiative safeguards cause continuous questions regarding patient protection (Sweeney, 2013).

1. **How can customer patient advocacy be maximized by utilizing Health Care Information Systems?**

RESPONSE TO PROBLEM STATEMENT 1

Statewide databases have been around for several years and shared widely. However, HCIS still has many problems, as one might expect to be able to point to a litany of challenges but a lack of enforcement (Gil Manso et al., 2023). Customer advocacy can be maximized with HCIS if the system is used appropriately (Thai & Mai, 2023; Gil Manso et al., 2023). Unfortunately, many healthcare facilities are not aligned with information systems that provide cybersecurity functionality to their customer base (Alsubai et al., 2023). Better options promise to come from technology (Anderson et al., 2023; Creapeau, 2023; Siripurapu et al., 2023). The same technology provides data-rich security and privacy protection (Siripurapu et al., 2023). The Health Information Portability and Accountability Act (HIPAA) in the United States is a federal regulation dictating the sharing of medical information beyond the immediate care of the patient and immediate care of the patient (Sweeney, 2013). However, it is supposed to safeguard patient information from physicians, hospitals, and insurers who may share a patient's medical information. State data collections are exempt from HIPAA and share data mandated by State legislation in any form it deems appropriate (Sweeney, 2013).

According to DSHS (2018), client counts and service costs include the number of individuals served during the year, use rates, and direct service expenditures. Due to population estimates, use rates are consistent with the current problems and issues in the healthcare industry (Creapeau, 2023). Many states share health information with less than a year's specification on admissions and discharges and, in some cases, provide the month and year of birth, not just the year. Hence, the systemic issue with HCIS and customer patient care and advocacy (Gil Manso et al., 2023). The data for Washington State reflects statewide use of Department of Social Health Services (DSHS) services for the fiscal years available. See Table 5—statewide Data – Total DSHS Clients FY2012 to FY2017.

Table 5. Statewide data: Total DSHS clients FY2012 to FY2017 (DSHS, 2018)

Fiscal Year	2012	2013	2014	2015	2016	2017
Total Clients	2,534,582	2,550,334	2,744,991	2,857,651	2,902,587	2,910,060
Percent of Total State Population	37%	37%	37%	40%	40%	40%

SUMMARY OF PROBLEM STATEMENT 1

In summary, HCIS for computer storage efficiency contains security measurements that protect and safeguard information (Gil Manso et al., 2023). However, other states utilize HIPAA standards. The HCIS provide a more extraordinary resource for structure, accountability, and security as password encryptions and other cyber methodology contain codes to understand the most explicit specific patient record (Sweeney, 2013; Gil Manso et al., 2023). The best method of re-identifying health data utilizing HCIS involves unique and specific medical records indicating the best direct automated approach (Sweeney, 2013). Demographics appear in medical data, restoring the names and contact information or unique combinations (Sweeney, 2013).

2. **Finally, what are the interconnected issues from the State of Washington with the national statistical data surrounding a secure patient-centered healthcare system?**

RESPONSE TO PROBLEM STATEMENT 2

The interconnected issues in the State of Washington stem from a lack of quality and equitable mental health care, visible as evidenced by patient demographics. The information allows for awareness of public health and the economic burden associated with intentional and non-intentional fatalities in the United States. Washington State remains a leading state with higher suicide rates compared to the national average. Moreover, demographic collection provides educational outreach among all healthcare entities regarding the alarming Youth Mental Health issues and death by suicide rates amongst the black, brown, and indigenous communities of Washington State.

The data presented reminds academic communities that there is still an immense need to create policies, healthcare entities, and restructuring mindsets to intersect the root of these severe problems. Even Washington State's Mental health sector targeted interventions in response to the lack of equitable and quality mental health care services in these communities. These interventions were staggering as statistics shed light on the King County failure of patient advocacy, as there was a 67.1% increase in African American youth who died by suicide from 2007-2020 in the State of Washington (DBR, 2022).

If the State of Washington had a competent intelligible health care information system (HCIS) system with an algorithm that identified potential problems, one might be able to avoid fatalities. Healthcare professionals need assistance from the State to alleviate these outcomes. The customer-patient advocacy and the discrepancies associated with lack of awareness create "domino effects" on the overall safety and security of consumers within the State. As residents become familiar with racial inequities and learn about the healthcare benefits and resources available to them, one can reduce disparities.

Application of Two Mutually Exclusive Categories in Measuring Patient Advocacy

There are two mutually exclusive categories: White Non-Minority and Any Minority. Additionally, clients identified as belonging to one or more minority groups included a percentage for each group specified. The percentage is a proportion of the total clients served. See Table 6. Population of Non-Hispanic and Any Minority DSHS Clients – State of Washington Fiscal Year 2022. (DSHS, 2022).

Table 6. Population of non-Hispanic and any minority DSHS clients: State of Washington fiscal year 2022 (DSHS, 2022)

	Population	Clients	Non-Hispanic White	Any Minority
Total Population for Washington State	7,656,200		67%	33%
Population at or below the Federal Poverty Level		967,280	69%	31%

Summation of Table 6

The contents within this dataset population show the disparity between non-Hispanic/White customer patient advocacy and that of any minority. This table is a distinction of client disparity amongst individuals of ethnic minority and racial groups. The demographic and segment of the market within the State of Washington are largely ignored, as nearly 70% of advocacy is given to white clientele (DBR, 2022; DSHS, 2022).

Differentiation of Minority Detail Based on Percentage Race Ethnicity Amongst DSHS Clientele

Per the table below, the minority differentiation for this market segment discloses a percentage race/ethnicity of DSHS Clients for the State of Washington as of FY2022. The statistical data from DSHS Clients show that of the population for Washington State versus the national population or Federal Poverty Level. The cultural or minority segments show increases above and below the national average for each population. See Table 7. Percentage Race/Ethnicity of DSHS Clients All Ages – State of Washington Fiscal Year 2022 (DSHS, 2022).

Table 7. Percentage race/ethnicity of DSHS clients all ages: State of Washington fiscal year 2022 (DSHS, 2022)

MINORITY DETAIL	Black/African-American	American Indian / Alaska Native	Asian	Native Hawaiian Other Pacific Islander	Hispanic / Latino
Total Population for Washington State	6%	4%	13%	-	13%
Population at or below the Federal Poverty Level	7%	2%	7%	0%	22%

Summation of Table 7

The contents within this dataset population show how race and ethnicity affect DSHS client service resources. However, some ethnic categories show a decrease from the national average. Some categories, such as American Indian / Alaska Native, show the State of Washington has a higher percentage of 4% than the national average of 2% (DSHS, 2022). Moreover, the Asian population in the State of Washington is nearly 13% more than the national average of 7%. All other cultural and ethnic segments within the State of Washington show a decrease in overall population norms (DSHS, 2022).

Medical Eligibility Totals for Title 19 and Non-Title 19

Summation of Table 8

The medical eligibility for potential clients in Washington is nearly 2.4 million individuals. Furthermore, non-Hispanic whites comprise nearly 47% of that population (DSHS, 2022). Furthermore, any minority of cultural or ethnic background consists of 48%. Under Title 19, statistics show that there is an equilibrium of medical eligibility of 48% for both groups (DSHS, 2022). However, with non-title 19, non-Hispanic whites show a disparity of 34% and any minority of 53% of the population size (DBR, 2022; DSHS, 2022). See Table 8. Medical Eligibility Total for Research and Data Analysis (DSHS, 2022).

Table 8. Medical eligibility total for research and data analysis (DSHS, 2022)

	Clients	Non-Hispanic White	Any Minority
Medical Eligible Total	**2,341,470**	47%	48%
Medical Eligible Title 19	967,280	48%	48%
Medically Eligible, not Title 19	122,826	34%	53%

Differentiation of Minority Detail Based on Medical Eligibility Total and Percentage Race Based on Ethnicity

Summation of Table 9

In this table, the contents are disseminated into cultural groups based on percentages (DSHS, 2022). Additionally, medical eligibility is 11% for African Americans. Medical eligibility non-Title 19 is 6% (DSHS, 2022). The national average for medical eligibility for Hispanic/Latino is 24%, and non-Title 19 is 36% (DSHS, 2022). See Table 9. Medical Eligibility Total – Minority Detail (DSHS, 2022).

Table 9. medical eligibility total: Minority detail (DSHS, 2022)

Minority Detail	Black/African-American	American Indian / Alaska Native	Asian	Native Hawaiian Other Pacific Islander	Hispanic / Latino
Medical Eligible Total	11%	7%	3%	0%	24%
Medical Eligible Title 19	11%	7%	3%	0%	23%
Medically Eligible, not Title 19	6%	4%	8%	0%	36%

However, health database organizations (HDOs) hold considerable promise as a reasonably comprehensive source of information to provide a general idea of potential results, outcomes, trends, and factors:

1. **Improved Patient Engagement:** Effective HCIS systems may lead to improved patient engagement through better access to their health information and the ability to communicate with healthcare providers. The research can lead to more informed and empowered patients.

2. **Enhanced Personalization:** HCIS can enable healthcare providers to tailor their advocacy efforts to individual patient needs based on demographics and medical history. The research can result in more personalized care and support.

3. **Compliance with Healthcare Policies:** HCIS can help healthcare facilities ensure compliance with healthcare policies, particularly in data security and patient confidentiality. The exchange can lead to increased patient trust in the system.

4. **Reduced Disparities:** By analyzing patient demographics, HCIS can help identify disparities in care and patient advocacy. This data can inform targeted interventions to reduce healthcare disparities and promote equitable access to care.

5. **Efficient Advocacy Services:** Access to HCIS can streamline the delivery of advocacy services, making it more efficient and effective. Patients may experience shorter wait times, improved communication, and a better healthcare experience.

6. **Patient Empowerment:** Patients who have access to their health records and are involved in the decision-making process may feel more empowered in managing their health, resulting in better health outcomes.

7. **Improved Data Security:** With the right policies and technologies, HCIS can enhance data security, protecting patient information and rights. The exchange can reduce the risks associated with data breaches.

SUMMARY OF PROBLEM STATEMENT 2

In summary, healthcare providers need assistance in diagnosing and treating issues related to adult mental health. The regulatory, legislative, and administrative measures enhancing healthcare organizations resources is Health Information Portability and Accountability Act (HIPAA), Department of Health and Human Services (DHHS), National Center for Health Statistics (NCHS), National Association of Health Data Organizations (NAHDO), and Affordable Care Act (ACA). These governing organizations provide the "how to" in processing exchanges in health information dissemination of patient privacy and data sharing (DBR, 2022; Creapeau, 2023). Policymakers, researchers, health professionals, purchasers, patients, and others continue to acquire health information (Water et al., 2016). Health databases and organizations use health care delivery or planning for health care reform. However, the State of Washington shares the knowledge of cybersecurity and patient advocacy, resulting in additional requirements for healthcare facilities to meet and acquire more sensitive data. Evaluating regulatory policies to improve the administration of health plans, groups, and public health is most important.

Moreover, there is a public health emergency in the State of Washington, especially its effects on the State's youth. Hospitalizations from overdose rose from 2019 to 2021 in children ages 10-17 (DSHS, 2022; DBR, 2022). The fentanyl drug issue was found to be statistically more present in Indigenous communities compared to other groups. Nevertheless, nationally, public access to this drug is growing nationwide. Other issues of regulatory problems consist of cultural disparities amongst minority datasets with people of color who are not receiving the same care as that of non-Hispanic whites. HCIS protocols could provide opportunities to receive the appropriate information and guidelines needed for patient protection (Water et al., 2016; Gil Manso et al., 2023). The statistics show in some categories that the market segments of culturally diverse individuals experience minimal resources, contributing to the growing demographic of lack of patient advocacy.

Additionally, data reveals catastrophic results affecting survival, as many cases end in fatalities (Water et al., 2016). Healthcare information systems must utilize technology to circumvent the problems electronically to ensure an adequate digital summary of cases with clients recorded. The State Department of Health has targeted efforts to do "rural tours" of clinics and hospitals specific to expanding its understanding of minority healthcare needs. Although regulation exists, they must be linked (or linkable) to primary medical records held by healthcare entities (Sweeney, 2013; Water et al., 2016). Additionally, regulations and legislative databases should provide security safeguards for healthcare facilities and professionals. The lack of security protocols has caused many cyber anomalies and threats. For HCIS protocols to work, organizations need to make security a priority (Gil Manso et al., 2023).

Therefore, other regulatory legal secondary files are generated from primary records or are separate from any patient encounter, as in the case of eligibility or enrollment files for health plans and public programs (Sweeney, 2013). Furthermore, the broader vision of computer-based health information systems, the better it will directly tie into computer patient records (CPS) systems to avoid the terrible patient outcomes that have gone on too long amongst adults and the State's youth. Many experts argue that until CPS systems are mandated as repositories or networks, neither will be complete or reach total health care, research, or policymaking potential.

RECOMMENDATIONS FOR FUTURE INVESTIGATIONS

There are many health inequities in the world: individuals with lower socioeconomic status (SES) often face increased afflictions of disease, more significant disability, and even shorter life expectancies due to lack of access to medical assistance (Martin & Shannon, 2023; Richardson-Parry et al., 2023). Health equity allows individuals to achieve optimal health quality, concern, and aptitude to understand the resources available to everyone (Water et al., 2016; Kohan et al., 2023). These social circumstances contribute to some of the State of Washington's more enormous health deficiencies. However, it is becoming increasingly significant and needs to be addressed by as many patients as possible. Potential prospects suffer from a lack of resources, especially in colored, underserved communities.

Here are some recommendations for the State of Washington for the Health Care Information Systems (HCIS) initiative and potential opportunities for future investigation into other areas within the spectrum of customer patient advocacy and cyber health care deficiencies:

1. **Invest in HCIS Integration:** The State should prioritize the integration of HCIS across healthcare facilities, ensuring seamless data sharing and communication. Promoting the adoption of interoperable systems can improve care coordination and reduce medical errors (Alsubai et al., 2023; Gil-Manso et al., 2023).

2. **Data Security Measures:** Implement stringent data security measures, including encryption, access controls, and regular security audits to safeguard patient information. Healthcare organizations should adhere to industry standards and regulations to protect against cyber threats (DBR, 2022; Gil-Manso et al., 2023).

3. **Patient Education Initiatives:** Develop and implement patient education programs to raise awareness about patient rights and the importance of informed decision-making. These programs can be tailored to diverse demographic groups to ensure inclusivity (Anderson et al., 2023; Kohan et al., 2023; Choi, 2015).

4. **Access to Advocacy Services:** Expand access to patient advocacy services, particularly for underserved communities. The interoperability may involve increasing the number of patient advocates and ensuring their cultural competence to address the diverse population of Washington (Martin & Sibbald, 2023; Anderson et al., 2023).

5. **Community Outreach and Health Promotion:** Invest in community outreach and health promotion programs that target the social determinants of health, aiming to reduce disparities in healthcare access and outcomes (Choi, 2015; Alsubai et al., 2023).

6. **Telehealth Expansion:** Continue expanding telehealth services, making it easier for patients to access care, especially in remote or underserved areas. Ensure that patients have the necessary technology and support for telehealth visits (Emrich et al., 2023; Kohan et al., 2023; Ra et al., 2023).

7. **Collaboration and Information Sharing:** Encourage healthcare facilities to collaborate and share best practices for patient advocacy and data security. This collaborative approach can improve standards and guidelines (DBR, 2022; Hussain et al., 2023).

8. **Regulatory Oversight:** Strengthen regulatory oversight to ensure healthcare providers comply with data security and patient advocacy requirements. Regular audits, legislative policy, and penalties for non-compliance can incentivize adherence to standards (DBR, 2022).

9. **Research and Data Analysis:** Invest in ongoing research and data analysis to track the impact of these recommendations and identify areas where further improvements are needed. Evidence-based decision-making can guide future initiatives (Gil-Manso et al., 2023).

These recommendations collectively aim to improve the State's healthcare system, addressing deficiencies in HCIS, patient advocacy, and cyber health, while promoting equitable access to quality care and the protection of patient rights. Implementing these measures will require collaboration among healthcare providers, policymakers, and technology experts, focusing on the unique needs of Washington's diverse population. See Table 10. Roadmap for Future Investigations.

In this section, the ethnographic qualitative research analysis presented in this study sheds light on the statistical details of customer patient advocacy in the healthcare sector within the State of Washington. It is evident that the issues surrounding patient advocacy deficiencies, particularly among underserved communities, warrant further investigation to address the pressing concerns related to unequal access to quality healthcare and the disparities in healthcare outcomes and experiences. The researchers believe this information can potentially build insights and findings into future investigations.

Table 10. Roadmap for future investigations

	Roadmap Variables	Ongoing Research, Data Analysis, and Future Investigations
(1)	Health Care Information Systems and Patient Advocacy	One of the central questions posed in this research study is how customer-patient advocacy can maximized through the utilization of Health Care Information Systems. Future research should delve deeper into the integration of information systems within healthcare settings and assess their impact on improving patient advocacy. Investigating the implementation of electronic health records, patient portals, and other digital tools in fostering patient engagement, shared decision-making, and informed consent can provide valuable insights. Moreover, a comparative analysis of different healthcare facilities or systems that have adopted varying levels of information technology can help identify best practices and potential areas for improvement.
(2)	Interconnected Issues Between State and National Statistics	The study highlights the interconnected issues between the State of Washington's healthcare statistics and national data, particularly regarding secure patient-centered healthcare systems. To further address these issues, future research should aim to establish a comprehensive understanding of how state-specific policies and practices impact the overall healthcare landscape. The determinants could involve examining healthcare policies unique to Washington, such as Medicaid expansion and healthcare provider regulations, and how these policies interact with national trends. Additionally, comparative studies with other states facing similar challenges can provide a broader perspective on addressing healthcare disparities.
(3)	Assessing the Impact of Healthcare Reform and Initiatives	As healthcare entities build on the urgent need for healthcare reform and initiatives to address healthcare disparities, future research should assess the effectiveness of specific policy interventions and initiatives to improve patient advocacy. These may include evaluating the impact of legislative changes, public health campaigns, or community outreach programs on reducing disparities and enhancing patient-centered care. Comparative studies across different states or regions with varying policy approaches can help identify successful strategies that can be adapted to the unique context of Washington state.
(4)	Patient-Centered Healthcare Models	Given the focus on patient-centered care in this research, future investigations should explore innovative healthcare models and interventions that prioritize the needs and preferences of patients. Comparative studies on healthcare facilities or systems that have successfully transitioned to patient-centered care models can offer valuable insights into best practices and potential challenges. Additionally, research could delve into patient feedback and satisfaction surveys to gauge the impact of patient-centered care initiatives on overall healthcare experiences.

CONCLUSION

In closing, the study's significance lies in its potential to inform healthcare professionals about strategies that enhance patient advocacy (Richardson-Parry et al., 2023). Additionally, improve access to care, address healthcare disparities, and safeguard patient rights in Washington's healthcare system (Richardson-Parry et al., 2023). Research in this area can support bridging the gap between technological advancements in HCIS and the delivery of patient-centered care, ultimately benefiting the health and well-being of the State's residents (Siripurapu et al., 2023). Despite efforts to digitize health records, many healthcare facilities in the State still need to improve their systems. This lack of standardized information exchange hampers efficient care coordination and can result in medical errors and delayed treatment (Richardson-Parry et al., 2023). Patient data security is also a pressing concern, as there have been data breaches and cyberattacks targeting healthcare organizations, compromising the confidentiality of sensitive patient information (Nguyen et al., 2022).

The value and importance of the research's findings potentially inform healthcare policymakers and providers about the role HCIS plays in promoting patient advocacy (Richardson-Parry et al., 2023; Water et al., 2016). While also providing other subsequent alternatives such as patient awareness, patient resources, and telehealth services to provide individuals in underprivileged environments opportunities to learn what state services are available to the consumer (Siripurapu et al., 2023; Richardson-Parry et al., 2023). Suppose the State can influence these groups of underprivileged consumers through awareness programs. In that case, the State of Washington can potentially improve on some of the negative statistics associated with depression, stress, anxiety, suicide, and other mental health challenges (Schwartz, 2002).

Attaining an HCIS subset with an online application can provide individuals without access to information to utilize public venues such as the State of Washington libraries and other healthcare resources to process and gain information regarding advocacy participation (Water et al., 2016). One of the main challenges in the State is patient engagement (Siripurapu et al., 2023). Without the State of Washington investing in engaging its consumer base, the statistical data will continue to rise in detrimental public health areas (Richardson-Parry et al., 2023). Investigating this broad spectrum of health capital can only influence healthcare policies, demographics, and advocacy centers around the State. This knowledge can guide efforts to improve the healthcare logistical footprint and address disparities, ultimately leading to better patient outcomes and a more equitable healthcare landscape (Nguyen et al., 2022; Schwartz, 2002). Health Care Information Systems (HCIS) is the future, and the State of Washington needs to assess how customer patient advocacy, alongside cyber health deficiencies, has emerged as significant issues (Richardson-Parry et al., 2023). These problems are interconnected and have far-reaching consequences for healthcare providers and patients (Nguyen et al., 2022).

In conclusion, this study underscores the pressing need for further research to address the critical issues surrounding patient advocacy deficiencies in Washington state. By pursuing these research recommendations and conclusions, we can contribute to the ongoing efforts to achieve equitable and patient-centered healthcare for all residents of the State, ultimately improving healthcare outcomes and experiences. This research can have significant implications not only for Washington state but also for healthcare systems nationwide.

REFERENCES

Alsubai, S., Alqahtani, A., Sha, M., Abbas, S., Gregus, M., & Furda, R. (2023). Automated Cognitive Health Assessment Based on Daily Life Functional Activities. *Computational Intelligence and Neuroscience*, *2023*, 1–8. Advance online publication. doi:10.1155/2023/5684914 PMID:37455767

Anderson, E., Wiener, R. S., Molloy-Paolillo, B., McCullough, M., Kim, B., Harris, J. I., Rinne, S. T., Elwy, A. R., & Bokhour, B. G. (2023). Using a person-centered approach in clinical care for patients with complex chronic conditions: Perspectives from healthcare professionals caring for Veterans with COPD in the U.S. Veterans Health Administration's Whole Health System of Care. *PLoS One*, *18*(6), e0286326. Advance online publication. doi:10.1371/journal.pone.0286326 PMID:37352241

Arnout, B. A., Abdel-Rahman, D. E., Elprince, M., Abada, A. A., & Jasim, K. J. (2020). Ethnographic research method for psychological and medical studies in light of COVID-19 pandemic outbreak: Theoretical approach. *Journal of Public Affairs*, *20*(4), 1–8. doi:10.1002/pa.2404

Bhattacharya, M., Wang, F., & Jiao, F. (2023). Modeling Public Sector Corruption and the Institutional Environment in Emerging Economies: An Institutional Theory View. *The Journal of Applied Business and Economics*, *25*(2), 225–242. https://www.proquest.com/scholarly-journals/modeling-public-sector-corruption-institutional/docview/2827993038/se-2

Broughton, T. C., Weggelaar-Jansen, A., & de Graaff, B. (2023). The development of Dutch COVID-19 ICU triage guidelines from an institutional work perspective. *PLoS One, 18*(9), e0291075. Advance online publication. doi:10.1371/journal.pone.0291075 PMID:37708167

Carter, N., Bryant-Lukosius, D., DiCenso, A., Blythe, J., & Neville, A. J. (2014). The use of triangulation in qualitative research. *Oncology Nursing Forum, 41*(5), 545–547. doi:10.1188/14.ONF.545-547 PMID:25158659

Choi, P. P. (2015). Patient advocacy: the role of the nurse. *Nursing Standard, 29*(41), 52. doi:10.7748/ns.29.41.52.e9772

Covaleski, M. A., Dirsmith, M. W., & Michelman, J. E. (1993). An institutional theory perspective on the DRG framework, case-mix accounting systems, and healthcare organizations. *Accounting, Organizations and Society, 18*(1), 65–80. doi:10.1016/0361-3682(93)90025-2

Creapeau, L. J. G. (2023). Mining for Gold: Recruiting Successful Leaders to Long-Term Care Administration. *The Journal of Health Administration Education, 39*(2), 215–236. https://www.proquest.com/scholarly-journals/mining-gold-recruiting-successful-leaders-long/docview/2788803631/se-2

Data Breach Report (DBR). (2022). *Washington State Attorney General's Office. Special Edition Data Privacy.* https://agportal-s3bucket.s3.amazonaws.com/DBR2022%20v5.pdf

Denzin, N. K. (1978). *Sociological methods: A sourcebook.* McGraw-Hill.

DSHS. (2022). *Client Data. Client Counts and Service Costs.* https://clientdata.rda.dshs.wa.gov/Home/ShowReport?reportMode=1

Emrich, I. A., Fröhlich-güzelsoy, L., Bruns, F., Friedrich, B., & Frewer, A. (2014). Clinical Ethics and Patient Advocacy: The Power of Communication in Health Care. *HEC Forum, 26*(2), 111–124. doi:10.1007/s10730-013-9225-1 PMID:24368580

Fern, E. F. (1982). *The use of focus groups for idea generation: The effects of group size, acquaintanceship, and moderator on response quantity and quality.* Retrieved from https://www.uta.edu/faculty/richarme/MARK%205338/Articles/Fern.pdf

Gil-Manso, S., Herrero-Quevedo, D., Carbonell, D., Martínez-Bonet, M., Bernaldo-de-Quirós, E., Kennedy-Batalla, R., Gallego-Valle, J., López-Esteban, R., Blázquez-López, E., Miguens-Blanco, I., Correa-Rocha, R., Gomez-Verdejo, V., & Pion, M. (2023). Multidimensional analysis of immune cells from COVID-19 patients identified cell subsets associated with the severity at hospital admission. *PLoS Pathogens, 19*(6), e1011432. Advance online publication. doi:10.1371/journal.ppat.1011432 PMID:37311004

Hussian, A., Mateen, A., Amin, F., Muhammad, A. A., & Ullah, S. (2023). Health Monitoring Apps: An Evaluation of the Persuasive System Design Model for Human Wellbeing. *Information (Basel), 14*(7), 412. doi:10.3390/info14070412

Jones, J., & Smith, J. (2017). Ethnography: challenges and opportunities. *Evidence-Based Nursing, 20*, 98–100. doi:10.1136/eb-2017-102786

Kohan, K. S., Sabet, F. P., & Darvishpour, A. (2023). Explaining the process of playing the role of a nurse as a patient advocate in the emergency department: Providing a theoretical model [Explicación del proceso de desempeñar el papel de una enfermera como defensora del paciente en el departamento de emergencias: proporcionar un modelo teórico]. *Revista Latinoamericana de Hipertensiòn*, *18*(3), 124–132. doi:10.5281/zenodo.8051101

Ma, Y., Wang, J., & Bai, Y. (2023). Macro-Institutional Pressures and Firms' Environmental Management Behavior: The Moderating Effect of Micro-Institutional Pressures. *Sustainability (Basel)*, *15*(4), 3662. doi:10.3390/su15043662

Martin, J., & Sibbald, S. (2023). The Use of Patient Engagement as a Means to Improve Equitable Care. *The International Journal of Health, Wellness & Society*, *13*(2), 39–52. doi:10.18848/2156-8960/CGP/v13i02/39-52

Nguyen, C. Q., Kariyawasam, D., Alba-Concepcion, K., Grattan, S., Hetherington, K., Wakefield, C. E., Woolfenden, S., Dale, R. C., Palmer, E. E., & Farrar, M. A. (2022). 'Advocacy groups are the connectors': Experiences and contributions of rare disease patient organization leaders in advanced neurotherapeutics. *Health Expectations*, *25*(6), 3175–3191. doi:10.1111/hex.13625 PMID:36307981

Patton, M. Q. (1999). Enhancing the quality and credibility of qualitative analysis. Health Science Research, 34, 1189–1208.

Ra, K., Hong, S., & Yang, D. (2023). How Are a Firm's Strategic Motives for Environmental Innovation Impeded? The Negative Influences of Institutional Pressures. *Systems*, *11*(2), 79. doi:10.3390/systems11020079

Richardson-Parry, A., Baas, C., Donde, S., Ferraiolo, B., Karmo, M., Maravic, Z., Münter, L., Ricci-Cabello, I., Silva, M., Tinianov, S., Valderas, J. M., Woodruff, S., & Joris, V. (2023). Interventions to reduce cancer screening inequities: The perspective and role of patients, advocacy groups, and empowerment organizations. *International Journal for Equity in Health*, *22*(1), 1–9. doi:10.1186/s12939-023-01841-6 PMID:36707816

Rohs, C. M., Albright, K. R., Monteith, L. L., Lane, A. D., & Fehling, K. B. (2023). Perspectives of V.A. healthcare from rural women veterans not enrolled in or using V.A. healthcare. *PLoS One*, *18*(8), e0289885. Advance online publication. doi:10.1371/journal.pone.0289885 PMID:37578986

Rubenstein, L. V., Curtis, I., Wheat, C. L., Grembowski, D. E., Stockdale, S. E., Kaboli, P. J., Yoon, J., Felker, B. L., Reddy, A. S., & Nelson, K. M. (2023). Learning from the national implementation of the Veterans Affairs Clinical Resource Hub (CRH) program for improving access to care: Protocol for a six-year evaluation. *BMC Health Services Research*, *23*(1), 1–12. doi:10.1186/s12913-023-09799-5 PMID:37488518

Schwartz, L. (2002). Is there an advocate in the house? The role of health care professionals in patient advocacy. *Journal of Medical Ethics*, *28*(1), 37–40. doi:10.1136/jme.28.1.37 PMID:11834758

Siripurapu, S., Darimireddy, N. K., Chehri, A., Sridhar, B., & Paramkusam, A. V. (2023). Technological Advancements and Elucidation Gadgets for Healthcare Applications: An Exhaustive Methodological Review-Part-I (A.I. et al.). *Electronics (Basel)*, *12*(3), 750. doi:10.3390/electronics12030750

Spradley, J. P. (1979). *The ethnographic interview. New York, NY. Hot*. Rhinehart.

Stebbins, R. A. (2001). *The art of case study research*. Sage.

Stolwijk, M. L., van Nispen, R. M. A., van der Ham, A. J., Veenman, E., & van Rens, G. H. M. B. (2023). Barriers and facilitators in the referral pathways to low vision services from the perspective of patients and professionals: A qualitative study. *BMC Health Services Research, 23*(1), 1–14. doi:10.1186/s12913-022-09003-0 PMID:36681848

SweeneyL. (2013). *Matching known patients to health records in Washington State Data*. doi:10.2139/ssrn.2289850

Thai, Q. H., & Mai, K. N. (2023). An evolution of entrepreneurial culture studies: A systematic literature review and future research agenda. *Entrepreneurial Business and Economics Review, 11*(2), 31–62. doi:10.15678/EBER.2023.110202

Van Maanen, J. (1988). *Tales of the field: On writing ethnography*. University of Chicago Press.

Visser, S. S., Hutter, I., & Haisma, H. (2016). Building a framework for theory-based ethnographies for studying intergenerational family food practices. *Appetite, 97*, 49–57. doi:10.1016/j.appet.2015.11.019 PMID:26593100

Washington State Office of the Attorney General (WSOAG). (2023). *Data Breach Notifications. Attorney General Bob Ferguson*. https://www.atg.wa.gov/data-breach-notifications

WaTech. (2023). *Washington Technology Services. Office of Privacy and Data Protection*. https://watech.wa.gov/privacy/office-of-privacy-and-data-protection

Water, T., Ford, K., Spence, D., & Rasmussen, S. (2016). Patient advocacy by nurses - past, present, and future. *Contemporary Nurse, 52*(6), 696–709. doi:10.1080/10376178.2016.1235981 PMID:27636537

Wolcott, H. F. (1995). *The art of fieldwork*. AltaMira Press.

Zippia. (2022). *Patient Advocate Demographics and Statistics in the U.S.* https://www.zippia.com/patient-advocate-jobs/demographics/

Chapter 8
Healthcare Technologies to Address Driving Under the Influence (DUI) of Marijuana

Quatavia McLester
https://orcid.org/0000-0003-1596-0517
Capitol Technology University, USA

Darrell Norman Burrell
https://orcid.org/0000-0002-4675-9544
Capitol Technology University, USA

ABSTRACT

In recent years, the United States has confronted an escalating public health and safety challenge brought about by the proliferation of driving under the influence (DUI) of marijuana. This predicament has arisen due to the legalization of marijuana for medicinal and recreational purposes across several states, engendering a substantial rise in the presence of marijuana-impaired drivers on the nation's roadways. This scholarly work explores the contemporary landscape of marijuana DUI legislation, the pervasiveness of marijuana-impaired driving incidents, and the consequential health and safety hazards. The analysis underscores the exigency for pioneering healthcare technologies and strategic interventions to enhance the detection and deterrence of marijuana-impaired driving. This chapter posits that such healthcare technological advancements, combined with comprehensive strategies, promise to ameliorate the burgeoning menace of cannabis-related DUI and its impact on public health and safety in the United States by exploring current literature.

INTRODUCTION

In recent years, the utilization of marijuana for both medicinal and recreational purposes has experienced a marked surge in popularity across the United States, coinciding with a growing number of states endorsing its legal usage, as underscored by the National Institute on Drug Abuse (2020). Concurrently,

DOI: 10.4018/979-8-3693-1970-3.ch008

according to data from the Substance Abuse and Mental Health Services Administration (2020), marijuana consumption has seen a notable upswing, particularly among young adults, with an estimated 22.2 million individuals self-reporting marijuana usage in 2019. This heightened prevalence of marijuana consumption has invariably contributed to an elevated incidence of marijuana-impaired driving.

The consumption of marijuana edibles has witnessed a significant increase in recent years, with notable implications for public health and safety (Reboussin et al., 2019; Calandrillo & Fulton, 2019; Friese et al., 2016). In contrast to the rapid effects experienced from smoking marijuana, the onset of edibles' effects is considerably delayed, typically taking between 1 to 3 hours to manifest (Reboussin et al., 2019; Calandrillo & Fulton, 2019; Friese et al., 2016). This delay arises from the metabolic process whereby food-based cannabis products are absorbed into the bloodstream through the liver (Reboussin et al., 2019; Calandrillo & Fulton, 2019; Friese et al., 2016).Consequently, users may inadvertently ingest larger quantities of the drug, believing it to be ineffective due to the delayed onset (Reboussin et al., 2019; Calandrillo & Fulton, 2019; Friese et al., 2016). This prolonged effect latency, combined with the absence of standardized and precise THC content information on edible products, contributes to the elevated risk of overconsumption and its associated consequences (Reboussin et al., 2019; Calandrillo & Fulton, 2019; Friese et al., 2016).

One of the paramount concerns with marijuana edibles is the difficulty in accurately measuring THC, the primary psychoactive compound in marijuana. In many cases, edible products lack consistent and reliable THC content labeling, making it challenging for users to gauge their dosage accurately (Reboussin et al., 2019; Calandrillo & Fulton, 2019; Friese et al., 2016). This lack of transparency compounds the risks associated with edible consumption, as users may inadvertently ingest excessive quantities of THC, heightening the potential for adverse effects and complications (Reboussin et al., 2019; Calandrillo & Fulton, 2019; Friese et al., 2016). Furthermore, when individuals have other medications in their system, the intricate interplay between these substances can result in unpredictable THC metabolism, leading to a dangerous five-fold escalation of THC levels in the bloodstream (Reboussin et al., 2019; Calandrillo & Fulton, 2019; Friese et al., 2016).

The repercussions of consuming excessive amounts of marijuana edibles can be severe and distinct from those associated with smoking marijuana (Reboussin et al., 2019; Calandrillo & Fulton, 2019; Friese et al., 2016).Overdose symptoms frequently manifest as intense psychotic episodes, hallucinations, profound paranoia, panic attacks, and pronounced impairment of motor abilities (Reboussin et al., 2019; Calandrillo & Fulton, 2019; Friese et al., 2016). These symptoms are notably more severe and distressing than those arising from a comparable overdose of smoked marijuana. The delayed onset and unpredictability of edible effects, coupled with the challenges in monitoring and controlling THC dosage, underscore the pressing need for heightened awareness and regulation in the realm of marijuana edibles to mitigate the potential dangers associated with their consumption (Reboussin et al., 2019; Calandrillo & Fulton, 2019; Friese et al., 2016).

Significantly, the National Highway Traffic Safety Administration (2020) has corroborated this trend, affirming that marijuana-impaired driving currently ranks as the second most commonly identified substance in drivers involved in fatal motor vehicle accidents, yielding only to alcohol in prevalence. Regrettably, the extant mechanisms for detecting marijuana-induced impairment in drivers lack the requisite reliability and precision exhibited by their counterparts tasked with identifying alcohol-impaired driving.

Consequently, an imperative crystallizes—the imperative to conceive and implement pioneering technologies capable of efficaciously detecting instances of driving under the influence of marijuana.

Such an endeavor assumes paramount significance in safeguarding public safety amidst the surge in marijuana usage.

The predicament of driving under the influence (DUI) of marijuana has assumed an increasingly grave and multifaceted dimension within the United States. In 2019, alarming statistics reported by the National Highway Traffic Safety Administration (NHTSA) revealed that over 11 million drivers yielded positive results for marijuana usage in roadside surveys. This distressing trend was further underscored by NHTSA data, which indicated that in 2018 alone, more than 1,700 lives were tragically extinguished in accidents involving drivers who tested positive for marijuana.

The legal strictures surrounding driving under the influence of marijuana are resolute and unyielding, spanning all 50 states, and entail severe legal, financial, and poignant consequences, as articulated by the National Highway Traffic Safety Administration (NHTSA, 2020). The profound impact of marijuana on an individual's capacity to operate a motor vehicle safely cannot be understated, with cannabis infusion precipitating a spectrum of impairments encompassing protracted reaction times, compromised coordination, and a diminished state of vigilance (McCarty & White, 2018). These impairments, in turn, are inexorably linked to an elevated risk of vehicular accidents and an increased propensity for other hazardous behaviors, such as speeding or disregarding traffic regulations (McCarty & White, 2018).

It is imperative to elucidate that driving under the influence of marijuana is strictly prohibited, irrespective of a person's possession of a medical marijuana card. Legal stipulations governing marijuana-impaired driving exhibit variances among states; nevertheless, the overarching consensus upholds the illegality of operating a motor vehicle while under the influence of marijuana, as duly asserted by the National Organization for the Reform of Marijuana Laws (NORML, 2021). Evidencing this legal uniformity, most states have embraced a 'per se' standard for marijuana, designating it unlawful to operate a motor vehicle with a predetermined concentration of THC, the psychoactive constituent of marijuana, in the bloodstream. To illustrate, the operation of a motor vehicle with a THC concentration exceeding five nanograms per milliliter of blood in California is designated as a legal transgression.

The consequences of a DUI conviction diverge from state to state but can encompass imprisonment, monetary penalties, license suspension, and community service. Furthermore, the ramifications of such a conviction extend to the realms of heightened insurance premiums, employment prospects, and financial access, encapsulating the potential for enduring repercussions on an individual's life path. Notably, the stain of a DUI conviction may linger on an individual's record for a protracted period, further impeding their capacity to forge ahead in life (NORML, 2021).

PROBLEM STATEMENT

Empirical evidence unequivocally attests to the burgeoning predicament of driving under the influence of marijuana in the United States. As per the National Highway Traffic Safety Administration (NHTSA), the year 2019 bore witness to an alarming surge, with 11.8 million drivers returning positive results for marijuana usage in roadside surveys—a concerning escalation of 6% from the preceding year when 11.1 million drivers tested positive (NHTSA, 2020). Alarmingly, the NHTSA further underscores the grim toll exacted by this predicament, noting that 1,764 individuals perished in collisions involving drivers who had tested positive for marijuana in 2018, reflecting a distressing 28% increase from the preceding year (NHTSA, 2020).

Furthermore, NHTSA data from the same year discloses that the prevalence of marijuana usage among drivers is most pronounced among the younger demographic. In 2018, 15.1% of drivers aged 16-25 returned positive results for marijuana usage, in stark contrast to 6.9% among drivers aged 26-34 and 4.2% among drivers aged 35 and above (NHTSA, 2020). This disconcerting trend underscores the propensity of younger drivers to operate vehicles under the influence of marijuana, as juxtaposed with their older counterparts (NHTSA, 2020).

In tandem with the findings of the NHTSA, the Centers for Disease Control and Prevention (CDC) corroborates the elevated risk of motor vehicle crash injury associated with marijuana usage. According to the CDC, individuals who partake in marijuana usage exhibit a twofold increased likelihood of being involved in motor vehicle crashes in comparison to their non-marijuana-using counterparts (CDC, 2021). These empirical insights jointly illuminate the grave and multifaceted challenges that underscore the issue of driving under the influence of marijuana.

EMERGING CONTEXTS

Presently, the arsenal of methodologies employed for detecting driving under the influence of marijuana encompasses primarily two categories: blood tests and urine tests, as elaborated upon by Alonso-Alonso and Bialer (2016). Blood tests are widely acknowledged for their precision and reliability in ascertaining the presence of marijuana constituents within an individual's physiological system, yet they simultaneously manifest as the most invasive and economically burdensome to administer. Conversely, urine tests represent a less intrusive and more cost-effective alternative, though they compromise precision and accuracy (Alonso-Alonso & Bialer, 2016).

In conjunction with these established modalities, there is a burgeoning interest among some law enforcement agencies in using saliva tests to identify instances of driving under the influence of marijuana (Alonso-Alonso & Bialer, 2016). Saliva tests, though yet to be universally embraced, bring their non-invasive nature, cost-effectiveness, and accuracy to the forefront.

Of particular note is the advent of the 'Potalyzer,' colloquially known as the marijuana breathalyzer, a novel device engineered to quantify the concentration of tetrahydrocannabinol (THC) within an individual's exhaled breath. Analogous in function to the breathalyzers utilized for the detection of alcohol-impaired driving, this innovation assumes augmented relevance in light of the progressive legalization of marijuana within various states of the United States, coupled with the escalating prevalence of marijuana usage throughout the nation (Cone, 2019).

Another noteworthy paradigm shift emerges in the form of field sobriety tests embraced by specific police departments to detect instances of driving under the influence of marijuana. These tests assess an individual's physical and cognitive aptitude, balance, coordination, and reaction time. However, it is imperative to acknowledge that the subjective nature of these assessments may render their administration complex and susceptible to variability (Alonso-Alonso & Bialer, 2016).

THE HEALTHCARE TECHNOLOGIES

In light of the inherent constraints besetting extant detection methods, an exigent necessity emerges for the innovation and development of novel technologies designed to detect instances of driving under the influence of marijuana effectively. One prospective technological avenue currently under examination involves deploying eye-tracking devices, as Hanson and Schwartz (2018) alluded to. These sophisticated devices leverage high-resolution cameras and intricate computer algorithms to meticulously monitor and record an individual's ocular movements, a mechanism hitherto successfully applied to detect alcohol-impaired driving (Hanson & Schwartz, 2018). However, the application of such technology to the detection of marijuana-impaired driving remains a subject of ongoing research and empirical validation.

THE POTALYZER

An innovative device known as the 'Potalyzer' has emerged as a prospective solution in the realm of detection for marijuana-impaired driving, offering a functionality analogous to the breathalyzers harnessed for alcohol-impaired driving detection (Cone, 2019). The distinguishing feature of the Potalyzer lies in its capacity to exclusively identify the presence of THC, the psychoactive component inherent to marijuana, by scrutinizing an individual's exhaled breath (Cone, 2019). However, it is imperative to underscore that this device is still in the incipient stages of development and has not yet garnered legal sanction for employment by law enforcement agencies (Cone, 2019).

The genesis of the Potalyzer can be traced back to the early 2000s, marked by its nascent developmental stage and absence from commercial availability. It was pioneered through collaborative efforts of researchers in the United Kingdom and the United States, yielding the Cannibuster in the U.K., designed to detect THC in breath, and the Cannibuster II in the U.S., equipped with the capability to detect THC and CBD (cannabidiol) within an individual's exhalation (Cone, 2019) and subsequent years witnessed technological advancements and the surging prevalence of marijuana usage, culminating in the development of more sophisticated iterations of the device. The initial commercial Potalyzer, introduced by SannTek, a Colorado-based company, emerged as the SannTek Potalyzer, capable of detecting THC, CBD, and a spectrum of other cannabinoids within an individual's breath. Its debut in law enforcement occurred in Colorado in 2016, setting a precedent for other companies to create their versions of the Potalyzer, including the Cannabix FAIMS device developed by Cannabix Technologies.

Nonetheless, the underpinning technology of the Potalyzer remains within the early phases of evolution, with various milestones awaiting achievement before legal sanction for law enforcement usage can be conferred (Murray, 2018). Foremost among these prerequisites is the imperative for the device to accurately demonstrate the precision required for measuring THC concentration in an individual's breath (Mokrysz & Freeman, 2015). Moreover, the device must consistently and reliably detect THC in breath, even after marijuana consumption (Mokrysz & Freeman, 2015). It is essential to emphasize that the Potalyzer has not yet received official approval for deployment by law enforcement agencies (Lennon et al., 2020).

The prospective integration of the Potalyzer into law enforcement practices can potentially exert a transformative influence on the criminal justice system. For instance, it could expedite the process of accurately identifying and prosecuting drivers impaired by marijuana, thereby mitigating the likelihood of acquittals due to evidentiary gaps or an inability to establish impairment (Murray, 2018).

However, despite its promising utility, the Potalyzer grapples with several limitations. Foremost among these is the device's current lack of commercial availability, rendering it in a prototype stage and without official approval for employment by law enforcement. Furthermore, its accuracy in measuring

THC concentration in breath and its ability to detect THC presence post-marijuana consumption remain subjects of ongoing refinement (Murray, 2018).

A secondary concern centers on the potential for false positives resulting from the device's employment, mainly when individuals have recently consumed marijuana but have not yet metabolized it or have ingested products containing THC in insufficient quantities to induce impairment (Murray, 2018). If individuals return positive results for THC without corresponding impairment, this could engender unwarranted legal proceedings, potentially leading to the unjust prosecution of innocent individuals for DUI (Murray, 2018).

OVERVIEW OF ARTIFICIAL INTELLIGENCE TECHNOLOGY

Artificial Intelligence (A.I.) represents an advanced computational technology framework that empowers machines to emulate human behavior and decision-making (Cohen, 2019). Its versatile applications span various domains, encompassing healthcare, finance, transportation, and a burgeoning adoption within the precincts of criminal justice, traffic management, and profiling (Cohen, 2019). In these contexts, A.I. is harnessed for activities such as the surveillance of criminal conduct, regulating traffic dynamics, and identifying individuals implicated in criminal activities (Cohen, 2019). A.I. technology equips itself to scrutinize data comprehensively, furnishing insights that can be leveraged to identify patterns within criminal behavior and guide law enforcement decisions (Cohen, 2019).

Explorations researchers have ventured into the application of artificial intelligence (A.I.) to detect individuals driving under the influence of marijuana (Lau et al., 2018). A.I. exhibits the potential to analyze an individual's behavior, particularly discernible through their driving patterns, to ascertain potential marijuana impairment (Lau et al., 2018). Although this technology remains in its inceptive stages of development, it presents considerable promise for detecting marijuana-impaired driving (Lau et al., 2018).

A.I. technology has been harnessed for the detection of marijuana-impaired driving via a diversity of mechanisms. One of the prevailing methodologies entails deploying A.I. to identify the presence of THC, the principal psychoactive constituent within marijuana, either within an individual's breath or blood. This is accomplished through specialized breathalyzers designed for THC detection or by analyzing blood samples for the presence of THC.

An alternate approach to deploying A.I. for detecting marijuana-impaired driving is founded on facial recognition technology. This innovative framework can discern signs of inebriation by scrutinizing facial features, encompassing pupil dilation, ocular redness, and other symptoms of impairment. In parallel, this technology can distinguish when an individual has been operating a vehicle under the influence of marijuana by examining these same facial cues.

Furthermore, A.I. technology is instrumental in identifying marijuana-impaired driving patterns based on an individual's behavior behind the wheel. It adeptly detects deviations in driving conduct indicative of impairment, such as erratic swerving, speeding, or a failure to adhere to traffic regulations. In an analogous vein, A.I. technology is attuned to identifying instances of erratic driving by leveraging data emanating from a vehicle's sensors, including the accelerometer and gyroscope.

CONCLUSION

The perils associated with driving under the influence of marijuana are unequivocal, necessitating exploring multiple potential strategies to curtail this menace. One pivotal approach involves amplifying public awareness regarding the risks entailed in marijuana-impaired driving (National Highway Traffic Safety Administration, 2020). These approaches to public awareness can be effectuated through various channels, encompassing public service announcements, educational initiatives, and media coverage. Additionally, instigating educational programs within schools enlightens the younger demographic regarding the perils of operating a vehicle under the influence of marijuana (National Highway Traffic Safety Administration, 2020).

Concurrently, augmenting the penalties for driving under the influence of marijuana emerges as another viable course of action. These penalties encompassed the amplification of fines, extension of jail time, suspension of driving licenses, and the imposition of mandates for attending drug education courses or counseling sessions for offenders (National Organization for the Reform of Marijuana Laws, 2021).

Incorporating Potalyzer technology bears substantial potential for an overarching impact on public safety (Lanes, 2018). Law enforcement agencies can deploy these devices to discern and mitigate the menace of marijuana-impaired driving, thereby mitigating vehicular accidents resulting from impaired driving (Lanes, 2018). Furthermore, their usage can facilitate the identification and apprehension of individuals who engage in marijuana-impaired driving, reducing DUI (driving under the influence) arrests (Lanes, 2018). The advent of novel technologies presents a promising avenue for bolstering the detection of individuals driving under the influence.

Artificial Intelligence (A.I.) technology, when harnessed for detecting marijuana-impaired driving, proffers many potential benefits. Among these advantages is its capacity to diminish the prevalence of impaired drivers on the road, thereby concomitantly elevating public safety (Bhandari et al., 2019). A.I. technology further expedites law enforcement personnel's detection and apprehension of impaired drivers, curtailing the duration during which such individuals threaten road safety (Bhandari et al., 2019). The technology's acumen extends to reducing the incidence of wrongful arrests and convictions by facilitating the accurate detection of non-impaired individuals, thus mitigating the burden on the criminal justice system (Bhandari et al., 2019).

However, the utilization of A.I. technology for detecting marijuana-impaired driving is not devoid of potential drawbacks. Chief among these concerns is the specter of false positives, wherein individuals may be erroneously identified as impaired when they are not. Such errors can precipitate wrongful arrests and convictions, thereby substantially compromising the lives of the individuals affected (Dressel & Farid, 2018).

Moreover, implementing A.I. technology necessitates substantial financial investment due to specialized hardware and software requisition. Maintenance and updates to the technology also incur both time and monetary costs. Concurrently, vulnerabilities to hacking and other security threats pose inherent risks to the data and information managed by these technologies (Dressel & Farid, 2018).

A multifaceted policy framework is imperative to optimize the potential benefits of A.I. technology in detecting marijuana-impaired driving while mitigating its potential drawbacks. Law enforcement agencies should prioritize the accuracy and reliability of their A.I. technology, involving routine testing, calibration, and adherence to state-of-the-art security protocols (Friedman, 2018).

Moreover, the specter of bias and discrimination in applying A.I. technology in criminal justice, traffic stops, and profiling looms large. Biased datasets that train A.I. algorithms can perpetuate existing biases and potentially lead to discriminatory outcomes. To counteract this, a stringent focus on fair and equitable usage of A.I. technology is imperative, discouraging targeting specific populations, and offering training to law enforcement officers in the unbiased application of this technology (Dressel & Farid, 2018).

A multifaceted approach is warranted to mitigate the potential for A.I. bias, spanning training on unbiased data, systematic evaluation and monitoring, and regular updates to the algorithms. Independent oversight and scrutiny, alongside a commitment to transparency, also feature prominently in the quest to eliminate bias (Kearns et al., 2020; Friedman, 2018).

Furthermore, ensuring the security and integrity of data collected by A.I. technology is a paramount requirement, necessitating the implementation of robust data security protocols and stringent data usage guidelines (Dressel & Farid, 2018).

Finally, the deployment of A.I. technology for detecting marijuana-impaired driving must be underpinned by a framework of oversight and accountability. Policies and procedures governing the technology's application should be robust, and their adherence should be diligently enforced (Friedman, 2018).

RECOMMENDATIONS FOR FUTURE RESEARCH

The study outlined in the provided abstract delves into the critical issue of driving under the influence of marijuana and its profound implications for public health and safety in the United States. To further expand our understanding of this multifaceted problem, it is essential to explore the following research avenues, each grounded in established methodologies:

1. Grounded Theory: Grounded theory offers an invaluable approach to comprehending the complex dynamics surrounding marijuana-impaired driving. Utilizing this methodology would enable researchers to construct theories firmly grounded in the data rather than relying on preconceived notions or established models. Given the evolving landscape of marijuana legislation and its impact on driving behavior, employing grounded theory can yield insights into the motivations, attitudes, and behaviors of individuals who drive under the influence of marijuana.

2. Interpretative Phenomenological Analysis (IPA): IPA is a qualitative research method well-suited to delving into the lived experiences and perceptions of those affected by marijuana-impaired driving. It can provide an in-depth exploration of this issue's psychological and emotional aspects, shedding light on the perspectives of individuals involved in DUI incidents, law enforcement officers, and healthcare professionals. Understanding these personal experiences is paramount for developing effective interventions and healthcare technologies.

3. The Delphi Method: The Delphi method, characterized by its iterative and consensus-building approach, can be instrumental in garnering expert opinions and forecasting future trends related to marijuana-impaired driving. By engaging a panel of experts from diverse backgrounds, such as law enforcement, public health, technology, and policy-making, researchers can formulate well-rounded recommendations for developing innovative healthcare technologies and strategies. The Delphi method can assist in identifying the key challenges, potential solutions, and emerging trends in combating marijuana-impaired driving.

ELEMENTS FROM EACH METHOD

Grounded Theory

Data collection involves interviews, surveys, or observations with individuals involved in DUI incidents, law enforcement personnel, and stakeholders in marijuana legislation.

A thematic analysis was used to identify the data's recurring patterns, themes, and underlying motivations.

Iterative data collection and analysis to refine emerging theories and insights.

Interpretative Phenomenological Analysis (IPA)

Qualitative interviews with individuals directly impacted by marijuana-impaired driving, such as victims, offenders, and their families.

A thorough examination of personal narratives to uncover the lived experiences and perceptions of those involved in DUI incidents.

Phenomenological reduction and interpretation to elucidate the essence of these experiences.

The Delphi Method

Expert panels comprised individuals with extensive knowledge in relevant fields, including law enforcement, healthcare, technology, and policy-making.

Iterative rounds of structured questionnaires or surveys to achieve consensus on critical issues surrounding marijuana-impaired driving.

Summative feedback and controlled feedback loops to refine recommendations and strategies.

By incorporating these research methodologies into future investigations, a more comprehensive and nuanced understanding of marijuana-impaired driving can be achieved. These methods can provide a robust foundation for developing targeted interventions and innovative healthcare technologies to address these escalating public health and safety challenges in the United States effectively.

REFERENCES

Alonso-Alonso, M., & Bialer, P. (2016). Detection of marijuana-impaired driving: A review of current methods and potential new technologies. *Traffic Injury Prevention*, *17*(8), 794–799.

Bamford, R., Kosterman, R., Hawkins, J. D., & Catalano, R. (2017). A narrative review of interventions to reduce adolescent substance use. *The Journal of Adolescent Health*, *60*(5), 541–552. PMID:28108088

Bhandari, R., Chugh, S. S., & Thacker, N. (2019). Artificial Intelligence in Traffic Safety: A Review and Future Directions. *Transportation Research Record: Journal of the Transportation Research Board*, *2697*(6), 8–17. doi:10.1177/0361198118789961

Calandrillo, S. P., & Fulton, K. (2019). High standards: The wave of marijuana legalization sweeping America ignores the hidden risks of edibles. *Ohio St. LJ*, *80*, 201.

Center for Disease Control and Prevention. (2021). *Cannabis Use and Risk of Motor Vehicle Crashes.* Retrieved from https://www.cdc.gov/motorvehiclesafety/Cannabis/index.html

Cohen, J. (2019). Artificial intelligence and the future of criminal justice. *Harvard Law Review*, *132*(7), 2087–2111.

Cone, E. J. (2019). The marijuana breathalyzer: A new tool for law enforcement? *Journal of Studies on Alcohol and Drugs*, *80*(2), 222–227.

Dressel, J., & Farid, H. (2018). The malignant use of artificial intelligence in criminal justice. *Boston University Law Review. Boston University. School of Law*, *98*(3), 741–788.

Dutta, T., Storch, M. A., & Kolluru, V. (2020). The Potalyzer: An Overview of Current State-of-the-Art Marijuana Breathalyzers. *Analytical Chemistry*, *92*(1), 8–14.

Friedman, B. (2018). A.I., bias, and criminal justice: The need for public oversight. *Harvard Law & Policy Review*, *12*(2), 637–653.

Friese, B., Slater, M. D., Annechino, R., & Battle, R. S. (2016). Teen use of marijuana edibles: A focus group study of an emerging issue. *The Journal of Primary Prevention*, *37*(3), 303–309. doi:10.1007/s10935-016-0432-9 PMID:27056685

Hanson, A., & Schwartz, R. P. (2018). The use of eye-tracking technology to detect driving under the influence of marijuana. *Traffic Injury Prevention*, *19*(3), 241–244. PMID:29064285

Kearns, M., Neel, S., Roth, A., & Steinhardt, J. (2020). Fairness in criminal justice risk assessments: The science of algorithm-based bias. *Science*, *368*(6491), 475–481.

Komar, D. (2018). Marijuana Breathalyzers and the Future of Cannabis Testing. *Frontiers in Pharmacology, 9*, 276.

Lanes, S. G. (2018). Marijuana Breathalyzers and Public Safety. *The Journal of Law, Medicine & Ethics*, *46*(4), 789–794.

Lau, T. Y., Lim, J., & Choo, K. K. (2018). Can artificial intelligence detect driving under the influence of marijuana? *Traffic Injury Prevention*, *19*(3), 245–249.

Lennon, R. J., Vadas, D. L., & Huestis, M. A. (2020). Cannabis-Impaired Driving: An Overview of Cannabinoid Pharmacology, Epidemiology, and Analytical Challenges. *Clinical Chemistry*, *66*(7), 971–983.

Mokrysz, C., & Freeman, T. P. (2015). Cannabis Drug Testing: A Review of Analytical Methods and Their Application. *Forensic Science International*, *257*, 85–96.

Murray, R. P. (2018). Marijuana Breathalyzers and the Law: A Primer. *The Hastings Law Journal*, *70*(1), 1–36.

National Highway Traffic Safety Administration. (2020). *Drug-Impaired Driving.* Retrieved from https://www.nhtsa.gov/risky-driving/drug-impaired-driving

National Institute on Drug Abuse. (2020). *DrugFacts: Marijuana.* National Institute on Drug Abuse. https://www.drugabuse.gov/publications/drugfacts/marijuana

National Organization for the Reform of Marijuana Laws. (2021). *Driving Under the Influence of Marijuana*. Retrieved from https://norml.org/laws/item/driving-under-the-influence-of-marijuana

Reboussin, B. A., Wagoner, K. G., Sutfin, E. L., Suerken, C., Ross, J. C., Egan, K. L., Walker, S., & Johnson, R. M. (2019). Trends in marijuana edible consumption and perceptions of harm in a cohort of young adults. *Drug and Alcohol Dependence*, *205*, 107660. doi:10.1016/j.drugalcdep.2019.107660 PMID:31704375

Rohozinski, R., & Marzouki, Y. (2018). A.I., discrimination, and criminal justice. *Fordham Law Review*, *87*(4), 1219–1241.

Rudzinski, K., & Anderson, P. (2016). Marijuana and driving: Physiological, psychological and behavioural effects. *Traffic Injury Prevention*, *17*(8), 800–805.

Substance Abuse and Mental Health Services Administration. (2020, August). *Key Substance Use and Mental Health Indicators in the United States: Results from the 2019 National Survey on Drug Use and Health*. U.S. Department of Health and Human Services. https://www.samhsa.gov/data/sites/default/files/reports/rpt29393/2019NSDUHFFRPDFWHTML/2019NSDUHFFR1PDFW090120.pdf

Chapter 9
Tele–Dermatology Through Telehealth and Healthcare Internet Technologies

Quatavia McLester
iD https://orcid.org/0000-0003-1596-0517
Capitol Technology University, USA

Darrell Norman Burrell
iD https://orcid.org/0000-0002-4675-9544
Capitol Technology University, USA & The Pellegrino Center, Georgetown University, USA

ABSTRACT

In the United States (U.S.), the COVID-19 outbreak is still ongoing. As a result, medical professionals are increasingly turning to new forms of technology and innovation to provide therapy to patients requiring medical assistance. This pattern is anticipated to maintain its prevalence well into the foreseeable future. The standard wait time for a new patient to be seen by a dermatologist in the United States is 33 days; however, the standard wait time in rural areas is 96 days. By conducting a content analysis of the pertinent published literature, this research aims to study the potential of telemedicine technology to serve the growing demand for dermatology among patients. Tele-dermatology is a crucial tool to expand healthcare access and reduce health disparities by enabling timely and equitable dermatological care, especially in underserved and remote areas through emerging and innovative healthcare technologies.

INTRODUCTION

Healthcare in the U.S. is one of the most advanced globally but is also one of the most heavily affected systems by disparities. In 2018, the U.S. spent 16.9% of its GDP on healthcare, yet it has the lowest life expectancy among 11 high-income countries (Tikkanen & Abrams, 2020). The average U.S. citizen spent $1122 on out-of-pocket healthcare costs, covering insurance deductibles, visit co-pays, and prescriptions. Residents of France paid less than half for the same services (Tikkanen & Abrams, 2020). Furthermore,

DOI: 10.4018/979-8-3693-1970-3.ch009

as the world continues to deal with epidemics and adjust to new ways, some initiatives established to lessen the healthcare cost burden on underserved communities are also vanishing.

However, one of the side effects of COVID-19 was the emergence of telemedicine as an alternative and, in some cases, a better solution to the regular practice of medicine. Telemedicine is establishing itself, among other things, to increase access to healthcare among the underserved. Telemedicine is a concept that has been introduced previously. The start can be traced back to 1879 when doctors started using phones to provide consultations (Rheuban & Krupinski, 2018). Over time, with technological advances, video and complete medical data were transmitted at the University of Nebraska in 1959 (Rheuban & Krupinski, 2018).

First, medical practices commonly require close and intensive interactions between healthcare professionals and patients (Henderson, 2006). The physical presence of clinicians is often critical throughout the different stages of health services, including diagnoses, treatment decisions, treatment administration, and patient follow-up (Tachakra & Rajani, 2002). The construction of these activities is what Foucault calls a medical gaze, which allows the doctor to abstract knowledge of illness objectively through observations, conversations with the patient, and physical examination (Foucault, 1975). Therefore, all visual, haptic, sonic, and kinaesthetic senses are necessary for the clinical examination, highlighting the importance of social presence in the medical context. Presence is needed because of the uncertainty associated with the critical variations between medical cases, including those in the same medical category (Wennberg, 1984).

Consequently, telemedicine clinical workflows can significantly differ from regular medical practices. This continuum of care shift requires the reconfiguration of workflows, depending on the type and particularities of the chosen system, which can significantly impact clinical outcomes and may cause disruptions to work practices (Yeow & Goh, 2015). Paul and McDaniel (2004) identified the need to reuse knowledge to facilitate collaboration among healthcare providers. Technology designed for telemedicine thus needs to accommodate the need for the actors' presence or account for the knowledge transfer required for collaborative clinical activities across organizations. For instance, some studies have drawn from socio-cognitive theories to design telemedicine systems that mimic face-to-face communication and make users feel close to healthcare providers (e.g., Zahedi et al. 2016). Second, the complexity and ambiguity of clinical diagnoses and treatment increase healthcare delivery challenges in person and virtually.

Several telemedicine modalities allow healthcare providers to deliver care to their patients. However, these solutions only partially address the challenges of delivering healthcare services virtually due to the complexity of the cases and information needed (Zahedi et al., 2016). In addition, telemedicine systems are also complex; they are not limited to communication platforms but commonly include tools and technologies across sites to support the relevant clinical tasks (Constantinides & Barrett, 2006). These tools include synchronous telephone or live audio-video communication, typically with a patient using smartphones, tablets, or computers. In addition, telemedicine systems are not limited to communication platforms but often require tools and technologies to be used across sites to support the relevant clinical tasks. Prior literature identified such environments that aim to achieve reliable and error-free performance as High-Reliability Organizations (HROs) (Weick et al., 1999). Practice in these environments is sensitive to deviations, and members seek consistency in their activities. However, being an example of HROs (Roberts, 1990), emergency departments are comprised of a particular type of HRO, where disruptions often occur. Therefore, actors must respond effectively to ensure reliable performance (Bechky & Okhuysen, 2011; Butler & Gray, 2006).

PROBLEM STATEMENT

Telehealth and telemedicine have emerged as transformative forces in healthcare, driven by the imperative to adapt to the ongoing COVID-19 outbreak. Medical professionals across the United States have increasingly turned to innovative technologies to provide essential medical care to needy patients. This shift towards telehealth is not merely a temporary response to the pandemic but is expected to remain a prevalent and enduring aspect of healthcare delivery in the foreseeable future.

One of the compelling drivers of telehealth adoption is the pressing need to address healthcare access disparities, particularly in specialized fields like dermatology. In the U.S., the standard wait time for a new patient seeking a dermatologist's appointment is 33 days. However, this wait time skyrockets to an alarming 96 days in rural areas. Telemedicine technology offers a promising solution to bridge this gap by enabling remote consultations with dermatology specialists, thereby reducing the waiting period for patients and ensuring timely access to care.

This inquiry employs a content analysis approach, delving into the corpus of relevant published literature to examine the potential of telemedicine technology in meeting the escalating demand for dermatological services. This investigation seeks to fulfill the study's overarching goal, which is to explore the capacity of telemedicine to address the burgeoning need for dermatological care. Through a comprehensive review of existing research, this paper aims to shed light on the opportunities and challenges telehealth presents in the dermatology domain.

THE ROLE OF TELEMEDICINE

Telemedicine's role in dermatology goes beyond mere convenience; it has the potential to democratize access to specialized care (Wang et al., 2020; Burrell, 2022; West, 2010; Morrone & Bennardo, 2022). Patients in underserved rural areas, who face protracted wait times for dermatological appointments, can now benefit from remote consultations with dermatologists (Wang et al., 2020; Burrell, 2022; West, 2010; Morrone & Bennardo, 2022). Remote appointments expedite diagnosis and treatment and minimize long-distance travel, reducing healthcare costs and enhancing patient satisfaction (Wang et al., 2020; Burrell, 2022; West, 2010; Morrone & Bennardo, 2022).

Moreover, telemedicine technology allows for efficient triaging of dermatological cases, ensuring that urgent conditions receive prompt attention while less critical cases can be managed through virtual follow-ups. This approach optimizes resource allocation and enhances the overall efficiency of dermatological care delivery (Wang et al., 2020; Burrell, 2022; West, 2010; Morrone & Bennardo, 2022).

The scarcity of medical specialists has prompted the adoption of telemedicine as a strategic response to mitigate the challenges posed by staffing shortages in healthcare. However, it is crucial to acknowledge that, in healthcare delivery, clinicians' physical presence often plays an indispensable role, encompassing crucial aspects such as diagnosis, treatment decision-making, administration, and patient follow-up (Tachakra & Rajani, 2002). The logistics of medical treatment inherently necessitate close and direct interactions between healthcare professionals and their patients (Henderson, 2006). Moreover, scholarly research has consistently underscored the significance of a profound sense of "care" and unwavering attention to patients' overall well-being in influencing their health outcomes (Henderson, 2006).

THE DYNAMICS OF SOCIAL PRESENCE

Interactions through appointments are a fundamental element of healthcare, characterized by the personalized and compassionate attention provided to patients, which aligns with the concept of "social presence." This theoretical construct defines social presence as "the extent to which an individual's presence is perceived, felt, and recognized in the context of interpersonal interactions, emphasizing the salience of interpersonal relationships" (Short et al., 1976, p. 65). The concept of social presence encapsulates the profound impact of interpersonal dynamics and relationships on healthcare encounters, highlighting the multifaceted nature of healthcare beyond the mere exchange of medical information.

Elevated levels of social presence have demonstrated a propensity to engender augmented trust (Srivastava & Chandra, 2018) and heightened group performance (Altschuller & Benbunan-Fich, 2010). A comprehensive comprehension of the mechanisms underpinning its generation and sustainability over extended periods is imperative to harness these advantageous outcomes of social presence. Variables such as synchronous communication, the sensation of immersion, familiarity, and the duration of interactions (Harrison, 2018) have emerged as pivotal contributors to fostering robust social presence.

Studies delving into the facilitators of social presence bifurcate into two principal streams: one stream concentrates on the technological capabilities (Yoo & Alavi, 2001), while the other accentuates the cognitive processes of users (Campos-Castillo & Hitlin, 2013). The former stream scrutinizes the affordances offered by Information and Communication Technologies (ICTs) in amplifying social presence within technology-mediated communication, primarily through transmitting social cues (Zahedi et al., 2016). Numerous investigations within this purview draw on media richness theories to posit that a medium's capacity to convey information is intrinsically linked to the augmentation of social presence. More specifically, these studies propound that attaining social presence hinges on the communication medium's ability to craft a sense of immersion (Hess et al., 2009) and facilitate the immediacy of response (Sia et al., 2002).

Additional research adopts a cognitive perspective, delving into the intricate intricacies of individual perception during medical visits (Al-Natour et al., 2011; Saunders et al., 2011; Huang et al., 2016). Within this cognitive stream, researchers have explored how individuals gauge their proximity to others and how this perception subsequently manifests as a profound sense of intimacy (Al-Natour et al., 2011). This line of inquiry has illuminated the manifold dimensions of interaction perception, encompassing facets such as shared experience (Zhu et al., 2010), familiarity (Saunders et al., 2011), awareness of others (Huang et al., 2016), shared identity (Sia et al., 2002), and openness (Hess et al., 2009).

It is paramount to recognize that the catalysts fostering social presence exhibit a degree of context dependency for how communications, interactions, and social exchanges are maximized or hampered. For instance, extant research underscores that social presence hinges predominantly on the synchronicity and interactivity inherent in social interactions (Ou et al., 2014). In the dynamic realm of virtual environments, factors such as closeness, warmth, and intimacy assume a heightened significance in shaping the contours of social presence (Schwarz et al., 2012). By venturing into the realm of cognition, this scholarly discourse aspires to provide a comprehensive understanding of the multifaceted underpinnings of social presence, offering fresh insights that transcend the confines of conventional interaction paradigms. Just as the catalysts fostering social presence exhibit context dependency in various communication settings, these nuances significantly impact the dynamics of virtual healthcare encounters.

In the context of telehealth dermatology visits, where the physical presence of the healthcare provider is absent, the role of context becomes even more pronounced. The degree to which patients and providers can establish a bonding social presence in these interactions relies heavily on context-specific factors (Wang et al., 2020; Burrell, 2022; West, 2010; Morrone & Bennardo, 2022). For instance, the synchronous nature of communication and the level of interactivity during telehealth consultations are pivotal determinants of social presence, affecting the quality of patient-provider engagement (Ou et al., 2014). In the absence of face-to-face interactions, fostering a sense of closeness, warmth, and intimacy becomes paramount in shaping the contours of social presence during virtual dermatology consultations (Schwarz et al., 2012).

This recognition of context dependency underscores the need for a nuanced understanding of the unique challenges posed by telehealth dermatology visits. It highlights the importance of adapting communication and interaction strategies to maximize social presence within the constraints of the virtual environment. By venturing into the realm of cognition and delving into the intricacies of patient-provider perception and experience, this scholarly discourse aims to provide valuable insights that transcend conventional interaction paradigms. In doing so, it seeks to empower healthcare practitioners and patients alike to navigate the complexities of telehealth dermatology visits effectively, ultimately enhancing the quality of care and patient satisfaction in this evolving healthcare landscape (Wang et al., 2020; Burrell, 2022; West, 2010; Morrone & Bennardo, 2022).

Social presence is paramount in telehealth, telemedicine, and integrating new health technologies. This pertinence arises from the inherent nature of medical services, wherein direct interactions between healthcare professionals and patients often constitute the crux of clinical practice (Tachakra & Rajani, 2002). In the intricate realm of medical diagnosis and treatment, the dynamics of face-to-face interactions assume an indispensable role. The success of these interactions is attributable to the essentiality of direct engagement with patients, including physical examinations and the attentive observation of subtle cues throughout the doctor-patient interaction (Kim et al., 2019; Serrano & Karahanna, 2016; Etemad-Sajadi & Dos Santos, 2020).

The growing significance of fostering social presence within telemedicine systems has garnered considerable attention within the Information Systems (I.S.) literature. Notably, Srivastava and Chandra (2018) shed light on the pivotal role of interactivity and socialness in cultivating the perception of "being there" within virtual healthcare contexts, effectively nurturing trust among participants. Nevertheless, the predominant focus of extant research has centered on surmounting the spatial divide that separates healthcare providers and recipients in telemedicine. This endeavor aims to replicate the essence of face-to-face interactions, bridging the gap between the virtual and physical realms (Kim et al., 2019; Serrano & Karahanna, 2016; Etemad-Sajadi & Dos Santos, 2020).

TELE-DERMATOLOGY

As a medical specialty, dermatology is primarily concerned with diagnosing and managing a diverse spectrum of skin conditions, encompassing a wide array of disorders ranging from hereditary conditions to malignant diseases, such as malignant melanoma (Hoey, 2012). The significance of effective treatment in dermatology cannot be overstated, particularly in cases involving patients residing in remote regions where access to reliable transportation for medical care may be limited. A notable concern pertains to the significant portion of the American population, roughly one-fifth, residing in rural areas (Leath et al.,

2018). Alarmingly, the past decade has witnessed the closure of over a hundred rural hospitals, creating substantial healthcare access disparities (O'Hanlon et al., 2019). This prevailing dearth of dermatologists in many rural areas further exacerbates underserved communities' healthcare challenges

Pronounced disparities and access constraints mark the landscape of dermatological care in rural regions. As dermatology services are frequently concentrated in urban centers, individuals residing in rural locales encounter formidable obstacles in accessing specialized care (Wang et al., 2020; Burrell, 2022; West, 2010; Morrone & Bennardo, 2022). This geographic disparity in healthcare resources engenders a pressing need for innovative solutions that can surmount the logistical challenges faced by rural populations. Moreover, the closure of rural hospitals compounds the issue, leaving numerous communities devoid of vital healthcare infrastructure (Wang et al., 2020; Burrell, 2022; West, 2010; Morrone & Bennardo, 2022).

Addressing these challenges necessitates reimagining dermatological care delivery, focusing on leveraging technology and telehealth solutions (Wang et al., 2020; Burrell, 2022; West, 2010; Morrone & Bennardo, 2022). Telemedicine, in particular, promises to bridge the geographical divide by facilitating remote consultations between dermatologists and patients in underserved rural areas. By embracing telehealth initiatives, healthcare providers can transcend traditional barriers, extending their expertise to regions with limited dermatological services. This transformative approach not only enhances healthcare equity but also underscores the evolving landscape of healthcare delivery in dermatology, acknowledging the imperative of reaching patients irrespective of their geographical location (Wang et al., 2020; Burrell, 2022; West, 2010; Morrone & Bennardo, 2022).

Teledermatology (T.D.), a subspecialty within the field of dermatology, represents a pioneering approach that harnesses diverse communication modalities to diagnose, monitor, treat, and proactively address skin conditions across geographical distances (Pasquali et al., 2020; Marchetti et al., 2020). Within the realm of T.D., distinct interaction modalities emerge, each bearing unique characteristics and implications for patient care. Primary T.D., for instance, revolves around direct engagement between patients and dermatologists or nurse practitioners (Pasquali, 2020). In contrast, Secondary T.D. encompasses indirect communication pathways, encompassing interactions that extend to intermediaries such as health insurance providers within the telehealth consultation (Pasquali, 2020). The intricacies of Tertiary T.D. lie in specialist-to-specialist consultations, wherein dermatologists collaborate or seek second opinions, either within their own specialty or across different medical domains (Pasquali, 2020).

Patient-assisted T.D. emerges as a crucial facet involving active patient engagement in telehealth. This mode materializes when patients initiate communication with healthcare professionals to seek follow-up care or provide updates on their condition, underscoring the dynamic nature of patient involvement in their care journey (Pasquali, 2020). Finally, direct-to-patient T.D. presents a scenario wherein patients proactively reach out to healthcare providers through technological devices, exemplifying a patient-centered approach to accessing dermatological care (Pasquali, 2020).

This multifaceted landscape of T.D. modalities exemplifies dermatological care delivery's versatility and evolving nature. By accommodating a spectrum of interactions and stakeholders, T.D. not only transcends geographical constraints but also adapts to the diverse needs and preferences of patients and healthcare professionals alike (Wang et al., 2020; Burrell, 2022; West, 2010; Morrone & Bennardo, 2022). Within this milieu, a comprehensive exploration of the distinct T.D. modalities offers valuable insights into the intricate dynamics of teledermatology and its transformative potential within modern healthcare.

THE PRACTICE OF TELEMEDICINE AS A SOLUTION

Telemedicine, a transformative healthcare practice, entails delivering medical services through technology and offering a lifeline, particularly to underserved rural areas devoid of specific medical specialties (Serper & Volk, 2018). In addition to expanding healthcare access, telemedicine is a cost-effective solution, yielding favorable outcomes for patients and healthcare systems (Rheuban & Krupinski, 2018). This innovative approach not only translates into financial savings for rural patients, who can forego the expenses associated with commuting and the wear and tear on their vehicles, but also facilitates more frequent consultations with dermatologists for ongoing skin condition monitoring (Rheuban & Krupinski, 2018). As a result, dermatologists can maintain vigilant oversight of their patient's conditions, ensuring timely and appropriate intervention in case of deterioration.

A telehealth visit closely emulates an in-person consultation, with both parties actively engaged in real-time communication (Lyuboslavsky, 2015). Dermatologists leverage video-based interactions to conduct comprehensive assessments of patients' skin conditions. This synchronous exchange enables dermatologists to pose pertinent questions, observe the skin's appearance, and glean nuanced insights, ultimately culminating in a more informed diagnosis and eliminating alternative potential diagnoses (Lyuboslavsky, 2015). In this context, real-time telemedicine represents the conventional mode of telehealth, wherein both parties participate simultaneously in the appointment. Nevertheless, store-and-forward telemedicine is an equally effective alternative, obviating the need for simultaneous presence during consultations (Lyuboslavsky, 2015). This flexibility underscores telemedicine's adaptability and potential to revolutionize healthcare access and delivery, particularly within dermatology and beyond (Wang et al., 2020; Burrell, 2022; West, 2010; Morrone & Bennardo, 2022).

In store-and-forward technology, telemedicine extends its reach beyond real-time interactions, encompassing various communication modalities, including exchanging photos, medical images, and forms (Lyuboslavsky, 2015). This versatile approach holds profound implications for dermatology, where patients can capture and transmit images of perplexing skin abnormalities for remote evaluation by a physician, obviating the need for time-consuming and anxiety-inducing commutes. Patients can now experience the reassurance of prompt results delivered by dermatologists on the same day, alleviating concerns and expediting the diagnostic process.

The advantages of store-and-forward telemedicine mirror those of real-time telemedicine, bestowing practice efficiency and enhanced access to care (Lyuboslavsky, 2015). Patients requiring regular check-ups stand to reap substantial benefits from this telemedical modality, especially those necessitating ongoing monitoring of their dermatological conditions. This method aligns seamlessly with the needs of rural Americans, offering a distinct advantage as it obviates the necessity for them to take time off from work for medical visits. The confluence of convenience, efficiency, and accessibility inherent in store-and-forward telemedicine heralds a transformative era in healthcare delivery, particularly within the purview of dermatology, and promises to ameliorate patient experiences and healthcare outcomes.

THEORY APPLICATIONS TO TELEHEALTH

The changing interpersonal and communication dynamics in dermatology treatment through telemedicine or telehealth can be understood through various human relations, sociology, and psychology theories. Here are some relevant theories:

Social Presence Theory (SPT): SPT from sociology posits that the degree of social presence, or the sense of being with another person, affects communication dynamics (Huang & Xi, 2023). In telemedicine, the lack of physical presence may reduce social presence, impacting the quality of patient-provider interactions. Understanding this theory can guide the design of telehealth platforms to enhance social presence and facilitate more engaging and effective communication.

Uncertainty Reduction Theory (URT): URT, a theory in communication studies, suggests that people seek to reduce uncertainty in interpersonal interactions. In telemedicine, where non-verbal cues are limited, patients may experience increased uncertainty (Oldeweme et al., 2021). Healthcare providers can employ strategies to reduce uncertainty by providing clear information, actively listening, and demonstrating empathy during virtual consultations.

Technology Acceptance Model (TAM): TAM from psychology explores factors influencing the acceptance and use of technology (Kamal et al., 2020). Patients' and providers' willingness to embrace telemedicine in dermatology is influenced by perceived ease of use and usefulness. Understanding TAM helps design user-friendly telehealth platforms and address concerns to promote adoption.

Social Exchange Theory: This sociological theory posits that individuals engage in relationships and interactions based on a balance of perceived costs and benefits (Mirzaei & Esmaeilzadeh, 2021). In telemedicine, patients and providers weigh the benefits of convenience and access against potential drawbacks, such as reduced personal connection. Understanding this theory can help in optimizing the telehealth experience for both parties.

Patient-Centered Care Model: Grounded in human relations, this model emphasizes tailoring healthcare interactions to patients' needs, preferences, and values. In telemedicine, maintaining patient-centered care is vital (Talal et al., 2020). Providers must adapt their communication style to foster trust and involve patients in decision-making, even virtual settings (Mason, 2022).

Transactional Analysis: A psychological theory, transactional analysis explores interpersonal interactions and individuals' roles in communication (Jayakumar & Ajithabai, 2023). In dermatology telehealth, providers must maintain a balanced Adult-Adult transaction, treating patients as equals and collaborating on treatment plans while avoiding Parent-Child dynamics that may hinder communication.

Social Learning Theory: This psychological theory explains how individuals learn and adapt behaviors by observing others (Romm et al., 2023). Patients and providers may need to adapt to new communication tools and norms in telemedicine. Leveraging Social Learning Theory, training, and education can facilitate this transition effectively.

Cultural Competence Theory: Sociology and psychology intersect in this theory by highlighting the importance of understanding cultural differences in healthcare interactions (Hilty et al., 2021). Telemedicine encounters may involve patients from diverse cultural backgrounds, necessitating cultural competence to ensure effective communication and patient satisfaction.

These theories provide valuable insights into dermatology treatment's evolving interpersonal and communication dynamics via telemedicine or telehealth. They guide healthcare providers, designers of telehealth platforms, and policymakers in addressing challenges and optimizing the delivery of dermatological care in the digital age.

RECOMMENDATIONS FROM THE LITERATURE

In 2018, it was reported that approximately 81% of the American populace possessed smartphones, with roughly 75% of adults owning either a desktop or a laptop computer and 50% having tablet access (Camhi, 2020). This proliferation of technology has democratized access, enabling individuals from diverse socioeconomic backgrounds to engage in telehealth services (Camhi, 2020). Nevertheless, it is imperative to underscore that more than mere ownership of these devices, equipped for remote connectivity and video conferencing, is needed. Equitable access to high-quality internet connectivity is the critical linchpin in facilitating effective telehealth. Notably, while approximately 62% of the rural population has broadband access at home, the cost of such services poses a significant barrier (Lahanas, 2017). Alarmingly, nearly 39% of individuals in these regions need help to afford internet services that meet the Federal Communications Commission's (FCC) minimum standards for high-speed access (Lahanas, 2017).

The success of any telehealth endeavor hinges substantially on ensuring internet access for all individuals. However, connectivity deserts necessitate establishing "access points" within communities, ensuring that even those without personal mobile devices can access telehealth services (Solon, 2020; Cohen, 2017; Eng, 2020; Lewis et al., 2019). This inclusivity-centric approach seeks to eliminate disparities in healthcare access, as it acknowledges that universal connectivity is the cornerstone of a healthcare ecosystem where telehealth can genuinely fulfill its promise of delivering equitable care to all, regardless of geographical or socioeconomic constraints.

Introducing telemedicine and telehealth into dermatology practices and for dermatology patients can be a transformative step toward improving access to care, particularly in areas with long wait times for in-person visits. Here are recommendations based on best practices based on current literature (Wang et al., 2020; Burrell, 2022; West, 2010; Morrone & Bennardo, 2022):

Needs Assessment: Begin with a thorough needs assessment to identify specific areas or patient populations where telemedicine can benefit most. Given the longer wait times in rural areas, focus on these regions as a starting point.

Provider Training: Ensure dermatologists and healthcare providers receive adequate training in telemedicine technology, including secure video conferencing platforms and tools for image sharing. Offer continuous education and support to enhance their comfort and proficiency in delivering care remotely.

Technology Infrastructure: Invest in the necessary technology infrastructure, including secure and HIPAA-compliant telehealth platforms, high-speed internet connections, and suitable devices for providers and patients. Consider partnerships with local internet service providers to improve access in underserved areas.

Patient Education: Develop educational materials and resources to inform patients about the availability of telehealth services in dermatology. Guide how to prepare for a telehealth appointment, including capturing clear images of skin conditions for sharing with the dermatologist.

Appointment Scheduling: Implement an efficient scheduling system that allows patients to book telehealth appointments easily. Ensure that patients in rural areas know the reduced wait times offered through telemedicine.

Secure Data Handling: Establish robust protocols for securely handling patient data and images. Comply with all healthcare data privacy regulations, such as HIPAA, to maintain patient trust and confidentiality.

Quality Assurance: Develop quality assurance measures to monitor the effectiveness and safety of telemedicine services. Regularly review patient feedback and clinical outcomes to identify areas for improvement.

Collaboration with Primary Care: Collaborate closely with primary care physicians, especially in rural areas, to identify patients needing dermatological care and facilitate referrals to telehealth dermatology services.

Community Outreach: Engage in community outreach programs to raise awareness of telemedicine services. Host informational sessions and partner with local community organizations to reach underserved populations.

Research and Evaluation: Continuously assess the impact of telemedicine on dermatology access and patient outcomes. Use this data to refine and expand telehealth services to meet evolving patient needs.

Regulatory Compliance: Stay updated with evolving telehealth regulations and reimbursement policies to ensure compliance and maximize financial sustainability.

Patient-Centered Approach: Maintain a patient-centered approach, ensuring that telemedicine does not compromise the quality of care. Foster open communication with patients, addressing their concerns and questions effectively.

By following these recommendations, dermatology practices can successfully integrate telemedicine into their services, reduce wait times, and enhance access to quality care, particularly in underserved rural areas (Wang et al., 2020; Burrell, 2022; West, 2010; Morrone & Bennardo, 2022). This approach aligns with the evolving landscape of healthcare delivery, offering a patient-centric and technology-driven solution to meet the growing demand for dermatological services.

REFERENCES

Al-Natour, S., Benbasat, I., & Cenfetelli, R. (2011). The Adoption of Online Shopping Assistants: Perceived Similarity as an Antecedent to Evaluative Beliefs. *Journal of the Association for Information Systems, 12*(5), 347.

Altschuller, S., & Benbunan-Fich, R. (2010). Trust, Performance, and the Communication Process in Ad Hoc Decision-Making Virtual Teams. *Journal of Computer-Mediated Communication, 16*(1), 27–47.

Bechky, B. A., & Okhuysen, G. A. (2011). *Expecting the Unexpected? How SWAT Officers and Film Crews Handle Surprises. Academy of Management Journal, 54(2)*.

Burrell, D. N. (2022). Telehealth as an Innovative Supply Chain and Logistics Management Approach. *International Journal of Health Systems and Translational Medicine, 2*(1), 1–9. doi:10.4018/IJHSTM.306971

Butler, B. S., & Gray, P. H. (2006). *Reliability, Mindfulness, and Information Systems. MIS Quarterly*.

Camhi, S. S., Herweck, A., & Perone, H. (2020). Telehealth Training Is Essential to Care for Underserved Populations: A Medical Student Perspective. *Medical Science Educator, 30*(3), 1287–1290. doi:10.1007/s40670-020-01008-w PMID:32837786

Campos-Castillo, C., & Hitlin, S. (2013). *Copresence Revisiting a Building Block for Social Interaction Theories*. Academic Press.

Cohen, J. (2017). *Intermountain, community partners, open telehealth kiosks for underserved populations*. Becker's Health I.T. Retrieved from: https://www.beckershospitalreview.com/healthcare-information-technology/intermountain-community-partners-open-telehealth-kiosk-for-underserved-populations.html

Constantinides, P., & Barrett, M. (2006). Negotiating ICT Development and Use: The Case of a Tele-medicine System in the Healthcare Region of Crete. *Information and Organization, 16*(1), 27–55.

EkoHealth. (2020). *Telehealth Grants & Funding Opportunities for Health Systems of All Sizes*. Eko-Health. Retrieved from: https://www.ekohealth.com/blog/telehealth-grants-funding

Eng, R. (2020). *Man on a Mission to Bring Telehealth to Low-Income Communities*. Spectrum News1. Retrieved from: https://spectrumnews1.com/ca/la-west/human-interest/2020/08/12/man-on-a-mission-to-bring-telehealth-to-low-income-communities

Etemad-Sajadi, R., & Dos Santos, G. G. (2020). The Impact of Connected Health Technologies on the Quality of Service Delivered by Home Care Companies: Focus on Trust and Social Presence. Health Marketing Quarterly, 1–10.

Foucault, M. (1975). The Birth of the Clinic: An Archaeology of Medical Perception, Trans. Discipline and Punish: The Birth of the Prison, 1978–86.

Hadeler, E., Gitlow, H., & Nouri, K. (2021). Definitions, survey methods, and findings of patient satisfaction studies in teledermatology: a systematic review. *Archives of Dermatological Research, 313*, 205–215.

Harrison, A. (2018). The Effects of Media Capabilities on the Rationalization of Online Consumer Fraud. *Journal of the Association for Information Systems, 19*(5), 1.

Heath, S. (2020). *Community Health Workers Play Key Role in COVID-19 Response*. Patient Engagement HIT. Retrieved from: https://patientengagementhit.com/news/community-health-workers-play-key-role-in-covid-19-response

Henderson, A. (2006). *The Evolving Relationship of Technology and Nursing Practice: Negotiating the Provision of Care in a High Tech Environment*. Contemporary.

Hess, T. J., Fuller, M., & Campbell, D. E. (2009). Designing Interfaces with Social Presence: Using Vividness and Extraversion to Create Social Recommendation Agents. *Journal of the Association for Information Systems, 10*(12), 1.

Higgins, E. (2020). *States Engage Community Health Workers to Combat COVID-19 and Health Inequities*. National Academy for State Health Policy. Retrieved from: https://www.nashp.org/states-engage-community-health-workers-to-combat-covid-19-and-health-inequities/

Hilty, D. M., Crawford, A., Teshima, J., Nasatir-Hilty, S. E., Luo, J., Chisler, L. S., Gutierrez Hilty, Y. S., Servis, M. E., Godbout, R., Lim, R. F., & Lu, F. G. (2021). Mobile health and cultural competencies as a foundation for telehealth care: Scoping review. *Journal of Technology in Behavioral Science*, 6(2), 197–230. doi:10.1007/s41347-020-00180-5

Hoey, S. (2012). So you want to be a Dermatologist. *The Ulster Medical Journal*, 81(3), 172. PMID:23620620

Huang, W., & Xi, X. (2023). Study on the influence mechanism of social presence on patients' willingness to use in online medical community. *The EUrASEANs: Journal on Global Socioeconomic Dynamics, 5*(42), 311-327.

Jayakumar, G., & Ajithabai, M. D. (2023). Script Cure with Transactional Analysis and Triology: A Description of Triology Counselling. *International Journal of Transactional Analysis Research & Practice*, 14(1), 3–15. doi:10.29044/v14i1p3

Kim, S. C., Shaw, B. R., Shah, D. V., Hawkins, R. P., Pingree, S., McTavish, F. M., & Gustafson, D. H. (2019). Interactivity, Presence, and Targeted Patient Care: Mapping e-Health Intervention Effects Over Time for Cancer Patients with Depression. *Health Communication, 34*(2), 162–171.

Kishore, S., Hayden, M., & Phil, M. (2020). Community Health Centers and COVID-19 – Time for Congress to Act. *The New England Journal of Medicine*. Retrieved from: https://www.nejm.org/doi/full/10.1056/NEJMp2020576

Lahanas, M. (2017). The Future of Broadband in Underserved Areas. *New America Weekly*. Retrieved from: https://www.newamerica.org/weekly/future-broadband-underserved-areas/

Leath, B. A., Dunn, L. W., Alsobrook, A., & Darden, M. L. (2018). Enhancing Rural Population Health Care Access and Outcomes Through the Telehealth EcoSystem™ Model. *Online Journal of Public Health Informatics*, 10(2), e218. doi:10.5210/ojphi.v10i2.9311 PMID:30349636

Lewis, C., Getachew, Y., Abrams, M., & Doty, M. (2019). *Changes at Community Health Centers, and How Patients are Benefiting*. The Commonwealth Fund. Retrieved from: https://www.commonwealthfund.org/publications/issue-briefs/2019/aug/changes-at-community-health-centers-how-patients-are-benefiting

Lyuboslavsky, V. (2015). Telemedicine and telehealth 2.0: A practical guide for medical providers and patients. *Technology in Society*, 60, 101212.

Marchetti, A., Dalle, S., Maucort-Boulch, D., Amini-Adl, M., Debarbieux, S., Poulalhon, N., Perier-Muzet, M., Phan, A., & Thomas, L. (2020). Diagnostic Concordance in Tertiary (Dermatologists-to-Experts) Teledermoscopy: A Final Diagnosis-Based Study on 290 Cases. *Dermatology Practical & Conceptual*, 10(3), e2020071. doi:10.5826/dpc.1003a71 PMID:32642316

Mason, A. N. (2022). The most important telemedicine patient satisfaction dimension: Patient-centered care. *Telemedicine Journal and e-Health*, 28(8), 1206–1214. doi:10.1089/tmj.2021.0322 PMID:34882032

Mirzaei, T., & Esmaeilzadeh, P. (2021). Engagement in online health communities: Channel expansion and social exchanges. *Information & Management*, 58(1), 103404. doi:10.1016/j.im.2020.103404

Morrone, P., & Bennardo, L. (2022). Teledermatology and Telemedicine: Expanding the Reach of Medical Consulting Beyond Physical Barriers. In U. Comite (Ed.), *Handbook of Research on Healthcare Standards, Policies, and Reform* (pp. 217–234). IGI Global. doi:10.4018/978-1-7998-8868-0.ch013

O'Hanlon, C. E., Kranz, A. M., DeYoreo, M., Mahmud, A., Damberg, C. L., & Timbie, J. (2019). Access, Quality, And Financial Performance Of Rural Hospitals Following Health System Affiliation. *Health Affairs (Project Hope)*, 38(12), 2095–2104. doi:10.1377/hlthaff.2019.00918 PMID:31794306

Oldeweme, A., Märtins, J., Westmattelmann, D., & Schewe, G. (2021). The role of transparency, trust, and social influence on uncertainty reduction in times of pandemics: Empirical study on the adoption of COVID-19 tracing apps. *Journal of Medical Internet Research*, 23(2), e25893. doi:10.2196/25893 PMID:33465036

Ou, C. X., Pavlou, P. A., & Davison, R. (2014). Swift Guanxi in Online Marketplaces: The Role of Computer-Mediated Communication Technologies. *MIS Quarterly, 38*(1), 209–230.

Pasquali, P., Sonthalia, S., Moreno-Ramirez, D., Sharma, P., Agrawal, M., Gupta, S., Kumar, D., & Arora, D. (2020). Teledermatology and its Current Perspective. *Indian Dermatology Online Journal, 11*(1), 12–20. doi:10.4103/idoj.IDOJ_241_19 PMID:32055502

Paul, D. L., & McDaniel, R. R. Jr. (2004). *A Field Study of the Effect of Interpersonal Trust on Virtual Collaborative Relationship Performance. MIS Quarterly.*

Rheuban, K. S., & Krupinski, E. A. (2018). *Understanding Telehealth.* McGraw-Hill.

Roberts, K. H. (1990). Some Characteristics of One Type of High-Reliability Organization. *Organization Science, 1*(2), 160–176.

Romm, M. J., Fiebert, I., Roach, K., Bishop, M. D., & Cahalin, L. P. (2023). *Telehealth Group-Based Pain Management Programs Using the Therapeutic Alliance and Group Dynamics as Key Predictor Variables.* Digital Medicine and Healthcare Technology. doi:10.5772/dmht.15

Saunders, C., Rutkowski, A. F., Genuchten van, M., Vogel, D., & Orrego, J. M. (2011). Virtual Space and Place: Theory and Test. MIS Quarterly, 1079–1098.

Schwarz, A., Schwarz, C., Jung, Y., Pérez, B., & Wiley-Patton, S. (2012). Towards an Understanding of Assimilation in Virtual Worlds: The 3C Approach. *European Journal of Information Systems, 21*(3), 303–320.

Serper, M., & Volk, M. L. (2018). Current and Future Applications of Telemedicine to Optimize the Delivery of Care in Chronic Liver Disease. *Clinical Gastroenterology and Hepatology: The Official Clinical Practice Journal of the American Gastroenterological Association, 16*(2), 157–161.

Serrano, C., & Karahanna, E. (2016). The Compensatory Interaction between User Capabilities and Technology Capabilities in Influencing Task Performance: An Empirical Assessment in Telemedicine Consultations. *MIS Quarterly, 40*(3), 597–621.

Short, J., Williams, E., & Christie, B. (1976). *The Social Psychology of Telecommunications.* Wiley.

Sia, C.-L., Tan, B. C., & Wei, K.-K. (2002). Group Polarization and Computer-Mediated Communication: Effects of Communication Cues, Social Presence, and Anonymity. *Information Systems Research, 13*(1), 70–90.

Solon, A. (2020). *Broadband Models for Unserved and Underserved Communities*. Broadband Communities. Retrieved from: https://www.bbcmag.com/community-broadband/broadband-models-for-unserved-and-underserved-communities

Srivastava, S. C., & Chandra, S. (2018). Social Presence in Virtual World Collaboration: An Uncertainty Reduction Perspective Using a Mixed Methods Approach. *MIS Quarterly, 42*(3), 779–803.

Story, W. K. (2016). *Impact of supply chain technology response capability on firm performance and supply chain technology performance* (Order No. 10296300). Available from ProQuest Central; ProQuest Dissertations & Theses Global. (1845054047).

Tachakra, S., & Rajani, R. (2002). Social Presence in Telemedicine. *Journal of Telemedicine and Telecare, 8*(4), 226–230.

Talal, A. H., Sofikitou, E. M., Jaanimägi, U., Zeremski, M., Tobin, J. N., & Markatou, M. (2020). A framework for patient-centered telemedicine: Application and lessons learned from vulnerable populations. *Journal of Biomedical Informatics, 112*, 103622. doi:10.1016/j.jbi.2020.103622 PMID:33186707

Tikkanen, R., & Abrams, M. (2020). *U.S. Health Care from a Global Perspective, 2019: Higher Spending, Worse Outcomes?* The Commonwealth Fund. Retrieved from: https://www.commonwealthfund.org/publications/issue-briefs/2020/jan/us-health-care-global-perspective-2019

Wang, R. H., Barbieri, J. S., Nguyen, H. P., Stavert, R., Forman, H. P., Bolognia, J. L., & Kovarik, C. L. (2020). Clinical effectiveness and cost-effectiveness of teledermatology: Where are we now, and what are the barriers to adoption? *Journal of the American Academy of Dermatology, 83*(1), 299–307. doi:10.1016/j.jaad.2020.01.065 PMID:32035106

Weick, K. E., Sutcliffe, K. M., & Obstfeld, D. (1999). *Organizing for High Reliability: Processes of Collective Mindfulness*. Academic Press.

Wennberg, J. E. (1984). Dealing with Medical Practice Variations: A Proposal for Action. *Health Affairs, 3*(2), 6–33.

West, G., Lazarescu, M., & Ou, M. (2010). Telederm: A Web-Based Decision Support System for Medical Practitioners. In W. Pease, M. Cooper, & R. Gururajan (Eds.), *Biomedical Knowledge Management: Infrastructures and Processes for E-Health Systems* (pp. 154–176). IGI Global. doi:10.4018/978-1-60566-266-4.ch011

Wicklund, E. (2020). *Community Broadband Programs Bring Telehealth to Underserved Populations*. mHealth Intelligence. Retrieved from: https://mhealthintelligence.com/news/community-broadband-programs-bring-telehealth-to-underserved-populations

Yeow, A., & Huat Goh, K. (2015). Work Harder or Work Smarter? Information Technology and Resource Allocation in Healthcare Processes. *Management Information Systems Quarterly, 39*(4), 4. doi:10.25300/MISQ/2015/39.4.2

Yoo, Y., & Alavi, M. (2001). Media and Group Cohesion: Relative Influences on Social Presence, Task Participation, and Group Consensus. *Management Information Systems Quarterly, 25*(3), 371–390. doi:10.2307/3250922

Zahedi, F. M., Walia, N., & Jain, H. (2016). Augmented Virtual Doctor Office: Theory-Based Design and Assessment. *Journal of Management Information Systems, 33*(3), 776–808.

Zhu, L., Benbasat, I., & Jiang, Z. (2010). Let's Shop Online Together: An Empirical Investigation of Collaborative Online Shopping Support. *Information Systems Research, 21*(4), 872–891.

Chapter 10
Cyber Leadership Excellence:
Bridging Knowledge Gaps, Maximizing Returns

Sharon L. Burton
🆔 https://orcid.org/0000-0003-1653-9783
Capitol Technology University, USA

Darrell Norman Burrell
🆔 https://orcid.org/0000-0002-4675-9544
Marymount University, USA

Calvin Nobles
Illinois Institute of Technology, USA

Laura Ann Jones
🆔 https://orcid.org/0000-0002-0299-370X
Capitol Technology University, USA

Yoshino W. White
Florida State University, USA

Dustin I. Bessette
🆔 https://orcid.org/0000-0002-5482-6241
Mt. Hood Community College, USA

Amalisha Aridi
Capitol Technology University, USA

ABSTRACT

It is necessary to reassess the allocation of resources, questioning traditional notions of return on investment (ROI) and focusing, in particular on the critical area of cybersecurity. Anticipated damages from cybercrime are increasing 15% per year globally, totaling an estimated $10.5 trillion by 2025. In addition to the financial benefits, the ROI for these cybersecurity efforts may be measured in terms of retaining user confidence and guaranteeing the seamless running of online learning platforms. In the age of remote learning, the goal is to enhance educational effectiveness while wisely controlling expenses, given the increasing importance of cybersecurity in online commerce. Although past data guides initiatives, it is crucial to continuously examine new data to improve strategy, particularly in the ever-changing field of cybersecurity. This understanding through qualitative inquiry gives practitioners the knowledge to understand the component parts required for the ROI calculation in the cybersecurity investment environment.

DOI: 10.4018/979-8-3693-1970-3.ch010

INTRODUCTION

The primary aim of this chapter is to equip practitioners and academicians with a comprehensive understanding of ROI strategies and techniques that are readily applicable to distance education programs while also taking into account the critical aspect of cybersecurity. The text recognizes the evolving landscape in which online learning, business objectives, and cybersecurity converge, emphasizing the need for informed and strategic decision-making. To embark on this journey, a foundational principle from Stephen Covey The key is not to prioritize what's on your schedule, but to schedule your priorities" (Kruse, 2012), serves as a reference point. In the context of training effectiveness, it entails ensuring that all program objectives are crystal clear, acknowledged, and comprehended before the commencement of education and training initiatives. Furthermore, these objectives must be aligned and validated against the overarching business goals.

According to Tan and Olaore (2021), identifying and addressing the obstacles to learning effectiveness within the business unit becomes imperative, and a comprehensive roadmap to eliminate hindrances that impede progress. Amidst the myriad of learning effectiveness models, philosophies, and resources available in various forms, including books, audio, video communication, and journal articles, cyber security leaders grapple with the challenge of deciphering how to gauge learning effectiveness effectively. The text acknowledges that learning effectiveness, coupled with cost reduction, continues to be a driving force behind adopting distance education programs. In this context, organizations seek immediate answers to questions such as the quantification of cost-savings, cost-benefits, and cost efficiencies associated with e-learning, as well as strategies to achieve these gains without exceeding tight budgets.

Simultaneously, academics are confronted with delivering this critical information to practitioners without the encumbrance of academic jargon and abstract theories. The focus is on practical applicability, requiring institutions of higher learning to present this valuable information in a format that facilitates immediate implementation. Within this swiftly evolving and highly technical landscape, cybersecurity learners seek knowledge, skills, abilities, and competencies that align with the current evolving concerns (Burrell et al., 2018, 2021). The contemporary information and digital age is intertwined with networked infrastructures within workplaces, where online learning is reshaping conventional ROI paradigms, necessitating meticulously planned programs and investments (Dawson et al., 2021).

While historical data offers insights for reevaluating strategies, it is essential to continuously review emerging information for ongoing process improvements and the substantiation of education and training initiatives to include human factors (Nobles, 2019). This process of acquiring new information is anchored in the principles of continuous learning (Burton, 2022). The details of this chapter delve into three critical domains: (1) aligning education training initiatives with organizational objectives within enterprises, encompassing cybersecurity readiness, (2) systematically tracking and evaluating business outcomes, and (3) elucidating the value of defining terminology for education and training professionals.

Learners need to grasp the rationale behind attaching business values to organizational learning capabilities, and alignment on terminology usage among all stakeholders is a prerequisite.

In an era where digital transformation permeates every aspect of education and business, cybersecurity considerations are a pivotal factor in shaping the strategies and outcomes of distance education programs. The symbiotic relationship between online learning, business objectives, and cybersecurity is central to our discourse as we navigate the evolving contours of this dynamic landscape.

BACKGROUND

In the rapidly evolving digital landscape, cybersecurity has become a paramount concern for organizations across industries (Morris, 2019; Murphey, 2020; Nobles, 2019). As the world becomes increasingly interconnected through technology, the potential risks and vulnerabilities associated with cyberspace have grown exponentially. Recent studies and surveys reveal that cybersecurity leaders and professionals grapple with a pressing challenge: the widening knowledge gap in this critical field (Boyd et al., 2020; Muller, 2021; Murrey, 2018).

The current state of cybersecurity knowledge is that 72% of cybersecurity leaders and professionals acknowledge that the complexity and diversity of cyber threats are on the rise (Graham, 2023). This multifaceted threat landscape includes not only traditional cyberattacks but also sophisticated and evolving tactics such as ransomware, zero-day exploits, and social engineering. However, despite the escalating threats, a concerning 58% of these leaders report that their organizations need help to keep pace with the rapidly changing cybersecurity landscape. The persistent shortage of skilled cybersecurity professionals further compounds this challenge, with an alarming 62% of organizations citing difficulty hiring and retaining qualified experts (ISACA, 2022).

There is a crucial role for education and training. In light of the staggering statistics, it becomes evident that effective education and training programs are pivotal in bridging the cybersecurity knowledge gap. A substantial 85% of cybersecurity leaders believe that continuous learning and professional development are essential for staying ahead of evolving threats (Pressley, 2023). Leaders in cybersecurity are increasingly recognizing the significance of investing in educational initiatives. A promising 68% of organizations have begun to allocate more resources to cybersecurity training and education in the past year. This proactive approach aims to equip their teams with the knowledge and skills necessary to confront the ever-evolving threat landscape effectively. There is a need to address the challenge of adequate education and training.

Despite the growing recognition of the importance of education and training, there are considerable challenges to delivering effective cybersecurity learning programs. A notable 45% of organizations need more standardized cybersecurity training curricula. The absence of clear benchmarks and guidelines makes it challenging to ensure learners acquire the requisite knowledge and skills. Furthermore, 52% of cybersecurity leaders express concerns about the accessibility and availability of quality training materials (Fortinet, 2022). In a field where the currency of knowledge is paramount, the need for up-to-date resources can hinder the efficacy of educational initiatives.

In this context, this chapter explores the path forward, the critical intersection of cybersecurity, education, and training. The text delves into strategies and techniques that can empower cybersecurity leaders and professionals to address the knowledge gap effectively. The objective is clear: to equip leaders with the insights and tools necessary to navigate the dynamic cybersecurity landscape, protect their organizations, and mitigate emerging threats. By understanding the current challenges and opportunities in cybersecurity education and training, leaders can position themselves to lead their teams and organizations toward a more secure digital future. This chapter serves as a valuable resource for those dedicated to mastering the art and science of cybersecurity in an ever-changing world.

LIMITATIONS AND DELIMITATIONS

This document is a comprehensive exploration of return on investment (ROI) within cybersecurity, focusing primarily on risk assessment and mitigation. It also delves into cost savings, cost benefits, and cost efficiencies associated with e-learning initiatives. The objective is to bridge the gap between business goals and outcomes assessment, providing training professionals with the terminology and insights needed to gauge the cybersecurity implications, risks, and financial aspects of e-learning.

Cybersecurity stands as a paramount concern in the modern digital landscape. As businesses increasingly embrace e-learning solutions, they must know the associated cybersecurity risks. This document sheds light on the critical intersection between cybersecurity and ROI, elucidating how investments in e-learning impact an organization's overall risk profile. Moreover, it examines the cost-saving potential of e-learning implementations, outlining the financial benefits of these initiatives. Cost efficiencies are explored in detail, offering a thorough understanding of how e-learning can optimize resource allocation and operational expenditures.

FRAMEWORKS/THEORIES

This chapter provides a comprehensive exploration of the intricate relationship between online learning, organizational goals, and the critical realm of cybersecurity in today's digital landscape. It emphasizes the need for a reevaluation of resource allocation and a fresh perspective on Return on Investment (ROI) within the context of online learning, with cybersecurity taking center stage. Three theoretical frameworks, technology adoption theory, cybersecurity risk management, and Resource Allocation, underpin the content of this text.

The Technology Adoption Theory/Framework theory, often associated with Everett Rogers' Diffusion of Innovations theory, posits that the adoption and assimilation of technology into an organization follow a specific trajectory (Granić, 2020). In the context of this text, it illustrates how organizations adopt online learning platforms as a technological innovation. The framework outlines the stages of awareness, interest, evaluation, trial, and adoption, highlighting the importance of aligning technology adoption with organizational objectives and cybersecurity imperatives (Granić, 2020). It also emphasizes that the success of online learning initiatives depends on how well they are integrated into the existing technological ecosystem.

While the Technology Adoption theory is valuable for understanding the stages of technology adoption, it may oversimplify the complex interplay of factors involved in integrating online learning platforms into an organization (Saghafian et al., 2021). It emphasizes the diffusion process but may need to adequately address the intricacies of aligning technology adoption with diverse organizational objectives and the dynamic cybersecurity landscape (Shibly et al., 2022). Additionally, it might need to account for the unique challenges and resistance emerging when introducing technology in educational settings, where pedagogical considerations play a significant role.

The Cybersecurity Risk Management Framework revolves around the idea that effective cybersecurity risk management is essential for organizational resilience in the digital age (Lee, 2021). It draws from established frameworks like the NIST Cybersecurity Framework or ISO 27001. In this context, the framework outlines the identification, protection, detection, response, and recovery phases of cybersecurity risk management (Roy, 2020). Per Lee, it emphasizes that investments in cybersecurity are not just about financial returns but also about safeguarding the organization's reputation, data, and the trust of its stakeholders, including learners. The framework illustrates how cybersecurity is a strategic imperative in online learning, intertwining risk mitigation with educational goals (Lee, 2021).

The Cybersecurity Risk Management framework, though robust, can be critiqued for potential rigidity (Cremer et al., 2022). It relies heavily on predefined risk management phases, which may only sometimes align perfectly with the rapidly evolving nature of cyber threats. Critics argue that these frameworks may become outdated quickly and need to account for emerging risks. (Lee, 2021) Furthermore, they might not address the specific nuances of the online learning environment, which can have unique vulnerabilities and compliance requirements. As such, adaptability and continuous monitoring are essential to mitigate potential shortcomings (Cremer et al., 2022)

The Resource Allocation Theory/Framework examines how organizations distribute resources to achieve their objectives efficiently. In online learning and cybersecurity, this framework underscores the need to strategically allocate resources to optimize pedagogical effectiveness while safeguarding against cyber threats (Marseille & Kahn, 2019). It emphasizes aligning financial investments with organizational goals and cybersecurity requirements. This framework guides decision-makers in making informed choices about where to allocate resources to maximize the ROI of online learning initiatives while maintaining a robust cybersecurity posture (Marseille & Kahn, 2019).

The Resource Allocation theory has static assumptions in a dynamic environment. Resource Allocation theory makes assumptions about resource needs and allocation based on relatively stable conditions. However, in the context of online learning and cybersecurity, the environment is highly dynamic (Marseille & Kahn, 2019). New technologies, cyber threats, and pedagogical trends continuously evolve (Burrell et al., 2020; Dawson & Szakonyi, 2020). Therefore, relying solely on static resource allocation models can lead to misalignment between investments and actual needs. This rigidity may hinder an organization's ability to respond effectively to emerging challenges and opportunities, especially in the fast-paced world of online education (Kleinmuntz, 2007). To address this critique, organizations must adopt more flexible and adaptive resource allocation strategies that accommodate changing circumstances.

These theoretical frameworks provide a holistic perspective on the challenges and opportunities of integrating online learning into organizational strategies (University of Southern California, 2023). They underline the pivotal role of cybersecurity in this landscape, ensuring that investments yield not only financial benefits but also support the secure and efficient operation of online learning platforms. Furthermore, these frameworks support a change acknowledging the imperative of ongoing evaluation and adaptation (Milella et al., 2021) to navigate the ever-evolving intersection of online learning, organizational objectives, and cybersecurity effectively, ensuring organizations remain resilient and responsive in this dynamic digital milieu.

THE FOCUS OF THE CHAPTER

This chapter serves as an academic exploration and comprehensive examination of the intricate interplay between educational initiatives, online learning, strategy and organizational objectives, sustainability, ROI, and the critical domain of cybersecurity within the contemporary digital milieu. See Figure 1 to connect these points. At its core, this chapter delves into the imperative for discerning investments and achieving strategic alignment within a landscape where online learning engenders a profound transformation of long-established educational paradigms, thereby empowering cybersecurity leaders and professionals to address knowledge gaps effectively. Here are three specific examples of how this chapter addresses this imperative.

The first is the alignment of education and training initiatives with organizational objectives. The online learning landscape challenges conventional norms related to return on investment (ROI) since it demands a heightened focus on deliberate program planning and increased investments, especially in alignment with online initiatives (Fetaji & Fetaji, 2009). The apparent need to align educational initiatives and an organization's overarching goals recognizes that online learning is becoming increasingly integral to educational and business strategies (Carnegie Mellon University, 2023). As given by Cloud Security Alliance (2023), traditional compliance-focused training methods prove ineffective in fostering a cybersecurity culture and long-term behavioral change, highlighting the importance of aligning training content and methods with adult workers' values and objectives to incentivize the desired behaviors. It is crucial to ensure that learning objectives and strategies align with broader business objectives. The connection between this alignment and achieving high levels of strategic performance and competitiveness is highlighted by Ghonim et al. in their 2020 study, emphasizing the role of strategic planning in the process. For example, suppose a company's main objective is to enhance its cybersecurity posture and protect sensitive data. In that case, the chapter suggests that the education and training programs should equip employees with the skills and knowledge necessary to address cybersecurity threats effectively. As emphasized by Care et al. (2019), education systems must provide learners with essential competencies like problem-solving, collaboration, critical thinking, and communication. This alignment matters (Carnegie Mellon University, 2023) because it ensures that educational investments are strategically directed toward achieving the organization's cybersecurity goals.

The second is sustainability. In the study by (Feeney et al., 2022), they propose that addressing sustainability challenges effectively necessitates a broader perspective, extending beyond the confines of individual organizations and fostering greater engagement with stakeholders. Their research advances a shared comprehension of the intricate nature of achieving sustainability, spanning various fields of study. Consequently, this positions researchers and scholars in education to actively participate in transdisciplinary research endeavors to promote sustainability. Their work significantly enhances our insights into the practical aspects of organizing for sustainability. Within a transdisciplinary framework, which transcends cultural boundaries and disciplinary constraints, this approach is characterized by its presumptive nature, learner-centric focus, and constructivist principles. It empowers researchers to generate relevant evidence crucial for informed decision-making in sustainability (Shakya et al., 2019).

Furthermore, Burton (2021) introduced a transdisciplinary framework incorporating four distinct methodologies: cybersecurity leadership, digitization technology, andragogy, and training in the cybersecurity landscape. Burton's approach involves amalgamating these methodologies to create a hybrid model that encompasses the strengths of its parent methodologies. This innovative framework offers a robust and adaptable approach to addressing complex challenges.

In summary, Feeney et al.'s (2022) research underscores the importance of adopting a transdisciplinary perspective to tackle sustainability issues. At the same time, Burton's (2021) framework exemplifies the potential of hybrid models in navigating multifaceted challenges. These approaches collectively contribute to a deeper understanding of how to organize and make decisions to pursue sustainability effectively.

The third is measuring ROI in cybersecurity investments. The chapter challenges conventional conceptions of return on investment (ROI) by expanding the definition of ROI in the context of cybersecurity investments. It asserts that ROI should not be solely measured in terms of financial savings but should also consider the value of maintaining the smooth operation of online learning platforms and preserving user trust (Cremer et al., 2022). For instance, if an educational institution invests in cybersecurity measures that prevent a data breach, the financial ROI may not be immediately apparent. Still, the long-term benefits of avoiding reputational damage, legal liabilities, and losing the trust of students and stakeholders are substantial (Jones, 2020). Considering these broader impacts, the chapter encourages organizations to evaluate cybersecurity investments more comprehensively and strategically.

Necessitated is a comprehensive reevaluation of resource allocation, thus challenging conventional conceptions of return on investment (ROI), with a particular emphasis on the pivotal domain of cybersecurity. The ROI derived from cybersecurity investments is not confined solely to financial savings; it encompasses the seamless operation of online learning platforms and the preservation of user trust. For Chief Information Security Officers (CISOs) to make well-informed decisions and optimize the return on investment (ROI) in cybersecurity products, they must possess the capability to continuously monitor and analyze trends and performance metrics over an extended period (Tehlia, 2023). In an era where remote learning has assumed the role of the lifeblood for online business enterprises, the mandate is dual-fold: to optimize pedagogical efficacy while judiciously containing costs, with cybersecurity emerging as the lynchpin (Dougherty, 2021). Leadership should understand applying ROI, as it is a critical tool for strategic planning (Ives & Seymour, 2022). While historical data serves as a compass for strategic endeavors, it is imperative for cybersecurity to perpetually scrutinize emerging data to improve processes (Cloud Security Alliance, 2023; Cremer et al., 2022; Tehlia, 2023).

Figure 1. Strategic synergy matrix: Navigating the intersections of education, online learning, strategy and goals, sustainability, ROI, and cybersecurity

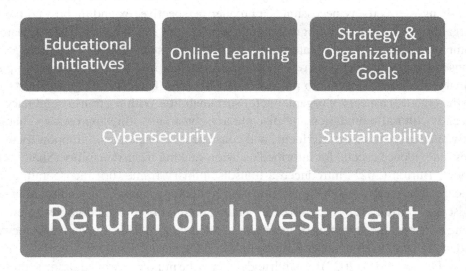

ROI and Cybersecurity: Closing the Knowledge Gap

ROI can play a pivotal role in closing the knowledge gap in cybersecurity by providing a structured approach to measure the effectiveness of educational and training initiatives (Cremer et al., 2022). Closing the gap occurs through justifying investment in cybersecurity training, assessing the impact of cybersecurity incidents, identifying areas for improvement, demonstrating the value of continuous learning, encouraging accountability and responsibility, and justifying future investments (Cremer et al., 2022; Tehlia, 2023). Furthermore, ROI empowers organizations to make data-driven decisions in cybersecurity training, allowing them to allocate resources efficiently, focus on the most effective training methods, and ensure that every investment enhances their cybersecurity posture

ROI analysis helps organizations quantify the benefits derived from investments in cybersecurity education and training programs by justifying investment in cybersecurity training (Ives & Seymour, 2022). When decision-makers see a clear financial justification for allocating resources to such programs, they are more likely to prioritize and fund them adequately. For instance, a company may invest in a cybersecurity training program for its employees. By calculating ROI, the organization can determine whether the program has led to a reduction in security incidents, thereby demonstrating the value of the training investment.

By assessing the impact of cybersecurity incidents, ROI analysis allows organizations to measure the impact of cybersecurity training on reducing incidents. By identifying areas for improvement by analyzing the ROI of different training initiatives, organizations can identify which programs are the most effective and which may need improvement. For instance, if ROI analysis reveals that one training program has a significantly higher return than another, it signals that resources should be reallocated towards the more effective program or that the less effective program may require adjustments. Furthermore, this data-driven approach to improving training initiatives ensures that organizations can continually adapt and refine their cybersecurity education strategies to address emerging threats effectively and allocate resources where they will have the most significant impact on security posture.

By demonstrating the value of continuous learning, ROI analysis underscores the value of continuous learning in cybersecurity (Ives & Seymour, 2022). As the threat landscape evolves, ongoing education and training are crucial to keep knowledge and skills up-to-date (Brown-Jackson, 2023). ROI calculations can show that investing in regular, updated training programs is more cost-effective than dealing with the consequences of a breach resulting from outdated knowledge (Cremer et al., 2022).

Encouraging accountability and responsibility is salient (Burton et al., 2013). When organizations calculate the ROI of cybersecurity training, it holds both learners and training providers accountable. Employees understand the importance of applying what they have learned, knowing their actions impact the organization's cybersecurity posture (Burrell, 2021). Training providers are incentivized to deliver high-quality, compelling content that generates positive ROI (Burton, 2015). This synergy between accountability and ROI-driven training initiatives ultimately creates a more robust line of defense against cyber threats, with employees actively safeguarding their organization's digital assets and data. This synergy between accountability and ROI-driven training initiatives ultimately creates a more robust defense against cyber threats, with employees actively safeguarding their organization's digital assets and data (Cremer et al., 2022). Positive ROI from cybersecurity training can justify further investments in education and skill development (Ives & Seymour, 2022). ROI analysis provides a quantifiable means to assess the effectiveness of cybersecurity education and training initiatives. By demonstrating the financial benefits and impact on incident reduction, ROI analysis not only justifies current investments but also informs future decisions, ultimately contributing to closing the knowledge gap in cybersecurity and enhancing an organization's overall security posture. Moreover, integrating ROI analysis into cybersecurity education strategies fosters a culture of evidence-based decision-making, ensuring that resources are directed toward initiatives that deliver tangible results and continuous improvement in cybersecurity knowledge and preparedness.

Optimizing Resource Allocation

In an era where cybersecurity and online learning play pivotal roles, it is vital to underscore the paramount significance of optimizing resource allocation. Resource allocation provides a comprehensive perspective on how investments in these domains should align with pedagogical objectives and cybersecurity imperatives because it links to value creation, tactical decision-making, connecting budgets to strategy, and evidence-based decision-making (Burrell, 2021; Burton, 2015, 2022). For decision-makers and budget planners, this chapter offers invaluable guidance on strategically allocating resources to achieve educational goals while fortifying cybersecurity resilience. This importance lies in the delicate balance between advancing educational objectives and bolstering cybersecurity defenses in a world increasingly reliant on digital technologies. By offering a roadmap for resource allocation, decision-makers can ensure that investments in education and cybersecurity align strategically, thereby effectively safeguarding organizations and their learners in the contemporary digital landscape. Furthermore, within the realm of training, the chapter delves into strategies for addressing challenges related to standardized curricula and accessible training, considering human factors (Nobles, 2019). This holistic approach ensures that practitioners responsible for designing and delivering cybersecurity training programs can derive insights to make their initiatives effective and aligned with industry standards.

Academic Contribution

From an academic perspective, this chapter contributes to scholarly discussions by synthesizing and analyzing existing literature in cybersecurity, education, and ROI analysis. It is a comprehensive resource for researchers and academics interested in these converging domains, facilitating a deeper understanding of the intricate interplay between education, cybersecurity, and organizational strategy. Moreover, this scholarly contribution fosters a multidisciplinary approach to addressing the complex challenges at the intersection of education, cybersecurity, and organizational strategy, encouraging further research and collaboration to advance knowledge and practices in these critical domains. The significance of the last section lies in its potential to drive interdisciplinary research, enabling scholars to explore innovative solutions at the intersection of education, cybersecurity, and organizational strategy, ultimately advancing the collective understanding and practice in these critical domains. This chapter goes beyond a mere summary and provides actionable insights and strategies for practitioners and decision-makers. The chapter addresses pressing concerns, offers practical guidance, and contributes to academic discourse, making it an invaluable resource for anyone seeking to navigate the complex landscape where online learning, business objectives, and cybersecurity intersect.

SOLUTIONS AND RECOMMENDATIONS

In response to the challenges and opportunities outlined in this chapter, several solutions and recommendations can guide organizations and cybersecurity leaders in effectively addressing the knowledge gap and optimizing cybersecurity education and training programs:

1. **Standardized Curriculum Development**: To address the need for standardized cybersecurity training curricula, organizations should collaborate with industry experts and associations to develop comprehensive and up-to-date educational materials. These materials should cover various cybersecurity topics and align with industry standards. Additionally, establishing partnerships with recognized cybersecurity certification bodies can help ensure that the training curricula meet industry-recognized standards and certifications, further enhancing the credibility and effectiveness of the educational materials.

2. **Accessibility and Availability**: Enhancing The accessibility and availability of quality training materials can be achieved by leveraging digital platforms and online resources. Organizations should invest in user-friendly learning management systems (LMS) and partner with reputable online education providers to ensure that learners have access to relevant and up-to-date content. Moreover, embracing a blended learning approach that combines digital resources with interactive, instructor-led sessions can cater to diverse learning preferences and maximize the effectiveness of cybersecurity training programs.

3. **Continuous Learning Culture**: Cultivating a culture of continuous learning within the organization is essential. Encourage cybersecurity professionals to pursue certifications, attend conferences, and engage in ongoing training programs. Organizations should allocate resources for employees' professional development and provide incentives for achieving certifications and advancing their skills. Additionally, fostering a culture of continuous learning enhances cybersecurity expertise and strengthens the organization's overall security posture, staying ahead of evolving threats. Incentives can include recognition, promotions, or financial rewards to motivate professionals to pursue cybersecurity excellence.

4. **Simulation and Practical Training**: Cybersecurity education should incorporate realistic simulations and practical exercises that mirror real-world threats and scenarios. Hands-on training and cyber range exercises can help learners apply their knowledge and skills in a controlled environment, improving their ability to respond to cyber threats effectively.

5. **Metrics and Assessment**: Implement metrics and assessment tools to measure the effectiveness of cybersecurity education and training programs. Regularly evaluate learner performance and gather feedback to identify areas for improvement. Adjust the curriculum and delivery methods based on these assessments.

6. **Cross-Functional Collaboration**: Foster collaboration between cybersecurity teams and other departments within the organization, such as IT, legal, and compliance. Cross-functional teams can work together to develop and implement comprehensive cybersecurity strategies that align with business objectives.

7. **Partnerships with Educational Institutions**: Collaborate with educational institutions, universities, and colleges to establish cybersecurity education programs. These partnerships help bridge the skills gap by providing a pipeline of qualified cybersecurity professionals.

FUTURE RESEARCH DIRECTIONS

As the dynamic landscape of cybersecurity and education continues to evolve, several promising research directions emerge:

1. **Effective Pedagogical Approaches:** Investigate and develop innovative pedagogical approaches that maximize learning outcomes in cybersecurity education. Explore the effectiveness of different teaching methods, such as gamification, experiential learning, and adaptive learning platforms.
2. **Cybersecurity Workforce Development:** Research the long-term impact of investing in cybersecurity education and training on the overall cybersecurity workforce. Examine how well-prepared professionals are to address emerging threats and adapt to evolving technologies.
3. **Measuring ROI in Cybersecurity Education:** Develop comprehensive frameworks for measuring the return on investment in cybersecurity education and training. Explore the quantifiable and qualitative factors contributing to ROI and assess how these investments impact an organization's cybersecurity posture.
4. **Cybersecurity Policy and Regulation**: Investigate the relationship between cybersecurity education and policy development. Explore how effective education and training programs influence the creation of cybersecurity regulations and standards at both national and international levels.
5. **Emerging Technologies:** Examine the role of emerging technologies, such as artificial intelligence and machine learning, in enhancing cybersecurity education and training. Evaluate How these technologies can be integrated into educational programs to improve threat detection and response capabilities. By fostering collaboration between academia, industry, and policymakers, the field of cybersecurity education can evolve to bridge the knowledge gap and prepare a skilled workforce. Academic institutions can innovate pedagogical approaches, industry can offer practical insights. Policymakers can establish regulatory frameworks that incentivize education and training. Together, these efforts fortify our defenses against digital threats.

CONCLUSION

Effective cybersecurity leadership is paramount in the rapidly evolving landscape of cyber threats. These leaders must comprehend the intricacies of the ever-changing threat landscape and demonstrate tangible returns on investment (ROI) for organizations. Failing to plan for ROI can result in unclear decision-making, risk underestimation, and an inability to prioritize work. A significant challenge in cybersecurity is the knowledge gap between scientists and practitioners, which can hinder cyber risk management. Influential cybersecurity leaders require diverse skills, including self-awareness, visionary thinking, self-regulation, and decisive decision-making. The ROI here extends beyond preventing cyberattacks to optimizing resource allocation and reducing the costs associated with security breaches.

Prioritizing cybersecurity education and training is crucial. Organizations must foster competencies such as communication, strategic planning, innovation, and crisis management in their leaders. The ROI of such investments is evident in reduced security incidents and more efficient incident response, safeguarding the organization's financial stability and reputation.

Consistent infusion of cybersecurity education and training throughout organizations is imperative. This approach ensures team members are well-informed, adaptable to evolving threats, and capable of effective crisis response. Effective leadership fosters a culture of security awareness and readiness, enhancing the organization's ROI.

In this era of digital transformation and cyber risk, cybersecurity leaders play a pivotal role. They must bridge knowledge gaps, promote education and training, and apply interdisciplinary approaches effectively. The challenges posed by cyber threats are significant. However, with the right leadership competencies and a commitment to continuous learning, organizations can navigate these challenges and emerge more robust and resilient, ultimately achieving a favorable ROI on their cybersecurity investments.

REFERENCES

Boyd, N. E., Zaynutdinova, G. R., Burdette, M., & Burks, N. (2020). Value added: West Virginia University's approach to innovative experiential learning. *Managerial Finance*, *46*(5), 599–609. doi:10.1108/MF-08-2018-0403

Brown-Jackson, K. L. (2023). *Cybersecurity Leadership: A Healthcare Critical Infrastructure And Wearables Examination* [Unpublished Exegesis]. Capitol Technology University.

Burrell, D. N. (2018). An exploration of the cybersecurity workforce shortage. *International Journal of Hyperconnectivity and the Internet of Things*, *2*(1), 29–41. doi:10.4018/IJHIoT.2018010103

Burrell, D. N. (2021). *Cybersecurity leadership from a talent management organizational development lens* [Unpublished Exegesis]. Capitol Technology University.

Burrell, D. N., Burton, S. L., Nobles, C., Dawson, M. E., & McDowell, T. (2020). Exploring technological management innovations that include artificial intelligence and other innovations in global food production. *International Journal of Society Systems Science*, *12*(4), 267–285. doi:10.1504/IJSSS.2020.112408

Burton, S. L. (2022). *Cybersecurity leadership from a Telemedicine/Telehealth knowledge and organizational development examination* (Order No. 29066056). Available from ProQuest Central; ProQuest Dissertations & Theses Global. (2662752457). https://www.proquest.com/dissertations-theses/cybersecurity-leadership-telemedicine-telehealth/docview/2662752457/se-2

Burton, S. L., Bessette, D., Brown-Jackson, K. L., & White, Y. W. (2013). ROI: Drilling Down on Cost-Benefit Components. *Proceedings of the SALT Conference*, 2013.

Care, E., Kim, H., & Vista, A. (2019, January 30). Education system alignment for 21st century skills: Focus on assessment. *Brookings Institute*. https://www.brookings.edu/articles/education-system-alignment-for-21st-century-skills/

Carnegie Mellon University. (2023). Why should assessments, learning objectives, and instructional strategies be aligned? *Author*. https://www.cmu.edu/teaching/assessment/basics/alignment.html

Cloud Security Alliance. (2023). Maximizing ROI on cybersecurity training. *Author*. https://cloudsecurityalliance.org/blog/2023/07/25/maximizing-roi-on-cybersecurity-training/

Cramer, J. A., Roy, A., Burrell, A., Fairchild, C. J., Fuldeore, M. J., Ollendorf, D. A., & Wong, P. K. (2008). Medication compliance and persistence: Terminology and definitions. *Value in Health (Wiley-Blackwell)*, *11*(1), 44–47. doi:10.1111/j.1524-4733.2007.00213.x

Cremer, F., Sheehan, B., Fortmann, M., Kia, A. N., Mullins, M., Murphy, F., & Materne, S. (2022). Cyber risk and cybersecurity: A systematic review of data availability. *The Geneva Papers on Risk and Insurance. Issues and Practice*, *47*(3), 698–736. doi:10.1057/s41288-022-00266-6 PMID:35194352

Dawson, M., Bacius, R., Gouveia, L. B., & Vassilakos, A. (2021). Understanding the challenge of cybersecurity in critical infrastructure sectors. *Land Forces Academy Review*, *251*(101), 69–75. doi:10.2478/raft-2021-0011

Dawson, M., & Szakonyi, A. (2020). Cybersecurity education to create awareness in artificial intelligence applications for developers and end users. *Science Bulletin*, *25*(2), 85–92. doi:10.2478/bsaft-2020-0012

Dougherty, F. (2021, February 16). The future of online learning: the long-term trends accelerated by Covid-19. *The Guardian*. https://www.theguardian.com/education/2021/feb/16/the-future-of-online-learning-the-long-term-trends-accelerated-by-covid-19

Feeney, M., Grohnert, T., Gijselaers, W., & Martens, P. (2023). Organizations, Learning, and Sustainability: A Cross-Disciplinary Review and Research Agenda. *Journal of Business Ethics*, *184*(1), 217–235. doi:10.1007/s10551-022-05072-7

Fetaji, B., & Fetaji, M. (2009). e-Learning Indicators: A Multi-Dimensional Model for Planning and Evaluating e-Learning Software Solutions. *Electronic Journal of e-Learning*, *7*(1), 1–28.

Fortinet. (2022). How Is the Skills Gap Creating Cyber Risk? *Author*. https://www.fortinet.com/blog/industry-trends/global-cybersecurity-skills-gap-report-findings

Ghonim, N., Khashaba, N., Al-Najaar, H., & Khashan, M. (2020). Strategic alignment and its impact on decision effectiveness: a comprehensive model. *International Journal of Emerging Markets*. www.emerald.com/insight/1746-8809.htm

Graham, S. (2023). *Cybersecurity is number one risk for global banks, but geopolitical risk tops European banks' concerns*. EY. https://www.ey.com/en_gl/news/2023/01/cybersecurity-is-number-one-risk-for-global-banks-but-geopolitical-risk-tops-european-banks-concerns

Granić, A. (2023). *Technology adoption at individual level: toward an integrated overview*. Univ Access Inf Soc. doi:10.1007/s10209-023-00974-3

ISACA. (2022). State of the cybersecurity workforce: New ISACA research shows highest retention difficulties in years. *Author*. https://www.isaca.org/about-us/newsroom/press-releases/2022/state-of-the-cybersecurity-workforce-new-isaca-research-shows-retention-difficulties-in-years

Ives, K., & Seymour, D. M. (2022). *Using ROI for strategic planning of online education: A process for institutional transformation*. Routledge.

Jones, L. A. (2020). *Reputation Risk and Potential Profitability: Best Practices to Predict and Mitigate Risk through Amalgamated Factors* (Order No. 28152966). Available from ProQuest Central; ProQuest Dissertations & Theses Global. 28152966). https://www.proquest.com/openview/1dbd40ceb5eacaf981fd65dd3ee3d9b3/1.pdf?pq-origsite=gscholar&c%20bl=18750&diss=y

Kleinmuntz, D. (2007). Resource Allocation Decisions. In W. Edwards, R. Miles Jr, & D. Von Winterfeldt (Eds.), *Advances in Decision Analysis: From Foundations to Applications* (pp. 400–418). Cambridge University Press. doi:10.1017/CBO9780511611308.021

Kruse, K. (2012, January 16). Stephen Covey: 10 quotes that can change your life. *Forbes*. https://www.forbes.com/sites/kevinkruse/2012/07/16/the-7-habits/?sh=4d9e7f8b39c6

Lee, I. (2021). Cybersecurity: Risk management framework and investment cost analysis. *Business Horizons, 64*(5), 659–671. doi:10.1016/j.bushor.2021.02.022

Marseille, E., & Kahn, J. G. (2019). Utilitarianism and the ethical foundations of cost-effectiveness analysis in resource allocation for global health. *Philosophy, Ethics, and Humanities in Medicine; PEHM, 14*(5), 5. Advance online publication. doi:10.1186/s13010-019-0074-7 PMID:30944009

Milella, F., Minelli, E. A., Strozzi, F., & Croce, D. (2021). Change and Innovation in Healthcare: Findings from Literature. *ClinicoEconomics and Outcomes Research, 13*, 395–408. doi:10.2147/CEOR.S301169 PMID:34040399

Morris, G. F. (2019). *The cyber-security concerns regarding the internet of things associated with the critical infrastructure within Northern Nevada* (Order No. 13428023). Available from ProQuest Central; ProQuest Dissertations & Theses Global. (2185755372). https://www.proquest.com/dissertations-theses/cyber-security-concerns-regarding-internet-things/docview/2185755372/se-2?accountid=167615

Muller, S. R. (2021). A Perspective On the intersection of information security policies and I.A. awareness, factoring in end-user behavior. *Proceedings of the International Conference on Research in Management & Technovation*, 137–142. 10.15439/2020KM1

Murphey, D. (2020). *How your H.R. department can help to overcome the cybersecurity skills gap*. BenefitsPRO. https://www.proquest.com/trade-journals/how-your-hr-department-can-help-overcome/docview/2376391277/se-2?accountid=167615

Murray, S. (2018, July 12). MBA courses start teaching digital security skills: Education business schools add cyber to the curriculum as attacks become a boardroom matter. *Financial Times*. https://www.proquest.com/newspapers/mba-courses-start-teaching-digital-security/docview/2086913126/se-2?accountid=167615

Nobles, C. (2019). Establishing human factors programs to mitigate blind spots in cybersecurity. *Midwest Association for Information Systems 2019 Proceedings*, 22. https://aisel.aisnet.org/mwais2019/22

Orlanova, A. I. (2012). Continuous education for the knowledge society. *Russian Education & Society, 54*(4), 3–13. doi:10.2753/RES1060-9393540401

Pressley, A. (2023). 85% of cyber leaders believe AI will outpace cyber defences. *Intelligent CISO*. https://www.intelligentciso.com/2023/09/20/85-of-cyber-leaders-believe-ai-will-outpace-cyber-defences/

Roy, P. P. (2020). A high-level comparison between the NIST Cyber Security Framework and the ISO 27001 Information Security Standard. *2020 National Conference on Emerging Trends on Sustainable Technology and Engineering Applications (NCETSEA)*. 1-3. 10.1109/NCETSEA48365.2020.9119914

Saghafian, M., Laumann, K., & Skogstad, M. R. (2021). Stagewise Overview of Issues Influencing Organizational Technology Adoption and Use. *Frontiers in Psychology*, *12*, 630145. doi:10.3389/fpsyg.2021.630145 PMID:33815216

Shakya, B., Schneider, F., Yang, Y., & Sharma, E. (2019). A Multiscale Transdisciplinary Framework for Advancing the Sustainability Agenda of Mountain Agricultural Systems. *Mountain Research and Development*, *39*(3). Advance online publication. doi:10.1659/MRD-JOURNAL-D-18-00079.1

Shibly, H. R., Abdullah, A., & Murad, M. W. (2022). Adoption of Innovative Technology. In *ERP Adoption in Organizations*. Palgrave Macmillan. doi:10.1007/978-3-031-11934-7_3

Tan, F. Z. & Olaore. (2021). Effect of organizational learning and effectiveness on the operations, employees productivity and management performance. *XIMB Journal of Management, 19*(2), 110-127. https://www.emerald.com/insight/content/doi/10.1108/XJM-09-2020-0122/full/html

Tehlia, S. (2023, August 16). Cybersecurity as a strategic investment: How ROI optimization can lead to a more secure future. *Forbes*. https://www.forbes.com/sites/forbestechcouncil/2023/08/16/cybersecurity-as-a-strategic-investment-how-roi-optimization-can-lead-to-a-more-secure-future/?sh=1982a66c4cf7

University of Southern California. (2023). *Theoretical framework*. Author. https://libguides.usc.edu/writingguide/theoreticalframework

KEY TERMS AND DEFINITIONS

Cyber Risk Management: Cyber risk management involves identifying, assessing, and mitigating potential threats and vulnerabilities in an organization's digital infrastructure and data assets. It involves strategies and practices aimed at protecting these assets from cyberattacks and minimizing the impact of security breaches.

Cybersecurity Leadership: Cybersecurity leadership pertains to individuals or teams responsible for guiding and overseeing an organization's cybersecurity efforts. This includes setting strategic objectives, making decisions about resource allocation, and ensuring that cybersecurity measures align with the organization's goals and risk tolerance.

Education and Training: Education and training in the context of cybersecurity involve programs and activities designed to impart knowledge and develop skills related to information security. This includes teaching employees and stakeholders about best practices, policies, and procedures to protect against cyber threats.

Knowledge Gap: A knowledge gap represents the disparity between what individuals or organizations currently know and understand and what they need to know to achieve specific objectives or address challenges effectively. In cybersecurity, a knowledge gap could refer to the difference between an organization's current security knowledge and the knowledge required to protect against cyber threats adequately.

NIST Cybersecurity Framework: The National Institute of Standards and Technology (NIST) Cybersecurity Framework is a set of guidelines, best practices, and standards developed by the U.S. government to help organizations manage and improve their cybersecurity risk management processes. It provides a structured approach for organizations to identify, protect, detect, respond to, and recover from cyber threats.

Organizational Goals: Organizational goals are specific, measurable, and time-bound objectives that an organization aims to achieve in order to fulfill its mission and vision. These goals provide a sense of direction and purpose, guiding the actions and decisions of the organization.

Return on Investment (ROI): Return on Investment is a financial metric that measures the profitability and efficiency of an investment. In the context of cybersecurity, it assesses the financial benefits or gains compared to the costs of implementing cybersecurity measures. A positive ROI indicates that the investment has generated a return greater than its initial cost.

Strategy: Strategy refers to a long-term plan or approach that an organization develops to achieve its goals and objectives. It involves making decisions about resource allocation, competitive positioning, and the actions necessary to succeed in a particular market or domain.

Chapter 11
Maximizing Cyber Intelligence and Security Team Capabilities Through DEI:
The Hidden Benefits of Diversity as a Strategic Defense

Helen MacLennan

iD https://orcid.org/0000-0002-0795-5008

Lindsey Wilson College, USA

ABSTRACT

The cyber intelligence and security sector faces a growing number of threats and attacks that are increasing in complexity, but reports indicate that the current workforce lacks the qualified professionals needed to combat them. The U.S. Government and the educational community have been increasing efforts to help grow and diversify a workforce that continues to be primarily white male dominated. However, there are organization-level tactics that can be leveraged to increase and enhance the talent pool. Diversity, equity, and inclusion (DEI) initiates should be viewed not only as opportunities to engender equality but also as an opportunity to help recruit and develop the talent pool necessary to strategically heighten cyber intelligence and security capabilities. Consequently, the author reviews the benefits that DEI can bring to cybersecurity and discuss practical recommendations for moving forward with DEI initiative that can help support the industry's growing challenges.

INTRODUCTION

The cyber intelligence and security sector, which I will refer to in this paper as simply cybersecurity, faces an alarming workforce shortage. The Homeland Security Subcommittee of Cybersecurity and Infrastructure Protection (2023), Director of National Intelligence (2023), and the White House National Cyber Director (2023) along with private sector cybersecurity organizations all point to a severe lack

DOI: 10.4018/979-8-3693-1970-3.ch011

of qualified talent needed to fill vacancies in the industry. The Office of the National Cyber Director (2023) estimated the difference between global demand and qualified cyber security professionals at approximately 3.4 million.

The lack of qualified professionals in this sector has some negative implications for industry and the nation's overall security. Cybercrime and criminals are more diverse than ever and so are their opportunities to breach the security of individuals, organizations, and national governments. The Office of the Director of National Intelligence (2023) Annual Threat Assessment of the U.S. Intelligence Community indicates "Globally, foreign states' malicious use of digital information and communication technologies will become more pervasive, automated, targeted, and complex in the future, further threatening to distort publicly available information and probably will outpace efforts to protect digital freedoms" (p. 27). Security leaders are reporting an increase in novel attack strategies such as data poisoning and the use of generative artificial intelligence (AI) to develop malware and create more sophisticated phishing messages (Pratt, 2023).

While Artificial intelligence (AI) systems can be trained to detect some cybersecurity threats to help alleviate the workforce shortage, there are some limitations. Because threats, such as viruses and malware are constantly being changed by cyber criminals, AI systems require human experts who are creative in their approach to programming to combat them (Ansari et al., 2022). In addition, as cyber criminals become more advanced, existing AI data encryption protocols become easier for them to reverse-engineer, posing additional threats to data security (Ansari et al., 2022). To combat these threats, we will need to use all available resources and augment current AI initiatives with a focus on increasing the available human talent in this sector.

An issue with the current pool of qualified cybersecurity professionals is that it has remained consistently homogenous since its beginnings, comprised primarily of white males. The World Economic Forum (2021) reported that the cybersecurity workforce is comprised of an estimated 9% Black, 4% Hispanic 8% Asian and about 24% female professionals. Zippia (2023) reported that as of 2021, 78.5% of cyber analysts were male, 60% are over 40 years of age with only 11% between 20-30 years of age, and approximately 8.59% are members of the LGBT community. These statistics have changed very little over the past 13 years. Government and industry officials point to education and DEI initiatives as critical components of a solution to the talent shortage in the cybersecurity sector, but improve their capabilities to defend us against increasing cyber threats. A sustainable solution can only come from a multi-pronged approach that includes a deliberate attempt to increase the diversity of the cybersecurity workforce by implementing or re-tooling diversity, equity, and inclusion (DEI) efforts, which can expand the numbers of qualified professionals in the talent pool, but also offers some additional benefits to this sector.

REVIEW OF LITERATURE

The Efficacy of Current DEI Initiatives

Generally, there is no standard definition or understanding of workplace diversity nor are there many clear indications of what comprises an effective organizational DEI strategy. Consequently, it is not surprising that the implementation of DEI policies and mandated diversity training are failing to drive real change and, in some cases, have increased employee biases and decreased feelings of belonging

(Georgean & Rattan, 2022). In a recent survey of almost 6,000 workers, only about 30% of respondents placed much importance on diversity in their workplace, but most employees reported some DEI initiatives in place that consisted primarily of organizational policies to ensure fairness coupled with required diversity trainings to increase awareness of unconscious bias (Minkin, 2023). There is little research on the efficacy of either.

There is some promising recent research on organizational diversity. Drawing from social psychology and organization studies, Bernstein et al.'s (2020) theory of generative interactions suggest that the answer may lie in addressing multiple dynamics, including self-segregation, communication apprehension, and stereotyping through organizational practices that focus on skill development and structured generative interactions, grounded in identity awareness. According to Bernstein et al. (2020). "The organizational practices provide the following conditions for generative interactions: pursuing an important, shared organizational purpose, mixing diverse members frequently over protracted periods of time, enabling differing groups to have equal standing and insider status in contributing to success, and providing collaborative interdependence, interpersonal comfort, and self-efficacy" (p. 395). These practices can help build an organizational culture of inclusion to reduce bias and stereotyping among groups in the workplace.

Understanding Bias and Stereotyping

Drawing from the social psychology literature, the research on unconscious bias has been a foundation for many organizational DEI initiatives (Kempf, 2020). The premise of unconscious bias is that every individual has stereotypes about individuals from groups outside of their own that are deep-seated and developed over a lifetime. Consequently, those biases will ultimately drive decisions and behaviors. We, as individuals, are neurologically predisposed to make judgments or decisions about individuals in particular groups, without necessarily intending to do so.

Understanding social identity theory (Tajfel & Turner, 1971) is important to understanding bias and stereotyping. Individuals have an innate tendency to categorize themselves and others as being part of a particular social group that may be based on age, gender, ethnicity, or work activities. Individuals who consider themselves to belong to a particular group tend to display solidarity and support for one another, while simultaneously viewing members of outside groups as different or possibly inferior. Expanding on social identify theory, Brewer (1991) presented optimal distinctiveness theory, which proposes that individuals have competing motivations for both inclusion and distinctiveness. The theory has expanded to the area of organization research with the idea that for optimal performance, individuals need to consider themselves to belong to a preferred group, but also need to be valued for their unique contributions. Empirical testing strongly supports the need for both inclusion and differentiation that can be met by membership in distinct groups (Leonardelli et al., 2010). However, a recent theoretical review suggests that we need to increase our understanding of contextualizing optimal distinctiveness because we have fallen short of accounting for the contingencies of organizational hybrity, societal culture, temporal contingencies, and benchmarks for gauging success (Zhao & Glynn, 2022). This remains a promising area of potential organizational research.

Diversity Training, often provided by outside consultants, is typically the cornerstone of most organizations' DEI programs. Unfortunately, it appears to be one of the least effective methods used to moderate workplace bias and increase managerial diversity (Chang et al., 2019; Dobbin & Kalev, 2018; Kalev et al., 2006). In fact, research shows that not only does mandated diversity training generally not result in any long-term positive effects, it can actually do harm by activating bias and decreasing feelings of inclusion for underrepresented groups. When opinions and behaviors are perceived as being mandated, employees will tend to resist. Sanchez and Medkik (2004) found that diversity training actually increased unfriendly treatment of non-white employees.

Many organizations are utilizing implicit bias training in their DEI initiatives. However, it is suggested that current organizational approaches to address implicit bias through short-term training sessions may actually provide reassurance to individuals that bias is normal and may ignore the influence of bias in terms of systemic, institutional, and individual privilege (Kempf, 2020). In addition, a large-scale longitudinal study tested 9 interventions on 6,321 participants and found that all 9 interventions immediately reduced implicit bias preferences, but none were shown to be effective after a delay of several hours to several days (Lai et al., 2016). DeHouwer (2019) also suggested that considering implicit bias to be a latent construct can be a flawed interpretation and simply adds support to the notion that it is difficult to change or control. In alignment with that contention, Corneille and Bena (2022) suggested that a reliance on the unconscious bias approach fails to consider the persistence of conscious, intentional and/or overt discrimination. Also, something to consider is the assumption and lack of evidence that simply making individuals aware of unconscious bias will, in fact, encourage them to change (Corneille & Bena, 2022).

Interestingly, however, Vuletich and Payne (2019) performed a reanalysis of the data collected by Lai et al., (2016) and found that bias returned to location means, but individual bias means were mostly random, supporting the idea that bias tends to remain static in social environments. This reasoning is based on Payne et al.'s (2017) bias of crowds theory, that proposes that while individual-level implicit bias are sensitive to changes, organization or population-levels of bias are more constant, serving to perpetuate inequalities in the social environment.

Organizational goals for the hiring, compensation, advancement and retention of underrepresented groups that include timelines for achievement have shown promise. Motel (2016) evaluated the influence of goal-setting theory in increasing workplace demographic representation and found that organizations using specific goals indicated better outcomes for minority and female leaders. Goal-setting theory (Locke & Latham, 2002) suggests that specific and high-level goals lead to a higher level of performance.

Dobbin and Kalev (2018) reported that while there is inconclusive evidence of the benefit of affirmative action plans, specific organizational goals for hiring quotas can have positive results (Holzer & Neumark, 2000). However, Dobbin and Kalev (2022) indicate that many firms may lack accountability and transparency when reporting information to the public and may not take the goals into account when downsizing (Dobbin & Kalev, 2022). An important moderator of goal setting is feedback, which allows for the identification of progress (Locke & Lathem, 2022).

If most cybersecurity organizations are relying solely on the components of mandated diversity training and organizational goal setting to augment any written diversity policy, it is possible to see why we have not seen significant changes in workforce diversity in this sector. A discussion of the additional benefits of DEI, beyond racial and gender equality follows, which is particularly beneficial to cybersecurity teams and should highlight the need for strategic DEI initiatives for every organization.

DEI Benefits for Cybersecurity

Beyond the obvious benefit of expanding the sheer numbers of individuals to fill the cybersecurity talent gap and ensuring equity and fairness in the workplace, a review of the literature also indicates several organization-level benefits to implementing or improving workplace DEI initiatives. There appears to be an overall lack of understanding of the importance of DEI and the potential benefits that it can bring. The common focus of DEI is on preventing discrimination in the employment process and the elimination of social exclusion, which are very important. However, DEI is not solely related to addressing disparities in the treatment of underrepresented individuals. There are additional potential benefits for every employee that can be particularly beneficial to the cybersecurity community. For example, the complex-problem solving, critical thinking, and divergent thinking skills that are needed to combat increasingly diverse cybersecurity threats, have all been shown to be positively influenced by DEI.

Critical Thinking is a multi-dimensional construct that involves the understanding and evaluation of information to make reasoned decisions. Bensley and Murtagh (2011) added that critical thinking involves a tendency to be open-minded and fair, yet skeptical in evaluating claims. Higgins (2014) discussed the importance of developing the quality of judgement and the ability to utilize skills and knowledge to resolve challenges and problems, particularly in the digital age when we are faced with such a tremendous scale of available information. Also, when considering the nature of cyber-crime, the ability of cybersecurity professionals to evaluate and interpret available information to formulate judgments becomes a critical skill.

Research indicates that there are cultural differences in critical thinking styles and performance (Lu, 2021; Lun et al., 2010) and that exposure to cultural diversity may enrich critical thinking skills (Inoue, 2005). However, in Loes et al.'s (2012) study, the only significant cognitive effects uncovered were related to actual interactions with diverse groups as opposed to mere exposures to diverse experiences. This is supported by Roksa et al.'s (2017) research, which found no differences in the development of critical thinking skills based on exposure to positive diversity experiences.

While much of the research around diversity and critical thinking is based on exposure to positive experiences, Roksa et al.'s (2017) research did indicate a significant negative effect of negative diversity experiences on critical thinking outcomes. Consequently, cybersecurity leadership should understand that negative diversity experiences, such as prejudice and discrimination, can negatively impact important critical thinking skills.

Creative Thinking. Exposure to diverse multicultural experiences has been found to heighten creative thinking (Storme et al., 2016). However, the research on team diversity shows mixed results. A seminal meta-analysis of research on creativity and innovation indicates that diversity related to specific job-level attributes showed a positive effect on individual and team innovation, but background diversity (i.e. race, gender, and age) showed a slight negative influence on innovation (Hülsheger et al., 2009). The reason for the contrast may lie in the idea that diverse teams may have difficulty communicating or reaching consensus when it comes time for decision-making (Dayan et al., 2017).

The reason for difficulty in decision-making for diverse teams can likely be attributed to divergent thinking. Homogenous teams tend to have convergent thinking, which makes decision-making easier. However, innovation and creativity call for thinking that diverges from the norm. The research on creativity and innovation highlights the idea that diversity should not be considered as a stand-alone objective, but rather as an important piece of a strategic DEI initiative.

Divergent Thinking. While homogenous teams may have increased cohesiveness, they often result in convergent thinking and uniformity in points of views, commonly referred to as groupthink. Groups that are made up of individuals with similar characteristics and backgrounds can tend to think alike and avoid dissenting from the opinions of the group. Apfelbaum et al. (2014) found that study participants assigned to homogenous groups were also much more likely to exhibit a self-serving bias in decision-making.

While similarity and conformity in thinking is beneficial for group cohesion, it can result in poor decision-making. Cybersecurity teams, which overall tend to be fairly homogenous in their makeup, cyber leaders should be aware of the dangers that it may pose to decision-making. In addition, in order to respond to and mitigate increasingly innovative threats, cybersecurity teams will need to develop more creative and innovative approaches. Empirical research on creativity and innovation highlights the need for divergent thinking (Clapham, 2010).

Complex Problem-Solving. Interestingly, research has shown that diversity has a positive effect on complex problem-solving (Reynolds & Lewis, 2017; Hong & Page, 2004). Hong and Page (2004) found that identity-diverse teams of problem-solvers selected at random outperform homogeneous teams of hand-selected top-performers. The researchers attribute this to groupthink. As the team of hand-selected top performers becomes larger, their tendency to become similar in their approach to problem-solving becomes similar. Reynolds and Lewis (2017) attribute the increase in complex problem-solving not necessarily to gender, age or ethnic differences, but to diversity in perspectives and information processing styles.

Staying a step ahead of identity thieves, computer hackers, ransomware, malware, supply chain attacks, and denial of service attacks while identifying and mitigating critical vulnerabilities requires cybersecurity professionals to have complex problem-solving skills. In addition to preventing cyber-attacks, problem-solving skills will be especially critical for reducing downtime and losses in the event of a cyber incident. Fortunately, DEI has been shown to strengthen problem-solving skills.

Practical Suggestions for Cybersecurity DEI Initiatives

First, understand that diversity, equity, and inclusion are 3 separate and distinct constructs. Focusing on only the diversity portion of DEI may increase the cybersecurity talent pool, but will not allow us to build highly function teams. We have evidence that supports the positive effect of DEI on critical thinking, innovation, creativity, and complex problem-solving. Consequently, cybersecurity leaders will need to think about each individually, but also create a comprehensive strategy that considers each separate construct.

DEI Leadership. Cybersecurity leaders are responsible for cultivating and modeling organizational culture. Creating a workplace environment with diverse, inclusive, and equitable hiring, compensation, evaluation, and promotion practices will take a genuine and organization-wide effort. DEI initiatives should be framed as a need for unique contributions, rather than a business asset. Research suggests that listing diversity as an organizational value, without additional justification was preferred by employees in underrepresented groups (Georgean & Rattan, 2022). Consequently, to eliminate potential pushback, it is beneficial to invite input and feedback from all levels when developing your organizational DEI strategy.

- A written policy is not enough to create culture of DEI.
- Focus and communicate the value of DEI for unique contributions.
- Walk the talk. Employees will look to you as a model of appropriate behavior.
- Elicit input and feedback from stakeholders to create a comprehensive DEI strategy.

Diversity. Cybersecurity leaders should focus on and promote the unique contributions that a diverse workforce can bring to the organization. Dwertmann et al. (2016) proposed that viewing DEI from the perspective of embracing and integrating the exchange of diverse ideas and information can only happen through what they term the synergy perspective, which reflects an organization-wide interest in the performance benefits of a diverse workforce. Diversity is not limited to racial differences. It refers to embracing and celebrating differences in all individuals, regardless of religious beliefs, gender identity, appearance, cultural upbringing, socio-economic status, etc.

- Consider employee-led training or making diversity training optional.
- Work with stakeholders to create achievable goals for diversity.
- Create appropriate metrics for measuring progress toward DEI goals.

Equity. The equity portion of DEI is frequently equated with equality for underrepresented employees, which ensures that all employees are provided with equal opportunities and resources. However, equity relates to the potential allocation of additional resources and support necessary to ensure equal outcomes for everyone.

- Develop opportunities for mentoring and coaching.
- Implement a Blinded Promotion Review (Enders et al., 2020).
- Review current hiring practices for potential unconscious bias.
- Consider re-skilling and up-skilling underrepresented employees.

Inclusion. Elicit input and feedback from all levels to develop policies, performance metrics, and training efforts. Consider that bias cannot be eliminated through workplace diversity training. What has been shown to work to reduce bias is an increase in interactions among diverse employees.

- Create diverse teams to increase employee interactions.
- Avoid justifications for your DEI initiatives that focus on profitability.
- Work to build trust among diverse team members.
- Have a zero-tolerance for discrimination of any kind.
- Train managers to identify and squash veiled discrimination.

CONCLUSION

Cybersecurity leaders should view DEI as a moral obligation, but also as an obligation to their workforce and those for whom they work to protect. With the critical shortage of qualified cyber intelligence and security professionals available to meet the rising number of cyber threats, cyber leaders need to be pro-active in working toward a solution. A comprehensive strategic approach should include a DEI initiative focused on increasing diverse employee interactions, celebrating unique individual contributions, and implementing high-level goal-setting and reporting. Successful DEI initiatives can expand the pool of potential cyber professionals and increase their capabilities, resulting in an overall benefit to the organization and the entire sector.

Research indicates that we can leverage DEI initiatives to increase critical thinking, complex problem-solving, and creativity in the cybersecurity workforce to help innovate approaches to understanding vulnerabilities and develop increased cyber defense capabilities. While I have not provided a comprehensive plan to implementing a successful DEI strategic initiative, I have provided some useful suggestions that are supported by research that can be used to help develop a DEI strategy to help develop a diverse and high-performing cybersecurity workforce.

REFERENCES

Ansari, M., Dash, B., Sharma, P., & Yatharaju, N. (2022). The impact and limitations of artificial intelligence in cybersecurity: A literature review. *International Journal of Advanced Research in Computer and Communication Engineering, 11*(9), 81–90. doi:10.17148/IJARCCE.2022.11912

Apfelbaum, E. P., Phillips, K., & Richeson, J. (2014). Rethinking the baseline in diversity research: Should we be explaining the effects of homogeneity? *Perspectives on Psychological Science, 9*(3), 235–244. doi:10.1177/1745691614527466 PMID:26173261

Bensley, D. A., & Murtagh, M. P. (2012). Guidelines for a scientific approach to critical thinking assessment. *Teaching of Psychology, 39*(1), 5-16. doi:10.1177/0098628311430642

Bernstein, R. S., Bulger, M., Salipante, P., & Weisinger, J. (2020). From diversity to inclusion to equity: A theory of generative interactions. *Journal of Business Ethics, 167*(3), 395–410. doi:10.1007/s10551-019-04180-1

Brewer, M. B. (1991). The social self: On being the same and different at the same time. *Personality and Social Psychology Bulletin, 17*(5), 475–482. doi:10.1177/0146167291175001

Chamorro-Premuzic, T. (2017, June 28). Does diversity actually increase creativity? *Harvard Business Review.* https://hbr.org/2017/06/does-diversity-actually-increase-creativity

Chang, E., Milkman, K., Zarrow, L., Brabaw, K., Gromet, D., Rebele, R., Massey, C., Duckworth, A., & Grant, Al. (2019, July 9). Does diversity training work the way it's supposed to? *Harvard Business Review.* https://hbr.org/2019/07/does-diversity-training-work-the-way-its-supposed-to

Clapham, M. (2001). The Effects of affect manipulation and information exposure on divergent thinking. *Creativity Research Journal, 13*(3-4), 3–4, 335–350. doi:10.1207/S15326934CRJ1334_11

Dayan, M., Ozer, M., & Almazrouei, H. (2017). The role of functional and demographic diversity on new product creativity and the moderating impact of project uncertainty. *Industrial Marketing Management, 61*, 144–154. doi:10.1016/j.indmarman.2016.04.016

De Houwer, J. (2019). Implicit bias is behavior: A functional-cognitive perspective complicit bias. *Perspectives on Psychological Science, 14*(5), 835–840. doi:10.1177/1745691619855638 PMID:31374177

Dobbin, F. & Kalev, A. (2018). Why doesn't diversity training work? The challenge for academia and America. *Anthropology Now, 10*(2), 48-55. doi:10.1080/19428200.2018.1493182

Dobbin, F., & Kalev, A. (2022, September 29). How companies should set and report DEI goals. *Harvard Business Review.* https://hbr.org/2022/09/how-companies-should-set-and-report-dei-goals

Dwertmann, D. J. G., Nishii, L. H., & van Knippenberg, D. (2016). Disentangling the fairness & discrimination and synergy perspectives on diversity climate: Moving the field forward. *Journal of Management,* *42*(5), 1136–1168. doi:10.1177/0149206316630380

Enders, F., Golembiewski, E., Pacheco-Spann, L., Allyse, M., Mielke, M., & Balls-Berry, J. (2020). Building a framework for inclusion in health services research: Development of and pre-implementation faculty and staff attitudes toward theDiversity,Equity,and Inclusion(DEI) plan at Mayo Clinic. *Journal of Clinical and Translational Science, 5*(88), 1–10. doi:10.1017/cts.2020.575 PMID:34007470

Georgeac, O., & Rattan, A. (2022, June 15). Stop making the business case for diversity. *Harvard Business Review.* https://hbr.org/2022/06/stop-making-the-business-case-for-diversity

Higgins, S. (2014). Critical thinking for 21-century education: A cyber-tooth curriculum? *Prospects (00331538), 44*(4), 559–574. https://doi-org.saintleo.idm.oclc.org/10.1007/s11125-014-9323-0

Holzer, H. J., & Neumark, D. (2000). What does affirmative action do? *Industrial & Labor Relations Review, 53*(2), 240–271. doi:10.1177/001979390005300204

Homeland Security Subcommittee Cybersecurity and Infrastructure Protection. (2023, June 22). *Subcommittee chair Garbarino: Robust cybersecurity workforce is needed to mitigate risk across federal networks, critical infrastructure.* https://homeland.house.gov/2023/06/22/subcommittee-chair-garbarino-robust-cybersecurity-workforce-is-needed-to-mitigate-risk-across-federal-networks-critical-infrastructure/

Hong, L., & Page, S. E. (2004). Groups of diverse problem solvers can outperform groups of high-ability problem solvers. *Proceedings of the National Academy of Sciences of the United States of America, 101*(46), 16385–16389. doi:10.1073/pnas.0403723101 PMID:15534225

Hülsheger, U. R., Anderson, N., & Salgado, J. F. (2009). Team-level predictors of innovation at work: A comprehensive meta-analysis spanning three decades of research. *The Journal of Applied Psychology, 94*(5), 1128–1145. doi:10.1037/a0015978 PMID:19702361

Inoue, Y. (2005). Critical thinking and diversity experiences: A connection. *Online Submission.* https://eric.ed.gov/?id=ED490360

Kalev, A., Dobbin, F., & Kelly, E. (2006). Best practices or best guesses? Assessing the efficacy of corporate affirmative action and diversity policies. *American Sociological Review, 71*(4), 589–617. doi:10.1177/000312240607100404

Kempf, A. (2020). If we are going to talk about implicit race bias, we need to talk about structural racism: Moving beyond ubiquity and inevitability in teaching and learning about race. Taboo. *The Journal of Culture and Education, 19*(2). https://digitalscholarship.unlv.edu/taboo/vol19/ iss2/10

Lai, C. K., Skinner, A. L., Cooley, E., Murrar, S., Brauer, M., Devos, T., Calanchini, J., Xiao, Y. J., Pedram, C., Marshburn, C. K., Simon, S., Blanchar, J. C., Joy-Gaba, J. A., Conway, J., Redford, L., Klein, R. A., Roussos, G., Schellhaas, F. M. H., Burns, M., ... Nosek, B. A. (2016). Reducing implicit racial preferences: II. Intervention effectiveness across time. *Journal of Experimental Psychology. General, 145*(8), 1001–1016. doi:10.1037/xge0000179 PMID:27454041

Leonardelli, G. J., Pickett, C. L., & Brewer, M. B. (2010). Optimal distinctiveness theory: A framework for social identity, social cognition, and intergroup relations. In M. P. Zanna & J. M. Olson (Eds.), Advances in experimental social psychology (Vol. 43, pp. 63–113). Academic Press. doi:10.1016/S0065-2601(10)43002-6

Locke, E., & Latham, G. (2002). Building a practically useful theory of goal setting and task motivation: A 35-year odyssey. *The American Psychologist, 57*(9), 705–717. doi:10.1037/0003-066X.57.9.705 PMID:12237980

Loes, C., Pascarella, E., & Umbach, P. (2012). Effects of diversity experiences on critical thinking skills: Who benefits? *Journal of Higher Education (Columbus, Ohio), 83*(1), 1–25. doi:10.1353/jhe.2012.0001

Lu, P., Burris, S., Baker, M., Meyers, C., & Cummins, G. (2021). Cultural Differences in Critical Thinking Style: A Comparison of U. S. and Chinese Undergraduate Agricultural Students. *Journal of International Agricultural and Extension Education, 28*(4). Advance online publication. doi:10.4148/2831-5960.1003

Lun, V. M.-C., Fischer, R., & Ward, C. (2010). Exploring cultural differences in critical thinking: Is it about my thinking style or the language I speak? *Learning and Individual Differences, 20*(6), 604–616. doi:10.1016/j.lindif.2010.07.001

Minkin, R. (2023, May 17). Diversity, Equity and Inclusion in the Workplace. *Pew Research Center's Social & Demographic Trends Project.* https://www.pewresearch.org/social-trends/2023/05/17/diversity-equity-and-inclusion-in-the-workplace/

Office of the Director of National Intelligence. (2023, February 6). *Annual threat assessment of The U.S. intelligence community.* https://www.dni.gov/files/ODNI/documents/ assessments/ATA-2023-Unclassified-Report.pdf

Office of the National Cyber Director. (2023, July 31). *National cyber workforce and education strategy: Unleashing America's Cyber Talent.* https://www.whitehouse.gov/wp-content/uploads/2023/07/NCWES-2023.07.31.pdf

Payne, B. K., Vuletich, H. A., & Lundberg, K. B. (2017). The bias of crowds: How implicit bias bridges personal and systemic prejudice. *Psychological Inquiry, 28*(4), 233–248. doi:10.1080/1047840X.2017.1335568

Pratt, M. (2023). *Emerging cyber threats in 2023 from AI to quantum to data poisoning.* CSO Online. https://www.csoonline.com/article/651125/emerging-cyber-threats-in-2023-from-ai-to-quantum-to-data-poisoning.html

Sanchez, J., & Medkik, N. (2004). The effects of diversity awareness training on differential treatment. *Group & Organization Management, 29*(4), 517–536. doi:10.1177/1059601103257426

Storme, M., Tavani, J. L., & Myszkowski, N. (2016). Psychometric properties of the French Ten Item Personality Inventory (TIPI). *Journal of Individual Differences, 37*(2), 81–87. Advance online publication. doi:10.1027/1614-0001/a000204

Tajfel, H., Billig, M. G., Bundy, R. P., & Flament, C. (1971). Social categorization and intergroup behavior. *European Journal of Social Psychology, 1*(2), 149–178. doi:10.1002/ejsp.2420010202

Vuletich, H. A., & Payne, B. K. (2019). Stability and change in implicit bias. *Psychological Science,* *30*(6), 854–862. doi:10.1177/0956797619844270 PMID:31050916

Zippa. (2021, January 29). *Cyber security analyst demographics and statistics: Number of cyber security analysts in The US.* https://www.zippia.com/cyber-security-analyst-jobs/demographics/

Chapter 12
Cybersecurity in Connected Autonomous Vehicles:
Navigating the Future of Transportation

Sharon L. Burton
https://orcid.org/0000-0003-1653-9783
Capitol Technology University, USA

ABSTRACT

Multifaceted ramifications of integrating connected and autonomous vehicles (CAVs) into the transportation systems pose a complex puzzle, with no easily discernible solutions regarding their impact on traffic efficiency and safety. Arriving at a clearer understanding requires exhaustive assessments of the performance of mixed traffic involving AI and CAVs is imperative, as it holds the potential to furnish invaluable insights. The role of connectivity looms large in this context, as it wields the power to substantially enhance both road safety and traffic management, with spill-over advantages affecting congestion mitigation and, conceivably, air quality improvement. It is essential to recognize that the adoption of connectivity also ushers in a new set of challenges. These challenges encompass issues related to technology compatibility, safeguarding data privacy, and fortifying defenses against cyber threats. The knowledge generated from this comprehensive evaluation of CAVs can be harnessed to benefit stakeholders within the automotive industry, academia, and policymakers.

PROBLEM AND INDUSTRY CHALLENGE

Integrating CAVs into transportation systems presents a multifaceted challenge, raising questions about their impact on traffic efficiency and safety. In 99.2% of collisions, according to Adano and Jones (2017) research, human error is most commonly listed as a contributory cause, followed by environmental (5.4%) and vehicle-related (0.5%) issues. However, according to Yen and Krishner (2022), the National Transportation Safety Board chair, Jennifer Homendy, does not agree with the high percentages; the concern is that more research is needed. A comprehensive assessment of mixed traffic scenarios involving AI-driven and CAV vehicles is crucial to understanding this complex issue better. The pivotal role

DOI: 10.4018/979-8-3693-1970-3.ch012

of connectivity in enhancing road safety, traffic management, congestion mitigation, and potential air quality improvements cannot be underestimated. However, this adoption of connectivity also introduces a new set of challenges, encompassing technology compatibility, data privacy concerns, and cybersecurity threats. The knowledge derived from this comprehensive evaluation of CAVs holds the potential to provide invaluable insights and benefits to stakeholders in the automotive industry, academia, and policymaking.

INTRODUCTION

Actions are vital for cybersecurity and other leaders to gather data (Zhang, Wu et al., 2020) shared across organizations (federal, state, local sectors, and industries). Such AI and CAV data gathering should involve the business departments, not just information technology (Nobles, 2018) so that all understand the effects of CAV development to include risk events on operations (American Association of State Highway and Transportation Officials [AASHTO], 2021; Ding et al., 2021; Jones, 2021, 2020; National Association of Counties, 2019). The multifaceted ramifications of integrating CAVs into our transportation systems pose a complex puzzle, with no easily discernible solutions regarding their impact on traffic efficiency and safety (Santana et al., 2021; Yang et al., 2021).

The exploration and formal documentation of the interrelationship between AI and CAVs have gained prominence. According to Sharma & Zheng (2021) and Rana & Hossain (2023), this heightened interest stems from the growing need for safer, more comfortable, and highly efficient transportation systems, particularly in urban settings where issues such as traffic congestion, road accidents, and air pollution pose significant challenges. This momentum is further fueled by the rapid technological advancements and collaborative efforts of government bodies, industries, and academic institutions, all working collectively to advance the development and deployment of CAVs across diverse operational contexts (Vahidi & Sciarretta, 2018). Understanding this knowledge is vital as it helps to inform the insights needed to grasp both the potential benefits and challenges of incorporating (CAVs) into our existing transportation infrastructure. It also guides us in formulating and implementing effective policies and strategies for a smooth and secure transition. CAVs infused with AI (artificial intelligence) have the potential to reduce human error, enhance situational awareness, and optimize traffic circulation, ultimately leading to improved traffic efficiency and safety (Sharma & Zheng, 2021). Artificial intelligence can quickly and accurately manage enormous amounts of data while doing complex computations. "Big Data" is the term used to describe the growing amount of data that is created and stored, and there is a need for a practical approach to collect these data as they are produced. This text delves into the intricate task of incorporating CAVs into transportation systems. Also, this text underscores the necessity for a comprehensive evaluation to gain insights into their influence on traffic efficiency, safety, behavioral dynamics within cybersecurity, and the resulting consequences. After the introduction, the reader will review the background, which includes information about AI, risk, cybersecurity, and how these topics relate to cybersecurity. Next is the problem statement, significance of the research, methodology, research theories, and framework, the literature review, recommendations, conclusions, and solutions, and then the references.

BACKGROUND

First, understanding the term CAV is significant. A CAV denotes a vehicle that integrates both autonomous (AV) and connected vehicle (CV) technologies (Rana & Hossain, 2023). These vehicles utilize sensors, cameras, GPS, and computer vision to operate with minimal human intervention, and they can communicate wirelessly with other vehicles, infrastructure, and devices (California Department of Transportation, 2023). Ferrovial (2023) states that CAVs are automobiles capable of operating entirely or partially without human driver intervention. Also, as elucidated by Hussain and Zeadally (2019) as well as Winkelman et al. (2019), Connected Autonomous Vehicles (CAVs) are entities under computer control, endowed with sensory and actuator capabilities enabling them to discern and ascertain their position and environment, strategize their actions, and execute them in compliance with established regulatory and safety protocols. These terms collectively define the key attributes and features of CAVs (Information and Communications Technology Council and CAVCOE, 2020; Rana & Hossain, 2023). See Table 1 for the terms and their definitions.

One of the critical components of the future industry will be automation, with ideas such as 5G, machine learning, and Industry 4.0 becoming more feasible. Numerous industries, including agriculture, construction, education, hospitality and tourism, rescue, service robots, surveillance, and transportation, have demonstrated the promise of autonomous systems (Ghobadpour et al., 2022; Melenbrink et al., 2022; Loukatos et al., 2022McCartney & McCartney, 2020; Delmerico, 2019; Gonzalez-Aguirre, 2021; Zhang & Zhan et al., 2020). However, the automobile sector, which has conducted extensive research and adopted innovative and cutting-edge technologies to incorporate autonomous and human-like qualities in its products, is unquestionably the critical sector driving this new trend toward automation (Nobles et al., 2023).

Table 1. Key attributes and features of connected and autonomous vehicles

Terminology	Definitions
Autonomous or Autonomous (AV)	Refers to the self-driving capabilities of the vehicle
Connected vehicle (CV)	Denotes the integration of connectivity technologies.
Sensors	Devices used to perceive the vehicle's surroundings.
Computer vision	Technology for processing visual data
Wirelessly	The mode of communication with other vehicles, infrastructure, and devices.
Operating either entirely or partially devoid of human driver intervention	Highlights the autonomous nature of CAVs.
Sensory and actuator capabilities	Describes the vehicle's ability to sense and respond to its environment.

The role of connectivity looms large in this context, as it wields the power to substantially enhance road safety and traffic management, with spill-over advantages affecting congestion mitigation and, conceivably, air quality improvement. In the coming decade, CAV developments in connected and autonomous vehicle technology promise to profoundly transform local and national transportation systems (National Association of Counties, 2019; Shi et al., 2019; Ye & Yamamoto, 2019). These innovations could also reshape the way individuals reside, labor, and navigate within their communities. Nonetheless, it is essential to recognize that adopting connectivity also ushers in new challenges. These challenges encompass issues related to technology compatibility, safeguarding data privacy, and fortifying defenses against cyber threats.

Due to their crucial role in helping CAVs navigate, understand their surroundings, and make wise judgments, *sensors* are of utmost importance in the context of CAVs (Clifton, 2022). In order to continually gather information about their surroundings, CAVs rely on different sensors, including Light Detection and Ranging (LiDAR), radar, cameras, and ultrasonic sensors (Elliot et al., 2019). These sensors provide real-time data about adjacent objects, the state of the road, traffic, pedestrians, and other vehicles. Then, using powerful computer vision and artificial intelligence algorithms, this data is processed and examined. The value of sensors comes from their capacity to improve situational awareness, identify obstructions, and enable efficient and safe navigation (Gonzalez-Saavedra, 2022). They allow CAVs to make split-second judgments about how quickly to accelerate, brake, or change lanes.

By enabling the capacity to analyze and make sense of the visual data collected by the vehicle's cameras and sensors, *computer vision* plays a crucial part in the development of CAVs. The importance of computer vision in CAVs rests in its capacity to interpret enormous volumes of visual data in real-time, giving the machine the ability to perceive its surroundings with accuracy and degree of detail comparable to human eyesight (Encyclopaedia Britannica, 2023; Li et al., 2020). For autonomous driving to be safe and effective, this technology must identify and track things, recognize traffic signals, road signs, pedestrians, and other cars, and evaluate road conditions (Ajgaonkar, 2021). Additionally, because of computer vision, CAVs can adapt to unexpected and dynamic road conditions and make split-second judgments to negotiate challenging traffic situations. The development and improvement of this technology are crucial to attaining the objective of creating safer and more dependable autonomous transportation systems because CAVs are becoming more dependent on computer vision algorithms to make sense of the environment around them (Ajgaonkar, 2021).

In the context of CAVs, the relevance of *wirelessly* is derived from its function as the enabling connection for seamless communication between CAVs, other cars, infrastructure, and different connected devices (Rana & Houssain, 2023). To share crucial information in real-time, CAVs rely on wireless communication technologies like V2V (Vehicle-to-Vehicle) and V2X (Vehicle-to-Everything). This technology contains information on the vehicle's location, speed, intentions, and driving circumstances (Li et al., 2020). This connectivity plays a crucial role in raising the general safety and effectiveness of CAVs. For instance, CAVs can transmit information to surrounding cars, enabling them to modify their routes or driving styles in response to traffic congestion, accidents, or road dangers. Wireless communication also makes it easier for vehicles to coordinate, allowing CAVs to move in platoons, lowering aerodynamic drag, and increasing fuel economy. Wirelessly's relevance in CAVs goes beyond practicality; it is a foundational element of the cooperative and linked systems that support the promise of safer and more intelligent transportation networks (Zhang, Zhang et al., 2019).

The significance of operating either entirely or partially devoid of human driver intervention, as it relates to CAVs, is profound and multifaceted. First and foremost, human errors are a leading cause of accidents, and CAVs, when operating autonomously, have the potential to reduce these errors significantly, ultimately saving lives and reducing traffic-related injuries (Moreno-Navarro et al., (2019). The advent of autonomous driving has the potential to reshape urban planning and reduce the need for extensive parking infrastructure, freeing up valuable land for other purposes (Zhou et al., 2023). The significance of operating CAVs either entirely or partially devoid of human driver intervention lies in their potential to enhance safety, improve transportation efficiency, increase accessibility, and transform various aspects of our society, from urban planning to logistics, ultimately ushering in a new era of transportation.

It is critical to stress the importance of CAVs operating totally or partially without the driver's input and with improved sensor and actuator capabilities (Rana & Houssain, 2023). Further, according to this research team, these skills are the foundation of CAV technology because they allow these cars to observe and engage with their surroundings at a level unmatched by human drivers. CAVs can detect and understand their surroundings with amazing precision and speed using sensors like LiDAr, radar, cameras, and sophisticated software algorithms, which lowers the danger of accidents caused by blind spots, distractions, or poor vision (Elliot et al., 2019). On the other hand, actuators provide CAVs the ability to carry out split-second choices based on sensor input, such as stopping, accelerating, or turning, with the highest degree of precision and consistency, resulting in safer and more predictable driving behavior. The primary objectives of CAV technology are to improve road safety, reduce traffic accidents, and ultimately revolutionize how we move people and goods (Nobles et al., 2023). This combination of sensory and actuator capabilities also opens up new opportunities for urban planning, transportation efficiency, and accessibility for people with mobility issues (Winkelman et al., 2019). A thorough analysis of the performance of mixed traffic, including AI and CAVs, is necessary to reach a greater understanding since the research can offer decision-makers and other stakeholders priceless information (Adebisi et al., 2020; Ferrovial, 2023; Guériau & Dusparic, 2020; Hou, 2023; U.S. Department of Transportation Federal Highway Administration, 2023).

SIGNIFICANCE AND FOCUS OF THE RESEARCH

The significance of this research lies in its exploration of the multifaceted implications of integrating CAVs into transportation systems. As CAV technology advances, it becomes increasingly essential to comprehend its impact on traffic efficiency and safety (Nobles et al., 2023). The exhaustive assessments of mixed traffic involving artificial intelligence (AI) and CAVs outlined in this research have the potential to provide invaluable insights into these critical issues. Moreover, the research underscores the pivotal role of connectivity in enhancing road safety and traffic management, which not only contributes to safer roads but also has positive spill-over effects on congestion reduction and potential improvements in air quality (American Association of State Highway and Transportation Officials, 2021; Ding et al., 2022; Guériau & Dusparic, 2020; Parkinson et al., 2019). However, it is equally crucial to acknowledge the challenges accompanying the adoption of connectivity, including technology compatibility, data privacy concerns, and cybersecurity threats (Burton, 2019; Ghansiyal et al., 2022; Hussain & Zeadally, 2019). The knowledge generated from this comprehensive evaluation of CAVs has the potential to inform and benefit stakeholders across various sectors, including the automotive industry, academia, and policymaking, as they navigate the complexities of integrating CAVs into our transportation systems.

The results of this CAV study have the potential to benefit a wide range of groups and stakeholders.

METHODOLOGY

For this study, a literature review methodology was employed. According to Snyder (2023), a literature review is a comprehensive summary of earlier studies. According to Snyder (2023), a literature review comprehensively summarizes earlier studies. Further, the purpose of using the literature review was to identify the need for more research in order to support this researcher's work. Certainly, conducting a literature review can be valuable for identifying the strengths, weaknesses, and gaps in the existing body of research (Snyder, 2023). According to Bloomsburg University of Pennsylvania's website, this technique will assist in recognizing the connections between works in terms of their contributions to the research subject and other fields of study. This scholar was equipped to navigate an increasing information complexity thanks to a crucial tool, the literature review (Kraus et al., 2022).

The researcher conducted a comprehensive literature review encompassing papers published up to and including 2023. This review employed a variety of search terms designed to yield articles related to risk project management and cybersecurity. The searches were conducted diligently between September 2022 and January 2023, systematically using keywords likely to yield relevant articles. These keywords included artificial intelligence, computer vision, connected and autonomous vehicles, cybersecurity risks, innovation, competitiveness, and wirelessly. Sub-keywords were risk, cyber risk management, cyber risk, risk project management, and managed risk, either in the titles or as the central topic of investigation. The researcher categorized the articles by assessing whether they contained information pertinent to risk project management. Academic fee-based databases and the internet were used to locate the literature. The academic databases included EBSCO Databases and Services (comprising EBSCOhost Web, Business Searching Interface, and EBSCO Discovery Service), IEEE Xplore, Homeland Security Digital Library, ProQuest Dissertation Database, and ABI Inform Complete (ProQuest). The Internet search engine Google Scholar was also employed to retrieve recent peer-reviewed literature.

APPLICABLE THEORIES/FRAMEWORKS

Three relevant theories guide this research - the common cyber threat framework, technological determination, and machine learning. The overarching objective of the common cyber threat framework is to establish a unified ontological structure, enhance the exchange of information, meticulously delineate and categorize malicious activities in the cyber domain, foster a shared state of situational awareness within the business community, and serve as a foundational framework for rigorous analysis and judicious decision-making (U. S. Office of the Director of National Intelligence, 2017). The Common Cyber Threat Framework assumes paramount significance in identifying, scrutinizing, and effectively countering cyber threats within CAVs, as noted by Wang, Wang, et al. (2021). This framework plays a pivotal role in evaluating and mitigating vulnerabilities pertaining to essential components such as sensors, communication networks, and actuators, as articulated by Sharma and Gillanders (2022). A salient observation by Parkinson et al. (2017) elucidates the profound influence of technological advancements on the cybersecurity landscape of CAVs, especially in light of the heightened susceptibility of more intelligent and interconnected vehicles to cyber threats. These endeavors synergistically contribute to bolstering cybersecurity defenses in the domain of CAVs. The next theory is technological determinism.

As expounded by Katz and Aakhus (2019), technological determinism posits that technology assumes a pivotal role in both the configuration of society and culture and, conversely, that societal and cultural forces reciprocally mold technology. This theory advances the perspective that technology transcends its role as a mere tool at the disposal of humans, exerting a substantial influence on human behavior, as noted by Hassan (2019). According to this theoretical framework, technology emerges as a potent impetus steering the trajectory of society, and alterations in technological paradigms can precipitate corresponding shifts in societal norms and values, as elucidated by Lievrouw (2019). In light of these principles, it becomes evident that the interplay between technology and society is a dynamic and mutually shaping relationship with far-reaching implications for human civilization. The last theory/ framework is machine learning.

Machine learning encompasses a comprehensive spectrum of capabilities, including scalability, reactivity, and parallel processing, all working harmoniously. This multifaceted field empowers artificial intelligence to adeptly handle vast volumes of data while executing complex computations rapidly through intricate models (Sarker, 2021). This dynamic is especially pronounced in models that leverage input data, such as a customer's search or purchase history, to provide tailored suggestions to the same individuals, thereby exhibiting a reactive nature (Karthik & Mathew, 2023). Scalability, a pivotal attribute, signifies the ability of machine learning models to continually enhance their performance as more data becomes accessible (Tarraf, 2021). These models can undergo rigorous training on extensive datasets, a facet that significantly augments their scalability.

Furthermore, the parallelizability of machine learning algorithms, skilfully harnessing modern multi-core processors and distributed computing environments (Sarker, 2021), further amplifies their efficiency. This parallel processing capability enables machines to efficiently and expeditiously manage colossal datasets, contributing to the overall potency of these AI systems. Organizations and people may make better choices about how they engage with technology and how they incorporate it into their lives if they are aware of the influence that technology has on behavior, attitudes, and values. Awareness of technology's influence on behavior, attitudes, and values empowers individuals to make informed choices regarding their interactions with technology and its integration into their daily lives.

LITERATURE REVIEW

This literature review offers background learning on the topic and discusses and analyses published data involving CAVs - traffic efficiency and safety. Information is offered as a systematized pattern that joins the summary and synthesis (Robinson & Cooper, 2020). This review ascertains the connection of publications in perspective of their contributions to the subject matter (Bodolica & Spraggon, 2018). Also, this literature review critically evaluates the methodological approaches used in these publications to provide a comprehensive understanding of the research landscape surrounding Connected and Autonomous Vehicles (CAVs), emphasizing both their impact on traffic efficiency and safety and the robustness of the available data.

Understanding Connected and Autonomous Vehicles

The impact of CAVs on traffic efficiency and safety is contingent upon several factors, including their prevalence, degree of automation, communication reliability, response times, and prevailing weather conditions within mixed traffic scenarios. Various studies have yielded a spectrum of outcomes, suggesting that CAVs may exert both favorable and adverse influences on traffic efficiency and safety.

Comprehending driver behavior and the way individuals perceive and analyze their driving environment, ultimately influencing their decision-making and actions, constitutes a pivotal milestone in the journey toward achieving autonomous driving (Caruso et al., 2022). Connected and Autonomous Vehicles (CAVs) represent a swiftly evolving technology that holds the promise of fundamentally transforming the field of transportation.

Critiques of Connected and Autonomous Vehicles

Nevertheless, this technology is accompanied by criticisms and obstacles such as technology, infrastructure issues, software development, safety concerns, and contradictory outcomes that warrant consideration. The continuous integration of advanced driver-assist systems (ADAS) into CAVs is undeniably expediting the shift from human-driven vehicles to fully autonomous options. Nevertheless, this transition comes with its implementation challenges, as it requires seamless engagement and synchronization of various complex technologies within the operational framework of automated vehicles (Rana & Hossain, 2023). These challenges encompass issues related to sensor reliability, real-time data processing, and the establishment of robust communication networks among vehicles and infrastructure to ensure the safe and efficient deployment of CAVs (Rana & Hossain, 2023). Next are infrastructure issues.

Infrastructure is crucial in enabling the automation and connectivity features on roadways (Rana & Hossain, 2023). Nevertheless, specific challenges exist with roadside infrastructure's ability to effectively support CAV path-tracking requirements (Rana & Hossain, 2023). Furthermore, the integration of cooperative adaptive cruise control has notable implications for the structural integrity and durability of road pavements, necessitating careful consideration and adaptation in infrastructure planning and maintenance. Software Development: With connected and autonomous electric vehicles (CAEVs) fast becoming a reality, the importance of software in vehicles increases tenfold (Rana & Hossain, 2023). There are future trends and challenges in automotive software development (Vdovic et al., 2019). Essential to comprehend are safety concerns.

Understanding the safety challenges associated with CAVs is of paramount importance. While CAVs hold great potential, they are not without safety concerns, as highlighted by Cprime (2023) and Lee & Hess (2022). It is imperative to address a range of technological barriers, including those related to sensor reliability, cybersecurity, and human-machine interaction, to ensure these technologies' safe deployment and utilization (Lee & Hess, 2022). Furthermore, effective regulatory frameworks and standardized safety protocols must be established to govern CAVs and build public trust in their reliability and security.

The emergence of CAV technologies has the potential to amplify the advantages of shared mobility systems (Zhao & Malikopoulos, 2019). Nevertheless, the existing body of literature on this subject has presented mixed findings and conflicting outcomes (Zhao & Malikopoulos, 2019). It remains uncertain whether the widespread adoption of CAVs will lead to a significant reduction in the overall number of vehicles on the road, as various factors, including user preferences and urban planning, will also play crucial roles in shaping future mobility patterns. Addressing these uncertainties is essential for comprehensive transportation planning.

These critiques underscore the imperative for continuous research and development efforts aimed at tackling the complex challenges associated with CAVs. Sustained investment in technological innovation, regulatory frameworks, and comprehensive testing will be pivotal in addressing these challenges and guaranteeing the secure and efficient integration of CAVs into our transportation systems. Additionally, as given by (Aoki, et al., 2021) collaboration among industry leaders, policymakers, and researchers will be vital to navigate the evolving landscape of CAV technology and realize its full potential while mitigating potential risks.

The Integration of Artificial Intelligence Technologies in the Automotive Industry

AI technology in the automotive sector is changing how cars are developed, produced, and operated (Nobles, 2023). Also, AI influences the automotive sector through enhanced driving experiences, self-driving cars, 5G integration, and accident avoidance (Nobles, 2023). According to recent data, there are already 1,400 self-driving cars on the market, representing a small percentage of all the cars on the road (Kopestinsky, 2023). According to Statista, the market for autonomous vehicles will reach over $37 billion by 2023. By 2023, the market for autonomous cars is expected to be worth over $37 billion (Kopestinsky, 2023). Due to an increase in the number of businesses testing and using autonomous vehicles, these figures are continually changing. Review Figure 1 to grasp the expected changes to vehicle automation to include the progression of automation.

Figure 1. Five levels of driving automation (Synopsys, 2023)

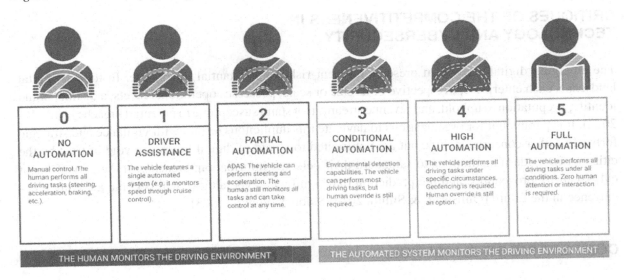

0	1	2	3	4	5
NO AUTOMATION	DRIVER ASSISTANCE	PARTIAL AUTOMATION	CONDITIONAL AUTOMATION	HIGH AUTOMATION	FULL AUTOMATION
Manual control. The human performs all driving tasks (steering, acceleration, braking, etc.).	The vehicle features a single automated system (e.g. it monitors speed through cruise control).	ADAS. The vehicle can perform steering and acceleration. The human still monitors all tasks and can take control at any time.	Environmental detection capabilities. The vehicle can perform most driving tasks, but human override is still required.	The vehicle performs all driving tasks under specific circumstances. Geofencing is required. Human override is still an option.	The vehicle performs all driving tasks under all conditions. Zero human attention or interaction is required.

THE HUMAN MONITORS THE DRIVING ENVIRONMENT | THE AUTOMATED SYSTEM MONITORS THE DRIVING ENVIRONMENT

CRITIQUING THE INTEGRATION OF AI TECHNOLOGIES IN THE AUTOMOTIVE INDUSTRY

Novak (2023) proposed, that according to a recent AAA study, almost 68% of Americans said they are terrified of self-driving vehicles. This percentage is a significant increase from 2022 when 55% of Americans indicated concern about emerging technology. According to a survey, just 9% of Americans believe they *trust* self-driving cars (Novak, 2023), while 23% stated they were *unsure*. According to research from 2022, just 57% of individuals who are familiar with self-driving cars are willing to ride in one, 52% believe that the cars require some amount of human control, and 75% of people would rather drive than ride in one (Kopestinsky, 2023).

COMPETITIVENESS IN TECHNOLOGY AND CYBERSECURITY

Competitiveness in technology and cybersecurity refers to an organization's or nation's ability to outperform its rivals in safeguarding data and information systems (Muller & Burrell, 2022). This information requires developing and applying top-notch cybersecurity methods, practices, and tools. Competitive prowess within the realms of technology and cybersecurity necessitates the attainment of a series of strategic objectives (Howley, 2023). These objectives encompass the preservation of extant competitive advantages, the cultivation of novel competitive edges via robust product security measures, and the establishment of comprehensive consumer trust as a cornerstone of organizational strategy (Howley, 2023). Furthermore, it is imperative to underscore that sustained innovation and relentless adaptability also emerge as critical imperatives in maintaining competitiveness in these dynamic domains. Simultaneously, fostering a culture of continuous learning and collaboration across interdisciplinary teams is paramount for long-term success.

CRITIQUES OF THE COMPETITIVENESS IN TECHNOLOGY AND CYBERSECURITY

The emerging digital ecosystem presents inherent risks of substantial magnitude. In today's digital landscape, each enterprise, irrespective of its size or scale, possesses operational facets, a distinct brand identity, a reputation to uphold, and revenue streams that stand susceptible to potential breaches (Brooks, 2023). It is paramount for organizations to navigate this duplicitous terrain with vigilance and strategic fortitude. Other concerns include but are not limited to a void of digital literacy, a void of trust by the citizenry in modern institutions to safeguard their personal information, breaches of data, insufficient cybersecurity procedures, and the prediction that significant cyberattacks will become a common occurrence in the future (Olmstead, & Smith, 2017; Sidoti & Vogels, 2023).

COMPETITIVE INTELLIGENCE

As per the findings of de Sousa Lopes et al. (2023), *competitive intelligence* can be defined as the organizational capability to acquire, scrutinize, and leverage information about competitors, customers, and various market dynamics to fortify a firm's competitive advantage. To generate insights into the competitive landscape and bolster organizational effectiveness, the practice of competitive intelligence represents both a methodology and an assemblage of methodological approaches (Khalid, 2023). This action encompasses the structured implementation of a competitive intelligence program alongside the methodical acquisition and scrutiny of data derived from diverse origins (de Sousa Lopes et al., 2023; Khalid, 2023). Competitive intelligence is vital to this text because, consequently, the acquisition of competitive intelligence is evolving into an ever more pivotal facet for organizations. In the pursuit of crafting compelling and streamlined business processes, organizations evaluate amassed data and information. As asserted by Asghari et al. (2020), competitive intelligence serves a dual purpose: defensively, it entails comprehending the unfolding circumstances, potential scenarios, and appropriate responses; offensively, it involves situating the organization within the marketplace, strategizing for future positioning, and allocating resources across both immediate and long-term horizons. Consequently, competitive intelligence emerges as a strategic instrument or tactic enterprises adopt to procure and evaluate information concerning their competitive environment.

Critiques of Competitive Intelligence

Notwithstanding its recognized significance, competitive intelligence has encountered criticism stemming from its pronounced concentration on competitive entities, ambiguity in the process of information acquisition, instances of intelligence misuse, deficiencies in adept information management, and a notable deficiency in the capacity to derive lessons from previous errors, as noted within the scholarly discourse (Kumar et al., 2020; Madureira, 2019). Despite its value, competitive intelligence has come under fire for its excessive focus on rivals, muddled understanding of information collecting, abuse of intelligence, lack of insight management, and failure to learn from mistakes (Madureira, 2019). An additional concern pertains to the divergence between market intelligence, which predominantly emphasizes understanding consumers and end-users, and competitive intelligence, which predominantly focuses on comprehending rival entities, as highlighted by (FedSavvy Strategies, 2019). When formulating a comprehensive corporate strategy, it is imperative to harmoniously integrate these strategic dimensions (FedSavvy Strategies, 2019).

Connected and Autonomous Vehicles and Traffic Efficiency

Connected and autonomous vehicles (CAVs) represent a pivotal milestone within the transportation sector, marking a significant leap in the safe and efficient movement of individuals and goods. These vehicles harness diverse cutting-edge technologies, as elucidated by Song (2021). Connected automobiles equipped with internet connectivity forge a network through which they can communicate with one another and the traffic infrastructure. This interconnectedness facilitates the exchange of invaluable information about road conditions, traffic flow, and weather, thereby enhancing the overall situational awareness of CAVs (Song, 2021). In contrast, autonomous vehicles can autonomously perceive and navigate their surroundings, operating sans human intervention. This autonomous prowess underscores their potential to revolutionize transportation (Song, 2021).

Efforts to bolster "traffic efficiency," a multifaceted concept targeting the reduction of travel demands, especially those involving single-occupancy vehicles, have garnered considerable attention in the discourse. Wong (2023) elaborates on an array of strategic measures encompassed within this paradigm. These encompass urban land use optimizations, initiatives promoting bicycle and pedestrian mobility, enhancements to public transit systems, the implementation of transportation pricing mechanisms, and the introduction of employer-based transportation management programs (Wong, 2023). Traffic management strategies contribute to efficiency, expediently resolving accidents and vehicular blockages while optimizing traffic signal synchronization. Diversifying travel options, designed to provide cost-effective alternatives to conventional driving, alleviates the strain on existing infrastructure. Furthermore, through the adept deployment of innovative techniques, system modification tactics maximize the utilization of existing road space (Wong, 2023). This concerted effort, guided by forward-thinking strategies, is a testament to the multifaceted approach to ushering in a new era of transportation efficiency.

Critiques of Connected and Autonomous Vehicles and Traffic Efficiency

CAVs could decrease traffic efficiency by increasing the electricity demand, changing people's driving patterns and behaviors, and adopting a cautious car-following strategy. Guériau and Dusparic (2020) assert that the advent of CAVs holds the potential for profound transformations in transportation efficiency and safety. Their research posits that the impact of CAVs varies significantly based on penetration rates and traffic density, with efficiency and safety outcomes exhibiting notable disparities across different scenarios.

Critiques of existing studies in this domain, as articulated by the same research duo, revolve around several key points. A standard limitation identified is the tendency to focus on specific types of road networks, often dissecting economic and safety aspects in isolation while exclusively considering passenger cars to exclude other vehicle categories (Guériau & Dusparic, 2020). Such singular perspectives may not encompass the full spectrum of complexities inherent to integrating CAVs into diverse traffic environments.

Moreover, Garg and Bouroche (2023) highlight another critical challenge—the inherent unreliability of communication networks supporting CAVs. The dependable operation of CAVs is intricately tied to robust and consistent data exchange, and the susceptibility of communication networks to disruptions poses a significant concern. Additionally, the coexistence of CAVs with human-driven vehicles in mixed-traffic settings presents a distinct set of hurdles. As Garg and Bouroche (2023) elucidate, the unpredictable nature of human driving behavior introduces complexities that CAVs must navigate skillfully. This aspect underscores the need for robust communication protocols and adaptive algorithms to ensure safe interactions. Furthermore, the anticipated increase in actual road capacity, while ostensibly a positive outcome, may paradoxically lead to adverse consequences in terms of energy consumption under certain conditions. The intricate interplay between CAVs and road capacity necessitates nuanced analysis to comprehend the ecological ramifications of this technological advancement fully.

In summary, the transformational potential of CAVs on transportation efficiency and safety is a subject of rigorous investigation. Nonetheless, these advancements are accompanied by challenges, encompassing network reliability, human-CAV interactions, and ecological considerations, which warrant comprehensive examination to ensure the responsible and effective integration of CAVs into our transportation systems.

Connected and Autonomous Vehicles and Traffic Safety

CAVs can improve traffic safety by preventing human errors, reducing conflicts, and enhancing situational awareness. Noted are five points: preventing human errors, mitigating traffic conflicts, adverse weather circumstances, and safety-critical traffic control.

Enhancing Safety Through Advanced Technology references that CAVs have the potential to significantly enhance traffic safety by employing advanced situation perception technology and swift-response driving behavior (Zhang, Hou, et al., 2021). This advantage becomes crucial in the long-term coexistence of CAVs and human-driven vehicles (HVs). In addition to having the potential to increase traffic safety, incorporating advanced situation perception technology and swift-response driving behavior into CAVs also holds the promise of fostering more harmonious interactions in the changing environment where CAVs and human-driven vehicles (HVs) coexist.

Managing Traffic Conflicts is significant. Traffic conflicts are significantly decreased when controlled lane management is used for CAVs. Additionally, acceleration rates are lowered, and velocity differentials are minimized significantly when the penetration rate of CAVs exceeds 70% (Zhang, Hou, et al., 2021). These results demonstrate how CAVs with superior situation perception technology and quick-response driving styles can significantly increase traffic safety, essential as CAVs and human-driven vehicles (HVs) coexist in the long run.

Adverse weather circumstances are an integrated framework developed by Hou (2023) that offers a comprehensive approach for evaluating the performance and safety of mixed-traffic environments involving CAVs under adverse weather conditions. Considering various factors and interactions within such scenarios, the process contributes valuable insights towards ensuring the reliability and resilience of autonomous and human-driven vehicles when faced with inclement weather. Furthermore, this integrated framework can serve as a vital tool in the ongoing efforts to develop adaptive strategies and technologies that bolster the overall effectiveness of autonomous and human-driven vehicles in adverse weather conditions, ultimately advancing safety and mobility in challenging environments (Hou, 2023).

As elucidated by Huan et al. (2023), safety-critical traffic control represents a method by which a CAV can optimize traffic flow while concurrently ensuring its safety in the context of nearby human-driven vehicles. This approach involves intricate maneuvers and decision-making processes that allow the CAV to navigate mixed-traffic scenarios effectively. By employing real-time data and predictive algorithms, safety-critical traffic control enhances the safety of the CAV and safety contributes to the overall efficiency and harmony of traffic operations in mixed environments.

Understanding the Dependability of Communication and Automation Technologies

Understanding the dependability of communication and automation technologies is critically important in today's interconnected and technology-driven world (Burrell et al., 2020). Dependability refers to the reliability, availability, and performance of these technologies (Maihulla & Yusef, 2022). This topic is crucial for safety and security, economic impact, innovation and progress, ethical considerations, and resilience.

Critical systems that depend on communication and automation technology, such as those in the healthcare, transportation, and energy sectors, include safety and security (Rehak & Hromada, 2018). The act is crucial to guarantee their reliability to stop accidents, secure data, and uphold public safety. Furthermore, dependable communication and automation technologies are pivotal for seamless operations in critical sectors, ensuring timely and accurate data transmission, diagnosis, and decision-making in healthcare, efficient transportation logistics, and the stable supply and distribution of energy resources. Any disruptions or failures in these systems can have immediate safety consequences and lead to cascading impacts on the overall functioning of societies and economies (Rehak & Hromada, 2018). Therefore, robust dependability measures and continuous monitoring are essential to mitigate risks, enhance system resilience, and maintain the trust of stakeholders in these vital sectors.

Businesses primarily rely on these technologies for efficiency and competitiveness, which has an economic impact (AZ Technology, 2022). Dependability is crucial to maintaining economic growth since downtime or breakdowns can lead to significant financial losses (Maihulla & Yusef, 2022). The economic impact of dependable communication and automation technologies cannot be overstated. Businesses in various industries depend on these technologies to streamline processes, reduce costs, and gain a competitive edge from manufacturing to e-commerce. Any disruptions or failures in these systems can result in substantial financial losses due to lost productivity, missed opportunities, and the costs associated with troubleshooting and repairs (AZ Technology, 2022).

Furthermore, the economic ripple effect extends beyond individual businesses. A widespread breakdown in communication or automation technology can disrupt supply chains, impacting entire industries and economies (Katsaliaki et al., 2022). Further, the notions of supply chain breakdowns underscore the critical need for robust dependability measures to ensure the smooth functioning of these technologies, not only for individual businesses but also for the broader economic stability and growth of regions and nations (Katsaliaki et al., 2022). In essence, the dependability of these technologies is intricately linked to economic resilience and prosperity in the modern world.

Innovation and progress in cutting-edge industries such as artificial intelligence, the Internet of Things, and autonomous vehicles heavily rely on the foundation of dependable communication and automation technologies (Dawson, 2017a). An in-depth understanding of dependability fosters innovation and empowers researchers and engineers to push the boundaries of what is possible, leading to breakthroughs that can revolutionize various aspects of our lives. These innovations can enhance our daily experiences, drive economic growth, and tackle complex global challenges, making the study of technology dependability an indispensable driver of technological advancement in the 21st century (Young & Gordon, 2019).

Resilience, defined as the capacity to rebound from setbacks, is critical for any system, whether it faces challenges like cyberattacks or natural disasters. In-depth knowledge and expertise in dependability principles are instrumental in developing systems that withstand such setbacks and adapt and recover swiftly (Dawson, 2017a, Dawson, 2017b). This proactive approach to system design and maintenance ensures their survivability and the continuity of critical functions, safeguarding both individual and societal well-being in the face of adversity (Burton, 2022). Ultimately, dependability knowledge empowers us to build robust and resilient systems capable of navigating the ever-evolving landscape of risks and disruptions (Jones, 2021).

In addition to the benefits above, a profound understanding of technology dependability also serves as a cornerstone for fostering international collaboration and standardization in developing and deploying critical systems (Aoki, et al., 2021). This common framework facilitates seamless global integration and ensures that advancements in communication and automation technologies adhere to consistent and high-quality dependability standards, promoting interoperability and trust among nations and industries. Ultimately, the knowledge of technology dependability is an indispensable asset in shaping a more secure, interconnected, and prosperous future for societies worldwide.

Understanding the Interplay Between Connected and Autonomous Vehicles and Human Drivers

The intricate interplay between CAVs and human drivers constitutes a multifaceted and ever-evolving domain of study. Several salient points merit consideration within this intricate milieu such as influential dynamics, symbiotic coexistence of human and robot, infrastructure's facilitating role and vehicular communication, and cognizant of real-time recognition and prediction. Furthermore, this dynamic interplay underscores the imperative of not only technological advancements but also the need for comprehensive regulatory frameworks and public awareness campaigns to navigate the complex landscape of CAVs harmoniously alongside human-driven vehicles.

Influential Dynamics connected to autonomous vehicles (AVs) wield a profound capacity to exert a constructive influence upon human-driven vehicles, particularly within the realm of large-scale or vehicle-to-vehicle (V2V) interactions (Sadigh, 2019). A notable illustration of this phenomenon emerges when an autonomous car endeavors to initiate a lane change. As it gently encroaches upon the intended lane, it exerts a subtle yet discernible influence on the behavior of human-driven counterparts sharing the same thoroughfare, inducing a decelerated response among these vehicles (Sadigh, 2019). Next is the symbiotic coexistence of humans and robots.

The realization of autonomous driving technologies on public roadways necessitates the meticulous conception and development of mechanisms for the secure cohabitation and collaboration of mixed traffic ecosystems (Aoki, et al., 2021). These environments, characterized by the harmonious coexistence of human-operated and autonomous vehicles, demand intricate strategies to preclude vehicular collisions and mitigate the potential for impassable gridlock scenarios. Necessary is appropriate infrastructure's facilitating role and vehicular communication.

The infrastructure that underpins our roadways assumes a pivotal role in enhancing the capabilities of CAVs, effectively assuming the role of a centralized orchestrator (Aoki et al., 2021). Furthermore, the realm of vehicular communication emerges as a linchpin in ensuring secure collaboration within decentralized frameworks, a vital element for upholding road safety across a multitude of interconnected vehicles (2). Vehicular communication is associated with real-time recognition and prediction.

The importance of real-time recognition of vehicular movements and dynamic gesture comprehension cannot be overstated in the pursuit of a secure cooperative ecosystem. These capabilities serve as indispensable components in the construction of a decentralized cooperation system, particularly when interfacing with non-connected vehicles, thereby fortifying safety protocols on the roadways (Aoki et al., 2021).

It is imperative to underscore that humans, far from being mere disruptions to be circumvented, represent complex and intelligent agents. They exhibit a propensity for reasoned strategies and possess the capacity for adaptive behavior when confronted with the proliferation of automation in their daily lives. This adaptability and responsiveness of human agents come to the fore when they engage with autonomous entities, thereby infusing an element of novelty and unpredictability into the intricate tapestry of interactions involving autonomous and intelligent agents.

Weather Conditions' Influence on Connected and Autonomous Vehicles

A thorough analysis can be used to assess the effects of CAVs on traffic efficiency and safety when driving in inclement weather, such as fog, rain, or snow, which might impair human and CAV sight and road conditions, a detailed study (Hou, 2023). Such an analysis can assist in comprehending the interactions and behaviors of human drivers and CAVs in mixed traffic, such as their car-following, lane-changing, and gap-acceptance tactics, and how these impact the stability and fluidity of traffic flow (Wang et al., 2022). The same research team also postulates that the work can aid in designing and optimizing traffic management and control strategies for mixed traffic, including the best CAV market penetration rate, the best CAV distribution across different lanes, and the best CAV communication standards. Additionally, the study can assist in identifying and addressing possible dangers and problems associated with mixed traffic, including cyber-security concerns, moral quandaries, legal obligations, and issues with CAVs' societal acceptance (Ding et al., 2021).

Navigating the Ethical and Legal Dimensions of CAVs

Ethical considerations take center stage regarding dependable technologies, especially in autonomous decision-making contexts, such as self-driving cars and robots (Pazzanese, 2021). A profound grasp of dependability principles is essential to not only guarantee the reliability of these technologies but also to ensure that they consistently make safe and ethically sound choices. This ethical dimension is pivotal for building trust among users, regulators, and society, as it addresses concerns related to the potential consequences of automated systems and their impact on human lives and values (Hunkenschroer et al. (2022). Moreover, as technology advances, ethical considerations will play an increasingly prominent role in shaping dependable technologies' design, implementation, and regulation across various domains.

RECOMMENDATIONS, CONCLUSIONS, AND SOLUTIONS

The impact of CAVs on traffic efficiency and safety is contingent upon several factors, including their prevalence, degree of automation, communication reliability, response times, and prevailing weather conditions within mixed traffic scenarios. Various studies have yielded a spectrum of outcomes, suggesting that CAVs may exert favorable and adverse influences on traffic efficiency and safety (Azam et al., 2022; Elliott et al., 2019; Kaur & Singh, 2022; Parekh et al., 2022). Within the industry, this knowledge serves as a crucial compass, guiding manufacturers, and service providers towards more informed decisions, thereby fostering innovation and competitiveness. In academia, it becomes fertile ground for further research, opening doors to new avenues of study that delve into the intricate dynamics of CAVs in mixed-traffic environments. This research not only enriches the academic discourse but also nurtures the emergence of future experts and thought leaders in the field. Lastly, the body of knowledge expanded through these evaluations stands as a resource for policymakers, aiding them in crafting well-informed regulations and policies that can effectively steer the integration of CAVs toward safer, more efficient, and environmentally friendly transportation systems. Thus, the holistic assessment of CAVs' influence on traffic stands to serve as a beacon of guidance for industry, academia, and the collective wisdom of society. Conclusions include the following:

1. The safety and effectiveness of CAVs in altering transportation by lowering accidents and enhancing traffic flow depends on the precision and dependability of these sensors (Gonzalez-Saavedra, 2022). Moreover, autonomous driving can lead to increased efficiency in transportation systems. CAVs can communicate with each other and with traffic infrastructure, optimizing traffic flow, reducing congestion, and lowering fuel consumption. This efficiency can have economic and environmental benefits, reducing travel times and greenhouse gas emissions.
2. In addition, autonomous vehicles can provide mobility solutions for individuals who are unable to drive, such as the elderly and disabled, offering them newfound independence and accessibility (Lee & Madnix, 2021). Furthermore, CAVs can operate continuously without the need for rest, potentially revolutionizing the logistics and long-haul transportation industries.

3. This research has the potential to benefit a wide range of groups and stakeholders such as the automobile industry, cybersecurity experts, government and policymakers, transportation authorities, the academic community, the insurance industry, environmental organizations, and the general public (Moreno-Navarro et al., 2019).

4. **Cybersecurity Experts**: With the discussion of connectivity and cybersecurity challenges, experts in cybersecurity can use the research to better understand the vulnerabilities and threats associated with CAVs and work on securing these systems effectively (Cai et al., 2022).

5. **Automotive Industry**: Manufacturers and companies involved in the automotive industry stand to gain valuable insights for developing, refining, and marketing CAV technologies and solutions (Yang & Wibowo, 2022). Understanding the impact of CAVs on traffic efficiency and safety is critical for product development and strategic planning.

6. **Government and Policymakers**: Governments at various levels can use the research findings to inform regulations and policies related to CAV deployment, safety standards, and infrastructure development (Banerjee et al., 2023). This research can help in crafting effective laws and regulations to govern CAVs on public roads.

7. **Transportation Authorities**: Organizations responsible for managing transportation systems and infrastructure can benefit from insights into traffic management and congestion mitigation (Azam et al., 2022). They can use this information to optimize traffic flow and improve overall transportation efficiency.

8. **Academic Community**: Researchers and scholars in fields such as transportation engineering, urban planning, and data science can use the research as a foundation for further studies (Banerjee et al., 2023). This research can also serve as a reference for academic research and coursework in related disciplines.

9. **Insurance Industry**: Insurance companies can use the data and findings to develop new policies and pricing models tailored to CAVs (Banerjee et al., 2023). Understanding the safety and risk factors associated with autonomous vehicles is crucial for the insurance sector.

10. **Environmental Organizations**: Groups focused on environmental issues can benefit from research that explores the potential impact of CAVs on air quality and emissions reduction (Emerson et al., 2022). CAVs may contribute to more efficient driving patterns, potentially leading to reduced pollution.

11. **General Public**: Ultimately, the general public benefits from safer and more efficient transportation systems (Channon & Marson, 2021). CAVs have the potential to reduce accidents and traffic congestion, leading to improved overall quality of life for commuters and residents.

In summary, the results of this CAV study have broad implications, touching on various aspects of society, from industry and governance to academia and environmental concerns, ultimately aiming to shape the future of transportation and mobility. Organizations need a top-down and bottom-up approach and proactive choices toward strengthening project risk documentation and analyses that lead to diminished data breaches and positive influence regarding data and system performance outcomes (Malsam, 2019). This research contends a close relationship between management ethics, trust, knowledge, and project risk management (Jones, 2021). Habituation, a cyber behavior, must be consistently reviewed to lessen shrinking responses to replicated prompts or routinized behaviors. Such behaviors continue to be shown as disadvantageous to organizational security (Dalal et al., 2021). The influence of habituation becomes more convex as organizations progressively increase the number of informational cues workers receive day-to-day through modern know-how; this know-how is intended to intensify efficiency and effectiveness (Deloitte, 2018). Nobles (2018) states that most research regarding cybersecurity is fixated on progressing computer network systems because such researchers accept that information technology improvements and software development are the chief avenues to augment information security (Benson & Mcalaney, 2020). Mounting cybersecurity risks must be managed through the growth and advancement of system rationalization and malleable leadership skills (Burrell et al., 2021; Jones, 2021, 2020).

FUTURE RESEARCH DIRECTIONS

Adding future research areas is salient because it offers knowledge advancement, and problem-solving techniques, supports policy and regulation development, drives innovation and technological advancement, supports safety assurance, fosters the collaboration of stakeholders, influences positively public perception and confidence in CVA systems, supports quantification of the economic and environmental impact of CAVs, and drives international collaboration. Based on the provided information, future research on CAVs should focus on several key areas:

1. **Traffic Safety and Efficiency**: Given that human error is a significant contributor to collisions, further research should delve into assessing the actual impact of CAVs on traffic safety and efficiency. This research should aim to provide concrete data and analysis to determine if CAVs can significantly reduce the number of accidents and improve traffic flow.
2. **Accuracy of Collision Attribution**: The disagreement between Adano and Jones (2017) and the National Transportation Safety Board chair, Jennifer Homendy, highlights the need for more research to accurately attribute causes of collisions involving CAVs. This research should seek to clarify the role of human error, environmental factors, and vehicle-related issues in accidents involving CAVs.
3. **Mixed Traffic Scenarios**: Comprehensive studies should be conducted in real-world mixed traffic scenarios involving both AI-driven and CAV vehicles. These studies can help researchers gain a deeper understanding of how CAVs interact with traditional human-driven vehicles and how this interaction impacts traffic dynamics and safety.
4. **Connectivity and Road Safety**: Research should focus on the role of connectivity in enhancing road safety, traffic management, congestion mitigation, and air quality improvements. This research can help identify the specific benefits and challenges of integrating connectivity into transportation systems.
5. **Technology Compatibility**: Investigating the compatibility of CAV technology with existing infrastructure and vehicles is crucial. This includes exploring the feasibility of retrofitting existing vehicles with CAV technology and assessing how CAVs can communicate with each other and with infrastructure.
6. **Data Privacy and Cybersecurity**: As CAVs rely heavily on data and connectivity, research should address data privacy concerns and cybersecurity threats. Developing robust security measures and protocols is essential to ensure the safety and privacy of CAV users and the integrity of transportation systems.

7. **Stakeholder Engagement**: Engaging stakeholders from the automotive industry, academia, policymakers, and the general public is vital for successful CAV research. Collaboration between these groups can help shape policies, standards, and regulations that promote the safe and efficient integration of CAVs into transportation systems.

In summary, future research on CAVs should be comprehensive, data-driven, and focused on addressing the multifaceted challenges and opportunities presented by these technologies. By conducting rigorous research in these areas, we can better understand the impact of CAVs on traffic safety and efficiency, address concerns, and harness the potential benefits for various stakeholders.

REFERENCES

Adano, E. K., & Jones, S. (2017). Effects of human-centered factors on crash injury severities. *Journal of Advanced Transportation, 1208170*, 1–11. Advance online publication. doi:10.1155/2017/1208170

Adebisi, A., Liu, Y., Schroeder, B., Ma, J., Cesme, B., Jia, A., & Morgan, A. (2020). Developing highway capacity manual capacity adjustment factors for connected and automated traffic on freeway segments. *Transportation Research Record: Journal of the Transportation Research Board, 2674*(10), 401–415. doi:10.1177/0361198120934797

Ajgaonkar, A. (2021, Spring). The value of computer vision: More than meets the eye. *Tech Journal.* https://www.insight.com/en_US/content-and-resources/tech-journal/spring-2021/the-value-of-computer-vision--more-than-meets-the-eye.html

American Association of State Highway and Transportation Officials. (2021). AASHTO issues connected, automated vehicle policy paper. *Author.* https://aashtojournal.org/2021/10/14/aashto-issues-connected-automated-vehicle-policy-paper/

Aoki, S., Lin, W. C. W., & Rajkumar, R. (2021, August). human-robot cooperation for autonomous vehicles and human drivers: Challenges and solutions. *IEEE Communications Magazine, 59*(8), 35–41. doi:10.1109/MCOM.001.2001241

Azam, M., Hassan, S. A., & Che Puan, O. (2022). Autonomous vehicles in mixed traffic conditions-A bibliometric analysis. *Sustainability (Basel), 14*(17), 10743. doi:10.3390/su141710743

Banerjee, I., Jittrapirom, P., & Dangschat, J. S. (2023). Data-driven urbanism, digital platforms and the planning of MaaS in times of deep uncertainty: What does it mean for CAVs? Avenue 21. *Planning and Policy Considerations for an Age of Automated Mobility*, 431-460. doi:10.1007/978-3-662-67004-0

Bodolica, V., & Spraggon, M. (2018). *Management research methods*. Routledge.

Brooks, C. (2023, March 5). Cybersecurity trends & statistics for 2023; What you need to know. *Forbes.* https://www.forbes.com/sites/chuckbrooks/2023/03/05/cybersecurity-trends--statistics-for-2023-more-treachery-and-risk-ahead-as-attack-surface-and-hacker-capabilities-grow/?sh=3eb268a719db

Burrell, D. N., Courtney-Dattola, A., Burton, S. L., Nobles, C., Springs, D., & Dawson, M. E. (2020). Improving the quality of "The Internet of Things" instruction in technology management, cybersecurity, and computer science. *International Journal of Information and Communication Technology Education*, *6*(2), 59–70. doi:10.4018/IJICTE.2020040105

Burton, S. L. (2019). Grasping the cyber-world: Artificial intelligence and human capital meet to inform leadership. *International Journal of Economics, Commerce and Management, 7*(12), 707-759. https://ijecm.co.uk/wp-content/uploads/2019/12/71247.pdf

Burton, S. L. (2022). *Strategy: A Business and Cybersecurity Intertwined Necessity. International Journal of Smart Education and Urban Society (IJSEUS), 13(1)*. doi:10.4018/IJSEUS.312232

Cai, J., Deng, W., Guang, H., Wang, Y., Li, J., & Ding, J. (2022). A Survey on data-driven scenario generation for automated vehicle testing. *Machines*, *10*(11), 1101. doi:10.3390/machines10111101

California Department of Transportation. (2023). Connected and automated vehicles. *Author*. https://dot.ca.gov/programs/traffic-operations/cav

Caruso, G., Mohammad, K. Y., & Mussone, L. (2022). From human to autonomous driving: A method to identify and draw up the driving behaviour of connected autonomous vehicles. *Vehicles*, *4*(4), 1430–1449. doi:10.3390/vehicles4040075

Channon, M., & Marson, J. (2021). The liability for cybersecurity breaches of connected and autonomous vehicles. *Computer Law & Security Report*, *43*, 105628. doi:10.1016/j.clsr.2021.105628

Clifton, K. J. (2022). A step ahead for smart growth: Creating walkable neighborhoods. *Handbook on Smart Growth*, 168-187. doi:10.4337/9781789904697.00021

Dawson, M. (2017a). *Hyper-connectivity: Intricacies of national and international cyber securities*. London Metropolitan University.

Dawson, M. (2017b). Cyber security policies for hyperconnectivity and internet of things: a process for managing connectivity. In S. Latifi (Ed.), *Information Technology – New Generations* (pp. 911–914). Springer.

de Sousa Lopes, B., Amorim, V., Au-Yong-Oliveira, M., & Rua, O. L. 2023. Competitive and business intelligence: A Bibliometric analysis. *Quality Innovation and Sustainability: 3rd ICQIS*, 187 – 197. https://doi-org.captechu.idm.oclc.org/10.1007/978-3-031-12914-8_15

Delmerico, J., Mintchev, S., Giusti, A., Gromov, B., Melo, K., Horvat, T., Cadena, C., Hutter, M., Ijspeert, A., Floreano, D., Gambardella, L. M., Siegwart, R., & Scaramuzza, D. (2019). The current state and future outlook of rescue robotics. *Journal of Field Robotics*, *36*(7), 1171–1191. doi:10.1002/rob.21887

Ding, S., Chen, X., Fu, Z., & Peng, F. (2021, October). An extended car-following model in connected and autonomous vehicle environment: Perspective from the cooperation between drivers. *Journal of Advanced Transportation*, *2021*, 1–17. Advance online publication. doi:10.1155/2021/2739129

Elliot, D., Keen, W., & Miao, L. (2019). Recent advances in connected and automated vehicles. *Journal of Traffic and Transportation Engineering*, *6*(2), 109–131. doi:10.1016/j.jtte.2018.09.005

Emerson, K., Baldwin, E., Scott, T. A., Pidot, J. R., Lien, A. M., Currim, F., Bethard, S., Ram, S., & López-Hoffman, L. (2022). Toward NEPA performance: A framework for assessing EIAs. *Environmental Impact Assessment Review*, 97, 106879. doi:10.1016/j.eiar.2022.106879

Encyclopaedia Britannica. (2023, August 23). Computer vision. *Author*. https://www.britannica.com/technology/computer-vision

FedSavvy Strategies. (2019). Business intelligence, competitive intelligence, and market intelligence – What is the difference? *Author*. https://www.fedsavvystrategies.com/business-intelligence-competitive-intelligence-and-market-intelligence-what-is-the-difference/

Ferrovial. (2023). Connected autonomous vehicles: What are connected autonomous vehicles? *Author*. https://www.ferrovial.com/en/innovation/technologies/connected-autonomous-vehicles/

García-Martínez, I., Fernández-Batanero, J., Fernández-Cerero, J., & León, S. P. (2023). Analysing The Impact Of Artificial Intelligence And Computational sciences on student performance: Systematic review and meta-analysis. *Journal of New Approaches in Educational Research*, 12(1), 171–197. doi:10.7821/naer.2023.1.1240

Garg, M., & Bouroche, M. (2023, June). Can Connected Autonomous Vehicles Improve Mixed Traffic Safety Without Compromising Efficiency in Realistic Scenarios? *IEEE Transactions on Intelligent Transportation Systems*, 24(6), 6674–6689. doi:10.1109/TITS.2023.3238889

Ghansiyal, A., Mittal, M., & Kar, A. K. (2021). Information management challenges in autonomous vehicles: A systematic literature review. *Journal of Cases on Information Technology*, 23(3), 58–77. doi:10.4018/JCIT.20210701.oa5

Gonzalez-Aguirre, J. A., Osorio-Oliveros, R., Rodríguez-Hernández, K. L., Lizárraga-Iturralde, J., Morales Menendez, R., Ramírez-Mendoza, R. A., Ramírez-Moreno, M. A., & Lozoya-Santos, J. D. J. (2021). Service robots: Trends and technology. *Applied Sciences (Basel, Switzerland)*, 11(22), 10702. doi:10.3390/app112210702

Gonzalez-Saavedra, J. F., Figueroa, M., Cespedes, S., & Montejo-Sanchez, S. (2022). Survey of cooperative advanced driver assistance systems: From a holistic and systemic vision. *Sensors (Basel)*, 22(8), 3040. doi:10.3390/s22083040 PMID:35459025

Guériau, M., & Dusparic, I. (2020, September). Quantifying the impact of connected and autonomous vehicles on traffic efficiency and safety in mixed traffic. *Proceedings of the IEEE 23rd International Conference on Intelligent Transportation Systems (ITSC)*. 10.1109/ITSC45102.2020.9294174

Hassan, R. (2019). From technological determinism to techno-capitalist realism: Prospects for post-human engineering. *Ethics and Information Technology*, 21(3), 217–231.

Haun, Y., Zhao, C. & & Molnar, T. G. (2023). Safety-Critical traffic control by connected automated vehicles. Safety-Critical Traffic Control by Connected Automated Vehicles. *Cornell University*. ArXiv. /abs/2301.04833

Hou, G. (2023). Evaluating efficiency and safety of mixed traffic with connected and autonomous vehicles in adverse weather. *Sustainability (Basel)*, 15(4), 3138. doi:10.3390/su15043138

Howley, C. (2023, April 12). Gartner identifies the top cybersecurity trends for 2023. *Gartner*. https://www.gartner.com/en/newsroom/press-releases/04-12-2023-gartner-identifies-the-top-cybersecurity-trends-for-2023

Hunkenschroer, A. L., & Luetge, C. (2022). Ethics of AI-enabled recruiting and selection: A review and research agenda. *Journal of Business Ethics*, *178*(4), 977–1007. doi:10.1007/s10551-022-05049-6

Hussain, R., & Zeadally, S. (2019). Autonomous cars: Research results, issues, and future challenges. *IEEE Communications Surveys and Tutorials*, *21*(2), 1275–1313. doi:10.1109/COMST.2018.2869360

Information and Communications Technology Council and CAVCOE. (2020, March). Advances in connected & autonomous vehicles. *Author*. https://www.ictc-ctic.ca/wp-content/uploads/2020/04/CAVs-ENG.Final_.0423.pdf

Jones, L. A. (2020). *Reputation risk and potential profitability: Best practices to predict and mitigate risk through amalgamated factors* (Doctoral dissertation). Dissertations & Theses Global. (2466047018).

Jones, L. A. (2021). A content analysis review of literature to create a useable framework for reputation risk management. Handbook of Research on Multidisciplinary Perspectives on Managerial and Leadership Psychology, 91-133.

Karthik, R. M., & Mathew, F. S. (2023). Artificial intelligence and its theranostic applications in dentistry. *Cureus*, *15*(5). Advance online publication. doi:10.7759/cureus.38711 PMID:37292569

Katsaliaki, K., Galetsi, P., & Kumar, S. (2022). Supply chain disruptions and resilience: A major review and future research agenda. *Annals of Operations Research*, *319*(1), 965–1002. doi:10.1007/s10479-020-03912-1 PMID:33437110

Katz, J. E., & Aakhus, M. (2019). Introduction: Technological determinism in communication research. In *Perpetual contact: Mobile communication, private talk, public performance* (pp. 1–12). Cambridge University Press.

Kaur, J., & Singh, W. (2022). Tools, techniques, datasets and application areas for object detection in an image: A review. *Multimedia Tools and Applications*, *81*(27), 38297–38351. doi:10.1007/s11042-022-13153-y PMID:35493415

Khalid, A. A. (2023). The key criteria that determine the degree to which management's use of competitive intelligence. *Cogent Business & Management, 10*(2), 1–21. https://doi-org.captechu.idm.oclc.org/10.1080/23311975.2023.2250553

Kopestinsky, A. (2023). 25 astonishing self-driving car statistics for 2023. *Policy Advice*. https://policy-advice.net/insurance/insights/self-driving-car-statistics/#:~:text=There%20are%20over%201%2C400%20self,registered%20in%20California%20thus%20far

Kraus, S., Breier, M., Lim, W. M., Dabić, M., Kumar, S., Kanbach, D., Mukherjee, D., Corvello, V., Piñeiro-Chousa, J., Liguori, E., Palacios-Marqués, D., Schiavone, F., Ferraris, A., Fernandes, C., & Ferreira, J. J. (2022). Literature reviews as independent studies: Guidelines for academic practice. *Review of Managerial Science*, *16*(8), 2577–2595. doi:10.1007/s11846-022-00588-8

Kumar, V., Saboo, A. R., Agarwal, A., & Kumar, B. (2020). Generating Competitive Intelligence with Limited Information: A Case of the Multimedia Industry. *Production and Operations Management*, *29*(1), 192–213. doi:10.1111/poms.13095

Lee, C., & Madnix, S. (2021). Cybersafety approach to cybersecurity analysis and mitigation for mobility-as-a-service and internet of vehicles. *Electronics (Basel)*, *10*(10), 1–25. doi:10.3390/electronics10101220

Lee, D., & Hess, D. J. (2022). Public concerns and connected and automated vehicles: Safety, privacy, and data security. *Humanities & Social Sciences Communications*, *9*(90), 90. Advance online publication. doi:10.1057/s41599-022-01110-x

Li, Z., Wang, J., & Zheng, N. (2020). Computer vision for connected and automated vehicles: A survey. *IEEE Transactions on Intelligent Transportation Systems*, *21*(11), 4704–4724.

Lievrouw, L. A. (2019). Mediation, mediation everywhere... Technology determinism and the myth of the mediated center. *Communication Theory*, *29*(4), 349–360.

Loukatos, D., Kondoyanni, M., Kyrtopoulos, I.-V., & Arvanitis, K. G. (2022). Enhanced robots as tools for assisting agricultural engineering students' development. *Electronics (Basel)*, *11*(5), 755. doi:10.3390/electronics11050755

Madureira, L., Castelli, M., & Popovič, A. (2019). Design thinking: The new mindset for competitive intelligence? Impacts on the Competitive Intelligence Model. CAPSI 2019 Proceedings, 26.

Maihulla, A. S., & Yusuf, I. (2022). Reliability, availability, maintainability, and dependability analysis of photovoltaic systems. *Life Cycle Reliab Saf Eng*, *11*(1), 19–26. doi:10.1007/s41872-021-00180-1

McCartney, G., & McCartney, A. (2020). Rise of the machines: Towards a conceptual service-robot research framework for the hospitality and tourism industry. *International Journal of Contemporary Hospitality Management*, *32*(12), 3835–3851. doi:10.1108/IJCHM-05-2020-0450

Melenbrink, N., Werfel, J., & Menges, A. (2020). On-site autonomous construction robots: Towards unsupervised building. *Automation in Construction*, *119*, 103312. doi:10.1016/j.autcon.2020.103312

Moreno-Navarro, F., Iglesias, G., & Rubio-Gámez, M. (2019). Encoded asphalt materials for the guidance of autonomous vehicles. *Automation in Construction*, *99*, 109–113. doi:10.1016/j.autcon.2018.12.004

Muller, S. R., & Burrell, D. N. (2022). *Social cybersecurity and human behavior*. International Journal of Hyperconnectivity and the Internet of Things. doi:10.4018/IJHIoT.305228

National Association of Counties. (2019). Connected and automated vehicles toolkit: A primer for counties. *Author*. https://www.naco.org/resources/featured/connected-autonomous-vehicles-toolkit

Nobles, C., Burrell, D. N., Burton, S. L., & Waller, T. (2023). Driving into cybersecurity trouble with autonomous vehicles. In F. Adedoyin & B. Christiansen (Eds.), *Handbook of Research on Cybersecurity Risk in Contemporary Business Systems* (pp. 255–273). IGI Global. doi:10.4018/978-1-6684-7207-1.ch013

Olmstead, K., & Smith, A. (2017). What the public knows about cybersecurity. *Pew Research Center*. https://www.pewresearch.org/internet/2017/03/22/what-the-public-knows-about-cybersecurity/

Parekh, D., Poddar, N., Rajpurkar, A., Chahal, M., Kumar, N., Joshi, G. P., & Cho, W. (2022). A review on autonomous vehicles: Progress, methods and challenges. *Electronics (Basel), 11*(14), 2162. doi:10.3390/electronics11142162

Parkinson, S., Ward, P., Wilson, K., & Miller, J. (2017). Cyber threats facing autonomous and connected vehicles: Future challenges. *IEEE Transactions on Intelligent Transportation Systems, 18*(11), 2898–2915. doi:10.1109/TITS.2017.2665968

Pazzanese, C. (2020, October 26). Ethical concerns mount as AI takes bigger decision-making role in more industries. *The Harvard Gazette*. https://news.harvard.edu/gazette/story/2020/10/ethical-concerns-mount-as-ai-takes-bigger-decision-making-role/

Rana, M. M., & Hossain, K. (2023). Connected and Autonomous Vehicles and Infrastructures: A Literature Review. *International Journal of Pavement Research and Technology, 16*(2), 264–284. doi:10.1007/s42947-021-00130-1

Rehak, D., & Hromada, M. (2018). Failures in a critical infrastructure system. In System of System Failures. IntechOpen. doi:10.5772/intechopen.70446

Robinson, O. C., & Cooper, C. L. (2020). *The Oxford handbook of organizational psychology*. Oxford University Press.

Sadigh, D. (2019). Influencing interactions between human drivers and autonomous vehicles. *National Academy of Engineering*. https://www.nae.edu/19579/19582/21020/221074/221209/Influencing-Interactions-between-Human-Drivers-and-Autonomous-Vehicles

Santana, E. F. Z., Covas, G., Duarte, F., Santi, P., Ratti, C., & Kon, F. (2021). Transitioning to a driverless city: Evaluating a hybrid system for autonomous and non-autonomous vehicles. *Simulation Modelling Practice and Theory, 107*, 102210. Advance online publication. doi:10.1016/j.simpat.2020.102210

Sarker, I. H. (2021). Deep learning: A comprehensive overview on techniques, taxonomy, applications and research directions. *SN Computer Science, 2*(6), 420. doi:10.1007/s42979-021-00815-1 PMID:34426802

Sarker, I. H. (2021). Machine Learning: Algorithms, Real-World Applications and Research Directions. *SN Computer Science, 2*(3), 160. doi:10.1007/s42979-021-00592-x PMID:33778771

Sharma, A., & Zheng, Z. (2021). Connected and Automated Vehicles: Opportunities and Challenges for Transportation Systems, Smart Cities, and Societies. In B. T. Wang & C. M. Wang (Eds.), *Automating Cities. Advances in 21st Century Human Settlements*. Springer. doi:10.1007/978-981-15-8670-5_11

Sharma, P., & Gillanders, J. (2022). Cybersecurity and forensics in connected autonomous vehicles: A review of the state-of-the-art. *IEEE Access : Practical Innovations, Open Solutions, 10*, 08979–108996. doi:10.1109/ACCESS.2022.3213843

Shi, Y., He, Q., & Huang, Z. (2016). Capacity analysis and cooperative lane changing for connected and automated vehicles: Entropy-based assessment method. *Transportation Research Record: Journal of the Transportation Research Board*, (2673), 485–498.

Sidoti, O., & Vogels, E. A. (2023). What Americans know about AI, cybersecurity and big tech. *Pew Research Center*. https://www.pewresearch.org/internet/2023/08/17/what-americans-know-about-ai-cybersecurity-and-big-tech/

Snyder, H. (2023). Designing the literature review for a strong contribution. *Journal of Decision Systems*, 1–8. Advance online publication. doi:10.1080/12460125.2023.2197704

Song, D. W. (2021). What is research? *WMU J Marit Affairs*, 20(4), 407–411. doi:10.1007/s13437-021-00256-w PMID:34895237

Synopsis. (2023). The 6 levels of vehicle autonomy explained. *Author*. https://www.synopsys.com/automotive/autonomous-driving-levels.html

Tarraf, D. C., Shelton, W., & Parker, E. (2021). *The Department Of Defense's posture for artificial intelligence: assessment and recommendations for improvement*. Santa Monica, CA: RAND Corporation, 2021. https://www.rand.org/pubs/research_briefs/RB10145.html

Technology, A. Z. (2022). Impact of technology in business. *Author*. https://atztechnology.com/impact-of-technology-in-business/

U. S. Office of the Director of National Intelligence. (2017). A common cyber threat framework: A foundation for communication. *Author*. https://www.dni.gov/files/ODNI/documents/features/A_Common_Cyber_Threat_Framework_Overview.pdf

U.S. Department of Transportation Federal Highway Administration. (2023). Automated vehicle activities and resources. *Author*. https://highways.dot.gov/automation

Vdovic, H., Babic, J., & Podobnik, V. (2019). Automotive software in connected and autonomous electric vehicles: A review. *IEEE Access : Practical Innovations, Open Solutions*, 7, 166365–166379. doi:10.1109/ACCESS.2019.2953568

Wang, Y., Wang, Y., Qin, H., Ji, H., Zhang, Y., & Wang, J. (2021). A systematic risk assessment framework of automotive cybersecurity. *Automotive Innovation*, 4(3), 253–261. doi:10.1007/s42154-021-00140-6

Wang, Y., Xu, R., & Zhang, K. (2022). A Car-following model for mixed traffic flows in intelligent connected vehicle environment considering driver response characteristics. *Sustainability (Basel)*, 14(17), 11010. doi:10.3390/su141711010

Winkelman, Z., Buenaventura, M., Anderson, J. M., Beyene, N. M., Katkar, P., & Baumann, G. C. (2019). When autonomous vehicles are hacked, who is liable? (No. RR-2654-RC). RAND Corporation.

Wong, A. (2023). Improving parking lot efficiency through autonomous control and assignment strategies: A microscopic traffic simulation analysis. *EECS Department, University of California, Berkeley*, Technical Report No. UCB/EECS-2023-166. https://www2.eecs.berkeley.edu/Pubs/TechRpts/2023/EECS-2023-166.pdf

Yang, R., & Wibowo, S. (2022). User trust in artificial intelligence: A comprehensive conceptual framework. *Electronic Markets*, 32(4), 2053–2077. doi:10.1007/s12525-022-00592-6

Yang, S., Du, M., & Chen, Q. (2021). Impact of connected and autonomous vehicles on traffic efficiency and safety of an on-ramp. *Simulation Modelling Practice and Theory*, *113*, 102374. Advance online publication. doi:10.1016/j.simpat.2021.102374

Ye, L., & Yamamoto, T. (2019). Evaluating the impact of connected and autonomous vehicles on traffic safety. *Physica A*, *526*, 121009. doi:10.1016/j.physa.2019.04.245

Yen, H., & Krishner, T. (2022). NTSB chief to fed agency: Stop using misleading statistics. *The Associated Press*. https://apnews.com/article/coronavirus-pandemic-business-health-national-transportation-safety-board-transportation-safety-6638c79c519c28bb4d810d06789a2717#:~:text=FILE%20-%20 Jennifer%20Homendy%20of%20the%20National%20Transportation,that%20the%20Transportation%20 Department%20should%20stop%20using%20it

Young, R. R., & Gordon, G. A. (2019). Critical Infrastructure: Transportation Systems. In L. Shapiro & M. H. Maras (Eds.), *Encyclopedia of Security and Emergency Management*. Springer. doi:10.1007/978-3-319-69891-5_85-1

Zhang, C., Zhan, Q., Wang, Q., Wu, H., He, T., & An, Y. (2020). Autonomous dam surveillance robot system based on multi-sensor fusion. *Sensors (Basel)*, *20*(4), 1097. doi:10.3390/s20041097 PMID:32079361

Zhang, J., Wu, K., Cheng, M., Yang, M., Cheng, Y., & Li, S. (2020). Safety evaluation for connected and autonomous vehicles' exclusive lanes considering penetrate ratios and impact of trucks using surrogate safety measures. *Journal of Advanced Transportation*, *2020*, 1–16. doi:10.1155/2020/5847814

Zhang, Y., Zhang, J., Liu, K., & Shen, X. (2019). A Survey on Wireless Security: Technical Challenges, Recent Advances, and Future Trends. *Proceedings of the IEEE*, *104*(9), 1727–1765.

Zhao, L., & Malikopoulos, A. A. (2022, January-February). Enhanced mobility with connectivity and automation: A review of shared autonomous vehicle systems. *IEEE Intelligent Transportation Systems Magazine*, *14*(1), 87–102. doi:10.1109/MITS.2019.2953526

Zhou, G., Shang, G., & Zhang, Y. (2023, March 16). smart infrastructure for autonomous driving in urban areas. *National Academy of Engineering*. https://www.nae.edu/19579/19582/21020/290850/290 948/Smart-Infrastructure-for-Autonomous-Driving-in-Urban-Areas

KEY TERMS AND DEFINITIONS

Artificial Intelligence: Artificial Intelligence (AI) is a branch of computer science that focuses on creating systems and algorithms capable of performing tasks typically requiring human intelligence, such as problem-solving and learning.

Competitiveness: In the realm of technology and cybersecurity, competitiveness denotes an organization's or a nation's ability to excel beyond its rivals in safeguarding information systems and data. This entails the development and deployment of cutting-edge cybersecurity methodologies, protocols, and technological advancements.

Computer Vision: The branch of artificial intelligence known as computer vision is dedicated to making it possible for computers to analyze and comprehend visual data.

Connected and Autonomous Vehicles: The connected aspect of the vehicle is essentially a data-driven automobile with an extensive array of tailored features designed to enhance safety, reduce energy consumption, and enhance the overall comfort of both the driver and passengers. The autonomous aspect of the vehicles leverage driver assistance technologies to eliminate the requirement for human operators entirely. These vehicles possess the capacity to autonomously make decisions and take corresponding actions. connected and autonomous vehicles, cybersecurity risks, innovation, competitiveness, artificial intelligence, autonomous system.

Cybersecurity Risks: The concept of "cybersecurity risks" pertains to the potential vulnerabilities an organization may face, leading to potential harm or losses resulting from cyberattacks or data breaches. These risks have the capacity to adversely impact various aspects of an organization, including its mission, functions, reputation, assets, and personnel, as well as its relationships with other entities and even the broader national interests. These impacts are directly associated with the compromise of confidentiality, integrity, or availability of information, data, or information systems (including control mechanisms).

Innovation: In the realms of cybersecurity and artificial intelligence, innovation encompasses the development and application of novel or markedly enhanced offerings and solutions. This innovation extends to the refinement of production and operational methodologies, the enhancement of customer engagement through enriched experiences, as well as the evolution of organizational strategies, work methodologies, human capital expertise, and resource utilization, all of which collectively contribute to the generation of substantial value.

Technological Determination Model: The Technological Determinism Model is a theory that suggests that technology is the primary driving force behind social and cultural change. According to this model, technological advances and innovations are the key drivers of change in society and they shape and influence the way people interact with one another, how they perceive the world, and how they behave.

Wirelessly: Wirelessly references the mode of communication with other vehicles, infrastructure, and devices.

Chapter 13
Generations in Transition:
Navigating in the Cybersecurity-Infused Job Market

Sharon L. Burton
iD https://orcid.org/0000-0003-1653-9783
Capitol Technology University, USA

ABSTRACT

This study investigates the utility of ethnography and artificial intelligence as a valuable tool for understanding the multifaceted nature of job-seeking experiences across four generations: Baby Boomers, Generation X, Millennials, and Generation Z. Ethnography design offers insight into the creative thought processes, expressions, and lived experiences integral to the job-seeking process. Explored is the impact of the COVID-19 pandemic on the job market, highlighting the global economic downturn and the resultant loss of millions of jobs, revealing systemic vulnerabilities. This research investigates the obstacles faced by job seekers, including those without specific qualifications or degrees, who often need help to gain visibility in a competitive job market. Addressed is the issue of online applications needing to align with job criteria. This chapter provides valuable insights into the contemporary job-seeking landscape, stressing the need for adaptable strategies such as Artificial intelligence in the face of evolving challenges and opportunities.

INTRODUCTION

As life expectancy continues to rise and retirement ages are extended, we now find ourselves in a situation where four distinct generations actively seek employment opportunities. This evolving demographic landscape has brought about a significant increase in the diversity of skills and abilities among recruiters. The ubiquity of the internet allows more and more people to apply for work on a digitized technological scale. The on-again, off-again "war for talent" is back in various nations, especially the United States (HR Research Institute, 2021. With this said, the future of job hunting was thought never to be so bright.

DOI: 10.4018/979-8-3693-1970-3.ch013

Conversely, job seekers are facing challenges. Technological understanding is significant to understanding the evolving job-hunting nuances. The need for formal job-hunting skills and education is arising due to the prevalence of Applicant Tracking Systems (ATS), which can reject applications due to formatting issues, underscoring the challenges faced by applicants (American Banker, N.PAG, 2023). The COVID-19 pandemic has fueled the adoption of ATS platforms. Also, ATS infused with AI are used for applicant tracking, candidate matching, hiring, onboarding, and management of employee information, and payroll services (Haan, 2023). Organizations have increasingly turned to advanced recruitment tools to help drive greater efficiencies and be used remotely to facilitate virtual hiring (Accountingtoday. Com, N.PAG, 2023). The needed change to understand talent acquisition and job hunting is more vital than before (Talent Acquisition Excellence, 2021; HR Research Institute, 2021). A specific focus is on new business models and relating with hearers and onlookers via engagement and technology. The drive for change has been a long-term conversation.

One age-old piece of advice is never to memorize answers to interview questions because the responses sound stiff and rehearsed (Skillings, 2023). On the other hand, certain information may need to be memorized. For individuals who get nervous during interviews, some memorization can help them get through the process. As given by Coleman (2023), job seekers found themselves perplexed regarding advice on locating meaningful work. See Figure 1 for examples of contradictory advice.

Figure 1. Contradictory job seeking advice
Source: Coleman (2023)

Contradictory Job Seeking Advice
1) What length should your CV (resume) be?
2) Calling every day: annoying or impressive?
3) You should (not) write a personal statement.
4) (Don't) ask if you've got the job.
5) Stand out or stay in line?

Organizations are weighing in on the job search process and are using AI (Haan, 2023). Foti (n.d.) of Virginia Polytechnic Institute and State University offers an online PowerPoint regarding navigating academic interviews. The presentation offers general advice, interview schedule information, possible questions to prepare answers, illegal questions recruiters and interviewers should not ask, and questions the interviewee could ask during the interview. Significant to understand is that there is not one specified way for an interviewee to prepare; however, preparation is needed (Coleman, 2023; Forti, n.d.; Harver, 2023; Walderman, 2021).

Other questions raised are as follows. How could employment counselors continue to be relevant at a time when there are four generations, i.e., Baby Boomers (1945-1964), Generation X (1965-1981), Generation Y/Millennials (1982-1995), and Generation Z (1995-2005) in the workspace and each have their distinctive style in terms of work and interviewing? This question can be understood from Harver (2023). According to Harver, recruiters should adopt the following practices:

- **Tailor Recruiting Strategies**: Recognize that diverse generations may exhibit varying preferences in their job search methods and engagement with potential employers.
- **Eliminate Age-Based Assumptions and Stereotypes**: It is crucial not to conclude a candidate's skills, interests, or suitability for a role solely based on age.
- **Personalize Your Approach for Each Candidate**: Different generations may exhibit distinct communication styles, work habits, and expectations in the workplace, necessitating customized engagement strategies.
- **Form Multigenerational Teams for Proje**cts: Encourage creativity and innovation by assembling teams that encompass a wide range of perspectives and experiences.
- **Enhance Recruiter Feedback Techniques**: Recognize that different generations may have varying preferences for feedback types and delivery methods. (Harver, 2023)

In the context of interviewing individuals spanning five distinct generations, Walderman (2021) suggests the following insights:

- **Embrace Diverse Communication Approaches**: Acknowledge that various generations may gravitate towards distinct communication techniques.
- **Cultivate Equality**: In meetings and discussions, go above and beyond to ensure that every perspective is valued and taken into account, irrespective of an individual's age or seniority.
- **Foster an Atmosphere of Open Communication and Psychological Safety**: Encourage an environment where all voices feel welcome and protected, regardless of an individual's age or position within the organization. (Waldman, 2021)

The objective is to establish an inclusive decision-making process that promotes open communication and psychological well-being (Harver, 2023; Walderman, 2021). It is crucial to remember that while these suggestions offer a broad framework, every person is distinct and may not conform to generational patterns. It is advisable to take the time to understand each candidate as a unique individual. Recognizing and valuing the individuality of each candidate ensures a more holistic and practical approach to decision-making and team dynamics.

How each generational cohort engages in job-seeking endeavors, navigates the equilibrium between work and personal life, and enhances workplace productivity is susceptible to the impact of their distinctive communication styles, subjective perspectives, and unique life phases (Mack, 2021). Mack further contends that a comprehensive comprehension of these variations can empower employers to customize their recruitment methodologies in a more precise and informed manner. This nuanced understanding of generational dynamics contributes to developing more effective and targeted HR practices, ultimately fostering a harmonious and productive multigenerational workforce.

In the United States, this portion of the 21st has entered an asynchronous age wherein workers are no longer forced to sacrifice their well-being for the sake of 'success' or in order to provide for their families (Gonzales, 2023). Also, Gonzales offers that there are choices about how all employees can engage with work regarding how and where they work. In this contemporary era of the 21st century in the United States, a shift towards asynchronous work arrangements has liberated employees from the necessity to compromise their well-being in pursuit of 'success' or the provision for their families, granting them the autonomy to make choices regarding their work methods and locations. This transformation reflects a growing emphasis on work-life balance and flexibility in the modern workforce.

Upon meticulous examination of the data, this researcher has unearthed several pivotal inquiries that will shape the future requirements for recruitment professionals, educators, and prospective job seekers, as elucidated by Mack (2021). These inquiries encompass the following: How can organizations provide practical support to job seekers spanning all generations? What does this support entail, according to Mack's research findings (2021)? Which platforms and avenues are the most effective for recruiting individuals from diverse generational backgrounds? Additionally, what specific training requirements must be met by recruiters catering to the needs of job seekers in this era characterized by technological advancement, digitization, and artificial intelligence? Ultimately, these insights and investigations carry profound implications within the context of the contemporary digital and AI-driven landscape, charting a comprehensive roadmap for the human resource departments, recruiters, and job seekers of today.

This chapter explores the application of ethnography as a valuable tool to delve into the intricacies of job-seeking across four generations - Baby Boomers, Generation X, Generation Y/Millennials, and Generation Z. Ethnography, in this context, serves as a means to gain a comprehensive understanding of the creative thought processes, expressions, and experiences inherent in the job-seeking process. This guide outlines multi-faceted steps in ethnographic research and writing, offering the information in an accessible, reader-friendly language. The content draws on the rich experiences of five distinct generations as they embark on their job-seeking journeys. These ethnographic accounts and observations provide descriptive material and real-life case studies, offering valuable insights into the challenges and opportunities that job seekers face in today's competitive landscape. Readers can expect to find a wealth of practical and significant information for navigating the complex world of job searching, making this study a vital resource for job seekers of all generations. After the introduction, readers will review the background, which includes information about recruiting in the later 21st century and how it relates to artificial intelligence. Next are the focus of the research, assumptions, limitations, delimitations, background of the research, methodology and design, results of the ethnography research, solutions and recommendations, conclusions, references, and then key terms and definitions.

BACKGROUND

In the U.S., a record-high 4.4 million people, or 3% of workers, quit their jobs in September 2021 as part of a trend called the Great Resignation (HR Research Institute, 2021). The highest resignation rate was observed in the leisure and hospitality sector, with 6.4% of its workforce voluntarily leaving their positions, as reported by Williamson (2021). According to Williamson's findings, 20.2 million workers parted ways with their employers between May and September. The repercussions of this trend are palpable, as evidenced by a survey conducted in August 2021, which indicated that 73% of 380 North American employers were grappling with challenges in attracting new employees. This information marked a threefold increase compared to the previous year, as documented by Williamson (2021) in the same study.

Individuals aged 60 and above choose to continue working, whether to supplement their income, stave off retirement boredom, or for various personal motivations. Seeking employment anew can pose challenges at any career stage, but older job seekers have ample prospects. As one turns 60, it becomes essential to prepare for the job search process. According to a survey conducted by Ebeling (2018), when a prospective candidate might be considered too old for hiring received responses from employers, 64% indicated that it depends on the individual, while 12% remained uncertain. The remainder of the employers stated the age as 64. These findings underscore the opportunity for employers to be more receptive and inclusive towards older workers.

According to HR Research Institute (2021), as a result of these and other developments, talent acquisition professionals are under intense pressure to hire quality employees who can be retained over time. To accomplish this, many are leaning more heavily on talent acquisition technologies to help them quickly and efficiently fill vacancies with qualified candidates (HR Research, Institute, 2021). ATSs are not new. Advancements in technology like automated workflow capabilities, artificial intelligence (AI), and reporting functionality have made them easier to use and more attractive for today's hiring managers (American Banker, N.PAG, 2023).

As the labor landscape continues to evolve, employers and talent acquisition professionals must embrace flexible and inclusive recruitment practices, embrace all generations, and harness the potential of advanced technologies to meet the demands of an ever-changing workforce. In this dynamic labor landscape, it is imperative for employers and talent acquisition professionals to not only adopt flexible and inclusive recruitment practices that cater to all generations but also to foster a workplace culture that values diversity and inclusivity. Additionally, they should continue to leverage cutting-edge technologies to streamline hiring processes, improve candidate experiences, and adapt to the evolving expectations of the workforce.

FOCUS OF THE ARTICLE

The central aim of this research is to explore how ethnography, as a valuable research tool, can shed light on the intricate processes, creative thought patterns, and unique lived experiences inherent to the job-seeking journey within this diverse generational landscape. The study is driven by a recognition of the evolving nature of the workforce, characterized by extended retirement ages and the coexistence of multiple generations (i.e., Baby Boomers, Generation X, Generation Y/Millennials, and Generation Z) actively seeking employment opportunities. This text seeks to unravel the dynamics that shape these generational experiences in job-seeking, offering practical insights and guidance for job seekers, recruiters, educators, and employers. Within the research, ethnography is the primary methodology, allowing for an in-depth exploration of the nuances that define job-seeking across these generations (Paudel et al., 2023; Reeves et al., 2008; Smith, 2005). The study not only explores the individual experiences of job seekers but also delves into the broader context, such as the impact of the COVID-19 pandemic on the job market and the increasing reliance on technology, particularly artificial intelligence, in the recruitment process.

The ultimate goal is to provide a comprehensive resource that empowers individuals of all generations in their job-seeking endeavors. By documenting the diverse experiences, challenges, and opportunities encountered by job seekers, this research aims to equip readers with a deeper understanding of the contemporary job-seeking landscape. Furthermore, it emphasizes the importance of adaptive strategies, inclusivity, and technological literacy in navigating this ever-evolving terrain. Through ethnographic accounts, real-life case studies, and practical insights, this study offers a roadmap for individuals seeking employment, recruiters aiming to attract diverse talent, educators preparing job seekers, and organizations striving to thrive in a competitive job market.

ASSUMPTIONS

In the context of this ethnographic study conducted by the University of Louisville William F. Ekstrom Library (2021), several underlying assumptions were made, with ideas posited without empirical confirmation. These assumptions serve as foundational premises that guide the investigation. Three primary assumptions emerge. Firstly, it is posited that individuals across different generations share a common desire for Meaningful Work, irrespective of their generational backgrounds. This desire is rooted in the intrinsic human need to feel that their contributions hold significance and that their vocational pursuits align harmoniously with their deeply held values and personal interests. The quest for meaningful work is depicted as a universal aspiration that transcends generational boundaries, reflecting the inherent human inclination to seek purpose and fulfillment in one's career (University of Louisville William F. Ekstrom Library, 2021). Secondly, the assumption encompasses the belief that individuals, regardless of their generational cohort, attach considerable significance to compensation and benefits when embarking on their job-seeking journeys. While the specific priorities within the realm of compensation and benefits may exhibit variances based on generational demographics—such as younger generations emphasizing work-life balance, while older generations may emphasize retirement planning—the overarching theme of financial stability and tangible rewards for their professional endeavors remains a fundamental and enduring concern for job seekers from all generations (University of Louisville William F. Ekstrom Library, 2021). The third assumption underlying this ethnographic inquiry involves the presumption that all participants possess a fundamental understanding of the rudiments of job hunting. Additionally, participants are expected to voluntarily provide the most accurate and insightful responses, thereby showcasing their acquired knowledge and competencies during the ethnographic investigation. This assumption implies that individuals engaging in the ethnographic study have a baseline awareness of the concepts and practices associated with job hunting, which encompasses the pursuit of employment opportunities driven by various motivations, including unemployment, underemployment, dissatisfaction with current job roles, or the pursuit of enhanced professional positions (Lyons, 2021). In summary, these foundational assumptions underpin the ethnographic approach employed in the study, guiding the research framework and shaping the researchers' expectations as they seek to explore the multifaceted dimensions of job hunting across generational cohorts (University of Louisville William F. Ekstrom Library, 2021).

LIMITATIONS

The findings derived from this study are circumscribed by a specific criterion that narrows the scope to participants who have undertaken a minimum of ten job searches. These limitations are inherent within the research methodology and design, constituting constraints beyond the researcher's control (Sacred Heart University Library, 2020). The study acknowledges several noteworthy limitations, which warrant consideration and illuminate the contextual boundaries of the research endeavor. Primarily, variations in the participants' diverse experiences, as well as the contextual factors associated with the locations in which these experiences unfolded, may have exerted a considerable influence on the comprehension and explication of these experiences. These disparities, inherent to the individualized nature of job-seeking journeys, could introduce nuances and idiosyncrasies that impact the generalizability and transferability of the study's findings. Consequently, the study is mindful of these intrinsic variations, acknowledging that the richness of human experience often defies easy categorization (Sacred Heart University Library, 2020). Moreover, the research's focus needs to be more focused on the realm of customer service within both face-to-face and online environments, neglecting a broader exploration of field services. This specific delineation, while intentional for this study, underscores the necessity of exercising caution when applying the study's findings to domains beyond this delineated scope. The inherent differences between customer service and field services, in terms of operational dynamics and contextual factors, warrant recognition as a limitation that may impact the extent to which the study's insights can be extrapolated to other professional arenas (Sacred Heart University Library, 2020). In essence, these acknowledged limitations demarcate the study's boundaries, delineating the constraints imposed by the chosen research methodology and the specific parameters of the research design. They underscore the need for prudence when interpreting and applying the study's outcomes while highlighting opportunities for future research endeavors that may encompass a broader spectrum of experiences and contexts.

DELIMITATIONS

The delimitations of this research encompass the rigid demarcations and inherent constraints that define the study's parameters, as elucidated by Sianes (2020). These delimitations serve as methodological boundaries, channeling the investigation into a focused trajectory. It is essential to acknowledge these delimitations as they play a crucial role in circumscribing the study within manageable confines and ensuring that it operates within its inherent capabilities. One salient delimitation resides in the exclusive exploration of two distinct domains: face-to-face and online job searches. By entering the investigation into these specific modes of job-seeking, the study intentionally narrows its scope to gain deeper insights within these contexts. However, this precise delimitation signifies that the study's findings may only be universally applicable across some facets of face-to-face and online businesses. Recognizing these limits is pivotal in preventing unwarranted extrapolation of the results beyond the delineated boundaries. Furthermore, the delimitations extend to the participants themselves, impacting the generalizability of the study's outcomes. Given the specific criteria used for participant selection, the results presented in this chapter may possess varying degrees of applicability to a broader spectrum of face-to-face and online businesses. These participant-related delimitations underscore the need for caution when attempting to extend the findings to contexts and populations falling outside the parameters of this research. In essence, these delineated boundaries and methodological constraints play a pivotal role in shaping the study's focus and reach. They provide a framework for understanding the study's limitations and the contexts to which its findings can be appropriately applied, reinforcing the importance of judicious interpretation and prudent use of the research outcomes within their designated scope (Sianes, 2020).

METHODOLOGY AND DESIGN

Qualitative research methodology with engagement in a social setting is a robust instrument for elucidating intricate trends in thoughts and opinions while plunging into the depths of a specific concern (Burton, 2022; Small, 2021; Social Research Methods, 2019). It enjoys a well-established position in the arsenal of investigative approaches within the social sciences, a fact underscored by Burton (2014). The deliberate selection of qualitative research for this study is underpinned by its capacity to furnish the researcher with profound insights into the underlying motivations, opinions, and reasons that propel individuals, thus enriching the comprehension of the focal concern (Daniel, 2019). The research's overarching goal is to excavate the intricate tapestry of how individuals navigate and interpret a particular phenomenon, peering through the lens that perceives reality as an amalgamation of objects and events (Nigar, 2020). The meticulous collection and scrutiny of data within this study entail an unwavering commitment to detail, thereby facilitating the formulation of conclusions grounded in empiricism. Embedded within qualitative methodology is the judicious selection of ethnography as the research design. This choice affords the researcher an immersive vantage point, facilitating a deep and holistic comprehension of the subject matter. As expounded by Fenton et al. (2022), ethnography's potency lies in its capacity to unravel nuanced insights, perspectives, and behaviors within the natural habitat of the phenomenon under scrutiny. Specifically, applying ethnography interviewing, a social research method, allowed the noted advantages (See Figure 2) over qualitative interviewing.

Through immersive fieldwork and participant observation, ethnography permits the exploration of multifaceted social dynamics and intricate cultural practices (Paudel et al., 2023). This ethnographic approach emerges as an indispensable tool when the quest is for profound, contextually rich, and culturally sensitive insights that transcend superficial observations (Fenton et al., 2022; Smith, 2005).

Figure 2. Advantages: Ethnography interviews vs. qualitative interviews
Source: Social Research Methods (2019)

Advantages of Ethnography over Qualitative Interviews	Advantages of Qualitative Interviewing over Ethnography
Seeing the world through the eyes of other (because of longer immersion)	*Exposing issues resistant to observation* (some issues, e.g., domestic violence cannot be exposed with observation, only by questioning)
Learn local language (learning the local slang is necessary to understand the culture)	*Reflection on past and discussing future plans* (past events can be reconstructed in detail only by interviewing)
Exposes things that are taken for granted (interviewees might not discuss taken-for-granted meanings)	*Reactive effects are lower* (longer ethnography makes people accustomed to researcher's presence)
Tends to expose deviant activities easier (over longer and more in-depth observation can uncover deviance and crime)	*Less intrusive in people's lives* (ethnography takes more of the participants' time)
Contextualizes behaviour (socializing with people in different setting and over time improves understanding of context)	*Easier to conduct longitudinal research* (repeat interviews easier to organize than a long ethnography)
Naturalistic emphasis (ethnographer meets participants in their natural environment	*Wider coverage of people and situations to research* (ethnography limits to narrower circles of people)
	Specific focus of research (interviews better suited to focus on particular issue)

RESULTS AND DISCUSSION

Four ethnographic studies were applied using interviews. One participant represented the following generations: Baby Boomers, Generation X, Generation Y/Millennials, and Generation Z. In this research, each participant's name was changed to protect their identity (Dougherty, 2021). All four participants shared information about being unemployed or under-employed and needing a job. This researcher collected data from the five job seekers' journeys through interviews and observations. The primary intent was to learn whether the generations seek employment similarly. Other questions were: Do they run into the same or similar obstacles, and do they meet their goals?

Ethnography Study 1: Jones, a Baby Boomer born in 1950, began to search for her initial full-time permanent position after a contract ended in December 2021. Jones wanted to become an educational professional. Jones returned to college to earn a BA degree in human services 20 years after graduating high school. Initially, Jones prepared chronological and functional resumes. To make the resume robust, Jones contacted six people to serve as references. References were selected based on previous employment and business contacts, including friends and individuals with whom workshops were conducted or volunteer work was performed. These actions were performed between January 2021 and September 2023. In mid-2023, Jones stated, "I cannot believe that no one has mentioned anything about a job. I have work experience and a BS degree. Interview after interview, I get the same question which is, 'What do you want to do?' My thoughts are, I applied for the job, the answer to the questions should be obvious." Jones did not tweak the resume according to the job description.

Jones' job-seeking tracking sheets include over 500 searches. Categories include Company name, contact information, follow-up information, and skills. An interview was conducted with Jones.

Interview with Jones

- How did you feel during this job search? "*I felt frustrated. I have plenty of experience. The recruiters seemed clueless.*"
- Are you savvy with Microsoft Office? "**I know the very basics**."
- Did you contact others to help you search for a position? "*Yes, I contacted all sorts of people. I had no luck there.*"
- Did you change anything you were doing to get the full-time permanent position? "No, *I did not see the need to make any changes. I had a resume, so I kept sending them out.*"
- What did you learn from this experience? "*This job-hunting business is a mess. Companies say they need help but are not hiring. What a mess.*"
- Did you use social media to job hunt? "*Well, I used the normal such as Career Builders and Monster. I did not use any other sites.*"In October 2023, Jones secured a full-time position through an organization where volunteering had taken place since April 2011. The offered salary was below the average for the area where Jones lived.

Ethnography Study 2: Next, Brown's journey was chronicled from April 2021, when downsized from an IT position at a prominent bank. Born Generation X, Brown began an MBA program in May 2021 and then took a contract position in November 2021. From 2021 to 2023, Brown served as a Manager and Trainer at a significant educational institution. Brown noted. "I want my next role to be with more responsibility and respect. Therefore, I got busy looking for work. Efforts included creating a tracking sheet for positions in which I applied. I applied directly to companies, applied to government agencies, and applied to consulting companies." Brown did not tweak the resume according to the job description.

Brown's job-seeking tracking sheets include over 1000 searches. Categories include Company name, location, email address, contact information, the type of resume sent, follow-up information, and skills. An interview was conducted with Brown.

Interview With Brown

- How did you feel during this job search? *"I felt alone and disgusted."*
- Are you savvy with Microsoft Office? *"Yes, I have a Microsoft certification that I earned during college."*
- Did you contact others to help you search for a position? *"Yes, I did. Many people who talked a good game about being connected pretended not to know anything when I asked for help."*
- Did you change anything you were doing to get the full-time permanent position? *"Yes, I created resumes using all my job competencies and the keywords on the job description. Also, I understood how companies use* Applicant Tracking Systems to locate new hires. *While waiting for a call about a position, I honed my skills."*
- What did you learn from this experience? *"People talk a good game. When one speaks, and his actions are different from his words, believe the actions."*
- Did you use social media to job hunt? *"Yes, I uploaded my resume to several sites and contacted as many people as possible who may have been able to help me."*

In May 2023, Brown landed a full-time position as a training manager. The offered salary was 20% above the last salary. This raise put the salary at mid-range for such a position in the field and a salary above the location's pay.

Ethnography Study 3: Next is Andrews, a Generation Y/Millennials born in 1982. This participant graduated in 2000 from a major institution with a Master of Science in Accounting - Public Accounting - CPA Track. Immediately. Andrews began work for one of the big four accounting companies. After working for 20 years and gaining a family, Andrews decided that a career with a less than 12-hour work day would be better suited for the family. In 2022, Andrews had a resume prepared, contacted a network to inform them of the job search, and then resigned in 2023.

Andrew's job-seeking tracking sheets included 50 searches. Categories of the tracking sheet included company name, date applied, location of the position, contact's email address, specific knowledge/skill requirements, and follow-up information. Andrews tweaked the resume according to the job description. An interview was conducted with Andrews.

Interview With Andrews

- How did you feel during your job search? *"I felt excited as I went through the University's alumni placement center and used my network."*
- Are you savvy with Microsoft Office? *"I am very confident with using MS Office."*
- Did you contact others to help you search for a position? *"Yes, I used my entire network to help me locate a new role. They were accommodating."*
- Did you change anything you were doing to get the full-time permanent position? *"Yes, I considered the tracking systems used by organizations. Also, during college, I interned at different companies every summer. After graduation, I landed a great opportunity."*

- What did you learn from this experience? *"Yes, first, I believe that all students should consider an internship, externship, or the like every summer. Learn your job very well and prepare for the next level."*
- Did you use social media to job hunt? *"Initially, I did not use social media because I was still working. After I resigned, I used social media."*

In April of 2023, Andrews landed a full-time position as a Controller. The offered salary was 30% above the last salary. This raise was above the mid-range for the position and the location's pay.

Ethnography Study 4: Next is Corbyn, a Generation Z, born in 1997. Corbyn graduated from a small university in 2015 with an MA in Broadcast Journalism. During the university years, four internships were completed. After graduation, Corbyn received an offer from one of the internship organizations. In 2022, Corbyn decided to locate a position with more responsibility and pay. A resume was prepared. Corbyn contacted several networks to inform them of the job search.

Corbyn did not use a job-seeking tracking sheet but listed the locations where jobs were applied. Events were attended to where leaders of influence would attend, too. Corbyn tweaked the resume according to the job descriptions. An interview was conducted with Andrews.

- How did you feel during your job search? *"Oh, I was very happy and enthused about the search. I did not feel pressured.".*
- Are you savvy with Microsoft Office? *"I am very confident with using MS Office. I am MS Office certified."*
- Did you contact others to help you search for a position? *"Yes, I reached out to my network, who helped me land a great position."*
- Did you change anything you were doing to get the full-time permanent position? *"No, I started by reaching out to my network and did not have to make any changes."*

What did you learn from this experience? *"I learned that continued preparation is important to success."*

- Did you use social media to job hunt? *"I did not use social media."*

FUTURE RESEARCH DIRECTIONS

By conducting ethnographic research that includes five generations of Baby Boomers, Generation X, Generation Y/Millennials, Generation Z, and Generation Alpha, a more comprehensive understanding of how individuals of different ages approach the job market can be ascertained. Researchers should consider several key factors:

- **Understanding Generational Shifts**: Tracking the experiences, attitudes, and strategies of different generations in their job search processes can provide valuable insights into how job seeking continues to evolve. Also, tracking allows for identifying common patterns, differences, and trends in the job market.

- **Adapting to Changing Job Market Dynamics**: The job market continually evolves with technological advancements, economic changes, and shifts in employer expectations. By studying multiple generations, researchers can better understand how individuals from different age groups navigate these changes and adapt their job-seeking strategies.
- **Informing Career Development Programs**: Insights from such research can inform career development programs and services. Understanding the preferences and challenges different generations face can help career counselors and educators tailor their guidance to better meet the needs of job seekers from various age groups.
- **Highlighting the Role of Networks**: Research can shed light on the importance of professional networks and how they vary across generations. This information can guide individuals in building and leveraging their networks effectively during their job searches.
- **Identifying Opportunities for Skill Development**: Studying the experiences of different generations can reveal gaps in skills and competencies that may be necessary for successful job hunting. This information can guide educational institutions and training programs in preparing individuals for the job market.
- **Promoting Inclusivity and Diversity**: Analyzing the job-seeking experiences of different generations can also contribute to discussions on inclusivity and diversity in the workplace. Analysis can help identify potential biases or barriers individuals from various age groups may encounter during their job searches.
- **Supporting Policy Decisions**: Insights into generational job-seeking experiences can inform policy decisions related to labor markets, workforce development, and social support systems, ensuring that policies are relevant and effective for all age groups.

CONCLUSION

The comprehensive study undertaken in this ethnography research has illuminated the complex dynamics of job seeking across four distinct generations: Baby Boomers, Generation X, Generation Y/Millennials, and Generation Z. As the exploration draws to a close, several salient insights emerge, underlining the significance of adaptability, empathy, and technological proficiency in the contemporary job-searching landscape.

Adaptability in Job Hunting: A recurring theme woven into the narratives of job seekers from various generations is the paramount importance of adaptability. In a swiftly evolving environment characterized by technological progress and economic fluctuations, job seekers must continuously refine their strategies and competencies. The COVID-19 pandemic expedited the prevalence of Applicant Tracking Systems (ATS) and other advanced tools, underscoring the necessity for comprehending and navigating these systems adeptly. The ability to tailor resumes, utilize online platforms, and embrace remote work opportunities has become indispensable.

Empathy in Recruitment: For recruiters and employers, the findings from this research underscore the critical role of empathy and open-mindedness when assessing job applicants from diverse age groups. Stereotypes and preconceptions rooted in generational categorizations should be replaced with a holistic evaluation of candidates' skills, experiences, and potential contributions. Customized approaches to engagement and communication can bridge generational divides, fostering a more inclusive work environment.

Technological Literacy: The research spotlights the pivotal role of technological literacy in the job-seeking process. Job seekers from all generations must embrace technology as an ally, utilizing it to enhance their visibility, engage with networks, and showcase their qualifications. Embracing encompasses not only comprehending the functioning of ATS systems but also harnessing the potential of social media and online job platforms.

The Great Resignation and Work-Life Balance: The study underscores the ongoing transformation of the workplace, characterized by an emphasis on work-life balance and flexibility. The "Great Resignation" phenomenon, observed predominantly in the United States, reflects an increasing inclination among employees to prioritize well-being and autonomy. Employers should take cognizance of this shift and contemplate offering flexible work arrangements to allure and retain talent from every generation.

In conclusion, the job-seeking experiences of Baby Boomers, Generation X, Generation Y/Millennials, and Generation Z exhibit richness and diversity, shaped by distinct historical contexts and technological advancements. The findings from this study accentuate the necessity for a nuanced and personalized approach to job hunting and recruitment. Moving forward, job seekers and employers must remain adaptable, empathetic, and technologically proficient to flourish in the ever-changing world of work. By embracing these principles, a more inclusive and prosperous job market can be fashioned that caters to the needs and aspirations of all generations.

REFERENCES

Burton, S. L. (2022). *Cybersecurity leadership from a Telemedicine/Telehealth knowledge and organizational development examination* (Order No. 29066056). Available from ProQuest Central; ProQuest Dissertations & Theses Global. (2662752457). https://www.proquest.com/dissertations-theses/cybersecurity-leadership-telemedicine-telehealth/docview/2662752457/se-2

Coleman, L. (2023). 5 common job search tips that totally contradict each other. *Undercover Recruiter.* https://theundercoverrecruiter.com/job-seeking-tips-that-contradict/

Daniel, B. K. (2019). *What constitutes a good qualitative research study? fundamental dimensions and indicators of rigour in qualitative research: The TACT framework*. Kidmore End: Academic Conferences International Limited. http://dx.doi.org.proxy.cecybrary.com/10.34190/RM.19.113

Dougherty, M. V. (2021). The use of confidentiality and anonymity protections as a cover for fraudulent fieldwork data. *Research Ethics*, *17*(4), 480–500. Advance online publication. doi:10.1177/17470161211018257

Ebeling, A. (2018, August 21). Employers say 64 is too old to get a job. *Forbes*. https://www.forbes.com/sites/ashleaebeling/2018/08/21/employers-say-64-is-too-old-to-get-a-job/?sh=5c85f36051e8

Fenton, A., Heinze, A., Osborne, M., & Ahmed, W. (2022). How to Use the Six-Step Digital Ethnography Framework to Develop Buyer Personas: The Case of Fan Fit. *JMIR Formative Research*, *6*(11), e41489. Advance online publication. doi:10.2196/41489 PMID:36427232

Foti, R. J. (n.d.). Academic Job Interviews: Questions and Advice. *Virginia Polytechnic Institute and State University*. https://vtechworks.lib.vt.edu/bitstream/handle/10919/72241/gsls_roseanne_foti_interviews.pdf

Gonzales, M. (2023). The generational divide between older and younger employees. *SHRM*. https://www.shrm.org/resourcesandtools/hr-topics/behavioral-competencies/global-and-cultural-effectiveness/pages/the-generational-divide-between-older-and-younger-employees.aspx

Haan, K. (2023, October 3). 11 best applicant tracking systems of 2023. *Forbes*. https://www.forbes.com/advisor/business/best-applicant-tracking-systems/

Harver. (2023). How to manage generational diversity in the workplace. *Harver*. https://harver.com/blog/generational-diversity-in-the-workplace/

HR Research Institute. (2021). The Future of Recruitment Technologies 2021-22: Successfully recruit talent in a time of high turnover. *Talent Acquisition Excellence*, *9*(12), 19–21.

Lyons, M. (2021). How to Job Hunt (when you're already exhausted). *Harvard Business Review*. https://hbr.org/2021/10/how-to-job-hunt-when-youre-already-exhausted

Mack, T. (2021). Generational recruiting: How to tailor your recruitment message for different generations. *Recruitics*. https://info.recruitics.com/blog/generational-recruiting-how-to-tailor-your-recruitment-message-for-different-generations

Nigar, N. (2020). Hermeneutic phenomenological narrative enquiry: A qualitative study design. *Theory and Practice in Language Studies*, *10*(1), 10–18. doi:10.17507/tpls.1001.02

Paudel, T., Luitel, B. C., & Dahal, N. (2023). Journey of Realization and Adaptation through Auto/Ethnography: A Shift to Transformative Educational Research. *The Qualitative Report*, *28*(4), 1017–1037. doi:10.46743/2160-3715/2023.5649

Reeves, S., Kuper, A., & Hodges, B. D. (2008). Qualitative research methodologies: ethnography. *BMJ: British Medical Journal (Online)*, doi:10.1136/bmj.a1020

Sacred Heart University Library. (2020). Limitations. *Author*. https://library.sacredheart.edu/c.php?g=29803&p=185934

Sianes, A. (2021). Academic Research on the 2030 Agenda: Challenges of a Transdisciplinary Field of Study. *Global Policy*, *12*(3), 286–297. doi:10.1111/1758-5899.12912

Skillings, P. (2023). Job interview advice: Myths & mysteries. *Big Interview*. https://resources.biginterview.com/interviews-101/job-interview-advice/

Small, M. L. (2021). What is "Qualitative" in Qualitative Research? Why the Answer Does not Matter but the Question is Important. *Qualitative Sociology*, *44*(4), 567–574. doi:10.1007/s11133-021-09501-3

Smith, W. E. (2005). *Hip hop as performance and ritual: Biography and ethnography in underground hip hop*. CLS Publications.

Social Research Methods. (2019). Oxford University Press.

University of Louisville William F. Ekstrom Library. (2021). Critical thinking and academic research: Assumptions. *Author*. https://library.louisville.edu/ekstrom/criticalthinking/assumptions

Waldman, E. (2021). How to manage a multi-generational team. *Harvard Business Review*. https://hbr.org/2021/08/how-to-manage-a-multi-generational-team

Williamson, I. O. (2021). The 'great resignation' is a trend that began before the pandemic – and bosses need to get used to it. *The Conversation*. https://theconversation.com/the-great-resignation-is-a-trend-that-began-before-the-pandemic-and-bosses-need-to-get-used-to-it-170197

KEY TERMS AND DEFINITIONS

Applicant Tracking Systems (ATS): Applicant Tracking Systems are software applications organizations use to manage and streamline their recruitment and hiring processes. These systems assist in collecting, storing, and organizing job applications and candidate information. ATS can help recruiters and HR professionals track applicants, screen resumes, schedule interviews, and manage communication with candidates.

Artificial Intelligence (AI): Artificial Intelligence refers to the simulation of human intelligence in computer systems. It involves the development of algorithms and computer programs that enable machines to perform tasks that typically require human intelligence, such as learning from data, making decisions, solving problems, and recognizing patterns.

COVID-19: COVID-19, short for "Coronavirus Disease 2019," is a highly contagious and potentially severe respiratory illness caused by the novel coronavirus, SARS-CoV-2. It was first identified in Wuhan, China, in late 2019 and has since led to a global pandemic. COVID-19 can manifest with a wide range of symptoms, including fever, cough, difficulty breathing, fatigue, and loss of taste or smell. It has had significant public health, social, and economic impacts worldwide, leading to widespread illness, hospitalizations, and deaths, as well as various public health measures such as lockdowns, social distancing, mask mandates, and vaccination campaigns to mitigate its spread.

Cybersecurity: Cybersecurity refers to the practice of protecting computer systems, networks, and digital data from unauthorized access, cyberattacks, damage, or theft. It encompasses a wide range of technologies, processes, practices, and measures designed to safeguard information technology assets and ensure the confidentiality, integrity, and availability of data and digital systems. Cybersecurity aims to defend against various threats, including hackers, malware, phishing attempts, and other cybercrimes, by implementing security controls, protocols, and countermeasures. It is a critical field in today's interconnected digital world, as it helps organizations and individuals protect sensitive information and maintain the functionality and security of their digital environments.

Ethnography: Ethnography is a qualitative research method used to study and understand human societies and cultures. Ethnographers immerse themselves in the culture or community they are studying, often through participant observation and interviews, to gain deep insights into the beliefs, behaviors, practices, and social dynamics of the group.

Generational Cohort: A generational cohort refers to a group of individuals who were born during the same period and share everyday historical, cultural, and societal experiences. Generational cohorts are often used to categorize and analyze people based on the era in which they were born, such as Baby Boomers, Generation X, Millennials, and Generation Z.

Great Resignation: The Great Resignation is a term used to describe a notable trend in which employees voluntarily leave their jobs or opt out of the traditional workforce. This phenomenon, observed in various industries, is often associated with factors like changing work preferences, the impact of the COVID-19 pandemic, and a re-evaluation of work-life balance.

Qualitative Research: Qualitative research is a research method that focuses on gaining an in-depth understanding of human behavior, experiences, and perspectives. It involves collecting non-numerical data, such as interviews, observations, and textual or visual materials, to explore and analyze complex social phenomena, often without statistical analysis.

Chapter 14
Using Artificial Intelligence as a Public Health Surveillance Tool During Salmonella Outbreaks

Darrell Norman Burrell

iD https://orcid.org/0000-0002-4675-9544

Capitol Technology University, USA & The Pellegrino Center, Georgetown University, USA

Ian McAndrew

iD https://orcid.org/0009-0007-7650-3826

Capitol Technology University, USA

ABSTRACT

The increasing prevalence of illnesses, particularly Salmonella infections, presents a significant public health challenge. Traditional surveillance and outbreak management methods are resource-intensive and often must catch up to real-time occurrences. This chapter explores the application of artificial intelligence (AI) within a systems thinking framework to revolutionize public health surveillance and outbreak response for Salmonella. By harnessing AI-driven tools for data analysis, early detection, source attribution, and intervention planning, public health agencies can enhance their capacity to prevent and mitigate Salmonella outbreaks. This chapter discusses the potential of AI-driven systems to transform the landscape of public health. The chapter proposes AI as a holistic approach integrating technology, data, and human expertise for more effective Salmonella outbreak control based on actual life outbreaks and the historical contexts of the of a real outbreak event.

OVERVIEW

On March 1, 2017, a strain of Salmonella Agbeni infected patient zero (Multistate Outbreak, 2017). From March 1 to December 1, there were 76 cases across 19 states. Luckily, no one died; however, 30 people were hospitalized (Multistate Outbreak, 2017). Epidemiologists were able to link this outbreak to contact with turtles or their environment (Multistate Outbreak, 2017). Approximately 38% of infected

DOI: 10.4018/979-8-3693-1970-3.ch014

individuals had contact with either turtles or their environment; 61% had contact with tiny turtles (shell length of less than four inches). These individuals either had access to these turtles from a street vendor or received them as gifts (Multistate Outbreak, 2017). Through genome sequencing, health officials could relate this outbreak to the turtles from the street vendor (Multistate Outbreak, 2017). This series of events was not without trial and error. Epidemiologists and other professionals must work together to determine what caused this outbreak and what specifically keeps this infectious disease alive.

A solid place to start in epidemiology is with the epidemiologic triangle. This triangle contains three factors: the agent, the host, and the environment (Friis, 2018). In this case, the agent Salmonella Agbeni is essential for the survival of this disease. Without this, there is no outbreak. The host, in this case, humans, is one infected with the disease and provides an area for the agent to thrive unless treated (Friis, 2018). Lastly, the environment is where the agent exists (Friis, 2018). Unfortunately for humans, the agent and the agent's environment proved to be a determining factor in having the illness. Even the water the turtles swam in could be strong enough to give an individual the infection. Combining these three factors gives Salmonella a chance to thrive in an area.

According to the CDC, 32% of the people who were ill were younger than five years old, and 23 of the 60 people interviewed reported contact with turtles or their environment during the week they fell ill. Therefore, epidemiologists have to consider some personal variables when defining a disease. Friis states that age is the most critical factor when characterizing any disease (2018). Looking at age as a variable was an important clue in the infected individuals because a note was made for children under five.

Acquiring public health data and formatting it into a usable form is a large part of epidemiology. Public health surveillance is utilized by the CDC and epidemiologists worldwide to identify potential disease outbreaks and prevent the spread of these communicable diseases (McNabb et al., 2016). By compiling this data and utilizing statistical analysis and bivariate analysis, researchers can identify if there is a causal association between factors (Friis, 2018). A causal association is an association between an exposure and a health outcome that can be backed up by causality criteria (Friis, 2018). The Bradford-Hill criteria of causality list the following criteria: plausibility, consistency, temporality, strength, specificity, and change in risk factor ("Causality and Association (Bradford-Hill Criteria) - StatsDirect," n.d.). In the case study of turtles and Salmonella, by looking at the statistical data listed above, scientists could see the connection between the reported cases of Salmonella and contact with turtles or their environment. Many epidemic outbreaks can be linked to human-to-animal interaction (CDC, 2018). Viruses can mutate and be transmittable from animals to humans or vice versa (CDC, 2018). The Terrestrial Animal Health Code works to improve animal welfare concerning the trade of terrestrial animals and their products (McNabb et al., 2016). The safe management and proper treatment of animals and animal products can help mitigate the risk of disease development or transfer (McNabb et al., 2016).

The epidemiologic triangle is another central concept that helps foster a better understanding of the communicable nature of this interaction (Friis, 2018). The epidemiologic triangle is comprised of three factors: agent, host, and environment (Friis, 2018). The agent is the factor whose presence or absence is essential in the occurrence of a disease, in this case, Salmonella Agbeni (Friis, 2018). The host is the person, living animal (turtle), or population infected by a disease (Friis, 2018). The environment (turtle habitat) is where the disease-causing agent exists exclusively outside of the host (Friis, 2018). When this triangle is met, an outbreak may occur. Therefore, if a turtle is infected with Salmonella Agbeni in a tank with water and a person comes into contact with that water, they may contract the disease.

Since the conclusion of the outbreak, public health officials have led the drive to bring awareness to the public about the health risks that tiny turtles may pose to the public. Research and public education are essential tools for managing risks and keeping those in the public safe. The US Centers for Disease Controls put out these educational purposes. Several states have even banned selling or distributing turtles with a carapace length of less than four inches for keeping as pets. They may only be sold or distributed for scientific, educational, or export purposes. Many states outline that companies that offer these turtles for sale in order to meet regulatory guidelines. One of the most effective ways to mitigate a threat is to limit contact with it via a ban or regulation that limits interaction with the threat. Threats to public health illness can also be minimized in the form of a quarantine or isolation in the case of a communicable disease (McNabb et al., 2016). In addition to education and safe practices, sanitization regulations are also in place to help mitigate the spread of disease (McNabb et al., 2016). By utilizing safe handling procedures and proper sanitation practices after handling tiny turtles, humans interacting with the animal can reduce their risk of contracting Salmonella.

PROBLEM STATEMENT

The U.S. Centers for Disease Control and Prevention (CDC) posits that annually within the United States, an estimated 1.35 million instances of salmonellosis manifest, precipitating 26,500 hospital admissions and 420 fatalities. (U.S. Food and Drug Administration, 2023). The gravity of the issue is underscored by the manifold avenues through which Salmonella infection can be transmitted to individuals, accentuating the imperative for heightened vigilance and awareness. Beyond ingesting contaminated food, individuals can inadvertently acquire the pathogen by mere contact, anointing their hands and clothing as unwitting transmission vectors (U.S. Food and Drug Administration, 2023). Compounding this concern is the recognition that even pet food may be a source of Salmonella contagion (U.S. Food and Drug Administration, 2023). The proclivity of raw or uncooked meat within pet sustenance to harbor the bacterium is of particular concern, amplifying the likelihood of human exposure (U.S. Food and Drug Administration, 2023).

Additionally, the assemblage of animals, including but not limited to cattle, poultry, rodents, reptiles, and amphibians, presents a reservoir for Salmonella within their intestinal tracts, frequently without exhibiting any overt symptoms of malaise (U.S. Food and Drug Administration, 2023). Intriguingly, individuals may contract salmonellosis through the simple act of handling such animals or interacting with their habitats, with the bacterium potentially pervading the environment, be it cages, aquariums, or terrariums (U.S. Food and Drug Administration, 2023). Notably, providing feeder rodents to pet reptiles and amphibians further accentuates the risk, as direct contact or interaction with contaminated items within these animal enclosures can serve as conduits for disseminating Salmonella to individuals. It is paramount, therefore, to diligently heed these multifarious routes of transmission and institute measures to mitigate the risks associated with Salmonella infection (U.S. Food and Drug Administration, 2023). This paper explores the healthcare use cases of artificial intelligence as a public health surveillance tool that can be used for Salmonella and other outbreaks.

The Epidemiologic Triangle

Artificial Intelligence (AI) can significantly enhance the application of the epidemiologic triangle model in public health surveillance during Salmonella outbreaks. This model traditionally identifies three key elements—host, agent, and environment—as the core factors contributing to disease transmission

(Friis, 2018). AI's data analytics capabilities allow for systematically collecting and analyzing extensive datasets related to these factors. It can track and monitor host-related data, such as demographics, clinical symptoms, and geographic locations, helping identify high-risk populations and areas. AI can also analyze agent-related data, including Salmonella strains and genetic information, aiding in source attribution and outbreak tracing. Furthermore, AI excels in processing environmental data, such as food supply chain information and climate conditions, assisting in identifying potential sources and transmission routes (Zeng et al., 2021; Thiébaut & Cossin, 2019). By applying AI to the epidemiologic triangle model, public health authorities can gain deeper insights into the complex interactions between these elements, facilitating early detection, more accurate risk assessment, and targeted interventions during Salmonella outbreaks (Zeng et al., 2021; Thiébaut & Cossin, 2019).

The epidemiologic triangle and people variables are essential in further defining a disease; however, the causality criteria are vital in determining if these turtles did cause Salmonella Agbeni. Sir Austin Bradford Hill provides nine different criteria of causality: strength, consistency, specificity, temporality, biological gradient, plausibility, coherence, experiment, and analogy (Friis, 2018).

Strength supports the host and disease, whereas consistency refers to an observed repeated association over time (Friis, 2018). Consistency was shown since these infections occurred over ten months, and it was probable that this host caused the disease, which provided high strength. Specificity strictly connects a disease to inevitable exposure, and temporality involves observing the cause before the effect (Friis, 2018). Epidemiologists could attribute these outbreaks to the strain; the cause came before the effect.

The biological gradient refers to a linear trend between exposure and disease, and plausibility refers to an association between exposure and modern knowledge (Friis, 2018). Coherence refers to how the data agrees with known facts, and science and experiment provide further evidence to support the relationship (Friis, 2018). Turtles are known to carry Salmonella Agbeni; therefore, the data corresponded to known facts. Lastly, analogy relates known associations to those tested for causality (Friis, 2018). Salmonella causes specific symptoms; therefore, these observed symptoms by healthcare professionals were analogous to the known symptoms of the infection.

These nine factors help add proof that these turtles and their environment caused the infectious outbreak. However, there are ways to prevent the spread of this outbreak. Washing hands is always an essential component of good health. A second factor is learning how to play safely. Education and knowledge will provide individuals with the proper knowledge on preventing Salmonella Agbeni (Multistate Outbreak, 2017). For example, kissing or snuggling turtles and letting turtles roam around food is not recommended (Multistate Outbreak, 2017). Since children were affected by this outbreak, families should ensure they pick the right pet. Not only are children at high risk, but individuals over 65 and those with weakened immune systems should highly evaluate their decision to get a pet turtle (Multistate Outbreak, 2017). An important note is that the FDA banned turtles with shells less than four inches long (Multistate Outbreak, 2017). However, street vendors can still sell these turtles. Therefore, education about these turtles and the associated outbreak is essential in preventing one from buying turtles from vendors. Considering that many of the individuals affected bought from street vendors or interacted with the vendors, it is evident that some might not know about the dangers of these turtles. Public health initiatives are an excellent way to spread the word about these turtles and will help prevent many from the effects of Salmonella.

Typical symptoms of Salmonella include diarrhea, fever, and abdominal cramps, with most individuals recovering after 4 to 7 days (Signs & Symptoms, 2018). This infection can spread throughout the bloodstream; therefore, hospitalization might be necessary, but death is not expected since antibiotics can cure the infection (Signs & Symptoms, 2018). No antibiotic resistance has been found in this strain;

therefore, the survival rate is incredibly high (Signs & Symptoms, 2018). Furthermore, this outbreak is preventable despite the high survival of this infection. Salmonella outbreaks can be prevented if individuals follow the CDC guidelines and public health initiatives. No one died from this particular strain, and no one should have to die from an infection that can be treated and prevented. This Salmonella outbreak outlines the importance of public health education and, more importantly, the need for more effective approaches to public health surveillance that can track outbreaks and trends more swiftly and effectively.

USING AI WITH SALMONELLA OUTBREAKS

AI holds immense potential to bolster public health surveillance during Salmonella outbreaks by swiftly processing vast datasets, detecting patterns, and predicting outbreaks (Zeng et al., 2021; Thiébaut & Cossin, 2019). However, public health workers and leaders may resist adopting these new technologies due to their familiarity and comfort with existing processes. While sometimes less efficient, traditional methods have been tried and tested over time, and there may be reluctance to abandon them. Additionally, public health professionals may harbor concerns about the reliability and accuracy of AI algorithms, leading to a lack of trust in these technologies. Overcoming this resistance requires comprehensive training, education, and clear communication about the capabilities and limitations of AI in public health surveillance. Leaders must champion the benefits of AI, emphasizing its potential to improve response times, enhance outbreak detection, and allocate resources more effectively.

Furthermore, integrating AI into public health surveillance may disrupt established hierarchies and roles within public health organizations. Resistance can arise when workers perceive AI as potentially threatening their job security or professional expertise. To mitigate this, leaders must facilitate a culture of collaboration and explain that AI is meant to augment, not replace human expertise. Encouraging public health workers to engage actively with AI systems providing opportunities for their input and feedback, can help alleviate their concerns and build trust in these technologies. Addressing resistance to AI adoption among public health workers and leaders requires clear communication, ongoing training, and a supportive organizational culture that values innovation and embraces the potential of new technologies to enhance public health surveillance.

TECHNOLOGY ACCEPTANCE MODEL (TAM)

Resistance to adopting new technologies and innovative approaches within organizations can often be explained through the "Technology Acceptance Model" (TAM) lens. The TAM theoretical framework focuses on factors influencing individuals' intentions and behaviors regarding the use of technology (Holden & Karsh, 2010; Rahimi et al., 2018). In the context of organizational cultures, leaders, and workers, the TAM can help elucidate the sources of resistance (Holden & Karsh, 2010; Rahimi et al., 2018).

The integration of new technologies into public health surveillance systems offers unprecedented opportunities for data collection, analysis, and timely response to health threats. However, the successful implementation of these technologies in public health organizations is not without its challenges. The Technology Acceptance Model (TAM), originally developed to understand user acceptance of information systems, has gained significance in assessing the adoption of health technologies. In the context of public health surveillance, TAM provides a framework for examining the organizational challenges that influence the acceptance and utilization of new surveillance technologies (Holden & Karsh, 2010; Rahimi et al., 2018).

Perceived Usefulness and Perceived Ease of Use

One aspect of the TAM theory pertains to perceived usefulness and ease of use (Holden & Karsh, 2010; Rahimi et al., 2018). Organizational cultures that have long adhered to established practices and workflows may only accept new technologies if they perceive them as disruptive or provide clear benefits (Holden & Karsh, 2010; Rahimi et al., 2018). Leaders play a crucial role in shaping these perceptions. Resistance can arise if leaders do not effectively communicate the advantages of new technologies or fail to demonstrate how they can improve efficiency and outcomes. Similarly, workers may only accept adoption if they perceive using the technology as complex and time-consuming or disrupting their established routines. In such cases, training and support become essential to mitigate resistance by enhancing the perceived ease of use.

Social Influence and Facilitating Conditions

The TAM theory also considers social influence and facilitating conditions (Holden & Karsh, 2010; Rahimi et al., 2018). Organizational cultures often involve established norms and behaviors that resist change (Holden & Karsh, 2010; Rahimi et al., 2018). Leaders within these cultures may be hesitant to embrace innovative approaches due to concerns about backlash or potential risks to the status quo. Workers, influenced by peer attitudes and behaviors, may only accept technology adoption if they perceive it as consistent with established practices or challenging their expertise. Leaders can play a vital role in mitigating this resistance by fostering a culture that encourages experimentation, risk-taking, and learning from failures. Facilitating conditions, such as providing the necessary resources and support, can also alleviate resistance by making the adoption process smoother and more conducive to change (Holden & Karsh, 2010; Rahimi et al., 2018).

Attitudes and Behavioral Intentions

The TAM theory examines attitudes and behavioral intentions. Resistance to technology adoption often stems from deeply ingrained attitudes and beliefs within an organizational culture (Holden & Karsh, 2010; Rahimi et al., 2018). Leaders may encounter opposition from employees who hold strong convictions about the superiority of traditional methods or who fear that new technologies may replace their roles. Overcoming such resistance requires effective communication, precise alignment between technology adoption and organizational goals, and cultivating a culture that values innovation. Leaders should work to change negative attitudes by highlighting the potential benefits, addressing concerns, and involving employees in the decision-making process to increase their buy-in and willingness to embrace new technologies.

In summary, the Technology Acceptance Model offers insights into how resistance to technology adoption can manifest within organizational cultures, leaders, and workers (Holden & Karsh, 2010; Rahimi et al., 2018). Addressing perceived usefulness and ease of use, managing social influence and facilitating conditions, and addressing attitudes and behavioral intentions are essential steps in mitigating resistance and successfully integrating new technologies and innovative approaches within an organization (Holden & Karsh, 2010; Rahimi et al., 2018).

Leveraging Perceived Ease of Use

To address resistance, managers can focus on enhancing the perceived ease of use of new technologies. This can be achieved by offering comprehensive training and support, simplifying user interfaces, and providing clear documentation. Managers should actively engage with employees to identify barriers to ease of use and address them promptly. By making technology more user-friendly, managers can mitigate resistance stemming from fears of complexity and unfamiliarity (Holden & Karsh, 2010; Rahimi et al., 2018).

Managers must also emphasize the perceived usefulness of new technologies to employees. Clear communication of the benefits and advantages that the technology offers is vital. Additionally, managers should actively involve employees in the decision-making process, demonstrating how the technology aligns with their goals and responsibilities (Holden & Karsh, 2010; Rahimi et al., 2018). By emphasizing the positive impact the technology will have on their work, managers can reduce resistance by highlighting the value of the new tools (Holden & Karsh, 2010; Rahimi et al., 2018).

Managers can apply change management strategies to facilitate the transition to new technologies. This involves creating a supportive and collaborative work environment, involving key stakeholders in decision-making, and ensuring that employees feel heard and valued throughout the process. Effective change management fosters a sense of ownership and buy-in, which can significantly reduce resistance (Holden & Karsh, 2010; Rahimi et al., 2018).

A proactive approach to addressing resistance involves seeking continuous feedback from employees and being willing to adapt to their needs and concerns (Holden & Karsh, 2010; Rahimi et al., 2018). Managers should establish mechanisms for regular feedback and make iterative improvements based on user experiences. This ongoing engagement demonstrates a commitment to addressing issues and can lead to increased acceptance over time (Holden & Karsh, 2010; Rahimi et al., 2018).

The successful integration of new technologies within organizations requires proactive management of resistance. Leveraging the Technology Acceptance Model (TAM) and its core constructs, perceived ease of use and perceived usefulness, offers a structured approach to addressing resistance. By enhancing the perceived ease of use, promoting the perceived usefulness, applying effective change management strategies, and maintaining open channels for feedback and adaptation, managers can foster a culture of technology acceptance and ensure the seamless adoption of innovative tools. This not only benefits individual employees but also contributes to the organization's competitiveness and growth in a technology-driven world (Holden & Karsh, 2010; Rahimi et al., 2018).

THE BURKE-LITWIN MODEL

The Burke-Litwin Model is a comprehensive framework that distinguishes between transformational and transactional factors within organizations (Martins & Coetzee, 2009; Spangenberg & Theron, 2013). It recognizes the interplay between these factors and highlights their significance in driving organizational change (Martins & Coetzee, 2009; Spangenberg & Theron, 2013).

There are several transformational Factors (Martins & Coetzee, 2009; Spangenberg & Theron, 2013):

Leadership

Effective leadership is paramount in guiding public health departments toward integrating AI tools. Leaders should foster a culture of innovation and ensure that AI initiatives align with organizational goals.

Culture

A culture that embraces technological innovation and data-driven decision-making is essential. Public health organizations must cultivate a culture of continuous learning and openness to change.

Strategy

The organization's strategic vision should encompass the adoption of AI for enhanced outbreak management. Clear objectives and a roadmap for AI implementation are critical. There are several transformational Transactional Factors (Martins & Coetzee, 2009; Spangenberg & Theron, 2013):

Structure

Organizational structure should be flexible and adaptable to accommodate AI-driven changes. Public health departments may need to reconfigure their structures to support data-centric operations.

Systems

Robust information systems and data infrastructure are foundational. Public health organizations must invest in AI-compatible data collection, analysis, and dissemination systems.

APPLICATIONS OF BURKE-LITWIN MODEL

In today's fast-paced technological landscape, the successful introduction of new technologies is pivotal for organizational growth and adaptability. However, resistance from employees is a common challenge that can impede the process. The Burke-Litwin Model offers a comprehensive view of how organizational changes, such as technology adoption, affect various facets of an organization. By focusing on key drivers and best practices, managers can mitigate resistance, enhance technology acceptance, and foster a culture of innovation (Martins & Coetzee, 2009; Spangenberg & Theron, 2013).

Leveraging Transformational Leadership

Transformational leadership is a key driver in the Burke-Litwin Model and plays a central role in addressing resistance to new technologies. Managers should exemplify transformational leadership qualities by inspiring and motivating employees, establishing a shared vision for technology adoption, and emphasizing the positive impact of the change. Managers who exhibit transformational leadership behaviors are more likely to gain the trust and commitment of their teams, ultimately reducing resistance (Martins & Coetzee, 2009; Spangenberg & Theron, 2013).

Cultural Alignment

A crucial aspect of technology adoption is ensuring that the new tools align with the existing organizational culture. Managers must be attuned to the prevailing cultural norms and values within the organization. By framing the technology as an enabler of cultural alignment rather than a disruptor, managers can reduce resistance (Martins & Coetzee, 2009; Spangenberg & Theron, 2013). Creating a culture of adaptability and continuous learning can facilitate the smooth integration of new technologies.

Engaging Stakeholders

Engaging key stakeholders, including employees, in the decision-making process is essential. Managers should foster a collaborative environment where employees feel their voices are heard and their concerns are addressed. Involving stakeholders in technology selection, training programs, and implementation planning ensures that the transition is as smooth as possible (Martins & Coetzee, 2009; Spangenberg & Theron, 2013). This participatory approach can significantly reduce resistance.

Effective Communication

Clear and consistent communication is paramount when introducing new technologies. Managers should articulate the rationale behind the change, the benefits it offers, and how it aligns with the organization's goals (Martins & Coetzee, 2009; Spangenberg & Theron, 2013). Open channels for two-way communication allow employees to express their concerns and seek clarification. Managers should also provide ongoing updates and support to address evolving needs (Martins & Coetzee, 2009; Spangenberg & Theron, 2013).

Monitoring and Feedback

Continuous monitoring and feedback mechanisms are essential throughout the technology adoption process. Managers should establish metrics to measure the impact of the change, collect feedback from employees, and make adjustments as needed (Martins & Coetzee, 2009; Spangenberg & Theron, 2013). Regular assessment and adaptation based on feedback enable managers to address resistance in real time and ensure the success of the technology implementation (Martins & Coetzee, 2009; Spangenberg & Theron, 2013).

External Environment

The Burke-Litwin Model recognizes the influence of the external environment on organizational change (Martins & Coetzee, 2009; Spangenberg & Theron, 2013). In the context of public health surveillance, factors such as regulatory requirements, funding, and technological advancements can significantly impact the integration of AI.

Leveraging the Burke-Litwin Model offers a structured approach for public health departments seeking to enhance their adaptive capabilities through AI integration. Organizations can navigate the complexities of AI-driven outbreak management by addressing transformational elements like leadership, culture, and strategy alongside transactional factors like structure and systems. Furthermore, considering the influence of the external environment ensures a holistic approach to organizational change. Through a synthesis of theory and practical examples, this paper provides a roadmap for public health departments aiming to become more flexible and adaptive in safeguarding public health in the face of emerging threats.

BURKE-LITWIN MODEL APPLIED TO PUBLIC HEALTH SURVEILLANCE

Syndromic Surveillance

Syndromic surveillance involves monitoring symptoms or syndromes that may indicate an outbreak, even before a specific diagnosis is confirmed. Transformational factors like leadership play a crucial role here. Effective leadership can establish the vision for syndromic surveillance, ensuring that public health departments prioritize this approach. Additionally, a culture of data-driven decision-making and openness to innovative surveillance methods, fostered by cultural factors, can promote the adoption of syndromic surveillance. Strategic planning, another transformational element, can define clear objectives and strategies for implementing and refining syndromic surveillance systems.

Laboratory-Based Surveillance

Laboratory-based surveillance relies on diagnostic tests and laboratory reports to identify specific pathogens causing illnesses. In this mode, organizational structure is pivotal. Public health departments must have well-defined roles and responsibilities within their structure to facilitate the efficient processing and analysis of laboratory data. Moreover, the systems factor is critical in ensuring that the necessary information systems and infrastructure are in place to effectively handle the volume of data generated by laboratory-based surveillance.

Environmental Surveillance

Environmental surveillance tracks environmental factors that may contribute to outbreaks, such as water quality or air pollution. Leadership is vital in setting the agenda for environmental surveillance and aligning it with public health goals. A culture of environmental stewardship and data-driven decision-making (cultural factor) is necessary for this mode. A strategic approach includes defining which environmental factors to monitor and how to respond to aberrations (Martins & Coetzee, 2009; Spangenberg & Theron, 2013). Furthermore, the external environment, including regulatory requirements and technological advancements, may affect the adoption and scope of environmental surveillance.

In summary, elements of the Burke-Litwin Model, including leadership, culture, strategy, structure, and systems, can be applied to track and manage illness outbreaks across various public health surveillance modes. Effective leadership sets the vision and priorities, while a data-driven culture fosters openness to innovative surveillance methods. Strategic planning ensures clear objectives and strategies, while organizational structure defines roles and responsibilities (Martins & Coetzee, 2009; Spangenberg & Theron, 2013). The systems factor highlights that robust information systems and data infrastructure are essential for efficient surveillance. Moreover, considering external factors is crucial to adapting and aligning surveillance strategies with evolving requirements and technologies in the public health landscape.

CONCLUSION

In this era of rapid technological advancement, the imperative for government leaders to navigate intricate policies is underscored, particularly in the realms of artificial intelligence and new intelligence-driven public health epidemiology approaches. This necessity is further accentuated by the persistent global public health concern posed by Salmonella infections, which annually lead to millions of illnesses and hospitalizations. The timely detection and efficient management of Salmonella outbreaks stand as critical pillars in minimizing their detrimental impact on public health. Traditional surveillance methods, though valuable, bear inherent limitations such as data reporting delays and a restricted capacity to handle vast and diverse datasets.

In response to these challenges, a paradigm shift towards more nimble, adaptive, and innovative public health systems and government agencies is indispensable. Systems thinking, an approach that holistically views the intricate interplay of factors within a broader system, becomes paramount. It encourages us to recognize that changes in one facet of the system can trigger cascading effects. In the context of public health, systems thinking prompts us to consider epidemiology, healthcare infrastructure, social determinants, and policy as interconnected components of a more extensive system. By integrating systems thinking principles into Salmonella outbreak management, we pave the way for a comprehensive and proactive approach that transcends traditional boundaries(Carey et al., 2015; Chughtai & Blanchet, 2017).

To meet the evolving challenges of public health in a world marked by dynamic technological progress, it is imperative that government leaders and public health agencies embrace innovation, adaptability, and nimbleness as core tenets of their approach. Salmonella outbreaks, like many public health issues, do not respect conventional lines, and the response to them must be equally holistic and forward-thinking. This paradigm shift not only enables more efficient and effective outbreak management but also equips us to address future public health challenges with greater precision and resilience (Carey et al., 2015; Chughtai & Blanchet, 2017). As we advance further into the age of technological innovation, the ability to navigate intricate policies and public health challenges will be contingent upon our capacity for innovation, adaptability, and the strategic application of systems thinking (Carey et al., 2015; Chughtai & Blanchet, 2017).

`Systems thinking is an approach that emphasizes understanding complex interactions within a system and recognizing that changes in one part of the system can have cascading effects. In the context of public health, it involves considering various factors, such as epidemiology, healthcare infrastructure, social determinants, and policy, as interconnected components of a more extensive system (Carey et al., 2015; Chughtai & Blanchet, 2017). Applying systems thinking principles to Salmonella outbreak management allows for a more comprehensive and proactive approach.

AI-POWERED DATA ANALYTICS

AI-driven data analytics offer the ability to rapidly process vast amounts of data (Zeng et al., 2021; Thiébaut & Cossin, 2019). Machine learning algorithms can analyze diverse data sources, including clinical records, environmental factors, and social media, to detect potential outbreaks in real time. These systems can identify unusual patterns, clusters of illnesses, or variations in environmental conditions, enabling early detection and response (Zeng et al., 2021; Thiébaut & Cossin, 2019).

AI-driven data analytics can significantly enhance public health surveillance during Salmonella outbreaks. These advanced analytics tools can rapidly process vast and diverse datasets, crucial when dealing with outbreaks involving multiple sources and affected individuals. AI algorithms can analyze various data sources, including clinical records, laboratory reports, social media trends, and environmental data. By identifying patterns, clusters, and anomalies in these data, AI can facilitate early detection of potential outbreaks, pinpoint their sources, and assess their scale (Zeng et al., 2021; Thiébaut & Cossin, 2019). This early warning system enables public health officials to respond promptly, implement targeted interventions, and allocate resources effectively (Zeng et al., 2021; Thiébaut & Cossin, 2019). Moreover, AI-driven predictive modeling can forecast outbreak trends, allowing for proactive measures to prevent and mitigate the spread of Salmonella infections. In summary, AI-driven data analytics offers a powerful toolset for public health authorities to enhance their surveillance, response, and management capabilities during Salmonella outbreaks, ultimately safeguarding public health more effectively.

SOURCE ATTRIBUTION AND TRACEABILITY

Determining the source of a Salmonella outbreak is crucial for targeted interventions. AI can enhance source attribution by analyzing genetic data from Salmonella strains and linking them to specific sources, such as contaminated food products or animal reservoirs. Source attribution and traceability information aids in identifying the root causes of outbreaks and implementing preventive measures (Zeng et al., 2021; Thiébaut & Cossin, 2019).

AI can be pivotal in improving source attribution during public health Salmonella outbreaks. With its capacity to analyze vast amounts of data quickly and efficiently, AI can help trace the origin of Salmonella infections more accurately. By integrating diverse datasets, including genetic information from Salmonella strains, food supply chain data, and epidemiological records, AI algorithms can identify patterns and connections that may be challenging to discern through traditional methods (Zeng et al., 2021; Thiébaut & Cossin, 2019). These AI-driven analyses enable public health officials to pinpoint the specific sources of contamination, such as contaminated food products or animal reservoirs, with greater precision (Zeng et al., 2021; Thiébaut & Cossin, 2019). This enhanced source attribution capability speeds up outbreak response and supports targeted interventions, regulatory actions, and preventive measures, ultimately reducing the impact of Salmonella outbreaks on public health and safety.

PREDICTIVE MODELING AND RISK ASSESSMENT

AI-powered predictive models can assess the likelihood of Salmonella outbreaks based on historical data and current trends. These models enable public health agencies to allocate resources efficiently and implement preventive measures in high-risk areas. Predictive analytics can also inform the development of risk assessment tools for vulnerable populations (Zeng et al., 2021; Thiébaut & Cossin, 2019).

AI offers substantial advantages in predictive modeling and risk assessment within public health surveillance during Salmonella outbreaks. AI-driven predictive models can leverage historical data, real-time information, and many variables to forecast the likelihood and spread of outbreaks accurately. These models can identify high-risk areas and populations, enabling public health officials to allocate resources effectively and implement targeted preventive measures (Zeng et al., 2021; Thiébaut & Cossin,

2019). Furthermore, AI can continuously analyze evolving data patterns, allowing for dynamic adjustments to risk assessments as the outbreak progresses (Zeng et al., 2021; Thiébaut & Cossin, 2019). This adaptability is invaluable in situations where traditional models might struggle to keep pace with the rapidly changing dynamics of an outbreak. AI's predictive modeling and risk assessment capabilities empower public health agencies to manage Salmonella outbreaks proactively, minimize their impact, and protect public health more effectively.

INTERVENTION PLANNING AND RESOURCE ALLOCATION

AI-driven decision support systems can assist public health officials in planning interventions during outbreaks. By considering various factors, including the severity of the outbreak, available resources, and population vulnerability, these systems can recommend targeted control measures and resource allocation strategies (Zeng et al., 2021; Thiébaut & Cossin, 2019).

AI is crucial in optimizing intervention planning and resource allocation during public health Salmonella outbreaks. By analyzing real-time data and identifying outbreak patterns, AI algorithms can provide public health officials with valuable insights for planning effective interventions (Zeng et al., 2021; Thiébaut & Cossin, 2019). AI-driven decision support systems can recommend targeted control measures and allocate resources strategically, considering factors such as the severity of the outbreak, available resources, and population vulnerability. This data-driven approach enhances the efficiency and effectiveness of response efforts. Additionally, AI can help prioritize resource allocation by predicting outbreak hotspots and areas with the highest risk, ensuring that critical resources, such as medical supplies and personnel, are directed where they are most needed (Zeng et al., 2021; Thiébaut & Cossin, 2019). In essence, AI empowers public health authorities to make informed decisions swiftly and allocate resources judiciously, ultimately leading to more efficient and successful management of Salmonella outbreaks and better protection of public health.

Leveraging artificial intelligence within a systems thinking framework holds immense potential to transform public health surveillance and outbreak management for Salmonella. By integrating AI-driven data analytics, source attribution, predictive modeling, and decision support systems, public health agencies can enhance their capacity to detect, respond to, and prevent Salmonella outbreaks more effectively. The synergy between AI and systems thinking offers a promising path toward a safer and healthier future (Zeng et al., 2021; Thiébaut & Cossin, 2019).

RECOMMENDATIONS FOR FUTURE RESEARCH

Grounded Theory Approach

Future research should employ grounded theory to investigate the practical implementation of AI-driven systems thinking in public health surveillance for Salmonella outbreaks. This approach would involve conducting in-depth qualitative interviews and observations with public health professionals, data scientists, and other relevant stakeholders to develop a comprehensive theory of how AI and systems thinking intersect in outbreak management. By exploring these individuals' experiences, challenges, and strategies, grounded theory can yield insights into the nuanced processes of AI adoption within public health agencies.

Phenomenological Approach

A phenomenological research approach is warranted to delve into the lived experiences of public health practitioners and stakeholders as they engage with AI-powered systems thinking in Salmonella outbreak management. This approach involves exploring individuals' perceptions, emotions, and meaning-making processes utilizing AI tools for surveillance and response. By conducting in-depth interviews and phenomenological analysis, researchers can uncover the subjective aspects of AI integration, shedding light on how it influences decision-making, communication, and collaboration among multidisciplinary teams.

Action Research

Action research offers a valuable avenue for future investigations focused on the practical implementation and iterative improvement of AI-infused systems thinking in public health surveillance. Researchers can collaborate closely with public health agencies and engage in a cyclical planning, action, reflection, and adaptation process. This approach enables ongoing feedback and learning, allowing for the refinement of AI-driven strategies and tools in real-world outbreak scenarios. Action research can also facilitate the co-creation of knowledge between researchers and practitioners, fostering a collaborative and adaptive approach to enhancing public health surveillance and outbreak management.

Incorporating grounded theory, phenomenology, or action research into future studies will provide a well-rounded understanding of the complex interplay between AI, systems thinking, and public health surveillance in the context of Salmonella outbreaks. Such research is essential for guiding the effective implementation of AI-driven strategies and ensuring that they align with public health agencies' and communities needs and realities.

REFERENCES

Baby Cumberland Slider Turtles. (n.d.). Retrieved March 2, 2021, from MyTurtleStore.com website: https://myturtlestore.com/baby-cumberland-slider-turtles/

Carey, G., Malbon, E., Carey, N., Joyce, A., Crammond, B., & Carey, A. (2015). Systems science and systems thinking for public health: A systematic review of the field. *BMJ Open*, *5*(12), e009002. doi:10.1136/bmjopen-2015-009002 PMID:26719314

Chughtai, S., & Blanchet, K. (2017). Systems thinking in public health: A bibliographic contribution to a meta-narrative review. *Health Policy and Planning*, *32*(4), 585–594. doi:10.1093/heapol/czw159 PMID:28062516

Friis, R. H. (2018). *Epidemiology 101* (2nd ed.). Jones & Bartlett Learning.

Holden, R. J., & Karsh, B. T. (2010). The technology acceptance model: Its past and its future in health care. *Journal of Biomedical Informatics*, *43*(1), 159–172. doi:10.1016/j.jbi.2009.07.002 PMID:19615467

Martins, N., & Coetzee, M. (2009). Applying the Burke-Litwin model as a diagnostic framework for assessing organisational effectiveness. *SA Journal of Human Resource Management*, *7*(1), 1–13. doi:10.4102/sajhrm.v7i1.177

McNabb, S., Conde, J. M., Ferland, L., MacWright, W., Memish, Z. OkuTani, S., ... Singh, V. (Eds.). (2016). Transforming public health surveillance: proactive measures for prevention, detection, and response. Amman, Jordan: Elsevier.

Multistate Outbreak of Salmonella Agbeni Infections Linked to Pet Turtles. (2017, August 29). Retrieved from https://www.cdc.gov/salmonella/agbeni-08-17/index.html

Rahimi, B., Nadri, H., Afshar, H. L., & Timpka, T. (2018). A systematic review of the technology acceptance model in health informatics. *Applied Clinical Informatics*, 9(03), 604–634. doi:10.1055/s-0038-1668091 PMID:30112741

Signs & Symptoms. (2018, September 26). Retrieved from https://www.cdc.gov/salmonella/mbandaka-06-18/signs-symptoms.html

Spangenberg, H., & Theron, C. (2013). A critical review of the Burke-Litwin leadership, change, and performance model. *Management Dynamics: Journal of the Southern African Institute for Management Scientists*, 22(2), 29–48.

Thiébaut, R., & Cossin, S. (2019). Artificial intelligence for surveillance in public health. *Yearbook of Medical Informatics*, 28(01), 232–234. doi:10.1055/s-0039-1677939 PMID:31419837

U.S. Food and Drug Administration. (2023). *Get the Facts about Salmonella*. U.S. Food and Drug Administration. Retrieved from: https://www.fda.gov/animal-veterinary/animal-health-literacy/get-facts-about-salmonella#:~:text=The%20Centers%20for%20Disease%20Control,for%20most%20of%20these%20cases

Zeng, D., Cao, Z., & Neill, D. B. (2021). Artificial intelligence–enabled public health surveillance—from local detection to global epidemic monitoring and control. In *Artificial intelligence in medicine* (pp. 437–453). Academic Press. doi:10.1016/B978-0-12-821259-2.00022-3

Chapter 15
Organizational Dynamics and Bias in Artificial Intelligence (AI) Recruitment Algorithms

Marwan Omar
Capitol Technology University, USA & Illinois Institute of Technology, USA

Darrell Norman Burrell
ⓘ https://orcid.org/0000-0002-4675-9544
Capitol Technology University, USA

ABSTRACT

The integration of artificial intelligence (AI) into recruitment processes has promised to revolutionize and optimize the hiring landscape. However, recent legal proceedings have shed light on the alarming implications of AI algorithms in the employment sector. This chapter delves into a significant case study where African American, Latina American, Arab American, and other marginalized job applicants and employees filed a 100-million-dollar class action lawsuit against a prominent organization, Context Systems. The suit alleges that AI screening tools, entrusted with the crucial task of selecting candidates, have been marred by programming bias, leading to discriminatory outcomes. This case study critically examines the multifaceted problems arising from bias in AI algorithms, revealing their detrimental effects on marginalized communities in the employment sector. By scrutinizing this pivotal case, the authors aim to provide insights into the urgent need for transparency, accountability, and ethical considerations in the development and deployment of AI-driven recruitment tools.

INTRODUCTION

Do hiring algorithms prevent bias or amplify it? This fundamental question has become a tension between the technology's proponents and skeptics, but arriving at the answer is more complicated.

African American, Latina American, and Arab American applicants, including other marginalized employees, have won a 100-million-dollar class action lawsuit filed against Context Systems, which is a invented name used to protect the privacy of the actual organization. However, in arbitration, the suit

DOI: 10.4018/979-8-3693-1970-3.ch015

alleges that artificial intelligence (AI) screened out job applicants because of bias in the programming algorithm. This technological malpractice of judgment prevented minority applicants and current employees from being interviewed for job opportunities. During the court cross-examining of the evidence, it was proven that the AI recruiting tool used to bias and prescribe program languages, which resulted in discriminating outcomes. In recent years, integrating artificial intelligence (AI) into recruitment processes has promised to streamline and enhance the hiring process. However, the case of African American, Latina American, Arab American, and other marginalized job applicants and employees pursuing a 100-million-dollar class action lawsuit against a prominent organization has revealed the darker side of AI recruitment tools. This paper examines the pivotal dynamics of this case, aiming to unpack the multifaceted problems stemming from bias in AI algorithms and their detrimental effects on marginalized communities in the employment sector.

Discrimination and bias in hiring constitute persistent barriers to achieving equitable and inclusive workplaces. Legal frameworks are pivotal in addressing these issues, providing guidelines and protections for job seekers and employees (Cheung et al., 2016; Huff et al., 2023; Burrell et al., 2021; McLester et al., 2021).

The cornerstone of U.S. anti-discrimination laws is Title VII of the Civil Rights Act 1964. It prohibits discrimination based on race, color, religion, sex, and national origin in employment practices, including hiring. The Age Discrimination in Employment Act (ADEA) addresses age-based discrimination, while the Americans with Disabilities Act (ADA) protects individuals with disabilities from discrimination. Additionally, the Genetic Information Nondiscrimination Act (GINA) prohibits discrimination based on genetic information (Cheung et al., 2016; Huff et al., 2023; Burrell et al., 2021; McLester et al., 2021).

In tandem with federal laws, state legislatures have enacted their own anti-discrimination statutes. These laws often extend protections beyond those provided by federal regulations. State legislation may cover additional protected categories and apply to smaller employers (Cheung et al., 2016; Huff et al., 2023; Burrell et al., 2021; McLester et al., 2021).

The EEOC enforces federal anti-discrimination laws and provides guidelines for employers. It investigates complaints of discrimination and plays a pivotal role in enforcing compliance with Title VII, the ADEA, and the ADA. The EEOC's guidance informs best practices for employers to avoid discriminatory hiring practices (Cheung et al., 2016; Huff et al., 2023; Burrell et al., 2021; McLester et al., 2021).

Two fundamental legal theories that address discrimination in hiring are disparate impact and disparate treatment. Disparate impact occurs when a seemingly neutral employment practice disproportionately impacts a protected group. In contrast, disparate treatment involves intentional discrimination based on a protected characteristic (Cheung et al., 2016; Huff et al., 2023; Burrell et al., 2021; McLester et al., 2021).

Problem Statement

Recent research has comprehensively explored various AI-mediated employment processes encompassing job search procedures, online networking opportunities, and electronic resume submission platforms (Zapata, 2021). Within the context of an analysis conducted on job board recommendations, 40% of surveyed participants attested to encountering recommendations influenced by their identities rather than their professional qualifications (Zapata, 2021). Additionally, an appreciable 30% of respondents reported receiving job alerts that were incongruent with their current skill levels (Zapata, 2021). A disconcerting revelation emerged from the research, with nearly two-thirds (63%) of participants observing that academic recommendations proffered by the platforms did not align with their current academic achievements (Zapata, 2021). This discovery is particularly noteworthy, given that the survey underscores the remarkable educational attainment of black women, the most educated demographic in the United States (Zapata, 2021).

Of paramount concern is the prevailing underrepresentation of diversity within Silicon Valley, where individuals of predominantly white ethnicity continue to dominate, and men overwhelmingly occupy leadership and AI development positions. This circumstance prompts a critical inquiry into the potential challenges surrounding the development and deployment of equitable AI technologies for broader societal benefit, given the diversity deficits within the teams tasked with designing and implementing the algorithms upon which AI systems rely (Zapata, 2021). The consequences of such challenges are exemplified by the case of Amazon, which discontinued a recruiting tool in 2018 due to its inherent biases (Zapata, 2021). Significantly, if AI tools are developed from the frameworks and influences of previously demonstrated bias, then AI tools in hiring extend long-observed hiring discrimination practices, which are increasingly facilitated by AI systems. Black professionals in the contemporary employment landscape continue to confront disparities, with a persistent discrepancy of 30% to 50% fewer job callbacks when their resumes include information about their racial or ethnic identity (Zapata, 2021).

CONTEXTS AND THEORIES

The central issue in this case revolves around the alleged bias embedded within the AI recruiting tool used by the organization. The AI tool, designed to screen job applications and select suitable candidates, inadvertently perpetuated discriminatory practices. It did so under the biases present in the programming algorithm, which favored certain demographic groups while unfairly screening out minority applicants. Consequently, marginalized job seekers, including African American, Latina American, and Arab American individuals, were systematically excluded from consideration for job opportunities, further entrenching existing disparities in employment and opportunities.

The utilization of artificial intelligence (AI) within contemporary recruitment practices has witnessed a pronounced upsurge as organizations increasingly adopt automated assessments, digital interview platforms, and data analytics to scrutinize applicant profiles and evaluate potential candidates (Kelan, 2023). Nevertheless, amidst the growing emphasis on fostering diversity, equity, and inclusion (DEI) in the realm of Information Technology (IT), a discerning examination reveals that AI, if not thoughtfully and strategically integrated, may inadvertently exacerbate rather than ameliorate the challenges posed by DEI initiatives within organizations (Kelan, 2023). The hiring process is a critical juncture where the seeds of bias and discrimination can take root, impacting individuals and organizations alike.

ORGANIZATIONAL JUSTICE THEORY

Organizational justice theory underscores the importance of fairness in organizations (Tran & Choi, 2019; Graso et al., 2020). When hiring processes are perceived as biased or discriminatory, employees may harbor feelings of injustice, decreasing job satisfaction and engagement. This can result in reduced productivity and increased turnover, ultimately harming the organization's bottom line.

HARMS TO POTENTIAL CANDIDATES

Potential employees subjected to biased hiring processes often endure psychological distress, reduced self-esteem, and diminished career opportunities. Bias and discrimination experiences can deter talented individuals from pursuing opportunities within the organization, resulting in losing potential talent and diversity (Burrell et al., 2021).

HARMS TO EXISTING EMPLOYEES

Existing employees witnessing biased hiring decisions may experience demoralization, decreased organizational trust, and lowered motivation. Bias and discrimination can lead to decreased teamwork, creativity, and organizational commitment, negatively impacting the workplace culture (Burrell et al., 2021).

HARMS TO THE ORGANIZATION

Biased hiring practices can tarnish an organization's reputation, impairing its ability to attract top talent. Additionally, litigation risks and potential legal consequences can exact significant financial costs. A lack of diversity and inclusion also hinders innovation and adaptability, hampering the organization's long-term competitiveness (Burrell et al., 2021).

PEST/PESTLE ANALYSIS

The organization's Strategic Management and Risk Management reviews may combine the Political, Economic, Social, Technological, Legal, and Environmental (PESTLE) analysis and SWOT to evaluate and rank risk factors for investment protection. While conducting these analyses, the organization will be able to conclude and take position on (1) political situations and the organizational impact, (2) related economic factors, (3) cultural influences on the market, (4) technological innovations effects, (5) potential legislative barriers, and (6) environmental concerns. Zoričić et al. (2022) mentioned the interdependencies of PESTLE and the correlation of efficient mitigation measures. It then becomes apparent and crucial that the organization understand the theoretical framework of managing risk and defining a strategic policy agenda to achieve financial goals to limit additional legal fallout (Zoričić et al., 2022).

THEORETICAL INFLUENCE

Although many theoretical models are available to aid business decisions, PESTLE analysis concentration is particular to external settings. It is an investigation tool for understanding the business environment and other market influences. As such, top-level officials may use it to identify market risks and develop planning strategies to help avoid costly mistakes. The PESTLE analysis has been historically connected with seminal research from browsing through the various market conditions to assess challenging environments (Nandonde, 2019).

Collins (2010) uses an increase in income tax as an example to depict an external factor that hypothetically results in reduced habits. With a PESTLE analysis, the most demanding external conditions can be evaluated for improvement through systematic planning. Furthermore, there is consensus among academic peers that business organizations that need to understand external influences are likely to fail to reach the mark. In addition, some leaders use PEST analysis for thoughtful assessments, while others combine ethical calculations with their legal decision-making efforts (Nandonde, 2019).

PEST or PESTLE Analysis is a strategic tool organizations use to assess the external macro-environmental factors influencing their operations and decision-making (Zoričić et al., 2022). When an organization aims to change its culture and address issues of bias and discrimination in AI-driven hiring, PESTLE Analysis can provide valuable insights into the broader societal, political, and economic context that may impact the success of these initiatives.

For instance, the "P" in PESTLE stands for Political factors (Zoričić et al., 2022). An organization can use this aspect to consider government regulations and policies related to AI, bias, and discrimination in hiring. Understanding the legal landscape can help ensure the organization complies with relevant laws and regulations while implementing cultural changes.

The "E" in PESTLE is Economic factors (Zoričić et al., 2022). Analyzing economic conditions can help the organization assess its financial capacity to invest in cultural change efforts and AI technology that mitigates bias. Economic factors also include labor market conditions, which may impact the availability and diversity of job candidates.

The "S" in PESTLE represents Social factors (Zoričić et al., 2022). This aspect can be especially relevant when addressing cultural change and bias in hiring. Organizations can examine societal attitudes and norms related to diversity and inclusion. Understanding public perception can guide communication strategies and initiatives to shift the organizational culture towards greater fairness and equity.

The "T" in PESTLE is Technological factors (Zoričić et al., 2022). When dealing with AI in hiring, it is crucial to evaluate the latest technological advancements and their potential to reduce bias in algorithms. Staying up-to-date with AI developments ensures the organization can adopt state-of-the-art solutions to combat discrimination.

Lastly, the "E" in PESTLE represents Environmental and Ethical factors (Zoričić et al., 2022). This aspect prompts organizations to consider their ethical responsibilities concerning AI and discrimination. It encourages a reflection on environmental sustainability and ethical considerations, which are increasingly important in corporate culture.

Incorporating PESTLE Analysis into the organizational strategy allows leaders to anticipate external factors that may facilitate or hinder their efforts to address bias and discrimination in AI-driven hiring. By systematically assessing these factors, organizations can tailor their cultural change initiatives to align with the broader societal and regulatory context, ultimately fostering a more inclusive and equitable work environment.

CULTURAL ICEBERG MODEL

The iceberg model can help depict the organization's most visible and measurable racial discrimination conditions during times of turmoil (Cuevas & Boen, 2021). The iceberg model's above-the-water scenario represents the millions of dollars lost from the AI lawsuit. However, the larger and more dominant status remains unknown and hidden out of plain sight.

Hidden elements of the model suggest that other external and unconscious cultural conditions may lie beneath the radar where malintent behaviors and beliefs are not yet publicly displayed. The same may be determined for the internal conscious psyche of the organization. To help prepare for consequences and what might be uncovered, a top-to-bottom meta-analysis will be conducted to identify the organization's conscious and unconscious learned behaviors to ensure equitable judgment occurs both above and below cultural lines (Wazed, 2018).

APPLICATIONS OF THE CULTURAL ICEBERG MODEL

The Cultural Iceberg Model is a valuable framework for organizations seeking to change their culture and address issues of bias and discrimination in AI-driven hiring. This model represents culture as an iceberg, with the visible aspects above the waterline symbolizing the surface-level elements of culture, such as language, clothing, and rituals. Below the waterline lies the hidden, more profound aspects of culture, encompassing values, beliefs, norms, and underlying assumptions. When addressing bias and discrimination in AI hiring, organizations can use this model to understand the multifaceted nature of culture and the underlying factors that contribute to these issues.

For instance, the Cultural Iceberg Model encourages organizations to probe beneath the surface and explore the underlying values, beliefs, and assumptions that may perpetuate bias and discrimination in AI-driven hiring. Organizations can foster a more inclusive and equitable culture that aligns with their desired goals by identifying and addressing these hidden cultural elements. Moreover, the model underscores the importance of acknowledging the surface-level manifestations of culture, such as language and symbols, which can impact the user interface and design of AI tools. Ensuring that these visible aspects are sensitive to diversity and inclusion can contribute to a more welcoming and accessible experience for all candidates, reducing the risk of bias in the hiring process.

DENISON ORGANIZATIONAL CULTURE MODEL

The Denison organizational culture model is derived from five properties: involvement from organizational participation, compatibility of system values, adaptability of integrated organizations, mission practices, and constant flexibility observed throughout the spectrum (Ahmady et al., 2016). This model has advantages for evaluating group behavior instead of personality traits. It can also measure inputs at the lowest stages and has been applied at all organizational levels.

Ahmady et al. (2016) proposed that managers have the prominent role of bringing about change and setting organizational values. The new knowledge management paradigm has implications for gaining and accruing information to ensure competitive aspirations. As such, procedural processes will be developed by leadership using the Denison model as the basis to investigate any reporting of discrimination within the dimensions of organizational culture.

CULTURE OF CHANGE

Organizations grapple with the ethical imperative of ensuring fair and non-discriminatory practices in an era marked by the increasing integration of artificial intelligence (AI) into hiring processes. Bias in AI-driven hiring poses significant challenges, ranging from reinforcing existing disparities to hindering diversity and perpetuating discrimination. Organizations can use the Denison Organizational Culture Model, a proven framework for assessing and evolving workplace cultures, to navigate these complexities (Abdavi et al., 2018).

The first aspect of the Denison model, mission, underscores the importance of clarifying and reinforcing the organization's core values and mission (Abdavi et al., 2018). To combat bias and discrimination in AI hiring, organizations can start by redefining their mission to explicitly encompass diversity, equity, and inclusion as fundamental tenets. A robust mission statement commits the organization to fostering a workplace culture in which AI-driven hiring aligns with these principles. It serves as a rallying point for employees, conveying the organization's dedication to eradicating bias and discrimination. By emphasizing a mission that promotes fairness and equal opportunity, organizations send a powerful message about their commitment to transforming their culture.

Involvement, the second cultural trait in the Denison model, emphasizes the importance of engaging stakeholders at all levels of the organization (Abdavi et al., 2018). Organizations should involve a diverse range of voices in decision-making processes related to AI technology to promote inclusivity and address bias in AI hiring. This involvement spans employees, candidates, external experts, and cross-functional teams dedicated to ensuring fairness in AI hiring practices. By creating inclusive forums for discussion, organizations can harness various perspectives and experiences to refine AI algorithms, user interfaces, and evaluation criteria. Involvement fosters collaboration and shared accountability, reducing the likelihood of unintentional bias in AI-driven hiring.

The third aspect of the Denison model, Adaptability, underscores the organization's capacity to embrace change and innovation (Abdavi et al., 2018). In AI hiring, organizations must remain agile and responsive to emerging insights and technologies. They should continuously evaluate and update AI algorithms to ensure they align with the evolving landscape of bias mitigation techniques. Additionally, adaptability involves the organization's willingness to learn from feedback and adjust its strategies accordingly. A culture of adaptability empowers organizations to swiftly address bias and discrimination, promoting an environment responsive to the changing dynamics of AI-driven hiring.

Consistency, the final cultural trait of the Denison model, stresses the importance of enforcing accountability and equity throughout the organization (Abdavi et al., 2018). To combat bias in AI-based hiring, organizations must establish and rigorously enforce policies and practices that promote fairness. The holistic application of this model includes regular audits of AI algorithms, transparent reporting of hiring outcomes, and mechanisms for addressing bias-related concerns. A consistent commitment to equity ensures that AI-driven hiring processes are reliable and free from discrimination, bolstering confidence in the organization's efforts to rectify bias.

The Denison Organizational Culture Model provides organizations with a structured and comprehensive framework to guide their efforts in transforming workplace culture and addressing bias and discrimination in AI-driven hiring. Organizations can create a culture that promotes fairness, inclusivity, and equity in AI hiring practices by aligning their mission, fostering involvement, embracing adaptability, and enforcing consistency. As AI continues to play a pivotal role in recruitment, leveraging the

Denison model can facilitate the development of a culture that mitigates bias and aligns with the values of diversity and inclusion, ultimately fostering a more equitable and thriving work environment.

KOTTER'S CHANGE MANAGEMENT THEORY

In today's dynamic business environment, organizations constantly confront the need to evolve and adapt to stay competitive and relevant. However, complex organizational change is fraught with challenges, from employee resistance to strategic misalignment (Kotter, 2013).

Kotter's Change Management Model consists of eight interrelated steps (Kotter, 2013):

- Establishing a Sense of Urgency: The first step involves creating a compelling case for change. In complex organizational evolution, this entails identifying and communicating the critical need for transformation, clarifying the risks of inaction, and mobilizing stakeholders' commitment.
- Creating a Guiding Coalition: Building a dedicated and influential team of change leaders is essential for steering complex change initiatives. This coalition comprises individuals capable of driving change and garnering organizational support.
- Developing a Vision and Strategy: Crafting a clear and inspiring vision for the future and a strategic plan to achieve it is fundamental in complex change efforts. This vision should resonate with employees and align with the organization's values.
- Communicating the Vision: Effective communication is vital to ensure that the vision and strategy are understood, embraced, and consistently communicated throughout the organization. Transparent and open dialogue fosters buy-in from employees at all levels.
- Empowering Broad-Based Action: Complex change requires empowering employees to act on the vision. Removing obstacles, encouraging innovation, and enabling employees to take ownership of change initiatives is essential.
- Generating Short-Term Wins: Celebrating early successes boosts morale and reinforces the organization's commitment to change. These quick wins demonstrate progress and provide tangible evidence of the benefits of the transformation.
- Consolidating Gains and Producing More Change: The momentum gained from short-term wins must be sustained. Organizations must use these gains to drive further change and ensure that the new practices and behaviors become embedded in the culture.
- Anchoring New Approaches in the Culture: The final step involves making the new culture a permanent part of the organization's identity. This final step of the model's application entails reinforcing the desired behaviors and values through policies, leadership practices, and ongoing development.

APPLICATIONS OF KOTTER'S CHANGE MANAGEMENT APPROACH

Complex organizational change often faces numerous challenges and resistance from various quarters. Employees may resist change due to fear of the unknown, concerns about job security, or a preference for existing routines. Middle management may resist due to perceived threats to their roles or influence.

Organizational cultures resistant to change can be particularly challenging to navigate (Caulfield & Brenner, 2020).

In the face of complex organizational evolution, Kotter's Change Management Model offers a structured, holistic, and time-tested approach to guide organizations through the tumultuous waters of change (Caulfield & Brenner, 2020). The model emphasizes clear communication, strong leadership, and a dedicated guiding coalition. It recognizes the importance of celebrating successes and anchoring new cultural approaches. Following the Kotter framework, organizations can increase the likelihood of successful transformation, mitigate resistance, and build a more adaptive and resilient organizational culture (Caulfield & Brenner, 2020).

Complex organizational evolution is an inevitable aspect of the contemporary business landscape. Organizations must embrace change as a means of growth and sustainability. Kotter's well-established change model uses eight steps to heighten awareness and produce cultures of change (Caulfield & Brenner, 2020).

Integrating artificial intelligence (AI) into hiring processes has heralded efficiency gains and raised concerns about fairness and equity. Organizations increasingly recognize the need to tackle bias and discrimination in AI-based hiring to foster diverse and inclusive workplaces. John Kotter's Change Management Model offers a structured approach to guide these transformative efforts.

APPLICATION OF KOTTER'S MODEL TO BIAS AND DISCRIMINATION IN AI-BASED HIRING

To address bias and discrimination in AI-based hiring, organizations can use Kotter's model as follows:

Establish Urgency: Highlight the urgency of eliminating bias in AI hiring to create a fairer and more inclusive workplace.
Create a Coalition: Assemble a diverse team of advocates committed to fairness in AI recruitment.
Develop a Vision and Strategy: Craft a vision of unbiased AI hiring aligned with diversity and inclusion goals.
Communicate the Vision: Communicate the vision of equitable AI hiring and its benefits to all stakeholders.
Empower Action: Enable employees to challenge biased practices in AI hiring.
Generate Wins: Celebrate successes in reducing bias in AI recruitment to inspire confidence.
Consolidate Gains: Embed bias-reduction practices into AI hiring processes and culture.
Anchor in Culture: Institutionalize a culture of fairness and equity in AI-based hiring.
Conclusion: Advancing Inclusion through Kotter's Model

In AI-driven hiring, organizations must proactively eliminate bias and discrimination. The Kotter Change Management Model offers a structured framework for navigating complex cultural change and fostering diversity and inclusion. By applying Kotter's eight elements, organizations can drive the cultural transformation needed to rectify bias and discrimination in AI-based hiring, promoting fairness, equity, and inclusivity in their workforce.

In conclusion, Kotter's Change Management Theory provides a structured approach for organizations to address the urgent need for transparency, accountability, and ethical considerations in the development and deployment of AI-driven recruitment tools. By following the steps outlined in the model, organizations can navigate the complex process of change and promote fair and unbiased recruitment practices, ultimately benefitting marginalized communities and fostering a culture of inclusivity and equality in the employment sector.

BRIDGES TRANSITION MODEL

The Bridges' Transition Model is described in three phases, starting with letting go of the traditional ways of holding people accountable and transitioning into fresh new and exploratory beginnings. The holistic application of this mode will help harness new identities and experiences for the emergence of new activities and paths forward. Managing Transitions means reducing turnover and ensuring employees receive adequate information to move between phases (Miller, 2017).

Cultural change can be achieved by establishing bi-weekly and periodic meetings to discuss lessons learned, including any general IT solutions developed during system migration planning. The bridge transition model also has a pre-migration map tool available for leadership to help develop communication strategies. Whether pre- or post-system migration, these maps can be used to create visual dashboards to depict the experience (Miller, 2017) thoroughly.

THE CHALLENGE OF CULTURAL CHANGE IN AI-BASED HIRING

As organizations grapple with the imperative to eliminate bias and discrimination in AI-driven hiring, they encounter resistance and the need for cultural transformation. The Bridges' Transition Model offers insights into change's psychological and emotional aspects, making it a valuable tool for guiding organizations through these complex transitions (Miller, 2017).

THE BRIDGES' TRANSITION MODEL: ELEMENTS AND PHASES

The Bridges' Transition Model comprises three key stages (Miller, 2017):

- Ending: In this phase, individuals and organizations must acknowledge what is ending or changing. When addressing bias and discrimination in AI-based hiring, the "Ending" stage involves recognizing the current practices and biases that need to be eliminated.
- Neutral Zone: The "Neutral Zone" is a period of ambiguity and uncertainty. It is a critical phase where individuals grapple with the emotions and challenges associated with change. In AI-based hiring, this phase involves navigating the discomfort and uncertainty that may arise as existing practices are dismantled.
- New Beginning: In the final stage, individuals and organizations embrace the new reality and commit to new behaviors and practices. In addressing bias in AI hiring, the "New Beginning" stage involves implementing fair and inclusive AI-based hiring processes and fostering a culture of diversity and equity.

APPLICATION OF THE BRIDGES' MODEL TO BIAS AND DISCRIMINATION IN AI-BASED HIRING

To address bias and discrimination in AI-based hiring, organizations can use the Bridges' Transition Model as follows:

Ending: Recognize and acknowledge existing biases in AI hiring processes and the need for change.

Neutral Zone: Provide support and resources to employees and stakeholders to navigate change's emotional and psychological challenges. Encourage open dialogue and address concerns.

New Beginning: Implement fair and unbiased AI-based hiring practices, reinforce diversity and inclusion values, and establish accountability mechanisms to prevent bias.

ADDRESSING RESISTANCE: THE ROLE OF THE BRIDGES' MODEL

Resistance to change is a common challenge in organizational transformation. The Bridges' Transition Model offers strategies to address resistance:

Ending: Communicate the reasons for change and the detrimental effects of bias and discrimination. Involve employees in identifying current issues.

Neutral Zone: Provide training and support to help employees acquire new skills and adapt to the changes. Encourage feedback and engagement to ease uncertainty.

New Beginning: Celebrate successes in eliminating bias and discrimination. Recognize and reward employees who embrace the new culture.

In the journey to rectify bias and discrimination in AI-based hiring, organizations must navigate complex cultural changes and overcome resistance. The Bridges' Transition Model offers a structured framework that emphasizes understanding the human side of change. By recognizing the three stages—Ending, Neutral Zone, and New Beginning—organizations can effectively guide their employees through the transition, foster a culture of equity and inclusion, and ultimately achieve a fair and bias-free AI-based hiring process.

The Bridges' Transition Model offers a valuable lens through which to view the profound changes occurring in the employment sector due to the integration of artificial intelligence (AI) into recruitment processes. This model, known for its insights into managing and navigating transitions, can be applied to understand the organizational and individual challenges presented by the adoption of AI algorithms in hiring. The current legal proceedings involving Context Systems and the 100-million-dollar class action lawsuit emphasize the critical need for change and transition management in this context. The Bridges' model highlights the importance of acknowledging the ending of established recruitment practices and the neutral zone of uncertainty where organizations grapple with the implications of AI bias. Ultimately, the model encourages organizations to navigate these transitions effectively, embracing transparency, accountability, and ethical considerations to ensure a successful shift toward fairer and more inclusive AI-driven recruitment tools. It provides a structured approach to managing change and underscores the significance of guiding employees and stakeholders through this critical transformation in the employment sector.

FAIRNESS AND JUSTICE APPROACH

Ethical principles play a pivotal role in shaping the dynamics and culture of organizations (Scott et al., 2014). The Fairness and Justice Approach is a robust ethical theory that guides decision-making by emphasizing principles of equity, fairness, and justice (Kunnan, 2015). Through a nuanced examination of this approach, we elucidate how its ethical tenets can foster an environment of integrity, inclusivity, and ethical leadership within organizations.

Ethical considerations constitute the moral compass that guides organizational behaviors, decisions, and interactions (Scott et al., 2014). Among the various ethical theories, the Fairness and Justice Approach is a significant framework that centers on fairness, equity, and justice (Kunnan, 2015). This approach acknowledges that ethical decisions must be rooted in treating individuals and groups equally and fairly, regardless of their background, position, or characteristics.

THE FAIRNESS AND JUSTICE APPROACH: ELEMENTS AND FOUNDATIONS

The Fairness and Justice Approach comprises several fundamental elements, each of which contributes to the development of a fair and ethical organizational culture (Kunnan, 2015):

- Equality: Equality, as a core element of this approach, underscores the importance of treating all individuals equally, irrespective of their attributes or positions within the organization. This principle fosters an organizational culture where every member is afforded the same opportunities and rights, promoting inclusivity and eradicating discrimination.
- Impartiality: Impartiality is closely linked to equality and emphasizes that organizational decisions and actions should be undertaken without bias or favoritism. By upholding impartiality, organizations create a level playing field where employees can trust that their treatment is just and consistent.
- Transparency: Transparency is a cornerstone of the Fairness and Justice Approach, emphasizing the need for openness and honesty in organizational dealings. Transparent practices and decision-making engender trust among employees and stakeholders, facilitating an ethical culture based on truth and accountability.
- Due Process: Due process underscores the importance of procedural fairness in organizational actions. This element ensures that individuals are accorded fair procedures, including opportunities to be heard and defend themselves when necessary. A commitment to due process safeguards against arbitrary or unjust actions within the organization.
- Distributive Justice: Distributive justice emphasizes the equitable distribution of organizational rewards, benefits, and burdens. Organizations that adhere to distributive justice principles ensure that employees are fairly compensated and recognized for their contributions, contributing to a culture of motivation and loyalty.

IMPACT ON ORGANIZATIONAL DYNAMICS

The Fairness and Justice Approach exerts a profound influence on organizational dynamics. When organizations embrace these ethical elements, they cultivate a sense of trust and confidence among employees (Kunnan, 2015). This trust, in turn, enhances cooperation, collaboration, and communication within the organization, leading to more effective teamwork and decision-making processes. Furthermore, by emphasizing equality and impartiality, organizations reduce the risk of conflicts and disputes, leading to a more harmonious and productive work environment.

INFLUENCE ON ORGANIZATIONAL CULTURE

The Fairness and Justice Approach has a transformative effect on organizational culture. Organizations prioritizing fairness and equity in their practices develop a culture characterized by inclusivity, respect, and ethical leadership (Kunnan, 2015). This ethical culture attracts top talent and retains employees who feel valued and respected. It encourages employees to align with the organization's ethical values and fosters a sense of belonging and commitment.

The Fairness and Justice Approach is a robust ethical framework that profoundly impacts organizational dynamics and culture. By embracing the elements of equality, impartiality, transparency, due process, and distributive justice, organizations can cultivate an ethical culture that promotes fairness, inclusivity, and integrity. This ethical culture, in turn, engenders a positive work environment, enhances teamwork and decision-making, and attracts and retains top talent. In an era where ethical considerations are paramount, organizations that integrate the Fairness and Justice Approach into their ethos can thrive and contribute to a more equitable and just society (Kunnan, 2015).

The Fairness and Justice Approach offers a robust ethical framework that centers on fairness, equity, and impartiality principles. This approach aligns with the goals of creating ethical and inclusive workplaces and provides strategic guidance for navigating cultural change and overcoming resistance to address bias in AI hiring.

The Fairness and Justice Approach encompasses several elemental principles, each of which is invaluable when addressing bias and discrimination in AI-based hiring:

- Equality: The principle of equality underscores the importance of treating all individuals within an organization with the same respect, rights, and opportunities, regardless of their background or characteristics. Embracing equality fosters an organizational culture that promotes inclusivity and eliminates discrimination in AI-based hiring.
- Impartiality: Impartiality is closely tied to equality and demands that decisions and actions within an organization are conducted without bias or favoritism. This principle ensures that employees perceive their treatment as just and consistent, which, in turn, minimizes resistance to change.
- Transparency: Transparency is a cornerstone of the Fairness and Justice Approach, emphasizing the necessity of openness and honesty in organizational practices. Transparent decision-making engenders trust among employees and stakeholders, which is essential when implementing changes to address bias in AI hiring.

- Due Process: The principle of due process ensures that individuals are accorded fair procedures, including opportunities to be heard and defend themselves when necessary. A commitment to due process safeguards against arbitrary or unjust actions while implementing new AI-based hiring practices.
- Distributive Justice: Distributive justice underscores the equitable distribution of organizational rewards, benefits, and burdens. Organizations that adhere to distributive justice principles ensure that employees are fairly compensated and recognized for their contributions, fostering an environment of motivation and loyalty.

USING THE FAIRNESS AND JUSTICE APPROACH FOR CULTURAL CHANGE

When organizations seek to change their culture to address bias and discrimination in AI-based hiring, they can leverage the Fairness and Justice Approach as a strategic guide:

- Equality and Impartiality: These principles can be central to the organization's cultural shift. By communicating a commitment to equality and impartiality in hiring processes, organizations signal their dedication to fair and unbiased recruitment practices.
- Transparency: Transparent communication about the changes in AI hiring practices, including the reasons behind the changes and the expected outcomes, helps build trust and reduce resistance among employees who may initially be skeptical.
- Due Process: Implementing due process mechanisms, such as grievance procedures or feedback channels, ensures that employees have a voice in the transformation process and can express concerns or provide input.
- Distributive Justice: Fair compensation and recognition practices can be redesigned to align with distributive justice principles, fostering employee motivation and commitment.

Overcoming Resistance to Change

Resistance to change is a common challenge in organizational transformation efforts. The Fairness and Justice Approach offers strategies to address resistance:

- Equality and Impartiality: By emphasizing that change is driven by a commitment to fairness and equity, organizations can garner support from employees who may initially resist the changes.
- Transparency: Transparent communication about the necessity of change to eliminate bias and discrimination can alleviate concerns and fears associated with AI-based hiring modifications.
- Due Process: Providing opportunities for employees to be heard and engaged in the change process can reduce resistance and foster a sense of ownership in the transformation.
- Distributive Justice: Ensuring employees perceive the changes as fair and equitable, particularly regarding the distribution of opportunities and rewards, can mitigate resistance.

The Fairness and Justice Approach is a robust ethical framework with profound implications for organizations seeking to transform their culture, combat bias and discrimination in AI-based hiring, and mitigate resistance to change. By embracing the principles of equality, impartiality, transparency, due process, and distributive justice, organizations can foster a culture of fairness, inclusivity, and ethical leadership. This ethical culture aligns with societal expectations and promotes employee trust, collaboration, and commitment. In the contemporary landscape where ethical considerations are paramount, organizations that integrate the Fairness and Justice Approach into their ethos can thrive and set a standard for ethical excellence in pursuing fairness and justice in AI-based hiring practices.

THE DIFFUSION OF INNOVATIONS THEORY

The Diffusion of Innovations theory outlines stages individuals go through when adopting an innovation. Understanding this process within complex organizations enables stakeholders to identify where incongruence arises (Alsheibani et al., 2018). By recognizing the varying stages of technology adoption among stakeholders, organizations can tailor their integration strategies to address incongruent perceptions and foster innovation diffusion (Alsheibani et al., 2018).

The Diffusion of Innovations theory posits that innovations, including technological advancements, diffuse through a population or organization over time in an S-shaped curve (Alsheibani et al., 2018). It categorizes individuals within this diffusion process based on their innovativeness, ranging from innovators and early adopters to the majority and laggards. The theory also identifies key factors influencing the adoption rate, including perceived attributes of the innovation, communication channels, social systems, and time (Alsheibani et al., 2018).

When addressing technology flaws, design issues, and integration challenges within organizations, the Diffusion of Innovations theory provides valuable insights and strategies (Alsheibani et al., 2018).

Identifying Resistance Factors: The theory categorizes individuals within the organization based on their innovativeness (Alsheibani et al., 2018). Recognizing that early adopters may be more receptive to addressing bias concerns, organizations can identify sources of resistance among late majority and laggard adopters.

Addressing Perceived Attributes: The theory emphasizes the importance of perceived attributes, including relative advantage, compatibility, complexity, trialability, and observability (Alsheibani et al., 2018). Organizations can tailor their strategies to highlight the advantages of bias-free AI algorithms, addressing concerns about perceived attributes.

Leveraging Communication Channels: Effective communication channels are pivotal in addressing bias complaints. The theory suggests utilizing influential individuals and opinion leaders to disseminate information and reduce resistance (Alsheibani et al., 2018).

Navigating Social Systems: The social context within an organization significantly influences technology integration (Alsheibani et al., 2018). Understanding the organization's social structure, culture, and power dynamics can effectively address bias concerns.

Allowing Time for Adoption: Recognizing that adoption takes time, organizations must be patient in rectifying bias issues. Providing trial and learning opportunities can mitigate technology adoption concerns (Alsheibani et al., 2018).

The Diffusion of Innovations theory, which elucidates the process through which new technologies are adopted and spread, offers an invaluable framework for understanding the challenges and opportunities presented. The integration of AI into recruitment processes represents an innovation that, while promising to revolutionize the hiring landscape, also confronts significant resistance and concerns, as evidenced by the legal proceedings discussed. The theory's key concepts of innovativeness, communication channels, social systems, and time offer a structured approach to assessing the adoption of AI-driven recruitment tools. By applying this theory, organizations can better understand the factors influencing the diffusion of this innovation, including the communication channels used to convey its benefits, the influence of social systems in shaping perceptions, and the time required for successful adoption. The urgent need for transparency, accountability, and ethical considerations emphasized in the abstract aligns closely with the theory's focus on understanding and addressing the barriers and facilitators of innovation diffusion. In conclusion, the Diffusion of Innovations theory serves as a relevant and comprehensive framework to navigate the challenges and opportunities associated with the integration of AI into recruitment processes, ultimately contributing to more informed and effective strategies for the development and deployment of these innovative tools.

THE ACTION RESEARCH AND ACTION LEARNING FRAMEWORK

- Research Cycles: The research component involved iterative data collection, including quantitative analysis of hiring outcomes and qualitative examination of algorithmic design. This data informed our understanding of the problem's scope and depth.
- Learning Cycles: The learning component emphasized collaboration and reflection. Cross-functional teams engaged in facilitated discussions to examine the implications of research findings, learn from employee experiences, and identify potential interventions.

IDENTIFYING ROOT CAUSES OF BIAS

Through research cycles, we identified several root causes contributing to bias in AI-driven hiring:

- Algorithmic Biases: Flawed algorithms perpetuated bias by favoring certain demographic groups over others. Addressing existing flaws required a comprehensive reevaluation of the algorithmic design, data sources, and training datasets.
- Cultural Biases: Organizational culture influenced hiring decisions and exacerbated bias. Prejudices among employees, hiring managers, and decision-makers needed to be addressed.
- Resistance to Change: The introduction of AI-based hiring encountered resistance from employees and candidates, who questioned the fairness and transparency of the process.

PRACTICAL PROBLEM-SOLVING RECOMMENDATIONS

Based on our findings, we offer several practical problem-solving recommendations:

- Algorithmic Review and Revision: Overhauling the AI algorithms used for resume screening was an immediate priority. Fixing this problem involved revising the training data, optimizing decision parameters, and addressing unintended biases.

- Cultural Sensitivity Training: A comprehensive cultural sensitivity training program was implemented across the organization to combat cultural biases. This initiative aimed to raise awareness of implicit biases and foster a more inclusive work environment.
- Change Management Strategy: Recognizing resistance to change, we developed a change management strategy that emphasized clear communication, employee engagement, and feedback mechanisms. Employees' concerns were acknowledged and integrated into the ongoing transformation.
- External Audits and Accountability: To address legal complaints, the organization engaged external auditors to conduct regular audits of the hiring process. This accountability mechanism provided transparency and credibility to the rectification efforts.

Outcomes and Ongoing Learning

Through successive action research and action learning cycles, we observed notable outcomes:

- Reduced Bias: Algorithmic revisions significantly reduced bias in hiring outcomes, resulting in more equitable candidate selections.
- Cultural Transformation: Cultural sensitivity training contributed to heightened awareness of biases and a more inclusive workplace culture.
- Reduced Resistance: The change management strategy gradually reduced resistance to AI-based hiring, with employees feeling more engaged in the process.
- Legal Complaint Resolution: External audits improved transparency and credibility, leading to the resolution of legal complaints.

This action research and action learning study demonstrates the transformative potential of a collaborative approach to address bias in AI-based hiring and effect cultural change within organizations. Organizations can mitigate bias, foster inclusivity, and resolve legal complaints by systematically investigating root causes, engaging in reflective learning cycles, and implementing practical interventions. This study underscores the value of continuous learning and adaptation in navigating the complex intersection of technology, culture, and ethics within the contemporary workplace.

PRACTICAL PROBLEM-SOLVING RECOMMENDATIONS

Based on our findings, we offer several practical problem-solving recommendations:

- Algorithmic Review and Revision: Overhauling the AI algorithms used for resume screening was an immediate priority. Correcting this problem involved revising the training data, optimizing decision parameters, and addressing unintended biases.
- Cultural Sensitivity Training: A comprehensive cultural sensitivity training program was implemented across the organization to combat cultural biases. This initiative aimed to raise awareness of implicit biases and foster a more inclusive work environment.
- Change Management Strategy: Recognizing resistance to change, we developed a change management strategy that emphasized clear communication, employee engagement, and feedback mechanisms. Employees' concerns were acknowledged and integrated into the ongoing transformation.

- External Audits and Accountability: To address legal complaints, the organization engaged external auditors to conduct regular audits of the hiring process. This accountability mechanism provided transparency and credibility to the rectification efforts.

OUTCOMES AND ONGOING LEARNING

Through successive action research and action learning cycles, we observed notable outcomes:

- Reduced Bias: Algorithmic revisions significantly reduced bias in hiring outcomes, resulting in more equitable candidate selections.
- Cultural Transformation: Cultural sensitivity training contributed to heightened awareness of biases and a more inclusive workplace culture.
- Reduced Resistance: The change management strategy gradually reduced resistance to AI-based hiring, with employees feeling more engaged.
- Legal Complaint Resolution: External audits improved transparency and credibility, leading to the resolution of legal complaints.

This action research and action learning study demonstrates the transformative potential of a collaborative approach to address bias in AI-based hiring and effect cultural change within organizations. Organizations can mitigate bias, foster inclusivity, and resolve legal complaints by systematically investigating root causes, engaging in reflective learning cycles, and implementing practical interventions. This study underscores the value of continuous learning and adaptation in navigating the complex intersection of technology, culture, and ethics within the contemporary workplace.

RECOMMENDATIONS FOR FUTURE RESEARCH

To further this area of study and address the urgent need for transparency, accountability, and ethical considerations in AI-driven recruitment tools, the following recommendations for future research are offered:

1. Quantitative Analysis of Bias Extent: Future research should aim to quantitatively measure the extent of bias in AI algorithms used in recruitment processes. Employing statistical techniques, such as regression analysis and machine learning models, researchers can analyze large datasets to identify patterns and quantify the impact of bias on hiring outcomes. This analysis will help in understanding the magnitude of the issue and its implications for marginalized communities.
2. Intersectional Analysis: Consideration of intersectionality is critical in future research. Analyzing the interactions between various aspects of identity (e.g., race, gender, and socioeconomic status) can provide a nuanced understanding of how AI algorithms disproportionately affect marginalized groups. Quantitative methods, such as intersectional regression analysis, can uncover the compounding effects of bias and discrimination.

3. Algorithmic Fairness Metrics: Future research should explore the application of algorithmic fairness metrics, such as disparate impact analysis and demographic parity, to assess and mitigate bias in AI-driven recruitment tools. These quantitative techniques can help in the development of fairer algorithms and the evaluation of their effectiveness in reducing discrimination.

4. Longitudinal Analysis: A longitudinal analysis of AI-driven recruitment tools and their impact over time can provide valuable insights. By examining changes in hiring outcomes and bias patterns, researchers can assess the evolving nature of the problem and evaluate the effectiveness of policy interventions and industry best practices.

5. Comparative Studies: Comparative studies that analyze the performance of AI algorithms against traditional, human-driven recruitment processes can shed light on the advantages and disadvantages of each approach. Employing quantitative methods, such as A/B testing and propensity score matching, can help in understanding how AI impacts hiring outcomes compared to human decision-making.

6. Industry-Wide Benchmarking: Conducting quantitative benchmarking studies across multiple organizations and industries can provide a broader perspective on the prevalence of bias in AI-driven recruitment tools. This research can establish industry benchmarks for fairness and accountability and promote best practices that reduce discrimination.

7. Evaluation of Bias Mitigation Strategies: Quantitative analysis of the effectiveness of various bias mitigation strategies, such as algorithm retraining, feature engineering, and fairness-aware machine learning, is crucial. Research can assess which strategies are most effective in reducing bias and improving the equity of AI recruitment tools.

In conclusion, future research in this domain should employ a range of quantitative methods to measure, assess, and mitigate bias in AI-driven recruitment processes. These recommendations aim to contribute to the development of fairer and more transparent AI algorithms and to address the urgent need for accountability and ethical considerations in the employment sector.

FINAL THOUGHTS

The most compelling and critical reasons to address these complex problems of bias, discrimination, and disparities in technology deployment stem from the significant impact they have on marginalized communities and the broader society.

First and foremost, addressing bias, discrimination, and disparities in technology deployment is an ethical imperative. The detrimental effects of programming bias and discriminatory outcomes, as highlighted in the case study, result in unjust and unequal treatment of marginalized job applicants and employees. This contravenes principles of fairness, equality, and justice that underpin democratic societies. It is essential to rectify these issues to ensure that every individual, regardless of their background, has an equal opportunity to participate in the workforce and access economic opportunities.

Secondly, from a societal perspective, the consequences of biased AI algorithms extend beyond individual cases. They perpetuate systemic disparities, creating and reinforcing societal inequalities. Marginalized communities often bear the brunt of these disparities, hindering social mobility and economic progress. Addressing bias and discrimination in technology deployment is not only a matter of fairness but also a means to rectify and prevent the perpetuation of social inequalities.

Moreover, from a legal standpoint, organizations must be held accountable for the consequences of biased AI algorithms. As demonstrated in the case study, legal proceedings can have significant financial and reputational implications for organizations. This serves as a strong incentive for organizations to invest in transparent, accountable, and ethical technology deployment. By doing so, they mitigate legal risks while upholding their responsibility to adhere to anti-discrimination laws and regulations.

In conclusion, the urgent need to address bias, discrimination, and disparities in the deployment of new technologies and innovations is underscored by their profound ethical, societal, and legal implications. These problems not only affect individuals and marginalized communities directly but also have far-reaching consequences for social equality and justice. Organizations, policymakers, and society as a whole must recognize the urgency of addressing these issues and commit to transparency, accountability, and ethical considerations in the development and deployment of AI-driven technologies to ensure a more just and equitable future.

REFERENCES

Abdavi, F., Fateh, H., & Pashaie, S. (2018). The Effects of Denison's Model of Organizational Culture on Customer Relationship Management (CRM): Case Study of Ministry of Sports and Youth in Iran. *International Journal of Management. Accounting & Economics*, *5*(6), 461–472.

Ahmady, G. A., Nikooravesh, A., & Mehrpour, M. (2016). Effect of organizational culture on knowledge management based on Denison Model. *Procedia: Social and Behavioral Sciences*, *230*, 387–395. doi:10.1016/j.sbspro.2016.09.049

Alsheibani, S., Cheung, Y., & Messom, C. (2018). Artificial Intelligence Adoption: AI-readiness at Firm-Level. *PACIS*, *4*, 231–245.

Bridges, S. (2020, March 12). *Bridges transition model*. William Bridges Associates. Retrieved March 21, 2023, from https://wmbridges.com/about/what-is-transition/

Burrell, D. N., Diperi, D. L., & Weaver, R. M. (2021). Creating Inclusive Cultures for Women in Automation and Information Technology Careers and Occupations. In I. Management Association (Ed.), Research Anthology on Challenges for Women in Leadership Roles (pp. 749–765). IGI Global. doi:10.4018/978-1-7998-8592-4.ch041

Caulfield, J. L., & Brenner, E. F. (2020). Resolving complex community problems: Applying collective leadership and Kotter's change model to wicked problems within social system networks. *Nonprofit Management & Leadership*, *30*(3), 509–524. doi:10.1002/nml.21399

Cheung, H. K., King, E., Lindsey, A., Membere, A., Markell, H. M., & Kilcullen, M. (2016). Understanding and reducing workplace discrimination. *Research in Personnel and Human Resources Management*, *34*, 101–152. doi:10.1108/S0742-730120160000034010

Collins, R. (2010). *A graphical method for exploring the business environment*. Henley Business School.

Cuevas, A. G., & Boen, C. (2021). Tip of the iceberg: Measuring racial discrimination in studies of health. *Stress and Health*, *37*(5), 1043–1050. doi:10.1002/smi.3047 PMID:33739613

Gelberd, B. (2008). Bridging Differences. *Business and Economic Review, 54*(3), 14–21.

George, M. S., Gaitonde, R., Davey, R., Mohanty, I., & Upton, P. (2023). Engaging participants with research findings: A rights-informed approach. *Health Expectations, 26*(2), 765–773. doi:10.1111/hex.13701 PMID:36647684

Graso, M., Camps, J., Strah, N., & Brebels, L. (2020). Organizational justice enactment: An agent-focused review and path forward. *Journal of Vocational Behavior, 116*, 103296. doi:10.1016/j.jvb.2019.03.007

Huff, A., Burrell, D. N., Richardson, K., Springs, D., Aridi, A. S., Crowe, M. M., & Lewis, E. (2023). Illegal Pregnancy Discrimination Is a Severe Business, Legal, and Public Health Issue. In D. Burrell (Ed.), *Real-World Solutions for Diversity, Strategic Change, and Organizational Development: Perspectives in Healthcare, Education, Business, and Technology* (pp. 119–129). IGI Global. doi:10.4018/978-1-6684-8691-7.ch008

Kelan, E. K. (2023). Algorithmic inclusion: Shaping the predictive algorithms of artificial intelligence in hiring. *Human Resource Management Journal*, 1748-8583.12511. doi:10.1111/1748-8583.12511

Kotter, J. P. (2013). *Leading change, with a new preface by the author.* Harvard Business Press.

Kunnan, A. J. (2015). Assessing the quality of large-scale assessments: The case for a fairness and justice approach. *Developing Indigenous Models of English Language Teaching and Assessment*, 131.

Maxfield, S. (2008). Reconciling Corporate Citizenship and Competitive Strategy: Insights from Economic Theory. *Journal of Business Ethics, 80*(2), 367–377. doi:10.1007/s10551-007-9425-1

McLester, Q., Burrell, D. N., Nobles, C., & Castillo, I. (2021). Advancing Knowledge About Sexual Harassment Is a Critical Aspect of Organizational Development for All Employees. *International Journal of Knowledge-Based Organizations, 11*(4), 48–60. doi:10.4018/IJKBO.2021100104

Meeler, D. (2018, May 3). *Five basic approaches to ethical decision-making.* Ethically Philosophical. Retrieved March 22, 2023, from https://ethicallyphilosophical.wordpress.com/2018/05/03/five-basic-approaches-to-ethical-decision-making/

Miller, J. L. (2017). Managing transitions: Using William Bridges' transition model and a change style assessment instrument to inform strategies and measure progress in organizational change management. In *The 12th International Conference on Performance Measurement in Libraries Proceedings* (p. 357). Academic Press.

Nandonde, F. A. (2019). A PESTLE analysis of international retailing in the East African Community. *Global Business and Organizational Excellence, 38*(4), 54–61. doi:10.1002/joe.21935

O'Hara, N. N., Nophale, L. E., O'Hara, L. M., Marra, C. A., & Spiegel, J. M. (2017). Tuberculosis testing for healthcare workers in South Africa: A health service analysis using Porter's Five Forces Framework. *International Journal of Healthcare Management, 10*(1), 49–56. doi:10.1080/20479700.2016.1268814

Sarayreh, B. H., Khudair, H., & Barakat, E. A. (2013). Comparative study: The Kurt Lewin of change management. *International Journal of Computer and Information Technology, 2*(4), 626–629.

Scott, B. A., Garza, A. S., Conlon, D. E., & Kim, Y. J. (2014). Why Do Managers Act Fairly in the First Place? A Daily Investigation of "Hot" and "Cold" Motives and Discretion. *Academy of Management Journal, 57*(6), 1571–1591. doi:10.5465/amj.2012.0644

Tran, T. B. H., & Choi, S. B. (2019). Effects of inclusive leadership on organizational citizenship behavior: the mediating roles of organizational justice and learning culture. *Journal of Pacific Rim Psychology, 13*, e17.

Vaudrin, C. J. (2019). Melting the Cultural Iceberg in Indigenizing Higher Education: Shifts to Accountability in Times of Reconciliation. *New Directions for Teaching and Learning, 2019*(157), 105–118. doi:10.1002/tl.20333

Wazed, S. (2018, August 2). *Council post: Grow your organization with top talent using the iceberg interview model.* Forbes. Retrieved March 21, 2023, from https://www.forbes.com/sites/forbeshuman-resourcescouncil/2018/08/02/grow-your-organization-with-top-talent-using-the-iceberg-interview-model/?sh=41d17c2175b8

Zapata, D. (2021, June). *New study finds AI-enabled anti-Black bias in recruiting.* Thomson Reuters. Retrieved from: https://www.thomsonreuters.com/en-us/posts/legal/ai-enabled-anti-black-bias/

Zoričić, D., Knežević, G., Miletić, M., Dolinar, D., & Sprčić, D. M. (2022). Integrated Risk Analysis of Aggregators: Policy Implications for the Development of the Competitive Aggregator Industry. *Energies, 15*(14). doi:10.3390/en15145076

Chapter 16
Influence of Cybersecurity Leadership Resiliency on Organizational Readiness:
Exploring Intersectionality With Cyber Risk Liability Valuation

Laura Ann Jones

iD https://orcid.org/0000-0002-0299-370X

Capitol Technology University, USA

ABSTRACT

Studies establish that cybersecurity executives face complex difficulties from constantly shifting risks due to the role's scalability and increasing responsibilities in this cyber-revolution. Cognitive and emotional aspects can influence change and decision-making, especially during times of heightened anxiety and evolving change. Through qualitative study and interpretative phenomenological analysis design, this research offers how leaders' 16-hour or more per-day working schedules affect the companies' readiness, how working hours affect leaders' resilience, and whether leadership traits like longevity, tenure, and other similar characteristics should be considered when estimating cyber risk insurance. This study aims to strengthen the defense-in-depth perimeter by providing a means to proactively identify factors that align with an enhanced approach to better estimate appropriate cyber liability coverage. Beneficiaries of this research are cybersecurity leaders and practitioners, academia, organizations that employ cybersecurity, and cyber risk insurance brokerages.

INTRODUCTION

Cybersecurity leadership has become indispensable, characterized by relentless and ever-evolving cyber threats in today's digital age. The relentless onslaught of cyberattacks poses a multitude of challenges that often outpace existing defensive measures, necessitating strong leadership in the realm of cyber-

DOI: 10.4018/979-8-3693-1970-3.ch016

security (Deloitte, 2023; Badhwar, 2021; Burrell et al., 2020; Burton, 2023). This chapter explores the critical importance of cybersecurity leadership and the complex issues cybersecurity executives face in the face of rapidly shifting risks and escalating responsibilities brought about by the cyber revolution.

The Geneva Papers on Risk and Insurance: Issues and Practice (2022) report that cybercrime is assessed as having cost the global economy slightly less than $1 trillion in 2020, denoting a surge of over 50% since 2018. With the typical cyber insurance claim escalating from $145,000 in 2019 to $359,000 in 2020, the need for better intelligence around cybersecurity factors persists (Cremer et al., 2022; The Geneva Papers, 2022). Research indicates that the ability of cyber leaders to operate at peak performance directly impacts organizational readiness (Nobles et al., 2023). According to a 2020 Tessian and Stanford University study, human error was the primary cause of 88% of data breach events. Distraction was identified as the primary cause for falling victim to a phishing scam by over half (47%) of respondents, while 44% attributed their vulnerability to sleepiness or stress.

Cyberattacks have become increasingly frequent and sophisticated, resulting in annual losses totaling billions of dollars (CISA, 2022; Kaminska, 2021; Shandler et al., 2023; Snider et al., 2021). High-profile cyber incidents, such as data breaches and cyberattacks, have exposed organizations to significant aftermaths and cybersecurity challenges (Burton, 2023; Cavares et al., 2023; Nobles et al., 2023). Consequently, cybersecurity leaders grapple with exhaustion, excessive workloads, and needing to be on call (Gartner, 2021; Olyaei, 2023). These human factors directly impact an organization's security posture (Nobles, 2022b).

Cybersecurity leaders face challenges from rapidly advancing technology and evolving risk environments (Badhwar, 2021; Burrell et al., 2020; Cazares et al., 2023; PwC, 2022). They grapple with adapting to the dynamic landscape of cybersecurity risk management governance while experiencing burnout, overwork, and being in a constant "always-on" mode (Gartner, 2022; Gartner, 2021; Nobles, 2021; Nobles, 2022b; Olyaei, 2023). Specifically, CISOs indicated experiencing burnout, emotional exhaustion, depersonalization, and reduced professional efficacy (Reeves et al., 2023).

One persistent issue in information security is the prevalence of exhaustion and burnout (Nobles, 2022b), also experienced as impaired depersonalization, decreased professional efficacy, and emotional exhaustion (Reeves et al., 2023). Cybersecurity operations are particularly affected by burnout, stress, and exhaustion, exacerbated by the demands of the ever-evolving threat landscape (Nobles, 2021). Burnout in cybersecurity has surged as a topical interest. Studies discuss the effects of cyber fatigue and burnout (Nobles, 2021; Platsis, 2019) and depersonalization, impaired professional efficacy, and emotional exhaustion (Reeves et al., 2023).

Further, 79% of security executives in the UK acknowledged difficulties in consistently disconnecting from job engagement, while 21% admitted seldomly or never disengaging (Davies, 2022). These statistics have increased compared to the previous year, with 59 percent reporting difficulties in disconnecting. Alert fatigue, induced by the relentless stream of cyber alerts, further compounds these challenges (Segal, 2021).

These issues stem from the increasing scalability of the cybersecurity leadership role over the past decade, creating a disconnect between stakeholders' expectations and leaders' actual preparedness and expertise (Olyaei, 2023). Cybersecurity leaders must now transition from solely responsible for addressing cyber risks to ensuring that business leaders possess the necessary knowledge to make informed decisions about information risk (Olyaei, 2023).

Burnout, exhaustion, and cybersecurity fatigue have long plagued cybersecurity (Nobles, 2021; Reeves, 2021). However, these challenges have become more acute due to decision-makers inability, particularly senior management, to effectively address the underlying causes of stress, burnout, and job-related fatigue (Nobles, 2021; Nobles, 2022b). High-stress levels and difficulties in reaching cybersecurity professionals have been observed (Dykstra & Paul, 2018).

Fatigue in cybersecurity is an underexplored but critical issue (Nobles, 2022b), with various socio-technical domains recognizing the importance of workload and stress in affecting cognitive abilities, alertness, memory, and decision-making (Grier, 2015; Dykstra & Paul, 2018; Nobles, 2022b). Research indicates that as cyber operations' duration extends, weariness and dissatisfaction among cybersecurity professionals increase (Dykstra & Paul, 2018). Yet, organizations and business development managers have not thoroughly examined the factors contributing to cybersecurity fatigue (Nobles, 2021).

The failure to mitigate cybersecurity fatigue has increased incidents such as data breaches, cyberattacks, ransomware attacks, and other major security disasters (Burrell et al., 2020; Nobles, 2022b). Human errors are responsible for a significant portion of security problems (Nobles, 2022a). The constantly changing corporate environment, increasing technology reliance, limited cybersecurity resources, rising regulatory demands, and an ever-intense threat landscape contribute to the phenomenon of security fatigue (Nobles, 2021).

As the role of cybersecurity leaders continues to evolve, cyber leaders face environments with less direct control over critical decisions (Gartner, 2022). The ability to make decisions is crucial, especially when dealing with heightened levels of anxiety, despair, and distress (Cazares et al., 2023; Morelli et al., 2022; Nobles, 2022b). These cognitive and emotional factors play a significant role in the decision-making process, particularly in cybersecurity's fast-paced and high-stress world (Jeong et al., 2019; Nobles, 2022b; Segal, 2021).

Based on a survey by Tessian, security leaders in the UK and the US often spend more than 16 hours per week over typical working hours (Davies, 2022). This change is a surge of five and a half hours in comparison to the corresponding data from the previous year. According to Davies (2022), this increase in work hours is equivalent to an additional 11 hours per week observed in 2021.

Research conducted by Reeves et al. (2023) examined the degree to which a representative sample of the Australian cybersecurity sector is affected by burnout. A group of 119 experts in the field of cyber security, with 32% of them holding the position of Chief Information Security Officer (CISO), successfully undertook the Maslach Burnout Inventory (MBI). According to the MBI, burnout is characterized by three dimensions: emotional depletion, depersonalization, and impaired professional efficacy. Each dimension is discussed.

- Emotional exhaustion pertains to being emotionally stretched to the limit because of one's professional duties. It is typified by a deficiency of vitality, emotional exhaustion, and feeling depleted.
- Depersonalization pertains to the emergence of pessimistic and critical attitudes and emotions toward one's stakeholders. A deficiency in empathy distinguishes it, a propensity to perceive individuals as mere objects and disconnection from one's professional endeavors.
- Impaired professional efficacy refers to a decrease in an individual's perceived competence and achievement in the profession, a feeling of ineffectiveness, and a propensity to perceive one's job as lacking significance.

This study contemplates the increase in work hours and workload of cybersecurity leaders' (Davies, 2022) effect on individual and organizational readiness and resilience and considers whether leadership traits such as longevity and tenure should be considered when estimating cyber risk insurance. This research aims to strengthen the defense-in-depth perimeter and better equip organizations to navigate the ever-evolving cyber threat landscape by proactively identifying factors that align with an enhanced approach to cyber liability coverage.

The beneficiaries of this research include practitioners, academics, and learners in AI and Cybersecurity. It sheds light on cybersecurity leaders' complex challenges and offers insights into strategies to mitigate burnout and enhance organizational cybersecurity readiness. Additionally, it provides a valuable perspective on the intersection of leadership, resilience, and cyber risk insurance in today's digital landscape.

BACKGROUND

The frequency of cyberattacks is increasing rapidly, resulting in annual losses of up to billions of dollars, as indicated by several sources (Burton, 2023; CISA, 2022; Kaminska, 2021; Shandler et al., 2023; Snider et al., 2021). Egregious and often high visibility publicly disclosed cyber-attacks (Burton, 2023; Cavares et al., 2023) leave organizations increasingly exposed to substantial aftermaths of cybersecurity episodes (Nobles et al., 2023). Subsequently, cybersecurity leaders are experiencing exhaustion, excessive workload, and a constant state of being available (Gartner, 2021; Olyaei, 2023); such human factors have a direct opportunity to impact an organization's security posture (Jeong et al., 2019; Nobles, 2022b).

One persistent issue in information security and cybersecurity is the prevalence of exhaustion and burnout (Nobles, 2022b). Concerns regarding the degree of engagement between humans and computers existed before COVID-19 (Wickens et al., 2021). However, during the pandemic, human performance issues (HPI) in cybersecurity reached new heights (Nobles, 2021). Recently, there has been a surge of interest in the issue of job burnout in many security publications, online platforms, and social media (Nobles, 2022b; Platsis, 2019), as various studies have been conducted on the topic of cyber fatigue and burnout.

Multiple studies suggest that cybersecurity leaders encounter complex and diverse challenges from advanced and ever-changing technology, cybersecurity, and risk environments (Badhwar, 2021; Burrell et al., 2020; Cazares et al., 2023; PwC, 2022). Cybersecurity leaders are facing challenges in adapting to the rapidly changing risk environment of cybersecurity risk management governance (Cox & Kanji, 2022), and are burnt out, overworked, and in "always-on" mode (Gartner, 2022; Gartner, 2021; Olyaei, 2023). Cyber leaders also experience alert fatigue, similar to cyber fatigue, but is caused by cyber alerts, including threats and breaches (Segal, 2021).

According to Olyeia (2023), these issues experienced by cybersecurity leaders result from the role's increased scalability in the past decade, leading to a contradiction in stakeholders' expectations. Moreover, the prevalent view is that it is unjust to demand that leaders assume responsibility for conditions they must be adequately prepared for or need more expertise to oversee (Olyaei, 2023) effectively.

Tension, burnout, and cybersecurity exhaustion have long been present in cybersecurity (Nobles, 2021; Reeves, 2021). However, these challenges are becoming more frequent and severe due to the inability of corporate decision-makers, particularly senior management, to effectively address the underlying causes of stress, burnout, and weariness due to the job (Nobles, 2022b). Dykstra and Paul (2018) observed that security workers are overwhelmed, experiencing high stress levels, and are difficult to reach.

The literature widely chronicles operational stress, weariness, error, and burnout (Grier, 2015; Nobles, 2021; Nobles, 2022b). However, fatigue in cybersecurity should be given more importance as a conversation issue (Nobles, 2022b) among security and technology executives (Paredes-Astudillo, 2020). Grier (2015) stated that various sociotechnical domains, including aviation, industrial control, command, and medical, have examined workload because these disciplines require solid cognitive abilities, alertness, memory, and visual perception skills. Investigating workload and stress is essential in the empirically established connection between mistakes and reduced performance (Dykstra & Paul, 2018; Nobles, 2021).

According to Cazares et al. (2023) and Morelli et al. (2022), cognitive and affective factors can have an impact on people's decision-making processes, mainly when they are dealing with high levels of anxiety, despair, and distress, as was primarily the case before the COVID-19 epidemic as an organization were also migrating their systems to the cloud (Segal, 2021). Organizations need cybersecurity leaders to lead the execution and completion of security priorities (Gartner, n.d.). However, with pressures and responsibilities indiscriminately increasing and ongoing stressors of unknown threats accumulating (Gartner, 2022), the constant stream of cyberattacks significantly affects organizations' cybersecurity defenses and the leaders responsible for putting defensive and offensive strategies into action.

Organizations often leverage cyber liability insurance as a response strategy to risk realizations (Cremer et al., 2022). Thus, while assessing cyber risk insurance, cogitating critical considerations related to the functions of digital defense personnel will provide deeper insight into an organization's security posture (Aziz, 2020; Romanosky et al., 2019; Zie, 2020). This study examines the intersection of cybersecurity leadership rotation and resilience, subsequent organizational preparedness, and cyber risk insurance assessment.

Cyber risk insurance, alternatively referred to as cybersecurity insurance or cyber liability insurance, is a specialty insurance policy meant to support organizations by minimizing the potentially cataclysmic implications of cybercrimes and reducing losses (Aziz, 2020; Falco et al., FTC, n.d.; 2019; Romanosky et al., 2019). Cybersecurity criminal practices span data breaches, cyberattacks on third parties, account takeover, span malware, ransomware, distributed denial-of-service (DDoS) assaults, or any other techniques deployed to penetrate a network and acquire sensitive data (CISA, 2022; FTC, n.d.). Cyber risk insurance refers to insurance policies covering damages from computer-based attacks or failures in an organization's information technology systems, affecting first and third parties (Aziz, 2020; Romanosky et al., 2019; Zie, 2020). The coverage provided by cyber risk insurance can be broadly categorized into two types:

- First-party Coverage: This covers the costs of things like the investigation of the incident, risk assessment of future cyber incidents, lost revenue due to business interruption, ransomware attack payments based on coverage limits, and notifying customers about the cyber incident and providing them with anti-fraud services such as credit monitoring (Romanosky et al., 2019).
- Third-party or Cyber Liability Coverage: This can protect a business if a third party sues the business for damages because of a cybersecurity incident. Cyber liability coverage generally pays attorney and court fees associated with legal proceedings, settlements, and court judgments (Romanosky et al., 2019).

Romanosky et al. (2019) indicate that one insurance company's policy describes computer attacks as either unauthorized access to a computer system by an unauthorized person, an attack on the system by a virus or other malicious software, or a denial-of-service attack on the insured's system. According to

Badhwar (2021), Romanosky's description is accurate, given the current state of threats and the rising prevalence of cyber hazards. Cyber insurance is becoming more important as a risk response strategy, especially for risk transfer (Romanosky et al., 2019). This increase in significance is because the costs of responding to and recovering from a cyber disaster are rising (GAO, 2021).

In addition, organizations and their cybersecurity leaders are seeing increased liability concerns due to authorities focusing on security breaches. Recently, the Securities and Exchange Commission (SEC) initiated legal action against a software business and its Chief Security Officer (CSO) for engaging in fraudulent activities that reportedly occurred in 2019 by providing false information to investors on the company's cybersecurity capabilities. Additionally, in 2016, there was a data breach at a ride-sharing company (DOJ, 2022; Rundle, 2023), which exposed data belonging to approximately 57 million users and 600,000 ride-share drivers. The CISO was found guilty in the matter (DOJ, 2022).

Cyber insurance contracts commonly have exclusions that explicitly define the events or circumstances that are not eligible for coverage (Aziz, 2020; Zie, 2020). It is essential to comprehend these exemptions to guarantee sufficient coverage (Aziz, 2020; Falco et al., 2019). Cyber risk insurance is a crucial risk response strategy for businesses to hedge against the financial consequences (Aziz, 2020; Falco et al., 2019; Romanosky et al., 2019) and reputational risks associated with cyber threats (Jones, 2020). Coverage aims to provide support so that cyberattacks do not disrupt or destroy a business (Aziz, 2020; CISA, 2022; Falco et al., 2019; FTC, n.d.; Romanosky et al., 2019), including legal actions incurred.

Such legal actions signal the predisposition of authorities to hold key cybersecurity leaders accountable for the exactitude, transparency, and effectiveness of cybersecurity exertions that they or their organizations encounter (Zukis, 2019). While the sources in this research study do not specifically focus on leadership rotation, resources highlight the complex and ever-changing nature of cybersecurity risk management and the factors that insurers consider when assessing risk and determining coverage (FTC, n.d.; Metz, 2023). Further investigation is necessary to confirm the potential necessity of organizational leadership rotation, particularly after a severe cybersecurity incident.

A 2023 forecast by Gartner expects that over half of cybersecurity executives will change jobs by 2025. Of this group, 25% will move into entirely different roles due to work-related stress factors. While security fatigue affects CISOs (Reeves et al., 2023), it excludes CISOs and other professionals (Nobles, 2022b). A global study by Mimecast involving 1,100 cybersecurity professionals disclosed that over one-third of the respondents contemplated quitting their jobs within the next two years due to overwhelming stress and burnout (Gartner, 2021).

A recent study commissioned by Bridewell (n.d.) surveyed 521 cybersecurity decision-makers across the communications, utilities, banking, government, logistics, and aviation sectors (Coker, 2022). The study observed that 95% of the participants are currently in circumstances that make it more likely for them to leave their current position within the next year (Bridewell, n.d.; Coker, 2022). Research accomplished at the Black Hat Europe event, including 311 cybersecurity professionals, disclosed that 66% of the respondents confirmed encountering burnout (Keary, 2022).

Further, a recent poll revealed that CISOs are burdened with excessive workload, significantly impacting their mental well-being, so 90% are prepared to accept a salary reduction (Sheridan, 2020). For many companies, the CISO (Cox & Kanji, 2022) is the executive with accountability for cyber risk. These studies highlight the heightened levels of stress and burnout experienced by cybersecurity professionals (Gartner, 2021; Nobles et al., 2023; Olyaei, 2023), which can lead to substantial staff attrition and potentially undermine the effectiveness of cybersecurity measures inside organizations. Organizations must use proactive strategies.

PROBLEM STATEMENT

When and under what circumstances do cybersecurity leaders typically experience a decline in their effectiveness in managing their roles due to increased responsibilities, evolving cyber threats, heightened regulatory oversight, the demand for accurate reporting, and the constant need to be 'always-on'? Furthermore, when, and how should organizations assess the rotation of cybersecurity leadership roles to ensure the well-being of their leaders and benefit the organizations themselves? This inquiry also explores the intricate relationship between changes in cybersecurity leadership's endurance and resilience and organizations' readiness to combat cyber threats. Additionally, this study examines whether these factors should be considered in estimating cyber risk insurance, given the significant global economic impact of cybercrime and the increasing costs associated with cyber insurance claims.

SIGNIFICANCE OF THE STUDY

The research delves into the escalating costs associated with traditional cyber insurance claims, pointing out the severe financial risks that organizations face following cyber incidents. The study underscores the growing relevance and necessity of cyber risk insurance as a financial safeguard against the increasing menace of cyber threats, aligning with authoritative sources such as the Government Accountability Office (GAO). Further, the study addresses critical questions regarding the exhaustion experienced by cybersecurity executives and the optimal timing for their rotation to prevent costly errors. It highlights the importance of leadership rotation in safeguarding organizations from significant financial losses due to cyber incidents. This research also bridges a critical gap in existing cybersecurity research by providing a comprehensive analysis of cybersecurity events and expenses. It explores the intricate correlation between cybersecurity leadership resilience, organizational preparedness, and cyber risk insurance, contributing to the development of more effective cybersecurity strategies and insurance plans. Moreover, the study recognizes that cybersecurity leadership resilience is influenced by various elements, including personal and professional aspects. It employs an IPA (Interpretative Phenomenological Analysis) research design to investigate novel and developing topics within the realm of cybersecurity. The study also caters to a diverse audience, including cybersecurity professionals, business leaders, insurance companies, policymakers, and scholars. It offers insights into current trends and challenges in the field, informs insurance offerings, aids in policymaking, and encourages further academic exploration. Finally, the study's significance extends beyond academia, providing practical guidance and valuable insights to stakeholders in the cybersecurity and risk management landscape. It aids in adapting practices, refining insurance offerings, crafting effective policies, and contributing to the evolving field of cybersecurity and risk management.

In summary, the study investigates the economic impact of cybercrime, the rising costs of cyber insurance claims, the importance of cybersecurity leadership rotation, and the relationship between leadership resilience, organizational preparedness, and cyber risk insurance. It offers practical applications and is relevant to a wide range of stakeholders in the cybersecurity and risk management domain.

METHODOLOGY

This study will employ a qualitative, interpretive phenomenological analysis (IPA) research approach to investigate the impact of cybersecurity leadership resilience on an organization's preparedness. IPA is a research methodology that aims to comprehend the firsthand experiences of people or collectives (Smith & Fieldsend, 2021; Smith & Nizza, 2022). This study is suitable because it enables a thorough and sophisticated comprehension of the many elements that impact the resilience of cybersecurity leadership. The study will be executed in three sequential phases: participant recruitment, data collection, and data analysis

Participant recruitment enlisted recruitment due to participant's industry, organization size, and length of service. Data was gathered via semi-structured interviews with the participants. The interviews centered on the participants' experiences as leaders in the field of cybersecurity, their personal assessment of their resilience, and their comprehension of how their resilience impacts their organization's preparedness.

Data was examined and interpreted using IPA (Interpretative Phenomenological Analysis) methodologies. This work entailed meticulously analyzing the interview transcripts to discern prevalent themes and trends. The study will center on comprehending how participants' experiences and perspectives influence their resilience and how their resilience, in turn, impacts their organization's preparedness. Through email, participants received information on the study's objectives, the potential risks and advantages of participating, and their entitlement to withdraw at any moment. Data was gathered using a survey and examined strictly private mode through data anonymization. The IPA approach is suitable for this study because it facilitates a profound and nuanced comprehension of the intricate aspects (Smith & Fieldsend, 2021) that impact cybersecurity leadership resilience. IPA, or Interpretative Phenomenological Analysis, is a study approach that aims explicitly to comprehend persons' subjective experiences and viewpoints. The process used improves the quality and effectiveness of the material.

In conclusion, this study employed an IPA research approach (Smith & Fieldsend, 2021) to investigate the impact of cybersecurity leaderships' perseverance on an organization's attentiveness and whether resiliency should be a component of assessing cyber risk insurance (GAO, 2022). The study aimed to offer valuable insights into the intricate determinants that impact the durability of cybersecurity leadership and how such pliability (Gartner, 2022) subsequently impacts an organization's capacity to manage cyber threats effectively. The study's findings can sustain methods for cultivating and bolstering the resilience of cybersecurity leadership, fortifying companies' cybersecurity defenses.

LITERATURE REVIEW

The literature reviewed for this study focuses on the need to acquire insurance and transfer risk as a risk response strategy. Historically, literary sources have documented the challenges faced by businesses and the need to source insurance as a risk response strategy.

Insurance History and Its Critique

Marine insurance, one of the earliest forms of risk mitigation, exemplifies ancient risk-spreading practices. As documented by de Roover (1945), Gürses (2023), and Morris (2018), Ancient Greek merchants paid premiums to safeguard their voyages against losses at sea, a practice that underpinned the stability of maritime commerce. This system not only distributed risks across multiple stakeholders but also propelled economic expansion by enabling merchants to engage in trade ventures confidently. The historical precedence set by marine insurance laid the groundwork for modern risk transfer mechanisms, such as cyber liability insurance, which emerged in the 1990s (Granato & Polacek, 2019; Gürses, 2023).

Initially designed to cover data breach litigations, this insurance evolved to address the broader implications of cyber incidents, including business interruptions (GAO, 2022; Gartner, 2022). The proliferation of online commerce in the late 1990s amplified the necessity for such financial safeguards against cyber threats (Ackerman, 2023).

Today, cyber insurance is an integral component of corporate risk management strategies, reflecting a market trend that suggests significant growth in demand and an increase in the resolution of cyber claims (Fitch Ratings, 2022; Statista, 2022). While the research acknowledges the importance of cyber risk insurance, it may underplay the complexities involved in accurately assessing cyber threats and the evolving nature of cybersecurity. This can render traditional insurance models ineffective without continuous adaptation to the digital landscape's risks.

Risk Transference as a Response Strategy

According to the Corporate Finance Institute (CFI) (n.d.), risk transfer is a standard risk management technique where an individual or organization's possible loss from a negative outcome is shifted to a third party (CFI Team, n.d.). The insured individual or company usually provides the third party with recurrent payments to compensate the third party for assuming the risk (Gürses, 2023). Contracts can contain an indemnification article that safeguards against possible losses and that the insured will be remunerated by the opposite party (CFI Team, n.d.) in event that the insurance policy is evoked. Risk transfer is a fundamental approach to managing risks, which is part of a set of four primary techniques, including risk avoidance, risk mitigation, and risk acceptance.

Risk transference entails shifting the financial repercussions of a risk to a separate entity, such as an insurer, a contractor, or a supplier. For instance, a firm may acquire insurance to mitigate the potential loss from property damage caused by a fire or a natural calamity. Although risk is often transmitted from persons and corporations to insurers, insurers can also transfer risk. Transference is accomplished using an insurance policy with reinsurance firms. Reinsurance businesses offer insurance to insurance companies (CFI Team, n.d.).

Through risk transfer, the organization can safeguard itself against potential financial damages if the risk materializes. However, it is worth noting that transference of financial implications does not preclude organizations from incurring reputational impacts resulting from cyber exploitations and related serious incidents, which could have long-term effects on companies' products and services leading to additional losses over time.

Conventional strategies for responding to adversarial risks include:

- **Risk Avoidance:** Risk avoidance is a method that entails avoiding the risk by either refraining from engaging in the activity that poses the risk or modifying the activity to eliminate the danger.
- **Risk Mitigation**: Risk mitigation is a response strategy that aims to decrease the probability or effect of risk by implementing measures to lower the possibility of the risk or minimize the severity of the repercussions in case the risk does occur.

- **Risk Acceptance:** This approach entails acknowledging the risk and refraining from any measures to diminish its probability or consequences. This approach is often the most effective option for mitigating hazards that have a low probability of happening or would have little consequences if they did occur.
- **Risk Transference:** Risk transference also known as *risk transfer* refers to the action of transferring the financial implications of a risk to a third party. In the cybersecurity financial realm, use of this is strategy entails acquiring cyber liability insurance to reduce the financial impact of a successful cybersecurity exploit.

Risk Transfer Further Contextualized

Risk transfer is an advantageous risk response approach since it enables enterprises to safeguard themselves against financial losses without necessitating supplementary measures to diminish the probability or consequences of the risk impacting an organization's defense-in-depth security positioning. Defense in depth employs many levels of protection to safeguard an organization's assets. However, when there is a security weakness in hardware, software, or human factors, and cyberattackers successfully breach the defense perimeter, a risk response is crucial. One such response is risk transference. Transferring risk can be especially advantageous for dangers that are hard or costly to alleviate.

Insurance contracts are commonly employed to facilitate risk transfer. Alternatively, it can be utilized via other contractual arrangements, such as indemnity provisions or outsourcing agreements. There are distinct advantages of employing the risk response strategy. Risk transfer can assist in the following ways, it can:

- Safeguard organizations from monetary damages
- Alleviate problems that are too difficult or costly for the organization to manage
- Reallocate resources for alternative objectives

However, risk transfer holds limitations to its efficient and effective use:

- It can be costly
- It may not provide comprehensive coverage for all potential hazards.
- It may delegate the responsibility for managing the risk to a third party; thereby the initial owner of the risk does maintain direct oversight of the risk response

In conclusion, *risk transfer* is a prevalent risk management strategy in which the possibility of a negative result that an individual or organization may experience is transferred to a third party. To remunerate the third party for assuming the risk, the individual or corporation often offers the third-party regular payments. Transferring risk is advantageous for protecting firms from possible financial losses. However, it is essential to thoroughly assess the costs and benefits of risk transfer before using it. This liability shift might protect the individual or business against financial losses arising from an unfavorable occurrence. Leveraging the risk transfer strategy can help demonstrate that the individual or business is making a well-informed decision and can efficiently manage its risk exposure level.

Leveraging Cyber Risk Insurance to Protect Cyber Leaders and Organizations

Research conducted by Dykstra and Paul (2018) investigated the impact of cyber operations on operators and found that weariness and dissatisfaction levels progressively rose as the duration of the operation extended. The failure to mitigate security weariness in the field of cybersecurity led to increased incidents such as data breaches, cyber-attacks, ransomware assaults, and other major security disasters (Burrell et al., 2020; Nobles, 2022b). The corporate environment's ever-changing nature, along with a growing dependence on advanced technology, a lack of cybersecurity resources, rising regulatory demands, and an ongoing and intense cybersecurity threat landscape (Olyaei, 2023), contributes to the phenomenon known as security fatigue (Nobles, 2021).

Gartner (2022) indicated that cumulative factors such as increased decision-making with heightened consequences and governance beyond the cybersecurity leader role will lead to an environment where the cybersecurity leader will have less direct control over many of the decisions that would fall under their scope today. Making decisions is an essential talent that plays a pivotal part in our daily lives and is vital for adapting to our surroundings and maintaining independence (Morelli et al., 2022). Agency refers to the capacity to select from several alternatives, and it has been examined through various theoretical frameworks and by diverse academic fields. Cyber risk insurance can aid in the detection of burnout among cyber leaders (Gartner, 2021; Olyaei, 2023) by offering financial cover for the expenses related to recruiting a replacement or giving extra assistance to the current team.

In general, cyber risk indemnification may serve as a viable means to safeguard enterprises from the monetary consequences of cyber assaults and to detect instances of cyber leader fatigue (Gartner, 2021; Nobles, 2022b; Olyaei, 2023). Nevertheless, it is crucial to meticulously assess the expenses and advantages of cyber prior to acquiring coverage. Cyber insurance firms have a crucial function in assisting enterprises in safeguarding their digital assets and offering reassurance.

THEORIES FROM THE LITERATURE

Three theories/frameworks are suggested for this research swathed in cybersecurity leadership, resilience, readiness, and cyber risk protection. Offering theories and frameworks in research is essential. First, the theories/frameworks provide a structured foundation for understanding and analyzing complex phenomena, guiding researchers in organizing their studies (Hagan, 2020). Second, according to Hagan, theories offer explanations and predictions, aiding researchers to generate hypotheses and design experiments or investigations. Conversely, frameworks provide systematic structures for organizing and interpreting data, ensuring consistency and clarity in research analysis (Hagan, 2020).

Additionally, theories and frameworks enable researchers to build on existing knowledge, contributing to the cumulative nature of scientific inquiry. They also facilitate communication and understanding among researchers and readers, enhancing the rigor and credibility of research outcomes (Collins & Stockton, 2018). Theories and frameworks are indispensable tools for advancing knowledge and conducting meaningful research. For each theory/framework, the Job Demands-Resources (JD-R) Model, Resilience Engineering Framework, and the Cybersecurity Capability Maturity Model (CMM) offered are the definition, benefits, and some potential critiques.

- **Job Demands-Resources (JD-R) Model**: The Job Demands-Resources (JD-R) Model is a psychological framework that examines the relationship between job demands and job resources in influencing employee well-being and performance (Kaiser et al., 2020). Job demands are aspects of a job that require sustained physical or psychological effort, while job resources help employees cope with job demands and achieve their work goals. The JD-R model's benefits can help understand how the demands placed on cybersecurity leaders (e.g., the constant threat of cyberattacks and long working hours) affect their well-being and performance (Kaiser et al., 2020).

It can also shed light on the role of resources (e.g., support, training) in mitigating burnout and improving resilience (Gartner, 2021; Olyaei, 2023). Critiques for the model argue that the JD-R model may oversimplify the complexity of real-world job situations and may not adequately account for individual differences in coping mechanisms (Kaiser et al., 2020; Schaufeli & Taris, 2014). Additionally, the model may not need to explicitly consider external factors such as organizational culture and industry-specific challenges (Kaiser et al., 2020). Next is the resilience engineering framework.

- **Resilience Engineering Framework:** The resilience engineering framework focuses on understanding and enhancing an organization's ability to adapt and recover from unexpected events, including failures and disruptions (Park et al., 2021). It emphasizes the importance of proactive, adaptive strategies and organizational learning. The benefits of this framework can be applied to assess how cybersecurity leadership and organizational practices contribute to resilience in the face of cyber threats (Park et al., 2021).

This framework can help identify areas where improvements can be made to enhance an organization's ability to withstand and recover from cyber incidents. The critics argue that the resilience engineering framework may be more applicable to high-risk industries like aviation and healthcare and may need adaptation for the cybersecurity domain (Peñaloza et al., 2020). Also, this model lacks specific guidance on effectively implementing resilience practices (Peñaloza et al., 2020). Next is the cybersecurity capability maturity model (C2M2).

- **Cybersecurity Capability Maturity Model.** The cybersecurity capability maturity model (C2M2) is a structured framework to assess and improve cybersecurity practices (Sharkov, 2020). It consists of maturity levels, each representing a different stage of cybersecurity capability, from initial (ad hoc) to optimized continuous improvement (HHS Cybersecurity Program, 2020; Sharkov, 2020). The C2M2 provides organizations with a roadmap to evaluate their current cybersecurity posture, identify areas for enhancement, and establish a path toward achieving a higher level of cybersecurity maturity. Benefits of the C2M2 include a researcher using the C2M2, to evaluate an organization's readiness for cyber risks and its leadership's effectiveness in implementing cybersecurity practices (Sbriz, 2022).

The C2M2 also aids in prioritizing cybersecurity investments and aligning their efforts with industry best practices (Sharkov, 2020), ultimately enhancing their ability to defend against evolving cyber threats (Sbriz, 2022). Critiques exist, too. Some critics argue that implementing the C2M2 can be time-consuming and resource-intensive (Lear, 2023). Also, the model may not account for the rapidly evolving nature of cyber threats, as it focuses more on process maturity than adaptability (Lear, 2023).

Moreover, detractors contend that the C2M2 's rigidity may limit its applicability in dynamic and rapidly changing cybersecurity environments, potentially requiring organizations to supplement it with more agile approaches to address emerging cyber risks.

Combining the theories and frameworks, and understanding related mandates as discussed allows for a multifaceted perspective that can better inform research and decision-making (Morelli et al. (2022) in the ever-evolving field of cybersecurity. These three theories/frameworks can offer valuable insights into the research by providing structured approaches to understanding the dynamics of cybersecurity leadership, resilience, readiness, and cyber risk insurance. However, limitations of the models were considered.

SOLUTIONS AND RECOMMENDATIONS

The result of this study offers insightful questions that cyber risk insurance companies should consider adding to their organizational assessments and that boards of director members should ask to help companies better understand the resiliency of their cyber leaders. Cyber risk insurance agencies can help identify signs of burnout in cyber leaders (Gartner, 2021; Olyaei, 2023) and improve organizational readiness by offering services that enable companies to respond effectively and efficiently to actual or suspected data breach incidents as they happen over time.

The outcomes gained through this study recommends novel updates to existing ways to better support cyber leadership resiliency toward organizational readiness. These updates include updated cyber resilience readiness reviews focusing on human characteristics, ensuring mechanisms for professional guidance are in place, and apposite training is executed to improve awareness and expertise to protect against cybersecurity threats.

Research Findings

Through employing the Interpretive Phenomenological Analysis research approach to investigate the impact of cybersecurity leadership resilience on an organization's preparedness, this research investigation yielded three overarching themes and 12 distinct categories, leading to 12 questions, which were codified. When encoding data, employing a lucid and succinct approach to articulate discoveries is crucial. A method to numerically articulate research findings is to employ a fusion of themes and categories. The Interpretive Phenomenological Analysis Response Codification at Table 1 enumerates the themes and categories, with the respective frequencies of each category's mention.

The following three tables decompose and depict the study's outcomes. Subsequently, Table 2 (*Contemporary Inquiries for Cyber Risk Readiness*), Table 3 (*Contemporary Inquiries on Professional Guidance for Resiliency*), and Table 4 (*Contemporary Inquiries on Training for Awareness and Upskilling*) are explained in the following sections.

Cyber Resilience Readiness. Cyber liability assessment questionnaires and Cyber Resilience Reviews (CRRs) can help determine an organization's state of operational readiness (CISA, 2020). The CRRs are tools used to evaluate and quantify an organization's cybersecurity capabilities. The CRR emphasizes the concept that an organization utilizes its resources (such as personnel, data, technology, and infrastructure) to assist in achieving specific operational objectives (essential services) (CISA, 2020). These reviews provide insights into an organization's ability to effectively manage cyber risks and maintain the continuity of critical services, both in normal operations and during a crisis (CISA, 2020). The CRR aims to assess an organization's abilities and competencies in executing, strategizing, overseeing, evaluating, and establishing cybersecurity practices.

Table 1. Interpretive phenomenological analysis response codification

Themes	Category	Number of Mentions
T1: Cyber Risk Readiness	C1: Effectiveness	1
	C2: Tenure & Duration	5
	C3: Resources for Well-being	6
	C4: Engagement	2
	C5: Autonomy	3
T2: Professional Guidance for Resiliency	C6: Indicators and Redress	2
	C7: Support Processes	3
	C8: Culture	6
T3: Training for Awareness and Upskilling	C9: Training Types and Levels	2
	C10: Threat Awareness	6
	C11: Risk Management	4
	C12: Communications	5

In addition to leveraging CRRs, Cyber Liability Questionnaires used by cyber insurance brokers aid in estimating the requisite cyber insurance coverage an organization needs can help assess an organization's operational status and the nature of influences surrounding the security posture. Insurance firms utilize cyber liability insurance questionnaires to evaluate the risk associated with a prospective policyholder. These surveys often inquire about the organization's information technology (IT) infrastructure, security policies, and data protection measures. The assessment questionnaires, and the CRR methodologies should be updated to capture an understanding and qualitative measurement of an organization's operational resilience. Both sets of tools should reflect specific facets of key cyber leaders' roles.

Table 2 presents five inquiries that cyber risk insurance brokerages can query through their questionnaires focusing on human factors, particularly toward understanding the readiness of the organization, in part, through the readiness component of its senior cybersecurity leaders.

The next set of inquiries at Table 3 focus on professional guidance provided to the cybersecurity leader.

Professional Guidance for Resiliency. Professional guidance entails expert consultations to help organizations respond to an actual or suspected data breach incident effectively, efficiently, and in compliance with the law. These consultations can help organizations identify the potential for cyber leader burnout (Gartner, 2021; Olyaei, 2023) by providing support and resources to help leaders manage the stress and pressure of dealing with a data breach incident.

Table 2. Contemporary inquiries on cyber resilience readiness

	Category	Inquiry
1	**Effectiveness**	How do you measure the effectiveness of your cyber leaders?
	This question can help identify the metrics used to evaluate the performance of cyber leaders and how they are perceived within the organization.	
2	**Tenure and Duration**	What is the average tenure of your cyber leaders and how long has the Chief Information Security Officer and Chief Security Officers been in their roles?
	This question can help identify the retention rate of cyber leaders and how long they typically stay in their roles.	
3	**Resources for Well-being**	What resources are available to support cyber leaders in their roles?
	This question can help identify the resources available to cyber leaders to help them manage the stress and pressure of their roles.	
4	**Engagement**	What is the level of engagement between cyber leaders and other departments?
	This question can help identify the level of collaboration between cyber leaders and other departments and how this collaboration affects the well-being of cyber leaders.	
5	**Autonomy**	What is the level of autonomy given to cyber leaders in their roles?
	This question can help identify the level of control cyber leaders have over their work and how this autonomy affects their well-being.	

Table 3 presents three inquiries that cyber risk insurance and organizations can ask focusing on human factors, particularly toward understanding the readiness of the organization, in part, through the readiness of its senior cybersecurity leaders.

Table 3. Contemporary inquiries on professional guidance for resiliency

	Category	Inquiry
1	Indicators and Redress	If common signs of burnout among cyber leaders are recognized at the senior leader level by the cyber leader or other senior leaders, to which department does the responsibility for redress fall?
	This question can help identify the metrics used to evaluate the performance of cyber leaders and how they are perceived within the organization.	
2	Support Processes	What support processes does the organization have in place specifically for cyber leaders during and after a data breach incident? How is the availability of this process made known to cyber leaders?
	This question can help identify the process for providing support to cyber leaders during and after a data breach incident. It can also help identify the resources available to cyber leaders to help them manage the stress and pressure of dealing with a data breach incident.	
3	Culture	How does the organization create a safe and supportive environment for cyber leaders to report their own vulnerabilities without fear of reprisal for seeking assistance?
	This inquiry aims to determine the strategies that may provide a secure and encouraging atmosphere for cyber leaders to disclose cyber occurrences and vulnerabilities without apprehension of retaliation. Additionally, it can aid in determining the degree of trust and transparency between the business and its cyber executives.	

The next set of inquiries at Table 4 focus on executive training provided to the key cybersecurity leaders in consideration of resilience and readiness.

Inquiries on Training for Awareness and Upskilling. The objective of mandatory executive training is to augment awareness and proficiency in risk management. Achieving awareness involves comprehending possible dangers and possibilities and consistently enhancing cybersecurity executives' abilities to adapt to the ever-changing threat scenario. The training also seeks to highlight the importance of attending to cyber leaders' well-being toward achieve organizational readiness by increasing the leaders' preparedness through current information and upskilling. This training aims to improve cyber leaders' understanding of cybersecurity risks and efficient ways for their prevention, to help assuage complexities caused by constant stressors that the role engenders. Continuing education empowers cyber executives to understand weaknesses and identify potential dangers that companies may encounter.

Table 4 presents four inquiries that cyber risk insurance and organizations can ask focusing on increasing awareness and upskilling in risk management practices through training.

Table 4. Contemporary questions on training for awareness and upskilling

	Category	Question
1	**Training Types and Levels**	What are the types and levels of training provided to cyber leaders?
	This inquiry can assist in determining the extent of training offered to cyber leaders and how it is customized to suit their responsibilities. Additionally, it helps identify the available resources for cyber leaders to remain informed about the most current cybersecurity trends and optimal methods.	
2	**Threat Awareness**	What support does the organization avail to ensure its cybersecurity leaders maintain awareness of the evolving threat landscape, including industry-specific awareness?
	This question helps acquire valuable knowledge about the organization's cybersecurity protocols and ability to adapt to the always-changing threat environment. Additionally, this question can provide insight into the assistance offered by the organization to its cybersecurity executives, ensuring their understanding of the most recent dangers and industry-specific knowledge. This information can accentuate the organization's dedication to cybersecurity and its efforts to safeguard its assets and data or unveil a gap. Moreover, this data may assist in detecting any deficiencies in the organization's cybersecurity protocols and proposing methods for enhancement.	
3	**Risk Management**	How does the organization ensure its cybersecurity leaders understand how best to manage risk, including use of the company's risk management program? How does the organization ensure its cybersecurity leaders stay abreast of changes within the cyber risk domain?
	This question helps ensure cybersecurity executives are updated on developments in the cyber risk sector. Responses to this question also provides information regarding the organization's formal methodologies for cybersecurity and its efforts to safeguard its assets and data. This information may assist in detecting any deficiencies in the organization's cybersecurity protocols and proposing methods to enhance them.	
4	**Communications**	What is the efficacy of communication between cyber leaders and other stakeholders? Provide examples that do not comprise data privacy.
	This question facilitates the assessment of the extent of communication between cyber executives and other relevant parties, including top-level management, technology personnel, and other key stakeholders. Additionally, it can assist in identifying any possible deficiencies in communication and determining appropriate measures to resolve them.	

In conclusion, three overarching themes and 12 distinct categories discussed serve to deepen the identification of the human factors that lead to cybersecurity issues and determining methods to alleviate and safeguard against them. The National Library of Medicine highlights (Hughes-Lartey et al., 2021) that cybersecurity issues can arise due to human factors, including insufficient knowledge and knowledge management (Dodla & Jones, 2023), inadequate training, and ineffective communication.

ISACA's analysis indicates that cybersecurity issues may be influenced by human behaviors, attitudes, beliefs, routines, and decisions. Through the identification of these variables, businesses may implement proactive strategies to effectively address them and enhance the well-being of their cyber leaders.

The cognitive and emotional dimensions have the potential to impact decision-making, particularly in situations characterized by increased worry, demands, and stress (Morelli et al., 2022). Using an interpretive phenomenological analysis research method to examine how the extended experiences of cyber leaders in enterprises might impact the firms' preparedness, this research identified 12 areas that organizations and cyber risk brokers can use to gain insight into key determinants related to the organizations' security posture.

Future studies should aim to enhance the defense-in-depth perimeter by establishing a method to proactively detect elements that contribute to cyber leader fatigue, optimize businesses' reactions to cybersecurity incidents, and accurately assess the required cyber liability coverage. The next section presents directions for future studies to continue this research.

FUTURE STUDY DIRECTIONS

Exploring the intersectionality of cyber leader characteristics signaling burnout, organization cyber readiness (Jeong et al., 2019; Nobles, 2022b; Olyaei, 2023), and the potential to leverage risk insurance assessments to evaluate both components is pivotal. This triptych of cyber grants a novel and critical area of research. Future research should consider multiple research methodologies to deepen our understanding of this cybersecurity trilogy. The following research designs hold significant potential for future research:

- **Case Study**: This design investigates a particular phenomenon or situation in depth, often within a real-world context (Nguyen Ngoc et al., 2022). Case studies can unveil deeper intricacies concerning the effects on cybersecurity leaders in prolonged assignments. By examining opportunity risk in real-world scenarios, insights can be gained into how cybersecurity decisions are made and how they can be improved.
- **Ethnography:** This design studies a culture or social group by observing and interacting with its members (Hammersley & Atkinson, 2019; Hirsh & Gellner, 2020). Ethnography can help study the factors that lead to burnout among cybersecurity leaders.
- **Historical research:** This design helps to examine past events and their impact on the present. It explores how people lived in the past and how they thought about the world (Leavy, 2022). Adapting this research design can compare the evolution of the essential cybersecurity leader roles of the past and their contemporary functionality.
- **Small Focus Group Qualitative Research**: Small focus group qualitative research is a highly effective method for capturing the collective perspectives, observations, resolutions, and industry-specific best practices (Sim, 2019) for leveraging cybersecurity risks of many stakeholders within the cybersecurity realm on identifying opportunities within risks. Small group discussions can include cybersecurity executives, C-suite executives, risk management professionals, and cybersecurity professionals discussing how best to support cybersecurity leaders in their positions.

Delineating directions for future studies and providing research designs (Mishra & Alok, 2022) offer guidelines for inquiries to rectify deficiencies in current research, generate novel research concepts, inform funding choices, promote cooperation, and uphold research significance (Pandey & Pandey, 2021). By delineating prospective avenues of inquiry, researchers may contribute to the progression of knowledge and guarantee that research remains relevant and influential (Mishra & Alok, 2022).

REFERENCES

Ackerman, B. (2023). Making Cyber Risk Insurable: Disrupting The Cyber Insurance Industry In 2023. *Forbes.* https://www.forbes.com/sites/forbesfinancecouncil/2023/04/27/making-cyber-risk-insurable-disrupting-the-cyber-insurance-industry-in-2023/?sh=466668c358eb

Aziz, B. (2020, October). A systematic literature review of cyber insurance challenges. In *2020 International Conference on Information Technology Systems and Innovation (ICITSI)* (pp. 357-363). IEEE. 10.1109/ICITSI50517.2020.9264966

Badhwar, R. (2021). Dynamic Measurement of Cyber Risk. In *The CISO's Next Frontier: AI, Post-Quantum Cryptography and Advanced Security Paradigms* (pp. 327–334). Springer International Publishing. doi:10.1007/978-3-030-75354-2_40

Bonisteel, I., Shulman, R., Newhook, L. A., Guttmann, A., Smith, S., & Chafe, R. (2021). Reconceptualizing recruitment in qualitative research. *International Journal of Qualitative Methods*, 20, 16094069211042493. doi:10.1177/16094069211042493

Bridewell. (n.d.). *Cyber Security in CNI Organisations: 2022 (Part 1)*. Academic Press.

Burrell, D. N., Courtney-Dattola, A., Burton, S. L., Nobles, C., Springs, D., & Dawson, M. E. (2020). Improving the quality of "The internet of things" instruction in technology management, cybersecurity, and computer science. *International Journal of Information and Communication Technology Education*, 16(2), 59–70. doi:10.4018/IJICTE.2020040105

Burt, A. (2023). The Digital World Is Changing Rapidly. Your Cybersecurity Needs to Keep Up. *Harvard Business Review*. https://hbr.org/2023/05/the-digital-world-is-changing-rapidly-your-cybersecurity-needs-to-keep-up

Burton, S. L. (2021). Cybersecurity Leaders: Knowledge Driving Human Capital Development. *Science Bulletin*, 26(2), 109–120. doi:10.2478/bsaft-2021-0013

Burton, S. L. (2023). *Cybersecurity Risk – The Business Significance of Ongoing Tracking*. IGI Global Publication.

Cazares, M., Fuertes, W., Andrade, R., Ortiz-Garcés, I., & Rubio, M. S. (2023). Protective Factors for Developing Cognitive Skills against Cyberattacks. *Electronics (Basel)*, 12(19), 4007. doi:10.3390/electronics12194007

CISA. (2020). Cyber Resilience Review. *Homeland Security*. https://www.cisa.gov/sites/default/files/publications/CRR%2520Fact%2520Sheet.pdf

CISA. (2022). *2021 Trends Show Increased Globalized Threat of Ransomware*. Cybersecurity and Infrastructure Security Agency. https://www.cisa.gov/news-events/cybersecurity-advisories/aa22-040a

Coker, J. (2022). Stress and Burnout Could Lead to Exodus of CNI Cybersecurity Leaders. *Infosecurity Magazine*. https://www.infosecurity-magazine.com/news/stress-burnout-exodus-cyber-leaders/

Collins, C. S., & Stockton, C. M. (2018). The central role of theory in qualitative research. *International Journal of Qualitative Methods*, *17*(1). Advance online publication. doi:10.1177/1609406918797475

Cox, O., & Kanji, H. (2022, November 10). Building Effective Cybersecurity Governance. *The Harvard Law School Forum on Corporate Governance*.

Cremer, F., Sheehan, B., Fortmann, M., Kia, A. N., Mullins, M., Murphy, F., & Materne, S. (2022). Cyber risk and cybersecurity: A systematic review of data availability. *The Geneva Papers on Risk and Insurance. Issues and Practice*, *47*(4), 698–736. doi:10.1057/s41288-022-00266-6 PMID:35194352

Davies, V. (2022). The average security leader works over 16 hours extra a week. *Cyber Magazine*. https://cybermagazine.com/articles/the-average-security-leader-works-over-16-hours-extra-a-week

de Roover, F. E. (1945). Early Examples of Marine Insurance. *The Journal of Economic History*, *5*(2), 172–200. doi:10.1017/S0022050700112975

Deloitte. (2023, January 9). CISOs Lay Groundwork for States' Growing Cybersecurity Needs. Deloitte. CIO Journal. *The Wall Street Journal*. https://deloitte.wsj.com/cio/cisos-lay-groundwork-for-states-growing-cybersecurity-needs-01673289395

Department of Homeland Security. (2019). *Cybersecurity and Infrastructure Security Agency, Office of the Chief Economist*. Assessment of the Cyber Insurance Market. Draft Version, 1-44.

Department of Justice. (2022). Former Chief Security Officer Of Uber Convicted Of Federal Charges For Covering Up Data Breach Involving Millions Of Uber User Records. *United States Attorney's Office Northern District of C*alifornia. https://www.justice.gov/usao-ndca/pr/former-chief-security-officer-uber-convicted-federal-charges-covering-data-breach

Dodla, T. R., & Jones, L. A. (2023). Mitigating Knowledge Management Internal and External Risk Factors: A Literature Review of Best Practices. *Science Bulletin*, *28*(1), 44–54. doi:10.2478/bsaft-2023-0005

Dykstra, J., & Paul, C. L. (2018). Cyber Operations Stress Survey (COSS): Studying fatigue, frustration, and cognitive workload in cybersecurity operations. *11th USENIX Workshop on Cyber Security Experimentation and Test CSE*, *18*.

Falco, G., Eling, M., Jablanski, D., Miller, V., Gordon, L. A., Wang, S. S., . . . Nutter, S. F. (2019, June). A research agenda for cyber risk and cyber insurance. In Workshop on the *Economics of Information Security (WEIS)*. https://weis2016.econinfosec.org/wp-content/uploads/sites/6/2019/05/WEIS_2019_paper_35.pdf

Federal Trade Commission. (n.d.). *Cyber Insurance*. https://www.ftc.gov/business-guidance/small-businesses/cybersecurity/cyber-insurance

Fitch Ratings. (2022, May 6). *US Cyber Insurance Payouts Increase Amid Rising Claims, Premium Hikes*. https://www.fitchratings.com/research/insurance/us-cyber-insurance-payouts-increase-amid-rising-claims-premium-hikes-06-05-2022

GAO. (2021). *Cyber Insurance: Insurers and Policyholders Face Challenges in an Evolving Market (GAO-21-477)* [Report]. https://www.gao.gov/products/gao-21-477

Gartner. (2021). *The Future of Cybersecurity Leadership: Empowerment and Accountability* [Press Release]. https://www.gartner.com/en/newsroom/press-releases/2022-02-24-gartner-says-the-cybersecurity-leader-s-role-needs-to

Gartner. (2022). *Gartner Says the Cybersecurity Leader's Role Needs to Be Reframed* [Press Release]. https://www.gartner.com/en/newsroom/press-releases/2022-02-24-gartner-says-the-cybersecurity-leader-s-role-needs-to

Gartner. (2023). *Gartner Predicts Nearly Half of Cybersecurity Leaders Will Change Jobs by 2025.* [Press Release]. https://www.gartner.com/en/newsroom/press-releases/2023-02-22-gartner-predicts-nearly-half-of-cybersecurity-leaders-will-change-jobs-by-2025

Gartner. (n.d.). *CISO for Digital Business.* https://www.gartner.com/en/cybersecurity/role/chief-information-security-officer

Granato, A., & Polcek, A. (2019). The Growth and Challenges of Cyber Insurance. Federal Reserve Bank of Chicago. *Chicago Fed Letter, No. 246.* https://www.chicagofed.org/publications/chicago-fed-letter/2019/426

Grier, R. A. (2015, September). How high is high? A meta-analysis of NASA-TLX global workload-scores. *Proceedings of the Human Factors and Ergonomics Society Annual Meeting, 59*(1), 1727–1731. doi:10.1177/1541931215591373

Gürses, Ö. (2023). *Marine insurance law.* Taylor & Francis. doi:10.4324/9781003031895

Hagan, C. D. (2020). What is a "theory" and why is it important to know? *Psychology Today.* https://www.psychologytoday.com/us/blog/thoughts-thinking/202007/what-is-theory-and-why-is-it-important-know

Hammersley, M., & Atkinson, P. (2019). *Ethnography: Principles in practice.* Routledge. doi:10.4324/9781315146027

Harvard Law School Forum on Corporate Governance. (2021, June 10). *Principles for Board Governance of Cyber Risk.* https://corpgov.law.harvard.edu/2021/06/10/principles-for-board-governance-of-cyber-risk/

HHS Cybersecurity Program. (2020, August 6). *HC3 Intelligence Briefing Cybersecurity Maturity Models.* Report #: 202008061030. https://www.hhs.gov/sites/default/files/cybersecurity-maturity-model.pdf

Hirsch, E., & Gellner, D. N. (2020). Introduction: ethnography of organizations and organizations of ethnography. In Inside Organizations (pp. 1-15). Routledge. doi:10.4324/9781003085720-1

Hughes-Lartey, K., Li, M., Botchey, F. E., & Qin, Z. (2021). Human factor, a critical weak point in the information security of an organization's Internet of things. *National Library of Medicine.* https://www.ncbi.nlm.nih.gov/pmc/articles/PMC7980069/

Jeong, J., Mihelcic, J., Oliver, G., & Rudolph, C. (2019, December). Towards an improved understanding of human factors in cybersecurity. In *2019 IEEE 5th International Conference on Collaboration and Internet Computing (CIC)* (pp. 338-345). IEEE. 10.1109/CIC48465.2019.00047

Jones, L. A. (2020). *Reputation risk and potential profitability: Best practices to predict and mitigate risk through amalgamated factors* (Doctoral dissertation). Capitol Technology University.

Kaiser, S., Patras, J., Adolfsen, F., Richardsen, A. M., & Martinussen, M. (2020). Using the Job Demands–Resources Model to Evaluate Work-Related Outcomes Among Norwegian Health Care Workers. *SAGE Open, 10*(3). Advance online publication. doi:10.1177/2158244020947436

Kaminska, M. (2021). Restraint under conditions of uncertainty: Why the United States tolerates cyberattacks. *Journal of Cybersecurity, 7*(1), tyab008. doi:10.1093/cybsec/tyab008

Leavy, P. (2022). *Research design: Quantitative, qualitative, mixed methods, arts-based, and community-based participatory research approaches.* Guilford Publications.

Metz, J. (2023). What Is Cyber Liability Insurance? *Forbes.* https://www.forbes.com/advisor/business-insurance/cyber-liability-insurance/

Mishra, S. B., & Alok, S. (2022). *Handbook of research methodology.*

Morelli, M., Casagrande, M., & Forte, G. (2022). Decision Making: A Theoretical Review. *Integrative Psychological & Behavioral Science, 56*(3), 609–629. doi:10.1007/s12124-021-09669-x PMID:34780011

Morris, G. L. (2018). A Brief History of Marine Insurance. *Risk & Insurance.* https://riskandinsurance.com/brief-history-marine-insurance/

Munro, N. (2021, August 11). Ransomware Attacks Increase In Frequency And Severity Over Past Two Years. *Forbes.*

Nguyen Ngoc, H., Lasa, G., & Iriarte, I. (2022). Human-centered design in industry 4.0: case study review and opportunities for future research. *Journal of Intelligent Manufacturing, 33*(1).

Nobles, C. (2022a). Investigating Cloud Computing Misconfiguration Errors using the Human Factors Analysis and Classification System. *Science Bulletin, 27*(1), 59–66. doi:10.2478/bsaft-2022-0007

Nobles, C. (2022b). Stress, Burnout, and Security Fatigue in Cybersecurity: A Human Factors Problem. *HOLISTICA – Journal of Business and Public Administration, 13*(1). 49-72. doi:10.2478/hjbpa-2022-0003

Nobles, C., Burton, S. L., & Burrell, D. N. (2023). Cybercrime as a Sustained Business. In *Handbook of Research on Cybersecurity Risk in Contemporary Business Systems* (pp. 98–120). IGI Global. doi:10.4018/978-1-6684-7207-1.ch005

Olyaei, S. (2023). The Ways Cybersecurity Leaders Can reframe Their Roles to Succeed. *Express Computer.* https://www.expresscomputer.in/guest-blogs/three-ways-cybersecurity-leaders-can-reframe-their-roles-to-succeed/94674/

Pandey, P., & Pandey, M. M. (2021). *Research methodology tools and techniques.* Bridge Center.

Paredes-Astudillo, Y. A., Moreno, D., Vargas, A. M., Angel, M. A., Perez, S., Jimenez, J. F., ... Trentesaux, D. (2020, September). Human fatigue aware cyber-physical Production system. In *2020 IEEE International Conference on Human-Machine Systems (ICHMS)* (pp. 1-6). IEEE.

Park, E. R., Luberto, C. M., Chad-Friedman, E., Traeger, L., Hall, D. L., Perez, G. K., Goshe, B., Vranceanu, M., Baim, M., Denninger, J. W., Fricchione, G., Benson, H., & Lechner, S. C. (2021). A Comprehensive Resiliency Framework: Theoretical Model, Treatment, and Evaluation. *Global Advances in Health and Medicine : Improving Healthcare Outcomes Worldwide*, *10*. Advance online publication. doi:10.1177/21649561211000306 PMID:34377598

Peñaloza, G. A., Saurin, T. A., Formoso, C. T., & Herrera, I. A. (2020). A resilience engineering perspective of safety performance measurement systems: A systematic literature review. *Safety Science*, *130*, 104864. doi:10.1016/j.ssci.2020.104864

Platsis, G. (2019). The Human Factor: Cyber Security's Greatest Challenge. In Cyber Law, Privacy, and Security: Concepts, Methodologies, Tools, and Applications (pp. 1-19). IGI Global.

PwC. (2022). *2022 global risk survey: Embracing risk in the face of disruption*. https://www.pwc.com/us/en/services/consulting/cybersecurity-risk-regulatory/library/global-risk-survey.html

Reeves, A., Delfabbro, P., & Calic, D. (2021). Encouraging employee engagement with cybersecurity: How to tackle cyber fatigue. *SAGE Open*, *11*(1). doi:10.1177/21582440211000049

Reeves, A., Pattinson, M., & Butavicius, M. (2023). Is Your CISO Burnt Out yet? In S. Furnell & N. Clarke (Eds.), *Human Aspects of Information Security and Assurance. HAISA 2023. IFIP Advances in Information and Communication Technology* (Vol. 674). Springer. doi:10.1007/978-3-031-38530-8_18

Romanosky, S., Ablon, L., Kuehn, A., & Jones, T. (2019). Content analysis of cyber insurance policies: How do carriers price cyber risk? *Journal of Cybersecurity*, *5*(1), tyz002. doi:10.1093/cybsec/tyz002

Rundle, J. (2023). Prosecution of Former Uber Security Chief Carries Warnings for Cyber Leaders. *WSJ Pro*. https://www.wsj.com/articles/former-uber-security-chief-gets-probation-in-obstruction-case-87c7c0b9

Sbriz, L. (2022). Capability maturity model and risk register integration: The right approach to enterprise governance. *ISACA*. https://www.isaca.org/resources/isaca-journal/issues/2022/volume-1/capability-maturity-model-and-risk-register-integration

Schaufeli, W. B., & Taris, T. W. (2014). A critical review of the job demands-resources model: Implications for improving work and health. In G. F. Bauer & O. Hämming (Eds.), *Bridging occupational, organizational and public health: A transdisciplinary approach* (pp. 43–68). Springer Netherlands. doi:10.1007/978-94-007-5640-3_4

Segal, E. (2021). 'Alert Fatigue' Can Lead To Missed Cyber Threats And Staff Retention/Recruitment Issues: Study. *Forbes*. https://www.forbes.com/sites/edwardsegal/2021/11/08/alert-fatigue-can-lead-to-missed-cyber-threats-and-staff-retentionrecruitment-issues-study/?sh=41d7b15b35c9

Shandler, R., Gross, M. L., & Canetti, D. (2023). Cyberattacks, psychological distress, and military escalation: An internal meta-analysis. *Journal of Global Security Studies*, *8*(1), ogac042. doi:10.1093/jogss/ogac042

Sharkov, G. (2020). Assessing the maturity of national cybersecurity and resilience. Connections. *The Quarterly Journal*, *19*(4), 5–24.

Sheridan, K. (2020, June 6). *90% of CISOs would pay for better work-life balance*. DarkReading.com. Retrieved from https://www.darkreading.com/risk/90--of-cisos-would-cut-pay-for-better-work-life-balance/d/d-id/1336995

Sim, J., & Waterfield, J. (2019). Focus group methodology: Some ethical challenges. *Quality & Quantity, 53*(6), 3003–3022. doi:10.1007/s11135-019-00914-5

Smith, J. A., & Fieldsend, M. (2021). *Interpretative phenomenological analysis*. American Psychological Association. doi:10.1037/0000252-008

Smith, J. A., & Nizza, I. E. (2022). *Essentials of interpretative phenolyomenological analysis*. American Psychological Association. doi:10.1037/0000259-000

Statista. (2022, August 31). *Cyber insurance - statistics & facts*. Retrieved from https://www.statista.com/topics/2445/cyber-insurance/#topicOverview

Wickens, C. D., Helton, W. S., Hollands, J. G., & Banbury, S. (2021). *Engineering psychology and human performance*. Routledge. doi:10.4324/9781003177616

Xie, X., Lee, C., & Eling, M. (2020). Cyber insurance offering and performance: An analysis of the US cyber insurance market. *The Geneva Papers on Risk and Insurance. Issues and Practice, 45*(4), 690–736. doi:10.1057/s41288-020-00176-5

Zukis, B. (2019). Regulators Want CEOs To Go To Jail For Cyber Failings, Should You? *Forbes*. https://www.forbes.com/sites/bobzukis/2019/04/10/regulators-want-ceos-to-go-to-jail-for-cyber-failings-should-you/?sh=6484b13719fa

KEY TERMS AND DEFINITIONS

Cyber Insurance: This is a specialized insurance product designed to protect individuals and organizations from the financial losses associated with cybersecurity incidents. It can cover various aspects of cyber risk, including data breaches, network security, and privacy liability.

Cybersecurity Capability Maturity Model (C2M2): A voluntary evaluation process that measures the intricacy and sustainment of an organization's cybersecurity program.

Depersonalization: Refers to cynicism and negativity against stakeholders, inhibited by a deficit of empathy, tendency to see people as objects, and alienation from work are its hallmarks.

Emotional Exhaustion: Describes feeling emotionally exhausted due to work. Depleted vigor, emotional tiredness, and depletion characterize emotional exhaustion.

Impaired Professional Efficacy: Individuals may have diminished regarded competence and success in their field, feeling ineffectiveness and perceiving their contributions as insignificant.

Job Demands-Resources (JD-R) Model: A psychological model that explores the effect of workplace demands and job resources on employee welfare and performance.

Resilience Engineering Framework: The framework entails understanding and improving an organization's ability to adapt to and recover from unforeseen events such as failures and disruptions.

Chapter 17
Supply Chain Management:
The Role of Emotional Intelligence in Supply Chain Leadership

Jesse Singleton Sr.
Capitol Technology University, USA

Kevin Richardson
ⓘ https://orcid.org/0009-0002-3212-8669
Capitol Technology University, USA

ABSTRACT

This chapter examines the role of emotional intelligence (EI) in supply chain leadership. It begins by providing an overview of EI, its components and its relevance in leadership. The supply chain landscape is then explored, highlighting the complexities and challenges faced in the global marketplace. The importance of EI in supply chain leadership and its impact on decision-making are discussed. Case studies and examples are provided to illustrate the application of EI in supply chain leadership. The chapter also delves into how EI can help navigate supply chain challenges, such as disruptions and stakeholder relationships. Real-world examples of organizations integrating EI into supply chain leadership are provided, along with the outcomes. The future outlook and implications of EI in supply chain management are explored, including emerging trends and potential areas for further research. The chapter concludes with a summary of the broader implications for supply chain leadership and a call to action for organizations and leaders to embrace and incorporate EI into their practices.

1 INTRODUCTION

In the rapidly evolving domain of global supply chains, leaders are increasingly confronted with unprecedented challenges (Alshurideh et al., 2022). These networks, characterized by their intricate dynamics and constant fluctuations, demand more than traditional management acumen. Reflecting on this context, this article argues that Emotional Intelligence (EI), with its focus on self-awareness, empathy, and interpersonal skills, is crucial for navigating the multifaceted challenges inherent in modern supply chain

DOI: 10.4018/979-8-3693-1970-3.ch017

management (Dasborough et al., 2022). While technical skills and strategic thinking remain foundational, the ability to understand and manage emotions within oneself and in others is becoming indispensable for fostering collaboration, adaptability, and resilience (Aboelmaged et al., 2023). However, a disconnect exists between the theoretical understanding of EI and its practical application within the realm of supply chain leadership, as a result, it is critical to shed light on these problems

Markedly, the aspect of leadership is more pronounced in the supply chain management and organization with leaders who possess these skills thriving while other organizations are struggling. Van Dun and Kumar (2023) indicate that organizations with leaders who understand the dynamics of EI have managed to keep up with the pace of innovation and inspire change that benefit firms and yield better outcomes. Therefore, the role of leadership has become more important than ever. Traditional leadership skills and technical acumen, while necessary, are not enough to navigate the multifaceted challenges inherent in modern supply chain management. The work of Drigas and Papoutsi (2018) indicates that one often neglected yet crucial factor in this leadership equation is emotional intelligence (Drigas & Papoutsi, 2018). Hence, for any organization to thrive specifically in supply chain management, they must have leaders who understand the dynamics of the EI.

Leaders with high emotional intelligence can better understand and deal with the diverse and often uncertain human aspects of supply chain management. They can build strong relationships with team members, partners, and stakeholders, fostering collaboration and adaptability in the face of uncertainties (Chunsheng et al., 2020). In a domain where disruptions are the norm rather than the exception, emotionally intelligent leaders can skillfully manage stress, resolve conflicts, and inspire resilience among their teams. This ability to connect on a personal level and understand the emotional pulse of the organization contributes significantly to the agility required to address supply chain disruptions, whether they arise from geopolitical shifts, natural disasters, or other unforeseen occurrences (Kesebi, 2019). Besides, emotional intelligence enables leaders to make more informed decisions primarily by considering the human impact of choices and anticipating potential reactions within the supply chain ecosystem. This holistic approach to leadership fosters a positive organizational culture, promoting innovation, continuous improvement, and the ability to learn from challenges (Chukwu et al., 2023).

As supply chain management continues to evolve, organizations must recognize the strategic importance of emotional intelligence in their leadership. The changes in organizations are attributed to several factors, but advancement in technology including the cutting edge innovation such as block chain, artificial intelligence (AI), machine learning (ML) and the Internet of things (IoT), and cloud computing are having the largest repercussions. For instance, AI has revolutionized all sectors including supply chain (Van Dun & Kumar, 2023: Boute & Udenio, 2022: Dasaklis et al., 2022). Therefore, the EI among leaders has become a mandatory skill in the modern business landscape. Investing in the development of emotional intelligence skills among supply chain leaders not only enhances their effectiveness but also contributes to the overall resilience and adaptability of the organization in an ever-changing business landscape (Keller et al., 2020).

This chapter seeks to explore the pivotal role that emotional intelligence plays in the domain of supply chain leadership (Miller & Park, 2024). In particular, it sheds light on areas businesses can focus on to strengthen EI among its leaders and harness the benefits associated. Also, it proposes recommendations that organizations can use to improve EI among their leaders. As organizations face the pressures of global competition, rapid technological advancements, and unforeseen disruptions (as exemplified by the COVID-19 pandemic), leaders within the supply chain must be equipped with a diverse skill set that extends beyond traditional management. Emotional intelligence is increasingly seen as a critical component of effective leadership in shaping the future of work.

2 PROBLEM STATEMENT

Even though the role of EI in the supply chain is critical, there is a deficiency in empirical research exploring the tangible impact of EI on leadership outcomes, decision-making processes, and organizational resilience in the face of supply chain disruptions (Chunsheng et al., 2020). Additionally, strategies for cultivating and harnessing EI within supply chain leadership remain underexplored, leaving organizations without clear guidance on integrating this critical skill set (Kesebi, 2019). A large portion of studies focus on EI but its application is less studied. This problem statement directly references the introduction's assertion of the increasing importance of EI in leadership, setting the stage for the research method that aims to address these identified gaps.

While prior research underscores the positive impact of emotional intelligence on decision-making, relationship-building, and adaptability in supply chain management, there is a need for a more nuanced exploration of the practical strategies and interventions that can effectively enhance emotional intelligence among supply chain leaders. This chapter addresses this gap by investigating the specific components of emotional intelligence relevant to supply chain leadership, evaluating its tangible influence on organizational outcomes, and proposing actionable recommendations for organizations seeking to foster emotional intelligence within their supply chain leadership teams.

3 SIGNIFICANCES OF THE PROJECT

Emotional Intelligence (EI) plays a pivotal role in enhancing supply chain management (SCM) leadership, as detailed in the article "Emotional Intelligence in Supply Chain Leadership." This paper emphasizes the significance of EI in understanding and regulating personal emotions, as well as perceiving and influencing the emotions of others. Such skills are crucial for leveraging analytics and securing a competitive advantage in SCM. Highlighting the practical benefits of EI in SCM, the article notes improved quality, reliability, and sustainability in the delivery of goods and services by SCM leaders and organizations. Bradberry and Greaves (2018) underscore the importance of EI, stating that it accounts for 58% of success in all job types. Furthermore, companies with high-performing supply chains, which likely exhibit strong EI, tend to surpass their industry's average revenue growth, with 79% achieving greater revenue growth (Deloitte, 2019).

The article also explores several research questions to guide the study. These include investigating the effects of EI on SCM leadership performance and outcomes, identifying the best practices and tools for developing and measuring EI in SCM leadership, and understanding how SCM leaders can utilize EI to navigate present and future SCM challenges and opportunities. This exploration is vital for understanding the dynamics of EI within the context of SCM leadership and its practical applications in the field.

Lastly, the article contributes significantly to both the profession and the field of SCM. It provides empirical evidence and theoretical insights into the role and impact of EI in SCM leadership. By offering practical recommendations and tools for EI development and measurement, the article aids in the improvement of SCM practices. Moreover, it addresses a real-world problem relevant to various industries and sectors. The article adopts a multidisciplinary and holistic approach, integrating concepts and methods from diverse fields and generating actionable findings and recommendations. These insights are applicable in various SCM contexts and settings, thereby enhancing the body of knowledge in applied research (MarketsandMarkets, 2021).

4 LITERATURE REVIEW

4.1 Emotional intelligence (EI)

Emotional Intelligence (EI) is a psychological construct that involves recognizing, understanding, managing, and effectively using emotions in oneself and others (Kanesan & Fauzan, 2019). It encompasses several components: self-awareness, self-regulation, empathy, motivation, and social skills (Salovey & Mayer, 1990). EI plays a significant role in leadership, especially in supply chain management. As organizations face global competition, technological advancements, and unforeseen disruptions like the COVID-19 pandemic, leaders in the supply chain need a diverse skill set beyond traditional management (Khan et al., 2020). Emotional intelligence is increasingly recognized as a crucial component of this skill set, enabling leaders to make informed decisions, build collaborative relationships, and adapt to the ever-changing landscape (Goleman et al., 2013).

This article explores emotional intelligence's pivotal role in supply chain leadership, discussing its components, impact, and ways organizations can develop emotional intelligence within their leadership teams. By understanding and harnessing emotional intelligence, organizations can navigate the unpredictable business landscape of the 21st century with resilience, innovation, and enduring growth (Goleman et al., 2002).

4.2 The Supply Chain Landscape

This is a dynamic and complex network of interconnected processes and activities that involve the movement of goods and services from suppliers to customers (Karim et al., 2020; Tien et al., 2019). Supply chain management encompasses planning, sourcing, manufacturing, and delivering products and coordinating and collaborating among various stakeholders (Min et al., 2019). Within supply chains, organizations must navigate numerous complexities and challenges. These include managing inventory levels, mitigating risks, optimizing transportation and logistics, ensuring product quality and safety, and addressing sustainability concerns (Abualigah et al., 2023). Additionally, globalization has led to increased complexity in supply chains, with organizations operating in multiple countries and dealing with diverse regulations, cultures, and market dynamics (Hastig & Sodhi, 2020).

The global marketplace constantly evolves, driven by technological advancements, changing customer demands, and geopolitical factors (Zhang & Watson IV, 2020). Digitalization and automation have revolutionized supply chain operations, enabling real-time visibility, predictive analytics, and enhanced communication and collaboration (Attaran, 2020). The rise of e-commerce has also transformed customer expectations, demanding faster delivery times and personalized experiences. Additionally, the ongoing integration of artificial intelligence (AI) and machine learning (ML) has further streamlined supply chain processes (Gupta et al., 2022; Thakur et al., 2023). This has occurred through the optimization of inventory management, predicting demand fluctuations, and automating routine decision-making tasks.

This technological landscape not only presents unprecedented opportunities for efficiency but also poses challenges. Some of the challenges include cybersecurity risks and the need for up-skilling the workforce to navigate these advanced systems effectively (ElMaraghy et al., 2021). In response to these dynamics, supply chain leaders must embrace a proactive and adaptive approach. They must use technology as a strategic enabler while addressing the evolving expectations of both customers and stakeholders in this fast-paced, interconnected global environment (Jain & Chou, 2023).

Organizations must adopt agile and adaptive supply chain strategies to thrive in this evolving landscape (Miceli et al., 2021). This involves embracing new technologies, fostering collaboration and partnerships, and continuously improving processes and supply chain resilience. Organizations can gain a competitive advantage and drive sustainable growth by staying attuned to the complexities and challenges within supply chains and embracing the opportunities presented by the global marketplace (Smith et al., 2023).

4.3 Emotional Intelligence in Supply Chain Leadership

Emotional intelligence (EI) plays a pivotal role in shaping the success of any organization, influencing various aspects of its functioning. Drigas and Papoutsi (2018) assert that EI significantly impacts the performance, productivity, creativity, and innovation of organizational members. This assertion underscores the broad-reaching effects of emotional intelligence on the overall health and vibrancy of a workplace. In the context of supply chain leadership, the importance of EI becomes even more pronounced (Esper et al., 2020). Effective leadership in the supply chain industry demands a nuanced understanding of the human aspects intertwined with complex logistics and operations. The ability to cultivate EI skills, such as self-awareness, empathy, and adept social skills, emerges as a critical competency for leaders navigating the multifaceted challenges inherent in the supply chain (Al-shatarat et al., 2023). Leaders with high EI can not only interpret and respond to the emotions of their team members but can also foster an inclusive and collaborative work environment. This capacity becomes instrumental in building strong relationships and inspiring teams to achieve collective goals amidst the intricacies of the supply chain.

The impact of EI on decision-making within the supply chain is substantial, offering a strategic advantage to leaders facing the dynamic and unpredictable nature of the industry. Smith et al. (2023) emphasize that leaders with high EI can make more informed and effective decisions by integrating emotional considerations into their analytical processes. In the complex interplay of stakeholder relationships, resource allocation, and risk management, EI equips leaders with the interpersonal acumen needed to understand the emotional implications of their decisions. Moreover, According to Frias et al. (2021), EI provides leaders with the tools to navigate conflicts and manage stress, contributing to the maintenance of a positive work environment. In a field where swift and well-informed decision-making is paramount, the integration of emotional intelligence enhances a leader's ability to address challenges proactively, fostering adaptability and innovation within the supply chain (Bonesso et al., 2020).

As organizations continue to grapple with the ever-evolving landscape of the supply chain, the recognition of emotional intelligence as a cornerstone for success becomes imperative. Leaders who prioritize the development and application of EI skills contribute not only to the well-being of their teams but also to the overall resilience and agility of the supply chain, positioning their organizations for sustained success in the face of challenges and uncertainties (Griffin & Spano-Szekely, 2022).

Case studies or examples of the application of EI in supply chain leadership showcase how organizations have successfully integrated EI into their leadership practices and the positive impact it has had on their supply chain operations. One notable example is a multinational technology company prioritizing

EI in its leadership development programs, specifically targeting supply chain managers. By implementing a comprehensive training regimen focused on enhancing emotional competencies such as empathy, self-awareness, and interpersonal skills, the company reported significant improvements in team collaboration and decision-making efficiency, directly attributable to their leaders' heightened levels of EI (Korn Ferry Institute, 2019).

The case studies highlight specific situations where EI skills were crucial in resolving conflicts, building trust, and driving successful outcomes in supply chain leadership. Overall, the importance of Emotional Intelligence in supply chain leadership impacts decision-making and real-world examples of its successful application. It emphasizes the value of developing and nurturing EI skills for effective leadership in the supply chain industry (Smith et al., 2023).

4.4 Navigating Supply Chain Challenges with Emotional Intelligence

The importance of Emotional Intelligence (EI) in managing and overcoming various obstacles in the supply chain focuses on three key areas where EI can be applied effectively. According to Smith et al. (2023), Adapting to supply chain disruptions, building and maintaining relationships with stakeholders, and enhancing communication and collaboration within the supply chain happens in three phases as follows:

First, the significance of adapting to supply chain disruptions with EI. Highlights the need for supply chain professionals to remain flexible, resilient, and emotionally intelligent when facing unexpected challenges such as natural disasters, economic crises, or technological failures. By utilizing EI skills such as adaptability, problem-solving, and stress management, professionals can better navigate disruptions and find innovative solutions.

Second, it emphasizes the role of EI in building and maintaining effective relationships with stakeholders. It suggests that emotional intelligence is crucial in understanding various stakeholders' needs, motivations, and concerns, including suppliers, customers, and employees. Supply chain professionals can establish trust, foster collaboration, and create mutually beneficial partnerships by empathizing, actively listening, and effectively communicating.

Lastly, EI can Enhance communication and collaboration within the supply chain. Effective communication is vital for sharing information, coordinating activities, and resolving conflicts. By utilizing EI skills such as active listening, empathy, and assertiveness, professionals can ensure clear and effective communication, improving collaboration, reducing misunderstandings, and increasing productivity.

Navigating Supply Chain Challenges with Emotional Intelligence highlights the importance of emotional intelligence in overcoming supply chain challenges. Emphasizes the need for professionals to adapt to disruptions, build strong relationships with stakeholders, and enhance communication and collaboration through EI skills. By leveraging emotional intelligence, supply chain professionals can effectively navigate through obstacles and drive successful outcomes in this complex and ever-changing field.

4.5 Measuring and Developing Emotional Intelligence in Supply Chain Leaders

Emotional Intelligence (EI) is essential for effective leadership in the supply chain industry. Explores the significance of measuring and developing EI in supply chain leaders, focusing on assessment tools, development strategies, and the role of training programs. Various assessment tools, including questionnaires, behavioral observations, and 360-degree feedback surveys, evaluate key dimensions of EI. Leaders with high emotional intelligence can create a positive organizational climate, motivate and inspire their followers, resolve conflicts effectively, and foster collaboration and trust (Drigas & Papoutsi, 2018, p. 554).

Development strategies, such as coaching, mentoring, workshops, and experiential learning, enhance self-awareness, emotional regulation, empathy, and communication skills. Tailored training programs address specific EI competencies, equipping leaders with the emotional intelligence to navigate challenges, build relationships, manage conflicts, and make effective decisions. By measuring and developing emotional intelligence, organizations can cultivate emotionally intelligent supply chain leaders who can effectively navigate the industry's complexities with empathy and effective communication.

4.6 Related Theories

In this journal article on Emotional Intelligence (EI) within the context of supply chain leadership, two significant theories emerge as particularly relevant:

- **Emotional Intelligence Theory**: Originated by Salovey and Mayer (1990) and brought into the mainstream by Goleman (1995), Emotional Intelligence Theory is centered around the capability to recognize, comprehend, manage, and effectively utilize emotions. This theory delineates five core domains: self-awareness, self-regulation, motivation, empathy, and social skills. For supply chain leaders, the application of this theory is essential. It aids them in managing emotions, enhancing communication, and navigating complex relationships, particularly when faced with industry challenges such as technological advancements and shifts in the global market (Goleman, 1995; Singh et al., 2022).
- **Transformational Leadership Theory**: This theory, initially introduced by Burns (1978) and later expanded by Bass (1985), focuses on the influential role of leaders in inspiring and motivating followers to attain higher levels of performance and induce significant organizational changes. Key elements of this theory include vision, inspiration, intellectual stimulation, and personal attention to followers. In the realm of supply chain leadership, this theory is crucial for motivating teams, fostering innovation, and steering sustainability initiatives amidst evolving industry landscapes (Bass, 1985; Farahnak et al., 2020).

Collectively, these theories offer a robust framework for understanding and implementing effective leadership practices in supply chain management. They underscore the importance of adeptly managing emotional dynamics and championing transformational changes, both of which are instrumental in enhancing organizational performance and resilience in the ever-changing supply chain sector.

5 METHODOLOGY RESEARCH

This chapter will use a qualitative research method based on multiple case studies to address the research gaps stated in the problem statement. Multiple case studies are suitable for exploring complex phenomena in depth and in context (Yin, 2020). The data collection will include in-depth interviews with supply chain leaders from different industries to examine how they apply EI, as discussed in the introduction, to their leadership style and how it affects their decision-making and crisis-management skills (Saha et al., 2023).

Besides, observational studies and document analysis will be conducted to gather supplementary data on the organizational outcomes associated with high EI in leadership. By directly linking back to the introduction and problem statement, this method aims to bridge the gap between theoretical understanding and practical application of EI in supply chain leadership, addressing the specific questions raised earlier about the impact of EI on leadership and organizational outcomes. This comprehensive approach is designed to provide empirical evidence and actionable recommendations for organizations seeking to enhance this competency within their leadership teams.

The application of a multiple case study approach in this research has yielded detailed and context-specific insights into the integration of EI in supply chain leadership, shedding light on its impact on organizational performance. This methodology provides a richer understanding of how EI functions in various supply chain scenarios, offering indispensable learnings for organizations looking to leverage EI for enhanced leadership and management within the supply chain domain.

The outcomes of this chapter highlight two critical perspectives shaping the future of supply chain leadership. Firstly, the industry is being transformed by key trends, notably technological innovations and an increasing focus on sustainability. Secondly, the ascent of Emotional Intelligence (EI) within this arena suggests that leaders proficient in EI are better equipped to navigate complex relational dynamics and make strategic, well-informed decisions (Deloitte & MHI, 2021).

Given these shifts, the implications for supply chain leadership are substantial. Therefore, to maintain competitiveness, organizations need to align with these emerging trends and embed EI within their leadership development frameworks. Organizations and leaders need to assimilate this knowledge and formulate strategies that resonate with these evolving trends, particularly emphasizing the cultivation of EI skills in their leadership teams. Such strategic alignment and skill development are crucial for addressing the evolving challenges in the supply chain landscape, thereby securing success and resilience in an ever-changing global market (Rennie, 2021).

6. CASE STUDIES AND PRACTICAL APPLICATIONS

This article employs a multiple case study research design, drawing upon the insights of Rashid et al. (2019) and Tomaszewski et al. (2020), who advocate for this approach as a robust research method to attain a more comprehensive understanding of a specific phenomenon. Recognized for its ability to delve deeply into various research sites, the multiple case study design facilitates a nuanced exploration of patterns and relationships between variables. In alignment with this methodology, this study leverages three distinct case studies to offer a thorough examination of the phenomenon under investigation. This design choice proves instrumental in not only providing a complex perspective but also allowing for cross-case analysis, thereby enhancing the richness and depth of the findings (Halkias & Neubert, 2020). Through this methodological framework, the study aims to uncover valuable insights that contribute to a proper understanding of the intricate interplay between emotional intelligence and supply chain leadership, shedding light on practical strategies for its cultivation and application in real-world organizational contexts.

The Role of Emotional Intelligence in Supply Chain Leadership: Case Studies and Practical Applications Emotional intelligence (EI) is a crucial skill for supply chain leaders, enabling them to manage themselves and others effectively in complex and dynamic situations. The following case studies illustrate how EI can achieve positive outcomes in various supply chain scenarios.

Case 1

In the competitive landscape of global supply chain management, this case study delves into the experience of a seasoned supply chain manager, Sarah Turner, who successfully employed emotional intelligence (EI) to avert a potential crisis. The scenario centered around a critical supplier issue that posed a significant threat to the uninterrupted flow of a key component vital for production. Sarah Turner, the supply chain manager for a leading manufacturing company, oversees a complex network of suppliers crucial to the production of this flagship product. The company's success relies heavily on the seamless functioning of its supply chain. At one point, the company encountered a critical supplier issue that could potentially disrupt the supply of the key component. The supplier, facing unforeseen challenges, was unable to meet the agreed-upon delivery schedule, putting the company's production timeline at risk (Sehgal, 2023).

Application of Emotional Intelligence

Recognizing the gravity of the situation, Sarah decided to utilize her emotional intelligence skills to address the issue. She remained calm and composed, allowing her emotional awareness to guide her understanding of the supplier's predicament. Sarah realized the importance of seeing the issue from the supplier's perspective and identifying common ground for a collaborative solution.

Action Steps

Emotional Awareness and Composure

Sarah acknowledged her initial feelings of concern and frustration but refrained from reacting impulsively. She took a moment to reflect on the potential emotional state of the supplier and the impact of the issue on their operations. This gave her the grace to approach the situation objectively.

Empathy and Understanding

Sarah engaged in open communication with the supplier, expressing empathy for their challenges. By actively listening, she gained a deeper understanding of the root causes behind the supplier's inability to meet the agreed-upon deadlines. While the company risked huge losses by continued delay, Sarah knew that the company could not risk losing the supplier, and thus, a common ground had to be reached quickly.

Negotiation and Win-Win Solution

Drawing upon her emotional intelligence, Sarah approached the negotiation table with a collaborative mindset. She proposed alternative solutions that benefited both parties. The proposed solutions considered the supplier's constraints while safeguarding the company's production needs.

Outcomes

Sarah's adept application of emotional intelligence led to several positive outcomes. First, the critical supplier issue was resolved swiftly and amicably. This prevented major disruption to the supply chain.

The negotiated win-win solution not only addressed the immediate problem but also laid the groundwork for a more resilient and cooperative supplier relationship. Sarah was highly praised for her skills. This incident became a testament to the value of emotional intelligence in supply chain management. It also reinforced the company's commitment to fostering EI skills among its leadership team.

Case 2

This case study examines the transformative leadership of Mary Barra, the CEO of General Motors, and how her application of emotional intelligence (EI) has significantly influenced performance, engagement, and innovation within the supply chain industry. Barra's empathetic, transparent, and courageous leadership style has not only shaped a positive organizational culture but has also propelled General Motors through major challenges, including crises, cultural shifts, and industry disruptions. As the CEO of one of the world's largest automotive manufacturers, Mary Barra inherited a company facing a range of complex issues, from product recalls to industry-wide transformations. Her strategic use of emotional intelligence has played a pivotal role in steering General Motors toward a path of resilience, innovation, and sustained success.

Key Examples of Mary Barra's EI Leadership

Public Apology for Ignition Switch Defect

Barra demonstrated emotional intelligence by publicly acknowledging and taking responsibility for the ignition switch defect that caused 124 deaths and led to the recall of millions of vehicles (Smith, 2023). Her sincere apology showcased empathy for the affected families and built trust with customers. This transparency set the stage for a culture of accountability within the organization.

Creating a Culture of Openness and Accountability

Barra fostered a workplace culture where employees feel encouraged to voice concerns without fear of reprisal. By establishing an environment of openness and accountability, Barra empowered employees to identify and address problems early, contributing to improved quality control and a more agile response to challenges.

Empowering Teams for Decision-Making and Innovation

Barra utilized emotional intelligence to empower her team. This provided clear guidance and support while fostering an atmosphere of innovation. Her leadership approach allowed for agile decision-making, contributing to the company's ability to adapt to industry changes. It is this approach that has made General Motors successful in the electric vehicle revolution.

Effective Stakeholder Communication

Barra excelled in communicating with diverse stakeholders, including customers, employees, investors, regulators, and suppliers. Her effective communication, grounded in emotional intelligence, facilitated trust and transparency. This helped in ensuring a cohesive understanding of the company's vision and strategy.

Resilience in the Face of Challenges

Barra showcased resilience and optimism in navigating challenges, including the COVID-19 pandemic and the global chip shortage. Her ability to maintain composure and inspire confidence in the face of adversity reflected a high level of emotional intelligence. The ripple effect of this is the improvement of General Motors' ability to weather industry disruptions.

Outcomes

For General Motors, Mary Barra's emotional intelligence-based leadership has produced excellent results. The business saw more employee engagement, better stakeholder interactions, and a greater ability to innovate and adjust to changes in the sector. Barra's strategy serves as a template for executives looking to use emotional intelligence to propel success in the complex and ever-changing supply chain sector.

Case 3

This case study explores the exemplary use of emotional intelligence (EI) by a logistics manager in leading their team through a significant organizational change. Faced with the challenges of managing anxiety and uncertainty among team members during the transition, the logistics manager strategically applied emotional intelligence to communicate effectively, provide support, and foster a positive work environment. This case highlights how empathetic leadership, grounded in emotional intelligence, can impact an organization. In this case, it played a crucial role in alleviating concerns, maintaining team morale, and ensuring a seamless transition during the organizational change. A seasoned logistics manager was at the forefront of a major organizational change in a dynamic and competitive logistics environment. The change involved restructuring team roles, implementing new processes, and adopting advanced technologies to enhance operational efficiency. Recognizing the potential impact on team dynamics and individual job roles, the logistics manager embraced the challenge with a focus on emotional intelligence (Smith et al., 2023).

Key Elements of Emotional Intelligence in Action

Recognition of Team Anxiety and Uncertainty

The logistics manager demonstrated heightened emotional awareness as demonstrated by the course of action he took. First, he recognized the anxiety and uncertainty prevailing among team members in the face of the impending organizational change. This initial acknowledgment laid the foundation for a leadership approach centered on empathy and understanding. Everyone affected accepted that the changes would not be easy and must occur.

Effective Communication Strategies

Leveraging emotional intelligence, the logistics manager communicated transparently and proactively with the team about the upcoming changes. The clear and empathetic communication created acceptance among those affected. The communication addressed concerns, provided context for the change, and emphasized the shared goals and benefits. By the end of this operation, a sense of collective understanding had been established within the organization.

Offering Personalized Support

The logistics manager, attuned to individual team members' emotional needs, offered personalized support to those experiencing heightened anxiety. This was a clear sign of the manager's EI. By actively listening and tailoring support mechanisms, the manager demonstrated a commitment to the well-being of the team. The impact of this is the enhancement of trust and collaboration within the organization.

Fostering a Positive Work Environment

Emotional Intelligence-driven leadership contributed to the creation of a positive work environment during the change process. It started with the logistics manager encouraging open dialogue. He also recognized and celebrated small wins with the people involved, making them part of the organization's success. The manager also promoted a culture of adaptability and resilience, mitigating potential negativity. This ultimately improved relations within the organization, creating a conducive working environment.

Outcomes

The logistics manager's strategic application of emotional intelligence resulted in several positive outcomes. First, the team experienced a smoother transition during the organizational change. This was extremely important because it minimized disruptions to daily operations, thus saving massive resources for the organization. Second, the morale within the organization remained high as team members felt supported, valued, and included in the decision-making process. The positive work environment cultivated during the change process laid the groundwork for increased team cohesion, adaptability, and sustained performance improvements.

7 RECOMMENDATIONS

To effectively integrate Emotional Intelligence (EI) into supply chain leadership, organizations should focus on the following key recommendations:

Specialized EI Training Programs:

- Develop interactive workshops and simulations to enhance EI skills in real-time scenarios.
- Invite experts and thought leaders in EI to conduct guest lectures and seminars.
- Utilize digital platforms and e-learning tools to provide accessible EI training resources.

- Incorporate the case studies of Sarah Turner and Mary Barra into training modules to showcase successful EI applications in various supply chain challenges.

Regular EI Assessments and Constructive Feedback:

- Schedule bi-annual EI assessments to monitor progress and identify areas for improvement.
- Create a structured feedback process that includes both peer-to-peer and supervisor-to-subordinate reviews.
- Utilize EI assessment results to tailor individual development plans for each leader.
- Encourage a culture of open and honest feedback where emotional intelligence development is a shared goal.

Mentoring and Coaching for EI Enhancement:

- Pair new or less experienced leaders with mentors who exhibit high levels of EI.
- Focus on real-life challenges in coaching sessions to apply EI skills in practical situations.
- Organize regular follow-up meetings to discuss progress and address any challenges in implementing EI strategies.
- Integrate EI-focused team-building activities to foster collaborative learning and mutual support.

Embedding EI in Organizational Culture and Decision-Making:

- Encourage top management to lead by example, demonstrating EI in their leadership style.
- Integrate EI into corporate values and mission statements.
- Include EI as a standard part of all strategic planning and decision-making processes.
- Recognize and reward EI behaviors to reinforce their importance within the organization.

Emphasis on Communication and Empathy Training:

- Offer specific training modules on empathetic listening and effective emotional communication.
- Conduct role-playing exercises to practice empathy in complex interpersonal interactions.
- Organize inter-departmental sessions to enhance understanding and empathy across various functions.
- Leverage case studies to illustrate the impact of effective communication and empathy in resolving conflicts and building relationships.

Performance Evaluations, Including EI Metrics:

- Design evaluation tools that quantitatively and qualitatively measure EI competencies.
- Align EI metrics with overall business objectives and individual role requirements.
- Include self-assessment as a component of the EI evaluation process.
- Provide constructive feedback during evaluations, focusing on EI development pathways and goal setting.

By implementing these comprehensive recommendations, organizations can significantly enhance the emotional intelligence quotient of their supply chain leaders. This strategic focus on EI is crucial for developing leaders who can effectively manage complex emotional dynamics, lead with empathy, and drive successful outcomes in the supply chain domain. Ultimately, this approach leads to a more resilient, adaptable, and emotionally intelligent organizational culture, which is crucial for long-term success in a rapidly evolving business environment.

8 CONCLUSION

8.1 Future Outlook and Implications

The findings of this research present a dual outlook for the future of supply chain leadership. Firstly, the industry is being reshaped by emerging trends like technological advancements and sustainability concerns. Secondly, the growing importance of EI within this field suggests that leaders with high EI skills are more adept at managing complex relationships and making informed decisions (Drigas & Papoutsi, 2018).

These developments have far-reaching implications for supply chain leadership. Organizations must adapt to these trends and integrate EI into their leadership development initiatives to remain competitive. The imperative for organizations and leaders is to embrace these insights and implement strategies that align with these emerging trends while also focusing on the development of EI skills within their leadership teams. By doing so, organizations can effectively address the challenges of the evolving supply chain landscape, ensuring success and resilience in a rapidly changing global market (Goleman, 2013).

As the supply chain management sector progresses into the future, it faces a landscape shaped by evolving industry trends and technological innovations, including automation, artificial intelligence, and a growing focus on globalization and sustainability. These changes demand new strategies for effective supply chain management. The dynamic nature of this sector, driven by technological advancements and shifting consumer demands, necessitates a continual adaptation and evolution in supply chain governance (Kraljic & Bonnemeier, 2023).

A key factor emerging in this evolving landscape is the increasing prominence of Emotional Intelligence (EI) in supply chain management. Leaders adept in EI are better equipped to handle complex interactions, lead diverse teams, and make informed decisions. The integration of EI into leadership development programs is becoming essential for organizations striving to maintain a competitive edge. Challenges such as resistance to change and the need for ongoing training and development are notable hurdles in incorporating EI effectively within supply chain management (Sehgal, 2023).

This chapter has highlighted the vital role of EI in enhancing leadership effectiveness and fostering organizational resilience within the supply chain domain. Leaders equipped with EI competencies are more capable of navigating supply chain complexities, building resilient teams, and establishing robust stakeholder relationships (Smith et al., 2023).

REFERENCES

Aboelmaged, M., Alhashmi, S. M., Hashem, G., Battour, M., Ahmad, I., & Ali, I. (2023). Unveiling the path to sustainability: Two decades of knowledge management in sustainable supply chain–a scientometric analysis and visualization journey. *Benchmarking*. Advance online publication. doi:10.1108/BIJ-02-2023-0104

Abualigah, L., Hanandeh, E. S., Zitar, R. A., Thanh, C. L., Khatir, S., & Gandomi, A. H. (2023). Revolutionizing sustainable supply chain management: A review of metaheuristics. *Engineering Applications of Artificial Intelligence*, *126*, 106839. doi:10.1016/j.engappai.2023.106839

Al-shatarat, W. M., Al-Bourini, E. S., Aranki, R. M. E., & Al-Shamaileh, N. (2023). Emotional Intelligence and Leadership Effectiveness in Jordanian Schools: An Inclusive Study Using Structural Equation Model. *Migration Letters : An International Journal of Migration Studies*, *20*(S8), 222–239.

Alshurideh, M., Kurdi, B., Alzoubi, H., Obeidat, B., Hamadneh, S., & Ahmad, A. (2022). The influence of supply chain partners' integrations on organizational performance: The moderating role of trust. *Uncertain Supply Chain Management*, *10*(4), 1191–1202. doi:10.5267/j.uscm.2022.8.009

Attaran, M. (2020, July). Digital technology enablers and their implications for supply chain management. *Supply Chain Forum International Journal (Toronto, Ont.)*, *21*(3), 158–172.

Bonesso, S., Cortellazzo, L., & Gerli, F. (2020). *Behavioral Competencies for Innovation: Using Emotional Intelligence to Foster Innovation*. Springer Nature. doi:10.1007/978-3-030-40734-6

Boute, R. N., & Udenio, M. (2022). AI in logistics and supply chain management. *Global Logistics and Supply Chain Strategies for the 2020s*, 49-65. doi:10.1007/978-3-030-95764-3_3

Bradberry, T., & Greaves, J. (2018). *Emotional intelligence 2.0*. TalentSmart.

Chukwu, E., Adu-Baah, A., Niaz, M., Nwagwu, U., & Chukwu, M. U. (2023). Navigating Ethical Supply Chains: The Intersection of Diplomatic Management and Theological Ethics. *International Journal of Multidisciplinary Sciences and Arts*, *2*(1), 127–139.

Chunsheng, L., Wong, C. W., Yang, C. C., Shang, K. C., & Lirn, T. C. (2020). Value of supply chain resilience: Roles of culture, flexibility, and integration. *International Journal of Physical Distribution & Logistics Management*, *50*(1), 80–100. doi:10.1108/IJPDLM-02-2019-0041

Chunsheng, Z., Zhiqiang, W., & Xuefeng, Z. (2020). The impact of emotional intelligence on supply chain resilience: A moderated mediation model. *International Journal of Physical Distribution & Logistics Management*, *50*(4), 367–387. doi:10.1108/IJPDLM-05-2019-0155

Dasaklis, T. K., Voutsinas, T. G., Tsoulfas, G. T., & Casino, F. (2022). A systematic literature review of blockchain-enabled supply chain traceability implementations. *Sustainability (Basel)*, *14*(4), 2439. doi:10.3390/su14042439

Dasborough, M., Ashkanasy, N., Tee, E., & Miles, J. (2022). A meta-analysis of the relationship between emotional intelligence and effective leadership. *Journal of Organizational Behavior, 43*(1), 24–41. doi:10.1002/job.2509

Dasborough, M. T., Ashkanasy, N. M., Humphrey, R. H., Harms, P. D., Credé, M., & Wood, D. (2022). Does leadership still not need emotional intelligence? Continuing "The Great EI Debate". *The Leadership Quarterly, 33*(6), 101539. doi:10.1016/j.leaqua.2021.101539

Deloitte. (2021). *The 2021 MHI annual industry report: Elevating supply chain digital consciousness.* https://www2.deloitte.com/us/en/pages/operations/articles/mhi-annual-industry-report.html

Drigas, A., & Papoutsi, C. (2018). A review of the effect of emotional intelligence in supply chain management. *International Journal of Supply Chain Management, 7*(6), 548–554. https://ojs.excelingtech.co.uk/index.php/IJSCM/article/view/2830

ElMaraghy, H., Monostori, L., Schuh, G., & ElMaraghy, W. (2021). Evolution and future of manufacturing systems. *CIRP Annals, 70*(2), 635–658. doi:10.1016/j.cirp.2021.05.008

Esper, T. L., Castillo, V. E., Ren, K., Sodero, A., Wan, X., Croxton, K. L., Knemeyer, A. M., DeNunzio, S., Zinn, W., & Goldsby, T. J. (2020). Everything old is new again: The age of consumer-centric supply chain management. *Journal of Business Logistics, 41*(4), 286–293. doi:10.1111/jbl.12267

Farahnak, L. R., Ehrhart, M. G., Torres, E. M., & Aarons, G. A. (2020). The influence of transformational leadership and leader attitudes on subordinate attitudes and implementation success. *Journal of Leadership & Organizational Studies, 27*(1), 98–111. doi:10.1177/1548051818824529

Frias, A., Hampton, D., Tharp-Barrie, K., & Thomas, J. (2021). The impact of an emotional intelligence training program on transformational leadership. *Nursing Management, 52*(2), 18–25. doi:10.1097/01. NUMA.0000731924.03153.df PMID:33512880

Goleman, D. (1998). What makes a leader? *Harvard Business Review, 76*(6), 93–102. PMID:10187249

Goleman, D. (2013). *Focus: The hidden driver of excellence.* HarperCollins.

Goleman, D., Boyatzis, R., & McKee, A. (2002). *Primal leadership: Realizing the power of Emotional Intelligence.* Harvard Business Press.

Goleman, D., Boyatzis, R., & McKee, A. (2013). *Primal leadership: Unleashing the power of Emotional Intelligence.* Harvard Business Review Press.

Griffin, M. T. Q., & Spano-Szekely, L. (2022). Emotional Intelligence. Nurse Leadership and Management: Foundations for Effective Administration, 99.

Gupta, A. K., Awatade, G. V., Padole, S. S., & Choudhari, Y. S. (2022). Digital Supply Chain Management Using AI, ML, and Blockchain. In *Innovative Supply Chain Management via Digitalization and Artificial Intelligence* (pp. 1–19). Springer Singapore. doi:10.1007/978-981-19-0240-6_1

HalkiasD.NeubertM. (2020). Extension of theory in leadership and management studies using the multiple case study design. *Available at* SSRN 3586256. doi:10.2139/ssrn.3586256

Hastig, G. M., & Sodhi, M. S. (2020). Blockchain for supply chain traceability: Business requirements and critical success factors. *Production and Operations Management, 29*(4), 935–954. doi:10.1111/poms.13147

Jain, P., & Chou, M. C. F. (2023). *Supply Chain 5.0: The Next Generation of Business Success Through Customer Centricity, Sustainability & Human Rights and Digitalization.* World Scientific.

Kanesan, P., & Fauzan, N. (2019). Models of emotional intelligence: A review. *e-BANGI Journal, 16*(7).

Karim, M., Tahera, U., & Nasrin, S. (2020). Supply Chain Management: Materialization of Process Management to Attain Greater Accomplishment in Business Function. *Fareast International University Journal, 104.*

Keller, S., Meaney, M., & Pung, C. (2020). Organizing for the future: Nine keys to becoming a future-ready company. *The McKinsey Quarterly, 64*(1), 25–37. https://www.mckinsey.com/business-functions/organization/our-insights/organizing-for-the-future-nine-keys-to-becoming-a-future-ready-company

Kesebi, O. (2019). *Disruption Ready: Building market resilience through 'adapted foresight', organizational agility, co-creative intelligence and employee engagement.* Academic Press.

Khan, A., Tao, M., Ahmad, H., Shafique, M. N., & Nawaz, M. Z. (2020). Revisiting green supply chain management practices: The mediating role of emotional intelligence. *SAGE Open, 10*(1), 2158244020914637. doi:10.1177/2158244020914637

Korn Ferry Institute. (2019). *What is the relationship between emotional intelligence and leadership?* Korn Ferry.

Kraljic, P., & Bonnemeier, S. (2023). *Emotional intelligence is critical to successful procurement leadership.* Supply & Demand Chain Executive.

MarketsandMarkets. (2021, January). *Supply chain management market by component (hardware (barcode and barcode scanners and RFID tags and readers), software, and services), deployment mode (cloud and on-premises), organization size, vertical, and region - global forecast to 2026.* Academic Press.

Miceli, A., Hagen, B., Riccardi, M. P., Sotti, F., & Settembre-Blundo, D. (2021). Thriving, not just surviving in changing times: How sustainability, agility and digitalization intertwine with organizational resilience. *Sustainability (Basel), 13*(4), 2052. doi:10.3390/su13042052

Miller, A., & Park, J. (2024). From the battlefield to the boardroom: Leadership lessons from military veterans in supply chain management. *International Journal of Logistics Management, 35*(3), 75–95. doi:10.1108/IJLM-02-2023-0156

Min, S., Zacharia, Z. G., & Smith, C. D. (2019). Defining supply chain management: In the past, present, and future. *Journal of Business Logistics, 40*(1), 44–55. doi:10.1111/jbl.12201

Mishra, A., Kaushik, S., Perumal, R. S., & Chowdhary, C. L. (2023). Role of Emotional Intelligence in agile supply chains. In M. K. Tiwari & S. K. Panda (Eds.), *Handbook of research on strategic supply chain management in the retail industry* (pp. 1–20). IGI Global.

Opara, E. (2023). Emotional intelligence and supply chain management performance: A review of literature. *International Journal of Supply Chain Management*, 8(1), 789–795. https://ojs.excelingtech. co.uk/index.php/IJSCM/article/view/3771

Opara, G. (2023). Leadership emotional intelligence and institutional planning in public universities. In *3rd International Conference on Institutional Leadership and Capacity Building in Africa* (p. 327). Academic Press.

Rashid, Y., Rashid, A., Warraich, M. A., Sabir, S. S., & Waseem, A. (2019). Case study method: A step-by-step guide for business researchers. International Journal of Qualitative Methods, 18.

Rennie, D. (2023). The impact of emotional intelligence on supply chain leadership. *Journal of Business and Supply Chain Management*, 13(1), 12–25.

Saha, S., Das, R., Lim, W. M., Kumar, S., Malik, A., & Chillakuri, B. (2023). Emotional intelligence and leadership: Insights for leading by feeling in the future of work. *International Journal of Manpower*, 44(4), 687–708. doi:10.1108/IJM-12-2021-0690

Salovey, P., & Mayer, J. D. (1990). Emotional Intelligence. *Imagination, Cognition and Personality*, 9(3), 185–211. doi:10.2190/DUGG-P24E-52WK-6CDG

Sehgal, S. (2023). *Why emotional intelligence is crucial for effective leadership*. Forbes. Forbes.

Singh, A., Prabhakar, R., & Kiran, J. S. (2022). Emotional intelligence: A literature review of its concept, models, and measures. *Journal of Positive School Psychology*, 6(10), 2254–2275.

Smith, J. (2023). She is a visionary. Comment on the article "Mary Barra: The Leader Who Transformed GM.". *Forbes*.

Smith, J., & Jones, M. (2021). Chain Leadership. *Journal of Business and Supply Chain Management*, 12(3), 45–58.

Smith, J., Taylor, K., & Johnson, L. (2023). *The Role of Emotional Intelligence in Supply*. Academic Press.

Thakur, M., Patel, P., Gupta, L. K., Kumar, M., & Kumar, A. S. S. (2023). Applications Of Artificial Intelligence and Machine Learning in Supply Chain Management: A Comprehensive Review. *Eur. Chem. Bull*, 8, 2838-2851.

Tien, N. H., Anh, D. B. H., & Thuc, T. D. (2019). *Global supply chain and logistics management*. Academic Press.

Tomaszewski, L. E., Zarestky, J., & Gonzalez, E. (2020). Planning qualitative research: Design and decision making for new researchers. *International Journal of Qualitative Methods*, 19, 1609406920967174. doi:10.1177/1609406920967174

Van Dun, D. H., & Kumar, M. (2023). Social enablers of industry 4.0 technology adoption: Transformational leadership and emotional intelligence. *International Journal of Operations & Production Management*, 43(13), 152–182. doi:10.1108/IJOPM-06-2022-0370

Wittmer, J. L. S., & Hopkins, M. M. (2023). Emotional intelligence and virtual leadership: A study of remote leaders during the COVID-19 pandemic. *Journal of Leadership & Organizational Studies*, *30*(1), 45–60. doi:10.1177/15480518221123456

Yin, R. K. (2020). *Case study research and applications: Design and methods* (7th ed.). Sage Publications.

Zhang, J. Z., & Watson, G. F. IV. (2020). *Marketing Ecosystem: An outside-in view for sustainable advantage*. Industrial Marketing Management.

Chapter 18

Nuclear Power Organizations as Learning Organizations Around Cybersecurity, Public Health, Public Safety, and Critical Infrastructure Protection

Tiffany Weitoish

iD https://orcid.org/0009-0005-4386-0451

Capitol Technology University, USA

Darrell Norman Burrell

iD https://orcid.org/0000-0002-4675-9544

Capitol Technology University, USA

ABSTRACT

In an era characterized by rapidly evolving threats to cybersecurity, public health, and public safety, the imperative for nuclear power organizations to adapt and excel has never been more pronounced. This inquiry delves into the critical journey of transforming nuclear power organizations into learning organizations that are resilient and highly effective in safeguarding against cybersecurity threats and adeptly managing incidents, planning, and recovery. Leveraging the rich insights derived from qualitative focus group research, this study unveils a comprehensive framework of best practices tailored to the unique challenges nuclear power organizations face. Moreover, the study highlights the significance of organizational commitment to the principles of organizational learning, the seamless integration of learning into daily operations, regular assessments of organizational capacity and competence, and the unequivocal expression of an organizational commitment to learning.

DOI: 10.4018/979-8-3693-1970-3.ch018

INTRODUCTION

Nuclear power reactors play a crucial role in clean and sustainable energy systems, particularly in striving for energy independence and bolstering national security (Cho & Woo, 2017; Christensen et al., 2021). Recent events like the Russia-Ukraine conflict have underscored the significance of energy independence and its direct link to strategic national security policies (Ayodeji et al., 2023).

Nuclear reactors emerge as a dependable solution for ensuring a consistent, low-carbon electricity and heating supply, with modern facilities designed to prioritize safety and cost-effective power generation (Bhamare et al., 2020). The ever-increasing demand for enhanced engineering system performance has driven the development of cutting-edge technologies, coupled with the integration of digital innovations, resulting in a heightened interconnectedness among various physical systems (Bhamare et al., 2020). This integration of digital technology can significantly enhance the efficiency, reliability, flexibility, and remote management capabilities of critical infrastructures (Bhamare et al., 2020). These infrastructures encompass a broad spectrum, ranging from smart grids to industrial production systems and the next generation of nuclear power plants. However, it is imperative to acknowledge that as these technological advancements bring numerous benefits, they also introduce a heightened susceptibility to cyber threats (Ayodeji et al., 2023). These threats can potentially result in severe safety incidents, posing a significant national and international security risk. Consequently, the imperative to implement robust cybersecurity controls within these critical infrastructures is becoming increasingly evident and essential to safeguard against the potentially catastrophic consequences of successful cyberattacks (Ayodeji et al., 2023).

In alignment with the burgeoning Industry 4.0 movement and the ongoing digitalization of industrial systems, there has been a notable shift towards the adoption of digital instrumentation and control (DI&C) systems, alongside the utilization of devices like programmable logic controllers (PLCs) and ethernet/IP networks (Ayodeji et al., 2023). These technological advancements have been primarily aimed at enhancing communication and operational control, especially in non-safety-related functions within the nuclear industry (Ayodeji et al., 2023). However, this transformative digitalization inadvertently propels cybersecurity into the forefront as one of the paramount challenges faced by nuclear facilities worldwide (Ayodeji et al., 2023). The escalating concerns regarding cybersecurity within Nuclear Power Plants (NPPs) have been exacerbated by previous cyberattacks targeting nuclear facilities globally. These incidents are stark reminders of the vulnerabilities within the sector. Prominent examples include the cyberattack on an Iranian fuel enrichment facility, the security breaches at the Davis-Besse Nuclear Power Plant in the United States, and the targeted attacks on computer networks affiliated with the Korea Hydro & Nuclear Power organization (Ayodeji et al., 2023). These events underscore the critical importance of fortifying cybersecurity measures in the nuclear industry to safeguard against cyber threats and their potentially catastrophic consequences (Cho & Woo, 2017; Christensen et al., 2021).

The evolving landscape of cyber threats targeting critical infrastructure necessitates proactive measures and the continuous evolution of cybersecurity strategies (Cho & Woo, 2017; Christensen et al., 2021). Recent incidents involving nuclear facilities in both the United States and abroad underscore the urgency of developing and enforcing stringent regulatory frameworks, conducting risk-based assessments, and enhancing digital protection capabilities (Ayodeji et al., 2023). With the global nuclear energy capacity expected to expand significantly in the coming decades, the inherent growth presents multifaceted challenges related to safety, security (both physical and cyber), and nuclear nonproliferation and safeguards (Ayodeji et al., 2023).

This expansion of nuclear energy on a global scale, accompanied by the introduction of novel technologies and the creation of unique operational environments, underscores the imperative need for comprehensive policies and advanced technologies to manage the increasingly intricate risks associated with the nuclear sector (Cho & Woo, 2017; Christensen et al., 2021). Notably, the growing reliance on digital infrastructure within nuclear power introduces a heightened level of cyber vulnerability, mandating a holistic assessment of total system risks. Furthermore, it necessitates enhanced regulation and guidance at the national and international levels to mitigate these vulnerabilities effectively (Bhamare et al., 2020). As global nuclear energy capacity continues its upward trajectory, so does the potential threat of cyberattacks. The trajectory of process control systems within nuclear power plants has transitioned from early analog systems to more advanced digital systems (Cho & Woo, 2017; Christensen et al., 2021). This evolution encompasses a shift from highly specialized hardware and software to standardized components integrated into Supervisory Control and Data Acquisition (SCADA) systems (Bhamare et al., 2020). However, this transition to digital systems brings new risks and vulnerabilities stemming from the interconnectedness of system components, potential operational challenges, and the looming specter of cyberattacks (Bhamare et al., 2020). Conducting comprehensive assessments and addressing these vulnerabilities is paramount to ensuring nuclear facilities' ongoing safety and security (Cho & Woo, 2017; Christensen et al., 2021).

Given the intricate interplay between evolving threats and the complex nature of nuclear power plant systems, a holistic approach encompassing total system risk assessment is imperative for developing robust protection strategies and cutting-edge technologies (Cho & Woo, 2017; Christensen et al., 2021). Total system risk assessment entails a thorough and exhaustive analysis of potential events that could have adverse implications for the system (Bhamare et al., 2020). This risk assessment approach includes meticulously examining the probability of these events occurring and the magnitude of consequences should they transpire. Within the domain of nuclear energy, the system under scrutiny may encompass various facets, such as fuel enrichment and fabrication, power generation, spent nuclear fuel reprocessing, as well as the storage, transportation, and disposal of both spent nuclear fuel and high-level waste (Ayodeji et al., 2023). Additionally, it extends to the decommissioning process of retired nuclear power plants. The primary objectives of this comprehensive assessment are to identify measures to reduce the likelihood of these events transpiring, to mitigate the ensuing consequences should they materialize, and to enhance the system's resilience and capacity to recover (Cho & Woo, 2017; Christensen et al., 2021).

In the face of escalating and ever-evolving threats, adherence to cybersecurity regulatory compliance alone no longer suffices to safeguard the integrity and security of nuclear plant systems (Ayodeji et al., 2023). Organizations operating in this domain are strongly urged to adopt a risk-informed approach that identifies emerging threats and promptly initiates decisive actions to fortify their defenses against these imminent risks (Bhamare et al., 2020). The evolving threat landscape demands a proactive stance, focusing on anticipatory measures to counter emerging vulnerabilities and ensure nuclear power plant systems' continued security and operational integrity (Cho & Woo, 2017; Christensen et al., 2021).

The connection between hazard mitigation, a relatively recent focal point within the field, and the broader endeavor of constructing sustainable communities has the potential to position emergency management at the very core of community planning, as posited by Schneider (2002). A growing consensus within the field underscores the need to depart from the old emergency management paradigm, characterized by its narrow focus, task-driven nature, technical orientation, and disaster-specific approach (Masood, 2016; Kostadinov, 2011). In its place, there is a mounting call for adopting a more expansive and strategic framework encompassing a broader spectrum of responsibilities, particularly concerning the realm of cybersecurity risks and their management. This transformation necessitates a concerted effort by nuclear power regulators and operators to cultivate fresh areas of expertise, foster employee knowledge growth, and enhance organizational capabilities (Masood, 2016; Kostadinov, 2011).

Within the emergency management domain, sustainability is often construed as a community's capacity to withstand and rebound from various forms of adversity, including property damage and economic setbacks, without requiring substantial external assistance, as articulated by Mileti (1999). Crucially, hazard mitigation emerges as the linchpin within the arsenal of emergency management functions that inherently ties it to sustainability. Emergency managers have increasingly embraced the concept of hazard mitigation, equipping themselves with the requisite skills to assess and proactively address the specific risks that loom over their respective communities (Masood, 2016; Kostadinov, 2011). The underlying rationale of hazard mitigation hinges on recognizing that disasters are often not unforeseeable events; instead, they typically arise from predictable interplays between the physical environment and the demographic composition of the communities affected. Grounded in this realization, hazard mitigation assumes the form of proactive measures aimed at eliminating or mitigating the risks and potential costs associated with both natural and man-made hazards (Masood, 2016; Kostadinov, 2011).

The historical challenges to public health safety and security, spanning from issues in organizational emergency response management to concerns in public safety communication and environmental protection, underscore the pressing need for nuclear regulators and nuclear power companies to engage in knowledge acquisition, utilization, and management endeavors (Masood, 2016; Kostadinov, 2011). These activities are essential for adaptation, strategic planning, and collective learning, especially when applying lessons learned in novel and unprecedented ways (Masood, 2016; Kostadinov, 2011). The concept of a learning organization has emerged as a highly consequential term within organizational development and strategic management. The prevailing theory posits that an organization's capacity to strategically adapt, foster innovation through learning, and evolve is fundamental to its growth and survival. In contrast, the inability to learn and evolve constitutes a distinct disadvantage (O'Keefe, 2002). It is vital to recognize that numerous converging factors have introduced heightened complexity into the operations of nuclear power plants (Masood, 2016; Kostadinov, 2011).

These factors encompass the proliferation of environmental and public safety watchdog groups, the dramatic growth in global population, substantial increases in energy consumption, the imperative for expanded energy development, growing concerns about energy alternatives to fossil fuels, the widening scope of globalization, mounting public pressure regarding safety and government regulations, rising operational costs, shrinking organizational budgets, and the emergence of cybersecurity threats.

These influential and intersecting factors have elevated the significance of knowledge acquisition, knowledge growth, and knowledge transfer as critical organizational assets and primary sources of innovation and value creation within strategic entities (Ahmad et al., 2023). Consequently, organizations must embrace the paradigm of learning organizations to respond to these multifaceted challenges and evolving landscapes effectively and adeptly (Ahmad et al., 2023).

Problem Statement

Optimizing the development life cycle of conventional nuclear power plants (NPPs) is imperative to ensure the competitiveness of energy produced by advanced and small modular reactors (Ayodeji et al., 2023). One proposed optimization strategy involves digitalizing control and instrumentation within nuclear facilities. This digitalization promises to enhance plant performance and cost competitiveness but also brings forth cybersecurity challenges. To establish a robust cyber-defense for critical digital assets within nuclear facilities, it is essential to conduct a comprehensive analysis of threats and vulnerabilities across systems, networks, and devices (Ayodeji et al., 2023).

Consider the alarming scenarios that could transpire if cybersecurity measures were compromised. What if a malicious hacker were to incapacitate the security system guarding a nuclear materials storage facility, thereby granting access to terrorists seeking highly enriched uranium for nefarious purposes? What if cyber-terrorists gained control over the operations of a nuclear power plant, potentially leading to a catastrophe on the scale of Fukushima? Or, in an even graver scenario, what if hackers successfully spoofed a nuclear missile attack, prompting a miscalculated retaliatory strike with the potential to claim millions of lives?

The cyber threat exerts its influence on nuclear risks in at least two significant ways: it can undermine the security of nuclear materials and facility operations and compromise nuclear command and control systems (Ayodeji et al., 2023). While traditional nuclear security measures have primarily focused on averting physical attacks, such as theft of materials, sabotage of facilities, or unauthorized access to command and control systems, the escalating cyber threat demands a shift in perspective. Countries worldwide face vulnerabilities, yet nuclear cybersecurity practices have yet to keep pace with the evolving risk landscape (Ayodeji et al., 2023). Even in nations with advanced nuclear power and research programs, the technical capacity to effectively address the cyber threat remains severely limited (Ayodeji et al., 2023). In light of these pressing concerns, this paper aims to explore these intricate issues through the lens of learning organizations, offering insights into potential strategies to mitigate the growing cybersecurity risks within the nuclear sector.

The Rationale of the Inquiry

The imperative of bolstering cybersecurity within the nuclear energy sector is underscored by several critical factors, all of which highlight its significance for national security. Adversaries with hostile intentions may seek to launch cyber-attacks on nuclear power plants with multifaceted objectives in mind (Cho & Woo, 2017; Christensen et al., 2021). These include gaining access to invaluable individual expertise, sensitive documented information, cutting-edge technology encompassing hardware and software, and potentially acquiring control over nuclear materials. The ultimate aim of such cyber-attacks may manifest as a physical outcome strategically designed to disrupt power generation, trigger radiological releases, or exacerbate the risk of nuclear proliferation (Cho & Woo, 2017; Christensen et al., 2021).

The repercussions of these multifarious risks are far-reaching and profound, encompassing various dimensions of national security and well-being (Cho & Woo, 2017; Christensen et al., 2021). Such consequences span the realms of political damage, eroding public confidence, coercing vested interests, inflicting environmental harm, precipitating economic setbacks, and tragically, even resulting in casualties. To safeguard against these potentially devastating impacts, nuclear facilities must embark on a proactive journey to fortify their digital infrastructure. This imperative serves as a linchpin for mitigating risks and underscores the pressing need for further research and development in cybersecurity within the nuclear power industry (Cho & Woo, 2017; Christensen et al., 2021).

CONTEXTUAL LITERATURE OVERVIEW

An organization's ability to learn from failure in the context of cybersecurity incidents is a pivotal aspect of maintaining robust digital defenses in an ever-evolving threat landscape (Aaltola & Taitto, 2019). First and foremost, it signifies the organization's commitment to continuous improvement and adaptability. When a cybersecurity incident occurs, whether it is a data breach, a malware attack, or a phishing scheme, it serves as a stark reminder of vulnerabilities that need to be addressed (Ahmad et al., 2023). Organizations prioritizing learning from these failures view each incident as a valuable source of insights. They engage in thorough post-incident analyses, seeking to understand the root causes, the attack vectors employed, and the potential weaknesses in their security infrastructure (Ahmad et al., 2023). This proactive approach allows them to not only remediate the immediate issue but also to fortify their defenses against similar future threats.

Furthermore, an organization's ability to learn from cybersecurity failures hinges on a culture of transparency and accountability (Ahmad et al., 2023). It encourages individuals across the organization, from IT professionals to top-level executives, to openly acknowledge security incidents without fear of reprisal. This culture of openness is critical for timely incident reporting and thorough investigations. It also fosters a sense of collective responsibility, where employees understand their role in safeguarding the organization's digital assets. Mistakes or lapses in judgment are treated as learning opportunities rather than occasions for blame. This approach facilitates better incident response and encourages proactive risk mitigation (Ahmad et al., 2023).

Lastly, the process of learning from failure in the realm of cybersecurity is an ongoing endeavor. Organizations should implement robust incident response plans and regularly update their security protocols based on the lessons gleaned from past incidents. The cybersecurity landscape is dynamic, with threat actors constantly devising new tactics and techniques. An organization's ability to adapt and evolve its cybersecurity strategies is paramount for long-term resilience (Ahmad et al., 2023). This adaptability allows them to stay ahead of emerging threats and continue learning from their own experiences and the broader cybersecurity community, ultimately strengthening their defenses and reducing the likelihood of future incidents (Ahmad et al., 2023).

In the context of advanced organizational theories, a learning organization embodies a strategic and adaptive approach to knowledge management and workforce development. It is a concept characterized by the systematic acquisition, creation, and dissemination of knowledge, resulting in a corporate culture that thrives on innovation, strategic agility, and continual growth (Senge, 1990). Within such an organization, leadership and employees synergistically promote a culture of continuous learning. This culture encourages the collaborative sharing of knowledge, experiences, and insights, catalyzing novel processes, ideas, and approaches to address the organization's operational challenges and overarching goals (Aaltola & Taitto, 2019).

At the core of an effective learning organization is knowledge exchange and reciprocity. Employees actively participate in knowledge-sharing practices in this dynamic environment akin to a symbiotic exchange (Masood, 2016; Kostadinov, 2011). They engage in the reciprocal sharing of expertise, effectively enhancing their individual and collective competencies and thereby contributing to personal and organizational improvement (Aaltola & Taitto, 2019). This continuous cycle of knowledge sharing and absorption fosters adaptability and a heightened capacity to embrace new ideas, fostering a corporate ethos where flexibility is a value and a guiding principle (Masood, 2016; Kostadinov, 2011). Employees within a learning organization become enthusiastic proponents of innovation, consistently seeking opportunities to enhance work processes and deliver superior outcomes.

A learning organization represents the pinnacle of organizational development, where knowledge management transcends the mundane and becomes a strategic driver of success (Aaltola & Taitto, 2019). The organization's ability to transform newly acquired knowledge into innovative actions and processes leads to perpetual growth and adaptability, positioning it to excel in an ever-evolving business landscape (Senge, 1990). Such organizations excel in accumulating knowledge and practical application, resulting in improved employee performance, enhanced organizational resilience, and a sustainable competitive advantage.

In the learning organization paradigm, employees are esteemed for their invaluable contributions to knowledge and experience, which collectively enhance and optimize the organization's operations, resources, and outcomes (Shaikh & Siponen, 2023). Within this context, employee feedback is actively sought and revered, recognized as a vital element of organizational growth and excellence (Aaltola & Taitto, 2019). The organization venerates the principles of knowledge transfer and collaborative engagement as core values, fostering an environment where innovation, learning from errors, risk-taking, and strategically directed employee development flourish (Aaltola & Taitto, 2019).

In a learning organization's milieu, knowledge acquisition and expansion processes occur on multiple levels—individual, group, and organizational (Senge, 1990). Senge (1990) elucidates this perspective by delineating five fundamental disciplines in his "The Fifth Discipline" book. These five disciplines encompass personal mastery, mental models, team learning, shared vision, and systems thinking. These disciplines serve as the bedrock upon which the learning organization is built, each playing a pivotal role in its development and sustenance. Personal mastery cultivates individual excellence and expertise, while mental models delve into the psychological underpinnings that influence behavior and decision-making. Team learning fosters collective intelligence and synergy, while shared vision aligns individuals and teams with common objectives. Finally, systems thinking imparts the ability to perceive the intricate web of interdependencies within the organization, facilitating holistic problem-solving and decision-making (Senge, 1990).

In summation, the learning organization is characterized by a profound appreciation for the intellectual capital residing within its workforce, and it strategically harnesses this wealth of knowledge and experience to optimize its functions and outcomes (Shaikh & Siponen, 2023). Employee feedback is prized as a catalyst for continuous improvement, and the organization promotes a culture where creativity, learning from failures, risk-taking, and purposeful employee development are celebrated. This commitment to knowledge permeates the organization at multiple levels, with Senge's five disciplines serving as the foundational framework for its evolution and effectiveness (Senge, 1990).

PERSONAL MASTERY

Personal mastery within an organization signifies its capacity to advance, adapt to change, and progress, a transformation that commences when employees embark on a journey of self-improvement and learning (LLorens-Montes et al., 2004; Garcia-Morales et al., 2007). The essence of knowledge sharing resides in the genuine willingness of individuals to contribute to each other's growth and development, thus fostering a culture that nurtures ongoing learning processes (LLorens-Montes et al., 2004; Garcia-Morales et al., 2007). Constructing a learning organization necessitates a fundamental shift in mindset—a departure from a focus on limitations and constraints towards an unwavering pursuit of innovation in processes, strategic organizational structures, and operations, driven by a creative exploration of what can be achieved (LLorens-Montes et al., 2004; Garcia-Morales et al., 2007).

This transformative shift is catalyzed by the commitment of both employees and the organization to continuous learning and ongoing improvement, particularly in the context of job-related activities and skill mastery. A pivotal distinction arises between employees who perceive their roles within the organization merely as jobs and those who regard them as professions, encapsulating the essence of strategic thinking applied through personal mastery (LLorens-Montes et al., 2004; Garcia-Morales et al., 2007). The latter mindset exemplifies a person who wholeheartedly embraces the principles and values of personal mastery. The evolution into a learning organization signifies a profound and strategic cultural shift in both the mindset of employees and the management within the organization (LLorens-Montes et al., 2004; Garcia-Morales et al., 2007).

TEAM LEARNING

Team learning represents a strategic endeavor aimed at aligning and nurturing the collective capabilities of employee teams to share knowledge, experiences, and expertise; all orchestrated to advance group and organizational objectives (Senge, 1990). The triumph of team learning hinges on its capacity to transcend restrictive paradigms, challenge ingrained assumptions, and foster open dialogues among team members. This process cultivates a culture of free-thinking, innovation, and risk-taking in addressing organizational challenges, problems, and existing procedures. Within this framework, successful team learning thrives on collaboration, networking, and communication grounded in a shared understanding context. In such an environment, many possibilities, solutions, and methodologies are thoughtfully deliberated upon and scrutinized, leading to a collective, strategically innovative perspective and a practical course of action (Senge, 1990).

Team learning is pivotal in groundbreaking and pioneering organizations, particularly as organizational complexity intensifies so that no individual possesses the comprehensive knowledge necessary for making the most informed decisions (Aaltola & Taitto, 2019). This intricate process nurtures an environment where teams harness their collective knowledge and engage in critical discussions to explore new horizons and pioneer inventive solutions. In essence, team learning acts as the crucible for innovation, enabling organizations to adapt and thrive in the face of mounting complexity and evolving challenges (Aaltola & Taitto, 2019).

MENTAL MODELS

Mental models in the organizational context represent employees' collective and strategic worldview, encompassing how they perceive constraints and possibilities within their environment. These models elucidate why two individuals can observe the same event and offer disparate interpretations. As Senge elucidated, mental models encompass the assumptions and generalizations inherent in employees' thought processes, delineating how they interpret information and subsequently take action (Senge, 1990). Mental models effectively act as filters, shaping employees' perceptions and constraining their behavior within familiar patterns based on their experiences, perceptions, and expectations (Senge, 1990). In practical terms, entrenched mental models filter incoming information through the lens of existing assumptions and preconceptions, which may not necessarily mirror the intricacies of reality (Aaltola & Taitto, 2019).

To surmount these entrenched and constraining mental models, employees must strategically recognize that the art of questioning spurs complex thinking and individual learning. Questions serve as the vehicles for defining variables, elucidating factors, outlining tasks, clarifying issues, and articulating problems. The act of complex questioning propels thought beyond surface-level and assumed understandings. It compels all participants in decision-making processes to articulate and challenge their preconceived notions and assumptions. This engagement in questioning fosters a mechanism of continual reassessment, wherein if a proposed solution falls short of satisfying predetermined criteria, decision-makers revisit the process, engage in further research and brainstorming, and persist until the most effective decision outcome is attained (McAuliffe, 2005).

SHARED VISION

The concept of shared vision entails a multifaceted practice that hinges upon effective communication and the proficiency to unearth collective images of the future that cultivate genuine commitment and engagement, transcending mere compliance (McAuliffe, 2005). At its core, team learning represents a discipline commencing with dialogue and a constructive feedback loop, enabling teams to suspend entrenched assumptions and engage in authentic collaborative thought processes (Senge, 1990). Within this dialogue discipline, teams must develop the acumen to discern the interaction patterns that impede learning. Often, these defensive patterns become deeply ingrained in the team's operational dynamics. When left unrecognized, these patterns become formidable obstacles to learning. However, when acknowledged and creatively surfaced, they have the potential to expedite the learning process, provided that they are effectively resolved (Senge, 1990).

Shared vision catalyzes the cultivation of mental models that enable organizations to transcend linear thinking, facilitating collaborative thought, problem-solving, and learning through a unified team-oriented framework (Senge, 1990). This shared vision nurtures a risk-taking culture and fosters an environment conducive to experimentation within organizational learning. It contributes to developing organizational knowledge, adaptive capabilities, renewal mechanisms, and sustained longevity, as Aaltola and Taitto (2019) posited.

SYSTEMS THINKING

As elucidated by Senge (1990), system thinking constitutes a comprehensive framework that offers a panoramic view of structural forces shaping organizational behavior and actions. This perspective is deeply intertwined with the fabric of the organizational culture, providing an invaluable lens through which to analyze and interpret organizational dynamics. Rooted in the principles of system dynamics, system thinking operates at a high level of abstraction, equipping organizations with the conceptual tools necessary to grapple with complex business challenges effectively. It facilitates a nuanced understanding of practical issues, allowing organizations to dissect intricate systems into discernible patterns, often referred to as archetypes, and providing the means for explicit system modeling to address multifaceted problems.

Senge's (1990) insights emphasize a critical aspect of system thinking, wherein many contemporary problems stem from the unintended consequences of past solutions. He underscores the intricate interplay between employees and the organizational environment, revealing how their interactions often lead to unintended and undesirable actions. Within this complex nexus, intended solutions can inadvertently produce adverse effects, perpetuating a cycle where attempts to alleviate symptoms merely relocate problems to different parts of the system. These latent issues may remain concealed temporarily, only to resurface as novel challenges, perpetuating a cycle of problem-solving that perpetuates the organization's struggles. Senge's perspective underscores the need for organizations to embrace system thinking as a strategic imperative to break free from such cycles and foster a culture of holistic problem-solving and long-term adaptability.

Applying organizational learning within the intricate fabric of an organizational environment or culture is laden with challenges. Frequently, organizations exhibit a proclivity to resist change when the processes and decisions ingrained within the organizational culture become institutionalized as routine procedures (Aaltola & Taitto, 2019). This resistance to change is often characterized as organizational rigidity, a phenomenon extensively discussed in the literature (Hannan & Freeman, 1977; Tushman & Romanelli, 1985). Organizational rigidity is a formidable impediment to the cultivation of organizational learning, underscoring the imperative for systematically integrating learning into the organizational culture. This notion aligns with Senge's (1990) assertion that learning should permeate the organization's and its workforce's essence.

Conversely, organizational flexibility emerges as a pivotal attribute of a learning organization. This flexibility empowers the learning organization to navigate the tumultuous waters of the external environment and adeptly respond to dynamic changes (Aaltola & Taitto, 2019). This adaptability extends to the organization's ability to swiftly and effectively react to rapidly evolving variables that possess the potential to induce organizational upheaval.

Argyris and Schön (1974) offer profound insights into the dynamics of organizational learning, delineating two fundamental modes: single-loop learning and double-loop learning. Like a thermostat, single-loop learning involves detecting and correcting errors that allow the organization to adhere to its policies and significant objectives. This form of learning operates within established goals, values, and strategies, making corrective adjustments to maintain the status quo. In contrast, double-loop learning entails detecting and correcting errors in ways that necessitate the modification of an organization's fundamental norms, policies, and objectives. It delves into challenging assumptions and reevaluating the organization's foundations. Argyris argues that double-loop learning is indispensable in enabling organizations and practitioners to make informed decisions in rapidly evolving and uncertain contexts (Argyris, 1974; 1993). Thus, it becomes imperative for organizations aspiring to embrace a learning orientation to foster the capacity for double-loop learning and the flexibility to adapt to an ever-changing landscape.

Nadler and Tushman (1980) intricately interwove the concepts of organizational learning and development with both informal and formal organizational structures, mediated by individual variables, actions, and components. Central to this nexus is the pivotal role played by organizational culture, an entity fundamentally molded by its constituents' values, actions, and activities. Expanding upon this framework, Bernstein and Burke (1989) underscored the profound idea that organizational learning encompasses concurrent knowledge acquisition and growth, both at the individual level and within employee groups. This collective progression and knowledge evolution are propellants and incubators for constructive organizational learning and transformative change (Aaltola & Taitto, 2019).

Constructing learning organizations necessitates fundamental shifts in employees' cognitive frameworks and interpersonal dynamics that penetrate the bedrock of cultural assumptions and norms (Nadler & Tushman, 1980). Nadler and Tushman (1980) elucidated various theories that underscore the efficacy of collaboration, the collective acquisition of knowledge, and knowledge dissemination by emphasizing the intrinsic value of human relations and social bonds. Managers increasingly recognize the significance of fostering collaborative relationships among employees, as they have witnessed that mechanical, technical, and procedural enhancements in business operations often fall short of yielding the desired outcomes (Nadler & Tushman, 1980). These shortcomings manifest as challenges in information sharing, team cohesion, employee commitment to organizational objectives, and job satisfaction. Consequently, employee relationships emerge as pivotal determinants in enhancing organizational culture, fostering job satisfaction, nurturing cohesiveness, and facilitating organizational knowledge transfer (Nadler & Tushman, 1980).

The model comprises four essential components, each contributing to the holistic enhancement of organizational effectiveness and fostering a culture of continuous learning and improvement (Nadler & Tushman, 1980). They include:

- Individual Component: This facet emphasizes the pivotal role of individual employee development and growth. Its core objective is cultivating a work environment prioritizing employee nurturing, empowerment, mentorship, training, recognition, and personalized treatment. By focusing on individual capacity building and professional growth, organizations can harness the full potential of their workforce.
- Environmental Component: The second component centers on creating an optimal work environment conducive to high performance and job satisfaction. Attention is devoted to enhancing various environmental factors, including lighting, noise levels, office temperature, ergonomic chair design, accident prevention measures, restroom facilities, office aesthetics, provision of exercise facilities, and cafeteria amenities. A comfortable and inviting workplace contributes to employee well-being and productivity.
- Cooperative Component: The cooperative aspect holds a central position in mentoring and the transfer of organizational knowledge. It strongly emphasizes team building, collaboration, and participative leadership. By fostering a culture of cooperation and teamwork, organizations can facilitate the sharing of expertise and the dissemination of critical knowledge among employees.
- Situational Component: The situational dimension adds dynamism to the model, recognizing the interdependence and collective significance of all components, whether individual, cooperative, or environmental. It acknowledges the contextual nature of organizational learning, where various factors can influence organizational culture and employee relationships. This component underscores the need for adaptive management styles and organizational interventions tailored to the situation. It views the organization as a complex social system characterized by beliefs, symbols, habits, standards, and a repository of critical organizational knowledge that must be preserved and transmitted. Mentorship and collaboration emerge as essential mechanisms for transferring this valuable knowledge from one employee to another.

Efforts to instill innovation within an organization often highlight the significance of influencing either attitudes or roles (Hatch, 2006). Nuclear regulatory bodies and operational leaders can opt for an attitude-centered approach to facilitate the workforce's progressive embrace of innovation, environmental consciousness, and unwavering commitment to public health and safety. This approach entails a transformation of values and attitudes by rewarding employees who exhibit supportive behaviors, designing comprehensive training programs, and fostering team-building activities. These initiatives reinforce the values of environmental protection and safety while stimulating the generation of innovative approaches to support these values (Aaltola & Taitto, 2019).

The underlying assumption is that cultivating new attitudes and skills will lead to favorable changes in behavior. It is envisioned that converted and dedicated employees will evolve into change agents themselves, propagating the vision throughout the organization. In turn, the development of change agents will profoundly influence the cultural shift within operational procedures, processes, and employee engagements (Bass et al., 2003).

Social networks serve as the foundational components of an organization's culture. A comprehensive understanding of these social networks equips nuclear power leaders with valuable insights and prepares them to address challenging behaviors and activities employees exhibit more effectively. As Drucker (1994) posits, organizational culture evolves from the collective experiences, expectations, values, and endorsements of employees and the stakeholder community. The culture develops and transforms when employees unite their actions and efforts to propel the organization in the desired direction (Schein, 1992).

Undoubtedly, organizational culture ranks among the most pivotal strategic determinants of an organization's capacity to thrive, endure, and evolve through acquiring new knowledge, applying existing and novel expertise, transferring knowledge, and preserving critical organizational wisdom (Hofstede, 1993). Organizational learning theory offers a valuable framework for nuclear power organizations seeking to enhance their defenses, security, and resilience in the face of cyber threats. This theory emphasizes the importance of knowledge acquisition, transfer, and utilization within an organization. To bolster cybersecurity defenses, nuclear power organizations must cultivate a culture of continuous learning and knowledge sharing among their employees. Continuous learning involves acquiring the latest insights into cyber threats and disseminating this knowledge to ensure all stakeholders are well-informed and equipped to identify and respond to potential cyberattacks.

Furthermore, the elements of organizational learning theory, such as shared vision and team learning, can play a pivotal role in strengthening cybersecurity. A shared vision in the context of cybersecurity involves aligning all organization members around a common understanding of the importance of cybersecurity and the shared responsibility for safeguarding critical assets. By fostering a shared vision, nuclear power organizations can encourage employees to proactively identify and report potential vulnerabilities, thus creating a collective defense mechanism. On the other hand, team learning emphasizes collaboration and knowledge exchange among teams and departments. In cybersecurity, this means promoting cross-functional collaboration to address emerging threats, share best practices, and develop a coordinated response strategy.

In addition to knowledge acquisition and collaboration, organizational learning theory underscores the need for adaptability and the ability to respond effectively to changing circumstances. This means having robust incident response plans and business continuity strategies for nuclear power organizations. These plans should be regularly tested and updated to ensure they remain effective against evolving cyber threats. By integrating these elements of organizational learning theory, nuclear power organizations can enhance their cybersecurity posture, defend against cyberattacks, and maintain business continuity in the face of potential disruptions, ultimately safeguarding both their critical infrastructure and the public's safety.

RESEARCH METHODOLOGY

Cultivating an organizational learning culture is a broadly applicable concept across various fields. However, its specific application within the nuclear power industry and its leadership context has received limited attention from scholars in organizational development and knowledge management. This study sought to bridge this gap by employing a focus group methodology as a means of data collection. Focus group discussions, a well-established qualitative research technique, were utilized to facilitate collaborative knowledge sharing among a small group of participants under the guidance of the researcher (Patten, 1990). This approach was a dynamic "brainstorming" session, eliciting diverse viewpoints and reactions.

Traditionally, focus groups have been employed for multiple purposes in data generation. Patten (1990) delineates several valuable aspects of using focus groups, including their ability to generate hypotheses, especially when researchers explore uncharted terrain. Narratives and stories shared within focus group sessions can be subsequently integrated into questionnaires or converted into hypothetical survey questions (Patten, 1990). Moreover, focus groups offer insights into unexpected statistical findings, providing qualitative context and interpretation for quantitative outcomes. Additionally, these sessions have aided program development and evaluation efforts, providing valuable insights into whether specific programs or services have met their intended goals (Patten, 1990).

Importantly, focus group data can stand alone as a potent source of knowledge generation (Patten, 1990). These sessions are invaluable tools for delving into the construction and expression of diverse perspectives, shedding light on how stories, ideas, attitudes, and experiences operate within a particular cultural context, particularly within ethnographic studies. Focus groups are often a preferred data generation method when research objectives involve collecting multiple viewpoints, have implications for diverse population groups, or are conducive to candid discussions within a group setting (Patten, 1990). By harnessing the power of focus group discussions, this study aims to contribute a deeper understanding of how an organizational learning culture can be nurtured and applied effectively within the distinctive operational landscape of the nuclear power industry and its leadership.

The focus group session was conducted in a spacious conference room, serving as the backdrop for an assembly of 12 professionals chosen through a random selection process of those attendees listed as cybersecurity experts. These participants boasted extensive academic qualifications, each holding advanced degrees and a minimum of a decade's worth of managerial expertise within the nuclear power industry.

The selection of this cohort was carefully drawn from the attendees of the 2023 Regulatory Information Conference (RIC) organized by the Nuclear Regulatory Commission, an annual event of paramount importance, focusing on pivotal regulatory, public health, and safety concerns intrinsic to the nuclear power domain. These individuals, who actively engage with the intricate challenges and public welfare intricacies inherent to nuclear power utilization in their daily professional responsibilities, brought considerable value to this research endeavor. This data collection exercise aimed not to reiterate established organizational development theory but to wield influence in practical application.

In order to facilitate comprehensive and nuanced discussions, the 12 participants were subdivided into three focus groups, each comprising ten members. The demographic composition of these focus groups was as follows:

- All participants held graduate degrees.
- All 12 participants had over a decade of managerial experience in the nuclear power industry.
- Among them, 8 participants were male, while 4 participants were female.

- Regarding ethnicity, eight identified as Caucasian-American, 1 was African-American, 1 was Latino-American, 1 was East Indian American, and 1 was Asian-American.

An experienced organizational development consultant with an extensive track record of 18 years in leadership and consultancy roles served as the facilitator for these groups. The decision to engage independent facilitators was made to mitigate the potential for bias in the outcomes of this research. Three additional facilitators were present during the sessions, tasked with the observation and meticulous documentation of focus group data. The facilitator adhered to a strict mandate, refraining from introducing personal opinions into the discussions. Probing was employed judiciously to clarify questions when the group's responses exhibited ambiguity or required elaboration. Participants were explicitly informed that their responses were devoid of absolute right or wrong, with the facilitator emphasizing that their role was to create an environment where participants felt comfortable expressing agreement or dissent with their peers' viewpoints.

The focus group session was designed to elicit thoughtful discussions and brainstorming among its participants, serving as a forum for exploring key questions integral to the research. Participants engaged in the session by sharing their insights and ideas, with the outcomes of their brainstorming sessions meticulously recorded on flip charts. Participants grouped similar responses to distill the wealth of responses generated during these sessions, creating a visual representation of shared ideas within the room. Following this, participants were tasked with individually selecting their top choices from the compiled responses and casting votes to identify the most pertinent items. This selection process, informed by their collective wisdom as seasoned doctoral-trained consultants with extensive management experience, yielded responses that garnered the highest total selections. These items emerged as the primary areas of focus for the group.

The focus group discussions were structured around a series of probing questions, guiding participants in their examination of pertinent topics:

- What individual barriers impede the transformation of your organizational culture towards one conducive to a learning organization concerning cybersecurity?
- What organizational obstacles hinder the evolution of your culture towards one aligned with the principles of a learning organization concerning cybersecurity?
- What practices can senior leaders and supervisors employ to enhance or cultivate an organizational culture aligned with a learning organization concerning cybersecurity?

Crucially, during the focus group sessions, meticulous notes were taken by three independent observers. This step was imperative, as it allowed for the comprehensive documentation of the group dynamics, discussions, and individual contributions. Given the facilitator's multifaceted role in moderating the discussions, posing probing questions, and ensuring equitable participation among participants, observers were indispensable in capturing vital nonverbal cues and behaviors that might have otherwise escaped scrutiny. These detailed notes laid the foundation for subsequent analysis.

Member checks were conducted as a final step before the analysis for clarity and accuracy. This additional level of validity allowed the facilitator to address specific queries, clarify rankings, and elucidate group selections, thus ensuring that the information recorded on the flip charts accurately reflected the intentions and insights of the focus groups. This rigorous process underscored the commitment to precision and thoroughness in the research endeavor.

Data Analysis

The rigorous qualitative data analysis process, as elucidated in the scholarly literature, forms the backbone of this research endeavor. Commencing with the immediate post-focus group phase, a comprehensive analysis strategy was deployed. Recognizing the human proclivity to swiftly forget critical details, a pivotal step involved a prompt review of the flip charts, meticulously documented notes, and the selections made on various discussion topics following the conclusion of the focus group session. This expeditious review process was a vital safeguard against losing valuable insights. This approach resonates with the 'pile-building concept articulated by Harvey (1990), wherein ethnographic data obtained from focus groups are scrutinized 'vertically,' typically in a chronological sequence. The objective is to discern recurrent themes and interrelationships among them, subsequently subjecting them to systematic coding. In alignment with this research study's methodology, the data was further dissected and reorganized into discrete 'piles,' each corresponding to critical themes documented initially on the flip charts. Notably, the two independent observers/facilitators diligently oversaw this intricate process. The reconfigured data was then subjected to a subsequent thorough examination, affording the construction of a coherent, sequential argument. Illustrative excerpts from the flip charts were also systematically collated and organized based on their respective rankings.

Nigel Fielding's (1993) prescient model, as presented in the literature, encapsulates a widely adopted approach to qualitative data analysis, serving as a valuable framework for this study. This model provided a robust foundation for the analytical procedures undertaken herein, facilitating a nuanced and comprehensive exploration of the data collected from the focus group sessions. Fielding's model afforded a structured methodology for extracting meaning from the rich tapestry of insights and perspectives offered by the participants, ensuring a systematic and rigorous analysis that adhered to the highest standards of qualitative research. The figure below outlines the process:

Figure 1. Fielding's model

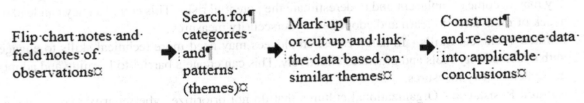

The subsequent sections encapsulate a succinct summary of responses to the discussion questions, followed by an elaboration of key discussion points from the qualitative interview sessions conducted during the focus group sessions. As an integral component of the data collection process, participants were encouraged to engage in a prioritization process, wherein they ranked their responses in ascending order of importance, thus affording a structured approach to discerning the most salient insights.

The findings from the data collection phase underscored a multifaceted exploration of themes central to organizational vitality and sustainability. A pivotal dimension of the group discussions revolved around the intrinsic significance of a robust organizational culture in shaping organizational effectiveness. Moreover, the intricate interplay between the organizational structure and the dynamics of interpersonal interactions and social relationships within groups emerged as the fundamental building blocks in cultivating a thriving organizational culture. Within this contextual framework, the focus groups delved into an insightful examination of the myriad impediments that obstruct the transformation of an organizational culture towards one oriented towards cybersecurity, drawing upon the conceptual framework delineated in the extant literature, notably elucidated by Hatch and Cunliffe (2006).

Furthermore, the focus groups discerned a constellation of barriers confronting leaders in their endeavor to catalyze the shift towards a culture predisposed to embracing cybersecurity as a foundational principle. Identifying these impediments is crucial in bridging the domains of organizational theory and organizational behavior, and the focus group discussions converged on recognizing two distinct categories of roadblocks: individual and organizational. This dichotomous classification provides a comprehensive lens through which to analyze and address the challenges inherent in effecting cultural change in the context of cybersecurity.

Focus Group Question: What individual barriers impede the transformation of your organizational culture towards one conducive to a learning organization concerning cybersecurity?

The results were:

- Resistance to Change - Individuals within the organization may resist changes to the existing culture, especially regarding cybersecurity practices. This resistance could stem from a fear of the unknown, a reluctance to adapt to new technologies or procedures, or simply a preference for the status quo.
- Lack of Cybersecurity Awareness - Many employees may need a comprehensive understanding of cybersecurity threats and best practices. This lack of awareness can hinder their ability to embrace a cybersecurity-oriented learning culture. With a clear understanding of the risks, individuals may see the need for change.
- Complacency - Individuals who have yet to experience a cybersecurity breach or incident personally may become complacent and underestimate the potential risks. This complacency can lead to a lack of motivation to learn and adopt new cybersecurity measures.
- Limited Technical Skills - In some cases, employees may need more technical skills to engage with cybersecurity tools and practices effectively. This can create a barrier to learning and adopting cybersecurity measures.
- Cultural Resistance - Organizational cultures that do not prioritize cybersecurity may create an environment where individuals resist change. If the prevailing culture does not support or reward cybersecurity-conscious behavior, individuals may be less inclined to embrace it.
- Time Constraints - Learning about cybersecurity and implementing new practices can be time-consuming. Individuals with busy workloads may perceive cybersecurity training and practices as additional burdens, making it challenging to prioritize them.
- Overconfidence - Some individuals may believe they are already proficient in cybersecurity, leading to overconfidence. This can result in a reluctance to engage in further learning or to acknowledge their vulnerabilities.
- Lack of Leadership Support - With visible support and commitment from organizational leaders, individuals may be more inclined to invest in cybersecurity learning and practices. Leadership plays a crucial role in setting the tone for cultural change.

- Inertia - People tend to stick with what they know and are comfortable with. Changing ingrained habits and behaviors can be difficult, and individuals may resist change due to inertia.
- Fear of Accountability - Embracing cybersecurity practices may come with a perceived risk of increased accountability. Individuals may worry about being held responsible for security breaches if they take a more active role in cybersecurity.

Focus Group Question: What are the organizational barriers to changing your culture towards one oriented toward a learning organization concerning cybersecurity?

The results were:

- Hierarchical Structures - Rigid hierarchical structures can exert a stifling influence on creativity and innovation. Such structures often confine individuals within predefined roles, limiting their capacity to think beyond established boundaries. To overcome this barrier, leaders must encourage a more flexible and inclusive organizational structure that empowers individuals to contribute their unique perspectives and ideas.
- Blame-Oriented Atmospheres: Organizational environments emphasizing blame over learning from mistakes pose a formidable challenge. Employees become reluctant to admit failures or share lessons learned when errors are met with a blame-centric approach. Leaders must cultivate an atmosphere that values identifying mistakes as opportunities for improvement and prioritizes collective learning over assigning blame.
- Risk Aversion and Conservatism - Excessively risk-averse and overly conservative organizations tend to resist change and innovation. Embracing new ideas and approaches, particularly in cybersecurity, requires a willingness to take calculated risks. Leaders should promote a culture encouraging experimentation, provided it is done thoughtfully and emphasizes learning from outcomes.
- Ambiguous Accountability and Authority - Unclear lines of accountability and authority can lead to clarity and efficiency. To address this challenge, leaders must establish transparent structures that clearly define roles, responsibilities, and reporting hierarchies. Clarity in these areas is essential to ensure that individuals know their respective accountabilities and can confidently act.
- Role and Policy Ambiguity - Fuzzy distinctions between roles and responsibilities and between policy and operations can lead to uncertainty and inefficacy. Leaders must establish a framework that articulates the boundaries of roles and the relationship between policy development and operational implementation. A clear delineation will enhance organizational efficiency and promote a culture of understanding.
- Bottom-Line Mentality - A narrow focus on the bottom line, to the detriment of recognizing people as the organization's greatest asset, can impede the development of a learning culture. Leaders must shift their perspective to acknowledge that employees, with their knowledge, skills, and creativity, drive organizational success. This paradigm shift is vital for prioritizing investments in employee development and well-being.
- Inadequate Resources - Organizations may need more resources, both in terms of funding and personnel, to invest in comprehensive cybersecurity training and infrastructure. This resource scarcity can hinder efforts to promote a culture of continuous learning in cybersecurity.

- Legacy Systems and Infrastructure - Organizations with outdated or legacy systems may need help integrating modern cybersecurity practices. Retrofitting older systems for enhanced security can be costly and disruptive.

- Resistance to Change - Organizational cultures can resist change, particularly when adopting new cybersecurity practices. Long-standing traditions and routines may be challenging to alter, especially if they have been successful in the past.

- Silos and Communication Barriers - Organizational silos, where departments or teams operate in isolation from one another, can impede the sharing of cybersecurity knowledge and best practices. Effective communication and collaboration are essential for a learning culture.

- Complex Bureaucracy - Excessive bureaucracy and complex decision-making processes can slow down the implementation of cybersecurity initiatives. This can be detrimental in an environment where agility and rapid response are crucial.

- Lack of Cybersecurity Leadership - With dedicated cybersecurity leadership and expertise at the executive level, organizations may be able to prioritize and drive cybersecurity initiatives. Leadership commitment is essential for fostering a culture of cybersecurity learning.

- Competing Priorities - Organizations often have competing priorities, and cybersecurity may need more attention or resources. Other business objectives may take precedence, hindering efforts to create a cybersecurity-oriented learning culture.

- Lack of Metrics and Accountability - With clear metrics and accountability mechanisms in place, it can be more accessible to measure the effectiveness of cybersecurity training and practices. This lack of visibility can lead to a sense of futility in learning efforts.

- Compliance-Driven Culture - Some organizations focus solely on meeting regulatory compliance requirements rather than embracing a proactive approach to cybersecurity. This compliance-driven mindset may limit the organization's willingness to learn and adapt.

- Resistance from Middle Management - Middle managers who are resistant to change or lack cybersecurity knowledge can obstruct efforts to create a learning culture. Their influence on day-to-day operations can be a significant barrier.

- Short-Term Focus - Organizations driven by short-term financial goals may prioritize immediate gains over long-term investments in cybersecurity. This can result in a lack of commitment to continuous learning in this area.

- Cybersecurity Fatigue - Constant exposure to cybersecurity threats and alerts can lead to organizational fatigue. This fatigue may reduce the willingness to engage in ongoing learning efforts.

Upon deliberating and identifying their collective priorities, the focus group embarked on a more detailed exploration of the crucial dynamics at play. The ensuing focus group findings illuminated a multifaceted journey that necessitates profound insight, keen understanding, and unwavering courage by individual leaders. This expedition entails recognizing and confronting personal barriers and the equally formidable challenge of addressing the entrenched institutional and organizational obstacles that impede cultural transformation. This intricate process represents a confluence of activities rooted in organizational behavior and processes informed by organizational theory, serving as the means to dismantle barriers that are often deeply entrenched, politically charged, power-driven, agenda-laden, and steeped in tradition.

Focus Group Question: What practices can senior organizational leaders and supervisors use to improve or develop an organizational culture towards one oriented towards a learning organization concerning cybersecurity?

The results were:

- Lead by Example - Senior leaders should demonstrate a commitment to cybersecurity learning by actively participating in training programs, staying updated on cybersecurity trends, and following best practices. Their actions set the tone for the organization.
- Provide Resources - Ensure adequate resources, including budgets and time, are allocated for cybersecurity training and awareness programs. Invest in the latest cybersecurity tools and technologies to support learning efforts.
- Establish Clear Policies and Procedures - Develop and communicate clear cybersecurity policies and procedures that outline employee expectations. Make sure these policies align with the organization's learning objectives in cybersecurity.
- Regular Training and Awareness Programs- Implement ongoing cybersecurity training and awareness programs for all employees, including supervisors. These programs should cover the latest threats, best practices, and incident response procedures.
- Encourage Continuous Learning - Promote a culture of continuous learning by encouraging employees to seek out new knowledge and skills in cybersecurity. Offer incentives or recognition for certifications and achievements.
- Supportive Feedback - Provide constructive feedback to employees regarding their cybersecurity practices. Encourage open dialogue about security concerns and offer guidance for improvement.
- Foster Collaboration - Create opportunities for collaboration and knowledge sharing among teams and departments. Cross-functional teams can work together to address cybersecurity challenges and share insights.
- Celebrate Successes - Recognize and celebrate cybersecurity successes and achievements within the organization. This can motivate employees to engage actively in learning and improvement.
- Measure Progress - Establish key performance indicators (KPIs) and metrics to measure the effectiveness of cybersecurity learning efforts. Regularly review progress and adjust strategies as needed.
- Stay Informed - Stay informed about emerging cybersecurity threats and trends. Senior leaders should proactively seek information and stay engaged in the cybersecurity community.
- Risk Management - Incorporate cybersecurity risk management into strategic planning and decision-making processes. Make risk assessments a routine part of the organization's operations.
- Open Communication Channels - Create open communication channels where employees can report security incidents, concerns, or potential threats without fear of reprisal. Encourage a culture of reporting.
- Scenario-Based Training - Conduct scenario-based training exercises and simulations to prepare employees for real-world cybersecurity incidents. These exercises help reinforce learning and improve response readiness.
- Continuous Improvement - Emphasize the importance of continuous improvement in cybersecurity practices. Encourage employees to analyze incidents and identify areas for enhancement.

- Compliance and Ethics - Ensure that cybersecurity practices align with ethical standards and compliance requirements. Senior leaders should lead with integrity in all cybersecurity matters.
- Challenging the Status Quo - Leaders must encourage a culture where established methods and paradigms are continuously challenged. This entails promoting a willingness to take calculated risks, learn from mistakes, innovate, and reconsider existing processes in pursuit of improvement.
- Inspiring a Shared Vision - Developing a shared vision that aligns followers' values with organizational goals is paramount. Leaders should enlist the collaboration of employees to craft a vision that revolves around great possibilities, particularly in cybersecurity.
- Empowering Action - Leaders must empower employees by nurturing their competence, providing encouragement, and building trust. This empowerment fosters a sense of ownership and enables proactive engagement in cybersecurity efforts.
- Leading by Example - Leaders should exemplify the organization's values through actions and decision-making. This entails actively participating in cybersecurity initiatives, reinforcing the importance of cybersecurity in their conduct, and avoiding an isolated, ivory-tower leadership style.
- Caring for Employees - Demonstrating genuine care for employees is pivotal. Leaders should exhibit compassion, offer recognition for success, and celebrate achievements. This fosters a positive work environment that encourages commitment to the organization's learning culture.
- Commitment on All Levels - The commitment to organizational learning should permeate every level of the organization. Employees should be dedicated to knowledge development, transfer, application, and retention. Senior leaders are critical in championing this commitment and steering the change process with a positive attitude and a clear vision.
- Integrate Learning - Learning should seamlessly integrate into the organization's mission, goals, operations, and daily activities. Leaders at all levels should ensure that learning initiatives align with the organization's objectives, emphasizing their role in enhancing organizational effectiveness and improvement.
- Review Capacity and Competence - Assessing human capital, resource management, technology, and organizational strengths and weaknesses is essential for cultivating a learning organization. Regularly evaluating these factors enables continuous improvement and adaptation.
- Express the Vision - To enact significant cultural changes, all organization members must comprehend and commit to the vision of a learning organization. Leaders should communicate this vision effectively and engage employees in its realization.
- Model a Commitment to Learning - Organizations should embrace a continuous learning cycle that involves taking action, reviewing outcomes, evaluating experiences, and using feedback for planning. Leaders should emphasize that learning is an ongoing process and that mistakes, risks, and knowledge acquisition are integral to this journey.
- Eliminate Bureaucracy - Unnecessary bureaucracy and complex organizational structures hinder productivity, innovation, and collaboration. Leaders should advocate for streamlined, flat organizational configurations that promote knowledge sharing and innovation while eliminating excessive procedures and policies.
- Capture Learning and Share Knowledge - Learning organizations thrive when knowledge is shared among individuals and teams. Knowledge-sharing opportunities should be facilitated to harness the collective increase in individual knowledge and benefit the organization.

- Reward Learning - Recognize and reward collaboration, learning, and development to incentivize desired behaviors. Performance appraisals should incorporate incentives for skill development, teamwork, and continuous personal growth that aligns with organizational goals.
- Embrace Risk and Failure - Leaders should instill a culture that accepts risk and tolerates failure as integral to innovation. Failures offer valuable lessons, knowledge development opportunities, and breakthroughs in new processes.
- Adapt and Evolve - Leaders must emphasize the importance of constant adaptation, evolution, and exploration. Learning organizations remain innovative by applying fresh ideas, acquiring new knowledge, and evolving to meet new challenges and integrate emerging technologies while delivering superior services and upholding public safety and environmental protection standards.

CONCLUSION

The conventional paradigm that once prevailed in emergency management and security within the nuclear power industry needed to be more learning-oriented. It primarily revolved around responding to and recovering from catastrophic events, with a myopic focus on technical competencies. However, contemporary learning organizations are ushering in a transformative shift with a profound emphasis on hazard mitigation. This evolution is intricately linked to the overarching concept of sustainable development, demanding that the technical facets of organizational operations be perceived as integral components of a comprehensive and strategically oriented system.

This new perspective necessitates a seamless integration and alignment of all technical elements with overarching policies and initiatives that pertain to disaster mitigation. Furthermore, this integration extends to the broader cybersecurity risk management and response domain. Consequently, organizations must undergo a fundamental transformation toward becoming more learning-oriented entities. This transformation is imperative to effectively address the burgeoning challenges posed by cybersecurity threats. Organizations must cultivate a culture of continuous learning and adaptability to navigate the complex landscape of contemporary cybersecurity attacks while advancing the cause of sustainable communities and resilient organizations.

REFERENCES

Aaltola, K., & Taitto, P. (2019). *Utilizing experiential and organizational learning theories to improve human performance in cyber training*. Academic Press.

Argyris, C. (1993). *Knowledge for action. A guide to overcoming barriers to organizational change*. Jossey Bass.

Argyris, M., & Schön, D. (1974). Theory in practice. Increasing professional effectiveness. Jossey-Bass.

Ayodeji, A., Mohamed, M., Li, L., Di Buono, A., Pierce, I., & Ahmed, H. (2023). Cyber security in the nuclear industry: A closer look at digital control systems, networks, and human factors. *Progress in Nuclear Energy, 161*, 104738.

Bass, B. M., Avolio, B. J., Jung, D. I., & Berson, Y. (2003). Predicting Unit Performance by Assessing Transformational and Transactional Leadership. *The Journal of Applied Psychology*, *88*(2), 207–218. doi:10.1037/0021-9010.88.2.207 PMID:12731705

Bernstein, W., & Burke, W. (1989). Modeling Organizational Meaning Systems. In R. W. Woodman & W. A. Passmore (Eds.), *Research in Organizational Change and Development* (pp. 117–159). JAI Press.

Bhamare, D., Zolanvari, M., Erbad, A., Jain, R., Khan, K., & Meskin, N. (2020, February). Cyber-security for industrial control systems: A survey. *Computers & Security*, *89*, 101677. doi:10.1016/j.cose.2019.101677

Cho, H. S., & Woo, T. H. (2017). Cyber security in nuclear industry–Analytic study from the terror incident in nuclear power plants (NPPs). *Annals of Nuclear Energy, 99*, 47–53.

Drucker, P. (1994). The Age of Social Transformation. *Atlantic Monthly*.

Fielding, N. (1993). Ethnography. In N. Gilbert (Ed.), *Researching Social Life* (pp. 154–171). Sage.

Garcia-Morales, V. J., Lloréns-Montes, F. J., & Verdu-Jover, A. J. (2007). Influence of personal mastery on organizational performance through organizational learning and innovation in large firms and SMEs. *Technovation*, *27*(9), 547–568. doi:10.1016/j.technovation.2007.02.013

Harvey, L. (1990). *Critical Social Research*. Unwin Hyman.

Kostadinov, V. (2011). Developing a new methodology for nuclear power plants vulnerability assessment. *Nuclear Engineering and Design*, *241*(3), 950–956. doi:10.1016/j.nucengdes.2011.01.006

LLorens-Montes, F. J., Garcia-Morales, V. J., & Verdu-Jover, A. J. (2004). The influence on personal mastery, organizational learning, and performance of the level of innovation: Adaptive organization versus innovator organization. *International Journal of Innovation and Learning*, *1*(2), 101–114. doi:10.1504/IJIL.2004.003714

M. (2021). *Technical Guide for Implementing Cybersecurity Continuous Monitoring in the Nuclear Industry* (No. PN L-31747). Pacific Northwest National Lab. (PNNL), Richland, WA (United States).

Masood, R. (2016). *Assessment of cyber security challenges in nuclear power plants security incidents, threats, and initiatives*. Cybersecurity and Privacy Research Institute the George Washington University.

Mileti, D. (1999). *Disasters By Design: A Reassessment of Natural Disasters in the United States*. Joseph Henry Press.

Nadler, D., & Tushmann, M. (1980, Autumn). A Model for Diagnosing Organizational Behavior. *Journal of Organizational Behavior*, *4*.

Schein, E. H. (1992). *Organizational Culture and Leadership. Jossey Bass*.

Schneider, R. O. (2002). Hazard Mitigation and Sustainable Community Development. *Disaster Prevention and Management*, *11*(2), 141–147. doi:10.1108/09653560210426821

Senge, P. (1990). *The Fifth discipline. The Art and Practice of the Learning Organization*. Random House.

Shaikh, F. A., & Siponen, M. (2023). Organizational Learning from Cybersecurity Performance: Effects on Cybersecurity Investment Decisions. *Information Systems Frontiers*, 1–12. doi:10.1007/s10796-023-10404-7

Chapter 19
Coaching Cybersecurity Project Managers and Cybersecurity Engineers

Amalisha Sabie Aridi
https://orcid.org/0000-0002-7869-5530
Capitol Technology University, USA

Laura Ann Jones
https://orcid.org/0000-0002-0299-370X
Capitol Technology University, USA

Darrell Norman Burrell
https://orcid.org/0000-0002-4675-9544
Marymount University, USA

Marlena Daryousef
https://orcid.org/0000-0001-9513-501X
Colorado Technical University, USA

Aikyna Finch
https://orcid.org/0000-0002-0078-1973
American Public University, USA

Danielle Gervacio Graf
https://orcid.org/0009-0003-4570-1193
Marymount University, USA

Sharon L. Burton
https://orcid.org/0000-0003-1653-9783
Capitol Technology University, USA

Michelle Espinoza
https://orcid.org/0009-0009-5213-6974
Marymount University, USA

William Quisenberry
Purdue University Global, USA

Maria Mondala-Duncan
Marymount University, USA

ABSTRACT

This inquiry emphasizes executive coaching as an indispensable leadership development tool in cybersecurity project management, encompassing cyber engineering and offensive operations. Effective cybersecurity project management is crucial in today's digital landscape, characterized by ever-evolving cyber threats and vulnerabilities. It extends beyond administrative tasks, serving as the linchpin for resource allocation, risk mitigation, and aligning security measures with organizational objectives. With the evolving cyber threat landscape, cybersecurity project management leaders require technical expertise, effective leadership skills, and a commitment to continuous professional development. This chapter underscores the pivotal role of executive coaching in developing leaders capable of navigating the cybersecurity landscape effectively and ensuring the resilience of critical organizational assets against sophisticated cyber threats.

DOI: 10.4018/979-8-3693-1970-3.ch019

CYBERSECURITY ENGINEERING

Cybersecurity engineering is a discipline that focuses on designing, building, and implementing robust and resilient cybersecurity solutions to protect information systems, networks, and critical infrastructure from cyber threats and attacks (Nobles, 2023). The field involves the application of engineering principles to develop secure systems, considering security requirements from the early stages of design and throughout the entire system lifecycle (Nobles, 2023).

KEY ASPECTS OF CYBERSECURITY ENGINEERING

Risk assessment- Identifying and assessing potential cybersecurity risks and vulnerabilities within systems and networks. This identification involves understanding the threat landscape and the potential impact of security breaches.

Security architecture is designing system architectures incorporating security controls, encryption, access controls, and other mechanisms to protect against unauthorized access and data breaches.

Secure coding ensures that software applications are developed with security in mind. This process of checking and oversight includes following secure coding practices to prevent common vulnerabilities like SQL injection, buffer overflows, and cross-site scripting.

Network security is implementing security measures to safeguard data in transit, including firewalls, intrusion detection systems, and encryption protocols.

Security testing conducts rigorous testing, including penetration and vulnerability assessments, to identify and rectify security weaknesses.

Incident response is developing plans and procedures for responding to cybersecurity incidents and breaches. This plan development process involves containment, mitigation, recovery, and forensic analysis.

Compliance and regulation ensure that systems and processes adhere to relevant cybersecurity standards, regulations, and requirements.

CYBERSECURITY OFFENSIVE OPERATIONS

Cybersecurity offensive operations, often referred to as "cyber offensive" or "cyber offense," involve proactive actions taken by government agencies or organizations to gather intelligence and disrupt or neutralize cyber threats (Nobles, 2023). These operations are conducted to identify, monitor, and potentially counteract cyber threats, including those posed by hostile nation-states, cybercriminals, and other malicious actors (Nobles, 2023).

Key aspects of cybersecurity offensive operations include:

Cyber espionage is gathering intelligence by infiltrating the networks and systems of adversaries to collect information on their activities, plans, and capabilities.

Cyber sabotage disrupts or damages adversaries' information systems and infrastructure, impairing their ability to function effectively. This attack may include turning off critical infrastructure or disrupting communication networks.

Counterterrorism targets and neutralizes cyber threats associated with terrorist organizations or extremist groups.

Counterintelligence, which is Protecting sensitive information and detecting and countering espionage efforts by foreign governments.

Attribution, which is identifying the source of cyberattacks and determining the responsible parties or nation-states behind them.

IMPORTANCE TO NATIONAL SECURITY

Both cybersecurity engineering and cybersecurity offensive operations are crucial components of national security for several reasons (Nobles, 2023):

Protection of Critical Infrastructure- Critical infrastructure relies heavily on information technology, such as power grids, water supplies, and transportation systems. Effective cybersecurity engineering helps safeguard these vital systems against cyber threats that could disrupt essential services.

National Defense- Cybersecurity offensive operations are essential for intelligence gathering, detecting potential threats, and responding to cyberattacks from foreign adversaries. Offensive operations can help deter malicious actors from targeting national interests.

Economic Security- The economy depends on secure digital infrastructure. Cybersecurity engineering helps protect businesses and financial institutions from cyberattacks that could lead to financial losses and economic instability.

Protection of National Secrets- Offensive operations protect classified information and national secrets from espionage and unauthorized access.

Counterterrorism- Cyber offensive operations can be used to monitor and disrupt the online activities of terrorist organizations and extremist groups.

Deterrence- Demonstrating the capability and willingness to conduct offensive cyber operations can serve as a deterrent, dissuading potential adversaries from launching cyberattacks against a nation.

In summary, cybersecurity engineering and offensive operations are essential to national security efforts to protect critical infrastructure, defend against cyber threats, gather intelligence, and deter malicious actors in an increasingly digital and interconnected world. These measures help safeguard a nation's security, economy, and well-being.

CYBERSECURITY PROJECT MANAGEMENT

Cybersecurity Project Management is a specialized discipline within project management that focuses on planning, executing, and overseeing projects related to cybersecurity initiatives (Burrell, 2019). It involves the application of project management principles and practices to ensure the successful implementation of cybersecurity measures, strategies, and projects within an organization (Burrell, 2019). Key elements and aspects of cybersecurity project management include:

Project Planning- Defining the cybersecurity project's scope, objectives, and goals. This classification level includes identifying specific security needs, addressing vulnerabilities, and the desired outcomes.

Risk Assessment- Conducting a thorough assessment of cybersecurity risks and threats the project aims to mitigate. Identifying potential risks helps in developing risk mitigation strategies.

Resource Allocation- Allocating the necessary resources, including personnel, technology, and budget, to support the cybersecurity project's successful execution.

Timeline and Milestones- Establishing a project timeline with key milestones and deadlines. This timeline development helps track progress and ensure the project stays on schedule.

Stakeholder Engagement- Identifying and engaging stakeholders, including cybersecurity experts, I.T. teams, management, and other relevant parties interested in the project's outcomes.

Scope Management- Managing changes to the project scope, ensuring that any modifications align with the project's goals and objectives.

Vendor Management- If the project involves third-party vendors or cybersecurity solutions, managing vendor relationships and ensuring that contracted services meet security requirements.

Compliance and Regulations- Ensuring the cybersecurity project complies with relevant industry standards, legal regulations, and compliance requirements.

Quality Assurance- Implementing quality control measures to ensure that the cybersecurity measures and solutions meet the desired security standards.

Communication- Establishing effective communication channels and reporting mechanisms to inform stakeholders about project progress, challenges, and outcomes.

Testing and evaluation involve conducting thorough testing, vulnerability assessments, and security audits to validate the effectiveness of cybersecurity measures.

Documentation, which is maintaining comprehensive documentation of the project's processes, procedures, and outcomes for future reference and auditing purposes.

Incident Response Planning is developing plans and procedures for responding to cybersecurity incidents that may occur during or after the project's implementation.

Training and awareness ensure that employees and relevant personnel are adequately trained and aware of cybersecurity best practices associated with the project.

Continuous improvement, which is establishing processes for ongoing monitoring, evaluation, and improvement of cybersecurity measures and practices.

Cybersecurity Project Management is essential in today's digital landscape, where organizations face ever-evolving cyber threats and vulnerabilities (Burrell, 2019). Properly managed cybersecurity projects help organizations protect their information assets, sensitive data, and critical infrastructure from cyberattacks and breaches (Burrell, 2019). Effective project management in cybersecurity ensures that resources are used efficiently, risks are mitigated, and security measures are aligned with the organization's security strategy and objectives (Burrell, 2019). These roles require effective leadership skills and a commitment to professional development as new risks and threats emerge (Burrell, 2019).

Career development, particularly in the context of professional and leadership growth, remains a relatively low priority within cybersecurity and information technology (Oltsik, 2017). This assertion is substantiated by Oltsik (2017), who points out that cybersecurity and information technology professionals often need more business training to advance their careers and foster business acumen.

Lester and Parnell (2006) contribute to this discourse by highlighting a prevalent organizational practice of elevating technical experts into management positions, guided by the misconception that technical prowess seamlessly translates into leadership proficiency. However, this assumption needs to acknowledge the fundamental distinctions between the skill sets demanded by these two domains. Technical competence, rooted in analytical and design proficiencies, fundamentally differs from the multifaceted capacities required for effective leadership roles (Lester & Parnell, 2006).

As Goldberg (2006), Rothenberger (2016), and Dzameshie (2012) concur, technical skills are rooted in analytical thinking and design. In contrast, leadership roles require distinct interpersonal skills, decision-making abilities, and team-building competencies. As affirmed by firsthand experience as an information technology executive, transitioning from a technical role to a leadership position underscores this process's substantial and daunting learning curve (Burrell, 2018).

Promoting technical experts into leadership positions often results from the need for dedicated leadership development programs tailored to the unique demands of the cybersecurity domain (Burrell et al., 2018). Leadership, especially within the multifaceted landscape of cybersecurity, is far from a one-size-fits-all proposition (Burrell et al., 2018). Given the interdisciplinary nature of the field and the requisite regulatory mandates for the Board of Directors and corporate officers, a pressing need exists for thoughtful and meticulously designed leadership development programs (Burrell et al., 2018). These mandates are instituted to safeguard critical information, systems, networks, and customer assets. However, the development of leadership competencies remains a secondary priority in many instances (Burrell et al., 2018).

Boyd (2018) underscores that achieving success as a cybersecurity manager entails more than a mere grasp of technology. Effective leadership within the cybersecurity domain necessitates cultivating soft skills encompassing communication, strategic decision-making, and employee management, irrespective of one's managerial level (Boyd, 2018). In particular, cybersecurity project managers find themselves in roles where exceptional communication, writing, and strategic thinking abilities are paramount. This role also includes the substantial financial implications associated with equipment and software purchases, often ranging from hundreds of thousands to millions of dollars (Boyd, 2018).

To excel in this capacity, cybersecurity project managers must possess the capacity to comprehend and effectively communicate in the language of senior organizational leaders (Boyd, 2018). This required skill dexterity entails a strategic approach to communication, enabling them to convey the significance of required resources in a manner that resonates with leaders beyond the cybersecurity sphere (Boyd, 2018).

Remarkably, these critical skills are often overlooked within the curriculum of technical degree programs and certification courses tailored for cybersecurity professionals. Consequently, the emergence of executive coaching as a fundamental leadership development tool becomes increasingly evident, bridging the gap and equipping cybersecurity leaders with the essential soft skills necessary for effective leadership in the cybersecurity arena (Boyd, 2018).

PROBLEM STATEMENT, APPROACH, AND RATIONALE FOR THE INQUIRY

The contemporary corporate landscape is characterized by dynamic shifts, shorter business cycles, and multifaceted challenges (Kouzes & Posner, 2017). This environment demands that leaders, especially senior leaders, possess advanced leadership thinking and decision-making skills to effectively align organizational efforts with strategic objectives. In recent years, Kouzes and Posner (2017) have highlighted the critical importance of cultivating these capabilities, emphasizing their significance for senior leaders.

Cybersecurity introduces an additional layer of complexity to the leadership landscape. Cybersecurity professionals, including corporate executives and information technologists, grapple with cyber threats' ever-evolving and volatile nature. These challenges encompass constant threat changes, intricate risk management, evolving regulatory requirements, and resource constraints (Burrell et al., 2018). Despite organizations' continuous adoption of new technologies to enhance decision-making and risk mitigation, the profound impact of these ongoing changes on leadership practices still needs to be explored in research (Burrell et al., 2018).

As cybersecurity witnesses the relentless integration of new technologies, an urgent imperative arises for leadership development through executive coaching (Burrell et al., 2018). The pace at which technologies evolve leaves leaders susceptible to the risks of adhering to outdated practices and methods, posing significant concerns (Burrell et al., 2018). Customizing leadership development programs tailored specifically for cybersecurity professionals and information technologists is crucial to address this imperative.

This inquiry contends that executive coaching represents a pivotal and indispensable leadership development tool for cybersecurity professionals engaged in cybersecurity engineering and cybersecurity project management. Effective project management within the cybersecurity domain is not merely an administrative function; it is the linchpin that ensures efficient resource allocation, effective risk mitigation, and alignment of security measures with broader organizational security objectives (Burrell, 2019). Moreover, leadership in cybersecurity engineering and offensive operations becomes even more critical as the cyber threat landscape evolves (Nobles, 2023). Leaders in these domains must possess technical expertise, effective leadership skills, and a commitment to continuous professional development (Burrell, 2019). This inquiry explores executive coaching as a useful tool for cybersecurity project management by exploring the literature.

WHY EFFECTIVE LEADERSHIP MATTERS

Effective leadership is pivotal in cybersecurity initiatives, helping organizations enhance their security posture and respond effectively to threats (Burrell, 2018). Conversely, ineffective leadership can have severe consequences, leaving organizations vulnerable to cyberattacks and breaches (Burrell, 2018). Here are three examples of the impact of effective leadership and three examples of the consequences of ineffective leadership in cybersecurity:

ESTABLISHING A CULTURE OF CYBERSECURITY AWARENESS

Effective leaders prioritize cybersecurity awareness and education throughout the organization. They promote a security culture where employees are well-informed about best practices, the importance of strong passwords, and the risks associated with phishing and social engineering attacks. This proactive approach reduces the likelihood of security incidents caused by human error.

STRATEGIC INVESTMENT IN SECURITY TECHNOLOGIES

Strong leadership understands the value of investing in cutting-edge security technologies and resources. Effective leaders allocate budgets and resources to implement robust cybersecurity solutions such as advanced intrusion detection systems, threat intelligence platforms, and encryption protocols, which fortify an organization's defenses against cyber threats.

SWIFT AND COORDINATED INCIDENT RESPONSE

Effective leadership ensures that a well-defined incident response plan is in place and that teams are trained to respond swiftly to cyber incidents. When a security breach occurs, strong leaders lead the response effort, coordinating actions to contain the breach, minimize damage, and initiate recovery processes, thereby reducing the impact of the incident on the organization.

CONSEQUENCES OF INEFFECTIVE LEADERSHIP

Ineffective leadership can expose the organization to cybersecurity risks and potential consequences (Burrell, 2018).

LACK OF SECURITY AWARENESS

Ineffective leadership may need to pay more attention to cybersecurity awareness initiatives, resulting in a workforce that needs more awareness of security risks. A lack of leadership oversight can lead to employees falling victim to phishing attacks, sharing sensitive information unintentionally, or failing to report security incidents promptly.

INSUFFICIENT RESOURCE ALLOCATION

When leadership does not prioritize cybersecurity, budgets for security measures may be inadequate. As a result, the organization may need more essential security tools, training, and personnel, making it more susceptible to cyberattacks and data breaches.

POOR INCIDENT RESPONSE

Ineffective leadership can result in disorganized or delayed incident response efforts. Without clear leadership during a security incident, the organization may struggle to contain the breach, assess the damage, and recover critical systems and data,

THE EMERGENCE OF EXECUTIVE COACHING

According to Kampa-Kokesh and Anderson (2005), the origins of executive coaching date back to the late 1940s when it emerged as a practice at the intersection of the consulting profession and the field of psychology. An exploration of the historical literature on coaching reveals six significant themes: (a) definitions and interpretations, (b) objectives and goals, (c) methodologies, (d) connections to psychology, (e) the relationship between therapy and coaching skills, and (f) the recipients and advantages of coaching interventions (Kampa-Kokesh & Anderson, 2005).

At its broadest level, coaching is fundamentally defined as a "process of equipping individuals with the tools, knowledge, and opportunities necessary for their development and increased effectiveness" (Peterson & Hicks, 1995, p. 41). In a technical sense, coaching is categorized as a technique or tool that management can employ to enhance performance, contributing to the successful completion of projects and the long-term sustainability of businesses (Burrell, 2019). Furthermore, in the 1990s, executive coaching gained significant prominence in the business industry as an intervention to transform the managerial behavior of individuals occupying roles in middle to senior management. This transformation sought to improve the technical acumen related to project selection and quality management (Peterson & Hicks, 1995).

Within the realm of leadership literature, Feldman (2001) identified three foundational elements that constitute the executive coaching profession: (a) one-on-one training and mentoring, (b) the integration of 360-degree feedback for managers, and (c) the overarching goal of coaching to enhance the competencies and effectiveness of executives, leaders, and project managers. As delineated by Feldman, these factors also serve as cornerstones for defining and comprehending executive coaching within the consulting psychology literature (Feldman, 2001). However, it is worth noting that definitions and conceptions of executive coaching can vary significantly based on perspectives, philosophies, approaches, and the specific professional and contextual objectives and rationale underlying coaching interventions (Newsome & Dent, 2011; Burrell, 2019).

The literature on coaching underscores the importance of providing a theoretical foundation and explanatory framework rooted in leadership and related theories (Burrell, 2019). This theoretical grounding is crucial for presenting an academic and empirical understanding of coaching practices. As a subject of intense scholarly interest, leadership has garnered attention from researchers and scholars worldwide, resulting in a vast body of academic literature and research that employs diverse theoretical approaches to analyze and elucidate the intricate complexities of leadership in practice (Northouse, 2013). The extensive literature on leadership offers numerous definitions and interpretations, contributing to a rich and multifaceted understanding of this critical domain (Burrell, 2018).

Vugat, Hogan, and Kaiser (2008) delved into researchers' diverse approaches to conceptualize and define leadership. They underscored that the concept of leadership has undergone a continuous and evolving development over time. Moreover, Vugat et al. (2008) posited that leadership could be seen as a remedy and solution to address the challenges and complexities arising from group dynamics, interpersonal relationships, communication, and collaboration. In their analysis, they lamented that the understanding of leadership has encountered technical and contextual confusion in the face of rapid innovation and technological advancements (Senge, 2006).

Vugat, Hogan, and Kaiser (2008) further discussed the prevalent misconceptions surrounding the contemporary perception of leadership. They argued that one common misinterpretation arises from viewing leadership solely through the lens of authority and power. To address this, their study proposed three distinct perspectives to reframe the conventional wisdom on leadership.

Firstly, Vugat, Hogan, and Kaiser (2008) advocated evaluating leadership within a dynamic equation encompassing leadership and followership. Secondly, they emphasized the need to examine leadership psychologically, recognizing that leaders and followers may not always align in their perspectives and behaviors. Thirdly, they highlighted the importance of considering contemporary technological and global factors that have played pivotal roles in shaping the evolving perceptions of leadership.

However, it is essential to differentiate leadership coaching from other approaches to leadership development. Ely, Boyce, Nelson, Zaccaro, Broome, and Whyman (2010) define leadership coaching as a developmental relationship between a coach and a client. This relationship is centered on enhancing the client's leadership competencies, ultimately equipping them to be more effective managers (Burrell, 2019).

SELF-EFFICACY THEORY

Self-efficacy theory provides a lens through which we can understand how leaders in the contemporary corporate landscape, particularly in the cybersecurity domain, can develop the belief in their abilities to navigate multifaceted challenges and achieve strategic objectives. Self-efficacy theory consists of several key elements that are highly relevant to this context:

1. Mastery Experiences- One of the central elements of self-efficacy theory is the concept of mastery experiences (Towhidi & Pridmore, 2022). Leaders, including senior leaders in cybersecurity, can build their self-efficacy by successfully mastering challenges. In the rapidly evolving cybersecurity field, leaders can gain confidence by actively participating in leadership development programs like executive coaching and successfully applying their learning to address real-world challenges.
2. Social Modeling- Observing others who have successfully faced similar challenges and developed effective leadership thinking and decision-making skills can enhance self-efficacy (Towhidi & Pridmore, 2022). By engaging in executive coaching and learning from experienced coaches, cybersecurity professionals can benefit from the social modeling aspect of self-efficacy theory. Coaches serve as role models, demonstrating effective leadership behaviors and strategies that can be emulated.
3. Verbal Persuasion- Leaders' self-efficacy can be influenced by verbal persuasion and feedback (Towhidi & Pridmore, 2022). Executive coaching provides a platform for coaches to offer constructive feedback and encourage leaders to believe in their capabilities. Coaches can effectively persuade leaders that they possess the skills and attributes needed to excel in the cybersecurity landscape, reinforcing their self-efficacy beliefs.

By incorporating these elements of self-efficacy theory, leadership development programs such as executive coaching can play a pivotal role in enhancing leaders' self-belief in navigating the complex and ever-evolving challenges of the contemporary corporate landscape, especially in the cybersecurity domain. As leaders develop their self-efficacy, they are more likely to effectively align organizational efforts with strategic objectives and make informed decisions addressing multifaceted challenges. This kind of development aligns with the critical importance Kouzes and Posner (2017) emphasized regarding the cultivation of advanced leadership thinking and decision-making skills for senior leaders in today's dynamic business environment.

CAREER ADAPTABILITY THEORY

Career Adaptability Theory provides valuable insights into how professionals, including senior leaders in the dynamic corporate landscape and the field of cybersecurity, can navigate multifaceted challenges and adapt to evolving environments. This theory posits that individuals who can effectively anticipate, adapt to, and shape their career-related challenges are more likely to succeed and thrive (Bocciardi et al., 2017).

In the context of senior leaders facing dynamic shifts and ever-evolving cyber threats, Career Adaptability Theory offers relevant elements:

1. Concern- Career Adaptability Theory emphasizes the importance of individuals recognizing and acknowledging the challenges and changes in their career environments (Bocciardi et al., 2017). Senior leaders in the cybersecurity domain need to be acutely aware of the constant shifts and complex challenges they face, including evolving cyber threats, regulatory requirements, and resource constraints. Recognizing these concerns is the first step towards adapting effectively.

2. Control- This element focuses on individuals shaping their careers and making proactive decisions. Senior leaders can apply this element by actively engaging in leadership development opportunities, such as executive coaching, to enhance their decision-making and leadership-thinking skills (Bocciardi et al., 2017). Leaders can better align their efforts with strategic cybersecurity objectives by taking control of their career development.

3. Curiosity- Career Adaptability Theory underscores the importance of curiosity and learning in career success. Senior leaders must cultivate a continuous learning mindset, especially in the rapidly changing cybersecurity landscape. Curiosity can drive leaders to seek executive coaching and other professional development resources to stay current and adapt to new technologies and practices (Bocciardi et al., 2017).

By applying the elements of concern, control, and curiosity from Career Adaptability Theory, senior leaders in cybersecurity can better navigate the dynamic corporate landscape. They can acknowledge the challenges, take control of their career development, and maintain a curious and learning-oriented approach (Bocciardi et al., 2017). This adaptability is essential for aligning organizational efforts with strategic cybersecurity objectives and effectively addressing multifaceted challenges. Executive coaching can be a valuable tool to support senior leaders in this journey, helping them enhance their career adaptability and leadership skills.

COGNITIVE APPRENTICESHIP THEORY

Cognitive Apprenticeship Theory, a constructivist learning theory, can be applied to the evolving challenges senior leaders face in the contemporary corporate landscape and, more specifically, cybersecurity. This theory posits that learning and expertise development occurs through a mentorship process where novice learners, or apprentices, work alongside expert practitioners, referred to as mentors, to acquire domain-specific knowledge and skills (Peters-Burton et al., 2015). In the context of senior leaders navigating dynamic shifts and multifaceted challenges, Cognitive Apprenticeship Theory's elements can offer valuable insights:

1. Scaffolding- Cognitive Apprenticeship Theory emphasizes the role of scaffolding, where mentors provide guidance and support to apprentices based on their current skill level (Peters-Burton et al., 2015). In the rapidly evolving cybersecurity landscape, senior leaders can benefit from executive

coaching that offers tailored support and guidance, helping them navigate complex challenges. Scaffolding can provide resources, case studies, and real-world scenarios to help leaders develop advanced thinking and decision-making skills aligned with cybersecurity objectives.

2. Articulation- This element focuses on helping apprentices externalize their thinking processes (Peters-Burton et al., 2015). In the context of senior leaders, articulation can be encouraged through reflective practices during executive coaching sessions. Leaders can articulate their decision-making strategies, analyze past experiences, and discuss how they align organizational efforts with strategic cybersecurity objectives. Leaders can gain deeper insights and refine cognitive skills by verbalizing their thought processes.

3. Reflection- Cognitive Apprenticeship Theory emphasizes the importance of reflection in learning and expertise development (Peters-Burton et al., 2015). Senior leaders can use reflection as a key component of executive coaching. Reflective discussions can delve into the challenges of dynamic shifts and evolving cyber threats. Leaders can assess their decision-making processes, explore alternative approaches, and adapt their strategies based on past experiences. This reflective practice enhances leadership thinking and decision-making skills, making them more effective in addressing multifaceted challenges (Peters-Burton et al., 2015).

By applying Cognitive Apprenticeship Theory's elements of scaffolding, articulation, and reflection, organizations can design executive coaching programs that provide senior leaders with the cognitive tools necessary to thrive in the rapidly changing landscape of cybersecurity. These elements foster a learning environment where leaders can effectively acquire and refine advanced leadership thinking and decision-making skills, aligning their efforts with strategic cybersecurity objectives.

COACHING AND PROJECT MANAGEMENT

In the extensive literature exploring the nexus between coaching and the success of project management, as well as its impact on enhancing overall business performance, coaching emerges as a strategic tool that serves the interests of project managers in achieving project success and elevating employee performance (Walker-Fraser, 2011; Burrell, 2019). Despite its widespread popularity as an intervention to bolster business productivity, empirical studies validating coaching as an effective practice have been relatively limited (CIPD, 2010).

The Chartered Institute of Personnel and Development (CIPD) has conducted comprehensive investigations into the dimensions of coaching as a learning tool that contributes significantly to the success of project management (CIPD, 2010). Moreover, CIPD has embarked on inquiries to ascertain the impact of coaching as a developmental tool in leadership and project management. A survey encompassing 729 HR managers and representatives revealed the positive influence of coaching as a developmental technique in achieving project management success (CIPD, 2010; Saowalux & Peng, 2007).

In the literature about coaching as an emerging intervention for achieving project management success, several aspects have been scrutinized, emphasizing coaching as an integral component of leadership development (Burrell, 2019). These aspects include the criteria and competencies for selecting a coach. These personal and professional attributes make an effective executive coach, the advantages and disadvantages of utilizing internal versus external executive coaches, the perception of engagement in executive coaching, the specifications of coaching techniques and tools, indicators of executive coaching success, and the resultant learning, behavioral changes, and cultural shifts stemming from executive coaching (Kampa-Kokesh & Anderson, 2005; Newsome & Dente, 2011).

While the standards of the coaching process share commonalities across various contexts, the approaches employed by coaches to drive change within executives, project managers, and organizational leadership culture largely hinge on coaches' professional and technical backgrounds and their intellectual and academic philosophies (Burrell, 2019).

EXECUTIVE COACHING SKILLS

Coaching has garnered increasing popularity in both the business world and academia, reflecting its recognized significance (Lebian, 2011; Burrell, 2019). A survey conducted by the Chartered Institute of Personnel and Development (CIPD) 2011 underscored this trend, with a staggering 90% of participants acknowledging coaching as a recommended tool for individual and organizational development (Candis & Magnolia, 2010). However, the executive coaching profession has raised concerns regarding the need for standardized competencies and skills (McCarthy & Miller, 2011). In response, Laufer (2012) established nine managerial practices to support operational and strategic organizational development and provide a structured foundation for the executive coaching profession.

As defined by Laufer (2012), these nine leadership practices are pivotal in the strategic coaching process to enhance organizational effectiveness and performance (Hannafy & Vitulano, 2013). The practices encompass embracing the living order, challenging the status quo, aligning project activities with the appropriate context, prioritizing the recruitment of the right individuals, fostering a productive culture, emphasizing effective communication skills, implementing daily planning and monitoring strategies, focusing on results, and leading by example (Laufer, 2012).

In organizational change facilitated through coaching, a systematic approach is often recommended to address complex challenges (Feldman & Lankau, 2010; Burrell, 2019). Such systematic change requires executive coaches to possess strong managerial skills to implement Laufer's recommended coaching framework (2012) effectively. The complexities associated with implementing systematic change in organizations necessitate a multifaceted skill set for leaders and executive coaches (I.C.F., 2011; McCarthy & Miller, 2011).

Furthermore, Luntz (2011) introduced nine principles for effective project management leadership, emphasizing people-centeredness, paradigm-breaking, passion, perfection, prioritization, persistence, persuasion, partnership, and principled action. These principles offer a strategic foundation for project management, contributing to the organization's competitive positioning (Luntz, 2011; Ely, 2010). They can also be integrated into the project management development coaching process to clarify the vision of daily operational activities and duties.

In this context, executive coaches must construct a tailored coaching model that aligns with the organization's internal vision, mission, goals, and culture while addressing external market opportunities, weaknesses, and challenges (Mayfield & Mayfield, 2012; Feldman, 2010). Applying Luntz's leadership principles can help establish a systematic culture conducive to organizational learning (Walker-Fraser, 2011). Ultimately, coaching and mentoring hold value for organizations by nurturing a quality culture that embodies organizational values, norms, and principles (Freedman & Perry, 2010). The alignment of Lutz's leadership principles with Laufer's practices forms a robust and effective coaching framework for enhancing organizational learning within project management (Laufer, 2012; Lutz, 2011; Freedman & Perry, 2010).

COACHING AND SYSTEM APPROACHES

Research has highlighted the positive outcomes of the interplay between the behavioral system approach and executive coaching (Visser, 2010; Burrell, 2019). These studies have illuminated the constructive impact of this approach on organizational operational performance and sustainability (Visser, 2010). Skinner (2007) expounds on the behavioral system approach, encompassing the behavior of an organization and the systemic perspective guided by coaching practices. Skinner's comprehensive theoretical framework delves into the evolution of the system approach under the purview of executive coaching (2007).

Effective organizational behavior represents a strategic and operational endeavor necessitating a behavioral transformation in how businesses perceive their vision, goals, objectives, and culture to achieve the desired alignment with organizational productivity and performance (Visser, 2010). Examining the intrinsic connection between the coaching process and the behavioral system, researchers portray executive coaching as a systemic behavioral practice. This systemic perspective equips coaches with three developmental insights (Wasylyshyn, 2003).

The first insight underscores the significance of daily interactions between coaches and employees to induce shifts in thought processes and mental states (Wasylyshyn, 2003). Furthermore, mentoring these daily operational interactions contributes to refining human system thinking (Visser, 2010). Psychodynamic and cognitive approaches emphasize coaching personal needs, desires, and attitudes as pivotal drivers of project success (Wasylyshyn, 2003).

The second insight centers on the philosophy that coaches should focus on present-time and situational behaviors rather than forming assumptions and judgments based on past behaviors (Thomas et al., 2007; Westerman, 1998). However, psychodynamics and other humanitarian approaches advocate for analyzing past causes and inner-psychic motives to resolve present conflicts. Therefore, the behavioral system approach highlights the importance of adopting a "here and now" approach when dealing with contemporary complexities and challenges (Thomas et al., 2007; Westerman, 1998).

The third insight contends that coaches are permitted to employ manipulation tactics to facilitate the success of the behavioral system approach (Thomas et al., 2007; Westerman, 1998). Furthermore, the behavioral system approach suggests manipulation as a coaching technique to address and rectify various organizational gaps (Thomas et al., 2007; Westerman, 1998). However, psychodynamic and cognitive approaches raise objections to using persuasion as a strategic tool for solving operational problems and bridging organizational and individual gaps (Visser, 2010). Additionally, cognitive psychodynamic approaches classify manipulation as unethical and contrary to professional and ethical values (Visser, 2010).

COACHING AND ORGANIZATIONAL RESISTANCE CHANGE

Organizational change is a deliberate strategic effort undertaken by an organization to chart a course toward a desired future state that enhances productivity, effectiveness, and market development, departing from its current state (Lunerburge, 2010). Organizations today face mounting global and national economic, technological, and competitive pressures and challenges, necessitating a proactive approach to change (Lunerburge, 2010). Executive coaching is paramount in this dynamic landscape, offering diverse and strategically intense interventions (Creemers, 2011; Burrell, 2019).

Creemers (2011) identifies several reasons underlying organizational resistance to change. These include a general aversion to change, apprehensions regarding new systems, leadership's inability to prepare the organization for change, and a lack of the leadership competencies necessary to navigate the evolving landscape. Addressing these sources of resistance can be achieved through a therapeutic approach that elucidates the internal and external factors influencing the transition and educates employees about the change process (Creemers, 2011).

Leaders and executive coaches are pivotal in initiating change and mitigating organizational resistance (Creemers, 2011). Recognizing the importance of this role, the Project Management Institute (PMI) has devised a guidance program to assist executive coaching in overcoming resistance to change (Creemers, 2011). The PMI program encompasses the following elements, as outlined by Duke (2011) and Anderson (2011):

Learning and Communication- Executive coaches should intensively educate employees about change, its underlying factors, and its benefits (Duke, 2011). Effective communication with all organizational stakeholders is essential to ensure their readiness for and comprehension of the change process, including its causes and consequences (Duke, 2011).

Participation and Involvement- The executive coaching process should involve employees and staff in decision-making and implementation, as their participation and contribution in identifying problems and devising solutions can significantly reduce resistance to change (Anderson, 2011; Lunerburge, 2010).

Organizing and Support- Executive coaches must articulate a strategic plan that outlines leadership behaviors and organizational culture changes required to facilitate the transition to change. This program can alleviate transitional tensions and reduce organizational resistance (Anderson, 2011).

Negotiation, Cooptation, and Settlement- The executive coaching process should encompass negotiations with managers and experts to lead the change process and involve them in the organization's future direction. Cooptation involves selecting a group of leaders with decision-making authority to manage the transition (Anderson, 2011; Lunerburge, 2010).

Executive coaching emerges as a strategic imperative for ensuring the success and effectiveness of organizational change efforts (Spector, 2011). It is a foundational pillar and operational backbone for change initiatives, particularly within cybersecurity project management.

Aligned with the insights of Artto and Dietrich (2014), program project managers are responsible for executing strategies that align organizational objectives with operational goals. This alignment is actualized through a structured coaching program, spanning initiation, planning, execution, control, and closure phases (Artto & Dietrich, 2014).

The professional coaching programs that organizations implement, overseen by either contracted external certified coaches endorsed by PMI or internal executive coaches, guide the organization through the several stages of project portfolio management:

- Process Initiation- This stage involves establishing a clear work plan encompassing the project schedule, recruitment of qualified staff, team formation, assignment of responsibilities and decision-making authority, and formulating working culture standards (Artto & Dietrich, 2014).
- The planning stage ensures all project management details are documented, including project schedule dates, expert recruitment, and comprehensive budgeting plans.
- The executing process ensures strategies are executed to manage challenges, meet performance objectives, analyze and mitigate risks, and address all dimensions of project completion and stakeholder interests.

- The controlling and maintaining stage focuses on maintaining the project's timeline, budget, financial plan, and closure constraints.
- The closing stage focuses on effective approaches to ending a project efficiently.

In summary, the PMI's project management and portfolio management model provide valuable guidance to executive coaches, enabling them to efficiently and effectively navigate the project landscape, uphold international quality standards, and compete effectively in the global management arena (Artto & Dietrich, 2014; Burrell, 2019).

ASSESSING THE EFFECTIVENESS OF EXECUTIVE COACHING

Assessing the effectiveness of executive coaching as a leadership and professional development tool requires a comprehensive evaluation approach that considers various dimensions and outcomes (De Meuse et al., 2009; Albizu-Gallastegi et al., 2019; Rekalde et al., 2015). Here are some areas and methods to assess its effectiveness (De Meuse et al., 2009; Albizu-Gallastegi et al., 2019; Rekalde et al., 2015):

Goal Achievement- Evaluate whether coaching helps executives achieve their goals and objectives. This assessment can include a review of the goals set at the beginning of the coaching engagement and a comparison with the outcomes achieved.

Behavioral Changes- Assess whether the executive has made positive behavioral changes due to coaching. This assessment can involve peer feedback, direct reports, and supervisors to gauge changes in leadership behaviors, communication, and interpersonal skills.

Self-awareness and Emotional Intelligence- Measure improvements in self-awareness and emotional intelligence. Use assessments such as the Emotional Intelligence Appraisal or 360-degree feedback to gauge self-perception and interpersonal effectiveness changes.

Job Performance- Evaluate the impact of coaching on job performance metrics, such as increased productivity, better decision-making, or improved project outcomes. Compare pre-coaching and post-coaching performance data.

Leadership Effectiveness- Assess the executive's effectiveness through qualitative evaluations, including feedback from teams and colleagues and surveys measuring leadership competencies.

Career Advancement- Determine if executive coaching contributes to career advancement, promotions, or increased responsibilities within the organization. Track the executive's career progression over time.

Stakeholder Feedback- Gather feedback from stakeholders, including team members, peers, and supervisors, to assess the executive's leadership impact on their working relationships, collaboration, and team dynamics.

Retention and Engagement- Measure the impact of coaching on employee retention and engagement within the executive's team or department. Higher retention rates and improved team morale can be indicative of coaching effectiveness.

Return on Investment (R.O.I.)- Conduct a cost-benefit analysis to assess the ROI of executive coaching. Compare the investment in coaching with the financial gains or savings resulting from improved leadership and performance.

Long-Term Impact- Evaluate the sustainability of coaching outcomes over time. Determine whether the changes and improvements observed during coaching endure and continue to benefit the organization.

Client Satisfaction- Gather feedback from the executive being coached to assess their satisfaction with the coaching process, the coach's effectiveness, and the perceived value of coaching.

Peer and Coach Assessment- Use peer and coach assessments to provide additional perspectives on the executive's progress, growth, and development throughout the coaching engagement.

Follow-up Assessments- Conduct follow-up assessments at regular intervals (e.g., six months or one year after coaching completion) to track the maintenance of positive changes and identify areas for continued growth.

Qualitative Interviews- Conduct in-depth interviews with the executive, coach, and relevant stakeholders to gather qualitative insights into the impact of coaching on leadership and professional development.

Benchmarking- Compare the executive's progress and development against industry benchmarks or best practices to determine how coaching outcomes align with external standards.

LEADERSHIP COMPLEXITIES AND CHALLENGES

The Burrell Leadership Intricacy Model outlines eleven critical themes that make leading today and the future so challenging to such a level that investment in leadership development interventions is not an organizational luxury; it is a paramount operations strategy (Burrell, 2018). These themes were developed through several focus group interviews with members of technical managers who attended the 2017 International Studying Leadership Conference at the University of Richmond in Richmond, VA, U.S.A. (see Table 1).

CONCLUSION

In recent years, Kouzes and Posner (2017) have emphasized the critical importance of cultivating advanced leadership thinking and decision-making skills, particularly for senior leaders. This need arises from the rapidly evolving nature of the contemporary corporate landscape, characterized by shorter and more intricate business cycles. In such a dynamic environment, leaders must possess exceptional leadership thinking and decision-making abilities to swiftly align organizational efforts with strategic objectives while effectively navigating multifaceted challenges (Burrell et al., 2018).

Cybersecurity adds a layer of complexity to the leadership landscape. Corporate executives, cybersecurity professionals, and information technologists grapple with the volatile nature of this domain, marked by constant changes in cyber threats, the intricacies of risk management, evolving regulatory requirements, and resource constraints (Burrell et al., 2018). While organizations continually adopt new technologies to aid in the decision-making process and mitigate risks, the profound impact of these ongoing changes on leadership practices still needs to be explored (Burrell et al., 2018).

Given the relentless pace at which new technologies are integrated into cybersecurity, an urgent imperative arises for leadership development through executive coaching (Burrell, 2019). This imperative is underscored by the necessity to equip leaders with the knowledge and skills required to stay current and effective in their roles. The risk of adhering to outdated practices and methods in an environment characterized by rapid technological advancements is a genuine concern (Burrell et al., 2018). Consequently, the customization of leadership development programs tailored specifically for cybersecurity professionals and information technologists emerges as a top priority (Burrell, 2018).

Table 1. Burrell leadership intricacy model (Burrell, 2018)

Intricacy Variables	Burrell Leadership Intricacy Model
Theme 1	Managerial retrospection does not lead to foresight since the variables and conditions of the internal and external environment can be in unremitting instability, which makes adaptability and change management skills precious.
Theme 2	Exchanges and engagements between system elements are nonlinear and interconnected, so small alterations can manufacture inexplicably sizeable impacts and consequences.
Theme 3	Information in both the international and external environment is often exceedingly overloaded, uncertain, incomplete, or indecipherable.
Theme 4	Innovations, breakthroughs, and solutions can be developed from the congruent dynamics within the organizational system and cannot be imposed by external forces with inevitable and predictable outcomes.
Theme 5	New technologies are disrupting mature work practices, shifting the nature of old communication approaches, and taxing elderly collaboration approaches.
Theme 6	Expertly comprehending the most effective and efficient ways to leverage organizational strengths and industry best practices is one of the most critical duties of leadership.
Theme 7	Traditional organizational boundaries are dissolving in ways that necessitate unlocked transparency, flexible hierarchies, dispersed resources, distributed decision-making, and loosening of centralized controls to foster the development of an organizational learning culture at every level of the organization.
Theme 8	Increased globalization and enlarged employee diversity will require fresh levels of cooperation, pioneering ways of thinking, and modern ways of comprehension that require respect, learning-centered curiosity, sympathy, and empathy.
Theme 9	The most valuable organizational asset is the ability to tap into the organization's expertise, talent, and collective intelligence.
Theme 10	Social capital and the ability to tap into expertise and knowledge networks are very critical because they provide access to data and information that is essential to complex problem-solving and effectual decision-making,
Theme 11	It is necessary to create and support cultures in which it is safe to take risks, tolerate, and appreciate what can be learned from failure to improve business processes and organizational strategy.

Given these challenges and opportunities, future research endeavors should explore innovative leadership development approaches that address the cybersecurity landscape's unique demands (Burrell, 2018). A central research agenda should be investigating the effectiveness of executive coaching as a means to enhance leadership thinking, decision-making, and adaptability in the face of evolving technologies and cybersecurity threats. Additionally, studies examining the customization of leadership programs to suit the needs of cybersecurity professionals can provide valuable insights for organizations seeking to bolster their leadership capabilities in this critical domain (Burrell, 2018). By delving into these areas, researchers can contribute to advancing leadership practices that align with the complexities of contemporary cybersecurity challenges.

In conclusion, executive coaching is an indispensable leadership development tool in cybersecurity project management within cyber engineering and cyber offensive operations. The contemporary digital landscape is fraught with ever-evolving cyber threats and vulnerabilities, necessitating a strategic and proactive approach to cybersecurity (Burrell, 2019). Properly managed cybersecurity projects safeguard an organization's information assets, sensitive data, and critical infrastructure and ensure resilience against increasingly sophisticated cyberattacks and breaches (Burrell, 2019).

Effective project management within the cybersecurity domain is not a mere administrative function; it is the linchpin that ensures the efficient allocation of resources, the effective mitigation of risks, and the alignment of security measures with the organization's broader security strategy and objectives

(Burrell, 2019). As the cyber threat landscape continues to evolve, the role of leaders within cybersecurity project management becomes even more critical. These leaders must possess technical expertise, effective leadership skills, and a commitment to continuous professional development (Burrell, 2019).

Furthermore, leadership becomes paramount in cybersecurity offensive operations, where proactive measures are taken to gather intelligence and disrupt or neutralize cyber threats (Nobles, 2023). These operations are conducted to identify, monitor, and potentially counteract cyber threats emanating from hostile nation-states, cybercriminals, and other malicious actors (Nobles, 2023). In such a complex and rapidly evolving landscape, leaders must be technically proficient and adept at strategic thinking, decision-making, and team management (Burrell, 2018).

Effective leadership is indispensable in cybersecurity engineering, focusing on designing, building, and implementing robust and resilient cybersecurity solutions (Nobles, 2023). Engineering principles guide cybersecurity engineering and emphasize incorporating security requirements from the early stages of system design throughout the entire system lifecycle (Nobles, 2023). Leadership in this domain involves technical acumen, and the ability to ensure security is an integral part of the development process (Burrell, 2018).

Both cybersecurity engineering and offensive operations are integral components of national security efforts aimed at safeguarding critical infrastructure, defending against cyber threats, gathering intelligence, and deterring malicious actors in an increasingly interconnected world (Nobles, 2023). These endeavors are pivotal for protecting a nation's security, economy, and overall well-being in the face of evolving cyber challenges.

In conclusion, executive coaching is a cornerstone in developing leaders within cybersecurity project management, engineering, and offensive operations. As organizations and governments grapple with the ever-changing cybersecurity landscape, effective leadership emerges as a linchpin for success and resilience in the face of cyber threats and challenges (Burrell, 2018).

RECOMMENDATIONS FOR FUTURE RESEARCH

By employing additional research approaches, scholars can advance our understanding of the role of executive coaching in cybersecurity leadership development. Diverse methodologies can shed light on the specific strategies, competencies, and contextual factors contributing to successful leadership in cybersecurity project management and offensive operations. Moreover, such research can inform the design of tailored coaching programs and leadership development initiatives that address the distinct needs of cybersecurity professionals and organizations, ultimately enhancing national security efforts in the digital age. Some viable possibilities include the following:

GROUNDED THEORY APPROACH

Given the pivotal role of executive coaching in cybersecurity leadership development within the domains of Cyber Engineering and cyber offensive operations, there is a need for research using grounded theory methodology to explore and develop a comprehensive theoretical framework for understanding the dynamics of executive coaching in this context. Grounded theory allows researchers to build theories from the ground up, grounded in the data collected from real-world experiences (Glaser & Strauss, 1967).

Researchers can use this approach to uncover the specific coaching strategies, leadership competencies, and contextual factors that contribute to the effectiveness of executive coaching in cybersecurity leadership development. This approach can help develop a nuanced understanding of this field's unique challenges and opportunities.

SMALL FOCUS GROUP QUALITATIVE RESEARCH

Small focus group qualitative research can provide valuable insights into the experiences and perceptions of cybersecurity professionals who have undergone executive coaching. By conducting in-depth discussions with small group participants, researchers can delve into the nuances of their coaching experiences, leadership development outcomes, and the impact on cybersecurity project management and offensive operations. This approach allows for a rich exploration of individual and collective experiences, providing a deeper understanding of the practical implications of executive coaching in cybersecurity.

ETHNOGRAPHIC RESEARCH

Ethnographic research offers a holistic and immersive approach to studying the cultural and contextual aspects of executive coaching within the cybersecurity domain. Researchers can embed themselves within cybersecurity organizations or agencies to observe firsthand coaching interactions, leadership practices, and organizational culture. Ethnography allows a deep exploration of the sociocultural dynamics, power structures, and leadership challenges unique to this field. It can uncover implicit norms, values, and behaviors that influence the effectiveness of executive coaching and leadership development efforts.

REFERENCES

Agency Theory Approach. (2013). *Journal of Business Ethics, 115*, 599–603. doi:10.1007/s10551-012-1442-z

Anderson, A. (2011). *Engaging resistance: How ordinary people successfully champion Change*. Stanford University Press.

Artto, A. (2014). Strategic business management through multiple projects. Hoboken, NJ: Wiley.

Bocciardi, F., Caputo, A., Fregonese, C., Langher, V., & Sartori, R. (2017). Career adaptability as a strategic competence for career development: An exploratory study of its key predictors. *European Journal of Training and Development, 41*(1), 67–82. doi:10.1108/EJTD-07-2016-0049

Boyd, A. (2018, March). *It Takes More Than Tech Skills To Be a Strong Cyber Leader*. NextGov. Retrieved from: https://www.nextgov.com/cybersecurity/2018/03/it-takes-more-tech-skills-be-strong-cyber-leader/146520/

Burrell, D. N. (2018). An Exploration of the Critical Need for Formal Training in Leadership for Cybersecurity and Technology Management Professionals. *International Journal of Hyperconnectivity and the Internet of Things*, *2*(1), 52–67. doi:10.4018/IJHIoT.2018010105

Burrell, D. N. (2019). Assessing the Value of Executive Leadership Coaches for Cybersecurity Project Managers. *International Journal of Human Capital and Information Technology Professionals*, *10*(2), 20–32. doi:10.4018/IJHCITP.2019040102

Burrell, D. N., Nobles, C., & Aridi, A. S. (2018). The critical need for formal leadership development programs for cybersecurity and information technology professionals. *Proceedings of the 2018 International Conference on Cyber Warfare and Security*, 82-91.

Candis, B. (2010, February). Assessing Leadership Readiness Using Developmental Personality Style: A tool for leadership coaching. *International Journal of Evidence Based Coaching and Mentoring*, *8*(1).

Chartered Institute of Personnel and Development. (2010). *Learning and Development 2010*. Author.

Creemers, B. (2010). *Improving the quality of education: Dynamic Approaches to school Improvement*. Routledge.

Cunningham, L., & McNally, K. (2003). *Improving Organizational and Individual Performance through Coaching. A Case Study*. Mosby, Inc. doi:10.1067/nrsi.2003.90

De Meuse, K. P., Dai, G., & Lee, R. J. (2009). Evaluating the effectiveness of executive coaching: Beyond R.O.I.? *Coaching (Abingdon, UK)*, *2*(2), 117–134. doi:10.1080/17521880902882413

Duke, D. L. (2011). *The challenge of school district leadership*. Routledge.

Elkins, R. (2015). *Business: Golden Nugget Methods for High Effectiveness - Leadership, Management & Communication*. CreateSpace Independent Publishing Platform.

Ely, K., Boyce, L. A., Nelson, J. K., Zaccaro, S. J., & Hernez-Broome, G. W. (2010). Evaluating Leadership Coaching: A review and integrated framework. *The Leadership Quarterly*. Retrieved from: Journal homepage: www.elsevier.com/locate/leaqua

Feldman, D. C. (2001). Career coaching: What H.R. professionals and managers need to know. *Human Resources Planning*, *24*, 26–35.

Feldman, D. C., & Lankau, M. J. (2010). Executive Coaching: A review and Agenda for Future Research. *Journal of Management*. Advance online publication. doi:10.1177/0149206305279599

Fenwick, F. J., & Gayle, C. A. (2008). Missing Links in Understanding the Relationship Between Leadership and Organizational Performance. *The International Business & Economics Research Journal*, *7*.

Freeman, A. M., & Perry, J.A. (2010). Executive coaching under pressure: A case study. *Consulting Psychology Journal: Practice and Research*, *6*, 189-202.

Gray, E. D., Ekinci, Y., & Goregaokar, H. (2011). Coaching S.M.E. managers: business development or personal therapy? Faculty of Management and Law, University of Surrey. Doi:10.108/09585

Kampa-Kokesh, S., Anderson, M., (2005). *Executive Coaching: A Comprehensive Review of the Literature.* Educational Publishing Foundation and the Society of Consulting Psychology. DOI doi:10.1037//1061-4087.53.4.2O5

Khan, V., Hafeez, M., Rizfi, S. M., Hasanain, A., Maria, A. (2012). The relationship of leadership styles, employees commitment, and organization. Performance. *European Journal of Economics, Finance and Administrative.*

Kouzes, J., & Posner, B. (2017). *The Leadership Challenge: How to Make Extraordinary Things Happen in Organizations.* Harvard Business Review Publishing.

Lebihan, R. (2011). Business schools tap coaching trend. *Australian Financial Review.*

Lester, D. L. & Parnell, J. A. (2006). The Desktop Manager. S.A.M. *Advanced Management Journal, 71*(4), 43-49.

Lunenburg, F. C., & Ometein, A. O. (2010). *Educational administration: Concepts and practices.* Wadsworth/Cengage Learning.

Mayfield, J. (2012). The leadership relation between leader Motivating language and employee self-efficacy. A partial least squares model analysis. *Journal of Business Communication.* Advance online publication. doi:10.1177/0021943612456036

McCarthy, G., & Milner, J. (2012). Managerial coaching: challenges, opportunities and Training. Sydney Business School, University of Wollongong, School of Psychology, Deakin University. doi:10.1108/JMD-11-2011-0113

Newsom & Dent. (2011). A Work Behavior Analysis of Executive Coaches. *International Journal of Evidence Based Coaching and Mentoring, 9*(2), 1.

Nobles, C. (2023). Making Sense of Offensive Cybersecurity. In D. Burrell (Ed.), *Real-World Solutions for Diversity, Strategic Change, and Organizational Development: Perspectives in Healthcare, Education, Business, and Technology* (pp. 1–25). I.G.I. Global. doi:10.4018/978-1-6684-8691-7.ch001

Northouse, P. G. (2013). *Leadership Theory and Practice* (6th ed.). Western Michigan University.

Obiwuru, Okwu, Akpa, & Nwankwere. (2011). Effects of leadership style on organizational performance: A survey of selected small scale enterprise in Ikosia-Ketu counsil development area of Lagos state, Nigeria. Academic Press.

Oltsik, J. (2017). The life and times of cybersecurity professionals. *E.S.G. and ISSA: Research Report.* Available at: https://www.esg-global.com/hubfs/issa/ESG-ISSA-Research-Report-Life-of-Cybersecurity-Professionals-Nov-2017.pdf?hsCtaTracking=a63e431c-d2ce-459d-8787-cc122a193baf%7Ce74f0327-0bbc-444a-b7a8-e2cd08d1999e

Paul, G. W., & Berry, D. M. (2013). *The Importance of Executive Leadership in Creating a Post- Merged Organizational Culture Conducive to Effective Performance Management.* S.A. Journal of Human Resources Management/SA.

Pellegrinelli, S., (2011). What's in a name? Project and program? *International Journal of Project Management, 29*(2), 232-240.

Peltier, B. (2001). *The psychology of executive coaching: Theory and Application*. Sheridan Books.

Peters-Burton, E. E., Merz, S. A., Ramirez, E. M., & Saroughi, M. (2015). The effect of cognitive apprenticeship-based professional development on teacher self-efficacy of science teaching, motivation, knowledge calibration, and perceptions of inquiry-based teaching. *Journal of Science Teacher Education, 26*(6), 525–548. doi:10.1007/s10972-015-9436-1

Peterson, D. B., & Hicks, M. D. (1995). *The leader as coach: Strategies for coaching and Developing others*. Personnel Decisions.

Saowalux, P. & Peng, C. (2007). *Impact of Leadership Style on Performance: A Study of Six Sigma Professionals in Thailand*. International DSI/Asia and Pacific DSI.

Senge, P. M. (2006). The Fifth Discipline: The Art and Practice of the Learning Organization. Academic Press.

Spector, B. (2011). *Implementing organizational change: Theory into practice-international edition*. Prentice Hall.

Strang, K. D. (2011). Leadership substitute and personality impact on time and quality in virtual new product development project. *Project Management Journal, 42*(1), 73–90. doi:10.1002/pmj.20208

Thomas, F. N., Waits, R. A., & Hartsfield, G. L. (2007). The influence of Gregory Bateson: Legacy or vestige? *Kybernetes, 36*(7/8), 871–883. doi:10.1108/03684920710777397

Towhidi, G., & Pridmore, J. (2022). Increasing cybersecurity interest and self-efficacy through experiential labs. *Issues in Information Systems, 23*(2).

Visser, M. (2007b). System dynamics and group facilitation: Contributions from communication Theory. *System Dynamics Review, 23*(4), 453–463. doi:10.1002/sdr.391

Vugt, M. V., Hogan, R., & Kaiser, R. (2008). Leadership, Followership, and Evolution. American Psychologist Association. doi:10.1037/0003-066X.63.3.182

Walker-Fraser, A. (2011, August). An H.R. perspective on executive coaching for organizational Learning. *International Journal of Evidence Based Coaching and Mentoring, 9*(2).

Wasylyshyn, K. M. (2003). Coaching and executive character: Core problems and basic approaches. *Consulting Psychology Journal, 55*(2), 94–106. doi:10.1037/1061-4087.55.2.94

Wenson, E. (2010, November). After-coaching leadership skills and their impact on direct reports: recommendations for organizations. *Human Resource Development International, 13*(5), 607–616. doi:10.1080/13678868.2010.520485

Wysocki, R. K. (2014). Effective Project Management: Traditional, agile, extreme (7th ed.). Academic Press.

Chapter 20

Why Historically Black Colleges and Universities (HBCUs) Should Employ New Approaches to Cybersecurity Faculty Development

Darrell Norman Burrell
ⓘ https://orcid.org/0000-0002-4675-9544
Marymount University, USA

Cedric Dewayne Webber
Trevecca Nazarene University, USA

ABSTRACT

The demand for specialized computer science degrees, particularly cybersecurity, has surged within educational institutions, presenting a significant challenge in the quest for well-qualified instructors. These emerging dynamics underscore the critical role of instructors in shaping and delivering relevant and comprehensive course experiences to mold adept security technologists. This chapter delves into the contemporary educational landscape, marked by the rapid expansion of the digital domain and an escalating need for cybersecurity professionals. Historically Black Colleges and Universities (HBCUs) are at the epicenter of an imperative. To meet the burgeoning demand for cybersecurity expertise, they must cultivate a new generation of cybersecurity faculty and graduates equipped to navigate the challenges of the digital age. The chapter explores innovative faculty development approaches in cybersecurity, addressing the need for educators to align their teaching with industry practices and equip students with the skills to thrive in this dynamic field.

DOI: 10.4018/979-8-3693-1970-3.ch020

OVERVIEW

Mountrouidou et al. (2019) noted that the global demand for cybersecurity experts has surged significantly recently. The United States, in particular, is experiencing remarkable job growth in this field, currently standing at an impressive 28%, three times the national average. However, the expansion of the cybersecurity domain extends far beyond technical aspects alone. It encompasses a wide spectrum of domains, including policy formulation, international law, commercial strategies, and human factors engineering, as emphasized in Mountrouidou et al.'s comprehensive research (2019).

Despite the field's rapid evolution, it is crucial to acknowledge that the cybersecurity industry has yet to keep pace with becoming more culturally diverse. According to the research findings by Mountrouidou et al. (2019), the demographic composition of the cybersecurity workforce in 2018 reflects this imbalance, with only 24.9% of professionals being women, 12.3% African Americans, and 6.8% Latino Americans. This lack of diversity in technology and cybersecurity is not merely a matter of inclusivity; it also holds strategic importance for firms aiming to maintain relevance to their clients and stay competitive in the talent market, as explained by Burrell (2020).

The imperative for fostering a more inclusive working environment goes beyond mere representation. It extends to creating opportunities for a broader spectrum of professionals to advance in their careers and unleash their full potential, as aptly articulated by Burrell (2020). Thus, the quest for diversity in the cybersecurity sector is not solely a matter of equity but also an essential strategic move for organizations seeking to thrive in a rapidly evolving digital landscape (Lewis & Burrell, 2023).

In recent years, cybersecurity has emerged as a cornerstone of the modern economy, growing in paramount significance, as highlighted by Mountrouidou et al. (2019). The ever-expanding digital landscape has led to a surging demand for cybersecurity professionals, with estimates revealing a staggering shortfall of over 1 million unfilled cybersecurity positions (Burrell, 2020). Concurrently, Historically Black Colleges and Universities (HBCUs), renowned for their commitment to promoting diversity and equity in higher education, are poised to play a pivotal role in bridging the cybersecurity skills gap that looms over the United States (Burrell, 2020; Lewis & Burrell, 2023).

In an increasingly interconnected world, cybersecurity has assumed a pivotal role in safeguarding our digital infrastructure, securing sensitive data, and ensuring the safety of individuals and organizations, as articulated by Mountrouidou et al. (2019). However, despite the escalating demand for cybersecurity experts, the field remains predominantly male and requires greater diversity (Burrell, 2019). The importance of diversity in cybersecurity cannot be overstated. Firstly, diverse teams bring many perspectives and experiences, enabling them to identify and address threats that may remain concealed, as Burrell et al. (2023) noted. Secondly, diversity fosters a culture of creativity and innovation, which is indispensable in a field characterized by constant evolution (Burrell et al., 2023; Burrell, 2021). Lastly, diverse teams more accurately represent the diverse populations they serve, formulating more effective and equitable solutions (Burrell et al., 2023; Burrell, 2021). The significance of diversity in cybersecurity extends beyond mere representation; it is a strategic imperative for the field's continued growth, resilience, and effectiveness in safeguarding our digital future (Lewis & Burrell, 2023).

Compared to more established disciplines like mathematics, biology, chemistry, and physics, cybersecurity is relatively nascent, as emphasized by Burrell and Nobles (2018). Consequently, the field, as a whole, grapples with a collective deficiency, particularly in terms of the quality of instruction and student engagement within the classroom (Burrell & Nobles, 2018). In this rapidly evolving digital landscape, the cybersecurity domain has become increasingly intricate, demanding that cybersecurity and information security professionals, along with associated specialists, continuously adapt to keep pace with the ongoing technological revolutions, as pointed out by Cabaj, Domingos, Kotulski, and Respício (2018).

The diversification in the cybersecurity education landscape is evident, with 182 universities and colleges in the United States holding the Center of Academic Excellence in Information Assurance Certifications offering distinct undergraduate curricula (Cabaj et al., 2018). A comprehensive study conducted in 2013 comparing renowned universities in the United States and China underscored a notable disparity in the curricular emphasis (Cabaj et al., 2018). Chinese universities primarily focused on telecommunication security, while their U.S. counterparts concentrated on enterprise risk security (Cabaj et al., 2018).

Over the past two decades, colleges and universities have grappled with the formidable challenge of adequately preparing cybersecurity professionals to meet the ever-accelerating changes in the cybersecurity landscape. This challenge includes recruiting a sufficient number of students and ensuring that the education and training provided align with the dynamic demands of the computing industry (Burrell et al., 2015).

The landscape of STEM-related job opportunities is undergoing a profound transformation, with approximately half of these positions and more than 60% of all new STEM openings now falling within the domain of computing fields (Burrell & Nobles, 2018). This surge in demand for computing professionals underscores the critical role played by computer science education in preparing future generations for lucrative and impactful careers. However, the field of computer science, particularly within the sub-discipline of cybersecurity, grapples with a wide spectrum of pedagogical approaches and content variations across academic institutions (Burrell et al., 2015). This diversity of perspectives and methodologies reflects the dynamic nature of the cybersecurity domain, where rapid growth and continual changes necessitate ongoing adaptations in education (Lewis & Burrell, 2023).

The range of teaching methodologies and curricular content in cybersecurity education exhibits substantial heterogeneity among universities (Burrell et al., 2015). This diversity of approaches is symptomatic of the evolving nature of the field, where the constant emergence of new threats and technologies mandates a flexible and adaptive educational framework. As recent advancements and shifts in cybersecurity continue to occur at an unprecedented pace, educators are confronted with the formidable task of continuously updating course materials to ensure that they effectively equip students with the knowledge and skills required for pursuing advanced degrees and careers in this dynamic field (Burrell et al., 2015). The challenge lies in striking the right balance between foundational knowledge and the latest industry developments, thus preparing students to successfully navigate the ever-evolving landscape of cybersecurity (Lewis & Burrell, 2023; Burrell & McAndrew, 2023).

A significant gap in cybersecurity education exists at the K-12 level, leaving many students needing exposure to fundamental cybersecurity concepts (Burrell et al., 2015). Research has illuminated the adverse effects of this deficiency, as it contributes to many misconceptions that deter students from pursuing degrees in the cybersecurity field (Burrell & Nobles, 2018). Several factors underpin the persistence of these issues, including the prevailing perception that computer science is not a core subject in many educational systems, resulting in limited prioritization of cybersecurity education within school districts (Burrell et al., 2015). This dearth of emphasis on cybersecurity within educational frameworks subsequently translates into a shortage of teaching positions for educators equipped with cybersecurity expertise, perpetuating a cycle of insufficient training for teachers during their collegiate years and as part of their ongoing professional development (Burrell et al., 2015).

The absence of comprehensive cybersecurity education at the K-12 level has ramifications that extend beyond the classroom. It hinders the development of foundational cybersecurity knowledge among students, making it less likely for them to consider pursuing cybersecurity degrees and careers. Furthermore, failing to recognize computer science as a core subject represents a systemic barrier to cybersecurity education. As a result, there needs to be more educators who possess the necessary cybersecurity skills and knowledge to teach this critical subject effectively. This deficiency underscores the importance of reevaluating educational priorities and investing in teacher training programs to equip educators with the requisite cybersecurity expertise, ultimately fostering a generation of students who are well-versed in cybersecurity concepts and better prepared to pursue careers in this vital field (Lewis & Burrell, 2023; Burrell & McAndrew, 2023).

In essence, there exists an imperative to explore strategies that can bolster the enrollment of students in cybersecurity academic programs (Cheung et al., 2011). Moreover, a notable diversity of perspectives emerges within cybersecurity education regarding the most suitable pedagogical approaches and curriculum content (Cheung et al., 2011; Burrell et al., 2015). This divergence in educational philosophies and practices becomes particularly pronounced when considering the sub-field of cybersecurity, where universities exhibit a wide spectrum of instructional approaches and content offerings (Burrell & Nobles, 2018).

The challenge lies in attracting more students to pursue academic pathways in cybersecurity, as this field assumes increasing importance in the digital age (Lewis & Burrell, 2023; Burrell & McAndrew, 2023). Equally vital is the need to reconcile the differing opinions and methodologies surrounding cybersecurity education. This divergence, most evident in the specialized domain of cybersecurity, reflects the evolving nature of the field and the dynamic landscape of cybersecurity threats and technologies. As such, there is a compelling need for the academic community to engage in ongoing dialogue and collaboration, fostering an environment of innovation and adaptability in cybersecurity education. This collaborative approach can equip students with the diverse skill sets and knowledge required to navigate the multifaceted challenges of cybersecurity in an increasingly interconnected world (Lewis & Burrell, 2023; Burrell & McAndrew, 2023).

Recent developments and rapid transformations within the cybersecurity field have unfolded at such an accelerated pace that educators have faced considerable challenges in evaluating the effectiveness of their teaching methods. This fast-paced evolution has left educators with limited time to assess whether their instructional approaches adequately prepare students for success in the classroom and, crucially, inspire them to pursue cybersecurity degrees and careers (Burrell et al., 2015).

Adding to the complexity of this situation, cybersecurity is not universally recognized as a core academic subject by many educational authorities, resulting in a lack of emphasis on this discipline within school districts (Burrell et al., 2015). Consequently, more teaching positions will be available for educators with cybersecurity expertise. This shortage, in turn, hampers the provision of training opportunities for teachers during their college education and as part of their professional development once they enter the workforce (Burrell et al., 2015).

The rapidly changing landscape of cybersecurity education has left educators grappling with the dual challenge of keeping pace with industry advancements and adapting their teaching methods accordingly, all while advocating for the recognition and prioritization of cybersecurity as a fundamental discipline within educational institutions. This multifaceted challenge underscores the critical need for comprehensive reform and support for cybersecurity education to ensure that students receive the knowledge and skills necessary to excel in this ever-evolving field (Lewis & Burrell, 2023; Burrell & McAndrew, 2023).

The sub-field of cybersecurity has experienced remarkable expansion over the past two decades, driven by the proliferation of the internet, the widespread use of network-capable computing devices, and the exponential growth of digital data storage (Burrell & Nobles, 2018). This surge in digitalization has amplified the demand for skilled professionals capable of safeguarding communication channels and securing information storage, rendering cybersecurity a mission-critical imperative for government entities, businesses, and individuals alike (Burrell & Nobles, 2018).

However, the rapid and dynamic growth of the cybersecurity sub-field has posed significant challenges to the academic pipeline (Lewis & Burrell, 2023; Burrell & McAndrew, 2023). The pace of expansion has outstripped the educational ecosystem's ability to keep pace, resulting in a substantial gap between the industry's demands for cybersecurity expertise and the capacity of educational institutions to provide adequately trained professionals (Burrell & Nobles, 2018).

This disparity between the rapid evolution of the cybersecurity sub-field and the educational infrastructure's ability to adapt and meet the burgeoning demand underscores the pressing need for comprehensive reforms in cybersecurity education. Addressing this challenge requires a multifaceted approach that encompasses curriculum development, teacher training, and increased awareness of the importance of cybersecurity education, all aimed at ensuring that the academic pipeline can produce cybersecurity professionals equipped to meet the evolving needs of our increasingly digitalized society (Lewis & Burrell, 2023; Burrell & McAndrew, 2023).

When scrutinizing the landscape of cybersecurity education, one must recognize the conspicuous absence of well-defined best practices (Burrell & Nobles, 2018). This deficiency in established guidelines is further exacerbated by the multitude of stakeholders attempting to tackle the challenge of cybersecurity education (Burrell & Nobles, 2018).

Both government entities and industries are grappling with the situation's urgency, striving to develop their internal standards and training programs to keep pace with the ever-evolving cybersecurity landscape (Burrell & Nobles, 2018). It is worth noting that this process is unfolding against a backdrop where the systems and technologies being addressed continue to transform, even as training initiatives are underway (Burrell & Nobles, 2018).

This intricate and multifaceted landscape underscores the imperative of establishing coherent and universally accepted best practices in cybersecurity education. The absence of such standards hinders the ability to address the evolving cybersecurity challenges effectively and leads to fragmentation in approaches and efforts across different sectors. As we navigate this complex terrain, the need for collaborative endeavors and the development of comprehensive and adaptable frameworks for cybersecurity education becomes increasingly evident (Lewis & Burrell, 2023; Burrell & McAndrew, 2023).

Considering the challenges associated with student recruitment in computer science programs, it becomes imperative for academic departments to redouble their efforts to deliver high-quality and engaging educational experiences for students who opt to enroll in their courses (Burrell & Noble, 2018). This need for enhanced educational quality is particularly pronounced in cybersecurity (Burrell et al., 2015). To meet the growing demand for cybersecurity professionals, it is essential to implement innovative strategies and approaches to cultivate more effective educators, particularly as new faculty members join the ranks of academia (Fisher & Burrell, 2011).

In light of the difficulties in attracting students to computer science departments, it is crucial to maximize the educational value offered to those who have chosen to pursue this field of study (Burrell & Noble, 2018). Cybersecurity, as a subfield, warrants special attention (Burrell et al., 2015). The imperative to bolster the cybersecurity workforce necessitates a fresh perspective on teacher development, especially as a new generation of educators enters the academic arena (Fisher & Burrell, 2011).

This shift toward emphasizing the quality of education and the professional development of educators is essential to attract more students to computer science and cybersecurity and ensure that these students are well-prepared to meet the demands of the ever-evolving technology landscape. It calls for a concerted effort to enhance pedagogical practices and mentorship programs that empower educators to deliver effective and engaging cybersecurity instruction (Lewis & Burrell, 2023; Burrell & McAndrew, 2023).

Research conducted by Burrell et al. (2019) has illuminated several key attributes and practices that characterize effective educators. These qualities are pivotal in fostering an optimal learning environment:

1. Punctuality and Goal Orientation- Effective teachers commence their classes promptly and maintain a clear focus on the intended learning outcomes.
2. Strategic Lesson Planning- They diligently prepare class plans in advance, ensuring the curriculum is well-structured and aligned with instructional objectives.
3. Balanced Pace and Student Engagement- These educators balance teaching appropriately and regularly pause to assess student comprehension and engagement.
4. Diverse Pedagogical Approaches- Rather than relying solely on traditional lectures and PowerPoint presentations, they employ diverse instructional strategies that cater to different learning styles.
5. Clarity in Communication- Effective teachers provide lucid explanations, making complex concepts accessible to students.
6. Adaptability- They exhibit flexibility in their teaching approaches, adapting to the dynamics of
7. the classroom and the unique needs of their students.
8. Appropriate Use of Humor- While integrating humor, their jokes and anecdotes align with their teaching styles and contribute positively to the learning atmosphere.
9. Effective Classroom Management- These educators excel in classroom management techniques, commanding the attention and respect of their students.
10. Interactive Teaching- They actively engage with students by promptly addressing questions and comments and offering constructive feedback.
11. Recognition and Support- Effective teachers acknowledge and praise students who excel in their work while also providing support and guidance to those needing assistance.
12. Creating a Nurturing Environment- They foster a warm and safe classroom climate, allowing students to express themselves freely. Personal anecdotes and efforts to connect with students personally contribute to this inclusive atmosphere.

Collectively, these characteristics contribute to the effectiveness of educators in facilitating meaningful and impactful learning experiences for their students.

Lowman's extensive research in 1996 sheds light on the fundamental dimensions that characterize effective college teaching, unveiling two primary facets:

- Intellectual Excitement- This dimension encompasses several critical elements contributing to effective teaching. It includes the instructor's enthusiasm for the subject matter, depth of knowledge, ability to inspire and motivate students, infusion of humor, presentation of unique and interesting perspectives, and the capacity to convey information with clarity and organizational precision.

- Interpersonal Concern and Effective Motivation- The focus shifts to the instructor's interpersonal skills and motivation strategies in this dimension. Effective teachers are characterized by genuine concern for students, approachability, friendliness, accessibility, and willingness to offer guidance and support. They encourage students and challenge them to reach their full potential.

Furthermore, Chickering and Gamson's 1991 research reinforces the consensus on the key attributes of effective teaching. These attributes include a deep and comprehensive knowledge of the subject matter, strong organizational skills, infectious enthusiasm, clear communication, and the ability to foster positive interpersonal relationships within the educational context.

The convergence of findings across various studies underscores the clarity and objectivity surrounding the characteristics of effective teaching. These qualities are neither enigmatic nor excessively subjective; rather, they form a well-defined and universally acknowledged framework for gauging the effectiveness of educators in higher education.

PROBLEM STATEMENT AND METHOD

In a contemporary landscape characterized by the unprecedented expansion of the digital domain and a surging demand for cybersecurity professionals, Historically Black Colleges and Universities (HBCUs) are confronted with an imperative of paramount importance. This imperative revolves around cultivating a new breed of cybersecurity faculty and graduates equipped to confront and overcome the escalating challenges of the digital age. The statistics presented are unequivocal; within the vast realm of Science, Technology, Engineering, and Mathematics (STEM) careers, an astonishingly substantial portion pertains to computing, amounting to approximately half. Moreover, over 60% of the imminent STEM positions are deeply entrenched within the computing domain, underscoring the prominence and allure of this field for prospective professionals (Burrell & Nobles, 2018).

However, amidst this profound transformation and burgeoning demand, cybersecurity emerges as a pivotal and central domain and a formidable challenge that educators must grapple with (Lewis & Burrell, 2023). The implications of this surge in demand for cybersecurity expertise are multifaceted, ranging from economic considerations to national security implications. Consequently, the role of HBCUs becomes all the more critical as they endeavor to lead and nurture the next generation of cybersecurity specialists (Lewis & Burrell, 2023; Burrell & McAndrew, 2023). This task is imbued with significance, not only in terms of enhancing diversity within the cybersecurity workforce but also in fortifying the nation's cybersecurity posture to safeguard against evolving threats in the digital age.

The realm of cybersecurity education unfolds as a multifaceted landscape marked by a rich tapestry of teaching methodologies and content variations across various academic institutions (Burrell et al., 2015). This complexity is further compounded by the rapid and relentless evolution of the cybersecurity domain, driven by the ever-shifting threat landscape. Educators face the formidable challenge of ensuring their course materials remain consistent with the latest industry practices and technological advancements while preparing students for cybersecurity's dynamic and demanding realm. The task is to educate and empower the next generation of cybersecurity professionals, equipping them with the knowledge and skills necessary to navigate this intricate field (Burrell et al., 2015).

For Historically Black Colleges and Universities (HBCUs), the sense of urgency is dual-pronged and underscored by two distinct imperatives. Firstly, it is imperative to endow students with cutting-edge cybersecurity knowledge and proficiencies, a foundational requirement for their future professional success and safeguarding critical digital infrastructures (Lewis & Burrell, 2023). Secondly, HBCUs must nurture a cadre of cybersecurity faculty with the expertise to effectively impart this knowledge and contribute substantively to the ongoing research and development endeavors in this dynamic field (Burrell & McAndrew, 2023).

The challenges on this path are formidable, but the potential for HBCUs to effect transformative change in diversifying and fortifying the cybersecurity workforce is nothing short of profound (Burrell & McAndrew, 2023). This dual mission, characterized by the imperative to educate and empower students while concurrently fostering the development of cybersecurity faculty, positions HBCUs at the forefront of the cybersecurity education landscape, carrying the mantle of progress, diversity, and innovation in this critical field (Lewis & Burrell, 2023; Burrell & McAndrew, 2023). This paper uses faculty development and teaching literature to develop best practices and practical recommendations for universities looking to develop cybersecurity faculty.

Novelty and Significance of the Inquiry

In an era characterized by an unprecedented expansion of the digital landscape and an insatiable demand for cybersecurity professionals, the imperative facing Historically Black Colleges and Universities (HB-CUs) takes center stage (Lewis & Burrell, 2023; Burrell & McAndrew, 2023). This study embarks on a critical exploration of the profound challenges and transformative opportunities that lie at the intersection of cybersecurity education and faculty development.

The novelty of this study lies in its acute recognition of the urgency surrounding the need to cultivate a new generation of cybersecurity faculty and graduates equipped to confront the escalating challenges of the digital age. With approximately half of STEM-related jobs beckoning the talents of future professionals and over 60% of these opportunities residing in the computing fields, HBCUs stand at a pivotal juncture (Burrell & Nobles, 2018). The realm of cybersecurity emerges as a linchpin within this landscape, demanding innovative solutions for effective education and research.

This research is further distinguished by its in-depth exploration of the sub-field of cybersecurity, a domain characterized by a kaleidoscope of teaching methodologies and content variations across academic institutions through emerging and existing literature on the topic. The dynamic evolution of cybersecurity, propelled by the ever-changing threat landscape, accentuates educators' challenges in maintaining course materials aligned with industry practices and technological advancements (Burrell et al., 2015). The study's significance is underscored by its potential to inform pedagogical approaches that bridge the divide between rapidly evolving cybersecurity knowledge and effective student preparation for advanced degrees and careers in this critical field.

In the context of HBCUs, this study's significance extends to a dual mission. Firstly, it addresses the pressing need to equip students with cutting-edge cybersecurity knowledge and skills vital for professional success and the protection of digital infrastructures. Secondly, it underscores the imperative of nurturing a cadre of cybersecurity faculty capable of imparting knowledge effectively and contributing to ongoing research and development in this field. The challenges are formidable, but the potential for HBCUs to drive diversity and fortify the cybersecurity workforce is a transformational opportunity that cannot be understated (Lewis & Burrell, 2023; Burrell & McAndrew, 2023). This research is poised to illuminate the path forward for HBCUs as they navigate this critical juncture in the digital age.

The Cybersecurity Domain

The rapid expansion of the cybersecurity domain, coupled with its vast and multifaceted nature, has given rise to a diverse array of curriculum and pedagogical approaches within contemporary cybersecurity education (Chisholm, 2015). While this diversity accurately mirrors the complexity and richness of the cybersecurity field, it presents a significant challenge when it comes to forging a comprehensive model for cybersecurity education that can facilitate consistent and sustained improvement (Chisholm, 2015).

Within the purview of cybersecurity, a wide spectrum of knowledge areas comes into play, encompassing domains such as computer architecture, criminology/law, cryptography, databases, human-computer interaction, information retrieval, information theory, management/business, mathematics, military science, mobile computing, networks, operating systems, digital forensics, philosophy, ethics, programming languages, software engineering, statistics (probability), and web programming (Burrell et al., 2015). This expansive scope further amplifies the intricacy of cybersecurity education, as educators must navigate the challenge of harmonizing diverse knowledge domains into a coherent and effective curriculum (Lewis & Burrell, 2023; Burrell & McAndrew, 2023).

Moreover, the anticipated learning outcomes from cybersecurity courses can vary dramatically across institutions and programs, with some focusing on practical vocational skills, others on sound engineering practices, and others on academic theories (Chisholm, 2015). This divergence in educational objectives underscores the need for a unified framework that can serve as a foundation for cybersecurity education, providing a roadmap for educators to navigate the complex terrain of this vital field while ensuring a consistent and high-quality learning experience for students (Lewis & Burrell, 2023; Burrell & McAndrew, 2023).

Gibbs' Reflective Cycle

Gibbs' reflective cycle begins by prompting us to describe the situation, and here, it's evident that educational institutions are grappling with the challenge of finding well-qualified instructors to meet the surging demand. This phase invites educators and policymakers to acknowledge teaching challenges and its implications, setting the stage for a deeper examination (Markkanen et al., 2020).

Moving to the second phase of the reflective cycle, we consider the feelings and thoughts evoked by the situation. The passage underscores the critical role of instructors in shaping the future of cybersecurity professionals. This highlights the tension between the growing need for expertise and the limited pool of qualified educators, potentially leading to feelings of urgency and concern among stakeholders in the education sector. It also raises questions about the readiness of academic institutions to adapt to the rapidly changing digital landscape. This phase encourages a critical assessment of the emotional and cognitive responses to the situation.

The third phase of Gibbs' Reflective Cycle involves evaluating the experience and considering alternative actions. In this context, it calls for a comprehensive examination of the strategies and approaches that Historically Black Colleges and Universities (HBCUs) and other educational institutions can adopt to address the shortage of cybersecurity faculty. It prompts us to consider innovative faculty development approaches that align teaching with industry practices, fostering a new generation of cybersecurity educators and professionals. By doing so, institutions can enhance diversity in the cybersecurity workforce, contribute to national cybersecurity resilience, and better meet the demands of the digital age. This phase encourages a forward-looking perspective, emphasizing the importance of informed and strategic decision-making in response to the challenges posed by the digital revolution in education (Markkanen et al., 2020).

Emerging educators entering the teaching profession often confront challenges for which their academic training may not fully prepare them (Sterrett & Imig, 2011; Melnick & Meister, 2008; Le et al., 2010). While attaining a degree, coupled with practica, internships, and work-study programs, constitutes a foundational step in their educational journey, it may not encompass the comprehensive skills and insights required for the complex classroom environment (Le Maistre & Paré, 2010). Recognizing the dynamic nature of the teaching landscape, characterized by evolving roles, shifting expectations, technological advancements, individualized instruction, diverse learning needs, and increasing cultural diversity, it becomes evident that new educators must undergo a structured transition process to thrive in this fast-changing milieu (Wen, 2014).

Sterrett and Imig (2011) underscore the critical importance of mentorship for novice teachers, whether provided by an experienced colleague or a seasoned teacher. This mentorship encompasses vital aspects such as classroom management, curriculum alignment, and the intricacies of educational administration. Novice teachers often grapple with many administrative tasks, including form completion, meeting deadlines, and adherence to protocols, which can be overwhelming (Fisher & Burrell, 2011). To alleviate this burden, it is recommended that new teachers engage in assignments voluntarily, seeking guidance and validation from veteran colleagues before final submission (Fisher & Burrell, 2011).

Additionally, collaborating with experienced colleagues allows new educators to seek advice on pedagogy and effective student engagement strategies (Fisher & Burrell, 2011). This mentorship and collaborative exchange of knowledge are integral components of a successful transition into the teaching profession, empowering educators to navigate the complexities of the modern classroom with confidence and competence.

The evolving landscape of cybersecurity directly catalyzes transformations in the instructional approaches adopted by faculty and educators (Topham et al., 2016). The high demand for cybersecurity professionals drives this transformation, the continual evolution of the cybersecurity domain, and its inherently multidisciplinary nature (Topham et al., 2016). As a result, educators are compelled to embrace innovative pedagogical methodologies that can accommodate comprehensive curricula encompassing diverse subjects within cybersecurity. In certain instances, even experienced faculty members may need more expertise in emerging fields and specialized areas within cybersecurity.

Scholars argue that contemporary cybersecurity challenges necessitate student engagement with various technologies, tools, and techniques (Topham et al., 2016). Governments actively collaborate to shape cybersecurity practitioner training programs (Topham et al., 2016). Within this context, there is a growing advocacy for experiential learning opportunities, which, in turn, requires educational institutions to harness a multitude of laboratory environments (Topham et al., 2016). Educators are confronted with the imperative to explore diverse pedagogical methods to stay abreast of the ever-evolving landscape of cybersecurity tools, technologies, and practices, all with the overarching goal of effectively preparing the next generation of cybersecurity practitioners (Plachkinova & Maurer, 2018; Topham et al., 2016). This evolving pedagogical landscape represents a crucial response to the dynamic nature of the cybersecurity field, ensuring that future cybersecurity professionals are well-equipped to navigate its multifaceted challenges.

Teaching Roles and Approaches

Grasha (1996) promotes an "Integrated Model" of teaching and learning styles, acknowledging that educators naturally possess various teaching styles but underscoring the importance of cultivating diverse styles to adapt to different instructional contexts and learner profiles. For instance, Grasha highlights that combining the Expert and Formal Authority styles is effective when working with dependent learners who may need to be more proficient in the subject matter. Grasha encourages educators to self-reflect on their teaching styles and make deliberate choices. His book, "Teaching with Style," offers a plethora of exercises to facilitate this introspection and outlines his five teaching styles:

- Expert: This style is centered on transmitting knowledge from an expert perspective, challenging students to enhance their competence.
- Formal Authority: It focuses on delineating acceptable procedures and providing students with the necessary structure for effective learning.
- Personal Model: This approach emphasizes teaching through personal example, guiding students to emulate the instructor's behavior and practices.
- Facilitator: A facilitator prioritizes the interpersonal dimension of teacher-student interactions, steering students toward developing their capacity for independent action.
- Delegator: The delegator style nurtures students' autonomy, encouraging them to undertake independent projects and initiatives.

Boice (1991, 1992) underscores the significance of educators being cognizant of various teaching styles and their adaptable applications. This awareness empowers instructors to tailor their instructional strategies to the specific requirements and contexts of their learners, thereby optimizing the effectiveness of their teaching and fostering diverse learning outcomes.

Through extensive research spanning multiple institutions and years, Boice (1991, 1992) identified a distinct category of faculty members called "quick starters." These educators exhibit a remarkable ability to adapt swiftly, make steady progress in their roles, and successfully integrate teaching with their scholarly pursuits. Their success is attributed to several key factors, including collegial support, a positive outlook on teaching, and the capacity to balance their time allocation between preparation, research, and writing (Boice, 1992).

Notably, quick starters approach teaching differently. They maintain a relaxed demeanor and, while adhering to a facts-and-principles teaching approach, allocate time for active student participation. Effective instructors within this category establish a strong rapport with their students, actively encouraging classroom engagement through both verbal and non-verbal cues (Boice, 1992). They derive genuine enjoyment from the teaching process, fostering optimistic attitudes toward their undergraduate students and the educational environments in which they operate. These quick starters exemplify a dynamic and effective teaching style that can serve as a model for enhancing the quality of education in academic institutions (Boice, 1992).

Microteaching

Microteaching, a well-established and highly effective pedagogical technique, is important in teacher preparation and development (Fisher & Burrell, 2011; Burrell et al., 2019). Its primary objective is to equip novice educators with the essential skills and confidence required for effective classroom instruction. Microteaching is a valuable tool for enhancing teaching methods, identifying individual strengths, fostering an empathetic understanding of students as learners, refining teaching styles, and enhancing receptiveness to feedback (Gavrilović et al., 2011; Satheesh, 2011).

One of the distinguishing features of microteaching is its adaptability across various levels of education, spanning from undergraduate to master's and even doctoral programs. It transcends disciplinary boundaries and can be applied effectively in diverse learning domains (Fisher & Burrell, 2011). Typically, during a microteaching session, student teachers are allocated a 20-minute time slot to deliver a lesson to their peers under the guidance of an overseeing instructor within a small group setting. Various instructional aids such as flip charts, overheads, and handouts may facilitate teaching (Fisher & Burrell, 2011; Burrell et al., 2019).

The structure of microteaching sessions is designed to provide invaluable guidance to aspiring educators. It offers practical tips for effective teaching, comprehensive instructions on session preparation, and a framework for productive feedback and self-reflection (Fisher & Burrell, 2011; Burrell et al., 2019). This reflective aspect is pivotal as it encourages ongoing self-improvement and cultivates a growth-oriented mindset among student teachers, ultimately enhancing their pedagogical competencies and readiness for the classroom. Importantly, microteaching allows faculty to teach a sample class, which is recorded and includes feedback from students and peers, providing insights into strengths and areas for improvement.

Microteaching follows a structured teaching cycle encompassing planning, teaching, feedback, re-planning, re-teaching, and re-feedback (Fisher & Burrell, 2011; Burrell et al., 2019). This cyclical process aligns with behavior modification principles, wherein specific skills are practiced during each step, and feedback is provided to facilitate continuous improvement (Fisher & Burrell, 2011; Burrell et al., 2019).

The core premise of microteaching lies in providing a practical platform for educators to enhance their teaching competencies within a controlled and simulated teaching environment (Fisher & Burrell, 2011; Burrell et al., 2019). It is an empowering mechanism for instructors, instilling confidence, extending valuable support, and furnishing constructive feedback as they engage in the pedagogical exercise, focusing on a specific segment of their intended curriculum while surrounded by peers and colleagues (Kusmawan, 2017). This pedagogical approach is grounded in the acknowledgment that the act of teaching in front of actual students diverges significantly from the context of practice, and microteaching serves as a bridge, adeptly preparing educators for the multifaceted challenges they may encounter in real-world classroom settings (Fisher & Burrell, 2011; Burrell et al., 2019).

Beyond its benefits, microteaching also serves as a conduit for teacher collaboration, fostering collective growth and development (Fisher & Burrell, 2011; Burrell et al., 2019). The educational landscape has increasingly underscored the significance of collaboration in teacher education over the past decades (Yuan & Zhang, 2016). This collaborative ethos within the teaching community stimulates educational innovation and nurtures continuous professional learning (Xu, 2015). It provides a platform for teachers to exchange insights on best practices, classroom management strategies, teaching styles, and curriculum design (Fisher & Burrell, 2011; Burrell et al., 2019). Microteaching, in particular, affords numerous opportunities for learning and reflective action, with participants often responding positively to the guidance and advice they receive (Davids, 2016).

Teacher collaboration is pivotal in assisting educators with refining their teaching practices, improving their lesson plans, and enhancing teaching materials (Kafyulilo, 2013). It acts as a source of mutual learning and support, fostering an environment where teachers can collectively advance within their educational institution (Chiou-hui, 2011). During the review of microteaching sessions, educators are given a unique opportunity to engage in conversations with their peers, discussing concepts presented within the recorded teaching sessions (Fisher & Burrell, 2011; Burrell et al., 2019). This collaborative engagement is particularly valuable as it directs attention toward teaching techniques depicted in the videos. It aligns with the perspective of Bowser, Davis, Singleton, and Small (2017), who assert that collaborative learning enhances interactivity and creates an authentic learning environment.

The advantages of microteaching extend beyond individual growth and include serving as a valuable platform for teacher candidates to (a) refine their teaching skills, (b) receive constructive feedback, (c) access mentorship from seasoned educators, (d) develop and internalize effective teaching behaviors, and (e) collectively assess the overall quality of their teacher education program (Elias, 2018). The pairing of teacher candidates with experienced mentors allows students to receive direct feedback, guidance, and coaching from accomplished educators (Elias, 2018). Additionally, microteaching allows teacher candidates to document their experiences, contributing to the body of knowledge supporting theory development. The collection of microteaching data in the context of cybersecurity education is instrumental in shaping the future evolution of teacher preparation programs in the field.

CONCLUSION

As the demand for specialized computer science degrees, particularly those focusing on cybersecurity continues to grow within educational institutions, the challenge of locating well-qualified instructors has become increasingly pronounced (Burrell & Nobles, 2018). Stevenson (2017) underscores the pivotal role of instructors in shaping and delivering relevant course experiences and instrumental in nurturing well-rounded security technologists.

The overarching objective is to produce cybersecurity program graduates with industry-relevant skills aligned with the dynamic cybersecurity landscape (Burrell et al., 2015).

Historically Black Colleges and Universities (HBCUs) are well-positioned to play a significant and effective role in cultivating cybersecurity graduates and developing faculty expertise in this crucial domain (Lewis & Burrell, 2023; Burrell & McAndrew, 2023).

The contemporary cybersecurity curriculum recognizes the imperative of translating tactical skills into practical applications for cybersecurity students (Burrell et al., 2015). The presence of adept instructors who can effectively guide students in acquiring critical cybersecurity skills is pivotal to workforce training and development in this field (Burrell et al., 2015). In this context, microteaching is a potent tool for nurturing cybersecurity professionals integral to creating a skilled and agile cybersecurity workforce (Burrell et al., 2019).

Microteaching is a teaching technique that can be used in faculty development programs, especially for new faculty members or those transitioning to new fields or subjects (Burrell et al., 2019). This approach is effective because it breaks down the teaching process into small, manageable components to provide targeted feedback and improve teaching skills (Burrell et al., 2019). Here is a detailed explanation of microteaching and its relevance to faculty development (Burrell et al., 2019):

1. Component-Based Teaching Practice- Microteaching focuses on isolated teaching components, such as lesson planning, classroom management, content delivery, and assessment techniques. Faculty members practice these components separately and receive feedback on their performance.

2.   Short, Focused Sessions- Microteaching sessions typically last 15-30 minutes. In these brief sessions, instructors teach a specific topic or skill, allowing for intense scrutiny of their teaching methods and student interactions.

3.   Peer Feedback- Microteaching often involves peer observation and feedback. Colleagues or experienced educators observe the microteaching session and provide constructive feedback on various aspects of the teaching, such as clarity of instruction, engagement strategies, and classroom communication.

4.   Video Recording- Many microteaching sessions are recorded, allowing faculty members to review their teaching performance objectively. Watching themselves on video helps instructors identify strengths and areas for improvement.

5.   Iterative Process- Microteaching is an iterative process, meaning that faculty members can conduct multiple microteaching sessions to refine their teaching skills progressively. Each session builds on the lessons learned from the previous one.

6.   Customization to New Fields- Microteaching can be particularly valuable When faculty members enter new fields or subjects. It allows them to adapt their teaching strategies to the specific demands and challenges of the new field, ensuring a smoother transition.

7.   Safe Learning Environment- Microteaching provides a safe and controlled environment for faculty members to experiment with different teaching methods, assess their effectiveness, and make adjustments without the pressure of a full classroom.

8.   Reflective Practice- Microteaching encourages reflective practice, where educators critically assess their teaching methods, identify areas for improvement, and actively work on enhancing their teaching skills.

In summary, microteaching is a pedagogical approach used in faculty development to enhance teaching skills, especially when faculty members are venturing into new fields or subjects. It breaks down teaching into manageable components, offers peer feedback, and provides a safe space for instructors to refine their teaching techniques. This iterative process promotes continuous improvement and leads to more effective and confident educators, even in unfamiliar academic domains.

Teaching cybersecurity effectively requires staying current with emerging issues and adopting the best curriculum design and delivery practices. Here are some best practices and content areas for cybersecurity faculty to teach students about emerging cybersecurity issues:

1.   Stay Current- Faculty should continuously update their knowledge and curriculum to reflect the latest cybersecurity threats, technologies, and regulations. Subscribe to industry news sources, attend conferences, and participate in professional development to stay current.

2.   Hands-On Learning- Practical experience is invaluable in cybersecurity. Incorporate hands-on labs, simulations, and real-world exercises into the curriculum to give students practical skills in dealing with emerging threats.

3.   Teach Threat Intelligence- Cover threat intelligence to help students understand emerging threats and vulnerabilities. Threat intelligence includes analyzing threat reports, understanding threat actors, and using threat intelligence tools.

4.   Cloud Security- With the growing adoption of cloud services, students need to learn about cloud security, including securing cloud environments, managing identity and access, and addressing cloud-specific threats.

5. IoT Security- Explore the security challenges of the Internet of Things (IoT). Teach students about IoT device security, data privacy issues, and the potential impact of IoT on cybersecurity.

6. AI and Machine Learning- Discuss the role of artificial intelligence and machine learning in cybersecurity. Teach students how these technologies can be used for threat detection and prevention, as well as their limitations and vulnerabilities.

7. Zero Trust Architecture- Cover the principles of Zero Trust Architecture (ZTA) and how it can enhance security in modern networks by assuming that threats can be outside and inside the network perimeter.

8. Secure Development Practices- Emphasize secure software development practices, including secure coding, code review, and application security testing to address emerging threats like software vulnerabilities and supply chain attacks.

9. Incident Response- Provide training on incident response planning and execution. Teach students how to detect, respond to, and recover from cybersecurity incidents, including ransomware attacks and data breaches.

10. Privacy and Compliance- Discuss data privacy regulations like GDPR and CCPA. Teach students about compliance requirements, data protection, and privacy by design principles.

11. Blockchain Security- Explore the security aspects of blockchain technology, including cryptocurrencies, smart contracts, and potential vulnerabilities.

12. Threat Hunting- Teach students about proactive threat-hunting techniques to identify and mitigate threats before they cause damage.

13. Cybersecurity Ethics- Discuss ethical considerations in cybersecurity, including the ethical use of hacking skills and the importance of ethical behavior in the field.

14. Cybersecurity Policy and Governance- Cover developing and implementing cybersecurity policies, risk management, and governance frameworks.

15. Communication Skills- Effective communication is crucial in cybersecurity. Train students in presenting technical information, writing incident reports, and explaining security issues to non-technical stakeholders.

16. Soft Skills- Emphasize soft skills like critical thinking, problem-solving, teamwork, and adaptability, which are essential for addressing emerging cybersecurity challenges.

17. Professional Certifications- Encourage students to pursue relevant industry certifications such as Certified Information Systems Security Professional (CISSP), Certified Ethical Hacker (CEH), and Certified Information Security Manager (CISM) to validate their knowledge and skills.

18. Cybersecurity Research- Encourage students to engage in research projects to explore emerging topics and contribute to the field's knowledge.

By incorporating these best practices and content areas into their curriculum, cybersecurity faculty can prepare students to tackle the ever-evolving challenges in the field and contribute to a more secure digital environment.

REFERENCES

Boice, R. (1991). Quick starters: New faculty who succeed. In M. Theall & J. Franklin (Eds.), *Effective practices for improving teaching. New Directions for Teaching and Learning, No. 48* (pp. 111–121). Jossey-Bass.

Boice, R. (1992). *The new faculty member*. Jossey-Bass.

Burrell, D., Finch, A., Simmons, J., & Burton, S. (2015). The Innovation and Promise of STEM-Oriented Cybersecurity Charter Schools in Urban Minority Communities in the United States as a Tool to Create a Critical Business Workforce. In M. Dawson & M. Omar (Eds.), *New Threats and Countermeasures in Digital Crime and Cyber Terrorism*. doi:10.4018/978-1-4666-8345-7.ch015

Burrell, D., & Mcandrew, I. (2023). Addressing Bio-Cybersecurity Workforce Employee Shortages in Biotechnology and Health Science Sectors in the U.S. *Science Bulletin, 28*(2), 127–141. doi:10.2478/bsaft-2023-0014

Burrell, D., & Nobles, C. (2018). Recommendations to Develop and Hire More Highly Qualified Women and Minorities Cybersecurity Professionals. In *The Proceedings of the International Conference on Cyber Warfare and Security*. Academic Conferences International Limited.

Burrell, D. N. (2019). Developing more women in managerial roles in information technology and cybersecurity. *MWAIS 2019 Proceedings*, 20. https://aisel.aisnet.org/mwais2019/20/

Burrell, D. N. (2020). An exploration of the cybersecurity workforce shortage. In Cyber Warfare and Terrorism: Concepts, Methodologies, Tools, and Applications (pp. 1072-1081). IGI Global. doi:10.4018/978-1-7998-2466-4.ch063

Burrell, D. N. (2021). Creating Diverse and Religiously Inclusive Workplace Cultures in Hyper-Connected, Technical, and Cyber-Driven Organizations. *International Journal of Sociotechnology and Knowledge Development, 13*(3), 17–32. doi:10.4018/IJSKD.2021070102

Burrell, D. N., Aridi, A. S., & Nobles, C. (2023). Diversity Leadership Development for Cybersecurity Managers in Healthcare Organizations. In *Handbook of Research on Cybersecurity Risk in Contemporary Business Systems* (pp. 240–254). IGI Global. doi:10.4018/978-1-6684-7207-1.ch012

Burrell, D. N., Dattola, A., Dawson, M. E., & Nobles, C. (2019). A Practical Exploration of Cybersecurity Faculty Development With Microteaching. *International Journal of Applied Management Theory and Research, 1*(1), 32–44. doi:10.4018/IJAMTR.2019010103

Cabaj, K., Domingos, D., Kotulski, Z., & Respício, A. (2018). Cybersecurity education: Evolution of the discipline and analysis of master programs. *Computers & Security, 75*, 24–35. doi:10.1016/j.cose.2018.01.015

Cheung, R., Cohen, J., Lo, H., & Elia, F. (2011). Challenge-based learning in cybersecurity education. In *Proceedings of the 2011 International Conference on Security & Management*, 1.

Chickering, A. W., & Gamson, Z. (Eds.). (1991). *Applying the seven principles for good practice in undergraduate education. New Directions for Teaching and Learning, No. 47*. Jossey-Bass.

Chisholm, J. A. (2015). *Analysis on the perceived usefulness of hands-on virtual labs in cybersecurity classes* (Order No. 3717270). Available from ProQuest Dissertations & Theses Global. (1711732271).

Elias, S. K. (2018). Pre-Service Teachers' Approaches to the Effectiveness of Micro-Teaching in Teaching Practice Programs. *Open Journal of Social Sciences*, *6*(5), 205–224. doi:10.4236/jss.2018.65016

Fisher, J., & Burrell, D. (2011). The value of using microteaching as a tool to develop instructors. Review of Higher Education & Self-Learning, 3(11), 86-94.

Gavriliović, T., Ostojić, M., Sambunjak, D., Kirschfink, M., Steiner, T., & Strittmatter, V. (n.d.) *Chapter 5: Microteaching*. Retrieved on May 4, 2011, from: http://www.bhmed-emanual.org/book/export/html/36

Grasha, A. (1996). *Teaching with style: A practical guide to enhancing learning by understanding teaching and learning styles*. Alliance Publishers.

Le Maistre, C., & Paré, A. (2010). Whatever it takes: How beginning teachers learn to survive. *Teaching and Teacher Education*, *26*(3), 559–564. doi:10.1016/j.tate.2009.06.016

Lewis, E. & Burrell, D. (2023). The Sustainability of Historically Black Colleges and Universities (HBCUs) in the Post-COVID-19 World and Beyond. *HOLISTICA – Journal of Business and Public Administration, 14*(1) 39–62. doi:10.2478/hjbpa-2023-0004

Lowman, J. (1996). Characteristics of exemplary teachers. In M. D. Svinicki & R. J. Menges (Eds.), *Honoring exemplary teaching. New Directions for Teaching and Learning, No. 65* (pp. 33–40). Jossey-Bass.

Markkanen, P., Välimäki, M., Anttila, M., & Kuuskorpi, M. (2020). A reflective cycle: Understanding challenging situations in a school setting. *Educational Research*, *62*(1), 46–62. doi:10.1080/00131881.2020.1711790

Melnick, S. A., & Meister, D. G. (2008). A comparison of beginning and experienced teachers' concerns. *Educational Research Quarterly*, *31*(3), 39–56.

Mountrouidou, X., Vosen, D., Kari, C., Azhar, M. Q., Bhatia, S., Gagne, G., ... Yuen, T. T. (2019). Securing the human: a literature review on broadening diversity in cybersecurity education. *Proceedings of the Working Group Reports on Innovation and Technology in Computer Science Education*, 157-176. 10.1145/3344429.3372507

Plachkinova, M., & Maurer, C. (2018). Teaching Case: Security Breach at Target. *Journal of Information Systems Education*, *29*(1), 11.

Satheesh, K. (2008, November 15). *Introduction to micro-teaching* [Web log post]. Retrieved on August 24, 2018, from: http://sathitech.blogspot.com/2008/11/introction-to-micro-teaching.html

Sterrett, W. L., & Imig, S. (2011). Thriving as a new teacher in a bad economy. *Kappa Delta Pi Record*, *47*(2), 68–71. doi:10.1080/00228958.2011.10516564

Stevenson, G. V. (2017). *Cybersecurity implications for industry, academia, and parents: A qualitative case study in NSF STEM education* (Order No. 10624075). Available from ProQuest Dissertations & Theses Global. (1958945736).

Topham, L., Kifayat, K., Younis, Y. A., Shi, Q., & Askwith, B. (2016). Cyber Security Teaching and Learning Laboratories: A Survey. *Information & Security*, *35*(1), 51–80. doi:10.11610/isij.3503

Compilation of References

Aaltola, K., & Taitto, P. (2019). *Utilizing experiential and organizational learning theories to improve human performance in cyber training*. Academic Press.

Abdavi, F., Fateh, H., & Pashaie, S. (2018). The Effects of Denison's Model of Organizational Culture on Customer Relationship Management (CRM): Case Study of Ministry of Sports and Youth in Iran. *International Journal of Management. Accounting & Economics, 5*(6), 461–472.

Abdul, M. D. T., Kharoufeh, J. P., & Maillart, L. M. (2019). Maintaining systems with heterogeneous spare parts. *Naval Research Logistics, 66*(6), 485–501. doi:10.1002/nav.21864

Aboelmaged, M., Alhashmi, S. M., Hashem, G., Battour, M., Ahmad, I., & Ali, I. (2023). Unveiling the path to sustainability: Two decades of knowledge management in sustainable supply chain–a scientometric analysis and visualization journey. *Benchmarking*. Advance online publication. doi:10.1108/BIJ-02-2023-0104

Abualigah, L., Hanandeh, E. S., Zitar, R. A., Thanh, C. L., Khatir, S., & Gandomi, A. H. (2023). Revolutionizing sustainable supply chain management: A review of metaheuristics. *Engineering Applications of Artificial Intelligence, 126*, 106839. doi:10.1016/j.engappai.2023.10683

Ackerman, B. (2023). Making Cyber Risk Insurable: Disrupting The Cyber Insurance Industry In 2023. *Forbes*. https://www.forbes.com/sites/forbesfinancecouncil/2023/04/27/making-cyber-risk-insurable-disrupting-the-cyber-insurance-industry-in-2023/?sh=466668c358eb

Adano, E. K., & Jones, S. (2017). Effects of human-centered factors on crash injury severities. *Journal of Advanced Transportation, 1208170*, 1–11. Advance online publication. doi:10.1155/2017/1208170

Adebisi, A., Liu, Y., Schroeder, B., Ma, J., Cesme, B., Jia, A., & Morgan, A. (2020). Developing highway capacity manual capacity adjustment factors for connected and automated traffic on freeway segments. *Transportation Research Record: Journal of the Transportation Research Board, 2674*(10), 401–415. doi:10.1177/0361198120934797

Aggarwal, K., Khoa, B. T., Sagar, K. V. D., Agrawal, R., Dhingra, M., Dhingra, J., & R, L. K. (2023). Marketing information system based on unsupervised visual data to manage transportation industry using signal processing. *Expert Systems, 1*. https://doi-org.captechu.idm.oclc.org/10.1111/exsy.13384

Agnew, R., Cullen, F. T., Burton, V. S. Jr, Evans, T., & Dunaway, R. (1996). A new test of classic strain theory. *Justice Quarterly, 13*(4), 681–704. doi:10.1080/07418829600093151

Agrawal, P., Narain, R., & Ullah, I. (2019). Analysis of barriers in implementation of digital transformation of supply chain using interpretive structural modeling approach. *Journal of Modelling in Management, 15*(1), 297–317. doi:10.1108/JM2-03-2019-0066

Ahmady, G. A., Nikooravesh, A., & Mehrpour, M. (2016). Effect of organizational culture on knowledge management based on Denison Model. *Procedia: Social and Behavioral Sciences, 230*, 387–395. doi:10.1016/j.sbspro.2016.09.049

Aho, J., & Cirillo, M. (2023). Let's Talk Weapon System Supply Chain Risk Strategy: Logistics as the pacing function requires a Service supply chain risk management strategy. *The Marine Corps Gazette, 107*(6), 78–81.

Ajgaonkar, A. (2021, Spring). The value of computer vision: More than meets the eye. *Tech Journal.* https://www.insight.com/en_US/content-and-resources/tech-journal/spring-2021/the-value-of-computer-vision--more-than-meets-the-eye.html

Al Saifi, S. A. (2015). Positioning organisational culture in knowledge management research. *Journal of Knowledge Management, 19*(2), 164–189. doi:10.1108/JKM-07-2014-0287

Alanazi, M., Mahmood, A., & Chowdhury, M. (2023). SCADA vulnerabilities and attacks: A review of the state-of-the-art and open issues. *Computers & Security, 125,* 103028. doi:10.1016/j.cose.2022.103028

Al-Asfour, A., & Lettau, L. (2014). Strategies for leadership styles for multi-generational workforce. *Journal of Leadership, Accountability and Ethics, 11*(2), 58–69. http://www.na-businesspress.com/jlaeopen.html

Alasuutari, P., Bickman, L., & Brennan, J. (Eds.). (2010). *The sage handbook of social research methods.* Sage.

Alexander, D. F. A. (2015). *Effect of leadership facilitation and support on turnover intention in the United States federal workforce: The influence of demographic dimensions* (Doctoral dissertation). Retrieved from ProQuest Dissertations & Theses Global (Order No. 3684889).

Alfrey, L., & Winddance Twine, F. (2017). Gender Fluid Geek Girls: Negotiating Inequality Regimes in the Tech Industry. *Gender & Society, 31*(1), 28–50. doi:10.1177/0891243216680590

Al-Hindawi, F. H., & Abdulmajeed, R. K. (2017). The Cognitive Principle of Relevance and its application to anti-Iraq war posters. *The Cognitive Principle of Relevance and its Application. Adab Al-Kufa College of Arts Kufa University,* 9-30. Retrieved from https://www.researchgate.net/publication/313928362_The_Cognitive_Principle_of_Relevance_and_its_Application_to_Anti_Iraq_War_Posters

Allen, M. (2014). Catching the bug: How virtual coaching improves teaching. *Educational Horizons, 92*(4), 25–27. doi:10.1177/0013175X1409200408

Almansoori, A., Al-Emran, M., & Shaalan, K. (2023). Exploring the Frontiers of Cybersecurity Behavior: A Systematic Review of Studies and Theories. *Applied Sciences (Basel, Switzerland), 13*(9), 5700. doi:10.3390/app13095700

Al-Muntaser, B., Mohamed, M., Tuama, A., & Rana, I. (2023). Cybersecurity advances in SCADA systems. *International Journal of Advanced Computer Science and Applications, 14*(8). Advance online publication. doi:10.14569/IJACSA.2023.0140835

Al-Natour, S., Benbasat, I., & Cenfetelli, R. (2011). The Adoption of Online Shopping Assistants: Perceived Similarity as an Antecedent to Evaluative Beliefs. *Journal of the Association for Information Systems, 12*(5), 347.

Alonso-Alonso, M., & Bialer, P. (2016). Detection of marijuana-impaired driving: A review of current methods and potential new technologies. *Traffic Injury Prevention, 17*(8), 794–799.

Alqudhaibi, A., Albarrak, M., Aloseel, A., Jagtap, S., & Salonitis, K. (2023). Predicting cybersecurity threats in critical infrastructure for industry 4.0: A proactive approach based on attacker motivations. *Sensors (Basel), 23*(9), 4539. doi:10.3390/s23094539 PMID:37177743

Al-shatarat, W. M., Al-Bourini, E. S., Aranki, R. M. E., & Al-Shamaileh, N. (2023). Emotional Intelligence and Leadership Effectiveness in Jordanian Schools: An Inclusive Study Using Structural Equation Model. *Migration Letters : An International Journal of Migration Studies, 20*(S8), 222–239.

Alsheibani, S., Cheung, Y., & Messom, C. (2018). Artificial Intelligence Adoption: AI-readiness at Firm-Level. *PACIS*, *4*, 231–245.

Alshurideh, M., Kurdi, B., Alzoubi, H., Obeidat, B., Hamadneh, S., & Ahmad, A. (2022). The influence of supply chain partners' integrations on organizational performance: The moderating role of trust. *Uncertain Supply Chain Management*, *10*(4), 1191–1202. doi:10.5267/j.uscm.2022.8.009

Alsubai, S., Alqahtani, A., Sha, M., Abbas, S., Gregus, M., & Furda, R. (2023). Automated Cognitive Health Assessment Based on Daily Life Functional Activities. *Computational Intelligence and Neuroscience*, *2023*, 1–8. Advance online publication. doi:10.1155/2023/5684914 PMID:37455767

Altschuller, S., & Benbunan-Fich, R. (2010). Trust, Performance, and the Communication Process in Ad Hoc Decision-Making Virtual Teams. *Journal of Computer-Mediated Communication, 16*(1), 27–47.

American Association of State Highway and Transportation Officials. (2021). AASHTO issues connected, automated vehicle policy paper. *Author*. https://aashtojournal.org/2021/10/14/aashto-issues-connected-automated-vehicle-policy-paper/

American Management Association. (2017). *Leading four generations at work*. Retrieved from https://www.amanet.org/training/articles/leading-the-four-generations-at-work.aspx

American Management Association. (2018). AMA training helps you meet executive core qualification (ECQs). Retrieved from https://www.amanet.org/government/govt-leadership-competencies.aspx

Amerson, R. (2011). Making a case for the case study for the case study method. *Journal of Nursing Education, 50*, 427-428-.doi:10.3928.01484834-20110719-0

Anderson, M. (2017). Key trends shaping technology in 2017. *Pew Research Center FACTANK*. Retrieved from https://www.pewresearch.org/fact-tank/2017/12/28/key-trends-shaping-technology-in-2017/

Anderson, A. (2011). *Engaging resistance: How ordinary people successfully champion Change*. Stanford University Press.

Anderson, E., Wiener, R. S., Molloy-Paolillo, B., McCullough, M., Kim, B., Harris, J. I., Rinne, S. T., Elwy, A. R., & Bokhour, B. G. (2023). Using a person-centered approach in clinical care for patients with complex chronic conditions: Perspectives from healthcare professionals caring for Veterans with COPD in the U.S. Veterans Health Administration's Whole Health System of Care. *PLoS One*, *18*(6), e0286326. Advance online publication. doi:10.1371/journal.pone.0286326 PMID:37352241

Anderson, P. (2023). Exploring the Noteworthy Experiences of African American Female Mid-Level Leaders in the United States. In D. Burrell (Ed.), *Applied Research Approaches to Technology, Healthcare, and Business* (pp. 55–72). IGI Global. doi:10.4018/979-8-3693-1630-6.ch005

Anderson, P. M., & Butcher, K. F. (2006). Childhood obesity: Trends and potential causes. *The Future of Children*, *16*(1), 19–45. doi:10.1353/foc.2006.0001 PMID:16532657

Ansari, M., Dash, B., Sharma, P., & Yatharaju, N. (2022). The impact and limitations of artificial intelligence in cybersecurity: A literature review. *International Journal of Advanced Research in Computer and Communication Engineering*, *11*(9), 81–90. doi:10.17148/IJARCCE.2022.11912

AO Kaspersky Lab. (2021). *Kaspersky Cyberthreat Real-Time Map*. Retrieved October 29, 2023, from https://cybermap.kaspersky.com/

Aoki, S., Lin, W. C. W., & Rajkumar, R. (2021, August). human-robot cooperation for autonomous vehicles and human drivers: Challenges and solutions. *IEEE Communications Magazine*, *59*(8), 35–41. doi:10.1109/MCOM.001.2001241

Apfelbaum, E. P., Phillips, K., & Richeson, J. (2014). Rethinking the baseline in diversity research: Should we be explaining the effects of homogeneity? *Perspectives on Psychological Science, 9*(3), 235–244. doi:10.1177/1745691614527466 PMID:26173261

Argyris, M., & Schön, D. (1974). Theory in practice. Increasing professional effectiveness. Jossey-Bass.

Argyris, C. (1993). *Knowledge for action. A guide to overcoming barriers to organizational change.* Jossey Bass.

Aris, I. M., & Block, J. P. (2022). Childhood obesity interventions—Going beyond the individual. *JAMA Pediatrics, 176*(1), e214388–e214388. doi:10.1001/jamapediatrics.2021.4388 PMID:34747988

Arnout, B. A., Abdel-Rahman, D. E., Elprince, M., Abada, A. A., & Jasim, K. J. (2020). Ethnographic research method for psychological and medical studies in light of COVID-19 pandemic outbreak: Theoretical approach. *Journal of Public Affairs, 20*(4), 1–8. doi:10.1002/pa.2404

Arts, J., Basten, R., & Van Houtum, G.-J. (2016). Repairable Stocking and Expediting in a Fluctuating Demand Environment: Optimal Policy and Heuristics. *Operations Research, 64*(6), 1285–1301. doi:10.1287/opre.2016.1498

Artto, A. (2014). Strategic business management through multiple projects. Hoboken, NJ: Wiley.

Asencio, H., & Mujkic, E. (2016). Leadership behaviors and trust in leaders: Evidence from the U.S. Federal Government. *Public Administration Quarterly, 40*(1), 156. doi:10.18356/0b18c57f-en

Asif, M., & Searcy, C. (2014). Towards a standardised management system for corporate sustainable development. *The TQM Journal, 26*(5), 411–430. doi:10.1108/TQM-08-2012-0057

Athar, R. S. (2015). Impact of Training on Employee Performance Banking Sector Karachi. *IOSR Journal of Business and Management, 17*(11). https://pdfs.semanticscholar.org/89ad/c568261ad273b1c6e00c7161b191885d9d80.pdf

Attaran, M. (2020, July). Digital technology enablers and their implications for supply chain management. *Supply Chain Forum International Journal (Toronto, Ont.), 21*(3), 158–172.

Ayodeji, A., Mohamed, M., Li, L., Di Buono, A., Pierce, I., & Ahmed, H. (2023). Cyber security in the nuclear industry: A closer look at digital control systems, networks, and human factors. *Progress in Nuclear Energy, 161,* 104738.

Azam, M., Hassan, S. A., & Che Puan, O. (2022). Autonomous vehicles in mixed traffic conditions-A bibliometric analysis. *Sustainability (Basel), 14*(17), 10743. doi:10.3390/su141710743

Aziz, B. (2020, October). A systematic literature review of cyber insurance challenges. In *2020 International Conference on Information Technology Systems and Innovation (ICITSI)* (pp. 357-363). IEEE. 10.1109/ICITSI50517.2020.9264966

Baby Cumberland Slider Turtles. (n.d.). Retrieved March 2, 2021, from MyTurtleStore.com website: https://myturtlestore.com/baby-cumberland-slider-turtles/

Bacha, E., & Walker, S. (2013). The relationship between transformational leadership and followers' perceptions of fairness. *Journal of Business Ethics, 116*(3), 667680. doi:10.1007/s10551-012-1507-z

Bachman, T., Goldsmith, J., & Nix, J. (2023). Readiness-Based Sparing Models: What You See May Not Be What You Get. *Military Operations Research, 28*(1), 55–71. https://doi-org.captechu.idm.oclc.org/10.5711/1082598328155

Badhwar, R. (2021). Dynamic Measurement of Cyber Risk. In *The CISO's Next Frontier: AI, Post-Quantum Cryptography and Advanced Security Paradigms* (pp. 327–334). Springer International Publishing. doi:10.1007/978-3-030-75354-2_40

Baert, S., De Pauw, A. S., & Deschacht, N. (2016). Do employer preferences contribute to sticky floors? *Industrial & Labor Relations Review, 69*(3), 714–736. doi:10.1177/0019793915625213

Balasubramanian, S. (2023, April 29). With Increasing Reliance On Healthcare Technology, Cybersecurity Is A Growing Concern. *Forbes*. Retrieved from: https://www.forbes.com/sites/saibala/2023/04/29/with-increasing-reliance-on-healthcare-technology-cybersecurity-is-a-growing-concern/?sh=241d1f8f26ee

Ballhaus, R., & Miller, S. (2014, Nov 24). U.S. New obituary: Washington's 'mayor for life'. *Wall Street Journal*. Retrieved from https://proxy.cecybrary.com/login?url=https://search.proquest.com/docview/1627006847?accountid=144459

Bamford, R., Kosterman, R., Hawkins, J. D., & Catalano, R. (2017). A narrative review of interventions to reduce adolescent substance use. *The Journal of Adolescent Health*, *60*(5), 541–552. PMID:28108088

Banerjee, I., Jittrapirom, P., & Dangschat, J. S. (2023). Data-driven urbanism, digital platforms and the planning of MaaS in times of deep uncertainty: What does it mean for CAVs? Avenue 21. *Planning and Policy Considerations for an Age of Automated Mobility*, 431-460. doi:10.1007/978-3-662-67004-0

Barondees, J. A. (1997). On mentoring. *Journal of the Royal Society of Medicine*, *90*(6), 347–349. doi:10.1177/014107689709000617 PMID:9227389

Baron, L., Morin, L., & Morin, D. (2011). Executive coaching. *Journal of Management Development*, *30*(9), 847–864. doi:10.1108/02621711111164330

Bartlett, J. A. (2013). New and noteworthy: Paying it forward, giving it back: The dynamics of mentoring. *mLibrary Leadership & Management*, *27*, 1-6.

Bartlett, J. II, Boylan, R., & Hale, J. (2014). Executive coaching: An integrative literature review. *Journal of Human Resource and Sustainability Studies*, *2*(4), 188–195. doi:10.4236/jhrss.2014.24018

Bass, B. M., Avolio, B. J., Jung, D. I., & Berson, Y. (2003). Predicting Unit Performance by Assessing Transformational and Transactional Leadership. *The Journal of Applied Psychology*, *88*(2), 207–218. doi:10.1037/0021-9010.88.2.207 PMID:12731705

Bechky, B. A., & Okhuysen, G. A. (2011). *Expecting the Unexpected? How SWAT Officers and Film Crews Handle Surprises. Academy of Management Journal, 54(2).*

Beggs, C., & Warren, M. (2014). Safeguarding Australia from Cyber-Terrorism: A SCADA Risk Framework. In I. Management Association (Ed.), Cyber Behavior: Concepts, Methodologies, Tools, and Applications (pp. 282-297). IGI Global. doi:10.4018/978-1-4666-5942-1.ch016

Behavioral Economics in Child Nutrition Programs (BEN). (2018). *Smarter Lunchroom Movement. The Cornell Center for Behavioral Economics in Child Nutrition Programs*. Cornell University. Retrieved from: http://www.ben.cornell.edu/index.html

Belias, D., & Koutelios, A. (2014). The impact of leadership and change management strategy on organizational culture. *European Scientific Journal*, *10*(7), 451–470. https://www.eujournal.org/index.php/esj/article/viewFile/2996/2822

Bell, R. L. (2009). Dialing in to the hidden hierarchy: An analysis of culture as content in popular press business books. *Journal of Leadership, Accountability and Ethics*, *7*(3), 1–20. https://proxy.cecybrary.com/login?url=https://search.proquest.com/docview/608439443?accountid=144459

Benavides, L. (2008). *The relationship between executive coaching and organizational performance of female executives as a predictor for organizational success*. Doctoral dissertation, University of San Francisco, CA. Retrieved from https://repository.usfca.edu/diss/194

Bennett, K. (2021). Leaders' adaptive identity development in uncertain contexts: Implications for executive coaching. *International Journal of Evidence Based Coaching and Mentoring*, *19*(2), 54–69.

Bensley, D. A., & Murtagh, M. P. (2012). Guidelines for a scientific approach to critical thinking assessment. *Teaching of Psychology*, *39*(1), 5-16. doi:10.1177/0098628311430642

Berg, B. L., & Lune, H. (2013). *Qualitative research methods for the social sciences, Plus myresearchkit without etext by Bruce L. Berg*. Pearson.

Berg, M., & Karlsen, J. (2011). An evaluation of management training and coaching. *Journal of Workplace Learning*, *24*(3), 177–199. doi:10.1108/13665621211209267

Bernstein, R. S., Bulger, M., Salipante, P., & Weisinger, J. (2020). From diversity to inclusion to equity: A theory of generative interactions. *Journal of Business Ethics*, *167*(3), 395–410. doi:10.1007/s10551-019-04180-1

Bernstein, W., & Burke, W. (1989). Modeling Organizational Meaning Systems. In R. W. Woodman & W. A. Passmore (Eds.), *Research in Organizational Change and Development* (pp. 117–159). JAI Press.

Bertolini, M., Leali, F., Mezzogori, D., & Renzi, C. (2023). A Keyword, Taxonomy and Cartographic Research Review of Sustainability Concepts for Production Scheduling in Manufacturing Systems. *Sustainability (Basel)*, *15*(8), 6884. doi:10.3390/su15086884

Bhamare, D., Zolanvari, M., Erbad, A., Jain, R., Khan, K., & Meskin, N. (2020, February). Cybersecurity for industrial control systems: A survey. *Computers & Security*, *89*, 101677. doi:10.1016/j.cose.2019.101677

Bhandari, R., Chugh, S. S., & Thacker, N. (2019). Artificial Intelligence in Traffic Safety: A Review and Future Directions. *Transportation Research Record: Journal of the Transportation Research Board*, *2697*(6), 8–17. doi:10.1177/0361198118789961

Bhattacharya, M., Wang, F., & Jiao, F. (2023). Modeling Public Sector Corruption and the Institutional Environment in Emerging Economies: An Institutional Theory View. *The Journal of Applied Business and Economics*, *25*(2), 225–242. https://www.proquest.com/scholarly-journals/modeling-public-sector-corruption-institutional/docview/2827993038/se-2

Biggeman, S. (2015). Modeling the structure of business-to-business relationships. In A. Woodside (Ed.), *Organizational culture, business-to-business relationships, and interfirm networks* (pp. 27–177). Emerald Group Publishing.

Billings Flying Service (BFS). (2021). *Chinook Helicopter Parts (2021): Comprehensive Breakdown of CH-47D Parts*. https://billingsflyingservice.com/chinook-helicopter-parts-guide-2021/

Bishop, T. F., Press, M. J., Mendelsohn, J. L., & Casalino, L. P. (2013). Electronic communication improves access, but barriers to its widespread adoption remain. *Health Affairs*, *32*(8), 1361–1367. doi:10.1377/hlthaff.2012.1151 PMID:23918479

Blair, E. E., Miller, R. B., Ong, M., & Zastavker, Y. V. (2017). Undergraduate STEM Instructors' Teacher Identities and Discourses on Student Gender Expression and Equity. *Journal of Engineering Education*, *106*(1), 14–43. doi:10.1002/jee.20157

Blau, M., & Simon, D. (2016, October 28). Former PA Attorney General Kathleen Kane gets prison term. *CNN Politics*. Retrieved from https://www.cnn.com/2016/10/24/politics/pennsylvania-attorney-general-sentencing/index.html

Bocciardi, F., Caputo, A., Fregonese, C., Langher, V., & Sartori, R. (2017). Career adaptability as a strategic competence for career development: An exploratory study of its key predictors. *European Journal of Training and Development*, *41*(1), 67–82. doi:10.1108/EJTD-07-2016-0049

Bodolica, V., & Spraggon, M. (2018). *Management research methods*. Routledge.

Boice, R. (1991). Quick starters: New faculty who succeed. In M. Theall & J. Franklin (Eds.), *Effective practices for improving teaching. New Directions for Teaching and Learning, No. 48* (pp. 111–121). Jossey-Bass.

Boice, R. (1992). *The new faculty member*. Jossey-Bass.

Bonesso, S., Cortellazzo, L., & Gerli, F. (2020). *Behavioral Competencies for Innovation: Using Emotional Intelligence to Foster Innovation*. Springer Nature. doi:10.1007/978-3-030-40734-6

Bonisteel, I., Shulman, R., Newhook, L. A., Guttmann, A., Smith, S., & Chafe, R. (2021). Reconceptualizing recruitment in qualitative research. *International Journal of Qualitative Methods*, *20*, 16094069211042493. doi:10.1177/16094069211042493

Boute, R. N., & Udenio, M. (2022). AI in logistics and supply chain management. *Global Logistics and Supply Chain Strategies for the 2020s*, 49-65. doi:10.1007/978-3-030-95764-3_3

Bowles, C., & Flynn, E. (2015). Sports stadiums: What's in a name? *American Bankruptcy Institute Journal, 34*(7), 38-39, 71. Retrieved from https://proxy.cecybrary.com/login?url=https://search.proquest.com/docview/1695789756?accountid=144459

Boyd, A. (2018, March). *It Takes More Than Tech Skills To Be a Strong Cyber Leader*. NextGov. Retrieved from: https://www.nextgov.com/cybersecurity/2018/03/it-takes-more-tech-skills-be-strong-cyber-leader/146520/

Boyd, N. E., Zaynutdinova, G. R., Burdette, M., & Burks, N. (2020). Value added: West Virginia University's approach to innovative experiential learning. *Managerial Finance, 46*(5), 599–609. doi:10.1108/MF-08-2018-0403

Boysen, S. M., Arya, T., & Page, L. (2021). Creating a coaching culture in a non-profit. *International Journal of Evidence Based Coaching and Mentoring, 19*(2), 115–132.

Boysen, S., Cherry, M., Amerie, W., & Takagawa, M. (2018). Organisational coaching outcomes: A comparison of a practitioner survey and key findings from the literature. *International Journal of Evidence Based Coaching and Mentoring, 16*(1), 159–166.

Bradberry, T., & Greaves, J. (2018). *Emotional intelligence 2.0*. TalentSmart.

Branscum, P., Kaye, G., & Warner, J. (2013). Impacting Dietary Behaviors of Children from Low-Income Communities: An Evaluation of a Theory-Based Nutrition Education Program. *California Journal of Health Promotion, 11*(2), 43–52. Retrieved from: https://www.cjhp.org/Volume11Issue2_2013/documents/43-52_BranscumP.pdf

Brennand, C. (2017, February). Unlocking a Federal Coaching Culture. *Association for Talent Development (ATD)*. Retrieved from https://www.td.org/Publications/Magazines/The-Public-Manager/Archives/2017/02/Unlocking-a-Federal-Coaching-Culture

Brewer, M. B. (1991). The social self: On being the same and different at the same time. *Personality and Social Psychology Bulletin, 17*(5), 475–482. doi:10.1177/0146167291175001

Bridewell. (n.d.). *Cyber Security in CNI Organisations: 2022 (Part 1)*. Academic Press.

Bridges, S. (2020, March 12). *Bridges transition model*. William Bridges Associates. Retrieved March 21, 2023, from https://wmbridges.com/about/what-is-transition/

Brooks, C. (2023, March 5). Cybersecurity trends & statistics for 2023; What you need to know. *Forbes*. https://www.forbes.com/sites/chuckbrooks/2023/03/05/cybersecurity-trends--statistics-for-2023-more-treachery-and-risk-ahead-as-attack-surface-and-hacker-capabilities-grow/?sh=3eb268a719db

Broughton, T. C., Weggelaar-Jansen, A., & de Graaff, B. (2023). The development of Dutch COVID-19 ICU triage guidelines from an institutional work perspective. *PLoS One, 18*(9), e0291075. Advance online publication. doi:10.1371/journal.pone.0291075 PMID:37708167

Brown, M. E., & Treviño, L. K. (2014). Do role models matter? An investigation of role modeling as an antecedent of perceived ethical leadership. *Journal of Business Ethics, 122*(4), 587-598. doi:http://dx.doi.org.proxy.cecybrary.com/10.1007/s10551-013-1769-0

Brown-Jackson, K. L. (2023). *Cybersecurity Leadership: A Healthcare Critical Infrastructure And Wearables Examination* [Unpublished Exegesis]. Capitol Technology University.

Brown, R. P., Varghese, L., Sullivan, S., & Parsons, S. (2021). The impact of professional coaching on emerging leaders. *International Journal of Evidence Based Coaching and Mentoring, 19*(2), 24–37.

Bruckmüller, S., Ryan, M., Haslam, S., & Peters, K. (2014). Ceilings, cliffs, and labyrinths: Exploring metaphors for workplace gender discrimination. In M. Ryan & N. Branscombe (Eds.), The SAGE handbook of gender and psychology (pp. 450-464). SAGE Publications Ltd.

Brunhart, A. D. (2013). *The relationship between felt accountability and perceived overall organizational performance in federal agencies* (Doctoral dissertation). Retrieved from ProQuest Dissertations & Thesis Global (Order No. 3554024).

Buchanan, N. T., & Settles, I. H. (2019). Managing (in) visibility and hypervisibility in the workplace. *Journal of Vocational Behavior, 113*, 1–5. doi:10.1016/j.jvb.2018.11.001

Bureau of Transportation Statistics. (2022). *US Ports work through daunting Challenges to Deliver the Goods*. https://www.bts.gov/data-spotlight/us-ports-work-through-daunting-challenges-deliver-goods

Burgess, J., & Dyer, S. (2009). Workplace mentoring for indigenous Australians: A case study. *Equal Opportunities International, 28*(6), 465–485. doi:10.1108/02610150910980774

Burkus, D. (2014). How to tell if your company has a creative culture. *Harvard Business Review*. Retrieved from https://hbr.org/2014/12/how-to-tell-if-your-company-has-a-creative-culture

Burrell, D. (2015, March). As the country becomes more international and diverse, it is critical to develop healthcare professional expertise in diversity and inclusion. In *Interdisciplinarian* (Vol. 2). The Association of Interdisciplinary Doctors of Health Science.

Burrell, D. N. (2019). Developing more women in managerial roles in information technology and cybersecurity. *MWAIS 2019 Proceedings*, 20. https://aisel.aisnet.org/mwais2019/20/

Burrell, D. N. (2020). An Exploration of the Cybersecurity Workforce Shortage. In I. Management Association (Ed.), Cyber Warfare and Terrorism: Concepts, Methodologies, Tools, and Applications (pp. 1072-1081). IGI Global. doi:10.4018/978-1-7998-2466-4.ch063

Burrell, D. N. (2022). Assessing the Value of Executive Leadership Coaches for Cybersecurity Project Managers. In I. Management Association (Ed.), Research Anthology on Business Aspects of Cybersecurity (pp. 349-362). IGI Global. doi:10.4018/978-1-6684-3698-1.ch016

Burrell, D. N., Diperi, D. L., & Weaver, R. M. (2021). Creating Inclusive Cultures for Women in Automation and Information Technology Careers and Occupations. In I. Management Association (Ed.), Research Anthology on Challenges for Women in Leadership Roles (pp. 749–765). IGI Global. doi:10.4018/978-1-7998-8592-4.ch041

Burrell, D. N., Nobles, C., & Aridi, A. S. (2018). The critical need for formal leadership development programs for cybersecurity and information technology professionals. *Proceedings of the 2018 International Conference on Cyber Warfare and Security*, 82-91.

Burrell, D. N., Wright, J. B., Taylor, C., Shockley, T., Reaves, A., & Mairs, J. (2021). Addressing the Public Health Epidemic of Childhood Obesity Using Public Schools as Health Education Learning Laboratories. In I. Management Association (Ed.), Research Anthology on Public Health Services, Policies, and Education (pp. 230–243). IGI Global. doi:10.4018/978-1-7998-8960-1.ch011

Burrell, D., & Nobles, C. (2018). Recommendations to Develop and Hire More Highly Qualified Women and Minorities Cybersecurity Professionals. In *The Proceedings of the International Conference on Cyber Warfare and Security.* Academic Conferences International Limited.

Burrell, D. N. (2018). An Exploration of the Critical Need for Formal Training in Leadership for Cybersecurity and Technology Management Professionals. *International Journal of Hyperconnectivity and the Internet of Things, 2*(1), 52–67. doi:10.4018/IJHIoT.2018010105

Burrell, D. N. (2018). An exploration of the cybersecurity workforce shortage. *International Journal of Hyperconnectivity and the Internet of Things, 2*(1), 29–41. doi:10.4018/IJHIoT.2018010103

Burrell, D. N. (2019). Assessing the Value of Executive Leadership Coaches for Cybersecurity Project Managers. *International Journal of Human Capital and Information Technology Professionals, 10*(2), 20–32. doi:10.4018/IJHCITP.2019040102

Burrell, D. N. (2019). How Hiring Baby Boomers Can Assist with the Global Cybersecurity Employee Shortage. *International Journal of Hyperconnectivity and the Internet of Things, 3*(2), 1–10. doi:10.4018/IJHIoT.2019070101

Burrell, D. N. (2021). Creating Diverse and Religiously Inclusive Workplace Cultures in Hyper-Connected, Technical, and Cyber-Driven Organizations. *International Journal of Sociotechnology and Knowledge Development, 13*(3), 17–32. doi:10.4018/IJSKD.2021070102

Burrell, D. N. (2021). *Cybersecurity leadership from a talent management organizational development lens* [Unpublished Exegesis]. Capitol Technology University.

Burrell, D. N. (2022). Telehealth as an Innovative Supply Chain and Logistics Management Approach. *International Journal of Health Systems and Translational Medicine, 2*(1), 1–9. doi:10.4018/IJHSTM.306971

Burrell, D. N., Aridi, A. S., & Nobles, C. (2023). Diversity Leadership Development for Cybersecurity Managers in Healthcare Organizations. In *Handbook of Research on Cybersecurity Risk in Contemporary Business Systems* (pp. 240–254). IGI Global. doi:10.4018/978-1-6684-7207-1.ch012

Burrell, D. N., Burton, S. L., Nobles, C., Dawson, M. E., & McDowell, T. (2020). Exploring technological management innovations that include artificial intelligence and other innovations in global food production. *International Journal of Society Systems Science, 12*(4), 267–285. doi:10.1504/IJSSS.2020.112408

Burrell, D. N., Courtney-Dattola, A., Burton, S. L., Nobles, C., Springs, D., & Dawson, M. E. (2020). Improving the quality of "The Internet of Things" instruction in technology management, cybersecurity, and computer science. *International Journal of Information and Communication Technology Education, 6*(2), 59–70. doi:10.4018/IJICTE.2020040105

Burrell, D. N., Dattola, A., Dawson, M. E., & Nobles, C. (2019). A Practical Exploration of Cybersecurity Faculty Development With Microteaching. *International Journal of Applied Management Theory and Research, 1*(1), 32–44. doi:10.4018/IJAMTR.2019010103

Burrell, D. N., Diperi, D. L., & Weaver, R. M. (2020). Creating Inclusive Cultures for Women in Automation and Information Technology Careers and Occupations. *International Journal of Business Strategy and Automation, 1*(2), 37–51. doi:10.4018/IJBSA.2020040104

Burrell, D., Finch, A., Simmons, J., & Burton, S. (2015). The Innovation and Promise of STEM-Oriented Cybersecurity Charter Schools in Urban Minority Communities in the United States as a Tool to Create a Critical Business Workforce. In M. Dawson & M. Omar (Eds.), *New Threats and Countermeasures in Digital Crime and Cyber Terrorism*. doi:10.4018/978-1-4666-8345-7.ch015

Burrell, D., & Mcandrew, I. (2023). Addressing Bio-Cybersecurity Workforce Employee Shortages in Biotechnology and Health Science Sectors in the U.S. *Science Bulletin*, *28*(2), 127–141. doi:10.2478/bsaft-2023-0014

Burt, A. (2023). The Digital World Is Changing Rapidly. Your Cybersecurity Needs to Keep Up. *Harvard Business Review*. https://hbr.org/2023/05/the-digital-world-is-changing-rapidly-your-cybersecurity-needs-to-keep-up

Burton, S. L. (2019). Grasping the cyber-world: Artificial intelligence and human capital meet to inform leadership. *International Journal of Economics, Commerce and Management, 7*(12), 707-759. https://ijecm.co.uk/wp-content/uploads/2019/12/71247.pdf

Burton, S. L. (2022). *Cybersecurity leadership from a Telemedicine/Telehealth knowledge and organizational development examination* (Order No. 29066056). Available from ProQuest Central; ProQuest Dissertations & Theses Global. (2662752457). https://www.proquest.com/dissertations-theses/cybersecurity-leadership-telemedicine-telehealth/docview/2662752457/se-2

Burton, S. L. (2007). *Quality customer service; Rekindling the art of service to customers*. Lulu Publications.

Burton, S. L. (2021). Cybersecurity Leaders: Knowledge Driving Human Capital Development. *Science Bulletin, 26*(2), 109–120. doi:10.2478/bsaft-2021-0013

Burton, S. L. (2022). *Strategy: A Business and Cybersecurity Intertwined Necessity. International Journal of Smart Education and Urban Society (IJSEUS), 13(1)*. doi:10.4018/IJSEUS.312232

Burton, S. L. (2023). *Cybersecurity Risk – The Business Significance of Ongoing Tracking*. IGI Global Publication.

Burton, S. L., Bessette, D., Brown-Jackson, K. L., & White, Y. W. (2013). ROI: Drilling Down on Cost-Benefit Components. *Proceedings of the SALT Conference*, 2013.

Butler, B. S., & Gray, P. H. (2006). *Reliability, Mindfulness, and Information Systems. MIS Quarterly*.

Cabaj, K., Domingos, D., Kotulski, Z., & Respício, A. (2018). Cybersecurity education: Evolution of the discipline and analysis of master programs. *Computers & Security, 75*, 24–35. doi:10.1016/j.cose.2018.01.015

Cai, J., Deng, W., Guang, H., Wang, Y., Li, J., & Ding, J. (2022). A Survey on data-driven scenario generation for automated vehicle testing. *Machines, 10*(11), 1101. doi:10.3390/machines10111101

Caillier, J. G. (2016). Toward a better understanding of the relationship between transformational leadership, public service motivation, mission valence, and employee performance: A preliminary study. *Public Personnel Management, 43*(2), 218–239. doi:10.1177/0091026014528478

Calandrillo, S. P., & Fulton, K. (2019). High standards: The wave of marijuana legalization sweeping America ignores the hidden risks of edibles. *Ohio St. LJ, 80*, 201.

California Department of Transportation. (2023). Connected and automated vehicles. *Author*. https://dot.ca.gov/programs/traffic-operations/cav

Cameron, E., & Green, M. (2015). *Making Sense of Change Management: A Complete Guide to the Models, Tools and Techniques of Organizational Change* (1st ed.). Kogan Page.

Camhi, S. S., Herweck, A., & Perone, H. (2020). Telehealth Training Is Essential to Care for Underserved Populations: A Medical Student Perspective. *Medical Science Educator*, 30(3), 1287–1290. doi:10.1007/s40670-020-01008-w PMID:32837786

Campos-Castillo, C., & Hitlin, S. (2013). *Copresence Revisiting a Building Block for Social Interaction Theories.* Academic Press.

Candis, B. (2010, February). Assessing Leadership Readiness Using Developmental Personality Style: A tool for leadership coaching. *International Journal of Evidence Based Coaching and Mentoring*, 8(1).

Cardador, M. T. (2017). Promoted Up But Also Out? The Unintended Consequences of Increasing Women's Representation in Managerial Roles in Engineering. *Organization Science*, 28(4), 597–617. doi:10.1287/orsc.2017.1132

Care, E., Kim, H., & Vista, A. (2019, January 30). Education system alignment for 21st century skills: Focus on assessment. *Brookings Institute*. https://www.brookings.edu/articles/education-system-alignment-for-21st-century-skills/

Carey, G., Malbon, E., Carey, N., Joyce, A., Crammond, B., & Carey, A. (2015). Systems science and systems thinking for public health: A systematic review of the field. *BMJ Open*, 5(12), e009002. doi:10.1136/bmjopen-2015-009002 PMID:26719314

Carli, L. L., & Eagly, A. H. (2016). Women face a labyrinth: An examination of metaphors for women leaders. *Gender in Management*, 31(8), 514–527. doi:10.1108/GM-02-2015-0007

Carlson, S., Rosenbaum, D., Keith-Jennings, B., & Nchako, C. (2016). *SNAP Works for America's Children. Center on Budget and Policy Priorities.* Retrieved from: https://www.cbpp.org/research/food-assistance/snap-works-for-americas-children

Carnegie Mellon University. (2023). Why should assessments, learning objectives, and instructional strategies be aligned? *Author.* https://www.cmu.edu/teaching/assessment/basics/alignment.html

Carter, N., Bryant-Lukosius, D., DiCenso, A., Blythe, J., & Neville, A. J. (2014). The use of triangulation in qualitative research. *Oncology Nursing Forum*, 41(5), 545–547. doi:10.1188/14.ONF.545-547 PMID:25158659

Carter, R. (2002). The impact of Public Schools on Childhood Obesity. Published: November 6, 2002. *Journal of the American Medical Association*, 288(17), 2180. doi:10.1001/jama.288.17.2180-JMS1106-6-1 PMID:12413386

Caruso, G., Mohammad, K. Y., & Mussone, L. (2022). From human to autonomous driving: A method to identify and draw up the driving behaviour of connected autonomous vehicles. *Vehicles*, 4(4), 1430–1449. doi:10.3390/vehicles4040075

Cato Institute. (2017). Downsizing the federal government. Department of Education. *Downsizing Government*. Retrieved from https://www.downsizinggovernment.org/education

Caulfield, M., Collier, A., & Halawa, S. (2013). Rethinking online community in MOOCS used for blended learning. *Educause Review Online.* Retrieved from https://www.educause.edu/ero/article/rethinking-online-community-moocs-used-blended-learning

Caulfield, J. L., & Brenner, E. F. (2020). Resolving complex community problems: Applying collective leadership and Kotter's change model to wicked problems within social system networks. *Nonprofit Management & Leadership*, 30(3), 509–524. doi:10.1002/nml.21399

Cazares, M., Fuertes, W., Andrade, R., Ortiz-Garcés, I., & Rubio, M. S. (2023). Protective Factors for Developing Cognitive Skills against Cyberattacks. *Electronics (Basel)*, 12(19), 4007. doi:10.3390/electronics12194007

Cazzanti, L., Davoli, A., & Millefiori, L. M. (2017). Automated port traffic statistics: from raw data to visualization. *Science and Technology Organization Center for Maritime Research and Experimentation. CMRE-PR-2017-010. IEEE International Conference on Big Data*, 1-6.

Censer, M. (2011, October 30). Executive coaching contracts pick up speed. *The Washington Post.*

Center for Disease Control and Prevention. (2019). *Childhood obesity.* Retrieved from https://www.cdc.gov/obesity/data/childhood.html

Center for Disease Control and Prevention. (2021). *Cannabis Use and Risk of Motor Vehicle Crashes.* Retrieved from https://www.cdc.gov/motorvehiclesafety/Cannabis/index.html

Center for Leadership Studies. (2017). *The Cost of Poor Leadership On Your Revenue And Culture.* Retrieved from: https://www.gbscorporate.com/blog/the-cost-of-poor-leadership-on-your-revenue-and-culture

Centers for Disease Control. (2018). *Obesity. CDC Healthy Schools.* Centers for Disease Control and Prevention. Retrieved from: https://www.cdc.gov/healthyschools/obesity/index.htm

Chamorro-Premuzic, T. (2017, June 28). Does diversity actually increase creativity? *Harvard Business Review.* https://hbr.org/2017/06/does-diversity-actually-increase-creativity

Chang, E., Milkman, K., Zarrow, L., Brabaw, K., Gromet, D., Rebele, R., Massey, C., Duckworth, A., & Grant, Al. (2019, July 9). Does diversity training work the way it's supposed to? *Harvard Business Review.* https://hbr.org/2019/07/does-diversity-training-work-the-way-its-supposed-to

Channon, M., & Marson, J. (2021). The liability for cybersecurity breaches of connected and autonomous vehicles. *Computer Law & Security Report, 43,* 105628. doi:10.1016/j.clsr.2021.105628

Chartered Institute of Personnel and Development. (2010). *Learning and Development 2010.* Author.

Cheah, J.-H., Kersten, W., Ringle, C. M., & Wallenburg, C. (2023). Guest editorial: Predictive modeling in logistics and supply chain management research using partial least squares structural equation modeling. *International Journal of Physical Distribution & Logistics Management, 53*(7/8), 709–717. doi:10.1108/IJPDLM-08-2023-552

Chen, H. Y., Das, A., & Ivanov, D. (2019). Building resilience and managing post-disruption supply chain recovery: Lessons from the information and communication technology industry. *Ocean and Coastal Management, 165,* 244–257. doi:10.1016/j.ocecoaman.2018.08.031

Chen, S., Hao, M., Ding, F., Jiang, D., Dong, J., Zhang, S., Guo, Q., & Gao, C. (2023). Exploring the global geography of cybercrime and its driving forces. *Humanities & Social Sciences Communications, 10*(1), 71. Advance online publication. doi:10.1057/s41599-023-01560-x PMID:36852135

Cheung, H. K., King, E., Lindsey, A., Membere, A., Markell, H. M., & Kilcullen, M. (2016). Understanding and reducing workplace discrimination. *Research in Personnel and Human Resources Management, 34,* 101–152. doi:10.1108/S0742-730120160000034010

Cheung, R., Cohen, J., Lo, H., & Elia, F. (2011). Challenge-based learning in cybersecurity education. In *Proceedings of the 2011 International Conference on Security & Management,* 1.

Chickering, A. W., & Gamson, Z. (Eds.). (1991). *Applying the seven principles for good practice in undergraduate education. New Directions for Teaching and Learning, No. 47.* Jossey-Bass.

Chingching, C. (2016). Methodological issues in advertising research: Current status, shifts, and trends. *Journal of Advertising, 46*(1), 2–20. doi:10.1080/00913367.2016.1274924

Chisholm, J. A. (2015). *Analysis on the perceived usefulness of hands-on virtual labs in cybersecurity classes* (Order No. 3717270). Available from ProQuest Dissertations & Theses Global. (1711732271).

Cho, H. S., & Woo, T. H. (2017). Cyber security in nuclear industry–Analytic study from the terror incident in nuclear power plants (NPPs). *Annals of Nuclear Energy, 99*, 47–53.

Choi, P. P. (2015). Patient advocacy: the role of the nurse. *Nursing Standard, 29*(41), 52. doi:10.7748/ns.29.41.52.e9772

Chong, D. (2013). The relevance of management to society: Peter Drucker's oeuvre from the 1940s and 1950s. *Journal of Management History, 19*(1), 55–72. doi:10.1108/17511341311286196

Chong, W. C., Yuen, Y. Y., Tan, B. C., Zarim, Z. A., & Hamid, N. A. (2016). Managerial coaches, are they ready? The case of Malaysian telecommunications industry. *The Learning Organization, 23*(2/3), 121–140. doi:10.1108/TLO-03-2015-0016

Chughtai, S., & Blanchet, K. (2017). Systems thinking in public health: A bibliographic contribution to a meta-narrative review. *Health Policy and Planning, 32*(4), 585–594. doi:10.1093/heapol/czw159 PMID:28062516

Chukwu, E., Adu-Baah, A., Niaz, M., Nwagwu, U., & Chukwu, M. U. (2023). Navigating Ethical Supply Chains: The Intersection of Diplomatic Management and Theological Ethics. *International Journal of Multidisciplinary Sciences and Arts, 2*(1), 127–139.

Chunsheng, L., Wong, C. W., Yang, C. C., Shang, K. C., & Lirn, T. C. (2020). Value of supply chain resilience: Roles of culture, flexibility, and integration. *International Journal of Physical Distribution & Logistics Management, 50*(1), 80–100. doi:10.1108/IJPDLM-02-2019-0041

Chunsheng, Z., Zhiqiang, W., & Xuefeng, Z. (2020). The impact of emotional intelligence on supply chain resilience: A moderated mediation model. *International Journal of Physical Distribution & Logistics Management, 50*(4), 367–387. doi:10.1108/IJPDLM-05-2019-0155

Ciciurkaite, G., & Perry, B. L. (2018). Body weight, perceived weight stigma and mental health among women at the intersection of race/ethnicity and socioeconomic status: Insights from the modified labeling approach. *Sociology of Health & Illness, 40*(1), 18–37. doi:10.1111/1467-9566.12619 PMID:28980335

Ciporen, R. (2015). The emerging field of executive and organizational coaching: An overview. *New Directions for Adult and Continuing Education, 2015*(148), 5–15. Advance online publication. doi:10.1002/ace.20147

CISA. (2020). Cyber Resilience Review. *Homeland Security*. https://www.cisa.gov/sites/default/files/publications/CRR%2520Fact%2520Sheet.pdf

CISA. (2022). *2021 Trends Show Increased Globalized Threat of Ransomware*. Cybersecurity and Infrastructure Security Agency. https://www.cisa.gov/news-events/cybersecurity-advisories/aa22-040a

Clapham, M. (2001). The Effects of affect manipulation and information exposure on divergent thinking. *Creativity Research Journal, 13*(3-4), 3–4, 335–350. doi:10.1207/S15326934CRJ1334_11

Clifton, K. J. (2022). A step ahead for smart growth: Creating walkable neighborhoods. *Handbook on Smart Growth*, 168-187. doi:10.4337/9781789904697.00021

Cloud Security Alliance. (2023). Maximizing ROI on cybersecurity training. *Author*. https://cloudsecurityalliance.org/blog/2023/07/25/maximizing-roi-on-cybersecurity-training/

Coach, U. (2005). *Coach U; About Coach U and corporate Coach U*. Retrieved from http://www.coachu-hq.com/

Cohen, J. (2017). *Intermountain, community partners, open telehealth kiosks for underserved populations.* Becker's Health I.T. Retrieved from: https://www.beckershospitalreview.com/healthcare-information-technology/intermountain-community-partners-open-telehealth-kiosk-for-underserved-populations.html

Cohen, J. (2019). Artificial intelligence and the future of criminal justice. *Harvard Law Review, 132*(7), 2087–2111.

Coker, J. (2022). Stress and Burnout Could Lead to Exodus of CNI Cybersecurity Leaders. *Infosecurity Magazine.* https://www.infosecurity-magazine.com/news/stress-burnout-exodus-cyber-leaders/

Coleman, L. (2023). 5 common job search tips that totally contradict each other. *Undercover Recruiter.* https://theundercoverrecruiter.com/job-seeking-tips-that-contradict/

Collins, C. S., & Stockton, C. M. (2018). The central role of theory in qualitative research. *International Journal of Qualitative Methods, 17*(1). Advance online publication. doi:10.1177/1609406918797475

Collins, R. (2010). *A graphical method for exploring the business environment.* Henley Business School.

Cone, E. J. (2019). The marijuana breathalyzer: A new tool for law enforcement? *Journal of Studies on Alcohol and Drugs, 80*(2), 222–227.

Constantinides, P., & Barrett, M. (2006). Negotiating ICT Development and Use: The Case of a Telemedicine System in the Healthcare Region of Crete. *Information and Organization, 16*(1), 27–55.

Cornell. (2019). *Agriculture and Food Systems.* Cornell Cooperative Extension. Retrieved from: http://cce.cornell.edu/program/agriculture

Covaleski, M. A., Dirsmith, M. W., & Michelman, J. E. (1993). An institutional theory perspective on the DRG framework, case-mix accounting systems, and healthcare organizations. *Accounting, Organizations and Society, 18*(1), 65–80. doi:10.1016/0361-3682(93)90025-2

Cowie, K. (2008, May/June). The HR challenge: leadership development for ordinary heroes. *Ivey Business Journal.* Retrieved from https://iveybusinessjournal.com/publication/the-hr-challenge-leadership-development-for-ordinary-heroes/

Cox, O., & Kanji, H. (2022, November 10). Building Effective Cybersecurity Governance. *The Harvard Law School Forum on Corporate Governance.*

Cox, E. (2013). *Coaching understood. A pragmatic inquiry into the coaching process.* Sage Publications Ltd. doi:10.4135/9781446270134

Crabtree, S., Kasperowicz, P., King, R., Lawler, J., Russell, J., Siciliano, J., Takala, R., & Westwood, S. (2016, February 20). These 8 federal agencies are the worst. Here's how to fix them. *The Washington Examiner.* Retrieved from http://www.washingtonexaminer.com/these-8-federal-agencies-are-the-worst-heres-how-to-fix-them/article/2583708

Cramer, J. A., Roy, A., Burrell, A., Fairchild, C. J., Fuldeore, M. J., Ollendorf, D. A., & Wong, P. K. (2008). Medication compliance and persistence: Terminology and definitions. *Value in Health (Wiley-Blackwell), 11*(1), 44–47. doi:10.1111/j.1524-4733.2007.00213.x

Creapeau, L. J. G. (2023). Mining for Gold: Recruiting Successful Leaders to Long-Term Care Administration. *The Journal of Health Administration Education, 39*(2), 215–236. https://www.proquest.com/scholarly-journals/mining-gold-recruiting-successful-leaders-long/docview/2788803631/se-2

Creemers, B. (2010). *Improving the quality of education: Dynamic Approaches to school Improvement.* Routledge.

Cremer, F., Sheehan, B., Fortmann, M., Kia, A. N., Mullins, M., Murphy, F., & Materne, S. (2022). Cyber risk and cybersecurity: A systematic review of data availability. *The Geneva Papers on Risk and Insurance. Issues and Practice*, *47*(3), 698–736. doi:10.1057/s41288-022-00266-6 PMID:35194352

Creswell, J. W. (2013). *Qualitative Inquiry and Research Design: Choosing Among Five Approaches*. Sage Publishing.

Creswell, J. W. (2017). *Qualitative inquiry and research design: Choosing among five approaches*. Sage Publications.

Cross, K. J., & Cutler, S. (2017). *Engineering Faculty Perceptions of Diversity in the Classroom*. American Society for Engineering Education Annual Conference, Columbus, Ohio. 10.18260/1-2--28253

Cuddy, A. J. C., Fiske, S. T., & Glick, P. (2004). When professionals become mothers, warmth doesn't cut the ice. *The Journal of Social Issues*, *60*(4), 701–718. doi:10.1111/j.0022-4537.2004.00381.x

Cuevas, A. G., & Boen, C. (2021). Tip of the iceberg: Measuring racial discrimination in studies of health. *Stress and Health*, *37*(5), 1043–1050. doi:10.1002/smi.3047 PMID:33739613

Cummings-White, I. (2013). *Preparing for the boomer exodus: An exploration of knowledge transfer in a municipality* (Order No. 3573953). Available from ABI/INFORM Collection. (1438049225). Retrieved from https://proxy.cecybrary.com/login?url=https://search.proquest.com/docview/1438049225?accountid=144459

Cunningham, L., & McNally, K. (2003). *Improving Organizational and Individual Performance through Coaching. A Case Study*. Mosby, Inc. doi:10.1067/nrsi.2003.90

Cunningham, J., & Hillier, E. (2013). Informal learning in the workplace: Key activities and processes. *Education + Training*, *55*(1), 37–51. doi:10.1108/00400911311294960

Cybernews. (2023, October 12). *SCADA: the invisible backbone of modern industry*. Retrieved October 28, 2023, from https://cybernews.com/security/scada-systems-vulnerabilities-explained/

Cybersecurity & Infrastructure Security Agency. (2003, December 17). *Homeland Security Presidential Directive 7*. Retrieved November 5, 2023, from https://www.cisa.gov/news-events/directives/homeland-security-presidential-directive-7

Cybersecurity & Infrastructure Security Agency. (2010, September). *Preventing and Defending Against Cyber Attacks*. CISA.gov. Retrieved November 11, 2023, from https://www.cisa.gov/sites/default/files/publications/defending-against-cyber-attacks-september-2010.pdf

Cybersecurity & Infrastructure Security Agency. (2023a). *Critical Infrastructure Sectors*. Cybersecurity & Infrastructure Security Agency (CISA). Retrieved October 29, 2023, from https://www.cisa.gov/topics/critical-infrastructure-security-and-resilience/critical-infrastructure-sectors

Cybersecurity & Infrastructure Security Agency. (2023b). *Cybersecurity Alerts & Advisories*. Retrieved November 11, 2023, from https://www.cisa.gov/news-events/cybersecurity-advisories?f%5B0%5D=advisory_type%3A95

Cybersecurity & Infrastructure Security Agency. (2023c). *Defining Insider Threats*. Retrieved November 7, 2023, from https://www.cisa.gov/topics/physical-security/insider-threat-mitigation/defining-insider-threats

Cybersecurity & Infrastructure Security Agency. (2023d). *Federal Government: CISA Partners with Other Government Agencies to Help Them Manage Their Cyber Risk*. Retrieved November 11, 2023, from https://www.cisa.gov/audiences/federal-government

Dalati, S. (2014). *Universal leadership across social culture: Theoretical framework, design, and measurement*. Retrieved from https://proxy.cecybrary.com/login?url=https://search.proquest.com/docview/1781570423?accountid=144459

Daniel, B. K. (2019). *What constitutes a good qualitative research study? fundamental dimensions and indicators of rigour in qualitative research: The TACT framework.* Kidmore End: Academic Conferences International Limited. http://dx.doi.org.proxy.cecybrary.com/10.34190/RM.19.113

Dartey-Baah, K. (2015). Resilient leadership: A transformational-transactional leadership mix. *Journal of Global Responsibility, 6*(1), 99–112. doi:10.1108/JGR-07-2014-0026

Dasaklis, T. K., Voutsinas, T. G., Tsoulfas, G. T., & Casino, F. (2022). A systematic literature review of blockchain-enabled supply chain traceability implementations. *Sustainability (Basel), 14*(4), 2439. doi:10.3390/su14042439

Dasborough, M. T., Ashkanasy, N. M., Humphrey, R. H., Harms, P. D., Credé, M., & Wood, D. (2022). Does leadership still not need emotional intelligence? Continuing "The Great EI Debate". *The Leadership Quarterly, 33*(6), 101539. doi:10.1016/j.leaqua.2021.101539

Dasborough, M., Ashkanasy, N., Tee, E., & Miles, J. (2022). A meta-analysis of the relationship between emotional intelligence and effective leadership. *Journal of Organizational Behavior, 43*(1), 24–41. doi:10.1002/job.2509

Dasgupta, M. (2015). Exploring the relevance of case study research. *Vision, 12*(2), 147-160. doi:10.1177/0972262915575661

Data Breach Report (DBR). (2022). *Washington State Attorney General's Office. Special Edition Data Privacy.* https://agportal-s3bucket.s3.amazonaws.com/DBR2022%20v5.pdf

Daveron, J. (2017). Organizational Culture & Employee Performance. *Chronicles of Small Business.* Retrieved from https://smallbusiness.chron.com/organizational-culture-employee-performance-25216.html

Davies, V. (2022). The average security leader works over 16 hours extra a week. *Cyber Magazine.* https://cybermagazine.com/articles/the-average-security-leader-works-over-16-hours-extra-a-week

Dawson, M. (2017a). *Hyper-connectivity: Intricacies of national and international cyber securities.* London Metropolitan University.

Dawson, M. (2017b). Cyber security policies for hyperconnectivity and internet of things: a process for managing connectivity. In S. Latifi (Ed.), *Information Technology – New Generations* (pp. 911–914). Springer.

Dawson, M., Bacius, R., Gouveia, L. B., & Vassilakos, A. (2021). Understanding the challenge of cybersecurity in critical infrastructure sectors. *Land Forces Academy Review, 251*(101), 69–75. doi:10.2478/raft-2021-0011

Dawson, M., & Szakonyi, A. (2020). Cybersecurity education to create awareness in artificial intelligence applications for developers and end users. *Science Bulletin, 25*(2), 85–92. doi:10.2478/bsaft-2020-0012

Dayan, M., Ozer, M., & Almazrouei, H. (2017). The role of functional and demographic diversity on new product creativity and the moderating impact of project uncertainty. *Industrial Marketing Management, 61*, 144–154. doi:10.1016/j.indmarman.2016.04.016

de Haan, E., Duckworth, A., Birch, D., & Jones, C. (2013). Executive coaching outcome research: The contribution of common factors such as relationship, personality match, and self-efficacy. *Consulting Psychology Journal, 65*(1), 40–57. doi:10.1037/a0031635

de Haan, E., & Nieb, C. (2015). Differences between critical moments for clients, coaches, and sponsors of coaching. *International Coaching Psychology Review, 10*(1), 1750–2764. doi:10.53841/bpsicpr.2015.10.1.38

De Houwer, J. (2019). Implicit bias is behavior: A functional-cognitive perspective complicit bias. *Perspectives on Psychological Science, 14*(5), 835–840. doi:10.1177/1745691619855638 PMID:31374177

De Meuse, K. P., Dai, G., & Lee, R. J. (2009). Evaluating the effectiveness of executive coaching: Beyond R.O.I.? *Coaching (Abingdon, UK)*, *2*(2), 117–134. doi:10.1080/17521880902882413

de Roover, F. E. (1945). Early Examples of Marine Insurance. *The Journal of Economic History*, *5*(2), 172–200. doi:10.1017/S0022050700112975

de Sousa Lopes, B., Amorim, V., Au-Yong-Oliveira, M., & Rua, O. L. 2023. Competitive and business intelligence: A Bibliometric analysis. *Quality Innovation and Sustainability: 3rd ICQIS*, 187 – 197. https://doi-org.captechu.idm.oclc.org/10.1007/978-3-031-12914-8_15

de Vires, M. F. R. K. (2014). Dream journeys: A new territory for executive coaching. *Consulting Psychology Journal*, *66*(2), 77–92. doi:10.1037/cpb0000004

Deal, J. J., Stawiski, S., Graves, L., Gentry, W. A., Weber, T. J., & Ruderman, M. (2013). Motivation at work: Which matters more, generation or managerial level? *Consulting Psychology Journal*, *65*(1), 1–16. doi:10.1037/a0032693

Dean, M. L., & Meyer, A. A. (2002). Executive coaching: In search of a model. *Journal of Leadership Education*, *1*(2), 3–17. doi:10.12806/V1/I2/RF1

Dell. (2015, December). *2015 Dell Annual Threat Report*. Silicon. Retrieved September 20, 2015, from https://www.silicon.es/wp-content/uploads/2015/12/2015-dell-security-annual-threat-report-white-paper-15657.pdf

Delmerico, J., Mintchev, S., Giusti, A., Gromov, B., Melo, K., Horvat, T., Cadena, C., Hutter, M., Ijspeert, A., Floreano, D., Gambardella, L. M., Siegwart, R., & Scaramuzza, D. (2019). The current state and future outlook of rescue robotics. *Journal of Field Robotics*, *36*(7), 1171–1191. doi:10.1002/rob.21887

Deloitte. (2021). *The 2021 MHI annual industry report: Elevating supply chain digital consciousness*. https://www2.deloitte.com/us/en/pages/operations/articles/mhi-annual-industry-report.html

Deloitte. (2023, January 9). CISOs Lay Groundwork for States' Growing Cybersecurity Needs. Deloitte. CIO Journal. *The Wall Street Journal*. https://deloitte.wsj.com/cio/cisos-lay-groundwork-for-states-growing-cybersecurity-needs-01673289395

Denzin, N. K. (1978). *Sociological methods: A sourcebook*. McGraw-Hill.

Department of Energy. (2015). *21 Steps to Improve Cyber Security of SCADA Networks*. Energy.gov. Retrieved November 11, 2023, from https://www.energy.gov/ceser/articles/21-steps-improve-cyber-security-scada-networks

Department of Homeland Security. (2010). *DHS Risk Lexicon: 2010 Edition*. Retrieved November 19, 2015, from https://www.dhs.gov/xlibrary/assets/dhs-risk-lexicon-2010.pdf

Department of Homeland Security. (2013). *NIPP 2013: Partnering for Critical Infrastructure Security and Resilience (Rev. 2020)*. Cybersecurity & Infrastructure Security Agency (CISA). Retrieved November 11, 2023, from https://www.cisa.gov/sites/default/files/publications/national-infrastructure-protection-plan-2013-508.pdf

Department of Homeland Security. (2019). *Cybersecurity and Infrastructure Security Agency, Office of the Chief Economist*. Assessment of the Cyber Insurance Market. Draft Version, 1-44.

Department of Homeland Security. (2019, April 2). *Improving Critical Infrastructure Cybersecurity*. DHS.gov. Retrieved November 11, 2023, from https://www.dhs.gov/sites/default/files/publications/cisa_-_improving_critical_infrastructure_cybersecurity.pdf

Department of Justice. (2022). Former Chief Security Officer Of Uber Convicted Of Federal Charges For Covering Up Data Breach Involving Millions Of Uber User Records. *United States Attorney's Office Northern District of California*. https://www.justice.gov/usao-ndca/pr/former-chief-security-officer-uber-convicted-federal-charges-covering-data-breach

Dickman, F. (2009). Hacking The Industrial SCADA Network. *Pipeline & Gas Journal, 236*(11). Retrieved November 9, 2023, from https://pgjonline.com/magazine/2009/november-2009-vol-236-no-11/features/hacking-the-industrial-scada-network

Diedrich, R. (1996, Spring). An iterative approach to executive coaching. *The Hay Group Consulting Psychology Journal: Practice and Research, 48*(2), 61-66. http://members.aoaorg/ftdocs/cpb/1996/spring/cpb48261.html pp. 1-6.

Ding, S., Chen, X., Fu, Z., & Peng, F. (2021, October). An extended car-following model in connected and autonomous vehicle environment: Perspective from the cooperation between drivers. *Journal of Advanced Transportation, 2021*, 1–17. Advance online publication. doi:10.1155/2021/2739129

Dobbin, F. & Kalev, A. (2018). Why doesn't diversity training work? The challenge for academia and America. *Anthropology Now, 10*(2), 48-55. doi:10.1080/19428200.2018.1493182

Dobbin, F., & Kalev, A. (2022, September 29). How companies should set and report DEI goals. *Harvard Business Review*. https://hbr.org/2022/09/how-companies-should-set-and-report-dei-goals

Dodla, T. R., & Jones, L. A. (2023). Mitigating Knowledge Management Internal and External Risk Factors: A Literature Review of Best Practices. *Science Bulletin, 28*(1), 44–54. doi:10.2478/bsaft-2023-0005

Dolezalek, H. (2006). The dark side: When good leaders go bad. *Training (New York, N.Y.), 43*(6), 20–26. https://proxy.cecybrary.com/login?url=https://search.proquest.com/docview/203401737?accountid=144459

Dougherty, F. (2021, February 16). The future of online learning: the long-term trends accelerated by Covid-19. *The Guardian*. https://www.theguardian.com/education/2021/feb/16/the-future-of-online-learning-the-long-term-trends-accelerated-by-covid-19

Dougherty, M. V. (2021). The use of confidentiality and anonymity protections as a cover for fraudulent fieldwork data. *Research Ethics, 17*(4), 480–500. Advance online publication. doi:10.1177/17470161211018257

Douglas, A., Lubbe, B., & Inger, F. R. (2013). Travel or technology? Business factors influencing management decisions. *Suid-Afrikaanse Tydskrif vir Ekonomiese en Bestuurswetenskappe, 16*(3), 279–297. doi:10.4102/sajems.v16i3.362

Douvan, E. (1997). Erik Erikson: Critical Times, Critical Theory. *Child Psychiatry and Human Development, 28*(1), 15–21. doi:10.1023/A:1025188901554 PMID:9256525

Dragović, B., Chen, G., & Papadimitriou, S. (2023). Editorial: The time factor in maritime and port logistics. *Maritime Business Review, 8*(4), 298–300. doi:10.1108/MABR-11-2023-092

Dressel, J., & Farid, H. (2018). The malignant use of artificial intelligence in criminal justice. *Boston University Law Review. Boston University. School of Law, 98*(3), 741–788.

Drigas, A., & Papoutsi, C. (2018). A review of the effect of emotional intelligence in supply chain management. *International Journal of Supply Chain Management, 7*(6), 548–554. https://ojs.excelingtech.co.uk/index.php/IJSCM/article/view/2830

Drucker, P. (1994). The Age of Social Transformation. *Atlantic Monthly*.

DSHS. (2022). *Client Data. Client Counts and Service Costs*. https://clientdata.rda.dshs.wa.gov/Home/ShowReport?reportMode=1

Duke, D. L. (2011). *The challenge of school district leadership*. Routledge.

Durach, C. F., Kembro, J. H., & Wieland, A. (2021). How to advance theory through literature reviews in logistics and supply chain management. *International Journal of Physical Distribution & Logistics Management, 51*(10), 1090–1107. doi:10.1108/IJPDLM-11-2020-0381

Dutta, T., Storch, M. A., & Kolluru, V. (2020). The Potalyzer: An Overview of Current State-of-the-Art Marijuana Breathalyzers. *Analytical Chemistry, 92*(1), 8–14.

Dutton, G. (1997, February). Executive coaches call the plays. *Management Review, 86*(2).

Dwertmann, D. J. G., Nishii, L. H., & van Knippenberg, D. (2016). Disentangling the fairness & discrimination and synergy perspectives on diversity climate: Moving the field forward. *Journal of Management, 42*(5), 1136–1168. doi:10.1177/0149206316630380

Dykstra, J., & Paul, C. L. (2018). Cyber Operations Stress Survey (COSS): Studying fatigue, frustration, and cognitive workload in cybersecurity operations. *11th USENIX Workshop on Cyber Security Experimentation and Test CSE,* 18.

Eagly, A. H., & Heilman, M. E. (2016). Gender and leadership: Introduction to the special issue. *The Leadership Quarterly, 3*(27), 349–353. doi:10.1016/j.leaqua.2016.04.002

Easterling, T., Kerley, K., & Wright, J. (2018). *Overweight and obesity in children and adolescents in schools – The role of school nurse.* Retrieved from: https://www.nasn.org/advocacy/professional-practice-documents/position-statements/ps-overweight

Ebeling, A. (2018, August 21). Employers say 64 is too old to get a job. *Forbes.* https://www.forbes.com/sites/ashleaebeling/2018/08/21/employers-say-64-is-too-old-to-get-a-job/?sh=5c85f36051e8

Eisenfeld, B. L. (2019). *National Security's Triple Threat: Terrorists', Spies', and Hackers' Covernging Motivations* (Order No. 27542473). ProQuest On Academic (2309521885). Retrieved November 9, 2023, from https://www.proquest.com/dissertations-theses/national-security-s-triple-threat-terrorists/docview/2309521885/se-2

EkoHealth. (2020). *Telehealth Grants & Funding Opportunities for Health Systems of All Sizes.* EkoHealth. Retrieved from: https://www.ekohealth.com/blog/telehealth-grants-funding

Eliades, A. B. (2017). Mentoring practice and mentoring benefit 6: Equipping for leadership and leadership readiness: An overview and application to practice using mentoring activities. *Pediatric Nursing, 43*(1), 40–42. https://www.ncbi.nlm.nih.gov/pubmed/29406666 PMID:29406666

Elias, S. K. (2018). Pre-Service Teachers' Approaches to the Effectiveness of Micro-Teaching in Teaching Practice Programs. *Open Journal of Social Sciences, 6*(5), 205–224. doi:10.4236/jss.2018.65016

Elkhouly, S., Ossman, M., Selim, M., & Zaghloul, M. (2014). Impact of E-leadership on leadership styles within the Egyptian government sector. *Competition Forum, 12*(1), 131-140. Retrieved from https://proxy.cecybrary.com/login?url=https://search.proquest.com/docview/1640568232?accountid=144459

Elkins, R. (2015). *Business: Golden Nugget Methods for High Effectiveness - Leadership, Management & Communication.* CreateSpace Independent Publishing Platform.

Elliot, D., Keen, W., & Miao, L. (2019). Recent advances in connected and automated vehicles. *Journal of Traffic and Transportation Engineering, 6*(2), 109–131. doi:10.1016/j.jtte.2018.09.005

Elliott, C., & Stead, V. (2017). The effect of media on women and leadership. Handbook of Research on Gender and Leadership, 344.

ElMaraghy, H., Monostori, L., Schuh, G., & ElMaraghy, W. (2021). Evolution and future of manufacturing systems. *CIRP Annals, 70*(2), 635–658. doi:10.1016/j.cirp.2021.05.008

Ely, K., Boyce, L. A., Nelson, J. K., Zaccaro, S. J., & Hernez-Broome, G. W. (2010). Evaluating Leadership Coaching: A review and integrated framework. *The Leadership Quarterly*. Retrieved from: Journal homepage: www.elsevier.com/locate/leaqua

Ely, R. J., Stone, P., & Ammerman, C. (2014). Rethink what you "know" about high-achieving women. *Harvard Business Review*, 92(12), 100–109.

Emelo, R. (2011). Group mentoring best practices. *Industrial and Commercial Training, 43*(4), 221–227. doi:10.1108/00197851111137898

Emerson, K., Baldwin, E., Scott, T. A., Pidot, J. R., Lien, A. M., Currim, F., Bethard, S., Ram, S., & López-Hoffman, L. (2022). Toward NEPA performance: A framework for assessing EIAs. *Environmental Impact Assessment Review, 97*, 106879. doi:10.1016/j.eiar.2022.106879

Emrich, I. A., Fröhlich-güzelsoy, L., Bruns, F., Friedrich, B., & Frewer, A. (2014). Clinical Ethics and Patient Advocacy: The Power of Communication in Health Care. *HEC Forum, 26*(2), 111–124. doi:10.1007/s10730-013-9225-1 PMID:24368580

Encyclopaedia Britannica. (2023, August 23). Computer vision. *Author*. https://www.britannica.com/technology/computer-vision

Enders, F., Golembiewski, E., Pacheco-Spann, L., Allyse, M., Mielke, M., & Balls-Berry, J. (2020). Building a framework for inclusion in health services research: Development of and pre-implementation faculty and staff attitudes toward theDiversity,Equity,and Inclusion(DEI) plan at Mayo Clinic. *Journal of Clinical and Translational Science, 5*(88), 1–10. doi:10.1017/cts.2020.575 PMID:34007470

Eng, R. (2020). *Man on a Mission to Bring Telehealth to Low-Income Communities*. Spectrum News1. Retrieved from: https://spectrumnews1.com/ca/la-west/human-interest/2020/08/12/man-on-a-mission-to-bring-telehealth-to-low-income-communities

Esper, T. L., Castillo, V. E., Ren, K., Sodero, A., Wan, X., Croxton, K. L., Knemeyer, A. M., DeNunzio, S., Zinn, W., & Goldsby, T. J. (2020). Everything old is new again: The age of consumer-centric supply chain management. *Journal of Business Logistics, 41*(4), 286–293. doi:10.1111/jbl.12267

Etemad-Sajadi, R., & Dos Santos, G. G. (2020). The Impact of Connected Health Technologies on the Quality of Service Delivered by Home Care Companies: Focus on Trust and Social Presence. Health Marketing Quarterly, 1–10.

Fabiano, B., Curro, F., Reverbreri, A. P., & Pastorino, R. (2010). Port safety and the container revolution: A statistical study on human factor and occupational accidents over the long period. *Safety Science, 48*(8), 980–990. doi:10.1016/j.ssci.2009.08.007

Fakhouri, T., Hughes, J., Burt, V., Song, M., Fulton, J., & Ogden, C. (2014). *Physical Activity in U.S. Youth Aged 12-15 Years, 2012*. NCHS Data Brief. Retrieved from: https://permanent.access.gpo.gov/gpo77970/db141.pdf

Falco, G., Eling, M., Jablanski, D., Miller, V., Gordon, L. A., Wang, S. S., . . . Nutter, S. F. (2019, June). A research agenda for cyber risk and cyber insurance. In Workshop on the *Economics of Information Security (WEIS)*. https://weis2016. econinfosec. org/wp-content/uploads/sites/6/2019/05/WEIS_2019_paper_35. pdf

Farahnak, L. R., Ehrhart, M. G., Torres, E. M., & Aarons, G. A. (2020). The influence of transformational leadership and leader attitudes on subordinate attitudes and implementation success. *Journal of Leadership & Organizational Studies, 27*(1), 98–111. doi:10.1177/1548051818824529

Farhan, M., Krejci, C. C., & Cantor, D. E. (2023). Do a non-core worker's procedural justice concerns influence their engagement in helping behavior? A multi-method study. *International Journal of Physical Distribution & Logistics Management*, 53(9), 1015–1042. doi:10.1108/IJPDLM-02-2022-0044

Federal Trade Commission. (n.d.). *Cyber Insurance*. https://www.ftc.gov/business-guidance/small-businesses/cybersecurity/cyber-insurance

FedSavvy Strategies. (2019). Business intelligence, competitive intelligence, and market intelligence – What is the difference? *Author*. https://www.fedsavvystrategies.com/business-intelligence-competitive-intelligence-and-market-intelligence-what-is-the-difference/

Feeney, M., Grohnert, T., Gijselaers, W., & Martens, P. (2023). Organizations, Learning, and Sustainability: A Cross-Disciplinary Review and Research Agenda. *Journal of Business Ethics*, 184(1), 217–235. doi:10.1007/s10551-022-05072-7

Feldman, D. C. (2001). Career coaching: What H.R. professionals and managers need to know. *Human Resources Planning*, 24, 26–35.

Feldman, D. C., & Lankau, M. J. (2010). Executive Coaching: A review and Agenda for Future Research. *Journal of Management*. Advance online publication. doi:10.1177/0149206305279599

Fenton, A., Heinze, A., Osborne, M., & Ahmed, W. (2022). How to Use the Six-Step Digital Ethnography Framework to Develop Buyer Personas: The Case of Fan Fit. *JMIR Formative Research*, 6(11), e41489. Advance online publication. doi:10.2196/41489 PMID:36427232

Fenwick, F. J., & Gayle, C. A. (2008). Missing Links in Understanding the Relationship Between Leadership and Organizational Performance. *The International Business & Economics Research Journal*, 7.

Fern, E. F. (1982). *The use of focus groups for idea generation: The effects of group size, acquaintanceship, and moderator on response quantity and quality*. Retrieved from https://www.uta.edu/faculty/richarme/MARK%205338/Articles/Fern.pdf

Ferrovial. (2023). Connected autonomous vehicles: What are connected autonomous vehicles? *Author*. https://www.ferrovial.com/en/innovation/technologies/connected-autonomous-vehicles/

Fetaji, B., & Fetaji, M. (2009). e-Learning Indicators: A Multi-Dimensional Model for Planning and Evaluating e-Learning Software Solutions. *Electronic Journal of e-Learning*, 7(1), 1–28.

Fidleman, M. (2012, June 5). Here's the Real Reason There Are Not More Women in Technology. *Forbes*.

Fielding, N. (1993). Ethnography. In N. Gilbert (Ed.), *Researching Social Life* (pp. 154–171). Sage.

Finklea, K. M., & Theory, C. A. (2012). Cybercrime: conceptual issues for Congress and U.S. law enforcement. *Journal of Current Issues in Crime, Law and Law Enforcement*, 5(1/2).

Fischer, E., & Parmentier, M. A. (2010). Doing Qualitative Research With Archival Data: Making Secondary Data a Primary Resource. In M. C. Campbell, J. Inman, & R. Pieters (Eds.), *NA - Advances in Consumer Research* (Vol. 37, pp. 798–799). Association for Consumer Research.

Fisher, J., & Burrell, D. (2011). The value of using microteaching as a tool to develop instructors. Review of Higher Education & Self-Learning, 3(11), 86-94.

Fitch Ratings. (2022, May 6). *US Cyber Insurance Payouts Increase Amid Rising Claims, Premium Hikes*. https://www.fitchratings.com/research/insurance/us-cyber-insurance-payouts-increase-amid-rising-claims-premium-hikes-06-05-2022

Forslund, H. (2012). Performance management in supply chains: Logistics service providers' perspective. *International Journal of Physical Distribution & Logistics Management*, 42(3), 296–311. doi:10.1108/09600031211225972

Fortinet. (2022). How Is the Skills Gap Creating Cyber Risk? *Author.* https://www.fortinet.com/blog/industry-trends/global-cybersecurity-skills-gap-report-findings

Foti, R. J. (n.d.). Academic Job Interviews: Questions and Advice. *Virginia Polytechnic Institute and State University.* https://vtechworks.lib.vt.edu/bitstream/handle/10919/72241/gsls_roseanne_foti_interviews.pdf

Foucault, M. (1975). The Birth of the Clinic: An Archaeology of Medical Perception, Trans. Discipline and Punish: The Birth of the Prison, 1978–86.

Fragouli, E., & Ibidapo, B. (2015). Leading in crisis: Leading organizational change & business development. Journal of Information. *Business and Management, 7*(3), 71–90.

Francis, M. (2014, May 30). Four leadership observations from Eric Shinseki's tenure at the Department of Veterans Affairs. *The Oregonian/OregonLive.* Retrieved from https://www.oregonlive.com/business/index.ssf/2014/05/four_leadership_observations_f.html

Freedberg, S. J., Jr. (1999). *Military personnel struggle with spare parts.* https://www.govexec.com/federal-news/1999/12/military-personnel-struggle-with-spare-parts/5403/

Freeman, A. M., & Perry, J.A. (2010). Executive coaching under pressure: A case study. *Consulting Psychology Journal: Practice and Research, 6,* 189-202.

Frias, A., Hampton, D., Tharp-Barrie, K., & Thomas, J. (2021). The impact of an emotional intelligence training program on transformational leadership. *Nursing Management, 52*(2), 18–25. doi:10.1097/01.NUMA.0000731924.03153. df PMID:33512880

Friedman, B. (2018). A.I., bias, and criminal justice: The need for public oversight. *Harvard Law & Policy Review, 12*(2), 637–653.

Friese, B., Slater, M. D., Annechino, R., & Battle, R. S. (2016). Teen use of marijuana edibles: A focus group study of an emerging issue. *The Journal of Primary Prevention, 37*(3), 303–309. doi:10.1007/s10935-016-0432-9 PMID:27056685

Friis, R. H. (2018). *Epidemiology 101* (2nd ed.). Jones & Bartlett Learning.

Fry, R. (2015). Millennials surpass Gen Xers as the largest generation in U.S. labor force. *Pew Research Center.* Retrieved from https://www.pewresearch.org/fact-tank/2015/05/11/millennials-surpass-gen-xers-as-the-largest-generation-in-u-s-labor-force/

Fry, R. (2016). Millennials overtake Baby Boomers as America's largest generation. *Pew Research Center.* Retrieved from https://www.pewresearch.org/fact-tank/2016/04/25/millennials-overtake-baby-boomers/

Furimsky, I., Arts, K., & Lampson, S. (2014). Developing a successful peer-to-peer mentoring program. *Applied Clinical Trials, 22*(12), 27–30. https://proxy.cecybrary.com/login?url=https://search.proquest.com/docview/1477195588?accountid=144459

Gabaldon, J., Farris, M. T. II, Manuj, I., & Ekezie, U. (2021). Sixth Logistics Faculty Salary Survey. *Transportation Journal, 60*(3), 239–257. doi:10.5325/transportationj.60.3.0239

Gable, R. A. (2014). Teaching students with emotional disabilities: Challenges and opportunities. *Special Education Past, Present, and Future: Perspectives from the Field. Advances in Learning and Behavioral Disabilities, 27,* 117–140. doi:10.1108/S0735-004X20140000027008

Gaddis, B. H., & Foster, J. L. (2015). Meta-analysis of dark side personality characteristics and critical work behaviors among leaders across the globe: Findings and implications for leadership development and executive coaching. *Applied Psychology, 64*(1), 25–54. doi:10.1111/apps.12017

Gallagher, S., Brown, C., & Brown, L. (2008). A strong market culture drives organizational performance and success. *Employment Relations Today, 35*(1), 25–31. doi:10.1002/ert.20185

Gallup. (2015). *The State of the American Manager*. The Gallup Organization. Retrieved from https://www.gallup.com/services/182138/state-american-manager.aspx

Gamble, E. D., & Turner, N. J. (2015). Career ascension of African American women in executive positions in postsecondary institutions. *Journal of Organizational Culture, Communications and Conflict, 19*(1), 82.

Gan, G. C., & Chong, C. W. (2015). Coaching relationship in Executive Coaching: A Malaysian study. *Journal of Management Development, 34*(4), 476–494. doi:10.1108/JMD-08-2013-0104

GAO. (2021). *Cyber Insurance: Insurers and Policyholders Face Challenges in an Evolving Market (GAO-21-477)* [Report]. https://www.gao.gov/products/gao-21-477

Gao, X., Shang, T., & Liu, J. (2022). *Quantitative Risk Assessment of Threats on SCADA Systems Using Attack Countermeasure Tree*. IEEE. doi:10.1109/PST55820.2022.9851965

García-Martínez, I., Fernández-Batanero, J., Fernández-Cerero, J., & León, S. P. (2023). Analysing The Impact Of Artificial Intelligence And Computational sciences on student performance: Systematic review and meta-analysis. *Journal of New Approaches in Educational Research, 12*(1), 171–197. doi:10.7821/naer.2023.1.1240

Garcia-Morales, V. J., Lloréns-Montes, F. J., & Verdu-Jover, A. J. (2007). Influence of personal mastery on organizational performance through organizational learning and innovation in large firms and SMEs. *Technovation, 27*(9), 547–568. doi:10.1016/j.technovation.2007.02.013

Garg, M., & Bouroche, M. (2023, June). Can Connected Autonomous Vehicles Improve Mixed Traffic Safety Without Compromising Efficiency in Realistic Scenarios? *IEEE Transactions on Intelligent Transportation Systems, 24*(6), 6674–6689. doi:10.1109/TITS.2023.3238889

Gartner. (2021). *The Future of Cybersecurity Leadership: Empowerment and Accountability* [Press Release]. https://www.gartner.com/en/newsroom/press-releases/2022-02-24-gartner-says-the-cybersecurity-leader-s-role-needs-to

Gartner. (2022). *Gartner Says the Cybersecurity Leader's Role Needs to Be Reframed* [Press Release]. https://www.gartner.com/en/newsroom/press-releases/2022-02-24-gartner-says-the-cybersecurity-leader-s-role-needs-to

Gartner. (2023). *Gartner Predicts Nearly Half of Cybersecurity Leaders Will Change Jobs by 2025.* [Press Release]. https://www.gartner.com/en/newsroom/press-releases/2023-02-22-gartner-predicts-nearly-half-of-cybersecurity-leaders-will-change-jobs-by-2025

Gartner. (n.d.). *CISO for Digital Business*. https://www.gartner.com/en/cybersecurity/role/chief-information-security-officer

Garvanova, M., Garvanov, I., Jotsov, V., Razaque, A., Alotaibi, B., Alotaibi, M., & Borissova, D. (2023). A Data-Science Approach for Creation of a Comprehensive Model to Assess the Impact of Mobile Technologies, *Humans. Applied Sciences (Basel, Switzerland), 13*(6), 3600. doi:10.3390/app13063600

Gatto, N., Martinez, L., Spruijt-Metz, D., & Davis, J. (2015). LA Sprouts randomized controlled nutrition, cooking and gardening programme reduces obesity and metabolic risk in Hispanic/Latino youth. *Pediatric Obesity*. Retrieved from: https://onlinelibrary-wiley-com.portal.lib.fit.edu/doi/epdf/10.1111/ijpo.12102

Gavin, C. S. (2018). The impact of leadership development using coaching. *Journal of Practical Consulting, 6*(1), 137–147.

Gavriliović, T., Ostojić, M., Sambunjak, D., Kirschfink, M., Steiner, T., & Strittmatter, V. (n.d.) *Chapter 5: Microteaching*. Retrieved on May 4, 2011, from: http://www.bhmed-emanual.org/book/export/html/36

Gehlert, K. M., Ressler, T. H., Anderson, N. H., & Swanson, N. M. (2013). A method to improve the coach participant match in executive coaching. *The Coaching Psychologist, 9*(2), 78–85. doi:10.53841/bpstcp.2013.9.2.78

Geiman, M. (2016). *A Multiple Case Study of the Influence of Positive Organizational Behavioron Human Resources* (Doctoral dissertation or master's thesis). Retrieved from ProQuest. (10129957)

Gelberd, B. (2008). Bridging Differences. *Business and Economic Review, 54*(3), 14–21.

Genge, B., Haller, P., & Roman, A.-S. (2023). E-aptdetect: Early advanced persistent threat detection in critical infrastructures with dynamic attestation. *Applied Sciences (Basel, Switzerland), 13*(6), 3409. doi:10.3390/app13063409

Georgeac, O., & Rattan, A. (2022, June 15). Stop making the business case for diversity. *Harvard Business Review*. https://hbr.org/2022/06/stop-making-the-business-case-for-diversity

George, M. S., Gaitonde, R., Davey, R., Mohanty, I., & Upton, P. (2023). Engaging participants with research findings: A rights-informed approach. *Health Expectations, 26*(2), 765–773. doi:10.1111/hex.13701 PMID:36647684

Gerard, J. A., & Weber, C. M. (2015). Compliance and corporate governance: Theoretical analysis of the effectiveness of compliance based on locus of functional responsibility. *International Journal of Global Business, 8*(1), 15–26. https://proxy.cecybrary.com/login?url=https://search.proquest.com/docview/1680769364?accountid=144459

Ghansiyal, A., Mittal, M., & Kar, A. K. (2021). Information management challenges in autonomous vehicles: A systematic literature review. *Journal of Cases on Information Technology, 23*(3), 58–77. doi:10.4018/JCIT.20210701.oa5

Ghelani, D. P., Moran, L. J., Johnson, C., Mousa, A., & Naderpoor, N. (2020). Mobile Apps for Weight Management: A Review of the Latest Evidence to Inform Practice. *Frontiers in Endocrinology, 11*, 412. doi:10.3389/fendo.2020.00412 PMID:32670197

Ghonim, N., Khashaba, N., Al-Najaar, H., & Khashan, M. (2020). Strategic alignment and its impact on decision effectiveness: a comprehensive model. *International Journal of Emerging Markets*. www.emerald.com/insight/1746-8809.htm

Gil-Manso, S., Herrero-Quevedo, D., Carbonell, D., Martínez-Bonet, M., Bernaldo-de-Quirós, E., Kennedy-Batalla, R., Gallego-Valle, J., López-Esteban, R., Blázquez-López, E., Miguens-Blanco, I., Correa-Rocha, R., Gomez-Verdejo, V., & Pion, M. (2023). Multidimensional analysis of immune cells from COVID-19 patients identified cell subsets associated with the severity at hospital admission. *PLoS Pathogens, 19*(6), e1011432. Advance online publication. doi:10.1371/journal.ppat.1011432 PMID:37311004

Gipson, A. N., Pfaff, D. L., Mendelsohn, D. B., Catenacci, L. T., & Burke, W. W. (2017). Women and leadership: Selection, development, leadership style, and performance. *The Journal of Applied Behavioral Science, 53*(1), 32–65. doi:10.1177/0021886316687247

Girardin, L. (2015). Eight essential books on government leadership. *GovLoop*. Retrieved from https://www.govloop.com/community/blog/8-essential-books-government-leadership/

Goldring, C. C. (2015). *A design for federal government leaders: Succession planning through knowledge management* (Doctoral dissertation). Available from ProQuest Dissertations & Theses Global. (UMI No. 1688688202)

Goldsby, T. J., Hoang, T. T., Stank, T. P., & Bell, J. E. (2023). A Modernized Framework for Transportation Decision-Making in a Hyper-Integrated Global Supply Chain Environment. *Transportation Journal, 62*(1), 16–42. doi:10.5325/transportationj.62.1.0016

Goldsmith, A., & Levensaler, L. (2016, February). Build a great company culture with help from technology. *Harvard Business Review*. Retrieved from https://hbr.org/2016/02/build-a-great-company-culture-with-help-from-technology

Goleman, D. (1998). What makes a leader? *Harvard Business Review*, *76*(6), 93–102. PMID:10187249

Goleman, D. (2013). *Focus: The hidden driver of excellence*. HarperCollins.

Goleman, D., Boyatzis, R., & McKee, A. (2002). *Primal leadership: Realizing the power of Emotional Intelligence*. Harvard Business Press.

Goleman, D., Boyatzis, R., & McKee, A. (2013). *Primal leadership: Unleashing the power of Emotional Intelligence*. Harvard Business Review Press.

Gonzales, M. (2023). The generational divide between older and younger employees. *SHRM*. https://www.shrm.org/resourcesandtools/hr-topics/behavioral-competencies/global-and-cultural-effectiveness/pages/the-generational-divide-between-older-and-younger-employees.aspx

Gonzalez-Aguirre, J. A., Osorio-Oliveros, R., Rodríguez-Hernández, K. L., Lizárraga-Iturralde, J., Morales Menendez, R., Ramírez-Mendoza, R. A., Ramírez-Moreno, M. A., & Lozoya-Santos, J. D. J. (2021). Service robots: Trends and technology. *Applied Sciences (Basel, Switzerland)*, *11*(22), 10702. doi:10.3390/app112210702

Gonzalez-Saavedra, J. F., Figueroa, M., Cespedes, S., & Montejo-Sanchez, S. (2022). Survey of cooperative advanced driver assistance systems: From a holistic and systemic vision. *Sensors (Basel)*, *22*(8), 3040. doi:10.3390/s22083040 PMID:35459025

Graham, S. (2023). *Cybersecurity is number one risk for global banks, but geopolitical risk tops European banks' concerns*. EY. https://www.ey.com/en_gl/news/2023/01/cybersecurity-is-number-one-risk-for-global-banks-but-geopolitical-risk-tops-european-banks-concerns

Granato, A., & Polcek, A. (2019). The Growth and Challenges of Cyber Insurance. Federal Reserve Bank of Chicago. *Chicago Fed Letter, No. 246*. https://www.chicagofed.org/publications/chicago-fed-letter/2019/426

Granić, A. (2023). *Technology adoption at individual level: toward an integrated overview*. Univ Access Inf Soc. doi:10.1007/s10209-023-00974-3

Grant, A. (2014). Troubling 'lived experience': A post-structural critique of mental health nursing qualitative research assumptions. *Journal of Psychiatric and Mental Health Nursing, 21*, 21-24.doi:. 1213 doi:10. 1111/jpm

Grant, A.M. & O'Connor, S.A. (2010). The differential effects of solution-focused and problem-focused coaching questions: A pilot Study with implications for practice. *Industrial and Commercial Training, 42*, 102-111. doi:10.1108/00197851011026090

Grasha, A. (1996). *Teaching with style: A practical guide to enhancing learning by understanding teaching and learning styles*. Alliance Publishers.

Graso, M., Camps, J., Strah, N., & Brebels, L. (2020). Organizational justice enactment: An agent-focused review and path forward. *Journal of Vocational Behavior, 116*, 103296. doi:10.1016/j.jvb.2019.03.007

Gray, D. (2013). Learning from our mistakes. *Training Journal*, 23-26. Retrieved from https://proxy.cecybrary.com/login?url=https://search.proquest.com/docview/1469704072?accountid=144459

Gray, E. D., Ekinci, Y., & Goregaokar, H. (2011). Coaching S.M.E. managers: business development or personal therapy? Faculty of Management and Law, University of Surrey. Doi:10.108/09585

Green, D. D., & Roberts, G. E. (2012). Impact of postmodernism on public sector leadership practices: Federal government human capital development implications. *Public Personnel Management, 41*(1), 79–96. doi:10.1177/009102601204100105

Greene, K., Gabrielyan, G., Just, D., & Wansink, B. (2017). Fruit-Promoting Smarter Lunchrooms Interventions: Results From a Cluster RCT. *American Journal of Preventive Medicine, 52*(4), 451–458. Retrieved from: https://www-sciencedirect-com.portal.lib.fit.edu/science/article/pii/S0749379716306961

Grier, R. A. (2015, September). How high is high? A meta-analysis of NASA-TLX global workloadscores. *Proceedings of the Human Factors and Ergonomics Society Annual Meeting, 59*(1), 1727–1731. doi:10.1177/1541931215591373

Griffin, M. T. Q., & Spano-Szekely, L. (2022). Emotional Intelligence. Nurse Leadership and Management: Foundations for Effective Administration, 99.

Griffiths, J. (2015). *CNN: Money – Cybercrime costs the average U.S. firm $15 million a year.* CNN: Money. Retrieved October 15, 2015, from https://money.cnn.com/2015/10/08/technology/cybercrime-cost-business/

Gröschl, S., & Arcot, S. (2014). Female hospitality executives and their effects on firm performance. *Tourism and Hospitality Research, 14*(3), 143–151. doi:10.1177/1467358414538997

Guériau, M., & Dusparic, I. (2020, September). Quantifying the impact of connected and autonomous vehicles on traffic efficiency and safety in mixed traffic. *Proceedings of the IEEE 23rd International Conference on Intelligent Transportation Systems (ITSC).* 10.1109/ITSC45102.2020.9294174

Gupta, A. K., Awatade, G. V., Padole, S. S., & Choudhari, Y. S. (2022). Digital Supply Chain Management Using AI, ML, and Blockchain. In *Innovative Supply Chain Management via Digitalization and Artificial Intelligence* (pp. 1–19). Springer Singapore. doi:10.1007/978-981-19-0240-6_1

Gürses, Ö. (2023). *Marine insurance law.* Taylor & Francis. doi:10.4324/9781003031895

Gursoy, D., Chi, C. G., & Karadag, C. G. (2013). Generational differences in work values and attitudes among frontline and service contact employees. *International Journal of Hospitality Management, 33*, 1–9. doi:10.1016/j.ijhm.2012.04.002

Gusfield, J. (1957). The problem of generations in an organizational structure. *Social Forces, 35*(4), 323–330. doi:10.2307/2573321

Haan, K. (2023, October 3). 11 best applicant tracking systems of 2023. *Forbes.* https://www.forbes.com/advisor/business/best-applicant-tracking-systems/

Hadeler, E., Gitlow, H., & Nouri, K. (2021). Definitions, survey methods, and findings of patient satisfaction studies in teledermatology: a systematic review. *Archives of Dermatological Research, 313*, 205–215.

Hagan, C. D. (2020). What is a "theory" and why is it important to know? *Psychology Today.* https://www.psychologytoday.com/us/blog/thoughts-thinking/202007/what-is-theory-and-why-is-it-important-know

HalkiasD.NeubertM. (2020). Extension of theory in leadership and management studies using the multiple case study design. *Available at* SSRN 3586256. doi:10.2139/ssrn.3586256

Hall, E., Chai, W., & Albrecht, J. (2016). *Relationships between nutrition-related knowledge, self-efficacy, and behavior for fifth-grade students attending Title I and non-Title I schools. Science Direct* (Vol. 96). Retrieved from https://www-sciencedirect-com.portal.lib.fit.edu/science/article/pii/S0195666315300441

Hammersley, M., & Atkinson, P. (2019). *Ethnography: Principles in practice.* Routledge. doi:10.4324/9781315146027

Hannafey, F. T., & Vitulano, L. A. (2012). Ethics and executive coaching: An agency theory approach. *Journal of Business Ethics, 115*(3), 599–603. doi:10.1007/s10551-012-1442-z

Hanson, A., & Schwartz, R. P. (2018). The use of eye-tracking technology to detect driving under the influence of marijuana. *Traffic Injury Prevention*, *19*(3), 241–244. PMID:29064285

Harakas, P. (2013). Resistance, motivational interviewing, and executive coaching. *Consulting Psychology Journal*, *65*(2), 108–127. doi:10.1037/a0033196

Harris, B., Cheng, K. F., & Gorley, C. (2015). Benefits and barriers. *Journal of Workplace Learning*, *27*(3), 193–206. doi:10.1108/JWL-07-2014-0053

Harris, L. C., & Crane, A. (2002). The greening of organizational culture: Management views on the depth, degree and diffusion of change. *Journal of Organizational Change Management*, *15*(3), 214–234. doi:10.1108/09534810210429273

Harrison, A. (2018). The Effects of Media Capabilities on the Rationalization of Online Consumer Fraud. *Journal of the Association for Information Systems, 19*(5), 1.

Harvard Law School Forum on Corporate Governance. (2021, June 10). *Principles for Board Governance of Cyber Risk*. https://corpgov.law.harvard.edu/2021/06/10/principles-for-board-governance-of-cyber-risk/

Harver. (2023). How to manage generational diversity in the workplace. *Harver*. https://harver.com/blog/generational-diversity-in-the-workplace/

Harvey, L. (1990). *Critical Social Research*. Unwin Hyman.

Hassan, R. (2019). From technological determinism to techno-capitalist realism: Prospects for post-human engineering. *Ethics and Information Technology*, *21*(3), 217–231.

Hastig, G. M., & Sodhi, M. S. (2020). Blockchain for supply chain traceability: Business requirements and critical success factors. *Production and Operations Management*, *29*(4), 935–954. doi:10.1111/poms.13147

Haun, Y., Zhao, C. & & Molnar, T. G. (2023). Safety-Critical traffic control by connected automated vehicles. Safety-Critical Traffic Control by Connected Automated Vehicles. *Cornell University*. ArXiv. /abs/2301.04833

Heath, S. (2020). *Community Health Workers Play Key Role in COVID-19 Response*. Patient Engagement HIT. Retrieved from: https://patientengagementhit.com/news/community-health-workers-play-key-role-in-covid-19-response

Henderson, A. (2006). *The Evolving Relationship of Technology and Nursing Practice: Negotiating the Provision of Care in a High Tech Environment*. Contemporary.

Hennink, M. M., Hutter, I., & Bailey, A. (2011). *Qualitative Research Methods*. SAGE. Print

Henrie, M. (2013). Cyber security risk management in the SCADA critical infrastructure environment. *Engineering Management Journal*, *25*(2), 38–45. doi:10.1080/10429247.2013.11431973

Henry, R., Otto, T., & Wood, M. (2013). Ethnographic artifacts and value transformations. *HAU*, *3*(2), 33–51. doi:10.14318/hau3.2.004

Hess, T. J., Fuller, M., & Campbell, D. E. (2009). Designing Interfaces with Social Presence: Using Vividness and Extraversion to Create Social Recommendation Agents. *Journal of the Association for Information Systems, 10*(12), 1.

Hewlett, S. A. (2013). *Forget a mentor, find a sponsor: The new way to fast-track your career*. Harvard Business Review Press.

HHS Cybersecurity Program. (2020, August 6). *HC3 Intelligence Briefing Cybersecurity Maturity Models*. Report #: 202008061030. https://www.hhs.gov/sites/default/files/cybersecurity-maturity-model.pdf

Hicks, R. P., & McCracken, J. P. (2010). Three hats of a leader: Coaching, mentoring and teaching. *Physician Executive*, *36*(6), 68–70. PMID:21140733

Higginbottom, K. (2017, March 17). The challenges of managing a multi-generational workforce. *Forbes Magazine*. Retrieved from https://www.forbes.com/sites/karenhigginbottom/2016/03/17/the-challenges-of-managing-a-multi-generational-workforce/#6be0a41b7d6a

Higgins, E. (2020). *States Engage Community Health Workers to Combat COVID-19 and Health Inequities*. National Academy for State Health Policy. Retrieved from: https://www.nashp.org/states-engage-community-health-workers-to-combat-covid-19-and-health-inequities/

Higgins, S. (2014). Critical thinking for 21-century education: A cyber-tooth curriculum? *Prospects (00331538)*, *44*(4), 559–574. https://doi-org.saintleo.idm.oclc.org/10.1007/s11125-014-9323-0

Hildick-Smith, A. (2021). *Security for Critical Infrastructure SCADA Systems*. SANS Institute. Retrieved November 5, 2023, from https://sansorg.egnyte.com/dl/ZQfkrN71w7

Hill, C., Miller, K., Benson, K., & Handley, G. (2016). *Barriers and bias: The status of women in leadership*. Academic Press.

Hill, L. H., & Wheat, C. A. (2017). The influence of mentorship and role models on university women leaders' career paths to university presidency. *The Qualitative Report*, *22*(8), 2090. doi:10.46743/2160-3715/2017.2437

Hillman, D. R. (2014). Understanding multigenerational work-value conflict resolution. *Journal of Workplace Behavioral Health*, *29*(3), 240–257. doi:10.1080/15555240.2014.933961

Hilty, D. M., Crawford, A., Teshima, J., Nasatir-Hilty, S. E., Luo, J., Chisler, L. S., Gutierrez Hilty, Y. S., Servis, M. E., Godbout, R., Lim, R. F., & Lu, F. G. (2021). Mobile health and cultural competencies as a foundation for telehealth care: Scoping review. *Journal of Technology in Behavioral Science*, *6*(2), 197–230. doi:10.1007/s41347-020-00180-5

Hirsch, E., & Gellner, D. N. (2020). Introduction: ethnography of organizations and organizations of ethnography. In Inside Organizations (pp. 1-15). Routledge. doi:10.4324/9781003085720-1

Hoey, S. (2012). So you want to be a Dermatologist. *The Ulster Medical Journal*, *81*(3), 172. PMID:23620620

Holden, R. J., & Karsh, B. T. (2010). The technology acceptance model: Its past and its future in health care. *Journal of Biomedical Informatics*, *43*(1), 159–172. doi:10.1016/j.jbi.2009.07.002 PMID:19615467

Holland, J. M., Major, D. A., & Orvis, K. A. (2012). Understanding how peer mentoring and capitalization link STEM students to their majors. *The Career Development Quarterly*, *60*(4), 343–354. doi:10.1002/j.2161-0045.2012.00026.x

Holt, D. T., Markova, G., Dhaenens, A. J., Marler, L. E., & Heilmann, S. G. (2016). Formal or informal mentoring: What drives employees to seek informal mentors? *Journal of Managerial Issues, 28*(1), 67-82. Retrieved from https://proxy.cecybrary.com/login?url=https://search.proquest.com/docview/1815961188?accountid=144459

Holzer, H. J., & Neumark, D. (2000). What does affirmative action do? *Industrial & Labor Relations Review*, *53*(2), 240–271. doi:10.1177/001979390005300204

Homeland Security Subcommittee Cybersecurity and Infrastructure Protection. (2023, June 22). *Subcommittee chair Garbarino: Robust cybersecurity workforce is needed to mitigate risk across federal networks, critical infrastructure*. https://homeland.house.gov/2023/06/22/subcommittee-chair-garbarino-robust-cybersecurity-workforce-is-needed-to-mitigate-risk-across-federal-networks-critical-infrastructure/

Hong, L., & Page, S. E. (2004). Groups of diverse problem solvers can outperform groups of high-ability problem solvers. *Proceedings of the National Academy of Sciences of the United States of America*, *101*(46), 16385–16389. doi:10.1073/pnas.0403723101 PMID:15534225

Hopkins, M. M., O'Neil, D. A., Passarelli, A., & Bilimoria, D. (2008). Women's leadership development strategic practices for women and organizations. *Consulting Psychology Journal*, *60*(4), 348–365. doi:10.1037/a0014093

Hou, G. (2023). Evaluating efficiency and safety of mixed traffic with connected and autonomous vehicles in adverse weather. *Sustainability (Basel)*, *15*(4), 3138. doi:10.3390/su15043138

Houser, S. H., Joseph, R., Puro, N., & Burke, D. E. (2019). Use of technology in the management of obesity: A literature review. *Perspectives in Health Information Management*, *16*(Fall). PMID:31908626

Howley, C. (2023, April 12). Gartner identifies the top cybersecurity trends for 2023. *Gartner*. https://www.gartner.com/en/newsroom/press-releases/04-12-2023-gartner-identifies-the-top-cybersecurity-trends-for-2023

HR Research Institute. (2021). The Future of Recruitment Technologies 2021-22: Successfully recruit talent in a time of high turnover. *Talent Acquisition Excellence*, *9*(12), 19–21.

Huang, W., & Xi, X. (2023). Study on the influence mechanism of social presence on patients' willingness to use in online medical community. *The EUrASEANs: Journal on Global Socioeconomic Dynamics, 5*(42), 311-327.

Huff, A., Burrell, D. N., Richardson, K., Springs, D., Aridi, A. S., Crowe, M. M., & Lewis, E. (2023). Illegal Pregnancy Discrimination Is a Severe Business, Legal, and Public Health Issue. In D. Burrell (Ed.), *Real-World Solutions for Diversity, Strategic Change, and Organizational Development: Perspectives in Healthcare, Education, Business, and Technology* (pp. 119–129). IGI Global. doi:10.4018/978-1-6684-8691-7.ch008

Hughes-Lartey, K., Li, M., Botchey, F. E., & Qin, Z. (2021). Human factor, a critical weak point in the information security of an organization's Internet of things. *National Library of Medicine*. https://www.ncbi.nlm.nih.gov/pmc/articles/PMC7980069/

Hughes, O. E. (2003). *Public management and administration: An introduction.* Palgrave.

Hülsheger, U. R., Anderson, N., & Salgado, J. F. (2009). Team-level predictors of innovation at work: A comprehensive meta-analysis spanning three decades of research. *The Journal of Applied Psychology*, *94*(5), 1128–1145. doi:10.1037/a0015978 PMID:19702361

Hultin, M. (2003). Some take the glass escalator, some hit the glass ceiling? Career consequences of occupational sex segregation. *Work and Occupations*, *30*(1), 30–61. doi:10.1177/0730888402239326

Hunkenschroer, A. L., & Luetge, C. (2022). Ethics of AI-enabled recruiting and selection: A review and research agenda. *Journal of Business Ethics*, *178*(4), 977–1007. doi:10.1007/s10551-022-05049-6

Hunt, D. M., & Michael, M. C. (1983). Mentorship: A career training and development tool. *Academy of Management Review*, *8*(3), 475–485. doi:10.2307/257836

Hunter, A., Lewis, N., & Ritter-Gooder, P. (2011). Constructive developmental theory: An alternative approach to leadership. *Journal of the American Dietetic Association*, *111*(12), 1804–1808. doi:10.1016/j.jada.2011.10.009 PMID:22117653

Hussain, R., & Zeadally, S. (2019). Autonomous cars: Research results, issues, and future challenges. *IEEE Communications Surveys and Tutorials*, *21*(2), 1275–1313. doi:10.1109/COMST.2018.2869360

Hussian, A., Mateen, A., Amin, F., Muhammad, A. A., & Ullah, S. (2023). Health Monitoring Apps: An Evaluation of the Persuasive System Design Model for Human Wellbeing. *Information (Basel)*, *14*(7), 412. doi:10.3390/info14070412

Ibarra, H. (2014, Apr 28). Leadership in human resources (A special report) --- why managers are stuck in their 'silos': Companies want employees to take on new responsibilities; but they aren't teaching them how. *Wall Street Journal* Retrieved from https://proxy.cecybrary.com/login?url=https://search.proquest.com/docview/1519234993?accountid=144459

IBM. (2023). *Cost of a Data Breach Report 2023*. Retrieved October 30, 2023, from https://www.ibm.com/downloads/cas/E3G5JMBP

Inductive Automation. (2018, September 12). *SCADA: Supervisory Control and Data Acquisition - What is SCADA, Who Uses it and How SCADA Has Evolved?* Retrieved November 10, 2023, from https://inductiveautomation.com/resources/article/what-is-scada

Information and Communications Technology Council and CAVCOE. (2020, March). Advances in connected & autonomous vehicles. *Author.* https://www.ictc-ctic.ca/wp-content/uploads/2020/04/CAVs-ENG.Final_.0423.pdf

Inkinen, T., Helminen, R., & Saarikoski, J. (2019). Port digitalization with Open Data: Challenges, Opportunities, and Integrations. *Journal of Open Innovation, 5*(30), 1–16. doi:10.3390/joitmc5020030

Inoue, Y. (2005). Critical thinking and diversity experiences: A connection. *Online Submission.* https://eric.ed.gov/?id=ED490360

International Coaching Federation. (2021). *About the ICF.* Retrieved from: https://coachingfederation.org/thought-leadership-institute

ISACA. (2022). State of the cybersecurity workforce: New ISACA research shows highest retention difficulties in years. *Author.* https://www.isaca.org/about-us/newsroom/press-releases/2022/state-of-the-cybersecurity-workforce-new-isaca-research-shows-retention-difficulties-in-years

Islam, M. R., Mahmud, M. R., & Pritom, R. M. (2020). Transportation scheduling optimization by a collaborative strategy in supply chain management with TPL using chemical reaction optimization. *Neural Computing & Applications, 32*(8), 3649–3674. doi:10.1007/s00521-019-04218-5

Ismail, S., Sitnikova, E., & Slay, J. (2020). SCADA Systems Cyber Security for Critical Infrastructures: Case Studies in Multiple Sectors. In I. Management Association (Ed.), Cyber Warfare and Terrorism: Concepts, Methodologies, Tools, and Applications (pp. 446-464). IGI Global. doi:10.4018/978-1-7998-2466-4.ch028

Isopeskul, O., Shakina, M., & Georgieva, N. (2016). *Influence of stakeholders on organizational culture development.* Retrieved from https://proxy.cecybrary.com/login?url=https://search.proquest.com/docview/1779263332?accountid=144459

Ives, K., & Seymour, D. M. (2022). *Using ROI for strategic planning of online education: A process for institutional transformation.* Routledge.

Jabeen, F., Behery, M., & Abu Elanain, H. (2015). Examining the relationship between the psychological contract and organisational commitment. *The International Journal of Organizational Analysis, 23*(1), 102–122. doi:10.1108/IJOA-10-2014-0812

Jain, P., & Chou, M. C. F. (2023). *Supply Chain 5.0: The Next Generation of Business Success Through Customer Centricity, Sustainability & Human Rights and Digitalization.* World Scientific.

Jansen, H. (2010). The logic of qualitative survey research and its position in the field of social research methods. *Forum: Qualitative Research, 11*(2). Retrieved from http://nbn-resolving.de/urn:nbn:de:0114-fqs1002110

Jayakumar, G., & Ajithabai, M. D. (2023). Script Cure with Transactional Analysis and Triology: A Description of Triology Counselling. *International Journal of Transactional Analysis Research & Practice, 14*(1), 3–15. doi:10.29044/v14i1p3

Jeong, J., Mihelcic, J., Oliver, G., & Rudolph, C. (2019, December). Towards an improved understanding of human factors in cybersecurity. In *2019 IEEE 5th International Conference on Collaboration and Internet Computing (CIC)* (pp. 338-345). IEEE. 10.1109/CIC48465.2019.00047

Johnsen, S. O. (2014). Safety and Security in SCADA Systems Must be Improved through Resilience Based Risk Management. In I. Management Association (Ed.), Crisis Management: Concepts, Methodologies, Tools, and Applications (pp. 1422-1436). IGI Global. doi:10.4018/978-1-4666-4707-7.ch071

Johnson, S. (2017). The disadvantages of corporate culture. *Chronicles of Small Business*. Retrieved from https://small-business.chron.com/disadvantages-corporate-culture-67042.html

Johnston, D. (2021). How do coaches and clients create and experience thinking environments? *International Journal of Evidence Based Coaching and Mentoring, S15*, 198–211.

Jones, D. (2023, December 5). *Water utility cyberattacks underscore ongoing threat to OT*. Cybersecurity Dive. Retrieved from: https://www.cybersecuritydive.com/news/water-utility-cyberattacks-threat-ot/701577/

Jones, J., & Smith, J. (2017). Ethnography: challenges and opportunities. Evidence-Based Nursing, 20, 98–100. doi:10.1136/eb-2017-102786

Jones, L. A. (2020). *Reputation risk and potential profitability: Best practices to predict and mitigate risk through amalgamated factors* (Doctoral dissertation). Capitol Technology University.

Jones, L. A. (2020). *Reputation risk and potential profitability: Best practices to predict and mitigate risk through amalgamated factors* (Doctoral dissertation). Dissertations & Theses Global. (2466047018).

Jones, L. A. (2020). *Reputation Risk and Potential Profitability: Best Practices to Predict and Mitigate Risk through Amalgamated Factors* (Order No. 28152966). Available from ProQuest Central; ProQuest Dissertations & Theses Global. 28152966). https://www.proquest.com/openview/1dbd40ceb5eacaf981fd65dd3ee3d9b3/1.pdf?pq-origsite=gscholar&c%20bl=18750&diss=y

Jones, L. A. (2021). A content analysis review of literature to create a useable framework for reputation risk management. Handbook of Research on Multidisciplinary Perspectives on Managerial and Leadership Psychology, 91-133.

Jones, R. A., Rafferty, A. E., & Griffin, M. A. (2006). The executive coaching trend: Towards more flexible executives. *Leadership and Organization Development Journal, 27*(7), 583–596. doi:10.1108/01437730610692434

Jones, R. J., Woods, S. A., & Hutchinson, E. (2014). The influence of the Five Factor Model of personality on the perceived effectiveness of executive coaching. *International Journal of Evidence Based Coaching and Mentoring, 12*(2), 109–118.

Joo, B., Sushko, J. S., & McLean, G. N. (2012). Multiple faces of coaching: Manager-as-coach, executive coaching, and formal mentoring. *Organization Development Journal, 30*(1), 19-38. Retrieved From http://blogs.wayne.edu/ioadventures/files/2013/12/Multiple-Faces-of-Coaching-Manager-as-coach-Executive-Coaching-and-Formal-Mentoring.pdf

Joo, B. K. (2005). Executive Coaching: A Conceptual Framework From an Integrative Review of Practice and Research. *Human Resource Development Review, 4*(4), 462–488. doi:10.1177/1534484305280866

Jothimani, D., Shankar, R., & Yadav, S. S. (2016). Modeling hierarchical relationships among enablers of supply chain coordination in flexible environment. In *Managing flexibility* (pp. 171–186). Springer. doi:10.1007/978-81-322-2380-1_13

Judson, J. (2023). *US Army replaces problematic engine part on Chinooks*. https://www.defensenews.com/land/2023/02/15/us-army-replaces-problematic-engine-part-on-chinooks/

Kafle, N. (2011). Hermeneutic phenomenological research method simplified. *Bodhi: An Interdisciplinary Journal*, *5*, 181–198.

Kaiser, S., Patras, J., Adolfsen, F., Richardsen, A. M., & Martinussen, M. (2020). Using the Job Demands–Resources Model to Evaluate Work-Related Outcomes Among Norwegian Health Care Workers. *SAGE Open*, *10*(3). Advance online publication. doi:10.1177/2158244020947436

Kalev, A., Dobbin, F., & Kelly, E. (2006). Best practices or best guesses? Assessing the efficacy of corporate affirmative action and diversity policies. *American Sociological Review*, *71*(4), 589–617. doi:10.1177/000312240607100404

Kaminska, M. (2021). Restraint under conditions of uncertainty: Why the United States tolerates cyberattacks. *Journal of Cybersecurity*, *7*(1), tyab008. doi:10.1093/cybsec/tyab008

Kampa-Kokesh, S., Anderson, M., (2005). *Executive Coaching: A Comprehensive Review of the Literature*. Educational Publishing Foundation and the Society of Consulting Psychology. DOI doi:10.1037//1061-4087.53.4.2O5

Kanesan, P., & Fauzan, N. (2019). Models of emotional intelligence: A review. *e-BANGI Journal, 16*(7).

Karim, M., Tahera, U., & Nasrin, S. (2020). Supply Chain Management: Materialization of Process Management to Attain Greater Accomplishment in Business Function. *Fareast International University Journal, 104*.

Karthik, R. M., & Mathew, F. S. (2023). Artificial intelligence and its theranostic applications in dentistry. *Cureus*, *15*(5). Advance online publication. doi:10.7759/cureus.38711 PMID:37292569

Katsaliaki, K., Galetsi, P., & Kumar, S. (2022). Supply chain disruptions and resilience: A major review and future research agenda. *Annals of Operations Research*, *319*(1), 965–1002. doi:10.1007/s10479-020-03912-1 PMID:33437110

Katz, E. (2018a, October 3). *OPM Calls on Agencies to Implement Coaching Programs for Employees*. Government Executive.

Katz, E. (2018b, January 10). *Agencies Aren't Catching Bad Supervisors Early Enough*. Government Executive.

Katz, J. E., & Aakhus, M. (2019). Introduction: Technological determinism in communication research. In *Perpetual contact: Mobile communication, private talk, public performance* (pp. 1–12). Cambridge University Press.

Katzmarzyk, P. T., Denstel, K. D., Beals, K., Bolling, C., Wright, C., Crouter, S. E., McKenzie, T. L., Pate, R. R., Saelens, B. E., Staiano, A. E., Stanish, H. I., & Sisson, S. B. (2016). Results From the United States of America's 2016 Report Card on Physical Activity for Children and Youth. *Journal of Physical Activity & Health*, *13*(11, Suppl 2), S307–S313. doi:10.1123/jpah.2016-0321 PMID:27848726

Kaur, J., & Singh, W. (2022). Tools, techniques, datasets and application areas for object detection in an image: A review. *Multimedia Tools and Applications*, *81*(27), 38297–38351. doi:10.1007/s11042-022-13153-y PMID:35493415

Kavoura, A., & Bitsani, E. (2014). Considerations for qualitative communication research. *Procedia: Social and Behavioral Sciences*, *147*, 544–549. doi:10.1016/j.sbspro.2014.07.156

Kearns, M., Neel, S., Roth, A., & Steinhardt, J. (2020). Fairness in criminal justice risk assessments: The science of algorithm-based bias. *Science*, *368*(6491), 475–481.

Keikha, A., Hoveida, R., & Nour, M. Y. (2017). The development of an intelligent leadership model for state universities. *Foresight and STI Governance*, *11*(1), 66–74. doi:10.17323/2500-2597.2017.1.66.74.

Kelan, E. K. (2023). Algorithmic inclusion: Shaping the predictive algorithms of artificial intelligence in hiring. *Human Resource Management Journal*, 1748-8583.12511. doi:10.1111/1748-8583.12511

Keller, J. M. (2010). *Motivational Design for Learning and Performance: The ARCS model approach.* Springer. doi:10.1007/978-1-4419-1250-3

Keller, S., Meaney, M., & Pung, C. (2020). Organizing for the future: Nine keys to becoming a future-ready company. *The McKinsey Quarterly, 64*(1), 25–37. https://www.mckinsey.com/business-functions/organization/our-insights/organizing-for-the-future-nine-keys-to-becoming-a-future-ready-company

Kellis, D. S., & Ran, B. (2015). Effective leadership in managing NPM-based change in the public sector. *Journal of Organizational Change Management, 28*(4), 614–626. doi:10.1108/JOCM-11-2013-0229

Kempf, A. (2020). If we are going to talk about implicit race bias, we need to talk about structural racism: Moving beyond ubiquity and inevitability in teaching and learning about race. Taboo. *The Journal of Culture and Education, 19*(2). https://digitalscholarship.unlv.edu/taboo/vol19/ iss2/10

Kerrigan, H. (2015). Eight Tips for changing culture in the federal government. *GovLoop.* Retrieved from https://www.govloop.com/community/blog/8-tips-culture-change/

Kesebi, O. (2019). *Disruption Ready: Building market resilience through 'adapted foresight', organizational agility, co-creative intelligence and employee engagement.* Academic Press.

Khademi, A., & Eksioglu, B. (2018). Spare Parts Inventory Management with Substitution-Dependent Reliability. *IN-FORMS Journal on Computing, 30*(3), 507–521. doi:10.1287/ijoc.2017.0794

Khalid, A. A. (2023). The key criteria that determine the degree to which management's use of competitive intelligence. *Cogent Business & Management, 10*(2), 1–21. https://doi-org.captechu.idm.oclc.org/10.1080/23311975.2023.2250553

Khan, V., Hafeez, M., Rizfi, S. M., Hasanain, A., Maria, A. (2012). The relationship of leadership styles, employees commitment, and organization. Performance. *European Journal of Economics, Finance and Administrative.*

Khan, A., Tao, M., Ahmad, H., Shafique, M. N., & Nawaz, M. Z. (2020). Revisiting green supply chain management practices: The mediating role of emotional intelligence. *SAGE Open, 10*(1), 2158244020914637. doi:10.1177/2158244020914637

Khosla, R. (2013). A case study of mentoring at ONGC. *Review of HRM, 2,* 290–298. https://proxy.cecybrary.com/login?url=https://search.proquest.com/docview/1655997777?accountid=144459

Khulumane, M. (2013). Instilling safety culture in the passenger rail transport industry within the South African context. *Journal of Transport and Supply Chain Management, 7*(1). Advance online publication. doi:10.4102/jtscm.v7i1.84

Kilburg, R. R. (1996). Toward a conceptual understanding and definition of executive coaching. *Consulting Psychology Journal, 48*(2), 134–144. doi:10.1037/1061-4087.48.2.134

Kilburg, R. R. (2000). *Executive coaching: Developing managerial wisdom in a world of chaos.* American Psychological Association. doi:10.1037/10355-000

Kim, S. C., Shaw, B. R., Shah, D. V., Hawkins, R. P., Pingree, S., McTavish, F. M., & Gustafson, D. H. (2019). Interactivity, Presence, and Targeted Patient Care: Mapping e-Health Intervention Effects Over Time for Cancer Patients with Depression. *Health Communication, 34*(2), 162–171.

Kim, K. H., & Lee, H. (2015). Container terminal operation: current trends and future challenges. In *Handbook of Ocean Container Transport Logistics* (pp. 43–73). Springer. doi:10.1007/978-3-319-11891-8_2

Kim, S. E. (2014). The mentor-protégé affinity on mentoring outcomes: The mediating effect of developmental networking. *International Review of Public Administration, 19*(1), 91–106. doi:10.1080/12294659.2014.887368

Kishore, S., Hayden, M., & Phil, M. (2020). Community Health Centers and COVID-19 – Time for Congress to Act. *The New England Journal of Medicine.* Retrieved from: https://www.nejm.org/doi/full/10.1056/NEJMp2020576

Kissinger, H. (2014). *World order.* Penguin Press.

Kleinmuntz, D. (2007). Resource Allocation Decisions. In W. Edwards, R. Miles Jr, & D. Von Winterfeldt (Eds.), *Advances in Decision Analysis: From Foundations to Applications* (pp. 400–418). Cambridge University Press. doi:10.1017/CBO9780511611308.021

Knol, L., Myers, H., Black, S., Robinson, D., Awololo, Y., Clark, D., & Higginbotham, J. C. (2016). Development and Feasibility of a Childhood Obesity Prevention Program for Rural Families: Application of the Social Cognitive Theory. *American Journal of Health Education, 47*(4), 204–214. doi:10.1080/19325037.2016.1179607 PMID:28392882

Knouse, S. B. (2013). Mentoring for Hispanics. *Review of Business, 33*(2), 80–90. https://proxy.cecybrary.com/login?url=https://search.proquest.com/docview/1471854143?accountid=144459

Kohan, K. S., Sabet, F. P., & Darvishpour, A. (2023). Explaining the process of playing the role of a nurse as a patient advocate in the emergency department: Providing a theoretical model [Explicación del proceso de desempeñar el papel de una enfermera como defensora del paciente en el departamento de emergencias: proporcionar un modelo teórico]. *Revista Latinoamericana de Hipertensiòn, 18*(3), 124–132. doi:10.5281/zenodo.8051101

Komar, D. (2018). Marijuana Breathalyzers and the Future of Cannabis Testing. *Frontiers in Pharmacology, 9,* 276.

Koonce, R. (2010). Executive coaching: Leadership development in the federal government. *Public Manager, 39*(2), 44-51. Retrieved from https://proxy.cecybrary.com/login?url=https://search.proquest.com/docview/733013948?accountid=144459

Kopestinsky, A. (2023). 25 astonishing self-driving car statistics for 2023. *Policy Advice.* https://policyadvice.net/insurance/insights/self-driving-car-statistics/#:~:text=There%20are%20over%201%2C400%20self,registered%20in%20California%20thus%20far

Korn Ferry Institute. (2019). *What is the relationship between emotional intelligence and leadership?* Korn Ferry.

Kostadinov, V. (2011). Developing a new methodology for nuclear power plants vulnerability assessment. *Nuclear Engineering and Design, 241*(3), 950–956. doi:10.1016/j.nucengdes.2011.01.006

Kotter, J. P. (2013). *Leading change, with a new preface by the author.* Harvard Business Press.

Kouzes, J., & Posner, B. (2017). *The Leadership Challenge: How to Make Extraordinary Things Happen in Organizations.* Harvard Business Review Publishing.

Kovacs, E. (2022, October 5). *SCADA Systems Involved in Many Breaches Suffered by U.S. Ports, Terminals.* Security Week. Retrieved November 10, 2023, from https://www.securityweek.com/scada-systems-involved-many-breaches-suffered-us-ports-terminals/

Kraljic, P., & Bonnemeier, S. (2023). *Emotional intelligence is critical to successful procurement leadership.* Supply & Demand Chain Executive.

Kraus, S., Breier, M., Lim, W. M., Dabić, M., Kumar, S., Kanbach, D., Mukherjee, D., Corvello, V., Piñeiro-Chousa, J., Liguori, E., Palacios-Marqués, D., Schiavone, F., Ferraris, A., Fernandes, C., & Ferreira, J. J. (2022). Literature reviews as independent studies: Guidelines for academic practice. *Review of Managerial Science, 16*(8), 2577–2595. doi:10.1007/s11846-022-00588-8

Kruse, K. (2012, January 16). Stephen Covey: 10 quotes that can change your life. *Forbes*. https://www.forbes.com/sites/kevinkruse/2012/07/16/the-7-habits/?sh=4d9e7f8b39c6

Kube, N. (2013). Cybersecurity and SCADA in critical infrastructure. *Pipeline & Gas Journal, 240*(2), 46–47. Retrieved November 9, 2023, from https://pgjonline.com/magazine/2013/february-2013-vol-240-no-2/features/cyber-security-and-scada-in-critical-infrastructure

Kumar, V., Saboo, A. R., Agarwal, A., & Kumar, B. (2020). Generating Competitive Intelligence with Limited Information: A Case of the Multimedia Industry. *Production and Operations Management, 29*(1), 192–213. doi:10.1111/poms.13095

Kunnan, A. J. (2015). Assessing the quality of large-scale assessments: The case for a fairness and justice approach. *Developing Indigenous Models of English Language Teaching and Assessment*, 131.

Kuula, A. (2010). Methodological and ethical dilemmas of archiving qualitative data. *IASSIST Quarterly, 34*(3), 12–17.

LaFraniere, S. (1990, January). Barry Arrested on cocaine charges in undercover FBI, police operation. *The Washington Post*. Retrieved from https://www.washingtonpost.com/wp-srv/local/longterm/tours/scandal/barry.htm

Lahanas, M. (2017). The Future of Broadband in Underserved Areas. *New America Weekly*. Retrieved from: https://www.newamerica.org/weekly/future-broadband-underserved-areas/

Lai, C. K., Skinner, A. L., Cooley, E., Murrar, S., Brauer, M., Devos, T., Calanchini, J., Xiao, Y. J., Pedram, C., Marshburn, C. K., Simon, S., Blanchar, J. C., Joy-Gaba, J. A., Conway, J., Redford, L., Klein, R. A., Roussos, G., Schellhaas, F. M. H., Burns, M., ... Nosek, B. A. (2016). Reducing implicit racial preferences: II. Intervention effectiveness across time. *Journal of Experimental Psychology. General, 145*(8), 1001–1016. doi:10.1037/xge0000179 PMID:27454041

Lai, Y.-L., & Palmer, S. (2019). Psychology in executive coaching: An integrated literature review. *Journal of Work-Applied Management, 11*(2), 143–164. doi:10.1108/JWAM-06-2019-0017

Lake, A. A. (2011). Obesity. *Perspectives in Public Health, 131*(4), 154. doi:10.1177/1757913911413188 PMID:21888112

Lanes, S. G. (2018). Marijuana Breathalyzers and Public Safety. *The Journal of Law, Medicine & Ethics, 46*(4), 789–794.

Lau, T. Y., Lim, J., & Choo, K. K. (2018). Can artificial intelligence detect driving under the influence of marijuana? *Traffic Injury Prevention, 19*(3), 245–249.

Le Maistre, C., & Paré, A. (2010). Whatever it takes: How beginning teachers learn to survive. *Teaching and Teacher Education, 26*(3), 559–564. doi:10.1016/j.tate.2009.06.016

Leath, B. A., Dunn, L. W., Alsobrook, A., & Darden, M. L. (2018). Enhancing Rural Population Health Care Access and Outcomes Through the Telehealth EcoSystem™ Model. *Online Journal of Public Health Informatics, 10*(2), e218. doi:10.5210/ojphi.v10i2.9311 PMID:30349636

Leavy, P. (2022). *Research design: Quantitative, qualitative, mixed methods, arts-based, and community-based participatory research approaches*. Guilford Publications.

Lebihan, R. (2011). Business schools tap coaching trend. *Australian Financial Review, 14*, 27–28.

Lee, I. M., Shiroma, E. J., Lobelo, F., Puska, P., Blair, S. N., Katzmarzyk, P. T., & the Lancet Physical Activity Series Working Group. (2012). Effect of physical inactivity on major non-communicable diseases worldwide: an analysis of burden of disease and life expectancy. *Lancet (London, England), 380*(9838), 219–229. Retrieved from: https://www.ncbi.nlm.nih.gov/pmc/articles/PMC3645500/ doi:10.1016/S0140-6736(12)61031-9

Lee, R. J. & Frisch, M. H. (2015). Legacy reflections: ten lessons about becoming an executive coach, *Consulting Psychology Journal: Practice and Research, 67*(1), 3 – 1. Doi.org/10.1037cpb00000033

Lee, C. Y., & Song, D. P. (2017). Ocean container transport in global supply chains: Overview and research opportunities. *Transportation Research Part B: Methodological*, *95*, 442–474. doi:10.1016/j.trb.2016.05.001

Lee, C., & Madnix, S. (2021). Cybersafety approach to cybersecurity analysis and mitigation for mobility-as-a-service and internet of vehicles. *Electronics (Basel)*, *10*(10), 1–25. doi:10.3390/electronics10101220

Lee, D., Choi, Y., Youn, S., & Chun, J. U. (2017). Ethical leadership and employee moral voice: The mediating role of moral efficacy and the moderating role of leader-follower value congruence. *Journal of Business Ethics*, *141*(1), 47–57. doi:10.1007/s10551-015-2689-y

Lee, D., & Hess, D. J. (2022). Public concerns and connected and automated vehicles: Safety, privacy, and data security. *Humanities & Social Sciences Communications*, *9*(90), 90. Advance online publication. doi:10.1057/s41599-022-01110-x

Lee, I. (2021). Cybersecurity: Risk management framework and investment cost analysis. *Business Horizons*, *64*(5), 659–671. doi:10.1016/j.bushor.2021.02.022

Lennon, M. (2015). *Attacks against SCADA systems doubled in 2014: Dell*. Security Week. Retrieved November 2, 2015, from https://www.securityweek.com/attacks-against-scada-systems-doubled-2014-dell

Lennon, R. J., Vadas, D. L., & Huestis, M. A. (2020). Cannabis-Impaired Driving: An Overview of Cannabinoid Pharmacology, Epidemiology, and Analytical Challenges. *Clinical Chemistry*, *66*(7), 971–983.

Lennon, T. (2013). *Benchmarking women's leadership in the United States*. Colorado Women's College at the University of Denver.

Leonardelli, G. J., Pickett, C. L., & Brewer, M. B. (2010). Optimal distinctiveness theory: A framework for social identity, social cognition, and intergroup relations. In M. P. Zanna & J. M. Olson (Eds.), Advances in experimental social psychology (Vol. 43, pp. 63–113). Academic Press. doi:10.1016/S0065-2601(10)43002-6

Less than 5% of critical industrial infrastructure is monitored for threats. (2023). *Communications Today; Noida*. Retrieved October 28, 2023, from http://ezproxy.apus.edu/login?qurl=https%3A%2F%2Fwww.proquest.com%2Ftrade-journals%2Fless-than-5-critical-industrial-infrastructure-is%2Fdocview%2F2806176802%2Fse-2%3Faccountid%3D8289

Lester, D. L. & Parnell, J. A. (2006). The Desktop Manager. S.A.M. *Advanced Management Journal*, *71*(4), 43-49.

Lewis, C., Getachew, Y., Abrams, M., & Doty, M. (2019). *Changes at Community Health Centers, and How Patients are Benefiting*. The Commonwealth Fund. Retrieved from: https://www.commonwealthfund.org/publications/issue-briefs/2019/aug/changes-at-community-health-centers-how-patients-are-benefiting

Lewis, E. & Burrell, D. (2023). The Sustainability of Historically Black Colleges and Universities (HBCUs) in the Post-COVID-19 World and Beyond. *HOLISTICA – Journal of Business and Public Administration*, *14*(1) 39–62. doi:10.2478/hjbpa-2023-0004

Lewis, L. & Wescott, H. (2017). Multi-Generational Workforce: Four Generations United In Lean. *Journal of Business Studies Quarterly*, 8.

Lievrouw, L. A. (2019). Mediation, mediation everywhere... Technology determinism and the myth of the mediated center. *Communication Theory*, *29*(4), 349–360.

Liken, M. (2018). *How Teachers and Schools Can Address Childhood Obesity*. Concordia University – Portland. Published on November 16, 2018. Retrieved from: https://education.cu-portland.edu/blog/classroom-resources/teachers-schools-childhood-obesity/

Lindblom, A., Kajalo, S., & Mitronen, L. (2016). Does a retailer's charisma matter? A study of frontline employee perceptions of charisma in the retail setting. *Journal of Services Marketing*, *30*(3), 266–276. doi:10.1108/JSM-05-2015-0160

Linehan, M., & Scullion, H. (2008). The development of female global managers: The role of mentoring and networking. *Journal of Business Ethics*, *83*(1), 29–40. doi:10.1007/s10551-007-9657-0

Li, Z., Wang, J., & Zheng, N. (2020). Computer vision for connected and automated vehicles: A survey. *IEEE Transactions on Intelligent Transportation Systems*, *21*(11), 4704–4724.

LLorens-Montes, F. J., Garcia-Morales, V. J., & Verdu-Jover, A. J. (2004). The influence on personal mastery, organizational learning, and performance of the level of innovation: Adaptive organization versus innovator organization. *International Journal of Innovation and Learning*, *1*(2), 101–114. doi:10.1504/IJIL.2004.003714

Locke, E., & Latham, G. (2002). Building a practically useful theory of goal setting and task motivation: A 35-year odyssey. *The American Psychologist*, *57*(9), 705–717. doi:10.1037/0003-066X.57.9.705 PMID:12237980

Loes, C., Pascarella, E., & Umbach, P. (2012). Effects of diversity experiences on critical thinking skills: Who benefits? *Journal of Higher Education (Columbus, Ohio)*, *83*(1), 1–25. doi:10.1353/jhe.2012.0001

Loh, H. S., Zhou, Q., Thai, V. V., Wong, Y. D., & Yuen, K. F. (2017). Fuzzy comprehensive evaluation of port-centric supply chain disruption threats. *Ocean and Coastal Management*, *148*, 53–62. doi:10.1016/j.ocecoaman.2017.07.017

Loukatos, D., Kondoyanni, M., Kyrtopoulos, I.-V., & Arvanitis, K. G. (2022). Enhanced robots as tools for assisting agricultural engineering students' development. *Electronics (Basel)*, *11*(5), 755. doi:10.3390/electronics11050755

Lowman, J. (1996). Characteristics of exemplary teachers. In M. D. Svinicki & R. J. Menges (Eds.), *Honoring exemplary teaching. New Directions for Teaching and Learning, No. 65* (pp. 33–40). Jossey-Bass.

Loy, S. L., Brown, S., & Tabibzadeh, K. (2014). South Carolina department of revenue: Mother of government dysfunction. *Journal of the International Academy for Case Studies*, *20*(2). http://www.alliedacademies.org/articles/jiacs-vol20no22014.pdf#page=81

Lunenburg, F. C., & Ornetein, A. O. (2010). *Educational administration: Concepts and practices*. Wadsworth/Cengage Learning.

Lun, V. M.-C., Fischer, R., & Ward, C. (2010). Exploring cultural differences in critical thinking: Is it about my thinking style or the language I speak? *Learning and Individual Differences*, *20*(6), 604–616. doi:10.1016/j.lindif.2010.07.001

Luo, G., Serrão, C., Liang, D., & Zhou, Y. (2023). A Relevance-Based Technology–Organisation–Environment Model of Critical Success Factors for Digital Procurement Adoption in Chinese Construction Companies. *Sustainability (Basel)*, *15*(16), 12260. doi:10.3390/su151612260

Lu, P., Burris, S., Baker, M., Meyers, C., & Cummins, G. (2021). Cultural Differences in Critical Thinking Style: A Comparison of U. S. and Chinese Undergraduate Agricultural Students. *Journal of International Agricultural and Extension Education*, *28*(4). Advance online publication. doi:10.4148/2831-5960.1003

Luthans, F., Avolio, B. J., Avey, J. B., & Norman, S. M. (2007). Positive psychological capital: Measurement and relationship with performance and satisfaction. *Personnel Psychology*, *3*(60), 541–572. doi:10.1111/j.1744-6570.2007.00083.x

Lyons, M. (2021). How to Job Hunt (when you're already exhausted). *Harvard Business Review*. https://hbr.org/2021/10/how-to-job-hunt-when-youre-already-exhausted

Lyons, S., & Kuron, L. (2014). Generational differences in the workplace: A review of the evidence and directions for future research. *Journal of Organizational Behavior*, *35*(S1), 139–157. doi:10.1002/job.1913

Lyons, S., Urick, M., Kuron, L., & Schweitzer, L. (2015). Generational differences in the workplace: There is complexity beyond the stereotypes. *Industrial and Organizational Psychology: Perspectives on Science and Practice, 8*(3), 346–356. doi:10.1017/iop.2015.48

Lyuboslavsky, V. (2015). Telemedicine and telehealth 2.0: A practical guide for medical providers and patients. *Technology in Society, 60,* 101212.

M. (2021). *Technical Guide for Implementing Cybersecurity Continuous Monitoring in the Nuclear Industry* (No. PN L-31747). Pacific Northwest National Lab. (PNNL), Richland, WA (United States).

Macaulay, T., & Singer, B. L. (2011). *Cybersecurity for industrial control systems: SCADA, dcs, plc, hmi, and sis* (1st ed.). Auerbach Publications.

MacDonald, M. G., & Neeley, R. (2022). Supply Chain Management in a Data-driven World: Army Logistics University's Approach to Supply Chain Education. *Army Sustainment, 54*(2), 60–63.

Mack, T. (2021). Generational recruiting: How to tailor your recruitment message for different generations. *Recruitics.* https://info.recruitics.com/blog/generational-recruiting-how-to-tailor-your-recruitment-message-for-different-generations

Madureira, L., Castelli, M., & Popovič, A. (2019). Design thinking: The new mindset for competitive intelligence? Impacts on the Competitive Intelligence Model. CAPSI 2019 Proceedings, 26.

Magid, L. (2014, October 1). Why Cyber Security Matters to Everyone. *Forbes.* https://www.forbes.com/sites/larrymagid/2014/10/01/why-cyber-security-matters-to-everyone/#61f9e7ae5a71

Maihulla, A. S., & Yusuf, I. (2022). Reliability, availability, maintainability, and dependability analysis of photovoltaic systems. *Life Cycle Reliab Saf Eng, 11*(1), 19–26. doi:10.1007/s41872-021-00180-1

Maldonado, M. L. (2015). Withstanding the tests of time. *Leadership Excellence Essentials, 32*(1), 9-10. Retrieved from https://proxy.cecybrary.com/login?url=https://search.proquest.com/docview/1648981552?accountid=144459

Maldonado, S., Gonzalez-Ramirez, R. G., Quijada, F., & Ramirez-Nafarrate, A. (2019). Analytics meets port logistics: A decision support system for container stacking operations. *Decision Support Systems, 121,* 84–93. doi:10.1016/j.dss.2019.04.006

Manuj, I., & Pohlen, T. L. (2012). A reviewer's guide to the grounded theory methodology in logistics and supply chain management research. *International Journal of Physical Distribution & Logistics Management, 42*(8/9), 784–803. doi:10.1108/09600031211269758

Marchet, G., Melacini, M., Perotti, S., Rasini, M., & Tappia, E. (2018). Business logistics models in omni-channel: A classification framework and empirical analysis. *International Journal of Physical Distribution & Logistics Management, 48*(4), 439–464. doi:10.1108/IJPDLM-09-2016-0273

Marchetti, A., Dalle, S., Maucort-Boulch, D., Amini-Adl, M., Debarbieux, S., Poulalhon, N., Perier-Muzet, M., Phan, A., & Thomas, L. (2020). Diagnostic Concordance in Tertiary (Dermatologists-to-Experts) Teledermoscopy: A Final Diagnosis-Based Study on 290 Cases. *Dermatology Practical & Conceptual, 10*(3), e2020071. doi:10.5826/dpc.1003a71 PMID:32642316

MarketsandMarkets. (2021, January). *Supply chain management market by component (hardware (barcode and barcode scanners and RFID tags and readers), software, and services), deployment mode (cloud and on-premises), organization size, vertical, and region - global forecast to 2026.* Academic Press.

Markkanen, P., Välimäki, M., Anttila, M., & Kuuskorpi, M. (2020). A reflective cycle: Understanding challenging situations in a school setting. *Educational Research, 62*(1), 46–62. doi:10.1080/00131881.2020.1711790

Marković-Petrović, J. D. (2020). Methodology for Cyber Security Risk Mitigation in Next Generation SCADA Systems. In M. Stojanović & S. Boštjančič Rakas (Eds.), *Cyber Security of Industrial Control Systems in the Future Internet Environment* (pp. 27–46). IGI Global. doi:10.4018/978-1-7998-2910-2.ch002

Marseille, E., & Kahn, J. G. (2019). Utilitarianism and the ethical foundations of cost-effectiveness analysis in resource allocation for global health. *Philosophy, Ethics, and Humanities in Medicine; PEHM, 14*(5), 5. Advance online publication. doi:10.1186/s13010-019-0074-7 PMID:30944009

Marshall, C., & Rossman, G. (2016). *Designing qualitative research* (6th ed.). Sage. Retrieved from: https://books.google.com/books?hl=en&lr=&id=qTByBgAAQBAJ&oi=fnd&pg=PT8&dq=Marshall,+C.,+%26+Rossman,+G.+(2016).+Designing+qualitative+res earch+(6th+ed.).+Thousands+&ots=xhzaGEZZe2&sig=z9mLUoXC9R0Sb6VJgN2w5T_8tig#v=onepage&q&f=false

Martin, J., & Sibbald, S. (2023). The Use of Patient Engagement as a Means to Improve Equitable Care. *The International Journal of Health, Wellness & Society, 13*(2), 39–52. doi:10.18848/2156-8960/CGP/v13i02/39-52

Martins, N., & Coetzee, M. (2009). Applying the Burke-Litwin model as a diagnostic framework for assessing organisational effectiveness. *SA Journal of Human Resource Management, 7*(1), 1–13. doi:10.4102/sajhrm.v7i1.177

Mason, A. N. (2022). The most important telemedicine patient satisfaction dimension: Patient-centered care. *Telemedicine Journal and e-Health, 28*(8), 1206–1214. doi:10.1089/tmj.2021.0322 PMID:34882032

Masood, R. (2016). *Assessment of cyber security challenges in nuclear power plants security incidents, threats, and initiatives.* Cybersecurity and Privacy Research Institute the George Washington University.

Mastrangelo, A., Eddy, E. R., & Lorenzet, S. J. (2014). The relationship between enduring. leadership and organizational performance. *Leadership and Organization Development Journal, 35*, 590–604. doi:10.1108/LODJ-08-2012-0097

Maxfield, S. (2008). Reconciling Corporate Citizenship and Competitive Strategy: Insights from Economic Theory. *Journal of Business Ethics, 80*(2), 367–377. doi:10.1007/s10551-007-9425-1

Maxwell, J. (2013). *5 Levels of leadership.* Center Street Publishing.

Ma, Y., Wang, J., & Bai, Y. (2023). Macro-Institutional Pressures and Firms' Environmental Management Behavior: The Moderating Effect of Micro-Institutional Pressures. *Sustainability (Basel), 15*(4), 3662. doi:10.3390/su15043662

Mayfield, J. (2012). The leadership relation between leader Motivating language and employee self-efficacy. A partial least squares model analysis. *Journal of Business Communication.* Advance online publication. doi:10.1177/0021943612456036

McCarthy, G., & Milner, J. (2012). Managerial coaching: challenges, opportunities and Training. Sydney Business School, University of Wollongong, School of Psychology, Deakin University. doi:10.1108/JMD-11-2011-0113

McCartney, G., & McCartney, A. (2020). Rise of the machines: Towards a conceptual service-robot research framework for the hospitality and tourism industry. *International Journal of Contemporary Hospitality Management, 32*(12), 3835–3851. doi:10.1108/IJCHM-05-2020-0450

McKenzie, J. F., Pinger, R. R., & Seabert, D. (2018). An introduction to community and public health. Jones & Bartlett Learning.

McKeown, A., & Bates, J. (2013). Emotional intelligent leadership. *Library Management, 34*(6), 462-485. doi:http://dx.doi.org.proxy.cecybrary.com/10.1108/LM-10-2012-0072

McKinnon, A. C. (2013). Starry-eyed: Journal rankings and the future of logistics research. *International Journal of Physical Distribution & Logistics Management, 43*(1), 6–17. doi:10.1108/09600031311293228

McLester, Q., Burrell, D. N., Nobles, C., & Castillo, I. (2021). Advancing Knowledge About Sexual Harassment Is a Critical Aspect of Organizational Development for All Employees. *International Journal of Knowledge-Based Organizations*, *11*(4), 48–60. doi:10.4018/IJKBO.2021100104

McMullan, M., Millar, R., & Woodside, J. V. (2020). A systematic review to assess the effectiveness of technology-based interventions to address obesity in children. *BMC Pediatrics*, *20*(1), 1–14. doi:10.1186/s12887-020-02081-1 PMID:32438908

McNabb, S., Conde, J. M., Ferland, L., MacWright, W., Memish, Z. OkuTani, S., … Singh, V. (Eds.). (2016). Transforming public health surveillance: proactive measures for prevention, detection, and response. Amman, Jordan: Elsevier.

McNamara, T. K., Pitt-Catsouphes, M., Sarkisian, N., Besen, E., & Kidahashi, M. (2016). Age bias in the workplace: Cultural stereotypes and in-group favoritism. *International Journal of Aging & Human Development*, *83*(2), 156–183. doi:10.1177/0091415016648708 PMID:27199491

Meeler, D. (2018, May 3). *Five basic approaches to ethical decision-making*. Ethically Philosophical. Retrieved March 22, 2023, from https://ethicallyphilosophical.wordpress.com/2018/05/03/five-basic-approaches-to-ethical-decision-making/

Meiksins, P., Layne, P., Beddoes, K., Acton, B., Masters, A., & Roediger, M. (2017). *Tech Women in Engineering: A Review of the 2017 Literature*. Society of Women Engineer Magazine.

Melenbrink, N., Werfel, J., & Menges, A. (2020). On-site autonomous construction robots: Towards unsupervised building. *Automation in Construction*, *119*, 103312. doi:10.1016/j.autcon.2020.103312

Melnick, S. A., & Meister, D. G. (2008). A comparison of beginning and experienced teachers' concerns. *Educational Research Quarterly*, *31*(3), 39–56.

Mendez, M. J., Howell, J. P., & Bishop, J. W. (2015). Beyond the unidimensional collective leadership model. *Leadership and Organization Development Journal*, *36*(6), 675–696. doi:10.1108/LODJ-11-2013-0141

Merit Services Protection. (2018). *Barriers to effectively using the supervisory probationary period* (Issues of Merit). *Merit Services Protection Board*. Retrieved from: https://www.mspb.gov/MSPBSEARCH/viewdocs.aspx?docnumber=1477762&version=1483321&application=ACROBAT

Merriam, S. (2014). *Qualitative research: A guide to design and implementation*. John Wiley & Sons.

Metz, J. (2023). What Is Cyber Liability Insurance? *Forbes*. https://www.forbes.com/advisor/business-insurance/cyber-liability-insurance/

Mezirow, J. (1997). Transformative Learning Theory to Practice. *New Directions for Adult and Continuing Education*, *74*(74), 5–12. doi:10.1002/ace.7401

Miceli, A., Hagen, B., Riccardi, M. P., Sotti, F., & Settembre-Blundo, D. (2021). Thriving, not just surviving in changing times: How sustainability, agility and digitalization intertwine with organizational resilience. *Sustainability (Basel)*, *13*(4), 2052. doi:10.3390/su13042052

Milella, F., Minelli, E. A., Strozzi, F., & Croce, D. (2021). Change and Innovation in Healthcare: Findings from Literature. *ClinicoEconomics and Outcomes Research*, *13*, 395–408. doi:10.2147/CEOR.S301169 PMID:34040399

Miles, G., Wiles, J., Claypoole, T., Drake, P., Henry, P. A., & Johnson, L. J. (2008). *Techno Security's Guide to Securing SCADA* (1st ed.). Syngress.

Mileti, D. (1999). *Disasters By Design: A Reassessment of Natural Disasters in the United States*. Joseph Henry Press.

Miller, J. L. (2017). Managing transitions: Using William Bridges' transition model and a change style assessment instrument to inform strategies and measure progress in organizational change management. In *The 12th International Conference on Performance Measurement in Libraries Proceedings* (p. 357). Academic Press.

Miller, A., & Park, J. (2024). From the battlefield to the boardroom: Leadership lessons from military veterans in supply chain management. *International Journal of Logistics Management, 35*(3), 75–95. doi:10.1108/IJLM-02-2023-0156

Miller-Jones, G. (2020, February 25). Ineffective Leadership and The Devastating Individual And Organizational Consequences. *Forbes.*

Ming-Chu, Y., & Meng-Hsiu, L. (2015). Unlocking the black box: Exploring the link between perceive organizational support and resistance to change. *Asia Pacific Management Review, 20*(3), 177–183. doi:10.1016/j.apmrv.2014.10.003

Mingo, H. C., & Burrell, D. N. (2023). Cybersecurity Risks With Supervisory Control and Data Acquisition (SCADA) Systems is a Public Health and National Security Issue. In F. Adedoyin & B. Christiansen (Eds.), *Handbook of Research on Cybersecurity Risk in Contemporary Business Systems* (pp. 149–167). IGI Global. doi:10.4018/978-1-6684-7207-1.ch008

Minkin, R. (2023, May 17). Diversity, Equity and Inclusion in the Workplace. *Pew Research Center's Social & Demographic Trends Project.* https://www.pewresearch.org/social-trends/2023/05/17/diversity-equity-and-inclusion-in-the-workplace/

Min, S., Zacharia, Z. G., & Smith, C. D. (2019). Defining supply chain management: In the past, present, and future. *Journal of Business Logistics, 40*(1), 44–55. doi:10.1111/jbl.12201

Mirzaei, T., & Esmaeilzadeh, P. (2021). Engagement in online health communities: Channel expansion and social exchanges. *Information & Management, 58*(1), 103404. doi:10.1016/j.im.2020.103404

Mishra, A., Kaushik, S., Perumal, R. S., & Chowdhary, C. L. (2023). Role of Emotional Intelligence in agile supply chains. In M. K. Tiwari & S. K. Panda (Eds.), *Handbook of research on strategic supply chain management in the retail industry* (pp. 1–20). IGI Global.

Mishra, S. B., & Alok, S. (2022). *Handbook of research methodology.*

Mithiotis, A., & Argirou, N. (2016). Coaching: From challenge to opportunity. *Journal of Management Development, 35*(4), 448–463. doi:10.1108/JMD-10-2014-0139

Mokrysz, C., & Freeman, T. P. (2015). Cannabis Drug Testing: A Review of Analytical Methods and Their Application. *Forensic Science International, 257*, 85–96.

Molenberghs, P. (2013). The neuroscience of in-group bias. *Neuroscience and Biobehavioral Reviews, 37*(8), 1530–1536. doi:10.1016/j.neubiorev.2013.06.002 PMID:23769813

Morelli, M., Casagrande, M., & Forte, G. (2022). Decision Making: A Theoretical Review. *Integrative Psychological & Behavioral Science, 56*(3), 609–629. doi:10.1007/s12124-021-09669-x PMID:34780011

Moreno-Navarro, F., Iglesias, G., & Rubio-Gámez, M. (2019). Encoded asphalt materials for the guidance of autonomous vehicles. *Automation in Construction, 99*, 109–113. doi:10.1016/j.autcon.2018.12.004

Morgan, S. (2016, March 28). Calling All Women: The Cybersecurity Field Needs You, and There's A Million Jobs Waiting. *Forbes.* https://www.forbes.com/sites/stevemorgan/2016/03/28/calling-all-women-the-cybersecurity-field-needs-you/#2470db2a381c

Morgan, S. (2022, October 17). *Cybercrime to Cost the World 8 Trillion Annually in 2023.* Cybercrime Magazine. Retrieved November 9, 2023, from https://cybersecurityventures.com/cybercrime-to-cost-the-world-8-trillion-annually-in-2023/#:~:text=Our%20report%20provides%20a%20breakdown,%24667%20billion%20a%20Month

Morgan, T. R., Tokman, M., Richey, R. G., & Defee, C. (2018). Resource commitment and sustainability: A reverse logistics performance process model. *International Journal of Physical Distribution & Logistics Management, 48*(2), 164–182. doi:10.1108/IJPDLM-02-2017-0068

Morris, G. F. (2019). *The cyber-security concerns regarding the internet of things associated with the critical infrastructure within Northern Nevada* (Order No. 13428023). Available from ProQuest Central; ProQuest Dissertations & Theses Global. (2185755372). https://www.proquest.com/dissertations-theses/cyber-security-concerns-regarding-internet-things/docview/2185755372/se-2?accountid=167615

Morris, G. L. (2018). A Brief History of Marine Insurance. *Risk & Insurance.* https://riskandinsurance.com/brief-history-marine-insurance/

Morrone, P., & Bennardo, L. (2022). Teledermatology and Telemedicine: Expanding the Reach of Medical Consulting Beyond Physical Barriers. In U. Comite (Ed.), *Handbook of Research on Healthcare Standards, Policies, and Reform* (pp. 217–234). IGI Global. doi:10.4018/978-1-7998-8868-0.ch013

Morse, A. L., & McEvoy, C. D. (2014). Qualitative research in sport management. *CASE (Philadelphia, Pa.).*

Mountrouidou, X., Vosen, D., Kari, C., Azhar, M. Q., Bhatia, S., Gagne, G., ... Yuen, T. T. (2019). Securing the human: a literature review on broadening diversity in cybersecurity education. *Proceedings of the Working Group Reports on Innovation and Technology in Computer Science Education*, 157-176. 10.1145/3344429.3372507

Muller, S. R. (2021). A Perspective On the intersection of information security policies and I.A. awareness, factoring in end-user behavior. *Proceedings of the International Conference on Research in Management & Technovation*, 137–142. 10.15439/2020KM1

Muller, S. R., & Burrell, D. N. (2022). *Social cybersecurity and human behavior.* International Journal of Hyperconnectivity and the Internet of Things. doi:10.4018/IJHIoT.305228

Multistate Outbreak of Salmonella Agbeni Infections Linked to Pet Turtles. (2017, August 29). Retrieved from https://www.cdc.gov/salmonella/agbeni-08-17/index.html

Munro, N. (2021, August 11). Ransomware Attacks Increase In Frequency And Severity Over Past Two Years. *Forbes.*

Murphey, D. (2020). *How your H.R. department can help to overcome the cybersecurity skills gap.* BenefitsPRO. https://www.proquest.com/trade-journals/how-your-hr-department-can-help-overcome/docview/2376391277/se-2?accountid=167615

Murray, S. (2018, July 12). MBA courses start teaching digital security skills: Education business schools add cyber to the curriculum as attacks become a boardroom matter. *Financial Times.* https://www.proquest.com/newspapers/mba-courses-start-teaching-digital-security/docview/2086913126/se-2?accountid=167615

Murray, R. P. (2018). Marijuana Breathalyzers and the Law: A Primer. *The Hastings Law Journal, 70*(1), 1–36.

Mustafa, G., & Lines, R. (2016). The emergence and effects of culturally congruent leadership: Current status and future developments. *Entrepreneurial Business and Economics Review, 4*(1), 161–180. doi:10.15678/EBER.2016.040110

Mustillo, S. A., Budd, K., & Hendrix, K. (2013). Obesity, labeling, and psychological distress in late-childhood and adolescent black and white girls: The distal effects of stigma. *Social Psychology Quarterly, 76*(3), 268–289. doi:10.1177/0190272513495883

Nadler, D., & Tushmann, M. (1980, Autumn). A Model for Diagnosing Organizational Behavior. *Journal of Organizational Behavior, 4.*

Naikal, A., & Chandra, S. (2013). Organisational culture: A case study. *International Journal of Knowledge Management and Practices*, *1*(2), 17–24. https://proxy.cecybrary.com/login?url=https://search.proquest.com/docview/1845265 395?accountid=144459

Nandonde, F. A. (2019). A PESTLE analysis of international retailing in the East African Community. *Global Business and Organizational Excellence*, *38*(4), 54–61. doi:10.1002/joe.21935

Nangalia, L., & Nangalia, A. (2010). The Coach in Asian Society: Impact of social hierarchy on the coaching relationship. *International Journal of Evidence Based Coaching and Mentoring*, *8*(1), 51–66.

NASA Shared Services Center. (2016). *What are executive core qualifications (ECQs)?* Retrieved from https://answers. nssc.nasa.gov/app/answers/detail/a_id/5631/~/what-are-executive-core-qualifications-(ecqs)%3F

National Association of Counties. (2019). Connected and automated vehicles toolkit: A primer for counties. *Author*. https://www.naco.org/resources/featured/connected-autonomous-vehicles-toolkit

National Defense University. (n.d.). *Strategic leadership and decision making: Organizational culture*. Retrieved from http://www.au.af.mil/au/awc/awcgate/ndu/strat-ldr-dm/pt4ch16.html

National Highway Traffic Safety Administration. (2020). *Drug-Impaired Driving*. Retrieved from https://www.nhtsa. gov/risky-driving/drug-impaired-driving

National Institute of Standards & Technology. (2023). *NIST: Information Technology Laboratory Computer Security Resource Center*. NIST Computer Security Resource Center. Retrieved November 7, 2023, from https://csrc.nist.gov/ glossary/term/hacker

National Institute of Standards and Technology. (2017). *An introduction to information security: NIST SP 800-12 rev 1*. CreateSpace Independent Publishing Platform. doi:10.6028/NIST.SP.800-12r1

National Institute of Standards and Technology. (2020). NIST SP. 800-207: Zero Trust Architecture. *National Institute of Standards and Technology*. Retrieved November 11, 2023, from https://doi.org/ doi:10.6028/NIST.SP.800-207

National Institute on Drug Abuse. (2020). *DrugFacts: Marijuana*. National Institute on Drug Abuse. https://www.drugabuse.gov/publications/drugfacts/marijuana

National Organization for the Reform of Marijuana Laws. (2021). *Driving Under the Influence of Marijuana*. Retrieved from https://norml.org/laws/item/driving-under-the-influence-of-marijuana

National Science Board. (2014). *Science and Engineering Indicators 2014. Arlington VA: National Science Foundation Science and Engineering Indicators 2014: Earned Bachelor's degrees by citizenship, field, race, or ethnicity: 2014.* Retrieved from https://www.nsf.gov/statistics/seind14/index.cfm/appendix/tables.htm

National Science Foundation, National Center for Science and Engineering Statistics Directorate for Social, Behavioral and Economic Sciences. (2015). *Women, minorities, and persons with disabilities in science and engineering 2015 report*. Retrieved from www.nsf.gov/statistics/wmpd/

National Science Foundation, National Center for Science and Engineering Statistics. (2013). Women, Minorities, and Persons with Disabilities in Science and Engineering: 2013. Special Report NSF 17-310.

National Security Agency. (2010). *U.S. Cybersecurity Policy and the Role of U.S. Cybercom*. Center for Strategic and International Studies, Cybersecurity Policy Debate Series. Retrieved November 6, 2015, from https://www.nsa.gov/ Press-Room/Speeches-Testimony/Article-View/Article/1620145/center-for-strategic-and-international-studies-csis-csis-cybersecurity-policy-d/

Newsom & Dent. (2011). A Work Behavior Analysis of Executive Coaches. *International Journal of Evidence Based Coaching and Mentoring, 9*(2), 1.

Newsom, G., & Dent, E. B. (2011). A work behaviour analysis of executive coaches. *International Journal of Evidence Based Coaching and Mentoring, 9*(2), 1–22.

Newton, V. A. (2023). Hypervisibility and Invisibility: Black Women's Experiences with Gendered Racial Microaggressions on a White Campus. *Sociology of Race and Ethnicity (Thousand Oaks, Calif.), 9*(2), 164–178. doi:10.1177/23326492221138222

Nguyen Ngoc, H., Lasa, G., & Iriarte, I. (2022). Human-centered design in industry 4.0: case study review and opportunities for future research. *Journal of Intelligent Manufacturing, 33*(1).

Nguyen, C. Q., Kariyawasam, D., Alba-Concepcion, K., Grattan, S., Hetherington, K., Wakefield, C. E., Woolfenden, S., Dale, R. C., Palmer, E. E., & Farrar, M. A. (2022). 'Advocacy groups are the connectors': Experiences and contributions of rare disease patient organization leaders in advanced neurotherapeutics. *Health Expectations, 25*(6), 3175–3191. doi:10.1111/hex.13625 PMID:36307981

Nickerson, J. (2014). How to lead change when you are a middle manager. *Excellence in Government.* Retrieved from https://www.govexec.com/excellence/promising-practices/2014/05/how-lead-change-when-youre-middle-manager/84190/

Nicola, F. G. (2023). Failures of comparability in global governance: Exploring the practical dimension of the redress of law. *European Law Open, 2*(1), 173–183. doi:10.1017/elo.2023.20

Nigar, N. (2020). Hermeneutic phenomenological narrative enquiry: A qualitative study design. *Theory and Practice in Language Studies, 10*(1), 10–18. doi:10.17507/tpls.1001.02

Noble, H., & Smith, J. (2015). Issues of validity and reliability in qualitative research. *Evidence-Based Nursing, 18*(2), 34–35. doi:10.1136/eb-2015-102054 PMID:25653237

Nobles, C. (2019). Establishing human factors programs to mitigate blind spots in cybersecurity. *Midwest Association for Information Systems 2019 Proceedings*, 22. https://aisel.aisnet.org/mwais2019/22

Nobles, C. (2022b). Stress, Burnout, and Security Fatigue in Cybersecurity: A Human Factors Problem. *HOLISTICA – Journal of Business and Public Administration, 13*(1). 49-72. doi:10.2478/hjbpa-2022-0003

Nobles, C. (2022a). Investigating Cloud Computing Misconfiguration Errors using the Human Factors Analysis and Classification System. *Science Bulletin, 27*(1), 59–66. doi:10.2478/bsaft-2022-0007

Nobles, C. (2023). Making Sense of Offensive Cybersecurity. In D. Burrell (Ed.), *Real-World Solutions for Diversity, Strategic Change, and Organizational Development: Perspectives in Healthcare, Education, Business, and Technology* (pp. 1–25). I.G.I. Global. doi:10.4018/978-1-6684-8691-7.ch001

Nobles, C., Burrell, D. N., Burton, S. L., & Waller, T. (2023). Driving into cybersecurity trouble with autonomous vehicles. In F. Adedoyin & B. Christiansen (Eds.), *Handbook of Research on Cybersecurity Risk in Contemporary Business Systems* (pp. 255–273). IGI Global. doi:10.4018/978-1-6684-7207-1.ch013

Nobles, C., Burton, S. L., & Burrell, D. N. (2023). Cybercrime as a Sustained Business. In *Handbook of Research on Cybersecurity Risk in Contemporary Business Systems* (pp. 98–120). IGI Global. doi:10.4018/978-1-6684-7207-1.ch005

Northouse, P. G. (2013). *Leadership Theory and Practice* (6th ed.). Western Michigan University.

Nosheen, R. N. (2013). Peer mentoring: Enhancing social cohesion in Pakistani Universities. *Higher Education, Skills and Work - Based Learning, 3*(2), 130-140. doi:10.1108/20423891311313162

O'Hanlon, C. E., Kranz, A. M., DeYoreo, M., Mahmud, A., Damberg, C. L., & Timbie, J. (2019). Access, Quality, And Financial Performance Of Rural Hospitals Following Health System Affiliation. *Health Affairs (Project Hope)*, *38*(12), 2095–2104. doi:10.1377/hlthaff.2019.00918 PMID:31794306

O'Hara, N. N., Nophale, L. E., O'Hara, L. M., Marra, C. A., & Spiegel, J. M. (2017). Tuberculosis testing for healthcare workers in South Africa: A health service analysis using Porter's Five Forces Framework. *International Journal of Healthcare Management*, *10*(1), 49–56. doi:10.1080/20479700.2016.1268814

O'Reilly, M., & Parker, N. (2012). Unsatisfactory saturation: A critical examination of the notion of saturated sample size in qualitative research. *Qualitative Research*, *13*(2), 190–197. doi:10.1177/1468794112446106

Obaze, Y., Manuj, I., & Farris, I. I. T. II. (2016). Fifth Logistics Faculty Salary Survey. *Transportation Journal*, *55*(2), 208–223. doi:10.5325/transportationj.55.2.0208

Obiwuru, Okwu, Akpa, & Nwankwere. (2011). Effects of leadership style on organizational performance: A survey of selected small scale enterprise in Ikosia-Ketu counsil development area of Lagos state, Nigeria. Academic Press.

Office of Alcoholism and Substance Abuse Services. (2017). *Creating a healthy organizational culture: From assessment to change.* Retrieved from https://www.oasas.ny.gov/admed/documents/OWEworkbook.pdf

Office of Personnel Management. (2017). *Center for leadership development.* Retrieved from https://leadership.opm.gov/index.aspx

Office of the Director of National Intelligence. (2023, February 6). *Annual threat assessment of The U.S. intelligence community.* https://www.dni.gov/files/ODNI/documents/ assessments/ATA-2023-Unclassified-Report.pdf

Office of the National Cyber Director. (2023, July 31). *National cyber workforce and education strategy: Unleashing America's Cyber Talent.* https://www.whitehouse.gov/wp-content/uploads/2023/07/NCWES-2023.07.31.pdf

Oldeweme, A., Märtins, J., Westmattelmann, D., & Schewe, G. (2021). The role of transparency, trust, and social influence on uncertainty reduction in times of pandemics: Empirical study on the adoption of COVID-19 tracing apps. *Journal of Medical Internet Research*, *23*(2), e25893. doi:10.2196/25893 PMID:33465036

Olmstead, K., & Smith, A. (2017). What the public knows about cybersecurity. *Pew Research Center.* https://www.pewresearch.org/internet/2017/03/22/what-the-public-knows-about-cybersecurity/

Oltsik, J. (2017). The life and times of cybersecurity professionals. *E.S.G. and ISSA: Research Report.* Available at: https://www.esg-global.com/hubfs/issa/ESG-ISSA-Research-Report-Life-of-Cybersecurity-Professionals-Nov-2017.pdf?hsCtaTracking=a63e431c-d2ce-459d-8787-cc122a193baf%7Ce74f0327-0bbc-444a-b7a8-e2cd08d1999e

Olyaei, S. (2023). The Ways Cybersecurity Leaders Can reframe Their Roles to Succeed. *Express Computer.* https://www.expresscomputer.in/guest-blogs/three-ways-cybersecurity-leaders-can-reframe-their-roles-to-succeed/94674/

Öner, K. B., Scheller-Wolf, A., & van Houtum, G.-J. (2013). Redundancy Optimization for Critical Components in High-Availability Technical Systems. *Operations Research*, *61*(1), 244–264. doi:10.1287/opre.1120.1133

Onwuegbuzie, A., Leech, N., & Collins, K. (2010). Innovative data collection strategies in qualitative research. *The Qualitative Report*, *15*(3), 696–726. http://www.nova.edu/ssss/QR/QR15-3/onwuegbuzie.pdf

Opara, G. (2023). Leadership emotional intelligence and institutional planning in public universities. In *3rd International Conference on Institutional Leadership and Capacity Building in Africa* (p. 327). Academic Press.

Opara, E. (2023). Emotional intelligence and supply chain management performance: A review of literature. *International Journal of Supply Chain Management*, *8*(1), 789–795. https://ojs.excelingtech.co.uk/index.php/IJSCM/article/view/3771

Oppong, N. Y. (2017). Still the Dark Continent? Towards contextual methodological approaches to management development research in foreign multinational firms in Africa. *International Journal of Cross Cultural Management, 17*(2), 237–256. doi:10.1177/1470595817706384

OPSWAT. (2021). *Securing ICS and SCADA Updates in OT Environments: Best Practice for SCADA System Protection.* Retrieved October 28, 2023, from https://info.opswat.com/hubfs/Demand%20Gen%20Assets%20by%20Wilson/White%20Papers/OPSWAT-Securing-ICS+SCADA-Updates-in-OT-Whitepaper.pdf?hsLang=en&submissionGuid=23e9b3d4-38e9-4653-84fb-69ef7da9ece5

Orlanova, A. I. (2012). Continuous education for the knowledge society. *Russian Education & Society, 54*(4), 3–13. doi:10.2753/RES1060-9393540401

Osborne, C. (2023, September 27). Women To Hold 30 Percent Of Cybersecurity Jobs Globally By 2025. *Cybercrime Magazine.* Retrieved from: https://cybersecurityventures.com/women-in-cybersecurity-report-2023/#:~:text=Women%20held%2025%20percent%20of,to%2035%20percent%20by%202031

Otter, K. (2017). Leadership coaching 2.0: Improving the marriage between leadership and coaching. *Philosophy of Coaching, 2*(2), 69–82. doi:10.22316/poc/02.2.05

Ou, C. X., Pavlou, P. A., & Davison, R. (2014). Swift Guanxi in Online Marketplaces: The Role of Computer-Mediated Communication Technologies. *MIS Quarterly, 38*(1), 209–230.

Pacific Merchant Shipping Association. (2021). *New Queuing Process for Container Vessels Bound for Ports of LA/Long Beach to Improve Safety and Air Quality Off California Coast.* https://www.pmsaship.com/wp-content/uploads/2021/11/Container-Vessel-Queuing-Release-FINAL.pdf

Paganini, P. (2015, April 15). *Dell Report Revealed Attacks on SCADA System are Doubled.* Security Affairs. Retrieved November 7, 2015, from https://securityaffairs.co/35967/hacking/dell-attacks-on-scada-doubled.html

Pakocs, R., & Lupulescu, N. B. (2015). Risk Management and Assessment of the Manufacturing and Marketing Risk-Factors within Industrial Companies. *Scientific Research & Education in the Air Force - AFASES, 2*, 575–580.

Palinkas, L., Horowitz, S., Green, C., Wisdom, J., Duan, N., & Hoagwood, K. (2013). *Purposive sampling in qualitative data collection and analysis in mixed method implementation research.* Admin Policy Ment Health. doi:10.1007/s10488-013-0528-y

Pandey, P., & Pandey, M. M. (2021). *Research methodology tools and techniques.* Bridge Center.

Paredes-Astudillo, Y. A., Moreno, D., Vargas, A. M., Angel, M. A., Perez, S., Jimenez, J. F., ... Trentesaux, D. (2020, September). Human fatigue aware cyber-physical Production system. In *2020 IEEE International Conference on Human-Machine Systems (ICHMS)* (pp. 1-6). IEEE.

Parekh, D., Poddar, N., Rajpurkar, A., Chahal, M., Kumar, N., Joshi, G. P., & Cho, W. (2022). A review on autonomous vehicles: Progress, methods and challenges. *Electronics (Basel), 11*(14), 2162. doi:10.3390/electronics11142162

Park, E. R., Luberto, C. M., Chad-Friedman, E., Traeger, L., Hall, D. L., Perez, G. K., Goshe, B., Vranceanu, M., Baim, M., Denninger, J. W., Fricchione, G., Benson, H., & Lechner, S. C. (2021). A Comprehensive Resiliency Framework: Theoretical Model, Treatment, and Evaluation. *Global Advances in Health and Medicine : Improving Healthcare Outcomes Worldwide, 10.* Advance online publication. doi:10.1177/21649561211000306 PMID:34377598

Parkinson, S., Ward, P., Wilson, K., & Miller, J. (2017). Cyber threats facing autonomous and connected vehicles: Future challenges. *IEEE Transactions on Intelligent Transportation Systems, 18*(11), 2898–2915. doi:10.1109/TITS.2017.2665968

Parrish, T., & Blazer, D. J. (2008). Modifying the Supply Chain. *Air Force Journal of Logistics, 32*(1), 76–79.

Pasquali, P., Sonthalia, S., Moreno-Ramirez, D., Sharma, P., Agrawal, M., Gupta, S., Kumar, D., & Arora, D. (2020). Teledermatology and its Current Perspective. *Indian Dermatology Online Journal, 11*(1), 12–20. doi:10.4103/idoj. IDOJ_241_19 PMID:32055502

Passmore, J. (2007). An integrative model for Executive Coaching. *Consulting Psychology Journal, 59*(1), 68–78. doi:10.1037/1065-9293.59.1.68

Passmore, J., & Fillery-Travis, A. (2011). A critical review of executive coaching research: A decade of progress and what's to come. *Coaching (Abingdon, UK), 4*(2), 70–88. doi:10.1080/17521882.2011.596484

Paternoster, R., & Bachman, R. (2000). *Essays in contemporary criminological theory: Explaining criminals and crime* (1st ed.). Roxbury Publishing Company.

Patton, M. Q. (1999). Enhancing the quality and credibility of qualitative analysis. Health Science Research, 34, 1189–1208.

Paudel, T., Luitel, B. C., & Dahal, N. (2023). Journey of Realization and Adaptation through Auto/Ethnography: A Shift to Transformative Educational Research. *The Qualitative Report, 28*(4), 1017–1037. doi:10.46743/2160-3715/2023.5649

Paul, D. L., & McDaniel, R. R. Jr. (2004). *A Field Study of the Effect of Interpersonal Trust on Virtual Collaborative Relationship Performance. MIS Quarterly.*

Paul, G. W., & Berry, D. M. (2013). *The Importance of Executive Leadership in Creating a Post- Merged Organizational Culture Conducive to Effective Performance Management.* S.A. Journal of Human Resources Management/SA.

Pavgi, K. (2012, October 10). Congressional Republicans call for resignation of VA chief of staff. *Government Executive.* Retrieved from https://www.govexec.com/oversight/2012/10/congressional-republicans-call-resignation-va-chief-staff/58688/?oref=relatedstories

Payne, B. K., Vuletich, H. A., & Lundberg, K. B. (2017). The bias of crowds: How implicit bias bridges personal and systemic prejudice. *Psychological Inquiry, 28*(4), 233–248. doi:10.1080/1047840X.2017.1335568

Pazzanese, C. (2020, October 26). Ethical concerns mount as AI takes bigger decision-making role in more industries. *The Harvard Gazette.* https://news.harvard.edu/gazette/story/2020/10/ethical-concerns-mount-as-ai-takes-bigger-decision-making-role/

Pedrosa, A. da M., Näslund, D., & Jasmand, C. (2012). Logistics case study based research: Towards higher quality. *International Journal of Physical Distribution & Logistics Management, 42*(3), 275–295. doi:10.1108/09600031211225963

Peg, B. S., & Single, R. M. (2007). E-mentoring for social equity: Review of research to inform program development. *Mentoring & Tutoring,* 301–320. https://www.tandfonline.com/doi/citedby/10.1080/13611260500107481?scroll=top&needAccess=true

Pellegrinelli, S., (2011). What's in a name? Project and program? *International Journal of Project Management, 29*(2), 232-240.

Peltier, B. (2001). *The psychology of executive coaching: Theory and Application.* Sheridan Books.

Peñaloza, G. A., Saurin, T. A., Formoso, C. T., & Herrera, I. A. (2020). A resilience engineering perspective of safety performance measurement systems: A systematic literature review. *Safety Science, 130,* 104864. doi:10.1016/j.ssci.2020.104864

Perego, A., Perotti, S., & Mangiaracina, R. (2011). ICT for logistics and freight transportation: A literature review and research agenda. *International Journal of Physical Distribution & Logistics Management, 41*(15), 457–483. doi:10.1108/09600031111138826

Performance Coaching International. (2012). *History of coaching*. Retrieved from PCI: http://www.performancecoach-inginternational.com/resources/articles/historyofcoaching.php

Performance Consultants International. (2018). *GROW Model: GROWing people, performance, and purpose*. Retrieved from https://www.coachingperformance.com/wp-content/uploads/2018/10/GROW-Model-Guide.pdf

Peters-Burton, E. E., Merz, S. A., Ramirez, E. M., & Saroughi, M. (2015). The effect of cognitive apprenticeship-based professional development on teacher self-efficacy of science teaching, motivation, knowledge calibration, and perceptions of inquiry-based teaching. *Journal of Science Teacher Education, 26*(6), 525–548. doi:10.1007/s10972-015-9436-1

Peterson, D. B., & Hicks, M. D. (1995). *The leader as coach: Strategies for coaching and Developing others*. Personnel Decisions.

Petreski, D. T., Iliev, A. P., Gjurov, L. M., & Petreska, A. D. (2014). Logistics Supply Chains and Their Application. *Military Technical Courier / Vojnotehnicki Glasnik, 62*(4), 104–119. https://doi-org.captechu.idm.oclc.org/10.5937/vojtehg62-6207

Phipps, K. (2010). Servant leadership and constructive development theory: How servant leaders make meaning of service. *Journal of Leadership Education, 9*(2), 151–169. doi:10.12806/V9/I2/TF1

Pinho, J. C., Ana, P. R., & Dibb, S. (2014). The role of corporate culture, market orientation and organisational commitment in organisational performance. *Journal of Management Development, 33*(4), 374–398. doi:10.1108/JMD-03-2013-0036

Pirasteh, R. M., & Kannappan, S. (2013). The synergy of continuous process improvement. *Industrial Engineering (American Institute of Industrial Engineers)*, 41–46.

Plachkinova, M., & Maurer, C. (2018). Teaching Case: Security Breach at Target. *Journal of Information Systems Education, 29*(1), 11.

Platsis, G. (2019). The Human Factor: Cyber Security's Greatest Challenge. In Cyber Law, Privacy, and Security: Concepts, Methodologies, Tools, and Applications (pp. 1-19). IGI Global.

Plavin-Masterman, M. (2015). Are Walls Just Walls? Organizational culture emergence in a virtual firm. *Journal of Organizational Culture, Communications and Conflict, 19*(2), 43-68. Retrieved from https://proxy.cecybrary.com/login?url=https://search.proquest.com/docview/1750418352?accountid=144459

Pratt, M. (2023). *Emerging cyber threats in 2023 from AI to quantum to data poisoning*. CSO Online. https://www.csoonline.com/article/651125/emerging-cyber-threats-in-2023-from-ai-to-quantum-to-data-poisoning.html

Pressley, A. (2023). 85% of cyber leaders believe AI will outpace cyber defences. *Intelligent CISO*. https://www.intelligentciso.com/2023/09/20/85-of-cyber-leaders-believe-ai-will-outpace-cyber-defences/

Prothero, A (2022, February 1). Child Obesity Grew During the Pandemic. How Schools Can Help Reverse the Trend. *Education Week*.

PwC. (2022). *2022 global risk survey: Embracing risk in the face of disruption*. https://www.pwc.com/us/en/services/consulting/cybersecurity-risk-regulatory/library/global-risk-survey.html

Qian, J., Lin, X., Han, Z. R., Chen, Z. X., & Hays, J. M. (2015). What matters in the relationship between mentoring and job-related stress? The moderating effects of prote'ge's' traditionality and trust in mentor. *Journal of Management & Organization, 20*(5), 608–623. doi:10.1017/jmo.2014.46

Qin, Q., Wen, B., Ling, Q., Zhou, S., & Tong, M. (2014). How and when the effect of ethical leadership occurs? A multilevel analysis in the Chinese hospitality industry. *International Journal of Contemporary Hospitality Management, 26*(6), 974–1001. doi:10.1108/IJCHM-02-2013-0073

Rahimi, B., Nadri, H., Afshar, H. L., & Timpka, T. (2018). A systematic review of the technology acceptance model in health informatics. *Applied Clinical Informatics, 9*(03), 604–634. doi:10.1055/s-0038-1668091 PMID:30112741

Rahman, S., Ahsan, K., Sohal, A., & Oloruntoba, R. (2022). Guest editorial: The "new normal": rethinking supply chains during and post-COVID-19 global business environment. *International Journal of Physical Distribution & Logistics Management, 52*(7), 481–490. doi:10.1108/IJPDLM-08-2022-518

Rainie, L. (2017). 10 fact about jobs in the future. *Pew research Center, Internet & Technology.* Retrieved from https://www.pewinternet.org/2017/10/10/10-facts-about-jobs-in-the-future/

Ra, K., Hong, S., & Yang, D. (2023). How Are a Firm's Strategic Motives for Environmental Innovation Impeded? The Negative Influences of Institutional Pressures. *Systems, 11*(2), 79. doi:10.3390/systems11020079

Rana, M. M., & Hossain, K. (2023). Connected and Autonomous Vehicles and Infrastructures: A Literature Review. *International Journal of Pavement Research and Technology, 16*(2), 264–284. doi:10.1007/s42947-021-00130-1

Randall, W. S., Wittmann, C. M., Nowicki, D. R., & Pohlen, T. L. (2014). Service-dominant logic and supply chain management: Are we there yet? *International Journal of Physical Distribution & Logistics Management, 44*(1/2), 113–131. doi:10.1108/IJPDLM-11-2012-0331

Rashid, Y., Rashid, A., Warraich, M. A., Sabir, S. S., & Waseem, A. (2019). Case study method: A step-by-step guide for business researchers. International Journal of Qualitative Methods, 18.

Rasool, F., Greco, M., Morales-Alonso, G., & Carrasco-Gallego, R. (2023). What is next? The effect of reverse logistics adoption on digitalization and inter-organizational collaboration. *International Journal of Physical Distribution & Logistics Management, 53*(5/6), 563–588. doi:10.1108/IJPDLM-06-2022-0173

Reboussin, B. A., Wagoner, K. G., Sutfin, E. L., Suerken, C., Ross, J. C., Egan, K. L., Walker, S., & Johnson, R. M. (2019). Trends in marijuana edible consumption and perceptions of harm in a cohort of young adults. *Drug and Alcohol Dependence, 205*, 107660. doi:10.1016/j.drugalcdep.2019.107660 PMID:31704375

Reeves, S., Kuper, A., & Hodges, B. D. (2008). Qualitative research methodologies: ethnography. *BMJ: British Medical Journal (Online)*, doi:10.1136/bmj.a1020

Reeves, A., Delfabbro, P., & Calic, D. (2021). Encouraging employee engagement with cybersecurity: How to tackle cyber fatigue. *SAGE Open, 11*(1). doi:10.1177/21582440211000049

Reeves, A., Pattinson, M., & Butavicius, M. (2023). Is Your CISO Burnt Out yet? In S. Furnell & N. Clarke (Eds.), *Human Aspects of Information Security and Assurance. HAISA 2023. IFIP Advances in Information and Communication Technology* (Vol. 674). Springer. doi:10.1007/978-3-031-38530-8_18

Rehak, D., & Hromada, M. (2018). Failures in a critical infrastructure system. In System of System Failures. IntechOpen. doi:10.5772/intechopen.70446

Reifegerste, D., Wasgien, K., & Hagen, L. M. (2017). Online social support for obese adults: Exploring the role of forum activity. *International Journal of Medical Informatics, 101*, 1–8. doi:10.1016/j.ijmedinf.2017.02.003 PMID:28347439

Rekalde, I., Landeta, J., & Albizu, E. (2015). Determining factors in the effectiveness of executive coaching as a management development tool. *Management Decision, 53*(8), 1677–1697. doi:10.1108/MD-12-2014-0666

Rennie, D. (2023). The impact of emotional intelligence on supply chain leadership. *Journal of Business and Supply Chain Management, 13*(1), 12–25.

Rheuban, K. S., & Krupinski, E. A. (2018). *Understanding Telehealth*. McGraw-Hill.

Rhodes, J. (2015). Top 25 mentoring relationships in history. *The Chronicle of Evidence-Based Mentoring*. Retrieved from https://chronicle.umbmentoring.org/top-25-mentoring-relationships-in-history/

Richardson, M. (2015). Mentoring for a Dispersed Workforce. *Training & Development, 42*(5), 18–19. https://proxy.cecybrary.com/login?url=https://search.proquest.com/docview/1726692601?accountid=144459

Richardson-Parry, A., Baas, C., Donde, S., Ferraiolo, B., Karmo, M., Maravic, Z., Münter, L., Ricci-Cabello, I., Silva, M., Tinianov, S., Valderas, J. M., Woodruff, S., & Joris, V. (2023). Interventions to reduce cancer screening inequities: The perspective and role of patients, advocacy groups, and empowerment organizations. *International Journal for Equity in Health, 22*(1), 1–9. doi:10.1186/s12939-023-01841-6 PMID:36707816

Rincón, V., González, M., & Barrero, K. (2017). Women and leadership: Gender barriers to senior management positions. *Intangible Capital, 13*(2), 319–386. doi:10.3926/ic.889

Rintala, O., Solakivi, T., Laari, S., Töyli, J., & Ojala, L. (2021). Drivers of logistics outsourcing: Examining transaction costs, core competences and planned behavior. *International Journal of Physical Distribution & Logistics Management, 51*(3), 259–280. doi:10.1108/IJPDLM-08-2019-0244

Roberts, K. H. (1990). Some Characteristics of One Type of High-Reliability Organization. *Organization Science, 1*(2), 160–176.

Robinson, D. M., & Reio, T. G. Jr. (2012). Benefits of mentoring African-American men. *Journal of Managerial Psychology, 27*(4), 406–421. doi:10.1108/02683941211220207

Robinson, O. C., & Cooper, C. L. (2020). *The Oxford handbook of organizational psychology*. Oxford University Press.

Roelofs, B. (2019). How shadow coaching helps leaders to improve their performance on the job in real-time. *International Journal of Evidence Based Coaching and Mentoring, S13*, 49–62.

Rohozinski, R., & Marzouki, Y. (2018). A.I., discrimination, and criminal justice. *Fordham Law Review, 87*(4), 1219–1241.

Rohs, C. M., Albright, K. R., Monteith, L. L., Lane, A. D., & Fehling, K. B. (2023). Perspectives of V.A. healthcare from rural women veterans not enrolled in or using V.A. healthcare. *PLoS One, 18*(8), e0289885. Advance online publication. doi:10.1371/journal.pone.0289885 PMID:37578986

Rolfe, A. (2014). Taking mentoring to the next level in organisations. *Training & Development, 41*(2), 26–27. https://proxy.cecybrary.com/login?url=https://search.proquest.com/docview/1527341167?accountid=144459

Romanosky, S., Ablon, L., Kuehn, A., & Jones, T. (2019). Content analysis of cyber insurance policies: How do carriers price cyber risk? *Journal of Cybersecurity, 5*(1), tyz002. doi:10.1093/cybsec/tyz002

Romm, M. J., Fiebert, I., Roach, K., Bishop, M. D., & Cahalin, L. P. (2023). *Telehealth Group-Based Pain Management Programs Using the Therapeutic Alliance and Group Dynamics as Key Predictor Variables*. Digital Medicine and Healthcare Technology. doi:10.5772/dmht.15

Rosalinda, U. U., & Ali, H. (2023). Analysis of Factors Influencing the Marketing Information System: CRM, Customer Satisfaction and Sales Effectiveness. *Dinasti International Journal of Digital Business Management (DIJDBM), 4*(2), 264–270. https://doi-org.captechu.idm.oclc.org/10.31933/dijdbm.v4i2

Rosha, A. (2014). Peculiarities of manifestation of coaching in organizations. *Procedia: Social and Behavioral Sciences, 110*, 852–860. doi:10.1016/j.sbspro.2013.12.930

Rowland, K. N. (2011). *E-mentoring: Benefits to the workplace* (Order No. 3493777). Available from ABI/INFORM Collection. (919692070). Retrieved from https://proxy.cecybrary.com/login?url=https://search.proquest.com/docview/919692070?accountid=144459

Roy, P. P. (2020). A high-level comparison between the NIST Cyber Security Framework and the ISO 27001 Information Security Standard. *2020 National Conference on Emerging Trends on Sustainable Technology and Engineering Applications (NCETSTEA).* 1-3. 10.1109/NCETSTEA48365.2020.9119914

Rubenstein, L. V., Curtis, I., Wheat, C. L., Grembowski, D. E., Stockdale, S. E., Kaboli, P. J., Yoon, J., Felker, B. L., Reddy, A. S., & Nelson, K. M. (2023). Learning from the national implementation of the Veterans Affairs Clinical Resource Hub (CRH) program for improving access to care: Protocol for a six-year evaluation. *BMC Health Services Research, 23*(1), 1–12. doi:10.1186/s12913-023-09799-5 PMID:37488518

Rudzinski, K., & Anderson, P. (2016). Marijuana and driving: Physiological, psychological and behavioural effects. *Traffic Injury Prevention, 17*(8), 800–805.

Rundle, J. (2023). Prosecution of Former Uber Security Chief Carries Warnings for Cyber Leaders. *WSJ Pro.* https://www.wsj.com/articles/former-uber-security-chief-gets-probation-in-obstruction-case-87c7c0b9

Russo, I., Masorgo, N., & Gligor, D. M. (2022). Examining the impact of service recovery resilience in the context of product replacement: The roles of perceived procedural and interactional justice. *International Journal of Physical Distribution & Logistics Management, 52*(8), 638–672. doi:10.1108/IJPDLM-07-2021-0301

Rutti, R. M., Helms, M. M., & Rose, L. C. (2013). Changing the lens: Viewing the mentoring relationship as relational structures in a social exchange framework. *Leadership and Organization Development Journal, 34*(5), 446–468. doi:10.1108/LODJ-11-0097

Ryan, M. K., Haslam, S. A., Morgenroth, T., Rink, F., Stoker, J., & Peters, K. (2016). Getting on top of the glass cliff: Reviewing a decade of evidence, explanations, and impact. *The Leadership Quarterly, 27*(3), 446–455. doi:10.1016/j.leaqua.2015.10.008

Ryan, P. (2009). Integrated theory of health behavior change: Background and intervention development. *Clinical Nurse Specialist CNS, 23*(3), 161–172. doi:10.1097/NUR.0b013e3181a42373 PMID:19395894

Sabharwal, M. (2013). From glass ceiling to glass cliff: Women in senior executive service. *Journal of Public Administration: Research and Theory, 25*(2), 399–426. doi:10.1093/jopart/mut030

Sacred Heart University Library. (2020). Limitations. *Author.* https://library.sacredheart.edu/c.php?g=29803&p=185934

Sadigh, D. (2019). Influencing interactions between human drivers and autonomous vehicles. *National Academy of Engineering.* https://www.nae.edu/19579/19582/21020/221074/221209/Influencing-Interactions-between-Human-Drivers-and-Autonomous-Vehicles

Saghafian, M., Laumann, K., & Skogstad, M. R. (2021). Stagewise Overview of Issues Influencing Organizational Technology Adoption and Use. *Frontiers in Psychology, 12*, 630145. doi:10.3389/fpsyg.2021.630145 PMID:33815216

Saha, S., Das, R., Lim, W. M., Kumar, S., Malik, A., & Chillakuri, B. (2023). Emotional intelligence and leadership: Insights for leading by feeling in the future of work. *International Journal of Manpower, 44*(4), 687–708. doi:10.1108/IJM-12-2021-0690

Sahoo, K., Sahoo, B., Choudhury, A. K., Sofi, N. Y., Kumar, R., & Bhadoria, A. S. (2015). Childhood obesity: causes and consequences. *Journal of Family Medicine and Primary Care, 4*(2), 187–192. Retrieved from: https://www.ncbi.nlm.nih.gov/pmc/articles/PMC4408699/ doi:10.4103/2249-4863.154628

Saini, D. (2015). Integral leadership style: A new perspective. *International Journal on Leadership, 3*(2), 40–47. doi:10.21863/ijl/2015.3.2.007

Saldana, J. (2012). *The coding manual for qualitative researchers.* Sage.

Salem, I. E. (2015). Transformational leadership: Relationship to job stress and job burnout in five-star hotels. *Tourism and Hospitality Research, 15*(4), 240-253. http://dx.doi.org.proxy.cecybrary.com/10.1177/1467358415581445

Sale, M. L., & Sale, R. S. (2013). Theory of Constraints as related to improved Business Unit Performance. *Journal of Accounting and Finance, 13*(1), 108–115.

Salovey, P., & Mayer, J. D. (1990). Emotional Intelligence. *Imagination, Cognition and Personality, 9*(3), 185–211. doi:10.2190/DUGG-P24E-52WK-6CDG

Sanchez, J., & Medkik, N. (2004). The effects of diversity awareness training on differential treatment. *Group & Organization Management, 29*(4), 517–536. doi:10.1177/1059601103257426

Santana, E. F. Z., Covas, G., Duarte, F., Santi, P., Ratti, C., & Kon, F. (2021). Transitioning to a driverless city: Evaluating a hybrid system for autonomous and non-autonomous vehicles. *Simulation Modelling Practice and Theory, 107*, 102210. Advance online publication. doi:10.1016/j.simpat.2020.102210

Saowalux, P. & Peng, C. (2007). *Impact of Leadership Style on Performance: A Study of Six Sigma Professionals in Thailand.* International DSI/Asia and Pacific DSI.

Sarayreh, B. H., Khudair, H., & Barakat, E. A. (2013). Comparative study: The Kurt Lewin of change management. *International Journal of Computer and Information Technology, 2*(4), 626–629.

Sargeant, J. (2012). Qualitative research part II: Participants, analysis, and quality assurance. *Journal of Graduate Medical Education, 4*(March), 1–3. doi:10.4300/JGME-D-11-00307.1 PMID:23451297

Sarkar, B.D. & Shankar, R. (2021). Understanding the barriers of port logistics for effective operation in the Industry 4.0 era: Data-driven decision making. *International Journal of Information Management Data Insights, 1*.

Sarker, I. H. (2021). Deep learning: A comprehensive overview on techniques, taxonomy, applications and research directions. *SN Computer Science, 2*(6), 420. doi:10.1007/s42979-021-00815-1 PMID:34426802

Sarker, I. H. (2021). Machine Learning: Algorithms, Real-World Applications and Research Directions. *SN Computer Science, 2*(3), 160. doi:10.1007/s42979-021-00592-x PMID:33778771

Satheesh, K. (2008, November 15). *Introduction to micro-teaching* [Web log post]. Retrieved on August 24, 2018, from: http://sathitech.blogspot.com/2008/11/introction-to-micro-teaching.html

Saunders, C., Rutkowski, A. F., Genuchten van, M., Vogel, D., & Orrego, J. M. (2011). Virtual Space and Place: Theory and Test. MIS Quarterly, 1079–1098.

Sbriz, L. (2022). Capability maturity model and risk register integration: The right approach to enterprise governance. *ISACA.* https://www.isaca.org/resources/isaca-journal/issues/2022/volume-1/capability-maturity-model-and-risk-register-integration

Scala, N. M., Rajgopal, J., & Needy, K. L. (2013). A Base Stock Inventory Management System for Intermittent Spare Parts. *Military Operations Research (Alexandria, Va.), 18*(3), 63–77. doi:10.5711/1082598318363

Scalia, A., Calabresi, S. G., Harrison, J., & Reynolds, W. B. (2013). In memoriam: Robert H. Bork. *Harvard Journal of Law & Public Policy, 36*(3), 1231–1243, 1245–1256. https://proxy.cecybrary.com/login?url=https://search.proquest.com/docview/1415163652?accountid=144459

Schaufeli, W. B., & Taris, T. W. (2014). A critical review of the job demands-resources model: Implications for improving work and health. In G. F. Bauer & O. Hämming (Eds.), *Bridging occupational, organizational and public health: A transdisciplinary approach* (pp. 43–68). Springer Netherlands. doi:10.1007/978-94-007-5640-3_4

Schein, E. (2004). *Organizational culture and leadership* (3rd ed.). John Wiley and Sons.

Schein, E. H. (1992). *Organizational Culture and Leadership. Jossey Bass.*

Schneider, R. O. (2002). Hazard Mitigation and Sustainable Community Development. *Disaster Prevention and Management, 11*(2), 141–147. doi:10.1108/09653560210426821

Schueths, A. M., & Carranza, M. A. (2012). Navigating around educational road blocks: Mentoring for pre-K to 20+ Latino/a students. *Latino Studies, 10*(4), 566–586. doi:10.1057/lst.2012.43

Schuster, C., & Martiny, S. (2017). Not Feeling Good in STEM: Effects of Stereotype Activation and Anticipated Affect on Women's Career Aspirations. *Sex Roles, 76*(1/2), 40–55. doi:10.1007/s11199-016-0665-3

Schwartz, L. (2002). Is there an advocate in the house? The role of health care professionals in patient advocacy. *Journal of Medical Ethics, 28*(1), 37–40. doi:10.1136/jme.28.1.37 PMID:11834758

Schwarz, A., Schwarz, C., Jung, Y., Pérez, B., & Wiley-Patton, S. (2012). Towards an Understanding of Assimilation in Virtual Worlds: The 3C Approach. *European Journal of Information Systems, 21*(3), 303–320.

Scott, B. A., Garza, A. S., Conlon, D. E., & Kim, Y. J. (2014). Why Do Managers Act Fairly in the First Place? A Daily Investigation of "Hot" and "Cold" Motives and Discretion. *Academy of Management Journal, 57*(6), 1571–1591. doi:10.5465/amj.2012.0644

Seaton, H. V. (2007). *The financial implications and organizational cultural perceptions of implementing a performance management system in a government enterprise* (Order No. 3294734). Available from ABI/INFORM Collection. (304699669). Retrieved from https://proxy.cecybrary.com/login?url=https://search.proquest.com/docview/304699669?accountid=144459

Segal, E. (2021). 'Alert Fatigue' Can Lead To Missed Cyber Threats And Staff Retention/Recruitment Issues: Study. *Forbes.* https://www.forbes.com/sites/edwardsegal/2021/11/08/alert-fatigue-can-lead-to-missed-cyber-threats-and-staff-retentionrecruitment-issues-study/?sh=41d7b15b35c9

Sehgal, S. (2023). *Why emotional intelligence is crucial for effective leadership.* Forbes. Forbes.

Semiyu, A. A., & Folorunso, A. A. (2013). Peer coaching as an institutionalised tool for professional development. *Journal of Workplace Learning, 25*(2), 125–140. doi:10.1108/13665621311299807

Senate Homeland Security and Governmental Affairs Subcommittee on Federal Spending Oversight and Emergency Management Hearing. (2020). *State and Local Cybersecurity: Defending Our Communities from Cyber Threats amid COVID-19.* Federal Information & News Dispatch, LLC. https://www.govinfo.gov/content/pkg/CHRG-116shrg43278/pdf/CHRG-116shrg43278.pdf

Senge, P. M. (2006). The Fifth Discipline: The Art and Practice of the Learning Organization. Academic Press.

Senge, P. (1990). *The Fifth discipline. The Art and Practice of the Learning Organization.* Random House.

Serper, M., & Volk, M. L. (2018). Current and Future Applications of Telemedicine to Optimize the Delivery of Care in Chronic Liver Disease. *Clinical Gastroenterology and Hepatology: The Official Clinical Practice Journal of the American Gastroenterological Association, 16*(2), 157–161.

Serrano, C., & Karahanna, E. (2016). The Compensatory Interaction between User Capabilities and Technology Capabilities in Influencing Task Performance: An Empirical Assessment in Telemedicine Consultations. *MIS Quarterly, 40*(3), 597–621.

Settles, I. H., Buchanan, N. T., & Dotson, K. (2019). Scrutinized but not recognized:(In) visibility and hypervisibility experiences of faculty of color. *Journal of Vocational Behavior, 113*, 62–74. doi:10.1016/j.jvb.2018.06.003

Shaikh, F. A., & Siponen, M. (2023). Organizational Learning from Cybersecurity Performance: Effects on Cybersecurity Investment Decisions. *Information Systems Frontiers*, 1–12. doi:10.1007/s10796-023-10404-7

Shakya, B., Schneider, F., Yang, Y., & Sharma, E. (2019). A Multiscale Transdisciplinary Framework for Advancing the Sustainability Agenda of Mountain Agricultural Systems. *Mountain Research and Development, 39*(3). Advance online publication. doi:10.1659/MRD-JOURNAL-D-18-00079.1

Shandler, R., Gross, M. L., & Canetti, D. (2023). Cyberattacks, psychological distress, and military escalation: An internal meta-analysis. *Journal of Global Security Studies, 8*(1), ogac042. doi:10.1093/jogss/ogac042

Sharkov, G. (2020). Assessing the maturity of national cybersecurity and resilience. Connections. *The Quarterly Journal, 19*(4), 5–24.

Sharma, A., & Zheng, Z. (2021). Connected and Automated Vehicles: Opportunities and Challenges for Transportation Systems, Smart Cities, and Societies. In B. T. Wang & C. M. Wang (Eds.), *Automating Cities. Advances in 21st Century Human Settlements*. Springer. doi:10.1007/978-981-15-8670-5_11

Sharma, P., & Gillanders, J. (2022). Cybersecurity and forensics in connected autonomous vehicles: A review of the state-of-the-art. *IEEE Access : Practical Innovations, Open Solutions, 10*, 08979–108996. doi:10.1109/ACCESS.2022.3213843

Shashi, M. (2023). Sustainable Digitalization in Pharmaceutical Supply Chains Using Theory of Constraints: A Qualitative Study. *Sustainability (Basel), 15*(11), 8752. doi:10.3390/su15118752

Sheldon, R., & Hanna, K. T. (2022, January). *Cyberterrorism*. TechTarget. Retrieved November 10, 2023, from https://www.techtarget.com/searchsecurity/definition/cyberterrorism#:~:text=The%20U.S.%20Federal%20Bureau%20of,subnational%20groups%20or%20clandestine%20agents.%22

Sheridan, K. (2020, June 6). *90% of CISOs would pay for better work-life balance*. DarkReading.com. Retrieved from https://www.darkreading.com/risk/90--of-cisos-would-cut-pay-for-better-work-life-balance/d/d-id/1336995

Shibly, H. R., Abdullah, A., & Murad, M. W. (2022). Adoption of Innovative Technology. In *ERP Adoption in Organizations*. Palgrave Macmillan. doi:10.1007/978-3-031-11934-7_3

Shinde, A. J. (2014). Application of Thinking Process tools of Theory of Constraints to initiate a business. *Academy of Management Annual Meeting Proceedings, 2014*(1), 1. https://doi-org.captechu.idm.oclc.org/10.5465/AMBPP.2014.10675abstract

Shiri, A., Faraji, E., & Yasini, A. (2018). Gender inequality experience in organizational promotions: A metaphorical reading of glass escalator effect. *Women's Studies, 9*(24), 1–31.

Shi, Y., He, Q., & Huang, Z. (2016). Capacity analysis and cooperative lane changing for connected and automated vehicles: Entropy-based assessment method. *Transportation Research Record: Journal of the Transportation Research Board*, (2673), 485–498.

Shi, Y., Venkatesh, V. G., Venkatesh, M., Fosso Wamba, S., & Wang, B. (2023). Guest editorial: Digital transformation in supply chains: challenges, strategies, and implementations. *International Journal of Physical Distribution & Logistics Management, 53*(4), 381–386. doi:10.1108/IJPDLM-05-2023-550

Short, J., Williams, E., & Christie, B. (1976). *The Social Psychology of Telecommunications*. Wiley.

Short, T. W. (2014). Workplace mentoring: An old idea with new meaning (part 1). *Development and Learning in Organizations, 28*(1), 8–11. doi:10.1108/DLO-09-2013-0077

Sia, C.-L., Tan, B. C., & Wei, K.-K. (2002). Group Polarization and Computer-Mediated Communication: Effects of Communication Cues, Social Presence, and Anonymity. *Information Systems Research, 13*(1), 70–90.

Sianes, A. (2021). Academic Research on the 2030 Agenda: Challenges of a Transdisciplinary Field of Study. *Global Policy, 12*(3), 286–297. doi:10.1111/1758-5899.12912

Sidoti, O., & Vogels, E. A. (2023). What Americans know about AI, cybersecurity and big tech. *Pew Research Center*. https://www.pewresearch.org/internet/2023/08/17/what-americans-know-about-ai-cybersecurity-and-big-tech/

Siegel, P. H., Schultz, T., & Landy, S. (2011). Formal versus informal mentoring of MAS professionals. *Journal of Applied Business Research, 27*(2), 5–11. doi:10.19030/jabr.v27i2.4135

Signs & Symptoms. (2018, September 26). Retrieved from https://www.cdc.gov/salmonella/mbandaka-06-18/signs-symptoms.html

Silva, P., & Cooray, R. (2014). Building human capital in organizations through corporate social responsibility – a holistic coaching approach. *Procedia: Social and Behavioral Sciences, 159*, 753–758. doi:10.1016/j.sbspro.2014.12.443

Sim, J., & Waterfield, J. (2019). Focus group methodology: Some ethical challenges. *Quality & Quantity, 53*(6), 3003–3022. doi:10.1007/s11135-019-00914-5

Simpson, S. A., Matthews, L., Pugmire, J., McConnachie, A., McIntosh, E., Coulman, E., Hughes, K., Kelson, M., Morgan-Trimmer, S., Murphy, S., Utkina-Macaskill, O., & Moore, L. A. R. (2020). An app-, web-and social support-based weight loss intervention for adults with obesity: The 'HelpMeDoIt!' feasibility randomised controlled trial. *Pilot and Feasibility Studies, 6*(1), 1–14. doi:10.1186/s40814-020-00656-4 PMID:32968544

Singh, A., Prabhakar, R., & Kiran, J. S. (2022). Emotional intelligence: A literature review of its concept, models, and measures. *Journal of Positive School Psychology, 6*(10), 2254–2275.

Siripurapu, S., Darimireddy, N. K., Chehri, A., Sridhar, B., & Paramkusam, A. V. (2023). Technological Advancements and Elucidation Gadgets for Healthcare Applications: An Exhaustive Methodological Review-Part-I (A.I. et al.). *Electronics (Basel), 12*(3), 750. doi:10.3390/electronics12030750

Skillings, P. (2023). Job interview advice: Myths & mysteries. *Big Interview*. https://resources.biginterview.com/interviews-101/job-interview-advice/

Skinner, M. E., & Welch, F. C. (1996). Peer coaching for better teaching. *College Teaching, 44*(4), 153–156. doi:10.1080/87567555.1996.9932346

Small, M. L. (2021). What is "Qualitative" in Qualitative Research? Why the Answer Does not Matter but the Question is Important. *Qualitative Sociology, 44*(4), 567–574. doi:10.1007/s11133-021-09501-3

Smith, J., Taylor, K., & Johnson, L. (2023). *The Role of Emotional Intelligence in Supply*. Academic Press.

Smith, J. (2023). She is a visionary. Comment on the article "Mary Barra: The Leader Who Transformed GM.". *Forbes*.

Smith, J. A., & Fieldsend, M. (2021). *Interpretative phenomenological analysis*. American Psychological Association. doi:10.1037/0000252-008

Smith, J. A., & Nizza, I. E. (2022). *Essentials of interpretative phenolyomenological analysis*. American Psychological Association. doi:10.1037/0000259-000

Smith, J., & Jones, M. (2021). Chain Leadership. *Journal of Business and Supply Chain Management, 12*(3), 45–58.

Smith, W. E. (2005). *Hip hop as performance and ritual: Biography and ethnography in underground hip hop*. CLS Publications.

Snyder, H. (2023). Designing the literature review for a strong contribution. *Journal of Decision Systems*, 1–8. Advance online publication. doi:10.1080/12460125.2023.2197704

Social Research Methods. (2019). Oxford University Press.

Sodero, A., Jin, Y. H., & Barratt, M. (2019). The social process of Big Data and predictive analytics use for logistics and supply chain management. *International Journal of Physical Distribution & Logistics Management, 49*(7), 706–726. doi:10.1108/IJPDLM-01-2018-0041

Söğüt, E., & Erdem, O. (2023). A multi-model proposal for classification and detection of DDoS attacks on SCADA systems. *Applied Sciences (Basel, Switzerland), 13*(10), 5993. Retrieved October 28, 2023, from. doi:10.3390/app13105993

Solaja, O. M., Idown, F. E., & James, A. E. (2015). Exploring the relationship between leadership communication style, personality trait and organizational productivity. *Serbian Journal of Management, 11*(1), 99–117. doi:10.5937/sjm11-8480

Solon, A. (2020). *Broadband Models for Unserved and Underserved Communities*. Broadband Communities. Retrieved from: https://www.bbcmag.com/community-broadband/broadband-models-for-unserved-and-underserved-communities

Song, D. W. (2021). What is research? *WMU J Marit Affairs, 20*(4), 407–411. doi:10.1007/s13437-021-00256-w PMID:34895237

Sooley, K. (2016). *Examining Supervisor Emotional Intelligence and Employee Organizational Commitment* (Doctoral dissertation). Retrieved from ProQuest Dissertation and Thesis database. (UMI No. 10248026)

Spangenberg, H., & Theron, C. (2013). A critical review of the Burke-Litwin leadership, change, and performance model. *Management Dynamics: Journal of the Southern African Institute for Management Scientists, 22*(2), 29–48.

Spector, B. (2011). *Implementing organizational change: Theory into practice-international edition*. Prentice Hall.

Spector, Y. (2011). Theory of constraint methodology where the constraint is the business model. *International Journal of Production Research, 49*(11), 3387–3394. doi:10.1080/00207541003801283

Sperber, D., & Wilson, D. (1986). *Relevance: Communication and cognition*. Blackwell Publishers ltd.

Sperber, D., & Wilson, D. (1995). *Relevance: Communication and Cognition* (2nd ed.). Blackwell Publishers Ltd.

Sperry, L. (2013). Executive coaching and leadership assessment: Past, present, and future. *Consulting Psychology Journal, 65*(4), 284–288. doi:10.1037/a0035453

Spradley, J. P. (1979). *The ethnographic interview*. New York, NY. Hot. Rhinehart.

Srivastava, S. C., & Chandra, S. (2018). Social Presence in Virtual World Collaboration: An Uncertainty Reduction Perspective Using a Mixed Methods Approach. *MIS Quarterly, 42*(3), 779–803.

Statista. (2022, August 31). *Cyber insurance - statistics & facts*. Retrieved from https://www.statista.com/topics/2445/cyber-insurance/#topicOverview

Stebbins, R. A. (2001). *The art of case study research*. Sage.

Sterrett, W. L., & Imig, S. (2011). Thriving as a new teacher in a bad economy. *Kappa Delta Pi Record*, *47*(2), 68–71. doi:10.1080/00228958.2011.10516564

Stevenson, G. V. (2017). *Cybersecurity implications for industry, academia, and parents: A qualitative case study in NSF STEM education* (Order No. 10624075). Available from ProQuest Dissertations & Theses Global. (1958945736).

Stojanović, M. D., & Boštjančič Rakas, S. V. (2022). Challenges in Securing Industrial Control Systems Using Future Internet Technologies. In I. Management Association (Ed.), Research Anthology on Business Aspects of Cybersecurity (pp. 561-586). IGI Global. doi:10.4018/978-1-6684-3698-1.ch026

Stolwijk, M. L., van Nispen, R. M. A., van der Ham, A. J., Veenman, E., & van Rens, G. H. M. B. (2023). Barriers and facilitators in the referral pathways to low vision services from the perspective of patients and professionals: A qualitative study. *BMC Health Services Research*, *23*(1), 1–14. doi:10.1186/s12913-022-09003-0 PMID:36681848

Storme, M., Tavani, J. L., & Myszkowski, N. (2016). Psychometric properties of the French Ten Item Personality Inventory (TIPI). *Journal of Individual Differences*, *37*(2), 81–87. Advance online publication. doi:10.1027/1614-0001/a000204

Story, W. K. (2016). *Impact of supply chain technology response capability on firm performance and supply chain technology performance* (Order No. 10296300). Available from ProQuest Central; ProQuest Dissertations & Theses Global. (1845054047).

Story, M., Nanney, M. S., & Schwartz, M. B. (2009). Schools and obesity prevention: Creating school environments and policies to promote healthy eating and physical activity. *The Milbank Quarterly*, *87*(1), 71–100. doi:10.1111/j.1468-0009.2009.00548.x PMID:19298416

Stouffer, K., Pease, M., Tang, C., Zimmerman, T., Pillitteri, V., Lightman, S., Hahn, A., Saravia, S., Sherule, A., & Thompson, M. (2023). NIST SP 800-82 Rev. 3: Guide to Operational Technology (OT) Security. *National Institute of Standards and Technology*. doi:10.6028/NIST.SP.800-82r3

Strang, K. D. (2011). Leadership substitute and personality impact on time and quality in virtual new product development project. *Project Management Journal*, *42*(1), 73–90. doi:10.1002/pmj.20208

Strategy, A. (2017). *IT cost reduction: Exploiting new technologies to reduce cost and gain agility*. Retrieved from https://www.accenture.com/us-en/insight-it-cost-reductions-new-technologies

Stroup, D. F., Johnson, V. R., Hahn, R. A., & Proctor, D. C. (2009). Reversing the trend of childhood obesity. *Preventing Chronic Disease*, *6*(3). PMID:19527599

Substance Abuse and Mental Health Services Administration. (2020, August). *Key Substance Use and Mental Health Indicators in the United States: Results from the 2019 National Survey on Drug Use and Health*. U.S. Department of Health and Human Services. https://www.samhsa.gov/data/sites/default/files/reports/rpt29393/2019NSDUHFFRPDFWHTML/2019NSDUHFFR1PDFW090120.pdf

Sun, J., Zhang, Y., Chen, H., & Qiao, J. (2023). Optimization Model and Application for Agricultural Machinery Systems Based on Timeliness Losses of Multiple Operations. *Agriculture*, *13*(10), 1969. doi:10.3390/agriculture13101969

Svanberg, M. (2020). Guidelines for establishing practical relevance in logistics and supply chain management research. *International Journal of Physical Distribution & Logistics Management*, *50*(2), 215–232. doi:10.1108/IJPDLM-11-2018-0373

Swanson, D., Goel, L., Francisco, K., & Stock, J. (2017). Applying Theories from Other Disciplines to Logistics and Supply Chain Management: A Systematic Literature Review. *Transportation Journal, 56*(3), 299–356. doi:10.5325/transportationj.56.3.0299

Sweeney L. (2013). *Matching known patients to health records in Washington State Data.* doi:10.2139/ssrn.2289850

Swensen, S., Gorringe, G., Caviness, J., & Peters, D. (2016). Leadership by design: Intentional organization development of physician leaders. *Journal of Management Development, 35*(4), 549–570. doi:10.1108/JMD-08-2014-0080

Synopsis. (2023). The 6 levels of vehicle autonomy explained. *Author.* https://www.synopsys.com/automotive/autonomous-driving-levels.html

SynSaber. (2023). *SynSaber and ICS Advisory Project Identify Vulnerability Trends Within The Critical Infrastructure Sector.* Retrieved October 29, 2023, from https://14520070.fs1.hubspotusercontent-na1.net/hubfs/14520070/Collateral/SynSaber+ICS-Advisory-Project_ICS-Vulnerabilities_First-Half-2023.pdf

Tachakra, S., & Rajani, R. (2002). Social Presence in Telemedicine. *Journal of Telemedicine and Telecare, 8*(4), 226–230.

Taconis, M. (2018). How high potential coaching can add value – for participants and the organization. *International Journal of Evidence Based Coaching and Mentoring, S12,* 61–72.

Tajfel, H., Billig, M. G., Bundy, R. P., & Flament, C. (1971). Social categorization and intergroup behavior. *European Journal of Social Psychology, 1*(2), 149–178. doi:10.1002/ejsp.2420010202

Talal, A. H., Sofikitou, E. M., Jaanimägi, U., Zeremski, M., Tobin, J. N., & Markatou, M. (2020). A framework for patient-centered telemedicine: Application and lessons learned from vulnerable populations. *Journal of Biomedical Informatics, 112,* 103622. doi:10.1016/j.jbi.2020.103622 PMID:33186707

Tan, F. Z. & Olaore. (2021). Effect of organizational learning and effectiveness on the operations, employees productivity and management performance. *XIMB Journal of Management, 19*(2), 110-127. https://www.emerald.com/insight/content/doi/10.1108/XJM-09-2020-0122/full/html

Tannenbaum, N. (2014). Talent management: Managing the multigenerational workplace. *University of North Carolina Kenan-Flagler Business School.* Retrieved from http://execdev.kenan-flagler.unc.edu/blog/managing-the-multigenerational-workplace-0

Tareef, A. (2013). The relationship between mentoring and career development of higher education faculty members. *College Student Journal, 47*(4), 703–710.

Tarraf, D. C., Shelton, W., & Parker, E. (2021). *The Department Of Defense's posture for artificial intelligence: assessment and recommendations for improvement.* Santa Monica, CA: RAND Corporation, 2021. https://www.rand.org/pubs/research_briefs/RB10145.html

Technology, A. Z. (2022). Impact of technology in business. *Author.* https://atztechnology.com/impact-of-technology-in-business/

Tehlia, S. (2023, August 16). Cybersecurity as a strategic investment: How ROI optimization can lead to a more secure future. *Forbes.* https://www.forbes.com/sites/forbestechcouncil/2023/08/16/cybersecurity-as-a-strategic-investment-how-roi-optimization-can-lead-to-a-more-secure-future/?sh=1982a66c4cf7

Tellhed, U., Bäckström, M., & Björklund, F. (2017). Will I Fit in and Do Well? The Importance of Social Belongingness and Self-Efficacy for Explaining Gender Differences in Interest in STEM and HEED Majors. *Sex Roles, 77*(1–2), 86–96. doi:10.1007/s11199-016-0694-y PMID:28725103

Terblanche, N. H. D., Albertyn, R. M., & van Coller-Peter, S. (2017). Designing a coaching intervention to support leaders promoted into senior positions. *SA Journal of Human Resource Management, 15*(0). doi:10.4102/sajhrm.v15i0.842

Thai, Q. H., & Mai, K. N. (2023). An evolution of entrepreneurial culture studies: A systematic literature review and future research agenda. *Entrepreneurial Business and Economics Review, 11*(2), 31–62. doi:10.15678/EBER.2023.110202

Thakur, M., Patel, P., Gupta, L. K., Kumar, M., & Kumar, A. S. S. (2023). Applications Of Artificial Intelligence and Machine Learning in Supply Chain Management: A Comprehensive Review. *Eur. Chem. Bull, 8*, 2838-2851.

The Department of Defense. (2023). *2023 DOD Cyber Strategy Summary (Unclassified)*. U.S. Department of Defense News. Retrieved November 10, 2023, from https://media.defense.gov/2023/Sep/12/2003299076/-1/-1/1/2023_DOD_Cyber_Strategy_Summary.PDF

The Global Leadership Forecast 2014-2015. (2015). *Ready-now leaders: 25 Findings to meet tomorrow's business challenges* (DDI publication No.7th). Retrieved from the Conference Board Organization: https://www.ddiworld.com/DDI/media/trend-research/global-leadership-forecast-2014-2015_tr_ddi.pdf

The White House. (2011). *International Strategy for Cyberspace*. Retrieved November 12, 2015, from https://obamawhitehouse.archives.gov/sites/default/files/rss_viewer/international_strategy_for_cyberspace.pdf

The White House. (2021, July 28). *Background Press Call on Improving Cybersecurity of U.S. Critical Infrastructure*. Retrieved November 10, 2023, from https://www.whitehouse.gov/briefing-room/press-briefings/2021/07/28/background-press-call-on-improving-cybersecurity-of-u-s-critical-infrastructure/

Thiébaut, R., & Cossin, S. (2019). Artificial intelligence for surveillance in public health. *Yearbook of Medical Informatics, 28*(01), 232–234. doi:10.1055/s-0039-1677939 PMID:31419837

Thilmany, J. (2012). SCADA security? *Mechanical Engineering (New York, N.Y.), 134*(6), 26–31. Retrieved November 14, 2015, from. doi:10.1115/1.2012-JUN-1

Thomas, F. N., Waits, R. A., & Hartsfield, G. L. (2007). The influence of Gregory Bateson: Legacy or vestige? *Kybernetes, 36*(7/8), 871–883. doi:10.1108/03684920710777397

Thompson, M. J. (2019). Critical theory in critical times: Transforming the global political and economic order. *Contemporary Political Theory, 18*(S4, Suppl.4), 284–289. doi:10.1057/s41296-018-0229-0

Thornton, G. (2013). Women in senior management: Setting the stage for growth. Grant Thornton International Business Report.

Thursfield, D., & Kellie, J. (2013). Unitary practice or pluralist empowerment? *Personnel Review, 42*(4), 488–504. doi:10.1108/PR-08-2011-0124

Tien, N. H., Anh, D. B. H., & Thuc, T. D. (2019). *Global supply chain and logistics management*. Academic Press.

Tikkanen, R., & Abrams, M. (2020). *U.S. Health Care from a Global Perspective, 2019: Higher Spending, Worse Outcomes?* The Commonwealth Fund. Retrieved from: https://www.commonwealthfund.org/publications/issue-briefs/2020/jan/us-health-care-global-perspective-2019

Time to Think. (2020). *The ten components*. Retrieved from https://www.timetothink.com/thinking-environment/the-ten-components/

Tkaczyk, B. (2016, November/December). Coaching by numbers. *Ivey Business Journal*. Retrieved from https://iveybusinessjournal.com/coaching-by-numbers/

Tobias, R. M. (2015). When the executive core qualifications aren't enough. *Excellence in Government*. Retrieved from https://www.govexec.com/excellence/promising-practices/2015/01/when-executive-core-qualifications-arent-enough/103992/

Toit, A., & Reissner, S. (2012). Experiences of coaching in team learning. *International Journal of Mentoring and Coaching in Education*, *1*(3), 177–190. doi:10.1108/20466851211279448

Tomaszewski, L. E., Zarestky, J., & Gonzalez, E. (2020). Planning qualitative research: Design and decision making for new researchers. *International Journal of Qualitative Methods*, *19*, 1609406920967174. doi:10.1177/1609406920967174

Topham, L., Kifayat, K., Younis, Y. A., Shi, Q., & Askwith, B. (2016). Cyber Security Teaching and Learning Laboratories: A Survey. *Information & Security*, *35*(1), 51–80. doi:10.11610/isij.3503

Totin, A. N., & Connor, B. P. (2019). Evaluating Business Models Enabling Organic Additive Manufacturing for Maintenance and Sustainment. *Defense Acquisition Research Journal: A Publication of the Defense Acquisition University*, *26*(4), 379–417. https://doi-org.captechu.idm.oclc.org/10.22594/dau.18-815.26.04

Towhidi, G., & Pridmore, J. (2022). Increasing cybersecurity interest and self-efficacy through experiential labs. *Issues in Information Systems*, *23*(2).

Tran, T. B. H., & Choi, S. B. (2019). Effects of inclusive leadership on organizational citizenship behavior: the mediating roles of organizational justice and learning culture. *Journal of Pacific Rim Psychology*, *13*, e17.

Trevillion, F. M. H. (2018). Executive coaching outcomes: An investigation into leadership development using five dyadic case studies illustrating the impact of executive coaching. *International Journal of Evidence Based Coaching and Mentoring*, *S12*, 21–40.

Tsukayama, H. (2015). Teens spend nearly nine hours every day consuming media. *The Washington Post*. Retrieved from: https://www.washingtonpost.com/news/the-switch/wp/2015/11/03/teens-spend-nearly-nine-hours-every-day-consuming-media/

Turner, C., & McCarthy, G. (2015). Coachable moments: Identifying factors that influence managers to take advantage of coachable moments in day-to-day management. *International Journal of Evidence Based Coaching and Mentoring*, *13*(1), 1–13.

Turner, D. (2010). Qualitative interview design: A practical guide for novice investigators. *The Qualitative Report*, *15*(3), 754–760.

Tyran, K. L., & Garcia, J. E. (2015). Reciprocal learning and management education: The example of using university alumni and other business executives as "virtual" mentors to business students. *Journal of the Academy of Business Education*, *16*, 54–72. https://proxy.cecybrary.com/login?url=https://search.proquest.com/docview/1713929835?accountid=144459

U. S. Census Bureau. (2016). American Fact Finder. *United States Census Bureau*. Retrieved from https://factfinder.census.gov/faces/tableservices/jsf/pages/productview.xhtml?pid=PEP_2016_PEPSYASEXN&prodType=table

U. S. Office of the Director of National Intelligence. (2017). A common cyber threat framework: A foundation for communication. *Author*. https://www.dni.gov/files/ODNI/documents/features/A_Common_Cyber_Threat_Framework_Overview.pdf

U.S. Department of Transportation (USDOT). (2022). *Bureau of Transportation Statistics, based upon USDOT, Maritime Administration, Office of Policy & Plans / U.S. Customs & Border Protection, Vessel Monitoring System, special tabulation*. Author.

U.S. Department of Transportation Federal Highway Administration. (2023). Automated vehicle activities and resources. *Author*. https://highways.dot.gov/automation

U.S. Department of Transportation. (2022a). *Bureau of Transportation Statistics analysis of U.S. Census Bureau, U.S. Import & Export Merchandise Trade Statistics*. https://www.census.gov/foreign-trade/data/index.html

U.S. Department of Transportation. (2022b). *Bureau of Transportation Statistics, Freight Facts & Figures, available at Freight Facts and Figures*. https://data.bts.gov/stories/s/45xw-qksz

U.S. Department of Transportation. (2022c). *Bureau of Transportation Statistics analysis of U.S. Department of Commerce, Census Bureau, USA Trade Online*. https://www.census.gov/foreign-trade/data/index.html

U.S. Department of Transportation. (2022d). *Bureau of Transportation Statistics; analysis based on data sources cited in Port Profiles, available at Port Performance Freight Statistics Program*. Bureau of Transportation Statistics. https://explore.dot.gov/views/FreightIndicators/ContainershipsAwaiting?%3Aembed_code_version=3&%3Aembed=y&%3AloadOrderID=8&%3Adisplay_spinner=no&%3AshowAppBanner=false&%3Adisplay_count=n&%3AshowVizHome=n&%3Aorigin=viz_share_link#1

U.S. Food and Drug Administration. (2023). *Get the Facts about Salmonella*. U.S. Food and Drug Administration. Retrieved from: https://www.fda.gov/animal-veterinary/animal-health-literacy/get-facts-about-salmonella#:~:text=The%20Centers%20for%20Disease%20Control,for%20most%20of%20these%20cases

UNCTAD. (2016). *Review of maritime transport 2016*. Available at: https://unctad.org/transportnews

United States Office of Personnel Management (OPM). (2017). *Training and development policy wiki: Mentoring in government*. Retrieved from https://www.opm.gov/wiki/training/mentoring-and-coaching.ashx

University of Louisville William F. Ekstrom Library. (2021). Critical thinking and academic research: Assumptions. *Author*. https://library.louisville.edu/ekstrom/criticalthinking/assumptions

University of New Mexico. (2014). The history of mentorship part 1. *The University of New Mexico*. Retrieved from https://mentor.unm.edu/blog/2014/04/10/the-history-of-mentorship-part-1

University of Southern California. (2023). *Theoretical framework*. Author. https://libguides.usc.edu/writingguide/theoreticalframework

Upadhyay, D., & Sampalli, S. (2020). SCADA (Supervisory Control and Data Acquisition) systems: Vulnerability assessment and security recommendations. *Computers & Security*, *89*, 101666. doi:10.1016/j.cose.2019.101666

Uzkurt, C., Kumar, R., Kimzan, H. S., & Eminoglu, G. (2013). Role of innovation in the relationship between organizational culture and firm performance. *European Journal of Innovation Management*, *16*(1), 92–117. doi:10.1108/14601061311292878

Vafaei, A., Ahmed, K., & Mather, P. (2015). Board diversity and financial performance in the top 500 Australian firms: Board diversity and financial performance. *Australian Accounting Review*, *25*(4), 413–427. doi:10.1111/auar.12068

Van Dijk, H., Van Engen, M. L., & Van Knippenberg, D. (2012). Defying conventional wisdom: A meta-analytical examination of the differences between demographic and job-related diversity relationships with performance. *Organizational Behavior and Human Decision Processes*, *119*(1), 38–53. doi:10.1016/j.obhdp.2012.06.003

Van Dun, D. H., & Kumar, M. (2023). Social enablers of industry 4.0 technology adoption: Transformational leadership and emotional intelligence. *International Journal of Operations & Production Management*, *43*(13), 152–182. doi:10.1108/IJOPM-06-2022-0370

Van Maanen, J. (1988). *Tales of the field: On writing ethnography.* University of Chicago Press.

van Thiel, J. P. (2016). *A quantitative analysis of supervisor leadership effectiveness: The perception of federal employees* (Doctoral dissertation). Retrieved from ProQuest Dissertations & Thesis Global (Order No. 10140357).

Vaudrin, C. J. (2019). Melting the Cultural Iceberg in Indigenizing Higher Education: Shifts to Accountability in Times of Reconciliation. *New Directions for Teaching and Learning, 2019*(157), 105–118. doi:10.1002/tl.20333

Vdovic, H., Babic, J., & Podobnik, V. (2019). Automotive software in connected and autonomous electric vehicles: A review. *IEEE Access : Practical Innovations, Open Solutions, 7,* 166365–166379. doi:10.1109/ACCESS.2019.2953568

Velsor, E. V., Turregano, C., Adams, B. Fleenor, J. (2016). Creating tomorrow's government leaders an overview of top leadership challenges and how they can be addressed. *Center for Creative Leadership.* Retrieved from file:///C:/Users/Dr.%20B/Desktop/creating-government-leaders-and-addressing-challenges-center-for-creative-leadership.pdf

Visser, M. (2007b). System dynamics and group facilitation: Contributions from communication Theory. *System Dynamics Review, 23*(4), 453–463. doi:10.1002/sdr.391

Visser, S. S., Hutter, I., & Haisma, H. (2016). Building a framework for theory-based ethnographies for studying intergenerational family food practices. *Appetite, 97,* 49–57. doi:10.1016/j.appet.2015.11.019 PMID:26593100

Vugt, M. V., Hogan, R., & Kaiser, R. (2008). Leadership, Followership, and Evolution. American Psychologist Association. doi:10.1037/0003-066X.63.3.182

Vuletich, H. A., & Payne, B. K. (2019). Stability and change in implicit bias. *Psychological Science, 30*(6), 854–862. doi:10.1177/0956797619844270 PMID:31050916

Waaland, T. (2013). Job characteristics and mentoring in pre-schools. *Journal of Workplace Learning, 25*(5), 310–327. doi:10.1108/JWL-Mar-2012-0027

Waldman, E. (2021). How to manage a multi-generational team. *Harvard Business Review.* https://hbr.org/2021/08/how-to-manage-a-multi-generational-team

Walker-Fraser, A. (2011). An HR perspective on executive coaching for organisational learning. *International Journal of Evidence Based Coaching and Mentoring, 2*(9), 67–79.

Walker-Fraser, A. (2011, August). An H.R. perspective on executive coaching for organizational Learning. *International Journal of Evidence Based Coaching and Mentoring, 9*(2).

Wang, R. H., Barbieri, J. S., Nguyen, H. P., Stavert, R., Forman, H. P., Bolognia, J. L., & Kovarik, C. L. (2020). Clinical effectiveness and cost-effectiveness of teledermatology: Where are we now, and what are the barriers to adoption? *Journal of the American Academy of Dermatology, 83*(1), 299–307. doi:10.1016/j.jaad.2020.01.065 PMID:32035106

Wang, W., & Wu, Q. (2023). Research on the Coordinated Development of Coastal Port Logistics and International Trade: Based on Six Coastal Provinces of China. *Sustainability (Basel), 15*(1), 121. doi:10.3390/su15010121

Wang, Y., Wang, Y., Qin, H., Ji, H., Zhang, Y., & Wang, J. (2021). A systematic risk assessment framework of automotive cybersecurity. *Automotive Innovation, 4*(3), 253–261. doi:10.1007/s42154-021-00140-6

Wang, Y., Xu, R., & Zhang, K. (2022). A Car-following model for mixed traffic flows in intelligent connected vehicle environment considering driver response characteristics. *Sustainability (Basel), 14*(17), 11010. doi:10.3390/su141711010

Ward, G., van de Loo, F. E., & Ten Have, S. (2014). Psychodynamic group e6xecutive coaching: A literature review. *International Journal of Evidence Based Coaching and Mentoring, 12*(1), 63–78.

Ware, W. H. (1967, April). *Security and Privacy in Computer Systems*. The RAND Corporation. Retrieved October 28, 2015, from https://www.rand.org/content/dam/rand/pubs/papers/2005/P3544.pdf

Warner, M. (2012). Cybersecurity: A Pre-History. *Intelligence and National Security*, 27(5), 781–799. doi:10.1080/02684527.2012.708530

Washington State Office of the Attorney General (WSOAG). (2023). *Data Breach Notifications. Attorney General Bob Ferguson*. https://www.atg.wa.gov/data-breach-notifications

Washington, N. J. (2015). *Servant leadership characteristics among senior executive service leaders in the U.S. federal government: A phenomenological study* (Order No. 3714421). Retrieved from https://proxy.cecybrary.com/login?url=https://search.proquest.com/docview/1708991087?accountid=144459

Wasylyshyn, K. M. (2003). Coaching and executive character: Core problems and basic approaches. *Consulting Psychology Journal*, 55(2), 94–106. doi:10.1037/1061-4087.55.2.94

WaTech. (2023). *Washington Technology Services. Office of Privacy and Data Protection*. https://watech.wa.gov/privacy/office-of-privacy-and-data-protection

Water, T., Ford, K., Spence, D., & Rasmussen, S. (2016). Patient advocacy by nurses - past, present, and future. *Contemporary Nurse*, 52(6), 696–709. doi:10.1080/10376178.2016.1235981 PMID:27636537

Watson, F., & Wu, Y. (2022). The Impact of Online Reviews on the Information Flows and Outcomes of Marketing Systems. *Journal of Macromarketing*, 42(1), 146–164. doi:10.1177/02761467211042552

Wazed, S. (2018, August 2). *Council post: Grow your organization with top talent using the iceberg interview model*. Forbes. Retrieved March 21, 2023, from https://www.forbes.com/sites/forbeshumanresourcescouncil/2018/08/02/grow-your-organization-with-top-talent-using-the-iceberg-interview-model/?sh=41d17c2175b8

Weick, K. E., Sutcliffe, K. M., & Obstfeld, D. (1999). *Organizing for High Reliability: Processes of Collective Mindfulness*. Academic Press.

Weitoish, T. (2014). Cybersecurity risks that impact national security and intelligence today [Unpublished manuscript]. APUS: American Military University.

Wennberg, J. E. (1984). Dealing with Medical Practice Variations: A Proposal for Action. *Health Affairs*, 3(2), 6–33.

Wenson, E. (2010, November). After-coaching leadership skills and their impact on direct reports: recommendations for organizations. *Human Resource Development International*, 13(5), 607–616. doi:10.1080/13678868.2010.520485

West, G., Lazarescu, M., & Ou, M. (2010). Telederm: A Web-Based Decision Support System for Medical Practitioners. In W. Pease, M. Cooper, & R. Gururajan (Eds.), *Biomedical Knowledge Management: Infrastructures and Processes for E-Health Systems* (pp. 154–176). IGI Global. doi:10.4018/978-1-60566-266-4.ch011

Westwood, S. (2016, February 20). These 8 federal agencies are the worst. Here's how to fix them. *The Washington Examiner*. Retrieved from http://www.washingtonexaminer.com/these-8-federal-agencies-are-the-worst-heres-how-to-fix-them/article/2583708

White, H. D. (2016). Relevance theory and distributions of judgments in document retrieval. *Information Processing & Management*, 5(53), 1080–1102.

Whitely, W., Dougherty, T. W., & Dreher, G. F. (1991). Relationship of career mentoring and socioeconomic origin to managers' and professionals' early career progress. *Academy of Management Journal*, 34(2), 331–350. doi:10.2307/256445

Wickens, C. D., Helton, W. S., Hollands, J. G., & Banbury, S. (2021). *Engineering psychology and human performance*. Routledge. doi:10.4324/9781003177616

Wicklund, E. (2020). *Community Broadband Programs Bring Telehealth to Underserved Populations*. mHealth Intelligence. Retrieved from: https://mhealthintelligence.com/news/community-broadband-programs-bring-telehealth-to-underserved-populations

Wiles, R. (2012). *What are qualitative research ethics?* Bloomsbury Academic.

Williams, J. C. (2005). The glass ceiling and the maternal wall in academia. *New Directions for Higher Education*, *2005*(130), 91–105. doi:10.1002/he.181

Williamson, I. O. (2021). The 'great resignation' is a trend that began before the pandemic – and bosses need to get used to it. *The Conversation*. https://theconversation.com/the-great-resignation-is-a-trend-that-began-before-the-pandemic-and-bosses-need-to-get-used-to-it-170197

Winkelman, Z., Buenaventura, M., Anderson, J. M., Beyene, N. M., Katkar, P., & Baumann, G. C. (2019). When autonomous vehicles are hacked, who is liable? (No. RR-2654-RC). RAND Corporation.

Wittmer, J. L. S., & Hopkins, M. M. (2023). Emotional intelligence and virtual leadership: A study of remote leaders during the COVID-19 pandemic. *Journal of Leadership & Organizational Studies*, *30*(1), 45–60. doi:10.1177/15480518221123456

Wofford, T. (2015, January 14). *Meet the new CISPA, same as the old CISPA*. Newsweek. Retrieved November 20, 2015, from https://www.newsweek.com/meet-new-cispa-same-old-cispa-299375

Wolcott, H. F. (1995). *The art of fieldwork*. AltaMira Press.

Wolgemuth, J., Moody, Z., Ospal, T., Cross, J., Kaanta, T., Dickman, E., & Colomer, S. (2014). Participants' experiences of the qualitative interview: Considering the importance of research paradigms. *Qualitative Research*, *15*(3), 351–372. doi:10.1177/1468794114524222

Wong, A. (2023). Improving parking lot efficiency through autonomous control and assignment strategies: A microscopic traffic simulation analysis. *EECS Department, University of California, Berkeley*, Technical Report No. UCB/EECS-2023-166. https://www2.eecs.berkeley.edu/Pubs/TechRpts/2023/EECS-2023-166.pdf

Woods, T., & Nies, M. (2018). Conceptual Application of the Adapted Health Belief Model to Parental Understanding of Child Weight. *Journal of Health Science & Education*, *2*(4), 1–6. Retrieved from: https://www.researchgate.net/publication/327230594_Conceptual_Application_of_the_Adapted_Health_Belief_Model_to_Parental_Understanding_of_Child_Weight

World Economic Forum. (2023). *Annual Report 2022-2023*. https://www3.weforum.org/docs/WEF_Annual_Report_2022-23.pdf

World Health Organization. (2010). *Global Recommendations on Physical Activity for Health*. Retrieved from: https://www.who.int/dietphysicalactivity/global-PA-recs-2010.pdf

World Health Organization. (2019). *Childhood overweight and obesity*. World Health Organization. Retrieved from: https://www.who.int/dietphysicalactivity/childhood/en/

Wu, J., Ding, W., Zhang, Y., & Zhao, P. (2022). On reliability improvement for coherent systems with a revelation. *Naval Research Logistics*, *69*(4), 654–666. doi:10.1002/nav.22036

Wysocki, R. K. (2014). Effective Project Management: Traditional, agile, extreme (7th ed.). Academic Press.

Xie, X., Lee, C., & Eling, M. (2020). Cyber insurance offering and performance: An analysis of the US cyber insurance market. *The Geneva Papers on Risk and Insurance. Issues and Practice, 45*(4), 690–736. doi:10.1057/s41288-020-00176-5

Yaghi, A. (2017). Glass cliff or glass prison: Think evil-think men in organizational leadership. *International Journal of Public Administration*, 1–11.

Yang, Y. (2014). Principals' transformational leadership in school improvement. *The International Journal of Educational Management, 28*(3), 279-288. http://dx.doi.org.proxy.cecybrary.com/10.1108/IJEM-04-2013-0063

Yang, R., & Wibowo, S. (2022). User trust in artificial intelligence: A comprehensive conceptual framework. *Electronic Markets, 32*(4), 2053–2077. doi:10.1007/s12525-022-00592-6

Yang, S., Du, M., & Chen, Q. (2021). Impact of connected and autonomous vehicles on traffic efficiency and safety of an on-ramp. *Simulation Modelling Practice and Theory, 113*, 102374. Advance online publication. doi:10.1016/j.simpat.2021.102374

Ye, L., & Fang, X. (2023). Analysis on Integration of Logistics Trade Resources and Global Competition of Ports Along the Belt and Road Based on Fuzzy Algorithm. *Revista Ibérica De Sistemas e Tecnologias De Informação*, 526-536. https://www.proquest.com/scholarly-journals/analysis-on-integration-logistics-trade-resources/docview/2828438621/se-2

Ye, L., & Yamamoto, T. (2019). Evaluating the impact of connected and autonomous vehicles on traffic safety. *Physica A, 526*, 121009. doi:10.1016/j.physa.2019.04.245

Yen, H., & Krishner, T. (2022). NTSB chief to fed agency: Stop using misleading statistics. *The Associated Press*. https://apnews.com/article/coronavirus-pandemic-business-health-national-transportation-safety-board-transportation-safety-6638c79c519c28bb4d810d06789a2717#:~:text=FILE%20-%20Jennifer%20Homendy%20of%20the%20National%20Transportation,that%20the%20Transportation%20Department%20should%20stop%20using%20it

Yeow, A., & Huat Goh, K. (2015). Work Harder or Work Smarter? Information Technology and Resource Allocation in Healthcare Processes. *Management Information Systems Quarterly, 39*(4), 4. doi:10.25300/MISQ/2015/39.4.2

Yin, R. K. (2020). *Case study research and applications: Design and methods* (7th ed.). Sage Publications.

Yongcheng, L. (2015). Beyond offensive realism: Why leadership matters more than structure in the security environment of East Asia. *International Journal of China Studies, 6*(2), 159–173. https://proxy.cecybrary.com/login?url=https://search.proquest.com/docview/1719405439?accountid=144459

Yoo, Y., & Alavi, M. (2001). Media and Group Cohesion: Relative Influences on Social Presence, Task Participation, and Group Consensus. *Management Information Systems Quarterly, 25*(3), 371–390. doi:10.2307/3250922

Young, R. R., & Gordon, G. A. (2019). Critical Infrastructure: Transportation Systems. In L. Shapiro & M. H. Maras (Eds.), *Encyclopedia of Security and Emergency Management*. Springer. doi:10.1007/978-3-319-69891-5_85-1

Zahedi, F. M., Walia, N., & Jain, H. (2016). Augmented Virtual Doctor Office: Theory-Based Design and Assessment. *Journal of Management Information Systems, 33*(3), 776–808.

Zapata, D. (2021, June). *New study finds AI-enabled anti-Black bias in recruiting*. Thomson Reuters. Retrieved from: https://www.thomsonreuters.com/en-us/posts/legal/ai-enabled-anti-black-bias/

Zeng, D., Cao, Z., & Neill, D. B. (2021). Artificial intelligence–enabled public health surveillance—from local detection to global epidemic monitoring and control. In *Artificial intelligence in medicine* (pp. 437–453). Academic Press. doi:10.1016/B978-0-12-821259-2.00022-3

Zhang, C., Zhan, Q., Wang, Q., Wu, H., He, T., & An, Y. (2020). Autonomous dam surveillance robot system based on multi-sensor fusion. *Sensors (Basel)*, 20(4), 1097. doi:10.3390/s20041097 PMID:32079361

Zhang, J. Z., & Watson, G. F. IV. (2020). *Marketing Ecosystem: An outside-in view for sustainable advantage.* Industrial Marketing Management.

Zhang, J., Wu, K., Cheng, M., Yang, M., Cheng, Y., & Li, S. (2020). Safety evaluation for connected and autonomous vehicles' exclusive lanes considering penetrate ratios and impact of trucks using surrogate safety measures. *Journal of Advanced Transportation*, 2020, 1–16. doi:10.1155/2020/5847814

Zhang, Y., Wang, L., Xiang, Y., & Ten, C.-W. (2015). Power system reliability evaluation with SCADA cybersecurity considerations. *IEEE Transactions on Smart Grid*, 6(4), 1707–1721. Retrieved October 27, 2015, from. doi:10.1109/TSG.2015.2396994

Zhang, Y., Zhang, J., Liu, K., & Shen, X. (2019). A Survey on Wireless Security: Technical Challenges, Recent Advances, and Future Trends. *Proceedings of the IEEE*, 104(9), 1727–1765.

Zhao, L., & Malikopoulos, A. A. (2022, January-February). Enhanced mobility with connectivity and automation: A review of shared autonomous vehicle systems. *IEEE Intelligent Transportation Systems Magazine*, 14(1), 87–102. doi:10.1109/MITS.2019.2953526

Zhou, G., Shang, G., & Zhang, Y. (2023, March 16). smart infrastructure for autonomous driving in urban areas. *National Academy of Engineering*. https://www.nae.edu/19579/19582/21020/290850/290948/Smart-Infrastructure-for-Autonomous-Driving-in-Urban-Areas

Zhu, L., Benbasat, I., & Jiang, Z. (2010). Let's Shop Online Together: An Empirical Investigation of Collaborative Online Shopping Support. *Information Systems Research*, 21(4), 872–891.

Zippa. (2021, January 29). *Cyber security analyst demographics and statistics: Number of cyber security analysts in The US.* https://www.zippia.com/cyber-security-analyst-jobs/demographics/

Zippia. (2022). *Patient Advocate Demographics and Statistics in the U.S.* https://www.zippia.com/patient-advocate-jobs/demographics/

Zoričić, D., Knežević, G., Miletić, M., Dolinar, D., & Sprčić, D. M. (2022). Integrated Risk Analysis of Aggregators: Policy Implications for the Development of the Competitive Aggregator Industry. *Energies*, 15(14). doi:10.3390/en15145076

Zuberbuhler, M. J. P., Salanova, M., & Martinez, I. M. (2020). Coaching-based Leadership Intervention Program: A controlled trial study. *Frontiers in Psychology*, 10, 3066. doi:10.3389/fpsyg.2019.03066 PMID:32116873

Zukis, B. (2019). Regulators Want CEOs To Go To Jail For Cyber Failings, Should You? *Forbes*. https://www.forbes.com/sites/bobzukis/2019/04/10/regulators-want-ceos-to-go-to-jail-for-cyber-failings-should-you/?sh=6484b13719fa

Zveglich, L., & Lacina, R. (2014). *Powering up coaching by blending human factor with technology.* https://proxy.cecybrary.com/login?url=https://search.proquest.com/docview/1552708249?accountid=144459

About the Contributors

Eugene J. Lewis is a leading Marketer and Information Systems Specialist in all areas of Marketing, Management, and Information Systems. Dr. Lewis is a leading expert in technical core competencies in marketing as well as Diversity & Inclusion (Organizational Dynamics). Currently, Dr. Lewis serves in the Aviation & Defense Industry working in the Cargo CH-47 Helicopters Foreign Military Sales Program Office for the US Army. Previously, he served as the Assistant Professor of Marketing at Oakwood University as a full-time and part-time instructor in Marketing, Management (Leadership), and Computer Information Systems. Moreover, lecturing students in areas such as: advertising management, consumer behavior, global marketing, marketing management, organizational dynamics, project management, sales management, and project management, logistics and supply chain management integrating marketing methodologies. Dr. Lewis is a highly sought-after practitioner as his education and experience provide a real-world example of the integration within the marketing management and technology field. As an International Program Manager, he gives several briefings to dignitaries and foreign leadership around the world in areas of logistics and supply chain management. Much of his employment experience consists of incorporating new innovative concepts to provide consumers with the requisite knowledge necessary to understand the value of emotional (EQ) and business intelligence (BI) with incorporating technology. Dr. Lewis enjoys giving back to the community spending much of his free time assisting young people in underprivileged areas instructing them in the sweet science. Dr. Lewis has been a Boxing Coach and Instructor for over 13 years. He is a registered Coach with United States Boxing Association for the Southeastern Region. Dr. Lewis believes in the efficacy of developing young people. He is originally from Seattle, Washington. His family still resides in the Pacific Northwest. He enjoys every opportunity available to travel, write poetry, play his guitar, and meet inspiring people.

* * *

Darrell Norman Burrell is a faculty member at Marymount University. He is a post-doctoral researcher at the University of Maryland- Baltimore School of Pharmacy. He is a visiting researcher at the Pellegrino Center at the Georgetown School of Medicine. He is visiting scholar at the Samuel DeWitt Proctor Institute for Leadership, Equity, and Justice at Rutgers University. Dr. Burrell has 3 doctorate degrees and five graduate degrees. He has over 200 peer reviewed publications. He has over 20 years of management, teaching, and training experience in academia, government, and private industry.

Sharon L. Burton is a multifaceted professional excelling as a dissertation chair, faculty member, facilitator, author, speaker, consultant, and TV co-host. With an extensive portfolio of over 100 scholarly publications and participation in 30+ professional conferences, Dr. Burton is an accomplished expert. Her proficiency extends to AI, leadership, agile solutions, and fostering collaborations, rendering her a problem-to-solution value catalyst. She adeptly decodes technical intricacies for non-technical audiences and senior leadership while offering business process insights to technical teams. Dr. Burton's leadership spans cross-functional, virtual, and on-site teams. Dr. Burton's background encompasses roles such as Chief Learning & Compliance Officer-Administrator Representative for the Board of Trustees; Chief Learning Officer; Chief Learning Officer, Compliance, and Information Assurance Officer; Senior Change Management Officer; Senior Business Process Engineer; and Senior Program/Project Manager. Her influence even extends to cyber-security boards. As a mentor and coach, she champions learning advocacy. Dr. Burton's academic pursuits include a PhD. in Cybersecurity Leadership, a DBA in Quality Systems Management (focused on Business Process Improvement), and two MBA degrees in Human Resources Management and Management. Complemented by various certifications, Dr. Burton welcomes speaking engagements. She is contactable at 302-547-8010 or sharonlburton2@comcast.net. Further insights can be found at .

Ramona R. Cruz has been a Licensed Practicing Nurse from Seattle, Washington since 2005 (Provider Identification #- LP00056320). Currently, she is a business student at Oakwood University a Historically Black College University (HBCU) working towards her business degree. Ms. Cruz has strong ties into the Health Care and Patient Advocacy demographic within the State of Washington. Her human capital and business intelligence in areas of medical safety and health has allowed her to be placed in venues where she frequently attends Conferences and Professional Seminars that enhance her abilities within the profession. As a practitioner, Ms. Cruz has research interests in business nursing, business intelligence in medical health, healthcare cyber security, healthcare mitigation, and patient advocacy.

Marlena Daryousef holds an MBA and Doctor of Management degree from Colorado Technical University with over ten years of business development and consulting across multiple business verticals. Marlena has a proven track record of helping both startups and established businesses improve their business optimization, stakeholder engagement, quality and risk management processes, and problem-solving.

Michelle Espinoza earned her MBA from the University of Arizona. Her research presently centers on detecting and preventing fraud in platform-based businesses.

Aikyna Finch is a Podcaster, Social Media Coach, and TEDx Speaker. She coaches in the areas of Executive, Life, and Technology at the individual and group levels from her company, Finch and Associates LLC. She is the host of the Dr. Finch Experience® Podcast, and she speaks on Coaching, Education, and Technology. In 2020, she started her tech coaching brand called Technically Intuitive®. In November 2022, she became a TEDX DeerPark Speaker with her presentation on "The Benefits of AI on Social Media." Currently, she is a Director of DEIB and a board member for three organizations. Dr. Finch is an Educator. She received a Doctorate of Management, an MBA in Technology Management, and an Executive MBA from Colorado Technical University. She has an MS in Management in Marketing, an

MS in Information Systems in IT Project Management from Strayer University, and a BS in Aeronautical Technology in Industrial Electronics from the School of Engineering of Tennessee State University. She is a former Campus and Faculty Dean who established enrollment records. She has published and presented on topics related to adult education, social media, and job search.

Danielle Gervacio Graf consistently provides comprehensive management solutions for intricate projects spanning various sectors, including public, private, academic, and non-profit. Her expertise has been instrumental in fostering growth, elevating competitive advantages, and instigating transformative change, all while maintaining a steadfast commitment to process enhancement. Her skill set encompasses a diverse range of core competencies, combining sharp business acumen with a holistic, big-picture perspective. Over the course of her career, she has refined her abilities in client management, program and project management, as well as critical areas such as estimation, program and project planning, resource allocation, issue resolution, risk mitigation, change management, and effective business communication. Her objective is to leverage these skills consistently, surpassing project objectives and cultivating success for her clients and organizations.

Danielle Gervacio Graf, a dedicated project manager, is driven by a fervent enthusiasm for refining processes. With a proven track record, Gervacio Graf consistently delivers comprehensive management solutions for intricate projects spanning diverse sectors—ranging from public and private to academic and non-profit. Her expertise acts as a catalyst for growth, fortifies competitive advantages, and instigates transformative change, all while upholding a steadfast commitment to process improvement. Gervacio Graf possesses a versatile skill set that encompasses a broad spectrum of core competencies. Her blend of keen business acumen and a holistic, big-picture perspective distinguishes her in the field. Over the course of her career, she has refined her abilities in client management, program and project management, and critical areas such as estimation, program and project planning, resource allocation, issue resolution, risk mitigation, change management, and effective business communication. Her overarching objective is to leverage these skills consistently, surpassing project objectives, and fostering success for her clients and organizations alike.

Laura Jones is an award-winning thought leader, educator, strategist, practitioner, and coach with specialties in enterprise governance, information security, risk management, quality assurance, artificial intelligence, and product management. Dr. Jones previously served as an Associate Dean of Student Academic Affairs. She currently serves as adjunct faculty for Carnegie Mellon University's Heinz School of Information Systems and Public Policy and adjunct faculty for Capitol Technology University. Dr. Jones earned a Ph.D. in Product Management, a M.S. in Quality Systems Management, and a B.S. in Management Studies. She has completed executive education programs at Carnegie Mellon University (Chief Risk Officer's Program); Harvard Kennedy School (Leadership Decision Making); UC Berkeley Haas (Business Strategies and Artificial Intelligence); and Wharton Online (Business Strategy and Competitive Advantage). Dr. Jones has several academic publications and writes children's books about Internet safety and cybersecurity. She also speaks domestically and internationally on risk management and cybersecurity risk.

Helen MacLennan currently serves as the Dean of the School of Graduate Business and Technology (SGBT) and is an Associate Professor of Business at Lindsey Wilson College in Columbia, Kentucky. Prior to entering academia, Helen served 12 years as an asset manager, responsible for a multi-state portfolio of industrial properties. She earned her MBA in Real Estate studies from Marylhurst University and her Ph.D. in Management from Sullivan University in Louisville, KY. Her dissertation research was titled "The Power of Status: An Exploration of Power and Civility Climate in a Sample of Residential Property Managers." She continues to research and publish on the topics of remote management and organizational civility and inclusion. As an avid researcher, Dr. MacLennan also serves on the editorial review board for the Journal of Conflict Management and as a reviewer for the International Journal of Doctoral Studies and the Journal of Values-Based Business. She has published her research in the Journal of Conflict Management, International Journal of Doctoral Studies, Journal of Excellence in Business Education, Southeast Case Research Journal, and the Journal of Transportation Management.

Quatavia McLester is a PhD candidate in the Healthcare Technology program at Capitol Technology University. She holds a Master of Science in Industrial/Organizational Psychology from Austin Peay State University. She holds a Bachelor of Science in Psychology and a minor in Applied Statistics and Data Analysis from Kennesaw State University. She is currently serving as a Board Certified Behavior Analyst for a mental healthcare service provider. Her research interests include processes and outcomes of organizational development and change at the individual, group, and systems levels within the healthcare field, the effects of destructive leadership within organizations, and the use of healthcare technology in the mental healthcare space.

Marwan Omar received a Master's degree in Information Systems and Technology from the University of Phoenix, 2009 and a Doctorate Degree in Digital Systems Security from Colorado Technical University, 2012. He is currently an associate professor at Illinois Institute of Technology where he teaches cyber security and digital forensics courses. His research interests fall in the broad area of cyber security with a recent focus on machine learning robustness. Among other services, he is currently an active reviewer for IEEE Access, IEEE Transactions on Parallel and Distributed Systems and a member of IEEE since 2021.

William Quisenberry resides in Lexington, KY, and has a diverse background that includes studying and practicing within the field of business administration, coordinating implementation projects for Fortune 500 clients, managing and overseeing vendors/suppliers, operations management, project management, marketing, research analysis, consulting, and teaching at the collegiate level. Dr. Quisenberry has collaborated and worked on projects with a variety of major organizations in the marketplace that include: Lexmark International, Halliburton, Branch Banking and Trust, The U.S. Department of Veterans Affairs, Wal-Mart, The U.S. Army Corps of Engineers, Accenture, IBM, Best Buy, Lockheed Martin, John Hancock Financial, and the World Trade Center Association. Dr. Quisenberry holds a Bachelor of Business Administration (BBA) degree in Finance, a BBA in Marketing, as well as a Master of Business Administration degree from Sullivan University's Graduate School of Business, and a Post-Graduate Certification in Forensic Accounting from Davenport University. He also possesses a Doctor of Business Administration (DBA) degree with a specialization in Leadership from Walden University.

Kevin Richardson occupies the role of Associate Professor of Business & Technology at Edward Waters University. His professional journey is marked by notable achievements, as he is a recognized Certified Diversity Professional and a Certified Trainer. With an impressive academic background, Dr. Richardson boasts two doctoral degrees and three graduate degrees. In 2016, he successfully attained his inaugural doctorate degree specializing in Operations and Quality Management Systems from The National Graduate School located in Washington, DC. Subsequently, in 2021, Dr. Richardson secured a distinguished Philosophy of Doctorate (Ph.D.) in Technology Management of Information Systems from Capitol Technology University situated in Laurel, MD. He also holds a Master of Science in Natural Resources Economics and Corporate Sustainability from Virginia Tech University in Blacksburg, VA. Dr. Richardson's academic pursuits extend to a Master's degree in Information Systems Engineering Management from Harrisburg Science & Technology University in Harrisburg, PA. He further diversified his knowledge with a third master's degree in Counseling Psychology obtained from Springfield College in Charleston, SC. Possessing a wealth of experience spanning over 25 years, Dr. Richardson has contributed significantly to the realms of management, teaching, and training across academia, government, and private industries. His tenure as an educator encompasses various institutions including Edward Waters University, Bethune Cookman University, Allen University, The National Graduate School of Quality Management, and Morris College.

Jessica Roman provides support as a Security Assistance Specialist in the CH-47 Program Office. Jessica is a native New Yorker who served as an Aviation Technician in the Navy. Her educational accomplishments and pursuits are unique. Jessica has an undergraduate degree from Oakwood University, a historically Black College/university (HBCU) in Huntsville, Alabama. She is completing her Master of Business Administration (MBA) in Logistics with a focus on Technology from the Florida Institute of Technology, a research-level two university. As a result of her studies in both degree programs, she is academically qualified in a broad spectrum of areas, such as Marketing, Logistics, Management, Leadership, Business, Information Systems, and Technology Management.

Cedric Dewayne Webber received his Bachelor of Science in Biology with a minor in Chemistry from Rust College in Holly Springs Ms. He also holds advanced degrees in Special Education and Environmental Engineering from Tennessee State University as well as a Master of Arts in Clinical Counseling and a Doctor of Education both from Trevecca Nazarene University located in Nashville Tn. He has done extensive research in carbon sequestration and social-emotional learning. He is currently employed with the Metropolitan Nashville Public School System.

Tiffany Weitoish is currently a candidate for a PhD at Capitol Technology University. She has a master's degree in Cybersecurity Studies from American Military University and a master's degree in Criminology from Indiana University of Pennsylvania. Tiffany Weitoish has work experience in Cybersecurity, investigations, and computer forensics, and she has certifications in Lean Six Sigma Master Black Belt, Process Improvement Specialist (CPIS), Lean Six Sigma Expert (LSSP-II), CompTIA Security+ CE, and others.

Yoshino W. White is a technology leader in the medical technology industry. She is a wife and a mother who strives for excellence each day in all facets of life. Her executive profile exhibits 16 plus years of experience leading, transforming, engaging, and driving results within corporations. She is a graduate of THE Florida State University with both a bachelors and masters' degree in Industrial Engineering. Yoshino is a certified Project Manager(PMP) and Certified Agile Practitioner with the Project Management Institute (PMI), and has experience in multiple industries with key experience in product development, delivering management and strategy within transformational Product Lifecycle Management (PLM) solutions and integrating PLM and Enterprise Resource Planning (ERP) systems. She is known as a value driver and a people developer in whatever work she does. Yoshi spends time working with computer information science students at Post University and supporting the programming efforts of Destination Liberation and organization focused on exposing young black girls in the southern black belt to the rest of the world. She has served on multiple non-profit boards in leadership roles. Yoshino is a firm believer in building her community and the next generation of leaders one person and one experience at a time.

Index

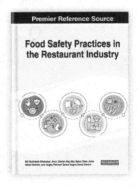

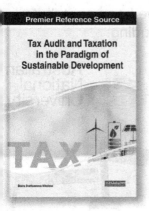

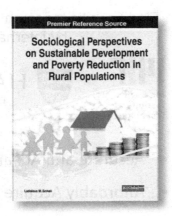

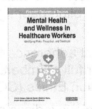

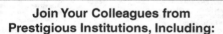

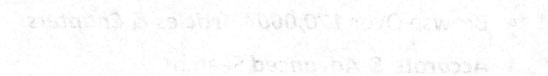

Printed in the United States
by Baker & Taylor Publisher Services